HPE ASE – Hybrid IT Solutions Architect V1
OFFICIAL CERTIFICATION STUDY GUIDE (EXAM HPE0-S57)

First Edition

Radek Zima

HPE Press
660 4th Street, #802
San Francisco, CA 94107

HPE ASE – Hybrid IT Solutions Architect V1
Official Certification Study Guide (Exam HPE0-S57)
Radek Zima

© 2019 Hewlett Packard Enterprise Development LP.

Published by:

Hewlett Packard Enterprise Press
660 4th Street, #802
San Francisco, CA 94107

ISBN: **978-1-7331277-0-7**

Printed in Mexico

WARNING AND DISCLAIMER
This book provides information about the topics covered in the Designing HPE Hybrid IT Solutions certification exam (HPE0-S57). Every effort has been made to make this book as complete and as accurate as possible, but no warranty or fitness is implied.

The information is provided on an "as is" basis. The author, and Hewlett Packard Enterprise Press, shall have neither liability nor responsibility to any person or entity with respect to any loss or damages arising from the information contained in this book or from the use of the discs or programs that may accompany it.

The opinions expressed in this book belong to the author and are not necessarily those of Hewlett Packard Enterprise Press.

Feedback Information

At HPE Press, our goal is to create in-depth reference books of the best quality and value. Each book is crafted with care and precision, undergoing rigorous development that involves the expertise of members from the professional technical community.

Readers' feedback is a continuation of the process. If you have any comments regarding how we could improve the quality of this book, or otherwise alter it to better suit your needs, you can contact us through email at hpepress@epac.com. Please make sure to include the book title and ISBN in your message.

We appreciate your feedback.

Publisher: Hewlett Packard Enterprise Press

HPE Contributors: Chris Bradley, Wilfred Brown, Darren Crawford, Chris Hornauer, Don McCracken, Norman Morales, Chris Powell, Kevin Spring

HPE Press Program Manager: Michael Bishop

About the Author

The author is an independent consultant who specializes in IT infrastructure design, implementation and maintenance for HPE servers, storage, networking, management and cloud software. He develops and delivers trainings, workshops, demonstrations, and conference presentations for HPE channel partners, customers and employees at training centers and events around the world. Radek has a Bachelor's degree and a Master of Science degree from the Faculty of Informatics and Statistics, University of Economics in Prague.

Introduction

This book is based on the Designing HPE Hybrid IT Solutions course and helps you prepare for the HPE ASE—Hybrid IT Solutions Architect V1 certification exam (HPE0-S57). The certification validates that you can expertly plan, design, recommend, and demonstrate the breadth and depth of HPE Hybrid IT solutions. Areas covered in this guide include compute, networking, storage, software-defined and cloud, hyperconverged, density, and mission critical solutions based on customer needs.

 Note

This certification also requires the HPE OneView product certification. Please visit the HPE ASE—Hybrid IT Solutions Architect V1 certification page for details:
https://certification-learning.hpe.com/tr/datacard/Certification/ASE-HITSolArcV1

Certification and Learning

Hewlett Packard Enterprise Partner Ready Certification and Learning provides end-to-end continuous learning programs and professional certifications that can help you open doors and accelerate your career.

We provide

- **Professional sales and technical training and certifications** to give you the critical skills needed to design, manage and implement the most sought-after IT disciplines; and

- **Continuous learning activities and job-role based learning plans** to help you keep pace with the demands of the dynamic, fast paced IT industry

- **Advanced training** to help you navigate and seize opportunities within the top IT transformation areas that enable business advantage today.

As a Partner Ready Certification and Learning certified member, your skills, knowledge, and real-world experience are recognized and valued in the marketplace. To continue your professional and career growth, you have access to our large HPE community of world-class IT professionals, trend-makers and decision-makers. Share ideas, best practices, business insights, and challenges as you gain professional connections globally.

To learn more about HPE Partner Ready Certification and Learning certifications and continuous learning programs, please visit:

http://certification-learning.hpe.com

Audience

This book is designed for presales solution architects involved in supporting the sale of HPE Hybrid IT solutions, including servers, storage, and networking devices.

Assumed Knowledge

The HPE ASE—Hybrid IT Solutions Architect V1 certification is an expert-level certification. It is assumed that you have the minimum of three years of design and/or operational experience or equivalent in at least one of the core HPE areas (Server, Storage, and Networking) and six months design and/or operational experience or equivalent in other HPE solutions and technologies.

Minimum Qualifications

The prerequisites for the HPE ASE—Hybrid IT Solutions Architect V1 certification are the HPE ATP - Hybrid IT Solutions V1 certification and HPE OneView product certification.

Relevant Certifications

After you pass the exam, your achievement may be applicable toward more than one certification. To determine which certifications can be credited with this achievement, log in to The Learning Center and view the certifications listed on the exam's More Details tab. You might be on your way to achieving additional certifications.

Preparing for Exam HPE0-S57

This self-study guide does not guarantee that you will have all the knowledge you need to pass the exam. It is expected that you will also draw on real-world experience and would benefit from completing the hands-on lab activities provided in the instructor-led training.

Recommended HPE Training

Recommended training to prepare for each exam is accessible from the exam's page in The Learning Center. See the exam attachment, "Supporting courses," to view and register for the courses.

Obtain Hands-on Experience

You are not required to take the recommended, supported courses, and completion of training does not guarantee that you will pass the exams. Hewlett Packard Enterprise strongly recommends a combination of training, thorough review of courseware and additional study references, and sufficient on-the-job experience prior to taking an exam.

The Designing Hybrid IT Solutions – Self-Directed Lab provides practical experience of how to design and implement HPE Hybrid IT solutions. For more information, go to:

https://hpepress.hpe.com/product/Designing+HPE+Hybrid+IT+Solutions+-+Self+Directed+Lab-eBook-19048

Exam Registration

To register for an exam, go to

https://certification-learning.hpe.com/tr/learn_more_about_exams.html

CONTENTS

1   Introduction to a Hybrid World

LEARNING OBJECTIVES

After completing this chapter, you should be able to:

✓ Introduce the benefits of Reference Architectures.

✓ Identify HPE as a company built on the idea of innovation.

✓ Identify the Hybrid IT vision.

✓ Explain hybrid business problems.

Reference Architecture

This class is wrapped around Reference Architectures and Reference Configurations. We do not want the class to start complex, as designing Hybrid IT solutions can be as easy as taking a Reference Architecture or Reference Configuration and build the customer solution based on best practices and guidelines in these documents.

Reference Architectures and Reference Configurations

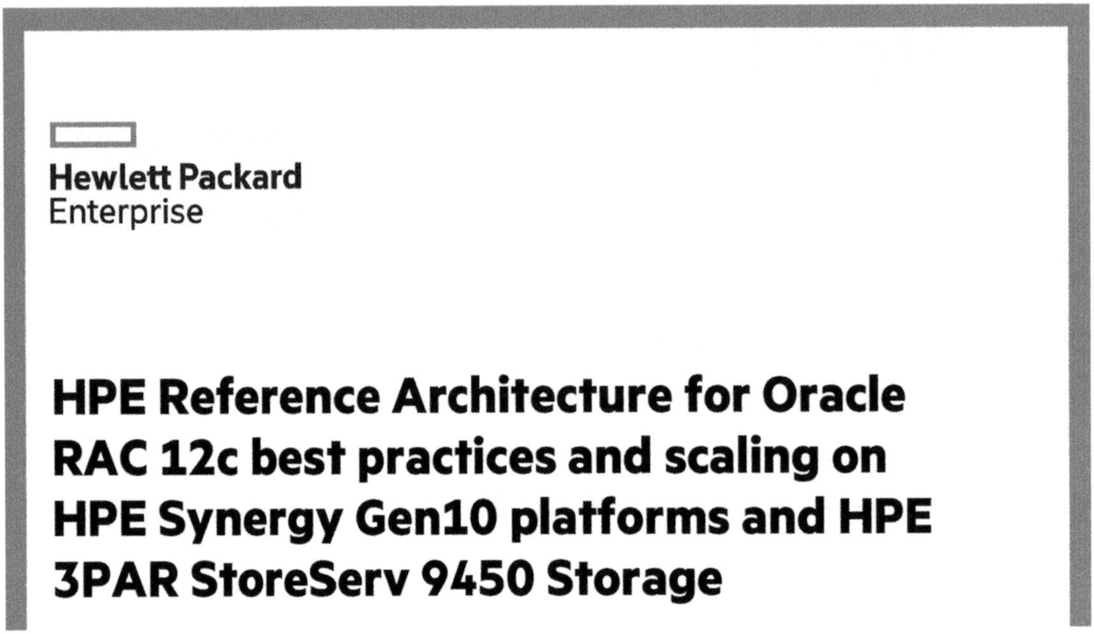

Hewlett Packard
Enterprise

HPE Reference Architecture for Oracle RAC 12c best practices and scaling on HPE Synergy Gen10 platforms and HPE 3PAR StoreServ 9450 Storage

Figure 1-1 Example of an HPE Reference Architecture

A reference architecture is a validated configuration for a specific workload, as indicated in Figure 1-1. HPE Reference Architectures and HPE Reference Configurations include complete configuration, sizing, bill of material (BOM), and deployment details. HPE is committed to development of these references.

 Note

A bill of materials or product structure (sometimes bill of material, BOM or associated list) is a list of the raw materials, sub-assemblies, intermediate assemblies, sub-components, parts, and the quantities of each needed to manufacture an end product (Wikipedia.org, April 2019).

 Note

To see an example of an HPE Reference Architecture, visit:

https://h20195.www2.hpe.com/V2/GetDocument.aspx?docname=a00049200enw

Synergy and 3PAR Reference Architecture: Contents of the "recipe"

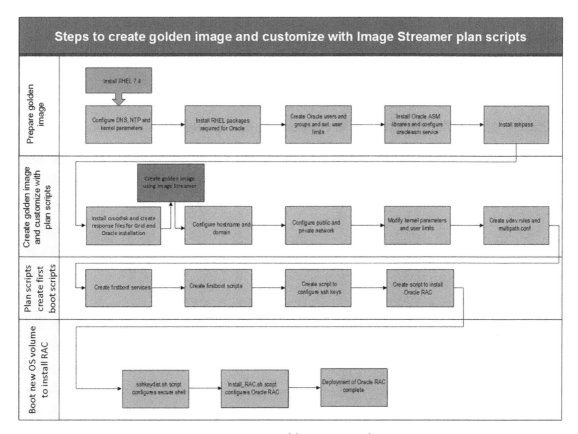

Figure 1-2 Steps to create a golden image with Image Streamer

Contents of Reference Architecture, as shown in Figure 1-2:

- Solution components

- Best practices

- Configuration guidance

- Capacity and sizing

- Implementing POC

- Appendices

Note

Proof of concept (PoC) is a realization of a certain method or idea in order to demonstrate its feasibility, or a demonstration in principle with the aim of verifying that some concept or theory has practical potential. A proof of concept is usually small and may or may not be complete (Wikipedia.org, April 2019).

Synergy and 3PAR Reference Architecture: Components of the solution

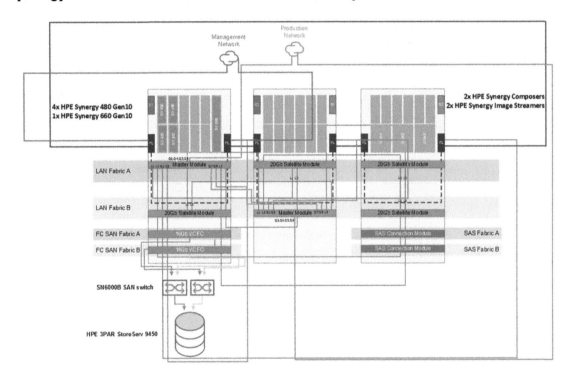

Figure 1-3 Components of the solution

Reference Architecture and Reference Configurations, as illustrated in Figure 1-3, usually contain a list of components of the recommended solution. For example, components of the Synergy and 3PAR Reference Architecture include:

- HPE Synergy Composer

- HPE Synergy Image Streamer

- HPE Synergy Gen10 Compute Modules

- HPE 3PAR StoreServ 9450 All-Flash Storage

- HPE Application Tuner Express

- Oracle Real Application Clusters

Activity: Synergy and 3PAR Reference Architecture

1. Download the Synergy Reference Architecture:
   https://h20195.www2.hpe.com/V2/GetDocument.aspx?docname=a00049200enw

2. Discuss the following questions:

   a. What is the best practice for BIOS configuration for the presented setup with Synergy Gen10 compute modules?

   _____

   _____

   _____

   b. What is the performance difference between RAID 1 and RAID 5 for redo logs on the 3PAR StoreServ 9450?

   _____

   _____

   _____

Learning check

1. What are the most important HPE components of the Reference Architecture for Oracle RAC 12c presented in this section?

   _____

   _____

   _____

   _____

   _____

   _____

   _____

   _____

HPE overview

HPE is a company built on the idea of innovation. From the beginning, we have always been about helping customers get more value out of their apps and data. Our mission has always been to help our customers use technology to improve the way we live and work. We have done that through innovation, expertise, and, most importantly, through a trusted partnership with our customers. For over seven decades, as illustrated in Figure 1-4, we have helped our customers through every major technology transition, including the shift from mainframe to industry standard servers, the virtualization revolution, and now to cloud and tomorrow, to the edge, and artificial intelligence (AI).

Innovation is in our DNA

Figure 1-4 Powering the world's apps and data for over 75 years

Today we face the biggest shift yet, digital transformation. Fueled by an explosion of data and a desire to unlock insights through AI and advanced analytics, a new generation of technology, apps, and data that is increasingly accessible to all, digital transformation is disrupting every industry—creating massive opportunities and challenges for enterprises of all sizes. Enterprises everywhere want to grow, to find new revenue streams, to become more efficient, and to gain a competitive edge.

They are starting to realize that the data generated by their business is not a burden, but a potent raw material. In that data is the vital insights that can transform their businesses.

We have all been talking about digital transformation for a while, but we are far from done. Companies are not slowing down, in fact their embracing of new technologies push businesses and governments to the edge of their capabilities and speed.

Advancing the way people live and work

Innovation is core to our DNA, and we are innovating to help enterprises redefine experiences and drive smarter, hyper-efficient operations:

- Redefining experiences at the intelligent edge for fans, museum goers, golfers, and more (for example, Tottenham Hotspur's new digital stadium)

- Speeding time to market with new cloud-based ventures (Virgin Money), creating smarter digital workplaces (Konica Minolta, an HPE OEM partner and customer), and enabling seamless experiences in every industry

Creating a world where everything computes

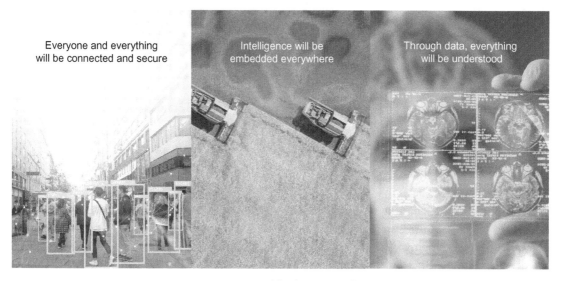

Figure 1-5 Creating a world where everything computes

We are creating a world where everything computes, a world that is hyperconnected, where everyone and everything share data. As illustrated in Figure 1-5, the possibilities to turn all that data into action and value—to create new experiences, products, and services, and drive efficiencies—is what is driving us to a faster, more intelligent world.

It is a world where billions of connected people, devices, and things are sharing data from our cars and homes, workplaces, museums, stadiums, hospitals, factory floors, and the data center—creating petabytes of data that bring new insights and actions—and where AI is used to make decisions faster and autonomously—with speed measured in nanoseconds.

We want to help customers connect all their data, across all their edges and all their clouds.

Driven by a new generation of apps and data—and a new speed of business

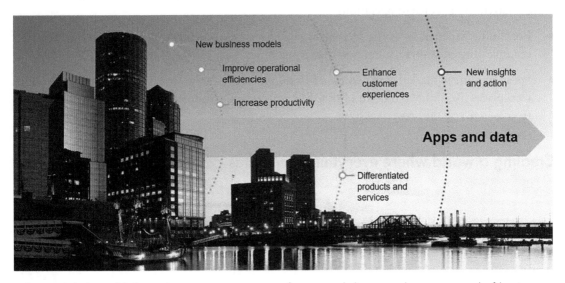

Figure 1-6 A world driven by a new generation of apps and data—and a new speed of business

The world is driven by a new generation of apps and data—and a new speed of business. In our connected world, expectations continue for more engaging, personal, and seamless experiences across platforms and channels, reflective of our context in a given moment.

Enterprises are capitalizing on new ways to engage and get closer to customers, thanks to deeper customer insights that drive smarter design and better experiences—with less friction at every step. Enterprises are also tapping machine learning, Internet of Things (IoT), and AI to create new services and drive operational efficiencies, using predictive insights to reduce downtime and keep the business running.

All of this is fueled by a new generation of apps and data, existing on multiple platforms, from the data center to the cloud—and increasingly at the edge of the network. This is where people, places, and things converge to create new intelligent digital experiences, based on massive amounts of data being collected, analyzed, and often acted upon instantaneously.

As indicated in Figure 1-6, the pace of business has never been faster—and accelerating time to value pays off. The possibilities are limitless—when optimally designed.

The edge has arrived

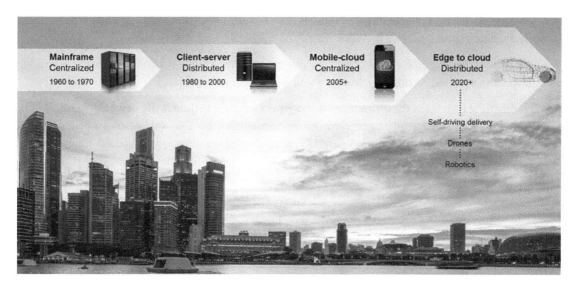

Figure 1-7 The edge has arrived

There is a shift underway—from data being highly centralized in large data centers to highly decentralized at the edge. It is shifting us to a whole new speed of business—measured in nanoseconds.

Let us take a look at where we have come from. We began with mainframe and super computers that solved complex issues, but they were enormous and slow. In the 1980s, we transitioned to the client-server and networked computing model, which was much more efficient, but still limited in capacity and speed. In the 2000s, we were introduced to a new way of computing with mobile devices with access to virtual/cloud data storage.

So, what do we really mean by the edge, as illustrated in Figure 1-7? The edge is where enterprises interact with their customers; where products are manufactured; where employees work each day; where everyday people interact, purchase, and explore; and where technology gets put into action. The edge employs AI, machine learning, and automation to continuously learn, predict, and adapt to changes, needs, and threats in real-time—and enables us to act locally, in the moment, in context—creating new possibilities in every industry. Connecting these new insights from edge to cloud across the enterprise, integrating the data with existing business systems (ERP, CRM, and more) is what is driving value and growth.

We have been at the forefront of developing technologies for the intelligent edge to help enable real-time insights, personalized experiences, and the ability to take action instantaneously. Recognizing the opportunity at the intelligent edge is why we acquired Aruba Networks—to deliver mobile-first solutions. Through Aruba, we acquired IntroSpect, to embed security with machine-learning capabilities that allow for rapid scale User and Entity Behavior Analytics (UEBA) at the edge and to indicate attacks among people—and things. Over the next four years, HPE will invest $4 billion in intelligent edge innovation. We will accelerate our investments in R&D to continue to advance and innovate new products, services, and consumption models across a number of domains including security, edge computing, automation, AI, and machine learning.

When it comes to data processing, HPE's capabilities span every scale. When it comes to the kind of data processing involved in machine learning and AI, we again lead.

Accelerating time to value is the ultimate goal in a world where real-time is the new just-in time. Time to action. Enterprises need to be obsessive about accelerating time to value—and hyper-efficient, ready to capture new opportunities and defend against disruption, increasingly in real-time.

In a data-driven world, speed matters more than ever—we believe enterprises that can act fast on a continuous stream of data—from everywhere—will win.

HPE: Accelerating your customer's digital transformation agenda

We created HPE to help your customers accelerate their digital transformation. We uniquely address the three biggest barriers to speed:

- **Transformation of technology for an edge-centric, cloud-enabled, data-driven world**—We help your customers create a software-defined, hybrid operating model that spans any cloud to multi-cloud, on- and off-premises, and the edge so they can create and deliver everything-as-a-service dynamically, everywhere.

- **Transformation of people and processes, creating a culture for growth and innovation**—The hardest part of any digital transformation involves people, their skills, processes, and culture.

- **Transformation of economics and technology investment strategy**—One of the most underappreciated aspects of any digital transformation is financial strategy. Capital trapped in underutilized fixed assets is a barrier to speed and innovation. With HPE Financial Services, we provide the right strategies and as-a-service consumption models to optimize IT investments.

Transform your customer's technology

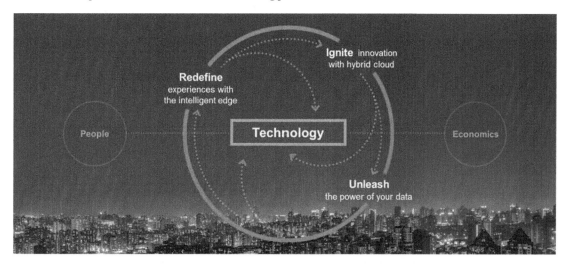

Figure 1-8 Accelerate with intelligent, software-defined solutions, edge to cloud

The explosion of connected things creates possibilities from the mobile, IoT edge to the cloud, and across the enterprise. We see a world that is edge-centric, cloud-enabled, and data-driven—where everything is created and delivered as-a-service. As illustrated in figure 1-8, we are helping enterprises transform to:

Redefine experiences with the intelligent edge

The revolution that is happening now is the explosion of data, powered by the edge. The explosion of data from connected things is driving data from large data centers to many small centers of data. By 2020, Gartner estimates 75% of data generated will never see a data center or cloud (Gartner, *Top 10 Strategic Technology Trends for 2018: Cloud to the Edge*, Published: March 8, 2018). It will be created at the edge in an oil rig, a retail store, a medical device, a self-driving car, and so on.

The edge is where billions of people and places and trillions of things intersect—generating unimaginable amounts of data. Data that has the potential value to drive insights and actions is where your customers interact with their customers, manufacture their products, where their employees work, where experiences can be personalized, local, and in the moment—enriched by context.

Ignite innovation with hybrid cloud

Enterprises must now create and deliver services across hybrid and multi-cloud environments in a hybrid reality. To do this effectively and efficiently, enterprises need to transform. It is not trivial. In fact, the biggest challenge is people adapting to the continuous change inherent in cloud.

HPE accelerates cloud transformation by addressing the toughest challenges from people and process, to economics and technology, with expertise and solutions to help enterprises get hybrid cloud right. We help your customers get the right mix of clouds for all of their apps and data—in public and private clouds—connected to their on-premises environments and unified with a common software-defined hybrid operating model, delivered as-a-service with pay-per-use models that span public and private clouds. We help your customers create an IT culture for growth, with the control, security, compliance, and governance behind it, so they can focus on what is next for their enterprise.

Unleash the power of customer data

Data is your intellectual property (IP), the new currency. To stay ahead, your customers must capture, keep, and refine every bit of their data. They cannot afford to throw anything away because all their data is valuable. It is all about speed to insights, everywhere from edge to cloud, and "real time" is the new "just-in-time."

Data is coming at us faster than ever before, and from new sources, like the intelligent edge. Enterprises can barely keep up with all this data—and the data explosion will continue.

We help enterprises process and analyze data from every edge to any cloud and at every scale. From intelligent storage to high-performance computing—and with our breakthrough innovations like Memory-Driven Computing, we help enterprises accelerate insights, action, and value—everywhere.

Transform your customer's people and processes

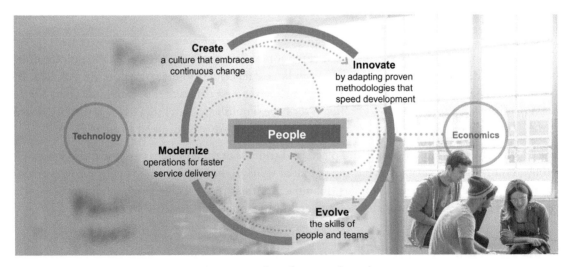

Figure 1-9 Create a culture for growth and innovation

Digital transformation comes down to how your customers drive business growth, ensuring you capitalize on their apps, data, people, and their capital to innovate and move faster. The hardest part of any digital transformation involves your customer's people: evolving skills, processes, and culture are the necessary components required to enable their teams to be successful through technology change. The challenge lies in helping people to understand how their roles change, why it matters, and equipping them with the skills that they need to be successful in their new roles. None of this is simple, especially in large-scale global organizations. With HPE Pointnext we help your customer's people to be successful through their unique digital transformation journey, as indicated in Figure 1-9:

- **Innovate by adopting** proven methodologies that speed development. When DevOps is combined with Agile methodology and cloud-native technologies, applications are built with a much shorter time to market, fewer issues, and improve quickly with frequent updates. This is frequently referred to as Continuous Integration/Continuous Delivery (CI/CD). HPE Pointnext helps enterprises establish and implement a CI/CD strategy, accelerating cloud-native development and leveraging a developer-ready infrastructure to help them embrace these new techniques, tools, and practices.

- **Evolve the skills** of your customer's people and teams: Modern IT systems are comprised of new technologies, new methodologies, new partners, and a new generation of staff. Keeping your customer's IT organization skilled to design, build, and operate these new environments requires a new approach. HPE Pointnext skills-based training is most effective in a team dynamic and at the time of need. HPE Digital Learner is our on-demand learning platform that provides online access to micro-learning courses everywhere, with real-time video feeds and collaborative mentoring services.

- **Modernize operations** for faster service delivery: IT complexity has exploded over the past few years, and an underfunded and overwhelmed IT Operations team is struggling to keep up. Public outages and security breaches are a rising trend. HPE Pointnext, with Datacenter Care, transforms your customer's IT operations. Working alongside their existing Ops team, we can help free them from the undifferentiated heavy lifting of infrastructure support, bringing a holistic view to service management and helping their team adopt new tools, processes, and approaches to manage a modern IT environment. By freeing up their people, we can help them shift these resources to other operational roles. We employ best practices from Information Technology Infrastructure Library (ITIL) and IT Service Management (ITSM).

 Note

ITSM stands for IT Service Management and refers to the total activities—directed by policies, organized and structured in processes and supporting procedures.

Enterprises dependent upon IT technology should ensure every aspect associated with IT technology is accomplished via proper planning and strategizing. Only then will they be able to get the best out of it. There are specific tools in the market which can help enterprises accomplish the planning and strategizing of IT technology effectively in a seamless and hassle-free manner. These tools are usually known as ITSM tools (ITarian.com, April 2019).

Note

The IT Infrastructure Library (ITIL) is a set of comprehensive practices that ensures to deliver commending IT services. ITIL has been through multiple revisions and is now comprised of five books—each book covers and focuses on a specific set of process and stage on the lifecycle of IT services. ITIL is the most welcomed approach to IT Service Management worldwide. The organized and structured approach of ITIL delivers efficient IT Service Management to enable businesses, manage risks, initiate affordable practices, raise a secure IT environment, and boost customer relations to therefore enhance scalable business growth.

ITIL was first developed by the Central Computer and Telecommunications Agency of the British Government during the 1980s while it is then first comprised of more than 30 books, which included best practices in IT gathered from various reliable sources from and around the world (ITarian.com, April 2019).

Transform your customer's economics

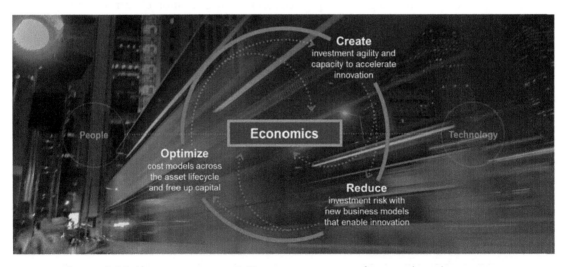

Figure 1-10 Align your customer's IT investment strategy for growth and innovation

Transforming IT investment strategies is key to successful digital transformation. As shown in Figure 1-10, HPE helps enterprises with three strategies to maximize your customer's IT investments: more power in their IT operational strategy today, future growth, and innovation.

Optimizing cost models and freeing up capital is focused on addressing existing operations. Today, 70 to 80% of most IT budgets is spent on simply maintaining the operational norm while only about 20% is available for investing in new areas of innovation or new applications. The challenge is how to reduce and optimize that maintenance spend.

HPE Financial Services can help by monetizing in-use and retired systems to fund new investments and by stabilizing legacy operations and spend aligned to in-use systems not ready to be retired. This increases profitability and minimizes new investments in old systems.

Your customers can create investment agility and capacity to accelerate innovation. Investing in innovation that your customer's business needs now requires significant up-front capital. However, their existing budgets do not always cover everything they need. Companies can create additional investment capacity from current systems by selling off assets, while continuing to use them. Oftentimes, IT leaders do not think about this, but in every IT asset they own, they have invested capital. That means the technology continues to have value for many years after its initial purchase.

Your customers can also look at better risk management. Risk has two forms. The first is that they have not invested in enough capacity or enough capability to handle the unexpected demand for a new market. It means turning away customers or giving them a bad experience. The other type of risk is equally bad, by which they build capacity and never use it. That ties up precious dollars that can be better used elsewhere.

HPE Financial Services can help with investment agility by creating an investment model that is designed for innovation, but right-sized to manage capacity risk. We can also remove infrastructure lock-in for systems that have not fully depreciated, but are holding up innovation initiatives. This frees up "trapped" capital, creating investment dollars that can be quickly aligned to new innovation investment.

Companies looking to implement new business models or run experimental deployments need to think about mitigating investment risk. Technology never stops changing, and most businesses must have a sharp eye on the future, looking at experimental technologies, rolling out products and services that are not ready for the mainstream. This can be the difference between being the disruptor or being disrupted, but it can be very risky. How do companies invest quickly while still managing the risk? If the innovation is successful, how do they scale quickly? If it fails, how do they make sure that the business is not impacted for years to come? There are many investment and asset lifecycle solutions that can help reduce risk, accelerate new model innovations, and help companies move into new spaces quickly.

HPE Financial Services can help in a number of ways. For example, in a phased deployment of new technology over a 12-month period, the customer can only pay when the systems are configured, tested, and turned on. This allows for a more gradual introduction of new technology. With our aggressively tailored investment models that are perfect for untested or experimental deployments, we provide peace of mind. You can step away (all or part, with no penalty) if the deployment is not successful, and continue or expand, based on project and business success.

With HPE Pointnext we help your customers assess where they are today, help them map their customer's apps and data to their optimal platforms to deliver speed and flexibility for their enterprise. HPE Pointnext provides a full spectrum of advisory, design, integration, migration, and operational consulting services to help our customers deploy and manage workloads across their entire IT estate.

At HPE, we continue to strategically build a portfolio that helps our customers take advantage of digital transformation and the resulting explosion of apps and data. We are focused on helping our customers accelerate business outcomes by extracting critical insights from their data, wherever it lives, from edge to core to cloud. HPE Pointnext provides customers with a truly comprehensive Hybrid IT strategy that includes private, managed, and public clouds, as well as traditional IT.

Accelerating our strategy with partnerships

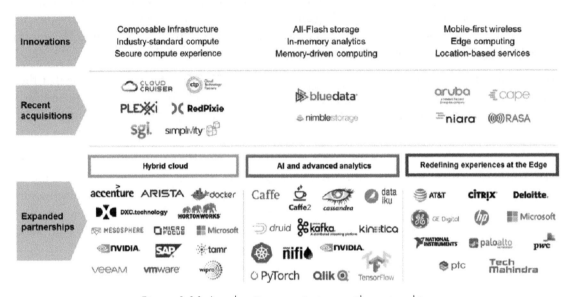

Figure 1-11 Accelerating our strategy with partnerships

It is important to be able to talk across hybrid/data/edge and be familiar with key technologies and recent acquisitions. If you look at Hybrid Cloud, as shown in Figure 1-11, we started with an industry-leading base of innovations, and our portfolio has never been stronger.

With Synergy, we introduced the world's first Composable Infrastructure to simplify and accelerate DevOps and business innovation. Our 3PAR storage line has been leading the way for customers to the all-flash data center, and of course, we maintain decades of leadership in industry-standard computing.

For data and analytics, we also lead the market in High-Performance Computing (HPC), in-memory analytics, and The Machine project from HPE Labs was out in front in planning the future of computing for when Moore's Law runs out of gas on current architectures.

Building on that foundation, we then put our cash to work to build on our strengths and to accelerate our roadmap and vision.

SimpliVity, Nimble, and Cloud Cruiser gave us an instant leadership position in hyperconverged, software-defined storage, and cloud and Hybrid IT management as well as radically simplifying on-premises environments in support of developers and business users, with a higher objective to help our customers accelerate insights and reduce time to value.

According to IDC, by 2022, the total addressable market for artificial intelligence/machine learning (AI/ML) and Big Data is expected to grow to approximately $160 billion.

 Note

By 2022, IDC projects Big Data/Analytics software investments will reach $90 billion (**https://www.idc.com/getdoc.jsp?containerId=prUS44215218**) and $77.6 billion for cognitive and artificial intelligence-based systems (**https://www.idc.com/getdoc.jsp?containerId=prUS44291818**).

However, we have recognized that not all organizations will have the AI and data literacy skills needed to extract business value and actionable insights from their data, and demand is increasing for faster and more cost-effective solutions that can easily deploy AI/ML and Big Data analytics.

To accelerate this opportunity, HPE acquired BlueData, a leading provider of software that transforms how enterprises deploy artificial intelligence and Big Data analytics in early 2019, expanding our offerings in these rapidly growing markets.

We also recently welcomed Plexxi and RedPixie into the fold, and HPE will continue to improve its hybrid cloud consulting capabilities that enable customers to deploy and manage workloads across environments seamlessly.

With Plexxi, we are delivering enhanced hyperconverged and composable solutions with a next-generation, software-defined data network fabric that can automatically create or rebalance bandwidth to workload needs, increasing agility, efficiency, and accelerating how quickly companies deploy applications and draw business value from their data. RedPixie, one of Europe's largest cloud specialists, expands our consulting capabilities to build and manage Microsoft Azure hybrid solutions for the financial sector.

We also acquired SGI, nearly doubling our market lead in HPC, which architecturally is forming the foundation for the future of HPE's approach to AI/ML and edge-to-core analytics. With SGI, we now have the perfect Big Data Analytics solutions for industry, government, research, energy, and healthcare.

As we have said, innovation in today's world is a team sport, and our relationship with our ecosystem partners is growing from strength to strength. In many ways, our partnerships today are much deeper, and in ways that previously were not possible; our services and software business was seen to be in competition with them. As a result, we have made many moves to extend partnerships, and not just with traditional names, but with a new breed of players who really understand the future of apps and data.

Through our venture investment and partnership program, called Hewlett Packard Pathfinder, we are using our deep expertise to curate the best emerging start-ups and help customers innovate and develop solutions faster. One example is Mesosphere, a data center operating system that enables customers to run modern apps in a hybrid infrastructure. Another is Chef, an infrastructure automation technology that we have integrated into our Proactive Care Service.

In addition, rather than trying to compete head-to-head in public cloud, we understood that HPE was uniquely positioned to help our customers take advantage of multi-cloud solutions, such as with our partnership with Microsoft Azure. We have also partnered with Docker and introduced the industry's first Docker-ready servers, which create the flexibility of a true hybrid solution. We also have a deep partnership with Arista for the software-defined data center (SDDC) networking that focuses on building application workloads for the cloud.

In the intelligent edge, we saw a huge new opportunity, but it was just emerging. We started with a core acquisition of Aruba that instantly put HPE at the front of the wireless first, mobility revolution. Because the edge is about data, and security is the biggest challenge, the next acquisitions we made were Rasa and Niara, to add to the strengths of the Aruba mobile-first platform with more analytics and AI for managing and securing networks. We have also recently acquired Cape Networks, and the team members have now joined Aruba to expand Aruba's AI-powered analytics and assurance capabilities with a sensor-based service assurance solution that gives a simple, proactive, and network-agnostic tool for measuring and monitoring Software as a Service (SaaS), application, and network services.

In IoT, we built on our own innovation in core-to-edge computing and storage and extended our partnerships with Deloitte, GE Digital, National Instruments, PTC, Tech Mahindra, Veeam, and more. Our aim is to complete our core-to-edge solution stacks that merge IT and operational technology (OT) data to drive a variety of industrial IoT solutions—to put IoT into action across multiple regions. Recently, Forbes magazine called us the "quiet giant of IoT" because of the depth of capability and the fact that we do not just "talk about IoT"—we know how to implement it and get outcomes for our customers.

Learning check

2. You are in a meeting with a customer, and they challenge you with a question: "What are the most important barriers of transforming IT environment for an edge-centric, cloud-enabled, data-driven world?"

   How should you respond?

   _____

   _____

   _____

   _____

   _____

HPE Hybrid IT

Although enterprises did not plan for a Hybrid IT world, it has become the answer to achieve speed and flexibility in our digital world.

Hybrid IT is the new normal and it is complex

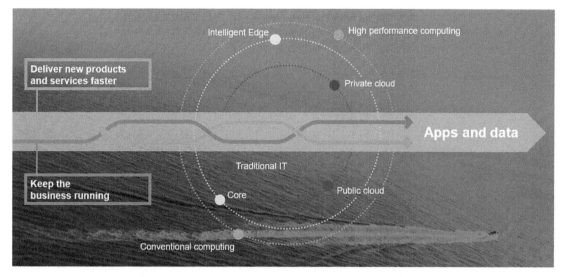

Figure 1-12 Operating customer apps and data across all technologies and platforms

To make Hybrid IT simple and optimal, as illustrated in Figure 1-12, enterprises must:

- Keep the business running and address the inefficiencies of **existing** environments (inflexible, legacy, siloes, overprovisioning, underutilization, capital-intensive) to free resources for innovation.

  - Enterprises continue to spend a disproportionate amount of budget keeping the lights on.

  - Rigid technology infrastructure was cited as the leading barrier preventing rapid innovation and speed to market (Source: HPE|Oxford Economics, January 2016).

- Deliver new products and services faster by speeding how you create **new** apps and services (agile, MVP strategies, containers, as a service) across mobile, IoT, AI, and more—amidst a growing ecosystem of partners.

  - HPE|Oxford Economics survey shows that companies leading their peers in pursuing rapid ideation also report superior financial results (Source: HPE Oxford Economics).

  - This demands a more experimental approach that is suited to the wealth of as-a-service models available, particularly pay-per use models that help accelerate innovation and growth.

Companies achieving growth do a lot of experimentation and build innovation into everyday operations. These companies take "lots of small steps" and readjust (Source: Professor Rita McGrath, Columbia University **https://hbr.org/2012/01/how-the-growth-outliers-do-it**).

- Create and deliver apps and data across multiple platforms and technologies, while understanding these critical new dimensions:

  - **Traditional, private, public cloud, multi-cloud**—Meeting control, cost, performance, and agility drivers

  - **Edge and core**—Aligned to responsiveness requirements (that is, a self-driving car cannot have decisions made in the cloud)

  - **Conventional and high-performance compute**—Systems must scale to new heights, and at the right performance; a central learning engine is needed as today's conventional computing architectures will not keep pace with the explosion of data

HPE believes achieving the optimal IT operating model for your customer's apps and data will enable their enterprise to move faster—with less risk. We make Hybrid IT simple for this reason:

- **As-a-service consumption, on-premises**

  - Pay-per-use consumption models and capacity planning strategies that limit risk and preserve capital

  - Pay for the resources you need, when you need them (whether you build or consume); this includes how you fund start-up ventures and new ideas—from experiment to strategic

- **Platforms from edge to core to cloud**

  - Modern Hybrid IT foundations that span the edge to cloud to core of the Hybrid IT environment

  - Software-defined infrastructure to speed development and delivery—and compose resources dynamically

  - Advanced data and analytics platforms that help turn data into insights and insights into action from all data

- **Invisible IT through automation and AI in the data center**—IT management that is AI driven from the edge to cloud to core

- **Ecosystem of partners**—Rich ecosystem of partners integrated across the Hybrid IT environment

- **Visibility across a multi-cloud environment**—Simplifying the complexity across the environment with unified management

- **Long-standing expertise to help bring it all together**—We help your customers bring it all together with HPE Pointnext, our services organization with the expertise to help them accelerate their Hybrid IT

How we make Hybrid IT simple

Figure 1-13 How we make Hybrid IT simple

HPE makes Hybrid IT simple with expertise, modern Hybrid IT foundations, software-defined infrastructure, advanced data and analytics platforms from core to edge and innovative IT consumption, and delivery models to help your customers get and pay for the resources they need, when they need them—with the control they need, as illustrated in Figure 1-13.

- **Define their Hybrid IT strategy** with expertise from HPE Pointnext and our partners to assess where your customers are today, map their apps and data to their optimal platforms, migrate to their right mix of Hybrid IT, and continuously evolve.

- **Power their Hybrid IT** with a modern Hybrid IT foundation, the benefits of software-defined infrastructure, and turn insights into action with advanced data and analytics platforms.

- **Optimize Hybrid IT with consumption and delivery models** that give your customers flexibility, speed, and on-premises control.

Define your customer's Hybrid IT strategy

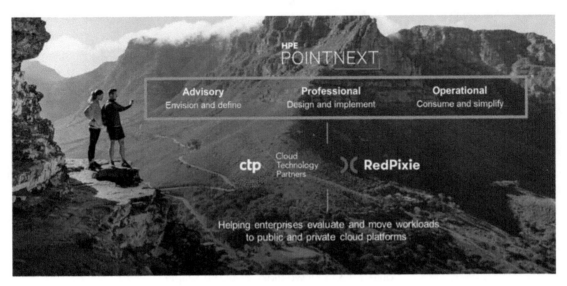

Figure 1-14 Expertise to help you accelerate your customer's Hybrid IT strategy

With HPE Pointnext we help you assess where you are today and help you map your customer's apps and data to their optimal platforms—that deliver speed and flexibility for their enterprise, as shown in Figure 1-14.

Deliver speed and flexibility from apps and data

As we assess your customer's current environment against their business goals, we help them drive efficiencies and free up resources. This includes modernizing, consolidating, and automating IT (address siloes, sprawl) to drive better utilization and simplify and reduce their IT footprint. Driving efficiencies by modernizing IT helps them free resources for growth.

At the same time, we assess how your customers can speed the creation and delivery of new services to their customers, developers, data scientists, and end users. This includes identifying ways to deliver app dev platforms with agility and speed, provide advanced data and analytics platforms to accelerate insights and action, adopt emerging technologies and methodologies.

The Right Mix of Hybrid IT enables your customers to pivot with the business

HPE believes achieving the optimal IT operating model for your customer's apps and data will enable their enterprise to move faster—with less risk. We call it the Right Mix of Hybrid IT when you optimize:

- **Cost model**—Pay for the resources they need (whether you build or consume). This includes how they fund start-up ventures and new ideas—from experiment to strategic.

- **Platforms and as-a-service models (on- and off-premises)**—Give them the resources at the right cost, performance, control, and agility across the data center, private cloud, public cloud and edge—securely.

- **Processes**—Simplify, automate, and accelerate the creation and delivery of your customer's services, combined with the enabling technologies.

- **People**—Free up your customer's resources for their most strategic initiatives, and tap new ways to drive collaboration in a digital workplace.

With HPE Pointnext, we do this with a 360-degree view across your customer's cost model, platforms, processes, and people.

Power your customer's Hybrid IT platforms

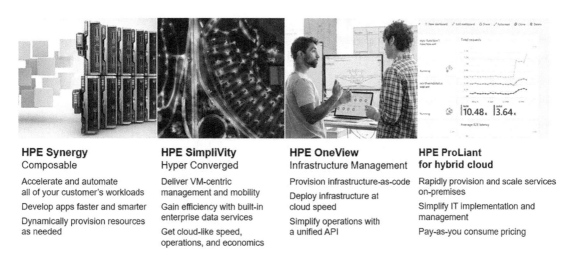

HPE Synergy	**HPE SimpliVity**	**HPE OneView**	**HPE ProLiant**
Composable	Hyper Converged	Infrastructure Management	**for hybrid cloud**
Accelerate and automate all of your customer's workloads	Deliver VM-centric management and mobility	Provision infrastructure-as-code	Rapidly provision and scale services on-premises
Develop apps faster and smarter	Gain efficiency with built-in enterprise data services	Deploy infrastructure at cloud speed	Simplify IT implementation and management
Dynamically provision resources as needed	Get cloud-like speed, operations, and economics	Simplify operations with a unified API	Pay-as-you consume pricing

← **Software-defined intelligence across apps and data** →

Figure 1-15 Power your customer's Hybrid IT platforms

Figure 1-15 shows how we help power your customer's apps and data with innovative HPE Hybrid IT platforms. To drive insights, speed, and action from their apps and data, enterprises must:

- Speed development and delivery with a software-defined infrastructure.

- Create a modern Hybrid IT foundation.

- Turn data into insights with advanced data and analytics platforms.

In a digital world, you must create and deliver services fast, and software-defined infrastructure helps your customers do just that.

Software-defined infrastructure is at the heart of HPE's strategy to make Hybrid IT simple, and we believe it is the foundation for Hybrid IT. HPE's software-defined infrastructure solutions enable your customers to create and deliver services dynamically, with the control they need for their business. It enables them to:

- Compose, teardown, recompose resources as needed. For example, HPE IT provisions resources in three minutes, not weeks.

- Repurpose resources dynamically from one workload to another. For example, HudsonAlpha reprovisions resources to teams of researchers in two hours, instead of four days.

- Infinitely scale resources.

Let us look at how important your customer's Hybrid IT platforms are in driving insights, speed, and action from their apps and data.

The ability to pivot with the business and compose resources as they are needed is key to thriving in a digital world. HPE software-defined infrastructure solutions help enterprises do just that.

HPE Synergy

HPE Synergy is the industry's first Composable Infrastructure and addresses challenges in your customer's existing environment **and** speeds the development and delivery of new services:

- Flexible resource pools of compute, storage, and fabric **in one infrastructure**

- Intelligently composes workloads across physical, virtual, and containers

- A single API that allows ops and developers to access the resources as code with developer environments and tools, including Docker, Mesosphere, Ansible, and Chef

HPE SimpliVity

The HPE SimpliVity hyperconverged infrastructure solution is designed from the ground up to meet the increased performance, scalability, and agility demands of today's data-intensive, highly virtualized IT environments. HPE SimpliVity technology transforms IT by virtualizing data and incorporating all IT infrastructure and services below the hypervisor into compact building blocks.

With three times total cost of ownership (TCO) reduction, HPE SimpliVity delivers the best of both worlds: the enterprise-class performance, protection, and resiliency that today's organizations require, with the cloud economics businesses demand.

HPE OneView

Simplify your customer's Hybrid IT environment with the HPE OneView management platform that transforms servers, storage, and networking into a software-defined infrastructure.

- Infrastructure-as-code

- Deploy infrastructure at cloud speed

- Simplify operations with a unified application programming interface (API)

HPE ProLiant for Microsoft Azure Stack

With Azure Stack, your customer's business will experience lower costs, more flexibility, and the increased business agility that the cloud offers. The public Azure variant, already implemented by many, has more than proven itself in recent years. Stack is its extension, with a smaller footprint within an on-premises data center. Azure Stack has the same user interface and APIs as the Azure public cloud.

Start with a foundation that is fast, always-on, secure—ready for anything

Figure 1-16 Start with platforms that are efficient, always-on, and secure

Start with platforms that are efficient, always-on, and secure. HPE solutions do just that, as illustrated in Figure 1-16:

- **Predictive analytics to anticipate and prevent issues with HPE All-Flash Storage and HPE InfoSight**—86% of issues automatically predicted and resolved

- **All-Flash Storage for fast and reliable access to data with HPE All-Flash Storage**—99.9999% proven availability

- **Speed application performance with HPE Gen10 Servers**—World's Most Secure Industry Standard Server

Predictive analytics provide continuous digital operations by anticipating and preventing issues across the infrastructure stack with HPE InfoSight and HPE All-Flash Storage. HPE All-Flash Storage is the only storage smart enough to predict and prevent issues and close the app-data gap.

Fast and reliable access to data with HPE All-Flash Storage Predictive analytics, coupled with cloud-ready flash storage, deliver fast and reliable access to data both on- and off-premises.

Optimize your customer's Hybrid IT financing and delivery

Figure 1-17 Optimize with as-a-service delivery and pay-per-use consumption

The fast pace of our digital world is driving change in how IT is delivered, paid for, and consumed. Today, too much capital is tied up in IT, making it difficult to get capital to fund new growth. Moreover, enterprises no longer want to (or have to) own IT assets.

As indicated in Figure 1-17, HPE is helping enterprises rethink the way they acquire, pay for, and consume IT to:

- Accelerate innovation with the right IT investment strategy (better align costs to revenues, monetize assets, smarter capital allocation).

- Start new projects faster, through pay-per-use and consumption-based models with on-premises control.

- Enhance the Hybrid IT service delivery with a global partner ecosystem.

Activity: Navigating the Hybrid IT portfolio at the HPE website

1. Open the Hybrid IT portfolio at: **https://www.hpe.com/us/en/products.html**

2. Answer the following questions:

    a. How many product categories and how many product families are presented at the website?

    _____

    _____

    _____

    _____

    _____

    _____

    b. What is the difference between categories and product families?

    _____

    _____

    _____

    _____

    _____

    _____

Learning check

3. Match the customer need with the HPE portfolio.

Always on availability	Storage and Big Data
Accelerate insight, data protection	Data center networking
Network agility and virtualization	HPC
Massive parallel computing	Mission critical

The world is now hybrid because business problems are hybrid

Customer Hybrid IT success stories include:

- EnterpriseDB (EDB)

- RioCan Real Estate Investment (RioCan)

- Sunkist Growers, Inc.

EnterpriseDB and HPE GreenLake Flex Capacity

EnterpriseDB (EDB) provides enterprises with the products, resources, and expertise required to confidently run large-scale and highly available deployments of the open source PostgreSQL (Postgres) database management system leveraging its EDB Postgres platform. The EDB Postgres platform integrates the core EDB Postgres database management system with adjacent technologies for hybrid cloud management, data integration, and data warehouse that can run across on-premises, hybrid, multi-cloud, and Database as a Service (DBaaS) environments.

EDB success story:

- **Industry challenge:** EDB's enterprise customers need to modernize their businesses to compete more effectively and efficiently in the digital age.

- **IT challenge:** EDB's customers are typically constrained by cost and have invested many years in developing applications, based on proprietary databases such as Oracle. Most of these customers cannot or do not want to run their proprietary solutions in a public cloud, yet they need the agility and efficiency that cloud offers.

- **Solution:** EDB adopted HPE GreenLake, a suite of consumption-based IT solutions designed, delivered, and operated by HPE Pointnext, which offers a simple, pay-per-use financial model leveraging HPE GreenLake Flex Capacity.

- **Results:** With HPE GreenLake, EDB can provide its customers the agility and efficiency of cloud with the control of an on-premises solution. EDB can drive innovation and meet its customers' needs to modernize while preserving their application investments. HPE GreenLake takes away the pain of modernizing and enables EDB's customers to accelerate their journey away from proprietary technologies to become more agile and grow more cost effectively by only paying for the infrastructure resources they use.

Daniel Williams, Director, Strategic Partners and Alliances, EnterpriseDB, says about HPE Pointnext:"HPE Pointnext is driving innovation with EDB. It has the skills, the infrastructure, and the resources and capabilities to really help enterprises move away from Oracle and other proprietary solutions, and re-platform in a consumption-based model which is innovative, leading-edge, and game-changing for the market."

Note

To see a short video about this case study, visit:

https://www.youtube.com/watch?v=Oc1bc_C28PQ&feature=youtu.be

RioCan Real Estate Investment and Synergy

RioCan Real Estate Investment (RioCan) is one of Canada's largest real estate investment trusts. It has leased, built, developed, and partnered with and renovated properties for recognizable retailers, grocery stores, movie theaters, restaurants, banks, and gyms. RioCan is now expanding its focus to residential properties.

- **Objective:** Increase operating margins and reduce data center footprint without sacrificing quality

- **Approach:** Implement HPE Synergy Composable Infrastructure as a flexible solution that allows for future platform growth

- **IT matters:**

  - Reduces host servers from 14 to eight

  - Lowers cost of hardware by $180,000 over three years

  - Eliminates a full rack in data center and saves $120,000 over three years in colocation costs through footprint reduction

- **Business matters:**

  - Improves ability to perform complex business analytics required for decision making

  - Alleviates the workload from the IT team to focus on other business-critical responsibilities

  - Increases total capacity of disk memory and CPU by 30%, leaving 20% of the total space free, which is crucial as the company is on a growth trajectory

- **Components of the solution:**

  - HPE Synergy 12000 Frame

  - HPE Synergy 480 Gen9 Compute Modules

  - HPE 3PAR StoreServ 8200

  - HPE Pointnext

  - HPE Proactive Care

  - HPE Factory Express Services

  - HPE Installation and Deployment Services

  - HPE Technical Training

Nadeem Hussain, Assistant Vice President, Technical Services and Engineering, RioCan, says about the solution: "We were looking to consolidate our hardware while reducing operational and capital costs. We've not only saved $300,000 over three years, we've gained performance, high availability, reliability, and consistency, and simplified management. HPE Synergy is the way to go."

 Note

To read the entire case study, visit:

https://www.hpe.com/h20195/v2/Getdocument.aspx?docname=a00058189enw

Sunkist Growers and HPE infrastructure components

Sunkist Growers, Inc., is a not-for-profit marketing cooperative, based in Valencia, Calif. Established in 1893, Sunkist is owned and operated by thousands of California and Arizona citrus growers who make up its membership. The Sunkist cooperative offers more than 40 fresh citrus varieties produced by family farms where traditional growing practices, stewardship of natural resources, and a dedication to innovation are proudly passed through the generations.

- **Industry challenge:** Sunkist is the largest citrus cooperative in the world, marketing millions of cartons of premium fresh citrus internationally each year. Like any business, Sunkist must keep the wheels of demand and supply moving in tandem. Unlike most businesses, in the fresh produce industry the cooperative's products are vulnerable to spoilage; fruit must not sit on docks waiting to ship.

- **IT challenge:** To keep produce fresh throughout the distribution process, Sunkist relies on its Fresh Fruit Marketing System, used by sales and shipping personnel to place, ship, track, and receive orders. Sunkist was migrating the Fresh Fruit Marketing application from its 25-year-old legacy platform to a new Microsoft SQL Server platform. Along with this upgrade, Sunkist wanted to strengthen its overall recovery capabilities for such a critical application by moving off tape and disk backup, and bring all network resources into a fast-recovery solution. Another key application is Sunkist's Microsoft Navision financial system.

- **Solution:** Sunkist turned to its trusted services provider Key Information Systems (KeyInfo) for KeyCloud Disaster Recovery as a Service (DRaaS) and Backup and Recovery as a Service (BRaaS).

- **Results:** With the HPE-powered DRaaS and BRaaS solutions, Sunkist has been able to automate approximately 95% of its recovery process. The cooperative's recovery time for its Fresh Fruit Marketing System has accelerated from four hours to 15 minutes and its financial system from 25 hours to 15 minutes. Before, if the Fresh Fruit Marketing System went down, Sunkist would have kept its business going with pen and paper order processing until systems were restored—and they would have to manually catch up on everything that had transpired since the previous night's backups. Now, they can restore to a state within 15 minutes of the present. This not only minimizes the impact on business operations, but also helps with security. For example, if the company were hit with ransomware, Sunkist could return rapidly to the state just before the malware hit. Internal audits are also no longer a resource challenge to Sunkist's IT staff. With

KeyInfo handling DR and backup, the IT staff can focus more time on projects that are more strategically important to the business.

- **Hardware:** HPE Apollo 2000 Systems with HPE ProLiant XL170 Servers, HPE ProLiant DL360 Servers, HPE ProLiant DL380 Servers, HPE 3PAR StoreServ 8440 Storage, HPE Altoline switches

- **Software:** Prophet PR3 supply chain management software (Sunkist Fresh Fruit Marketing System), Microsoft SQL Server, Microsoft Navision

- **Services:** KeyCloud DRaaS and KeyCloud BRaaS from KeyInfo

Clayton Weise, Director of Cloud Services, KeyInfo, says: "Sunkist is completely virtualized in its production environment; they can grow resources as needed. In contrast, its DR environment was based on an older style of restoring from backups onto machines that are in place. Now with KeyInfo Cloud Services, they can scale dynamically based on their needs."

 Note

To read the entire case study, visit:

https://h20195.www2.hpe.com/V2/GetDocument.aspx?docname=a00040401enw

---

How to get to the solution like this?

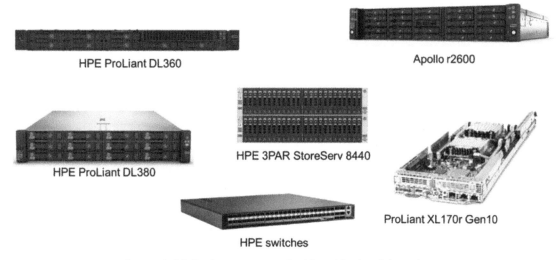

HPE ProLiant DL360

Apollo r2600

HPE ProLiant DL380

HPE 3PAR StoreServ 8440

HPE switches

ProLiant XL170r Gen10

Figure 1-18 Sunkist growers—Building blocks of the solution

How to get to a solution with the building blocks shown in Figure 1-18? You may not have the tools or knowledge to help these clients, but the next chapters will walk you through the day in the life of a typical Solutions Architect and along the way we will provide you with all the skills, knowledge, and tools you need from HPE to be your next customer's hero!

Learning check

4. Name the consumption-based IT model from HPE Pointnext.

_____

_____

_____

_____

_____

5. Write a summary of the key concepts presented in this chapter.

_____

_____

_____

_____

_____

_____

_____

_____

_____

_____

_____

_____

_____

_____

_____

_____

_____

_____

_____

_____

_____

Summary

- HPE Reference Architectures and HPE Reference Configurations include complete configuration, sizing, bill of material, and deployment details.

- HPE is a company built on the idea of innovation. HPE is accelerating the customer's digital transformation agenda: transformation of technology, people and processes, and economics.

- Achieving the optimal IT operating model, Hybrid IT for apps and data will help enterprises to move faster and with less risk. HPE makes Hybrid IT simple for this reason.

- The world is now hybrid because business problems are hybrid.

Prelearning check

Before proceeding with this section, answer the following question to assess your existing knowledge of the topics covered in this chapter. Record your answers in the space provided.

1. You are in a meeting with a customer, and they challenge you with a statement: "I heard that the configuration process required to prepare a quote is time consuming, with a high risk of errors and risk of ordering incompatible components"

   How should you respond?

   _____

   _____

   _____

   _____

   _____

   _____

   _____

   _____

   _____

   _____

   _____

   _____

2 Understanding the customers' Hybrid IT requirements

LEARNING OBJECTIVES

After completing this chapter, you should be able to:

✓ Describe how to assess each customer's requirements and environment to develop an HPE server solution, including how to perform:

- Needs analyses

- Requirements, segment, and workloads analyses

- Site surveys

✓ Explain the benefit of Reference Architectures.

✓ Name the design considerations that should be taken into account when planning Hybrid IT solutions.

✓ Identify typical decision trees when selecting Hybrid IT solution platform.

✓ Identify the HPE tools that can be used to select solution components when designing a solution.

✓ Describe the process of developing solution proposals.

✓ Describe possibilities for solution installation, configuration, and setup.

Architecting Hybrid IT solutions

We are presented with our course protagonist, a solution architect (SA), who has just been hired at one of HPE's top partners. The SA gets a phone call at the desk from the sales team, and they are presenting a new opportunity to help a customer. They give the customer scenario and the problem. What would they do first to help the customer?

This chapter will guide you through how and what to think about when gathering customer requirements, which tools to use, and how to make platform decisions.

Assessing the customer's requirements and environment

When planning and developing an IT solution, the business and IT needs of the customer should be assessed. These assessment results should be used to guide the implementation planning process. When all customer information has been gathered, your experience and knowledge can be used to recommend the best possible solution. The IT recommendation is ultimately described in the statement of work (SOW). However, before a solid SOW can be developed, the specific needs, expectations, and environment for the solution must be understood. Thorough planning helps to avoid potential costly mistakes and prepares an upgrade path for the future.

Understanding the scope and constraints of the design

Before starting to assess customer requirements, understand the scope and constraints of the design, including the:

- General scope and purpose
- Implementation time lines and time frames
- Budget

If budget is a constraint, consider presenting multiple solutions—an optimal solution that exceeds the budget and a solution that meets the budgetary requirements.

Assessing the customer's requirements and environment

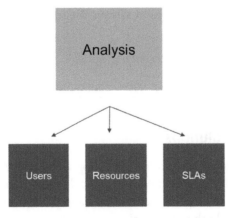

Figure 2-1 Analyzing a customer's infrastructure

When you are planning an HPE Hybrid IT solution, one of the first tasks to perform is an analysis of the customer's current infrastructure and the applications the customer plans to run on the infrastructure, as indicated in Figure 2-1. Several factors should be considered, including:

- **The number of users for the application**—The number of users has a direct impact on the amount of CPU, memory, networking, and storage resources that will be required.

- **IT resources required by the application**—The application installation or user guide should offer recommendations regarding the amount of CPU, memory, networking, and storage resources that will be required for the application.

- **Applications that can be consolidated**—Are there any applications that no longer provide business value? If so, could they be retired, or could a different application deliver better results?

- **Service-level agreements (SLAs) in place for the various business organizations**—SLAs have a direct impact on the hardware and software that will be required. For example, a solution capable of achieving 99.999% availability will need to be designed with no single points of failure (SPOFs) and will require redundant components, duplicated systems, and clustering software. If the solution is not considered business critical and will only be expected to achieve 99% availability, redundant components, duplicated systems, and clustering software will not normally be required.

- **Customer's current methodology**—Assess the customer's current infrastructure and processes to ensure that any new solution will integrate with their existing framework.

 Note

A service-level agreement (SLA) is a commitment between a service provider and a client. Particular aspects of the service—quality, availability, responsibilities—are agreed between the service provider and the service user. The most common component of SLA is that the services should be provided to the customer as agreed upon in the contract (Wikipedia.org, April 2019).

Conducting a needs analysis

A needs analysis starts with a customer interview. Ask questions to determine current challenges, ways to address those challenges, and business goals. Understanding a customer's needs is crucial to developing a positive, long-term relationship.

If a customer has experience with server, storage, and networking technologies, ask questions about intended solutions. Consider asking questions in the following categories:

- Future plans
  - What are the business goals?
  - What is the projected role of the server?

- – What is the projected operating system?

- – To which kind of network will the server be connected?

- Business requirements

  - – What are the capital expenses?

  - – Are there any total cost-of-ownership (TCO) requirements?

  - – Are there any return on investment (ROI) requirements?

  - – How does a solution impact the users?

  - – How does a solution help business analytics?

- Current environment

  - – How much storage is currently used?

  - – Have storage needs grown over the last 12 months?

  - – If networking is part of the solution, what is the technology (speed, port type) used today?

- Technical requirements

  - – What is the expected availability of the solution?

  - – Is price more important than functionality?

  - – Is a rack or tower configuration preferred?

  - – Will backups be performed? How long does the backup need to be stored? What is the daily change rate?

  - – How are the storage needs to be accessed? File-based or block-based?

  - – Is power protection needed?

  - – Does the storage capacity need to be on premise?

  - – Which kinds of system management tools are needed?

  - – Does the solution need to be configured from the component level, or does it need to be ready to install out of the box?

  - – What level of maintenance and support is desired?

- Obstacles

  - – What is the biggest IT problem facing the business today?

  - – What does the customer believe are possible solutions?

  - – What are the barriers to the solution?

- Resources

    – Is the customer willing to commit resources to achieving these goals?

    – Is the customer willing to let technical professionals help guide the way?

- Nontechnical considerations

    – Are there any open service calls or other customer sensitivities?

    – Who is the contact person for IT solution implementation within the customer's organization?

    – Are the customer's applications standardized?

    – Is there a long-term IT strategy in place?

    – Are there any rules in place for hardware isolation among business units?

Based on answers to these questions, recommendations can be made about which solution components are required and which are optional. For example, if file and print is the projected role for the server, storage capacity and transfer rate are important selection factors. Alternatively, if the server will be a database server, processor speed and memory are the primary considerations. The required port count and port speed will be considered for the selecting network device. Capacity, availability, and performance parameters are usually the most important selection factors for storage components.

It is important to align the right solution by workload and use case. Even with self-selection, there is workload affinity to certain classes of infrastructure.

- For small deployments, consolidating a few applications with good price/performance, but limited SLA requirements, start with MSA2x00 and consider SimpliVity or Nimble for more data services.

- For a virtual machine (VM) and virtual desktop infrastructure (VDI) environment, productivity and collaborations, small private cloud for VMs, or moderate Structured Query Language (SQL) database (DB) demands, start with SimpliVity and consider Nimble if your customer is open to a new approach but has physical hosts and non-hyper-converged needs.

- For DBs, emerging applications, Storage-as-a-Service with VMs, Microsoft applications, or container environments, start with Nimble and consider 3PAR for greater configurability, performance, and multi-tenant, multi-arrays scale.

- For a large private cloud, performance DBs, HPE Synergy-attach, IT-as-a-Service (ITaaS), VMs, and online transaction processing (OLTP) analytics, start with 3PAR and consider XP7 for extreme availability and/or mainframe connectivity.

For a cost- and performance-optimized solution for data protection ingest and recovery with extensive independent software vendor (ISV)/app support to consolidate backup from multiple sources, start with StoreOnce/Recovery Manager Central (RMC). StoreOnce and RMC is a comprehensive and low-cost backup solution.

To understand business value and value selling, this simple formula is a good starting point:

Profits = Revenue – Expenses

Demonstrating business value consists of creating additional profit for customers by influencing the components of this equation. This can mean a growth in revenue, a reduction in expenses, or both.

Value selling is the process of helping customers connect IT to their business and measuring the potential improvement in business value if they decide to change their IT strategies. This process leads to a much stronger customer relationship and, ultimately, increased sales.

IT has become a significant part of corporate spending. Large IT budgets require executives to be involved in IT spending decisions. Business executives focus on revenue, profitability, and ROI.

To guide customers' IT purchasing decisions, solution architects should assume the role of business consultant.

To make the best decisions for their companies, business executives need to understand the impact of IT investments on their business.

Rationalize IT investments relative to other strategic investments (such as research and development, plant, and equipment). Evaluate the financial case for investing in new technology.

Disruption is affecting the storage industry

Figure 2-2 Current trends in storage industry

Always consider current trends when assessing customer requirements, such as indicated in Figure 2-2:

- The all-flash data center
- The software-defined data center
- Multiple consumption models

 Note

Does the storage solution design consider current trends?

Similarly, current trends need to be assessed for other components of the solution, such as servers and networking. If they are not, a reasoning needs to be prepared for customers' question related to why a specific modern technology is missing.

Focus on business requirements

For solutions that address business needs, focus on business requirements when assessing storage requirements.

- Reduce risk

  – Ensure compliance with regulations

  – Protect data

  – Ensure data integrity

- Address current deficiencies

  – Provide more space

  – Ensure scalability

  – Improve performance

- Improve efficiency

  – Fit the same capacity in a smaller space

  – Reduce power consumption

  – Provide centralized management

Assess customer requirements

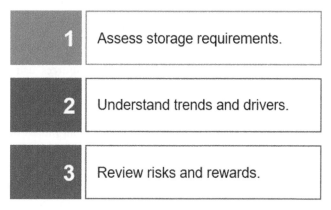

Figure 2-3 Key steps to understanding customer storage requirements

Powerful trends drive enterprise information and data storage, forcing organizations to review current-generation tools and strategies to find the ideal balance between data storage, cost, and performance. It is also increasingly important, as indicated in Figure 2-3, to assess storage requirements and rationalize, standardize, and consolidate data placement in a multi-tier storage environment.

Data poses real challenges to many organizations because of its dramatic growth in volume and diversity. As a result, companies and government agencies struggle to understand their true data requirements, and optimize the crucial data storage environment.

Understand trends and drivers

In a global economy that remains sluggish and less than predictable, executives are under pressure to generate growth, control costs and risk, and meet customer and constituent demands for innovation, transparency, and anywhere, anytime interactions. Savvy leaders seek to build organizations capable of responding instantly and cost-effectively to meet those challenges and opportunities.

This puts tremendous pressure on technology units at a time when IT is facing its own unique set of hurdles. Mergers and acquisitions continue to test the adaptive capabilities of many IT shops. Disruptive technologies such as cloud computing, ubiquitous mobility, and social media are reverberating across all industry sectors. In addition, applications are proliferating at an unprecedented rate.

These tectonic forces are driving explosive growth in the volume and diversity of enterprise information and present significant data storage challenges to organizations of all kinds. A 20% or greater annual growth in the amount of data to be stored is not unusual, and for many organizations, rates of data growth are even higher.

This growth is causing many organizations to investigate cloud storage options to accommodate some of this nonmission-critical storage growth. Gartner points out these key challenges to choose the right storage for cloud-native applications:

- Overprovisioning storage resources by "prematurely optimizing" without identifying key application characteristics and scalability requirements can result in high platform costs.

- Misconfiguration and mismanagement are the leading causes of data breaches for applications deployed and data stored using public cloud.

- Mobile applications typically communicate with remote resources using HTTP, rather than Network File System (NFS) and Common Internet File System (CIFS), complicating deployments using traditional protocols.

There are many reasons—external and internal—for this exceptional rate of data growth and why it will continue. More stringent and numerous government regulations require organizations of nearly every kind to collect and keep data in specific formats for longer time periods. Examples of these include Sarbanes-Oxley reforms of 2002, the Health Insurance Portability and Accountability Act (HIPAA), SEC rules 17a-3 and 17a-4 governing transaction related data, the Federal Rules of Civil Procedure, and other information-retention laws.

Business mergers and expansions can contribute to creating data storage silos that hinder easy access and information sharing. Disruptive new technologies and users generate vast amounts of unstructured data, leading to storage, duplication, and information management problems across organizations.

To better serve customers and constituents, organizations collect and retain information in greater volumes and in more detail. Further increasing data volumes and duplication, companies tend to share more data between departments and across global supply and value chains. Internal data policies often contribute to these difficulties. As users cancel their accounts, many organizations continue to maintain account-specific information, sometimes for extended time periods. That and other poor processes yield orphaned data for which owners cannot be identified. Even when organizations have good data retention policies, they all too frequently fail to communicate, implement, or enforce these important rules.

Executives typically recognize the value of well-managed storage, but lack the time, resources, or expertise to pursue that objective. Even when an organization makes the effort to analyze storage requirements, it might lack the resources and commitment needed to execute the resulting recommendations.

Storage-specific issues can exacerbate these data challenges. Data storage is typically the part of infrastructure environments least understood by organizations. Because they often lack the system engineering expertise needed to successfully plan and manage modern storage architectures, organizations can become reactive, which often leads to uncontrolled data placement through storage growth, over performance, and higher-than-needed storage costs.

To keep pace with growth and cover spikes, for example, companies tend to over-build and under-use storage environments—much like buying a luxury car to make once-a-week trips to the grocery store. Many have adopted a hardware-centric view of storage—a perspective that can produce overly complex storage environments. By opting for the "cheapest box" at every refresh cycle, organizations can create inconsistent environments that lack standardized tools. Globalization puts additional stress on traditional—and often rigid—IT, storage infrastructure, and operations. Mergers and acquisitions have forced many IT groups to deal with multiple inherited storage environments, difficult server consolidations, and market-specific requirements for data retention.

All those challenges are compounded by significant and ongoing budget constraints. There is a widespread belief that storage is getting cheaper, because hardware costs are indeed declining. This perception, however, ignores the 50 to 60% of non-hardware costs that drive up the total cost of storage ownership. Furthermore, because storage is rarely seen as a strategic issue, organizations tend to resist storage-related capital investments.

At the same time, information is recognized as the highest valued enterprise asset. Stakeholders expect and demand improvements in storage performance and greater data access, confidentiality, and integrity.

Review risks and rewards

Without an adequate assessment and rationalization, data storage can be a difficult and costly challenge. An inefficiently planned storage strategy is often focused primarily on application volumetric consumption as opposed to application requirements based on strategic business objectives.

Storage assessment and rationalization provides visibility into how data is actually used, where information is and should be stored, along with the relative costs and advantages of available storage tiering. Other issues can include reduced hardware use, redundant software licenses, and higher-than-needed staffing costs.

On the other hand, a carefully analyzed, rationalized data environment follows a forward-looking strategy designed to correctly balance true storage costs and requirements. A robust storage rationalization assessment can help to:

- Reduce total cost of storage ownership through standardization, consolidation, and business-optimized data placement.

- Leverage multiple storage tier options and a rational placement strategy to ensure high performance for crucial data, and cost efficiency for less critical information.

- Improve the return on storage investment by maximizing hardware and software use.

- Gain visibility and insight into enterprise data and storage environments, and open a roadmap to a more effective and cost-efficient future state.

- Drive operational consistency while reducing expenses and improving cash flow.

- Leverage standardization to reduce storage complexity, while enhancing data classification and management capabilities.

- Align storage tiers closer to actual application business data requirements.

Meet challenges with storage lifecycle management

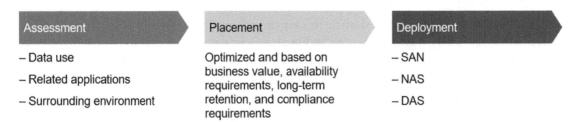

Figure 2-4 Meet challenges with storage lifecycle management

To meet data-related challenges and opportunities, a comprehensive information management and storage lifecycle management strategy is needed. Based on balanced and rationalized storage resources governance, a lifecycle model provides a sound methodology for assessing true data storage requirements, as shown in Figure 2-4. The process leverages a set of sophisticated toolsets to rationalize optimal data placement. This approach then recommends specific deployment strategies across enterprise and departmental storage tiers and generates validated storage governance rules.

This model can be used within an existing architecture or across a proposed storage architecture, including private storage utility, cloud-based Storage as a Service, hybrid storage, or traditional enterprise storage environments.

Assessment

To ensure optimal results from any storage rationalization program, the effort must begin with a thorough storage assessment, including data use, related applications, and the surrounding enterprise environment.

The purpose of a storage rationalization assessment is twofold: First, identifying the current placement of data across storage tiers; and, second, recommending initial classification and information placement based on the data's true performance requirements. Simply put: Storage rationalization assessment categorizes where data should be.

A robust, three-phase approach to storage assessment is recommended.

- An initial phase should establish the scope and assessment objectives.

- The substantive collection and collation phase should focus on collection, validation, and interpretation of relevant data points, and typically includes face-to-face interviews with storage instance experts.

- A third phase presents the results of the storage strategy, including a description of the current state, recommended optimal data placement in the desired future state, and expected results of the planned migration.

By creating a snapshot of current data placement and establishing a roadmap for the transition to a rationalized storage environment, an assessment should make a clear business case for any and all recommended changes. A reliable assessment will identify costs and challenges, potential savings, payback periods, ROI projections, and performance benefits of situating data in higher-performing storage tiers.

As with most analytics, the quality of a storage rationalization assessment depends heavily on the methods and granularity of the evaluation. A comprehensive approach is recommended for any storage assessment. A robust assessment should examine and interpret any interdependency that might affect storage, including:

- Workload profiles to determine storage characteristics of various applications and associated data

- Storage platform characteristics to best match storage devices, configurations, and connection modes to application requirements

- Standardized storage solution sets capable of supporting multiple workloads

- Methods to select optimized storage placement

A good assessment examines tactical details such as input/output (IO) rates, read/write ratios, data age, availability requirements, and other historical technical metrics. Any reliable analysis should also address more strategic business-level measurements, such as expectations for data growth, security requirements, migration considerations, latency tolerances, cost, and potential outages impact.

Depending on an organization's needs, a storage assessment might be done in association with data center modernization, as part of a larger storage management program, or in relation to backup, recovery, or email archiving initiatives.

Placement

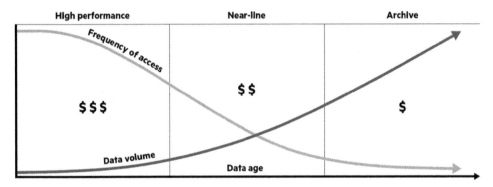

Figure 2-5 Relationship among data age, access, and volumes, and the general variables used to determine data placement

How to determine where best to locate data? In general, data placement should be optimized based on its underlying business value, availability requirements, and long-term retention or compliance requirements. To better understand where and why information should be stored, it might help to review the basic variables of enterprise data, as illustrated in Figure 2-5.

As data ages from minutes to days, months, and then years, the probability of it being used again declines dramatically. Data created in the last few minutes has a high probability of being accessed in the near future, while data that is several years old has a near-zero probability of reuse. Even though data volume grows over time, far more data is several years old than data that is several minutes old.

Cloud computing, ubiquitous mobility, and social media are reverberating across all industry sectors. Moreover, applications are proliferating at an unprecedented rate. These tectonic forces are driving explosive growth in the volume and diversity of enterprise information and present significant data storage challenges to most organizations.

Those two key variables—volume and access requirements—guide many data placement decisions. Because recently created data is likely to be needed again soon, and there is far less of it, that information is best located on high-performance, higher cost storage tiers. Conversely, much larger volumes of older, seldom-needed data can and should be situated on lower-cost, lower-performance storage tiers.

A storage rationalization assessment provides organizations with storage governance to determine initial data placement and an optimum middle ground, which maximizes data performance while minimizing storage costs. By reducing data clutter on higher-end and more expensive enterprise-class storage tiers, this approach optimizes the balance of performance and cost.

A detailed storage roadmap provides the tactical details needed to position data for initial placement and the strategic ability to adapt to changing business or regulatory requirements over time.

Beyond these broad principles, organizations must make granular decisions about precisely which data should be deployed on a given storage tier.

Deployment

Based on assessment and placement evaluations results, an organization can choose from a number of data storage tiers. These tiers offer various levels of reliability, functionality, cost, and availability.

- **Enterprise SAN (E-SAN)**—Storage area network (SAN) infrastructures can meet a range of storage requirements. E-SANs are director-based, feature block-level IO and are ideally suited to meet large database, data warehouse, and high-performance requirements. When compared to network-attached storage (NAS) environments, SAN offers higher availability and performance.

- **Enterprise NAS (E-NAS)**—Organizations can consolidate file data through a dedicated NAS infrastructure. E-NAS leverages file-level IO to deliver reduced costs and improve use in a large file server environment.

- **Departmental SAN (D-SAN)**—Switch-based D-SANs feature block-level IO and are well suited to smaller database and messaging environments.

- **Departmental NAS (D-NAS)**—D-NAS, featuring file-level IO, is an appliance-based solution for departmental file and print servers.

- **Direct-attached storage (DAS)**—DAS provides digital storage to single or multiple computers in a non-networked environment.

Multiple tiers enable optimized data placement, based on an organization's business, technical, and compliance requirements.

SAN solutions can be implemented at an organization's location or at a site operated by a storage services provider. NAS is used to consolidate storage from multiple remote locations in a single data center, gaining improvements in management efficiency and storage use.

Utility pricing and provisioning, available in a managed storage service environment, enable the organization to pay only for the storage needed, when it is needed. This pay-as-you-go model eliminates hardware-related capital spending requirements. Managed storage providers typically offer a range of options, based on an organization's volume, performance, and functional requirements.

Because utility capacity can be added or removed in just hours, customers do not need to build, maintain, or pay for excess storage capacity. SAN-based utility services, in particular, can be reprovisioned quickly to handle data storage growth, reallocation, or reconfiguration requirements. Managed services deliver well-known economies of scale, further reducing overall data storage costs. This model also gives the organization access to current technologies and best practices on a predictable operating cost basis.

Capacity calculations

Basic capacity calculations include:

- **Primary data**—GB stored by OS

- **Annual growth rate**—5 to 30%

- **Primary capacity**— Data x $(1+Growth\ rate)^{Years}$

- **Protection data**—Number of snap retention days

- **Daily change rate**—1 to 2%

- **Protection capacity**—Primary capacity x #Snap x Change rate

- **Array capacity required**—(Primary capacity + Protection capacity)/Data reduction rate

Matching customers to the best platforms

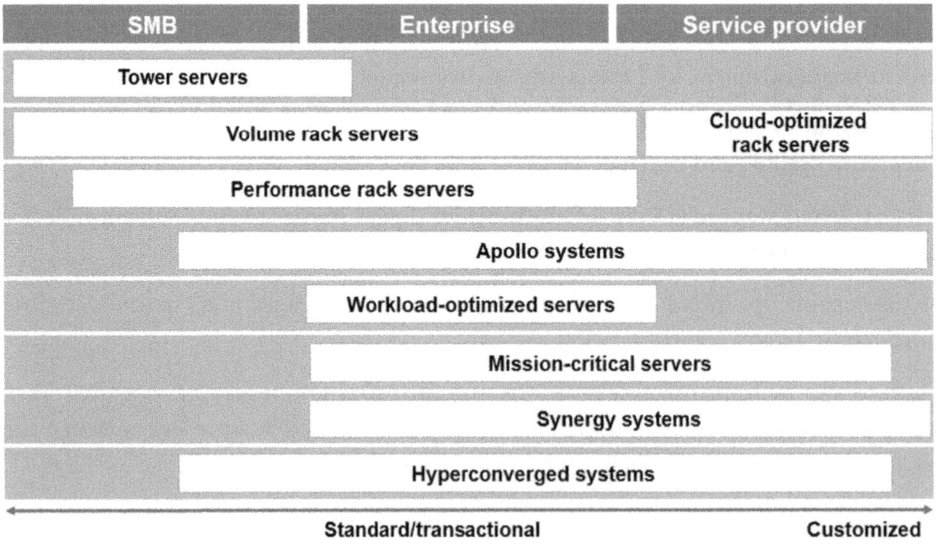

SMB	Enterprise	Service provider
Tower servers		
Volume rack servers		Cloud-optimized rack servers
Performance rack servers		
Apollo systems		
Workload-optimized servers		
Mission-critical servers		
Synergy systems		
Hyperconverged systems		

Standard/transactional   Customized

Figure 2-6 High-level guidance regarding which HPE servers might be suitable for SMBs

All customers have different needs, and there is no substitute for completing a full needs analysis. However, Figure 2-6 provides useful high-level guidance regarding which HPE servers might be suitable for small- to medium-sized businesses (SMBs), enterprises, and service providers.

There are different types of service providers, such as telecommunications, application, storage, and internet service providers (ISPs). There are three tiers of ISPs, including:

- **Tier 1** service providers are considered the highest ISP class. A Tier 1 ISP has its own IP network in a particular region connected with the primary internet backbone or other Tier 1 ISP. Typically, a Tier 1 ISP sells bandwidth to Tier 2 and Tier 3 ISPs, which provide internet connectivity to businesses and individual customers.

- **Tier 2** ISPs purchase their internet service from a Tier 1 ISP and tend to cover a specific region, and focus on business customers.

- **Tier 3** ISPs also purchase their internet service from Tier 1 ISPs. Tier 3 ISPs tend to cover a specific region and focus on the retail market.

Evaluating the business requirements

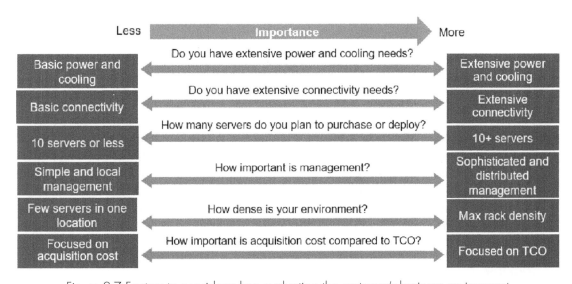

Figure 2-7 Factors to consider when evaluating the customer's business environment

When evaluating the customer's business environment, the factors listed in Figure 2-7 should be assessed and the importance of power and cooling, connectivity, deployment scale, management tools, server density, and TCO focus should be recorded.

Examples of questions that can be asked are:

- **Infrastructure**—Are there extensive power and cooling and interconnect needs?

- **Node count**—How many servers is the customer buying?

- **Management tools**—How important are management tools? Does the customer provide in-house training on these tools?

- **Deployment density**—How dense is the environment?

- **Price**—How important is acquisition cost compared to TCO and ROI?

Analyzing the business requirements

Three analyses should be performed to thoroughly assess each customer:

- **Requirements analysis**—Using the answers to the business environment evaluation can guide the selection of a particular HPE server portfolio. For example, if the customer has a need for a deployment on a massive scale, HPE Synergy and HPE Apollo solutions should be explored. If the customer has a need for very high server density, HPE BladeSystem, Apollo, and Synergy products should be considered. Specific factors to evaluate include power/cooling requirements and interconnectivity.

- **Segment analysis**—Customer segment analysis can also be used to guide the selection of a particular server family. For example, customers in need of a High-Performance Computing (HPC) solution might benefit from Apollo, BladeSystem, and rack servers. For Tier 3 service providers, rack and BladeSystem solutions should be considered.

- **Workload analysis**—Analysis of the types of workloads the customer is running can also provide guidance in selecting a server family. It is important to find out if the customer needs support for virtualization, cloud, web infrastructure, database, app development, and so on. For example, SMB customers requiring servers for a small IT infrastructure should consider the HPE ProLiant ML family. Enterprise customers who need large deployments of servers in an application development environment should consider the BladeSystem family.

Conducting a site survey

After the needs analysis interview, it is important to conduct a site survey to assess the facility and evaluate its suitability for the proposed IT solution. Factors to consider include:

- **Site/facility suitability**—Server room size, layout, limitations, and interference

- **Site services/utilities**—Power delivery, fire suppression, and environmental controls

- **Physical security**—Key locks and card, code, or fingerprint access

- **IT integration**—Existing computing infrastructure

- **Applications/software**—Loads and availability
- **Human resources**—Ownership and internal or external support
- **Projected growth**—Computer, employee, and business expansion

To evaluate these factors, survey questions can be used to gather data. Example questions include:

- How large is the facility?
- Does the facility currently have any radio frequency interference problems?
- Is there any extra space available?
- Will an existing space need to be modified?
- Are adequate utility outlets available in the proposed space?
- Are the electrical circuits of sufficient capacity?
- Are the electrical circuits shared or isolated? Are they properly grounded?
- Are there additional electrical circuits available in the facility?
- What type of fire-suppression system is in place, if any?
- If overhead sprinklers are installed, are they water- or halon-based?
- What type of floors or floor coverings exist?
- Does the ceiling allow cabling to be run easily?
- Is there adequate ventilation for the space?
- Is extra cooling capacity available?
- Is the proposed space in the interior of the building, or does it have an outside window?
- Does the facility already use keypads, card readers, or other physical security devices to control access?
- How many workstations does the company have now?
- How many servers are in use?
- Is a recent inventory of company IT assets available?
- If there is an existing network, what is its topology?
- What kinds of IT equipment purchases are planned for the next 12 months?
- What kinds of software are used regularly?
- Is the software workstation- or server-based?
- What software purchases are planned for the next 12 months?

- How are IT support issues currently handled?

- Who is responsible for IT issues at the company?

- Will any IT staff be added?

- How many other employees will be added in the next 12 months?

- Does the company plan to open other offices in the next 12 months?

This list is not complete, but it should serve as a guide to effectively define a specific customer's environment. It is important to identify existing resources, such as network capacity or IT assets, which might be required during the transition to the new environment. The availability of resources also affects the implementation timeline. For instance, if no network cabling exists in the facility, the plan must include time to install the wires.

Although the plan can recommend simultaneous tasks, it is inefficient to have servers and workstations in place, waiting for interconnectivity to complete their configuration. The amount of time needed to set up the server and address dependencies must be determined.

Service-level agreements drive the solution

Figure 2-8 SLA example

SLAs provide a common understanding about services, priorities, responsibilities, guarantees, warranties, and penalties. When necessary, the SLA, as shown in Figure 2-8, can be modified to enable the deployment of less equipment and, therefore, reduce costs.

Several factors need to be determined and agreed upon with the customer:

- What performance levels are expected? Consideration needs to be given to CPU, memory, networking, and storage performance.

- What availability is expected? How will it be calculated?

- Are there any legal compliance requirements?

- How will the systems and data be secured?

- What are the data-retention policies?

  - Where is the data located?

  - What are the legal implications of storing data in a different jurisdiction?

  - When data is deleted (either accidentally or on purpose), can it be recovered?

Solution design considerations

The information gathered during the needs analysis and site survey should narrow the choices for the solution recommended to the customer. When applying the data, the following areas should also be considered:

- **Servers**—Will the solution consist solely of physical servers or a mix of physical and virtual servers? If the latter, what virtualization technology will be used? For physical servers, memory and processor technology components are important. Fault-tolerant memory or redundant processors are less crucial to a file and print server than they are to a database server, which primarily performs computations and requires temporary storage. Determining the relative importance of server technologies, together with the server's projected role, narrows the focus to a server with the required capabilities.

- **Storage**—Every server has storage, but deciding on a RAID or non-RAID configuration depends on factors such as cost, storage availability, and fault tolerance. For a file and print server, a non-RAID configuration leaves data vulnerable to disk failure or data corruption. This would be less important to a network-centric firewall server.

- **Networking**—Depending on the existing network topology or the decision for a new topology, server networking capabilities must also be determined. Current corporate networks are usually at 1 Gb/s; however, corporate backbones can exceed 10 Gb/s (Ten Gigabit Ethernet), and remote offices can remain at 100 Mb/s (Fast Ethernet).

- **Operating system**—The choice of operating system directly affects the server components. Generally, the more recent (and thus more advanced) the operating system, the greater its demands on system hardware. Certain operating system features can also steer the decision. Potential server purchases should be made based on careful consideration for meeting or exceeding the highest minimum system requirements.

- **Applications**—Often referred to as **workloads**, the applications that the customer needs to use will have a major impact on several design considerations. For example, if the main application is a mission-critical, multi-petabyte database application, it will be necessary to make sure that the server solution is designed with minimal SPOFs and with sufficient storage, networking, memory, and processor resources to ensure the smooth operation of the database application. Availability clustering should also be considered to make sure that in the event of a catastrophic failure, the application can continue to run (by failing over to a standby or secondary system).

- **Availability**—Workloads should be assessed for their level of business importance and housed on an appropriately available server solution. There might be applications that are not considered mission critical and can therefore be unavailable without significant business impact. These might be located on non-clustered virtual or physical servers.

- **Security**—When planning where to place the server and how it should be configured, it is important to consider security. Be alert for physical and virtual security holes. When an employee leaves an organization, it is important to recover any keys and access cards. It might be necessary to change locks and codes. Disabling the user account and changing high-level passwords to which an employee had access are good practices.

  - **Physical**—Security measures also involve locks, codes, and location. Deciding to place a server in an interior room with a locked door sufficiently addresses most physical security needs. Because the temperature and humidity in a windowless interior room remain relatively constant, there should be no need to keep the door open to enhance airflow. A closed and locked door ensures that only individuals with authority and access can enter.

  - **Virtual**—Passwords, permissions, and access control lists should also be secured. Setting up users, groups, and permissions addresses virtual security needs. Each user needs a password to access project files stored on the server, and being a member of a particular group allows or denies access to other network resources. Grant each user only as much access as they typically need using access control lists. All passwords should be changed regularly; meet a minimum length (as defined by the operating system); and include letters, numbers, and special characters.

BTO and CTO product SKUs

When designing a solution, it is important to understand two different approaches:

- **Build to order**—BTO products are prepackaged bundles kept in stock by HPE partners. They provide competitive pricing, off-the-shelf fast delivery, and worldwide availability; however, they only offer field integration of components. They are typically available from HPE within five to eight days, or immediately, if in stock at the distributor.

- **Configure to order**—HPE partners or customers can request CTO products directly from HPE. This approach offers maximum flexibility in product customization and factory integration of components. There are two disadvantages to CTO products: reorderable configurations are not possible across regions, and they carry longer quote and order cycle times. Availability ranges from 10 to 15 days, depending on the country and availability of components.

Physical or virtual servers?

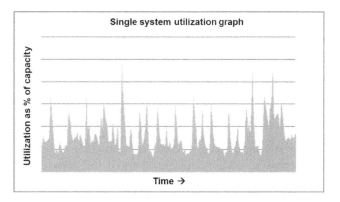

Figure 2-9 Each physical system is an isolated island of resources

Traditionally, servers have been acquired and deployed on an application basis. Each environment was configured to handle peak—not average—workload requirements. As a result, utilization rates could be as low as 30%. Although not an issue from a technical perspective, business leaders view this situation as a waste of valuable resources.

Many workloads exhibit utilization patterns similar to the workload shown in Figure 2-9. The peaks vary by time of day, and they tend to be for short durations. This means that most of the time resources are idle, but when they are required by a workload, they are required instantly.

Server virtualization enables customers to multiply their resource utilization by consolidating multiple applications onto a single server and dynamically balancing processing resources among applications. Server virtualization can optimize the use of available, and often limited, space. Technology surveys from Tech Pro and Gartner found that 75% of businesses either currently use server virtualization or plan to implement it in the near future, with respondents citing benefits such as a significant reduction in the time needed to deploy new applications, system downtime, and overall IT spending.

Note

- To read the full report on the Tech Pro Research survey, visit this site:

  http://www.techproresearch.com/downloads/research-smbs-discuss-current-status-and-future-adoption-plans-of-new-technologies/

- To read the full report on the Gartner survey:

  https://www.gartner.com/newsroom/id/3315817

IT departments are also frequently asked to provide more storage using budgets that are not increasing. Virtualization software residing between server hardware and software allows more applications to run on the server, and related hypervisor software enables the operating system and applications to move between servers. This allocates more resources where they are needed during periods of high demand. These server virtualization features also provide important redundancy capabilities and might be deployed as part of a comprehensive IT resiliency strategy.

Virtual machine design goals

VMs should be designed without bottlenecks so they can adequately meet the needs of users. To assist in the sizing process, it is possible to use an equivalent of the Amazon Compute Cloud (EC2) Compute Unit (ECU) VM instance. All Amazon EC2 instances are priced based on hourly usage and instance type. Each instance type consists of a certain number of ECUs and a set RAM size. The EC2 Standard instances, which are well suited for many applications, are:

- **Small**—One ECU (one virtual core with one ECU), 1.7 GB memory

- **Large**—Four ECUs (two virtual cores with two ECUs each), 7.5 GB memory

- **Extra large**—Eight ECUs (four virtual cores with two ECUs each), 15 GB memory

One ECU provides the equivalent CPU capacity of a 1.0 GHz to 1.2 GHz 2007 AMD Opteron or 2007 Intel® Xeon® processor (roughly equivalent to a PassMark CPU score of 400). The EC2 equivalent of a particular processor can be calculated by taking the PassMark CPU score for the 2.00 GHz Xeon® E5-2620, which is 9081. Divide this by 400 to get a score of 22 ECU. This means that the Xeon® E5-2620 processor in this example should be able to host approximately 22 small, five large, or two extra-large EC2-equivalent VMs.

Instance types above (T1 instances in Amazon terminology) were replaced by T2 instances in EC2 cloud. T2 instances are designed to provide moderate baseline performance and the capability to burst to a significantly higher performance as required by the workload. They are intended for workloads that do not use the full CPU often or consistently, but occasionally need to burst. T2 instances are well suited for general purpose workloads, such as web servers, developer environments, and small databases. The ratio between CPU and memory is very similar: the small model is one vCPU and 2 GB, the large model is two vCPUs and 8 GB, and the extra-large model is four vCPUs and 16 GB of memory.

 Note

For more information on PassMark CPU scores, visit:

http://www.cpubenchmark.net/cpu_list.php

According to Gartner, the recommended network bandwidth for each VM should be at least 100 Mb/s for IP traffic and 200 Mb/s for SAN traffic. Internet Small Computer Systems Interface (iSCSI) handles only IP traffic, so the bandwidth becomes 300 Mb/s for IP traffic.

Although 100 Mb/s for IP traffic is not always considered ideal, it is generally sufficient as a starting point. In a highly virtualized environment, there is a large amount of IP traffic coming from the system, and this can result in many cables emerging from a single enclosure. In this scenario, it might be necessary to specify a switch such as the HPE 59xx or HPE 125xx to provide top-of-rack (ToR) functions.

VM design guidelines

When designing a VM oversubscription ratio, there are four aspects to consider:

- Processing capacity per VM

- Memory per VM

- IO per VM

- Licensing cost

Together, these elements create a balanced virtualization design for the data center.

Processing capacity per VM

To enable customers to make a fair comparison of VM solutions, HPE has made use of an absolute VM processing capability. This is equal to a former ECU m1.small (one ECU, one CPU core, and 1.7 GB RAM) and close to the ratio that customers often use. A ratio of 36:1 works well with loads that typically use 2% to 3% of a dedicated server. If there are loads with lower typical use and no correlated peaks in traffic, then customers sometimes use in excess of 100:1; however, this can cause an imbalance with other design constraints. Also, using very high virtualization oversubscription ratios requires consideration of the number of threads supported. This depends on the CPU choice and knowledge of the workloads.

Memory per VM

Initially, HPE recommends using guidance from the virtualization platform provider (VMware, Microsoft, Citrix, and others) to size memory. Additional memory might be required to satisfy the needs of the applications being hosted on the VM.

 Note

> Dropping under the VMware-recommended memory per VM might cause instability with some workloads.

Use caution when specifying memory, because increasing server memory to support more VMs has two significant downsides:

- The use of high-density, high-power devices to achieve very large amounts of memory can significantly increase the cost of memory. High-density dual in-line memory modules (DIMMs) such as 64 GB and 128 GB are relatively expensive when compared with lower-density DIMMs such as 16 GB and 8 GB. The current and future requirements for RAM need to be assessed, and the most cost-effective DIMMs should be selected.

- The cost of VM licenses can increase significantly with very large memory configurations. Microsoft recommends accounting for overhead required by Hyper-V by configuring an additional 10% to 25% of hardware resources.

The minimum memory size for VMware vSphere is 4 MB (for VMs using BIOS); the maximum size depends on the host. VMs that use Extensible Firmware Interface (EFI) require at least 96 MB of RAM, or they cannot power on the server. The memory size is required to be in increments of 4 MB. The maximum size for best performance represents the threshold beyond which the host's physical memory is insufficient to run the VM at full speed. This value changes in alignment with host conditions (as VMs are powered on or off, for example). In addition to a complete portfolio of VMware licenses, HPE offers HPE OneView for VMware vCenter, which seamlessly integrates the manageability features of ProLiant and BladeSystem servers, Virtual Connect, and storage solutions with VMware products.

 Note

For more information on ESX and ESXi VM memory overhead, visit:

https://docs.vmware.com/en/VMware-vSphere/6.5/com.vmware.vsphere.vm_admin. doc/GUID-81E25CBB-16D9-416B-AD6F-5A96D7CD0A2D.html

With Citrix XenServer, three factors determine the memory size of a XenServer host. These include memory consumed by the:

- Xen hypervisor itself

- Control domain on the host

- XenServer crash kernel

 Note

For more information, refer to the *Citrix XenServer 7.2 Administrator's Guide*. To download the guide, visit:

https://docs.citrix.com/content/dam/docs/en-us/xenserver/current-release/downloads/xenserver-administrators-guide.pdf

---

IO per VM

The final technical constraint on oversubscription of VMs is on the IO bandwidth from the server to the core switch. HPE recommends 200 Mb/s storage and 100 Mb/s IP for each VM. With converged network adapters (CNAs) in a dual-resilient, high-availability configuration, each 10 Gb/s port pair can support 33 VMs. HPE uses dual CNAs on server blades; therefore, each blade can support 66 VMs in high-availability configurations. Additional CNAs can be added, if required.

The HPE Helion CloudSystem design splits off the Fibre Channel traffic in a BladeSystem c7000 enclosure. As a result, with 50 Gb/s resilient uplinks to the core switch and approximately 20% local IP traffic, 40 VMs per server blade can be supported. Adding a second pair of HPE Virtual Connect modules in the rear of the enclosure increases this limit to 65 VMs per blade. More VMs per blade can be supported if the demand for IP traffic is lower than the recommendation.

Licensing cost

The cost constraint on VM oversubscription is based on the cost of the hypervisor licenses. The licenses can dominate the cost of the raw compute elements and might be more expensive than the servers on which they run. In this case, a joint calculation on hypervisor and server costs will reveal the best oversubscription ratio.

Highly available designs

There are several approaches to designing a highly available IT environment. Most highly available environments use some form of hardware redundancy. The most basic form of hardware redundancy in a rack and tower server solution revolves around having redundant power supplies, fans, network interface cards (NICs), and more, so that if one component fails, the server continues running applications without interruption. In an HPE BladeSystem or Synergy environment, redundant power supplies, fans, NICs, and other elements should be complemented by redundant Onboard Administrator, Frame Link Modules, and Virtual Connect modules. Storage systems contain multiple/redundant array controllers and nodes, to provide load balancing and high available design. The network infrastructure also contains multiple switches/routers at the same layer for redundancy purposes.

Beyond protecting hardware resources with redundant components, software-based clustering solutions such as VMware high availability and Hyper-V clustering are available. These options can provide greater levels of availability instead of solely using the hardware redundancy method.

With software-defined data centers (SDDCs), high availability can be implemented using programmatic software control that can move server personalities (profiles) between servers automatically to maintain the required level of performance and availability.

Learning check

1. Which hardware components can increase availability of the server?

_____

_____

_____

_____

_____

_____

_____

Reference Architectures

HPE Reference Architectures deliver validated configurations for a wide range of customer use cases. Built on decades of HPE technical innovation and ISV expertise, these documents enable solution architects to find the right solution for customer business needs, as illustrated in Figure 2-10.

Driving tangible value

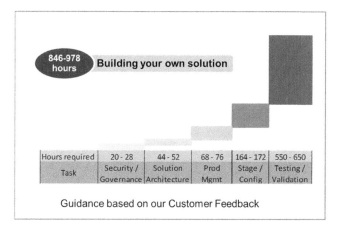

Figure 2-10 Reference architecture can significantly shorten the time to build and implement the solution

Based on HPE Core Enterprise Vertical Workload Research, 98% of IT decision makers use Reference Architectures for their infrastructure projects. Value of Reference Architecture includes risk mitigation, shorter time to value, TCO reduction, and improving business outcomes.

 Note

For more information on Reference Architectures, visit:

https://www.hpe.com/info/RA

Aligning RAs with business outcomes

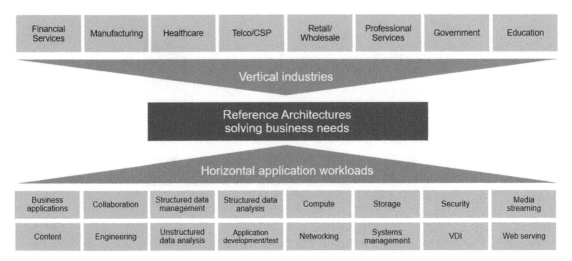

Figure 2-11 Reference Architectures solve business needs

Reference Configurations/Architectures are aligned with business outcomes, taking vertical industries and aligning them to application workloads. Reference Configurations and Architectures help solve business needs, as illustrated in Figure 2-11.

Two core deliverables: Reference Configurations and Architectures

HPE provides two core deliveries: Reference Configurations and Architectures.

Reference Configuration is a 10 to 15-page document that addresses the business problem and HPE's solution to the problem. It covers a high-level functional solution, with compelling use cases for the customer to consider the solution and covers infrastructure for new products, corner cases, and where Tier 1 coverage is not available. Limited or focused engineering testing may be required to create the paper.

When to use Reference Configurations:

- Breadth of workload coverage for new product launches

- New/smaller ISVs (start small and validate use case)

- Use cases/platform combinations where technical validation is not difficult

- Rapid response to competitive situations or field-identified solutions

Reference Configurations are primarily written for business decision makers and high-level technical decision makers (less technical content).

Reference Architecture is a 30 to 50-page document that covers the business problem, HPE's solution to the problem and proof with validation of test results. It covers both a functional and technical solution, with capacity sizing and limits of the configuration and targets use cases where more than one part of stack is in play (compute, storage, networking, converged system, and so forth). It also contains guidance and best practices for the workloads that cover all the layers of the workload and is often wrapped with automation scripts for services enablement.

When to use Reference Architectures:

- Tier 1 workloads that maximize revenue impact

- Customer problems with viable and proven solutions that can be implemented using HPE Pointnext or partners

- Difficult technical challenges that require clear articulation of configuration needs

Reference Architectures are primarily written for technical decision makers (highly technical content).

How do today's IT customers buy—Buyer's journey

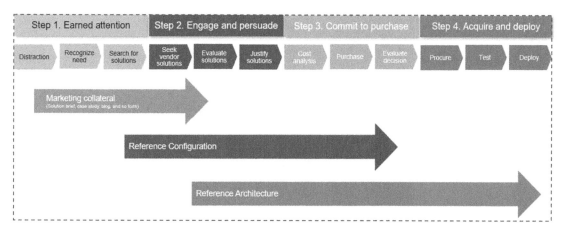

Figure 2-12 Steps of a buyer's journey

As indicated in Figure 2-12, typical customer's stages along the buying journey are:

- Earned attention

- Engage and persuade

- Commit to purchase

- Acquire and deploy

Reference Configurations are useful when customers are searching for solutions, seeking, evaluating, and justifying vendors.

 Note

Visit the links below to download additional documentation:

- Reference Configuration for VMware Horizon 7 on HPE ProLiant Gen10 servers:

  http://h20195.www2.hpe.com/V2/GetDocument.aspx?docname=a00018552enw

- Reference Configuration for Exchange 2016, SharePoint 2016, Skype for Business 2015, Windows Server 2016 on HPE ProLiant DL380 Gen10:

  http://h20195.www2.hpe.com/V2/GetDocument.aspx?docname=a00022804enw

- Reference Configuration for building a VMware AlwaysOn Digital Workspace with HPE ProLiant DL380 Gen10 servers:

  http://h20195.www2.hpe.com/V2/GetDocument.aspx?docname=a00019928enw

---

Learning check

2. HPE Reference Configurations are primarily targeted to business decision makers.

   ☐ True

   ☐ False

Selecting an HPE platform

Depending on workload, performance, capacity, and features required following decision trees can be used to select appropriate server, storage, and networking platforms, as illustrated in Figures 2-13 and 2-14:

Selecting HPE server platform—Synergy, ProLiant, Hyper-converged

Modular infrastructure? High amount of servers needed?	HPE Synergy
Traditional infrastructure? Lower amount of servers needed?	HPE ProLiant ML/DL
Integrated solution with storage, networking, compute, and virtualization?	HPE SimpliVity

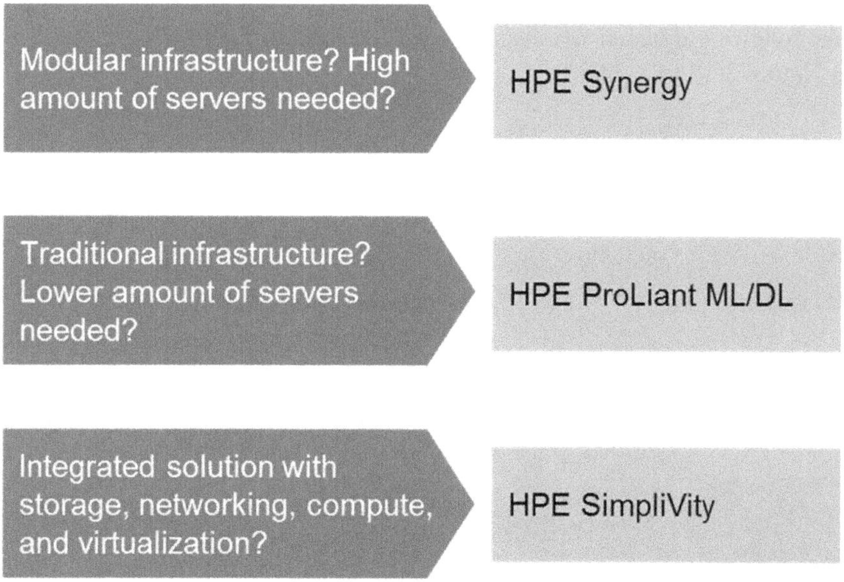

Figure 2-13 Selecting HPE server platform—Synergy, ProLiant, Hyper-converged

Selecting HPE server platform—Converged System, Apollo, Integrity

Integrated and optimized solution for specific workloads?	HPE Converged System
Purpose-built platform for HPC workloads?	HPE Apollo, HPE Superdome Flex
Purpose-built platform for Big Data?	HPE Apollo 4200/4500
Mission critical environment?	HPE Integrity portfolio, HPE Superdome Flex

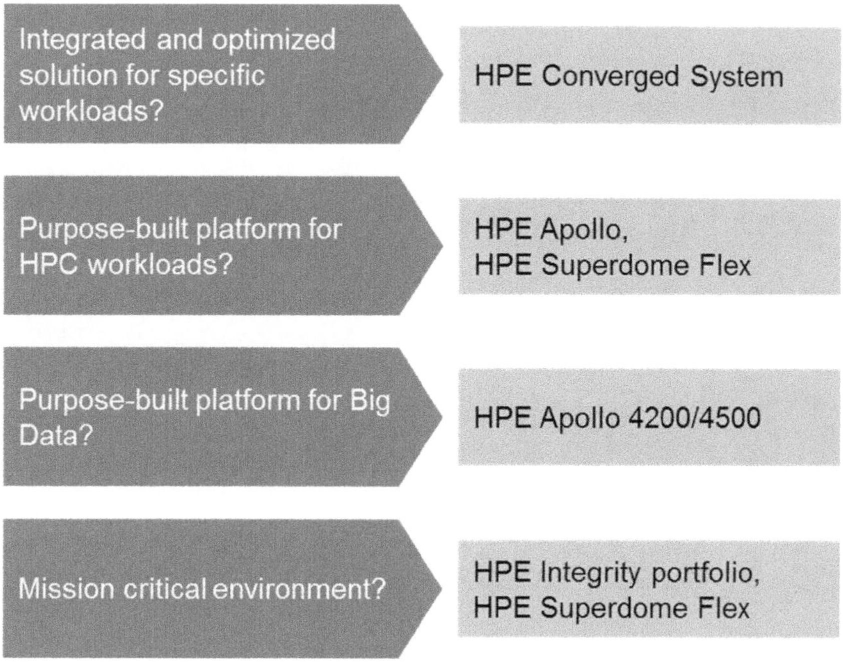

Figure 2-14 Selecting HPE server platform—Converged System, Apollo, Integrity

Selecting a Gen10 DL server

Depending on workload, performance, memory and storage requirements, and requirements for expansion, the following decision trees can be used to select an appropriate Gen 10 DL server, as illustrated in Figures 2-15 to 2-23:

Workload

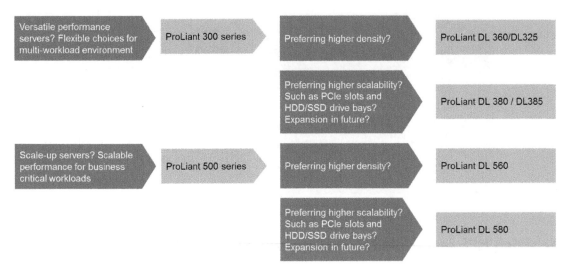

Figure 2-15 Selecting a Gen10 DL server

Performance and memory requirements

Figure 2-16 Selecting a Gen10 DL server

Internal storage requirements and PCIe expansion

Figure 2-17 Selecting a Gen10 DL server

Smart Array controllers

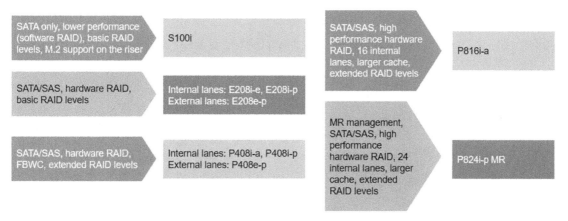

Figure 2-18 Selecting a Gen10 DL server

Network cards—Type of the network card

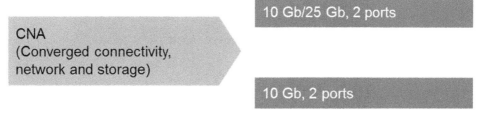

Figure 2-19 Selecting a Gen10 DL server

Network cards—Ethernet

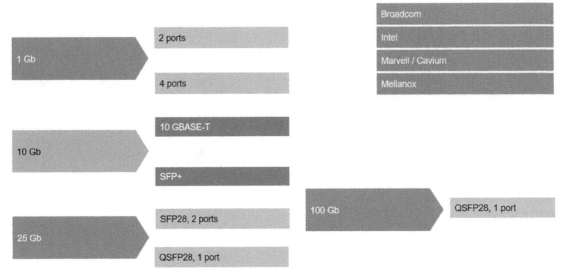

Figure 2-20 Selecting a Gen10 DL server

PCIe riser for DL325/DL360 Gen10

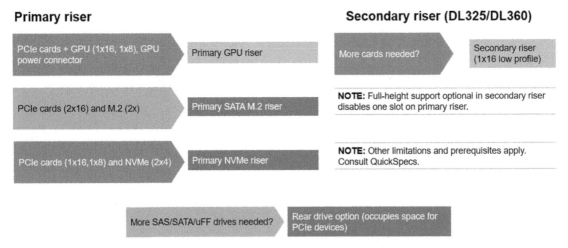

Figure 2-21 Selecting a Gen10 DL server

 Note

Full-height support, optional in the secondary riser, disables one slot on primary riser. A secondary riser requires two CPUs. Other limitations and prerequisites apply. Consult QuickSpecs.

PCIe riser for DL38x/DL560 Gen10

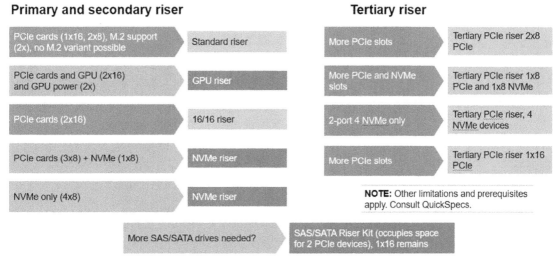

Figure 2-22 Selecting a Gen10 DL server

 Note

A secondary riser requires two/four CPUs. Other limitations and prerequisites apply. Consult QuickSpecs.

Selecting a density-optimized platform

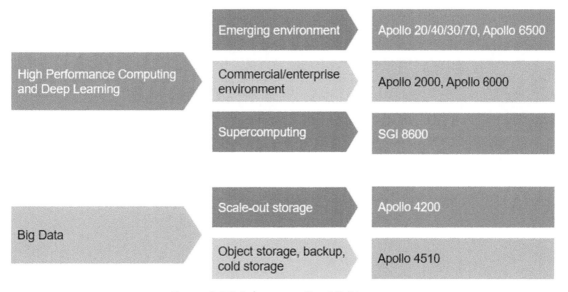

Figure 2-23 Selecting a Gen10 DL server

Selecting an HPE Storage platform

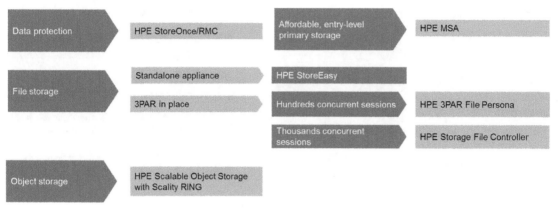

Figure 2-24 Selecting an HPE Storage platform

 Note

Consult the QuickSpecs for the full portfolio.

Selecting an HPE Storage platform: Nimble or 3PAR?

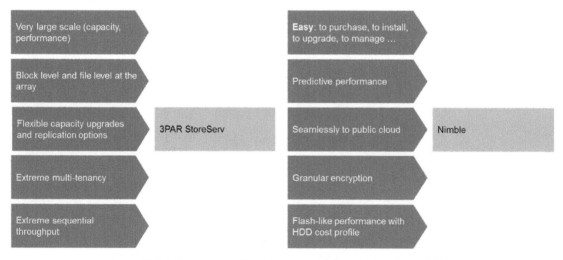

Figure 2-25 Selecting an HPE Storage platform: Nimble or 3PAR?

Selecting the Nimble All-Flash model

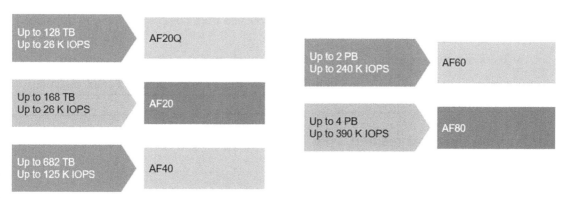

Figure 2-26 Selecting the Nimble All-Flash model

Note

- Effective capacity is based on a 5X data reduction from compression and dedupe on a single node.
- The maximum capacity numbers reflect what each model is capable of handling.
- Performance is based on a random mixed 50/50 R/W on 4 KB blocks, 2X dedupe.

Selecting the Nimble Adaptive Flash model

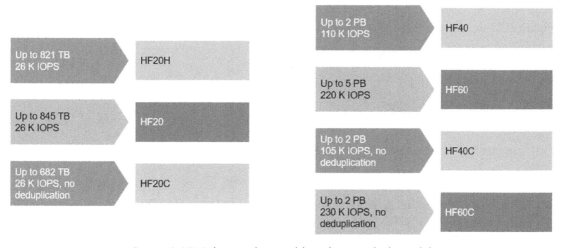

Figure 2-27 Selecting the Nimble Adaptive Flash model

Note

- Effective capacity is based on a 5X data reduction from compression and dedupe on a single node.

- The maximum capacity numbers reflect what each model is capable of handling.

- Performance is based on a random mixed 50/50 R/W on 4 KB blocks, 2X dedupe.

Configuring the most resilient HPE 3PAR configuration

> Use the presales processes, tools, and other information documented in this presentation to determine the proper solution based on the customer requirements

Determine proper array model	**Add resiliency features**	**Reach the next level with multi-site capabilities**
– Performance plus growth – Capacity plus growth – Compaction expectations – Availability considerations	– Resiliency features – Sizing adjustments – Performance under failure and upgrade scenarios	– Adding backup – Adding replication – Adding automated failover – Ensuring proper support levels – Other data protection features

Figure 2-28 Configuring the most resilient HPE 3PAR configuration

Figure 2-28 shows steps in 3PAR Configuration process:

- Determine proper array model.

- Add resiliency features.

- Add multi-site capabilities.

Determine the proper array model

Select the proper array model, based on these considerations:

- What type of provisioning: Fully Provisioned Virtual Volumes (FPVV), thinly provisioned virtual volume (TPVV), TPVV deduped, TPVV compressed, or TPVV DECO (deduplication and compression)?

- What are the expected data reduction ratios based on proper analysis, including data types?

- What are the random or sequential/block size, read/write ratio, and response time expectations?

- What is the initial capacity requirement and the yearly growth?

- What is the initial performance requirement in input/output operations per second (IOPS), MBs, and response time plus the yearly growth?

- Set the compaction ratio expectation using the NinjaSTARS thin scan, NinjaCrawler, Get Thinner, and Adaptive Data Reduction (ADR) spreadsheet.

- Choose a four-node system and one ending in a 40- or 50-model number for the extra CPU/cache.

Add resiliency features

Consider following best practices to add resiliency to the solution:

- Change to four nodes to increase performance under failure/upgrade and avoid write-through mode.

- Change to a highly available (HA) enclosure to protect against enclosure failure.

- Add eight drives to even the drive count per cage, and avoid unusable space due to HA enclosure.

- Understand the pros and cons of HA enclosure regarding the additional availability versus the effects of large solid-state drives (SSDs).

- Check the planned initiator count against per port, per node, and per system limits in Single Point of Connectivity Knowledge (SPOCK).

- Check the port count against the performance limits per port, and adjust for persistent ports/replication.

- Check the spare space to see if you have enough space to rebuild under a failed enclosure.

- Check the performance overhead for use of advanced software features in addition to compression already added.

- Check whether changing to a smaller drive can improve performance from the node count installed.

- Make sure to order the direct-connect version for the enclosures.

Reach the next level with multi-site capabilities

Consider following best practices to add extra value to the solution:

- Add the All-Inclusive Multi-System Software license to enable replication (Remote Copy) and automated failover (Peer Persistence), if needed.

- Add the Data at Rest encryption license, if needed, and change to Federal Information Processing Standards (FIPS) drives.

- Add StoreOnce, if needed, as a backup target for RMC included in the all-inclusive base-system license.

- Add a target 3PAR system if needed for replication, choose the mode, and size the link.

- If a zero Recovery Point Objective/Recovery Time Objective (RPO/RTO) with automated failover is desired (Peer Persistence), check on additional link, cluster, and quorum witness requirements.

- If an end-to-end Persistent Checksum is desired, check SPOCK for supported operating systems and host bus adapters (HBAs).

- Choose the proper level of support, based on customer needs.

- Be sure the customer understands the benefit of setting up and paying attention to the call home functionality.

- Check on the environmental requirements where the arrays will be installed.

Selecting an HPE Networking platform

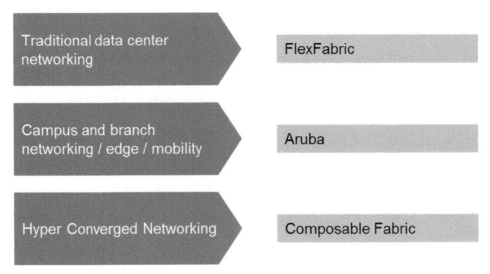

Figure 2-29 Selecting an HPE Networking platform

Which FlexFabric ToR/Leaf Switch should I use?

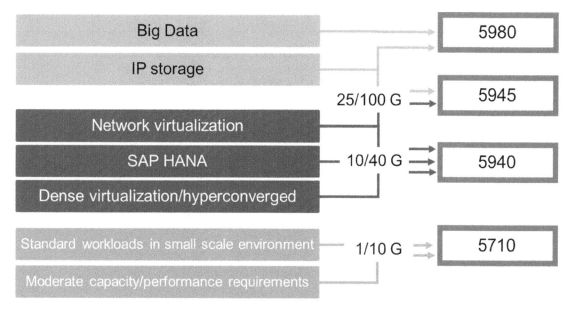

Figure 2-30 Know your application use case

Figure 2-30 illustrates quick specifications of selected HPE FlexFabric switches:

- **HPE FlexFabric 5980**—Big Data/Analytics, HPC, Scalable Packet Processing 1/10 G access, 40/100 G uplinks

- **HPE FlexFabric 5945**—Highest Performance ToR 10/25/40/50/100 G leaf, use 5950 32x100 GbE FOR small DC spines

- **HPE FlexFabric 5940**—DC Optimized ToR, 10/40 G access, 40/100 G uplinks, 4G/8 G FC module, VXLAN

- **HPE FlexFabric 5710**—Lowest TCO, 1/10 G access, 40/100 G uplinks

Learning check

3. Which HPE ProLiant Gen10 series should you recommend to a customer requiring multiple general-purpose servers with traditional 1U/2U/4U form factors?

    A. DL servers

    B. Apollo servers

    C. ML servers

    D. CL servers

4. Which parameters can be used to select a network card for a Gen10 DL server?

_____

_____

_____

5. Match the amount of processor sockets to the HPE ProLiant Gen10 server.

1 socket	DL380
2 socket	DL385
2 socket	DL580
4 socket	DL325

6. Which HPE ProLiant Gen10 series should you recommend to a customer requiring 6 TB of RAM and 10 PCIe 3.0 slots?

   A. MicroServer

   B. DL380 Gen10

   C. DL385 Gen10

   D. DL580 Gen10

7. Which Nimble storage solution should you recommend to a customer requiring 4 PB of effective capacity and 200,000 IOPS for random workloads?

   A. HPE Nimble AF20Q

   B. HPE Nimble AF60

   C. HPE Nimble HF60

   D. HPE Nimble HF60C

8. Which storage platform should you recommend to a customer requiring an affordable, entry-level primary storage?

   A. HPE Scalable Object Storage with Scality RING

   B. HPE 3PAR File Persona

   C. HPE MSA

   D. HPE 3PAR StoreServ

9. Which HPE networking device should you recommend to a customer requiring an affordable, data center switch supporting 1 Gb downlink ports and 40 Gb uplinks for a small-scale environment?

A. FlexFabric 5710

B. FlexFabric 5940

C. Aruba 8325-32C

D. HPE Altoline 9960

HPE tools for selecting solution components

HPE helps partners and customers create the best solution for each IT problem by providing multiple sizing and planning tools. Access to some tools might require registration. HPE offers a variety of configurator tools to guide you in developing appropriate IT solutions for customers. These tools streamline the ability to select and configure HPE products and to create quotes for you and your customers.

HPE Partner Ready Portal

Figure 2-31 HPE Partner Ready Portal

The HPE Partner Ready Portal delivers easy-to-find, personalized sales tools and resources to provide a faster and more collaborative sales engagement, training, demand generation, and business management experience, as shown in Figure 2-31.

It is a secure and trusted portal for resources including information in the following areas:

- Solution sizing and assessment

- Software downloads and licenses

- Software quoting tools

- Accessories, supplies, and services

Note

To access the Partner Ready Portal using an HPE Passport account, visit:

https://partner.hpe.com/

HPE Switch Selector

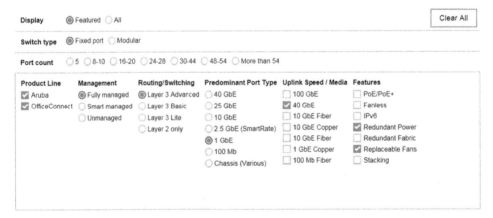

Figure 2-32 Filtering in HPE Switch Selector Tool

For Ethernet and TCP/IP-based storage solutions, an adequate switch might be needed. The HPE Switch Selector Tool, shown in Figure 2-32, can help architects to narrow product family selections based on network needs, infrastructure requirements, or competitive equivalents. The HPE Switch Selector allows you to view the complete HPE line of switches at a glance, and you can also sort the switches by port counts and speed.

Note

To access the HPE Switch Selector tool, visit:

http://h17007.www1.hpe.com/us/en/networking/products/switches/switch-selector. aspx

HPE Networking Online Configurator

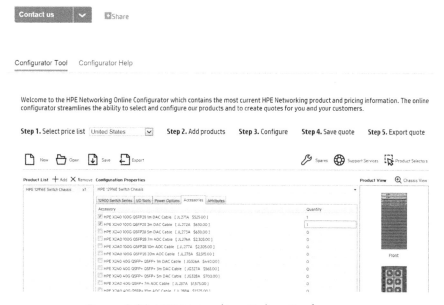

Figure 2-33 HPE Networking Online Configurator

The HPE Networking Online Configurator, shown in Figure 2-33, contains the most current HPE Networking product and pricing information. The online configurator streamlines the ability to select and configure our products and to create quotes.

The HPE Networking Online Configurator enables architects to quickly and easily create quotations of HPE products using web browser (Internet Explorer and Firefox are supported). Quotation files can be saved locally and can be exported in several formats, including Excel.

Product families included in the configurator:

- Aruba

- FlexFabric

- Routers

- Mobility controllers and access points

- Management tools

- Services

- And much more (Arista, Altoline, network virtualization …)

 Note

To access the HPE Networking Online Configurator tool, visit:

http://h17007.www1.hpe.com/us/en/networking/products/configurator/

HPE Proposal Web

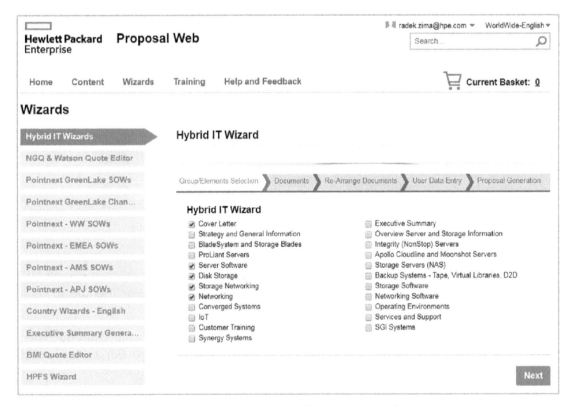

Figure 2-34 Hybrid IT Wizard at HPE Proposal Web

The portal also includes access to the HPE Proposal Web, shown in Figure 2-34. Proposal Web is an easy-to-use, web-based resource. You can create strong customer proposals quickly and easily using the HPE standard, global, online proposal platform. It offers a comprehensive library of up-to-date proposal boilerplate content along with a powerful tool suite for automated proposal assembly. This tool is used worldwide by sales representatives, proposal bid teams, and channel partners. It is structured around country- and region-specific portals with localized and translated content. Proposal Web content includes HPE products, services, and solutions as well as corporate and general information.

Figure 2-35 Selecting language variant

HPE Proposal Web, shown in Figure 2-35, offers the right resources to help with all your proposal-related sales activities. You can use this tool to:

- Prepare unsolicited proposals.

- Respond to customer request for information (RFI) or request for proposal (RFP) requests.

- Add boilerplate content to quotes or configurations.

 Note

To access the Partner Ready Portal using an HPE Passport account, visit:

https://proposalweb.ext.hpe.com

HPE One Configuration Advanced

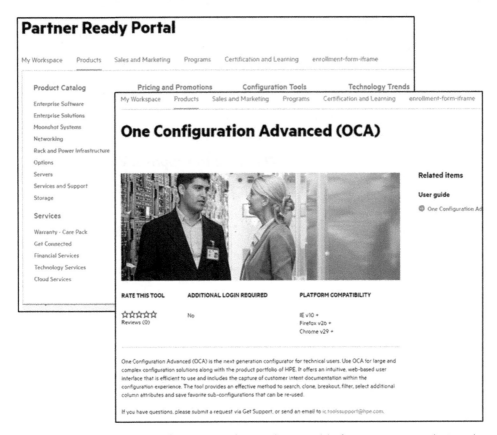

Figure 2-36 HPE One Configuration Advanced accessible from Partner Ready Portal

One Configuration Advanced (OneConfig Advanced, or OCA) is targeted to HPE internal, HPE distributor, and HPE partner use. New products are available to partners as a result of the recent SGI, SimpliVity, and Nimble acquisitions. To accelerate access, these new products are only configured on the new One Config Advanced (OCA) platform (not in Watson or SBW configuration tools), as shown in Figure 2-36.

 Note

- To download training slides for the One Configuration Advanced, visit:

    https://www.dropbox.com/sh/zpufstj6yqti9ip/AACrFOG63grHm_uFZc81T2GQa?dl=0

- To open the hyperlink to a video about the One Configuration Advanced, visit:

    https://www.dropbox.com/sh/rnylg57c60bwomz/AABzjgUyt3wr8wLs3DUQi0Xya?dl=0

Advantages of OCA:

- Allows a user to run multiple concurrent sessions

- Reliable performance supported by Akamai accelerators around the globe

- Minor configuration edits can be made without having to start over

- Ability to build configuration starting with any product (rack, server, blade, enclosure, switch, storage) and integrate them as required

- Automatic updates to Knowledge Base, which allows for real-time issue resolution rather than relying on large weekly downloads

- "Where Used" function finds instances where a Unique Configuration ID (UCID) or stock keeping unit (SKU) was used

- Visibility to recommended SKUs enables business units (BUs) to steer demand and meet delivery commitments

- Ability to configure on the go using a tablet (using supported browsers Chrome, Firefox, and IE)

- Configurations automatically save as you work

- Context-sensitive messaging throughout the application

- View into all saved configurations (not just orders) allows for detailed SKU demand analysis (by geography, by customer, and so forth)

- Comprehensive services view and edit capabilities for complete configuration or individual products therein

- Reverse engineers a configuration solution from an imported bill of materials (BOM) or SKU list

- Prevents unbuildable configurations by using "CLIC Check" functionality

- Provides configuration wizards for complex products, ensuring accuracy of products and services

- Power consumption report available for most configured products

- Reduces factory cycle times for select complex solutions by sending Config-to-Build (C2B) instructions when needed

- Eliminates memory and storage requirements for user's machine

- Eliminates timeouts and enables new business models like cloud services (for example: CS 500 appliances)

- Quickly scales solutions, from one rack to 55 racks in 3.5 minutes or less

- Share configurations within OCA directly with a distributor

- Share and reuse templates with "My Library"
- Set up work groups to share configurations easily
- Quote all existing HPE configuration types

Navigating the user interface: New Configuration, Open Configuration

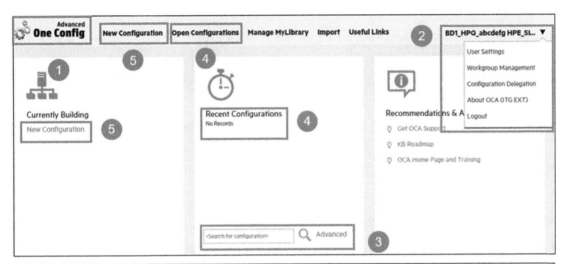

Figure 2-37 Navigating the user interface

The numbers, as illustrated in Figure 2-37, correspond to the information below regarding navigating the user interface:

1. **Home page**—Click the icon to go to OCA home page.

2. **User settings**—Click the login name to access the user setting page, to manage the workgroup, and to delegate your config.

3. **Simple Search/Advanced Search**—Use the search section for quick search and advanced searches.

4. **Open Configurations**—Open the local config file saved as ".oca" format, and view recent configs that are also displayed in the Recent Configurations section.

5. **New Configuration**—Click this tab to create a new config. You can also click the New Configuration link to initiate the process.

6. **Manage MyLibrary**—Click this tab to view and manage saved configurations, user-defined SKUs, and customer intent documents. Customer Intent Document (CID) can contain extra instructions such as special packaging, BIOS configuration, or OS patches installations.

7. **Import**—Click this tab to upload configs in a certain file format.

Other useful OCA links:

- **Currently Building**—OCA remembers your last configuration you saved and offers it in the Currently Building section.

- **Useful Links**—This tab provides links to useful configuration-related information.

- **Recommendations & Alerts**—This tab provides links to trainings, support, and a knowledge base roadmap.

Navigating the user interface: Managing MyLibrary, Import

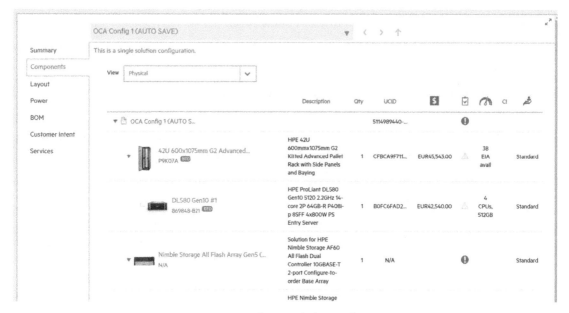

Figure 2-38 Working with the configuration

Working with the configuration, as shown in Figure 2-38:

- **Summary**—Provides an overview of the configured solution and shows users a picture of the product, summary of the configuration for this product, as well as any messages.

- **Components**—Provides physical or subconfiguration view of the configured solution with the possibility to change the configuration of the individual components.

- **Layout**—Provides a graphical representation of components inside a rack and enables specific customer-intent for memory cards, PCI cards, drives, servers in enclosures or racks, and so forth, to be conveyed.

- **Power**—Section provides estimates about power consumption (W, BTU/h, A) and other physical parameters like weight.

- **BOM**—Displays the BOM for the selected context; for the top level, the BOM shows the full solution.

- **Customer intent**—Various sections are available such as asset tag, BIOS configuration, or extra configuration instructions.

- **Services**—This tab allows users to customize the Care Pack Service for each product.

HPE Power Advisor

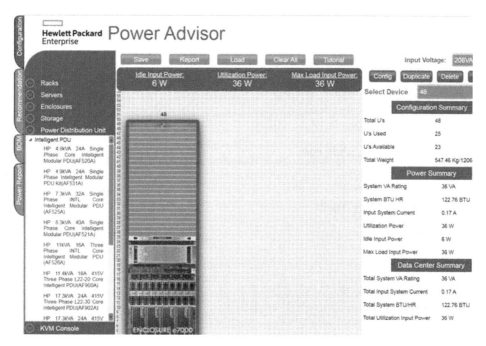

Figure 2-39 HPE Power Advisor

As information technology evolves and system density increases, systems housed in a single rack can now consume the amount of power once required for several racks. Effective sizing of a compute infrastructure while managing IT costs involves estimates of current and future power and cooling requirements. Accurately estimating the power consumption of a server can define power distribution requirements at the rack level and can be the starting point for estimating the total power consumption and cooling needs for a data center. This is one of many important factors when designing and expanding data centers or even planning rack deployments.

HPE has created the HPE Power Advisor utility that provides meaningful estimates of the power needs for HPE ProLiant, Hyperscale, Synergy, and Integrity servers. Our tool is used for estimating power use of the major components within a rack to determine power distribution, power redundancy, and battery backup requirements for computer facilities. Power Advisor allows you to configure each individual server or node. You can then duplicate the server configuration as often as necessary to populate an enclosure or rack, and then duplicate a rack. The outcome is that you can build a complete data center quickly.

Version 8.8 includes ProLiant Gen10 servers and options. A downloadable version for Windows and an online application are available. The Power Advisor online tool supports Google Chrome and Mozilla Firefox. As illustrated in Figure 2-39, this tool allows you to:

- Accurately estimate power consumption of HPE server and storage products.

- Select the appropriate power supplies and other system components.

- Configure and plan power usage at a system, rack, and multi-rack levels.

- Access useful tools, including a cost-of-ownership calculator, power report, and BOM.

 Note

To access the HPE Power Advisor, visit:

https://paonline56.itcs.hpe.com

HPE Synergy Planning Tool

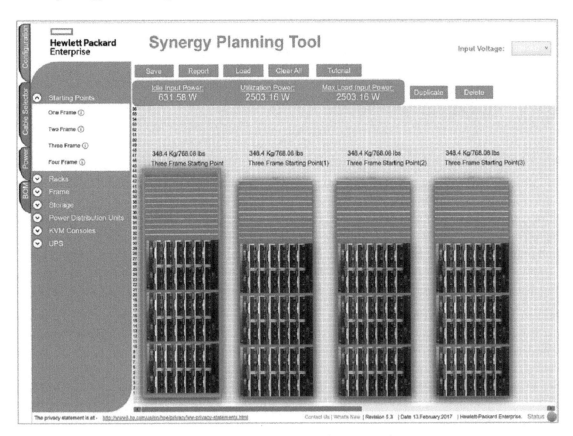

Figure 2-40 HPE Synergy Planning Tool

The HPE Synergy Planning Tool is an easy-to-use tool that helps in planning a Synergy solution by providing a configurator based on HPE Synergy product rules and best practices. The HPE Synergy Planning Tool provides a configuration, cable selection, and a BOM along with weight and power reports for data center planning.

When designing and expanding data centers or even planning rack deployments, it would be very helpful to have a tool that helps you in the design and uses the proper rules associated with the options installed. You also need to be able to estimate your power and weight requirements to ensure the appropriate levels of power and cooling as well as to determine weight-related requirements for the data center. HPE has created the HPE Synergy Planning Tool that provides meaningful information for build outs and installation verifications as well as power and weight needs for HPE Synergy solutions.

Features of the HPE Synergy Planning Tool, as shown in Figure 2-40:

- An easy-to-use tool for planning a Synergy solution

- Builds rack, frames, compute, storage, fabric, and power based on a set of rules for correct configuration

- Provides estimated power consumption and weights of the solution

- Offers both a system BOM and cables list for a given solution

- Provides access to useful tools, including a cost-of-ownership calculator, power report, and BOM

- Is downloadable and runs on the user's personal computer

 Note

To download the HPE Synergy Planning Tool, visit:

https://sizersllb.itcs.hpe.com/sb/installs/HPESynergyPlanningTool.zip

HPE SimpliVity sizing tools

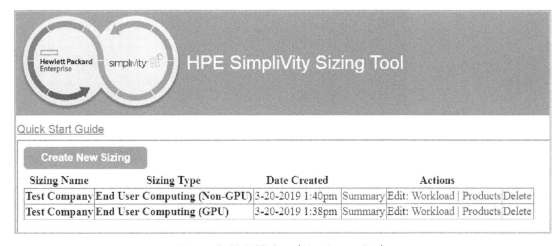

Figure 2-41 HPE SimpliVity Sizing Tool

The HPE SimpliVity Sizing Tool, shown in Figure 2-41, derives an optimal HPE SimpliVity Hyperconverged Infrastructure configuration for a specific set of customer requirements. It is a web-based utility that evaluates customer workloads and data protection policies across one or more physical locations, and then provides suitable SimpliVity-based product configurations.

After completing the sizing workflow, the tool provides a simple summary report of the specified customer requirements and selected infrastructure configuration.

To accurately size and build a SimpliVity configuration, it is critical to understand the footprint (current) and growth (future) needs of workloads that will be provisioned on or migrated to the new SimpliVity infrastructure. There are four general resources that need to be captured for each workload—CPU, memory, storage capacity, and storage performance.

There are two methods of collecting this information:

- Customer communication/conversation, with key technical and business contacts. This will derive quick estimates for certain resources, but will likely be insufficient to complete an accurate sizing.

- Programmatic data gathering, to instrument the existing customer infrastructure and profile workloads.

In most cases, conversation alone will not provide enough granularity to size effectively. A combination of both methods is recommended, especially in environments expected to yield large configurations (four or more hosts) to minimize margin of error.

 Note

To access the HPE SimpliVity Sizing Tool, visit:

https://hc4w01606.itcs.hpe.com/HPESizing/

Lanamark Data Gathering Tool

Lanamark Data Gathering Tool—Assessment of VMware infrastructure

The Lanamark Data Gathering Tool can be used to gather necessary performance and capacity information from current VMware, non-VMware, and physical environments.

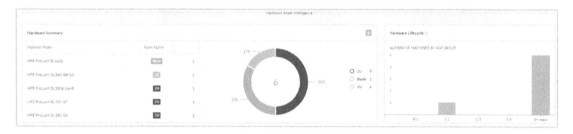

Figure 2-42 Lanamark Data Gathering Tool—Hardware summary

The typical sizing process, shown in Figure 2-42, includes:

- Install Lanamark snap or Lanamark Explorer on a windows host and point to the environment.

- Visit the Lanamark portal to review assessment.

- Extract data from Lanamark.

- Import data from Lanamark to the HPE SimpliVity Sizer.

- Produce possible configurations.

- An optimal configuration is selected and quoted.

 Note

To access the Lanamark Data Gathering Tool, visit:

https://hpe.lanamark.one/login

HPE Server Memory Configurator

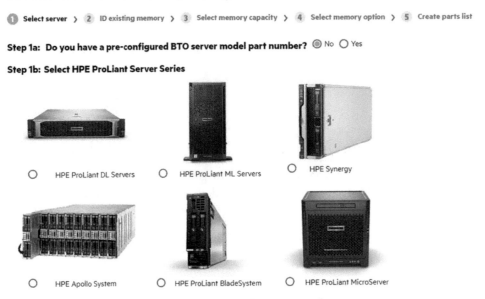

Figure 2-43 HPE Server Memory Configurator

The HPE Server Memory Configurator is a web-based tool used to assist with populating double data rate (DDR) memory in ProLiant servers. This tool provides optimal configurations based on memory population guidelines, as indicated in Figure 2-43. Non-optimal configurations are also shown for customers who require a specific memory configuration. The guidance provided is based on customer-provided information and does not guarantee specific performance.

This tool includes a five-step process that provides recommended memory configurations and RAM module installation locations:

1. Select the relevant ProLiant server.

2. Identify the existing memory (auto-detect memory with HPE Insight Diagnostics or manually enter current memory).

3. Select the memory capacity.

4. Select the memory option.

5. Create the parts list.

Note

To access the Server Memory Configurator, visit:

https://memoryconfigurator.hpe.com

SSD Availability Matrix

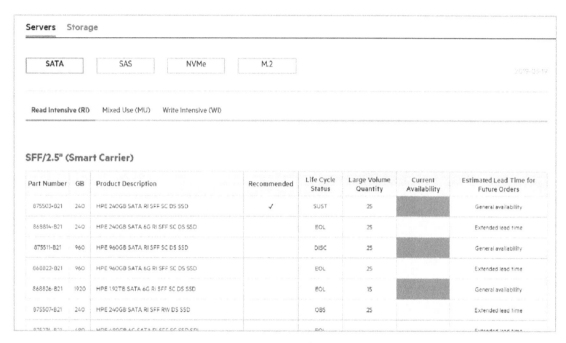

Figure 2-44 SSD Availability Matrix

The SSD Availability Matrix, shown in Figure 2-44, is a tool that can be used to find a suitable SSD model that is currently available.

In addition to servers and storage, now more products industry-wide use NAND flash technology, while SSDs progressively decrease in availability. Consequently, the suppliers that have been able to meet our demand are now no longer able to fulfill vendor's needs.

To prevent long lead times, please steer away from certain SKUs to ones with better availability. The recommended options depicted in the chart have a more robust stocking strategy, which means orders containing these options will have more predictable fulfillment times.

Availability status for each SSD part number:

- **Green**—Supply available

- **Yellow**—Constrained supply with extended lead times

- **Red**—Little or no supply. Incoming SSDs will be allocated to existing orders

Note

The SSD Availability Matrix is accessible from HPE Partner Ready Portal:

https://partner.hpe.com

SSD Selector Tool

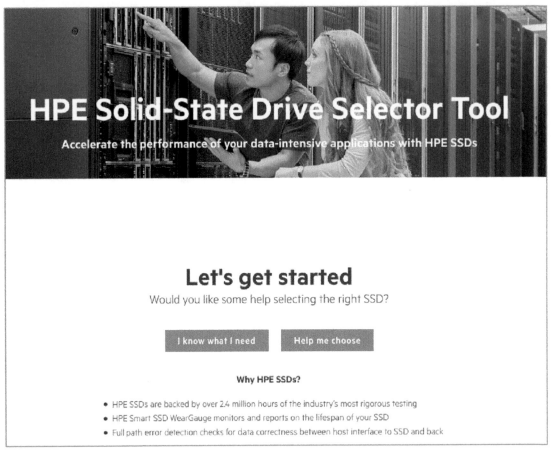

Figure 2-45 SSD Selector Tool

If you need help selecting solid-state drives for a customer solution, use the HPE SSD Selector Tool, as shown in Figure 2-45. This tool is a self-guided, online guide that leads you through drive options that can help accelerate the performance of a customer's data-intensive applications.

The SSD Selector Tool allows you to choose the SSD type, server type, drive capacity, interface type, and form factor. It also lets you select SSDs based on the qualities a customer might need from their SSDs, depending on the workload.

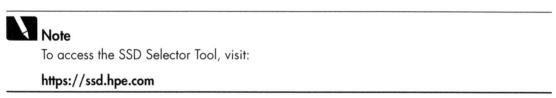

Figure 2-46 Filtering on the SSD Selector Tool

The SSD Selector Tool, shown in Figure 2-46, allows you to choose the SSD type, server type, drive capacity, interface type, and form factor. It also lets you select SSDs based on the qualities a customer might need from their SSDs, depending on workload.

Note

To access the SSD Selector Tool, visit:

https://ssd.hpe.com

HPE solution sizers

Sizers (31)	Type	Size	Date
HPE Storage Sizer	📄 PDF	123 KB	Nov 2018
HPE Sizer for ConvergedSystems Virtualization	📄 PDF	108 KB	Oct 2018
HPE Converged Infrastructure Solution Sizer Suite - installation file	⊞ ZIP	279 MB	Jan 2018
HPE Insight Management Sizer - installation file	⊞ ZIP	141 MB	Jan 2018
HPE Power Advisor - installation file	⊞ ZIP	79 MB	Jan 2018
HPE SAP Sizing Tool - installation file	⊞ ZIP	140 MB	Jan 2018
HPE Sizer for ConvergedSystems Virtualization - installation file	⊞ ZIP	201 MB	Jan 2018
HPE Sizer for Microsoft Exchange Server 2016 - installation file	⊞ ZIP	146 MB	Jan 2018
HPE Sizer for Microsoft SharePoint 2016 - installation file	⊞ ZIP	141 MB	Jan 2018
HPE Sizer for Microsoft Skype for Business Server 2015 - installation file	⊞ ZIP	141 MB	Jan 2018
HPE Sizer for the Elastic Platform for Big Data Analytics - installation file	⊞ ZIP	63 MB	Jan 2018

Figure 2-47 HPE solution sizers at the Hewlett Packard Enterprise Information Library

HPE offers several automated tools that assist with recommending a solution environment. The sizing information and algorithms in HPE solution sizers have been developed using testing and performance data on a wide range of HPE servers running solutions from partners such as Citrix, Microsoft, SAP, and VMware, as illustrated in Figure 2-47. These tools provide a consistent methodology to help determine a "best fit" server for the environment. Sizers are downloaded and run on the user's personal computer. Updates with the latest information on HPE hardware and solution software are available automatically when the user is connected to the internet and may optionally be installed by the user.

There are several solutions sizers available through the Hewlett Packard Enterprise Information Library, including:

- **HPE Converged Infrastructure Solution Sizer Suite (CISSS)**—Solution sizers from HPE are conveniently available through the CISSS. This suite provides an easy way to install sizers, consolidate the BOM generated by multiple sizings, access reference architectures, and more. You can use the CISSS to:

- List the HPE solution sizers, and select which ones to install through the Sizer Manager.

- Size an application solution using one of the installed solution sizers.

- Combine application solutions after two or more solutions have been sized and saved.

- Size an HPE ConvergedSystem solution.

- Calculate power requirements for a solution using Power Advisor.

- **HPE Sizer for Server Virtualization**—This automated, downloadable tool provides quick and helpful sizing guidance for HPE server and storage configurations running in VMware vSphere 5.0 or Hyper-V R2 environments. The tool allows users to create new solutions, open existing solutions, or use other types of performance data collecting tools, such as the Microsoft Assessment and Planning (MAP) Toolkit to build virtualized configurations based on HPE server and storage technologies. It enables the user to quickly compare different solution configurations and produce a customizable server and storage solution complete with a detailed BOM that includes part numbers and prices.

- Other sizers include:

  - Citrix Mobile Workspace

  - Microsoft Exchange Server 2016

  - Microsoft SharePoint 2016

  - Microsoft Skype for Business Server 2015

  - VMware ESXi on HPE Synergy Platform

 Note

To access solution sizers, visit:

https://hpe.com/info/sizers

HPE Storage Sizer

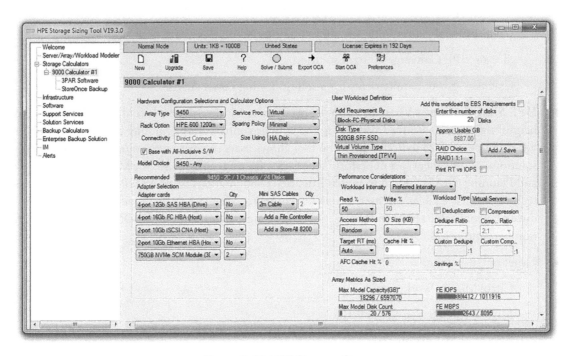

Figure 2-48 HPE Storage Sizer

The HPE Storage Sizer, as shown in Figure 2-48, is a sizing tool that helps you design a storage infrastructure to meet the needs of a customer. This is an important feature because it keeps the sizer current and any configuration prepared using this tool will be a valid, fully supported configuration.

The Storage Sizer supports the disk storage subsystem and other storage solutions such as backup systems, NAS solutions, and other storage components. The Storage Sizer requires a license.

Storage Sizer provides the following features and benefits:

- Simplifies the process of designing a storage solution

- Applies storage design, licensing, and services rules

- Provides output as a valid, supported configuration that can be imported directly into One Configuration Advanced (OCA) for a quotation

- Provides localized parts and pricing for different geographic regions

- Includes HPE Smart Update Technology, which brings new products or functionality through an internet connection

- Encompasses the HPE storage family

- Initiates an update for every product launch as part of the new product introduction process

- Includes new functionalities, which was added based on user input, annual surveys, and quarterly focus groups

The Storage Sizer enables you to work with your customers to design a storage infrastructure that will meet their online and offline needs. You can define customer requirements, such as:

- Performance requirements with specific metrics

- Business requirements, such as server consolidation

- Pure capacity requirements

For example, additional requirements might include raw capacity, estimated IOPS, replication and backup criteria, and the number of host ports.

Because the tool applies all the HPE SAN design rules, it provides a valid, supported storage infrastructure to meet the requirements of your customer. Use the Storage Sizer when you are not sure which combination of products will best address customer requirements. This tool lets you try different solutions.

A helpful wizard interface guides you through the process of sizing a SAN by asking a series of questions about the proposed configuration. This wizard is intended for those who have less experience using the Storage Sizer.

 Note

- For more information about the HPE Storage Sizer, visit:

  https://sizersllb.itcs.hpe.com/swdsizerweb/

- To download the HPE Storage Sizer, visit:

  https://sizersllb.itcs.hpe.com/sb/installs/StorageWorksSizer.zip

---

HPE iQuote Universal

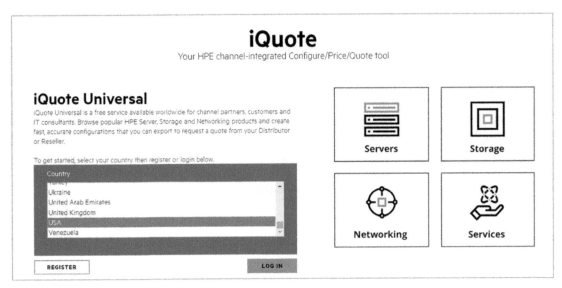

Figure 2-49 HPE iQuote Universal

iQuote Universal, shown in Figure 2-49, is a cloud-based service for channel partners that provides sales configuration and quoting features. This service simplifies the process of selling HPE products and helps users maximize revenue and margin on every sale. iQuote Universal generates quotes for products across the HPE portfolio, including ProLiant servers as well as HPE servers, storage, networking, and services. This includes Smart Buy Promotions.

This subscription-based software guides HPE partners through each step of the configuration process, includes real-time information on promotional pricing and stock, and notifies users of technical errors. Resellers and IT providers can select a product, create a configuration, export the information, and send a validated BOM to the distributor or supplier.

 Note

To access iQuote Universal, visit:

https://iquote.hpe.com/aspx/signin.aspx

HPE Product Tour

Figure 2-50 HPE Product Tour

HPE Product Tour is a downloadable application designed to demonstrate various HPE products, such as rack-based servers, the Apollo platform, Synergy, BladeSystem, and much more, as illustrated in Figure 2-50. It includes a demo loop mode and 3D models with the ability to drill down.

 Note

To download instructions for the HPE Product Tour, visit:

http://hpeservertour.com/Instructions_Guide_HPE_3D_Product_Tour.pdf

VisioCafe—Stencils for design documentation

Figure 2-51 VisioCafe

Some customer configurations can be complex and hard to present. The VisioCafe website, as shown in Figure 2-51, provides graphics that you can use with any version of Microsoft Visio to create diagrams and schemas for your proposed solutions. HPE not only provides storage subsystem graphics in this tool, but also provides graphics of servers or HPE networking devices. All graphics are free to download from the VisioCafe website.

VisioCafe can be especially useful when you are presenting the proposal, enabling you to show to the customer a graphical representation of a future solution, not just part numbers and quotations. This representation can enhance the selling process and influence the decision makers.

◤ Note

To access the HPE VisioCafe site, visit:

http://www.visiocafe.com/hpe.htm

HPE Product Bulletin

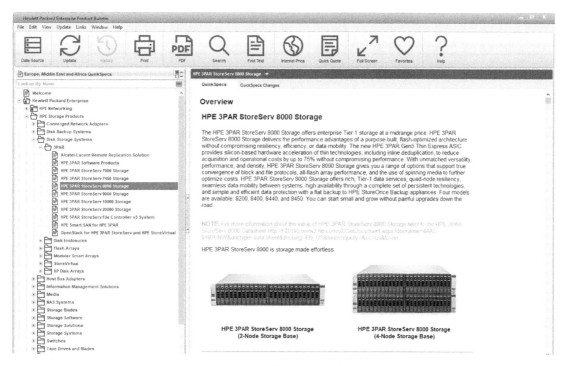

Figure 2-52 HPE Product Bulletin

The HPE Product Bulletin website, shown in Figure 2-52, is a convenient central resource that provides technical overviews and specifications for HPE hardware and software. The downloadable HPE Product Bulletin application is loaded with features to aid with the purchase, sale, and support of HPE products. The Product Bulletin contains the following useful features:

- Updated QuickSpecs

- Quick Quote

- Product photos

- "Locate by Name" search feature

- Advanced search capabilities

- Favorites

- Retired products

- Tip of the Day

Note

To access the HPE Product Bulletin, visit:

https://www.hpe.com/info/qs

HPE SAN certification and support

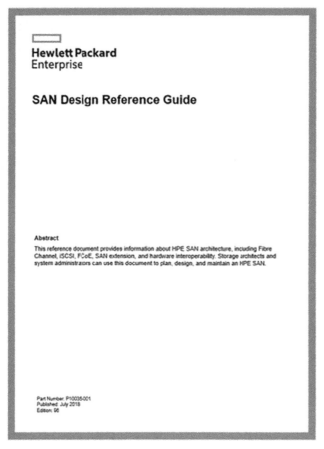

Figure 2-53 SAN Design Reference Guide

The SAN Design Reference Guide, shown in Figure 2-53, is the single source for SAN configuration support, interoperability, and best practices. The guide provides access to HPE multi-vendor, end-to-end storage networking architectural information, including:

- SAN design rules
- SAN topologies and supported configurations

- SAN design philosophies, security, and management

- HPE best practices

- SAN components

  - Architecture

  - Configurations

  - Implementation

  - New technologies

The SAN Design Reference Guide:

- Includes IP Storage implementations like iSCSI, NAS/SAN Fusion, Fibre Channel over IP (FCIP), Fibre Channel over Ethernet (FCoE), Data Center Bridging (DCB), and so forth

- Provides the benefit of HPE engineering when building a scalable, highly available enterprise storage network

- Documents HPE Services SAN integration, planning, and support services

 Note

To access the SAN Design Reference Guide, visit:

https://h20566.www2.hpe.com/hpsc/doc/public/display?docId=c00403562

 Note

Data center bridging (DCB) is a set of enhancements to the Ethernet local area network communication protocol for use in data center environments, in particular for use with clustering and storage area networks (Wikipedia.org, April 2019).

HPE Storage interoperability: SPOCK

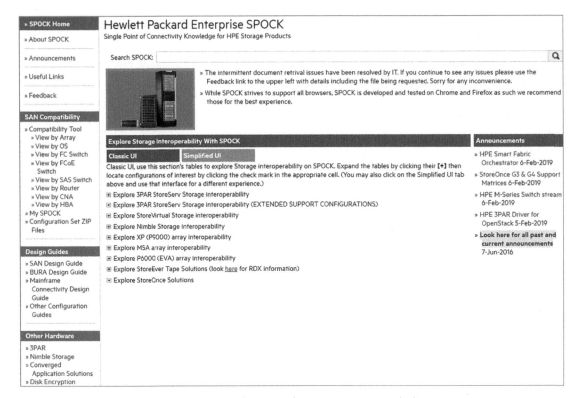

Figure 2-54 Single Point of Connectivity Knowledge

HPE Single Point of Connectivity Knowledge (SPOCK) is the primary portal used to obtain detailed information about supported HPE Storage product configurations, as shown in Figure 2-54. In SPOCK, you will find details of supported configurations (hardware and software) as well as other useful technical documents.

SPOCK provides the information to determine interoperability for integration of new products and features and maintaining active installations. HPE customers and partners require an HPE Passport to access.

 Note

An HPE Passport account is needed to access SPOCK. To access SPOCK, visit:

https://h20272.www2.hpe.com/spock/

HPE Assessment Foundry

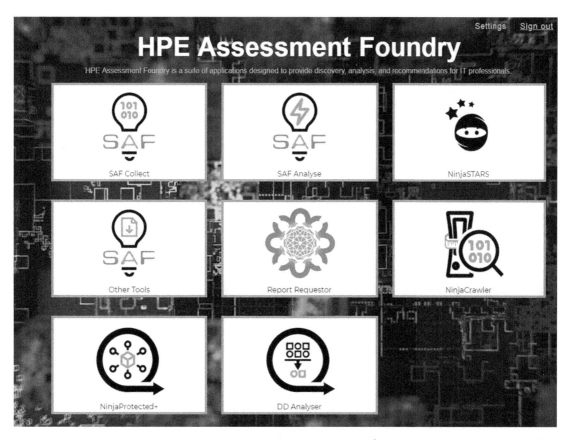

Figure 2-55 HPE Assessment Foundry

HPE Assessment Foundry, as shown in Figure 2-55, is a suite of tools for presales and internals only; it comprises several components that can be used for sizing, including Storage Assessment Foundry (SAF) Collect and SAF Analyze.

The collector is a lightweight and agentless tool that would be run against a customer's storage array to access the performance and configuration information from the array. Then, the data is securely uploaded to HPE and automatically analyzed.

When that is complete, you can go to the SAF self-service portal, view the summary, and drill-down into the analysis reports. This can be used to create a NinjaSTARS configuration.

The collector currently supports HPE 3PAR and EMC VMAX and VNX arrays. Additional third-party storage arrays are under development, and there is the potential to collect information from host systems as well as from the storage directly.

Note

To access HPE Assessment Foundry and all its tools, visit:

https://saf.itcs.hpe.com

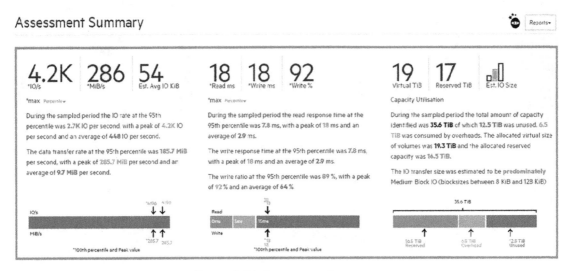

Figure 2-56 Assessment Summary

After the data is analyzed, a summary screen displays, shown in Figure 2-56. You can look at the information from a single storage array, or if your customer has, for example, multiple VNX storage arrays, you can combine them into a single view. The tool is interactive—you can drill down further into this information, or you can just use this summary to input directly into NinjaSTARS.

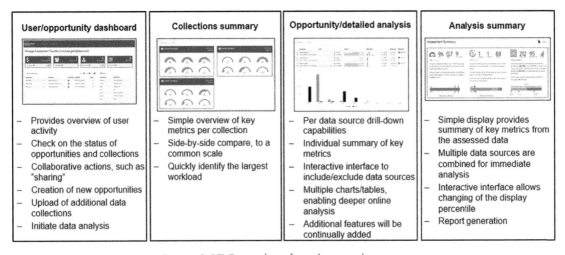

Figure 2-57 Examples of analysis and reports

The collector must be run from a command prompt to be able to add the required arguments to the collector, as indicated in Figure 2-57; however, it does not need to be run with admin rights (assuming the user is allowed to write to the current directory).

To collect capacity and configuration data and/or performance statistics for HPE StoreServ 3PAR arrays, use SAFcollector SS3PAR with the required options, for example:

```
C:\Storage Assessment Foundry>safcollector SS3PAR -u 3paradm -p 3par-
data -i 15.ip.ip.183
```

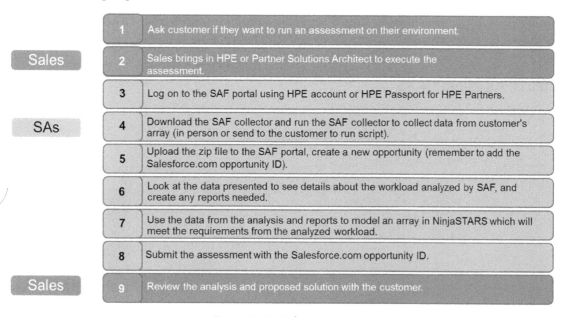

Figure 2-58 Sales process

 Note

To access the HPE Assessment Foundry, visit:

https://saf.itcs.hpe.com

NinjaSTARS and the Nimble Config Sizer are storage sizing tools for HPE Storage arrays. They can be used to size and configure cost-effective and performance-optimized solutions for both HPE 3PAR and HPE Nimble Storage. Using a basic set of capacity and performance metrics (requirements) from an existing storage environment, as illustrated in Figure 2-58, you can use these tools to interactively change the requirements and see the change in capacity and performance characteristics of the target storage array. In addition, both tools provide guidance on the anticipated capacity reduction benefits of a given application profile on each storage array.

The HPE Nimble Space Savings Estimator (NimbleSSE) is a command-line utility that provides an estimate for how much space a user could save on a disk or volume. The dataset can reside on any storage that is accessible to a host on which NimbleSSE is installed. The tool runs on a Windows host (either physical or a VM), scans one or more disks or volumes, and calculates the amount of space a user might save by using deduplication, compression, and zero block pruning.

NinjaCrawler is a tool that reads actual raw data on a host and determines the possible capacity savings that could be achieved with data deduplication and compression. NinjaCrawler relies on HPE 3PAR deduplication and compression technologies to emulate the amount of data reduction the specified volume(s) would benefit from if they were stored on a 3PAR array with those technologies enabled. NinjaCrawler works on both Linux and Windows platforms.

HPE 3PAR NinjaSTARS

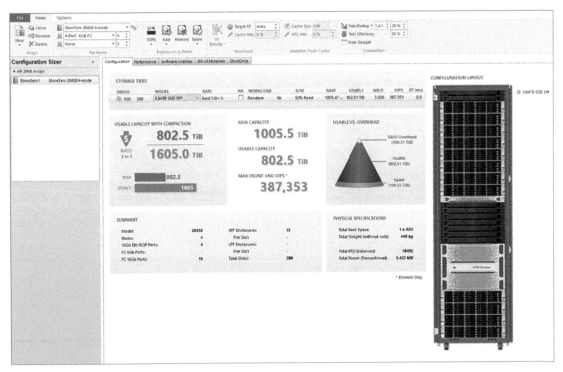

Figure 2-59 HPE 3PAR NinjaSTARS

HPE NinjaSTARS Tool, as shown in Figure 2-59, is an interactive storage sizing tool for HPE 3PAR StoreServ Storage and HPE Nimble Storage arrays. It can size and configure a cost-effective and performance-optimized HPE 3PAR StoreServ or HPE Nimble Storage that can replace existing legacy arrays. Based on a set of basic capacity and performance metrics (requirements) from an existing storage environment, it converts these requirements into a ready-to-order BOM list.

HPE NinjaSTARS for Nimble/StoreOnce

Figure 2-60 HPE NinjaSTARS for Nimble

As illustrated in Figure 2-60, the tool has different ways of accepting the sizing requirement, including using a set of standard templates, inputting a desired usable capacity number (with percentages per tier), or completely customizing the array. Users can interactively change the requirements to see the change in capacity and performance characteristics of the target storage system. NinjaSTARS also provides options for licensing and software components.

NinjaSTARS uses a flow-based approach in the following sequence:

- Gather configuration and sizing requirements.

- Interactively customize the target storage system.

- Select licensing and software components for final configuration.

- Generate a BOM for the selected configuration.

Installing NinjaSTARS

NinjaSTARS is an agentless, standalone tool, designed to run on any Windows machine, including a laptop, workstation, or server. It is compiled as a portable application, designed to run from a USB stick with no installation required. Scanning of the target systems does not examine any individual file, require a host agent, or leave behind any information. Network traffic generated is negligible.

NinjaCrawler

```
Administrator: C:\Windows\System32\cmd.exe - cmd - ddcrawler.exe --esx_ip 192.168.19.30 --esx_uid root --esx_pwd ChangeMe123!  /vmfs...

c:\ClassFiles\NinjaCrawler.3.1.2_WINDOWS64>ddcrawler.exe --esx_ip 192.168.19.30 --esx_uid root --esx_pwd ChangeMe123!  /vmfs/devic
es/disks/naa.6001405efd84505d51ded3631da794d4

3PAR DedupCrawler v3.1.2
(c) 2017 Hewlett Packard Enterprise. All rights reserved.
2019-02-16, 10:02:55 AM

Connecting to 192.168.19.30 via SSH
Connection successful!

Valid tested ESX version: 6.0.0.2

Configuring destination and deploying 6 files... SUCCESS

Opened a port in the ESX firewall: 1514

Scan Source         : /vmfs/devices/disks/naa.6001405efd84505d51ded3631da794d4
Scan Path           : /vmfs/devices/disks/naa.6001405efd84505d51ded3631da794d4
Estimated Capacity  : 100.0 GB
Throughput Limit    : 500 Mb/s
Deduplication       : ON
Compression         : ON
ESX IP:             : 192.168.19.30
Port:               : None

Scan:     1x !  1.0 GB !                    ! ETA:   0:39:19 ! 43.0 MB/s ! Q:--_
```

Figure 2-61 NinjaCrawler examining VMware datastore

NinjaCrawler is a tool that reads actual raw data on a host and determines the possible capacity savings that could be achieved with data deduplication and compression. NinjaCrawler, as shown in Figure 2-61, relies on HPE 3PAR deduplication and compression technologies to emulate the amount of data reduction the specified volume(s) would benefit from if they were stored on a 3PAR array with those technologies enabled. NinjaCrawler works on Linux, Windows, and VMware platforms.

NinjaProtected tool

Figure 2-62 NinjaProtected tool

Achieve better data protection by using the HPE StoreOnce NinjaProtected backup assessment and the Get Protected Guarantee program, shown in Figure 2-62.

Backup assessments have become one of the most popular storage services from HPE. The process takes less than an hour, depending on the size of the environment. HPE captures metadata from the backup application itself, and thus accesses no real customer data.

Each assessment analyzes key industry backup metrics from all the backup jobs and provides a backup window, backup success rate, failed backups, number of restores, failed restores, and the potential saving through data deduplication.

After HPE analyzes the data, the customer receives an executive report with an overall assessment of their backup environment and a benchmark for any future assessments.

Features include:

- **Lightweight and non-invasive**—The assessment tool is an agentless, non-invasive script tool. No installation is required on the system.

- **Simple, powerful, and efficient**—The tool automates the gathering of the existing backup environment data. It assesses the overall backup health of the environment, and it leverages historical stats from backup servers.

- **Get Protected Guarantee (GPG) Program**—By performing a free NinjaProtected backup assessment, HPE and its partners can demonstrate how customers can reduce the amount of backup data they need to store by 95% as compared to a fully hydrated backup.

The GPG program applies to **any** new HPE StoreOnce System including StoreOnce Virtual Storage Appliance (VSA):

- Data types include file servers, Microsoft Exchange, and VMs (using agentless backup methods).

- Audio and video files cannot exceed 10% of the total data within a backup.

- If the guarantee is not met, HPE will make up the difference with additional capacity and support.

GPG program requirements:

- Complete the NinjaProtected assessment to determine whether your customer qualifies for the GPG.

- The backup applications supported are Micro Focus Data Protector and Veritas NetBackup.

- Customers must perform daily and weekly full backups to qualify for the 95% guarantee.

- Customers must retain their stored data for a minimum of 90 days.

- Customer data might not be encrypted or precompressed.

- Only specific data types are applicable for GPG; see the "Terms and Conditions" for details.

Note
- Access the process description at **https://saf.itcs.hpe.com**
- For more information about the GPG, visit: **http://hpe.com/storage/getprotected**

HPE Demonstration Portal

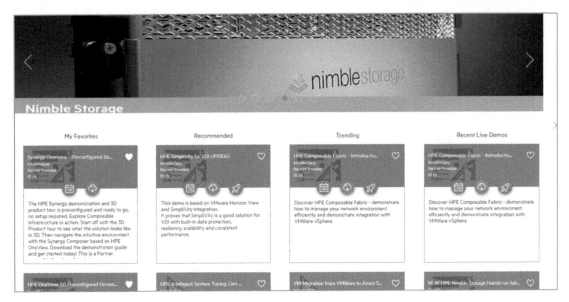

Figure 2-63 HPE Demonstration Portal

The HPE Demonstration Portal contains recorded and live demonstrations of HPE technology. As illustrated in Figure 2-62, it showcases how HPE technologies lead, innovate, and transform businesses by providing a central location for all demonstrations, webinars, and supporting collateral. Live and prerecorded demos feature HPE hardware, software, services, and partnerships in an exciting multimedia format to show how HPE can help solve your customer's business and IT problems.

The HPE Demonstration Portal is an interactive tool that allows your customers to navigate quickly and easily to find the information most relevant to them. The subject areas show trending, recommended, recent live demos, and recent recorded demos.

Your customers can choose the area they are interested in, and then select a category within the area to view all available prerecorded and live demonstrations as well as supporting collateral. Prerecorded demonstrations, or demos, provide high-level overview demonstrations of products and solutions, and they are an excellent way to learn more about HPE and partner products or solutions. Many live environments are available and can be used to become familiar with individual HPE solutions.

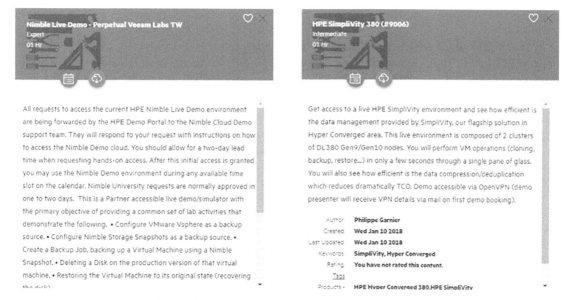

Figure 2-64 HPE Demonstration Portal: Live demo

 Note

To access the HPE Demo Portal, visit: **https://hpedemoportal.ext.hpe.com**

Using TCO and ROI tools

It is important to understand qualitative and quantitative data about the entire lifecycle cost of a technology project and the impact it will have on business processes. TCO measures cost, and ROI measures benefit. TCO data should feed ROI data, and ROI data should feed the overall business case for business technology decisions.

TCO

TCO costs can be difficult to quantify. It is important to ask the customer meaningful questions about why a technology initiative exists and what impact it will have on the business.

TCO represents total direct and indirect costs over the entire lifecycle of a hardware or software product. The simple approach to TCO data collection and assessment is a template that requires collecting specific hard and soft data. Hard data is always preferred over soft data, but soft data should be analyzed if it can be monetized (for example, generating a premium for a company's stock price or enhancing the brand). Examples of soft costs include the cost of downtime, consulting from indirect sources, and costs connected with standardization.

ROI

ROI can be difficult to calculate. For example, companies developed websites for a variety of reasons in the mid-to-late 1990s. First-generation sites were essentially company marketing displays, but very few transactions took place. What was the ROI for these sites? They did not reduce costs; in fact, they increased them. They did not generate revenue. Companies built them to convince customers, Wall Street analysts, investors, and others that they understood that the World Wide Web (WWW) was important. The ROI for this endeavor provided an intangible benefit, meaning the companies might have improved their credibility or reputation, which could have affected downstream profits.

There are many factors to consider when calculating ROI. Research suggests that although many ROI methods are used, the most popular approaches calculate cost reduction, customer satisfaction, productivity improvement, and contributions to profits and earnings. Most business technology executives consider two years to be a reasonable timeline for measuring ROI.

A few methods of calculating ROI are:

- Payback is one simple approach to ROI data collection and assessment. This method calculates the time it takes to offset the IT investment through increased revenues or reduced costs. If the payback period is short and the offsets are great, then the ROI is significant. Payback should be defined by using internal metrics. The payback for some projects will be a year, but others might take three years. Most IT projects should achieve a positive ROI within three years.

- Another way to determine ROI is based on a simple calculation that starts with the amount of money needed to purchase an IT solution (including TCO and other data). Then, the increased revenue or reduced costs that the investment would generate are projected. If a project costs $1 million but saves $2 million, then the ROI is healthy.

- Additional ROI methods are based on financial metrics such as economic value analysis (or economic value added), internal rate of return (IRR), net present value (NPV), total economic impact (TEI), rapid economic justification (REJ), information economic (IE), and real options valuation (ROV), among others.

Alinean ROI and TCO analysis

Alinean is a well-known ROI and TCO calculator and template designer. The company has developed more than 100 ROI sales tools for HPE and several other companies. It created the industry-standard software for chief information officer (CIO) budgeting, planning, and ROI and TCO benchmarking.

Alinean offers a proprietary database of financial and IT performance information for 20,000 worldwide corporations. It also has proprietary research methodologies to quantify the costs and benefits of IT projects. Alinean software helps users demonstrate ROI, TCO, and the overall value of IT solutions.

Note

To access the Alinean tools, visit:

https://www.hpe.com/us/en/solutions/tco-calculators.html

Alinean analysis tools use this data to perform calculations and determine the benefits of migrations to HPE solutions:

- Server, power and cooling, and operating system and database license costs
- Operations and administration costs

Financial metrics

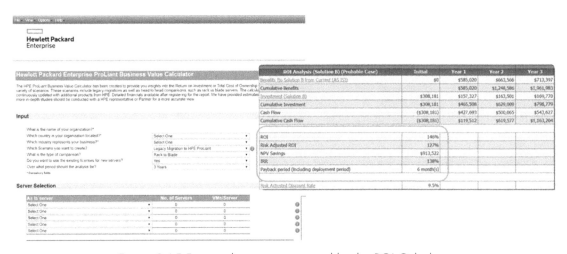

Figure 2-65 Financial metrics generated by the ROI Calculator

Figure 2-65 shows financial metrics generated by the ROI Calculator. The top half of the chart on the right shows the year-by-year cash flow and the cumulative cash flow. The rows highlighted in orange show the ROI, NPV, IRR, and the payback period. Remember that the output charts within the Alinean tool are based on the customer's information, which is important to know when developing or proposing an HPE solution.

Alinean customer deliverables

The ROI Calculator allows you to create a complete business value report. Using key inputs from your customer, you can generate a report that has third-party credibility along with the ability to dig deeper when necessary.

PowerPoint presentations, interactive surveys, assessment summaries, and blueprints can be generated using Alinean tools. These customer deliverables include information such as customer data, financial metrics, and competitive analysis.

Learning check

10. Which tool can you use to demonstrate the 3D model of a server solution to a customer?

_____

_____

_____

_____

11. Describe the purpose and functions of the HPE OneConfig Advanced tool.

_____

_____

_____

_____

_____

_____

_____

Developing the proposal

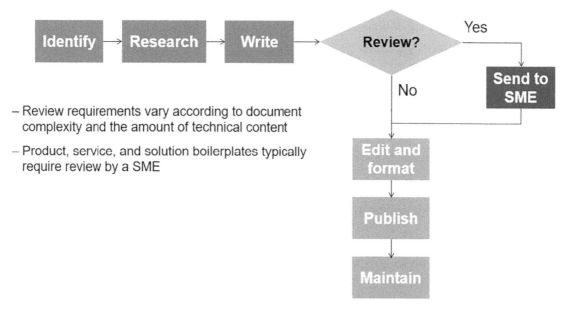

Figure 2-66 Simple flowchart for developing the proposal

After assembling the business and technical information from the customer, as illustrated in Figure 2-66, work can begin on the solution proposal. The creation of timely, accurate, high-quality, proposal-ready content requires a rigorous development and maintenance process. At this point, you should focus on various aspects of the solution, including addressing architectural and transitional issues such as functional and technical design, organizational design, technology governance, and change management.

Matching the challenge with the opportunity

When designing a solution, it is not enough to present the technical aspects. Remember that you want to present the value of the solution in business terms that matter to the customer. Frame the technology in terms of how it addresses business drivers and initiatives, how it overcomes obstacles, and how it meets the customer's goals. You will architect the solution to meet the customer's business, technical, and financial needs by:

- Developing a logical architecture that will host the solution, including:

    - Network devices and layout

    - Server requirements

- – Application services

- – Storage requirements

- Incorporating licensing options based on current QuickSpecs

- Outlining how to integrate your solution into the customer's IT infrastructure

- Describing the business value for the customer

From a content perspective, proposal-ready documents typically include:

- Key benefits and differentiators

- Latest HPE marketing messages

- Customer and analysis quotes

- High-level technical information

- Proof points

The order in which you present information might be dictated by points of focus in the RFI or RFP. Depending on the solution you are proposing and the resources required, you might also include support information from channel partners, program managers, special interest groups, and others.

The majority of proposal-ready content must be reviewed before publication to ensure accuracy. Reviewers can include:

- Product managers

- Program managers

- Marketing specialists

- Special interest groups

- – HPE Solution Architect (SA) community

- – Ambassador program

 Note

Proposal-ready content that is based on non-technical, external sources such as the HPE website does not require review by a subject-matter expert (SME).

After review, changes need to be incorporated from the reviewers to ensure that the content passes a final editing process.

Writing a scope of work

A **scope of work** is a pre-project overview you prepare for the proposal. This document captures the plan, time frame, required resources, and completion milestones of a project. It is crucial for ensuring a mutual understanding with the customer. Executive support is essential. Without leadership support, it can be difficult to implement an IT project.

 Note

A scope of work should not be confused with a statement of work (SOW), which is a final project overview prepared for billing.

The scope of work should provide a summary of the plan you create for the solution, including:

- Overall time frame
- Completion milestones for each aspect of the solution
- Resources required

  – Channel partners, HPE sales representatives, HPE services, and any other parties involved in delivering the solution

  – Executive support for the project (name, position, and so on)

Learning check

12. Proposal-ready content that is based on non-technical, external sources such as the HPE website does not require review by an SME.

    ☐ True

    ☐ False

Solution installation, configuration, and setup

Options to install a Hybrid IT solution:

- Customer self-install
- Installation and startup service

Installation options

Figure 2-67 Datasheet for Installation and Startup Service

Installation and Startup Service, shown in Figure 2-67, provides:

- Proper installation and integration

- Service includes all activities necessary to deploy the solution

- Benefits:

    - Allows IT staff to stay focused on core tasks and priorities

    - Enables a business to meet its configuration requirements

    - Reduces implementation time, impact, and risk to the storage environment

    - Facilitates a successful implementation for complex deployments

    - Effectively uses HPE products

    - Provides a service delivered by a trained specialist and based on HPE recommended configurations and best practices

    - Every startup service has different components and prerequisites

Example of Installation and Startup Service: HPE StoreOnce single-node System Installation and Startup Operational Service:

HPE StoreOnce single-node System Installation and Startup Operational Service provides planning, service deployment, installation verification testing (IVT), and an orientation session to help your customers deploy the features and functionality of the HPE StoreOnce Systems in their network environment. This operational service covers the installation and configuration of the HPE StoreOnce 2xxx, 3xxx, 4xxx, 51xx, and 55xx Gen3 single-node systems and the 36xx, 5200, 5250, and 5650 Gen4 single-node systems.

Service features include:

Service planning—An HPE service specialist contacts the customer to review expectations and validate that all pre-delivery requirements have been or will be met before installation of the service. The service planning activities includes:

- Communication and verification of the hardware and environmental prerequisites for the installation of the HPE StoreOnce System

- Collection, using a pre-delivery checklist, of the information needed to plan the deployment, including:

  - A check for the backup software that will be used (the software's installation or configuration is not included; however, if it is present, it can be used for verification)

  - Confirmation that the host to be used for the host setup demonstration meets the required specification

- Agreement on the proposed configuration and review of the service completion criteria

- Creation of a written installation plan, which will serve as the project plan for this service

- Scheduling of the service delivery at a time on which both HPE and the customer mutually agree

Service deployment—The deployment activities will include the following:

- Installation of the hardware into a customer-supplied rack, including any capacity expansion kits and network cards

- Connection of customer-supplied and pre-run network cabling to the hardware

- Validation of the StoreOnce System operation, and installation of any required licensing (including capacity expansion licenses)

- SAN integration, in which the StoreOnce System may require some additional configuration onto the SAN via its fiber connections

- Setup and demonstration of the configuration of one host

- Provision of configuration documentation to the customer

Installation verification tests— HPE will run the appropriate IVT required to verify the operation of the configuration

Customer orientation session—After completing the installation, the HPE service specialist will conduct an orientation session of up to one hour on product usage and HPE support. Subject areas for the orientation session may include:

- An overview of the expectations for the deduplication technology

- Information about how to set up email alerts

- Further information about network-attached libraries and tape drives

- Advice on backup strategies

The orientation session is informal and is not intended as a classroom activity or a substitute for formal product training.

 Note

Other limitations and prerequisites apply.

Installation, configuration, and setup documentation

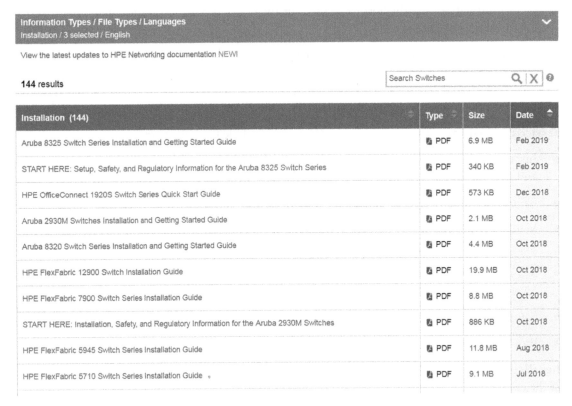

Installation (144)	Type	Size	Date
Aruba 8325 Switch Series Installation and Getting Started Guide	PDF	6.9 MB	Feb 2019
START HERE: Setup, Safety, and Regulatory Information for the Aruba 8325 Switch Series	PDF	340 KB	Feb 2019
HPE OfficeConnect 1920S Switch Series Quick Start Guide	PDF	573 KB	Dec 2018
Aruba 2930M Switches Installation and Getting Started Guide	PDF	2.1 MB	Oct 2018
Aruba 8320 Switch Series Installation and Getting Started Guide	PDF	4.4 MB	Oct 2018
HPE FlexFabric 12900 Switch Installation Guide	PDF	19.9 MB	Oct 2018
HPE FlexFabric 7900 Switch Series Installation Guide	PDF	8.8 MB	Oct 2018
START HERE: Installation, Safety, and Regulatory Information for the Aruba 2930M Switches	PDF	886 KB	Oct 2018
HPE FlexFabric 5945 Switch Series Installation Guide	PDF	11.8 MB	Aug 2018
HPE FlexFabric 5710 Switch Series Installation Guide	PDF	9.1 MB	Jul 2018

Figure 2-68 Installation, configuration, and setup documentation

Locate the information for specific product and scenario, as indicated in Figure 2-68:

● Filter the product or solution.

● Specify the model or keep all.

● Select the required information type:

   – Getting Started/Quick Start Guide

   – Installation

   – Configuration

 Note

Installation documents can be located at the Hewlett Packard Enterprise Information Library: **https://docs.hpe.com**

Quick Start Guide/Quick Setup Guide

Figure 2-69 HPE StoreEasy 1x60 Storage Quick Start Guide

Quick Start Guides are product specific and contain the minimum requirements and instructions to configure an HPE product, an example of which is shown in Figure 2-69. The usual contents of the Quick Start Guide include:

● Preinstallation requirements and preparation steps

● Specifications and cabling requirements

- Installation steps

- Initial configuration

- Links to additional documentation

Factory Express

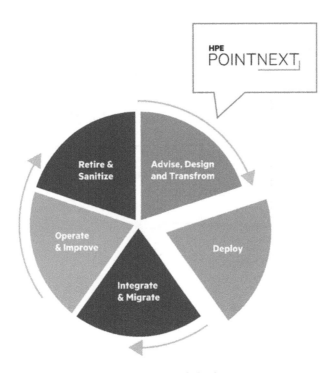

Figure 2-70 HPE Pointnext and deployment services

With HPE Factory Integration Services, all the build, integration, and testing are done at the HPE Factory. Customer receives a ready-to-deploy, custom IT solution built to specific requirements. Services cover the entire HPE portfolio from a single server to multi-rack solutions and multiple levels of customization, including image loading, custom system settings, solution integration, asset tagging/labeling, custom cabling, and third-party component integration, as indicated in Figure 2-70. The service is coupled with project management to oversee the service and delivery.

Customer benefits include:

- Quicker time to deploy

- Minimal onsite disruption

- Benefits of IT investment

- Quicker ROI

Learning check

13. Which resource contains installation steps required to setup an HPE device?

_____

_____

_____

_____

_____

14. You are in a meeting with a customer, and they challenge you with a statement: "I heard that the configuration process required to prepare a quote is time-consuming, with a high of risk of errors and risk of ordering incompatible components". How should you respond?

_____

_____

_____

_____

_____

_____

_____

15. Write a summary of the key concepts presented in this chapter.

_____

_____

_____

_____

_____

_____

_____

_____

_____

_____

_____

_____

Summary

- When you are planning an HPE server solution, it is crucial to thoroughly evaluate the customer's requirements. Factors that need to be examined include the number of users, existing SLAs, future plans, business requirements, obstacles, site specifications, and so on. This information can be used to determine the best HPE platform for each customer. When designing a solution, specific considerations range from basic server, storage, networking, and operating system requirements to VM design goals and guidelines. These factors are important to building a compelling business case.

- HPE Reference Architectures and HPE Reference Configurations include complete configuration, sizing, bill of material, and deployment details.

- Individual HPE platforms can be selected based on various parameters: workload, performance, capacity, and features.

- HPE helps partners and customers create the best solution for each IT problem by providing multiple sizing and planning tools.

- The creation of timely, accurate, high-quality, proposal-ready content requires a rigorous development and maintenance process.

- HPE provides installation services for its Hybrid IT products. To help customers with self-installation, various documentation resources are available.

Prelearning check

Before proceeding with this section, answer the following questions to assess your existing knowledge of the topics covered in this chapter. Record your answers in the space provided here.

1. You are in a meeting with a customer, and they challenge you with a question: "Is it possible to select the type of a local storage and the amount of drives, type of drive and physical size?"

   How should you respond?

   _____

   _____

   _____

   _____

   _____

   _____

   _____

_____

_____

_____

_____

_____

3 Recommending Hybrid IT compute solutions for customer use cases

LEARNING OBJECTIVES

After completing this chapter, you should be able to:

✓ Recommend and position HPE Hybrid IT products, solutions, tools, and appropriate services for customer use cases.

✓ Identify and position key HPE solutions and workload offerings with the key alliance partner ecosystem components to the appropriate customer use case.

✓ Differentiate and position HPE products and services products for the appropriate customer use case.

✓ Describe, differentiate, and apply industry-standard architectures and technologies.

✓ Explain the HPE approach to converged management for the infrastructure lifecycle.

HPE has it all!

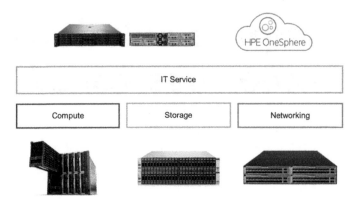

Figure 3-1 HPE has it all

Looking for industry-leading enterprise servers, storage, networking, software, or integrated systems products? Whether the IT service consumption model includes public cloud, private cloud, hyperconverged solutions, or traditional systems, there are always compute, storage, and networking components in the data center that provide necessary resources, as shown in Figure 3-1. In addition, HPE is providing any data center Hybrid IT component that is necessary for a successful deployment of IT service.

Why a single partner for compute, storage, and networking?

Using a single vendor at the rack level for compute, storage, and networking simplifies operations:

- **Plug-and-play integration**—No interoperability issues

- **Simplified logistics**—Single point of contact for procurement

- **Simplified support**—Single point of contact for server, OS, hypervisor, storage, and networking

- **Simplified management**—Unified administration

Using a single vendor for compute, storage, and networking improves business outcomes:

- **Lower operations expenses**—Unified management simplifies administration and reduces support burden

- **Faster time-to-value**—Reference architectures and plug-and-play integration simplifies planning and accelerates deployment

- **Lower risk/higher service levels/faster problem resolution**—No vendor squabbles or finger-pointing

The solution design can be simplified by using validated HPE Reference Designs and Proactive Care Services.

Scenario 1: Microsoft Exchange Server 2016 on HPE ProLiant DL380 Gen10 Server

The wide HPE portfolio of data center products can be introduced using customer scenarios and recommended, validated configurations, based on HPE Reference Architecture or HPE Reference configuration.

Introducing the customer scenario

WRT company will be used as a story line through this scenario. We will introduce the company using an interview:

- What is your primary business?

    - Global automotive supplier

- How many employees do you currently have?

    - 10,000 employees

- How does your selling and delivery channel look like?

    - Long-term contracts with selected car producers, limited marketing, no direct sales

- Where are you currently storing data, and how do you access files?

    - Mix of NAS and SAN devices, mainly HPE

- What does your server and network infrastructure look like?

    - Two data centers, hundreds of devices

- How much data do you currently have on servers and workstations?

    - Unknown

- Do you have an IT department?

    - Yes, every location has an IT team and both data center operations team

- What are your current plans?

    - Consolidating messaging solution in short term, better automation and vendor consolidation in long term

Customer requirements

As an HPE presales consultant or partner, your primary goal is to find and convey value to your customers. You need to learn as much as you can about the customer's business situation and needs. To fully understanding their needs, you should be able to:

- Communicate value by providing business insights.

- Identify other ways to support the customer through cross-selling.

- Develop and maintain long-term relationships that can lead to more business.

- Distinguish HPE from its competitors.

- Be the customer's first call when they need support.

It is so important that we make every single customer interaction as valuable as it can be. We can do this by knowing our customers, understanding our values, making ourselves relevant to our customers, and delivering meaningful business outcomes.

There are five stages to the consulting process. Keep these notes in mind as you progress through each stage:

1. Prepare

    – Learn as much as possible before you begin to engage a customer.

    – Research the company and the people, find out about areas of concern, and decide who is the best person to contact.

2. Interview

    – Know what you want to learn before the initial interview with the customer.

    – Consider the person's position at the company and anticipate their concerns accordingly.

    – Listen to what the customer has to say.

    – Use time effectively and address their concerns in a timely manner.

3. Plan

    – Determine which solutions are closely aligned with the customer's business needs.

    – Plan the next steps in the project, including who to add to your team when the time comes.

4. Propose

    – Design the solution that meets the customer's needs and successfully conveys value.

    – Do not propose products only; recommend a complete solution that demonstrates value at all levels of the organization.

5. Present

  – Articulate the recommended solution, positioning it in terms that the customer understands.

  – Ensure that the customer knows HPE has the solutions to meet their needs.

As a result of multiple interviews and gathering information about customer plans and customer's current infrastructure, the following requirements emerged for the new solution:

- On premise, highly resilient communication solution

- Spans two data centers

- 10,512 users

- 21.5 GB mailboxes

- Utmost performance and reliability

- Microsoft Exchange Server 2016 as the messaging platform

- Multi-copy database design with Exchange Database Availability Groups

- Security is top priority

Activity: Microsoft Exchange Server information resources

1. Download these information resources:

  – HPE Reference Architecture for Microsoft Exchange Server 2016 on HPE ProLiant DL380 Gen10 Server

    https://h20195.www2.hpe.com/V2/GetDocument.aspx?docname=a00048480enw

  – The Exchange 2016 Preferred Architecture

    https://blogs.technet.microsoft.com/exchange/2015/10/12/the-exchange-2016-preferred-architecture/

  – Exchange Server Role Requirements Calculator v9.1

    https://gallery.technet.microsoft.com/office/Exchange-2013-Server-Role-f8a61780

  – Ask the Perf Guy: Sizing Exchange 2016 Deployments

    https://blogs.technet.microsoft.com/exchange/2015/10/15/ask-the-perf-guy-sizing-exchange-2016-deployments/

  – HPE Migration Service for Exchange

    https://h20195.www2.hpe.com/v2/GetPDF.aspx/4AA6-7523ENW.pdf

2. Answer the following questions:

    a. What are the recommended commodity servers by the application vendor engineering team?

    _____

    _____

    –   How many rack units? _____

    –   How many processors and cores per processor? _____

    –   What is the minimum number of drives? _____

    –   Are physical or virtual servers recommended? Why?

    _____

    _____

    _____

    _____

    _____

    _____

    b. What is the recommended server platform by HPE in Reference Architecture?

    _____

    _____

    c. What is the recommended storage platform by HPE in Reference Architecture?

    –   DAS? _____

    –   NAS? _____

    –   SAN? _____

    –   What is the recommended HPE service to mitigate risks connected to Microsoft Exchange migration?

    _____

    _____

    _____

    _____

    _____

_____

_____

_____

_____

Building blocks of the solution

This Reference Architecture for Microsoft Exchange Server 2016 demonstrates a highly resilient solution that provides large mailboxes for users that expect the utmost in performance and reliability. The solution is based on a building block approach with four servers per site, and 10,512 users per building block, which was tested and validated at 21.5 GB mailboxes with a messaging profile of 150 emails sent and received, per user, per day.

Portfolio: HPE servers and server systems

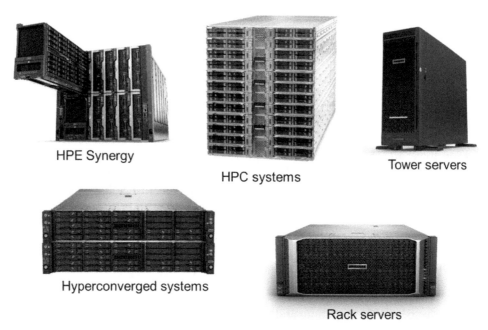

Figure 3-2 Selected HPE server platforms

HPE is offering multiple server platforms for various workloads, as illustrated in Figure 3-2. The selected reference architecture provides a validated configuration based on HPE rack servers.

HPE ProLiant Gen10 workload-based positioning: Select the series

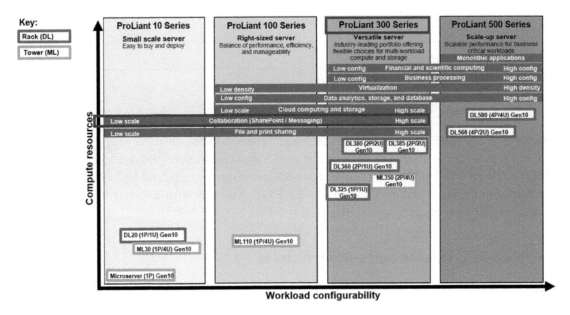

Figure 3-3 HPE ProLiant Gen10 workload-based positioning

Reference Figure 3-3 displays the positioning of various HPE ProLiant series to workloads. Since the customer is looking for a large-scale messaging solution, we can select ProLiant 300 series as a preferred hardware platform.

HPE ProLiant tower and rack-mounted servers provide a complete infrastructure that supports both business objectives and business growth. With the broadest server portfolio in the industry, HPE offers ProLiant servers that focus on the needs of all customer segments, including small and medium businesses (SMBs), enterprises, and High-Performance Computing (HPC).

The ProLiant rack and tower portfolio delivers flexible, reliable, secure, and performance-optimized server solutions for a range of workloads and budgets. It features versatile and flexible designs along with improved energy efficiencies to help reduce total cost of ownership (TCO).

The ProLiant rack portfolio is performance optimized for multi-application workloads to significantly increase the speed of IT operations and enable IT to respond to business needs faster. Integrated with a simplified yet comprehensive management suite and industry-leading support, the ProLiant Gen10 rack server portfolio enables customers to accelerate business results with faster compute, memory, and IO performance, coupled with increased storage and networking performance—including lower latency.

Gen10 servers are key to infrastructure modernization, accelerating business insights across a hybrid world of traditional IT, public cloud, and private cloud.

We are living in an era of digital disruption, where the accessibility and adoption of Big Data, mobility, Internet of Things, and cloud-native technologies are enabling companies to transform their businesses in exciting new ways. At the heart of these technologies are applications and data, and this has placed IT at the center of business innovation. IT needs to operate at the speed of today's business to be an accelerator of new ideas, products, and services. For IT to be successful in speeding time to value, a Hybrid IT infrastructure is needed to deliver the Right Mix of infrastructure and services to develop and deploy applications on a continuous basis and draw insights and make decisions from data. For IT decision makers who must define their Right Mix of Hybrid IT across on-premises dedicated and cloud environments as well as hosted cloud, a new compute experience is required to obtain cloud economics and agility with the security of an on-premises data center.

ProLiant servers provide:

- **Agility**—A better way to deliver business results with a software-defined infrastructure that delivers intelligent automation and high-performance reducing operational complexity for traditional applications while increasing velocity for the new breed of applications

- **Security**—A better way to protect business and data with an infrastructure that has security designed in from the start

- **Economic control**—A better way to consume IT that allows customers to pay for only what they use, scaling on demand without overprovisioning or incurring exponentially escalating costs

Differentiating innovations in HPE Gen10 servers include:

- The World's Most Secure Industry-Standard Servers

    - Unmatched threat protection through Hardware Root of Trust, extensive standards compliance, and supply chain attack detection

    - Unparalleled ability to recover firmware and OS after denial of service attempt or detection of compromised code

- Unprecedented high-speed memory capacity with persistence

    - High-capacity data acceleration with flash-backed Persistent Memory at multi-terabyte capacities for large data-intensive workloads

    - Second generation of memory-centric compute innovation on the path to the machine

- Intelligent System Tuning (IST)

    - Performance tuning to enable more workloads on more cores at a given CPU frequency for greater application licensing efficiency

    - Predictable latency reduction and balanced workload optimization

- New levels of compute

  - Next-generation industry-standard CPUs with faster processing, higher-speed memory access, enhanced software-defined management, and security

  - Enhanced GPU levels of performance and choice

- Increased in-server storage density

  - Substantially greater non-volatile memory express (NVMe) capacity for large write-intensive workloads needing advanced caching/tiering

  - Enhanced storage density in servers with more small form factor (SFF) and large form factor (LFF) drives for collaboration and database workloads

- More efficient and easier server management

  - Enables large-scale firmware deployment

  - Improved graphical user interface (GUI) to simply management with industry-standard application program interfaces (APIs)

  - Easy system debug access

  - Convenient warranty entitlement validation

HPE ProLiant DL380 Gen10

Figure 3-4 HPE ProLiant DL380 Gen10

Adaptable for diverse workloads and environments, the secure 2P 2U HPE ProLiant DL380 Gen10 delivers world-class performance with the right balance of expandability and scalability. Designed for supreme versatility and resiliency, as illustrated in Figure 3-4, while being backed by a comprehensive warranty makes it ideal for multiple environments from containers to cloud to Big Data.

HPE ProLiant DL380 Gen10 offers:

- Flexible design

  - Optimized performance for highly parallel workloads—image processing, app dev/test, cloud computing

- – Greater NVMe capacity all NVMe drive options allowing up to 20 Peripheral Component Interconnect express (PCIe) solid disk drives (SSDs) (128 TB max. capacity) direct connect drives per system

- – More LFF capacity—new modular LFF chassis supporting up to 19 LFF and 2 SFF drives

- – Enhanced solid-state drive (SSD) support—new M.2 backplane option supporting up to 30 SATA SSDs in 2U

- – Greater IO with eight PCIe 3.0 slots and expanded GPU support

- – Choice of HPE Flexible Smart Array or HPE Smart HBA Controllers for performance or additional features

- Industry-leading performance

  - – Up to 27x faster checkpoint operations enabling significantly faster business operations, compared checkpoint on persistent memory vs. SSD

  - – Up to 20x reduction in database recovery time preserving maximum system uptime, comparing scalable persistent memory vs. SSD and disk drives

  - – Improved speed with up to two Intel® Xeon® Processor Scalable Family, up to 28 cores and enhanced graphics processing unit (GPU) support

  - – Faster memory with 24 HPE Smart Memory DDR4 2666 MHz; (3.0 TB max)

  - – Persistent Memory—double the capacity of non-volatile dual in-line memory modules (NVDIMMs) over prior generation, delivers fastest storage tier supporting up to 192 GB per system

  - – Persistent Memory up to 12 NVDIMM options

  - – Dynamically Tune Server performance using with IST

  - – Improve performance with next generation of HPE Dynamic Smart Array S100i

- Agile, secure infrastructure

  - – Reducing risk of cyber or physical attacks with asset and data protection

  - – Up to 58% more storage capacity making it ideal for Big Data, bulk storage, email analytics, and NoSQL databases, compared to previous generation

  - – Enhanced security with HPE Secure Encryption, Trusted Platform Module (TPM) option, Digitally Signed Firmware, tamper-proof secure preboot environment with SecureStart, Hardware Root of Trust, HTTPS boot, and Intrusion detection

  - – Advanced system management with HPE iLO 5

  - – Boot options supporting Unified Extensible Firmware Interface (UEFI) and legacy boot modes

  - – Standard 3-3-3 warranty

Key selling points of the DL380 Gen10 include:

- Increased performance with IST, Persistent Memory, and greater NVMe capability

- "Future proof" design keeps up with business needs

- Huge storage footprint for large storage workloads

- PCIe expansion with HPE FlexLOM and HPE Flexible Smart Array

Ideal workloads include:

- Enterprise customers

- Virtualization and containers

- Big Data, storage-centric applications, and data warehousing

- Analytics, customer relationship management (CRM), enterprise resource planning (ERP), virtual desktop infrastructure (VDI), SAP

- Large storage capacity, such as Microsoft Exchange

The solution in the selected Reference Architecture for this scenario is designed using HPE ProLiant DL380 Gen10 servers and Exchange Server 2016 in a building block approach, with a multi-copy database design with Exchange Database Availability Groups (DAGs). This Reference Architecture testing is designed to validate that the storage, CPU, and memory subsystems can support this workload in both normal and peak operations, even in a failover scenario, where one of the servers in the primary site is offline. The solution is designed to withstand an outage of either a server within the site or the failover of the entire site, and maintain availability to all users. Optimal sizing is done for the failover scenario, such that the CPU load is handled effectively even when the secondary site is unavailable and one of the servers in the primary site is offline, for either planned or unplanned downtime. The solution adequately handles the normal and peak loads for 3504 users per server with three of four active servers in one site of the building block.

The solution uses direct-attached disk storage for Exchange databases. Each HPE ProLiant DL380 Gen10 server is configured with 21 total drives; two small form factor (SFF) SSDs (800 GB) in a RAID 1 configuration for the operating system and Exchange Transport files, and 19 large form factor (LFF) hard disk drives, 10 TB each, in a RAID-less JBOD configuration. This provides the entire capacity of the 10 TB drives for several Exchange databases (four databases per volume, given a maximum set size of 1.8 TB databases). The design and testing shown here in this document cover the importance of understanding how either two or three of the four database copies on a single disk are activated in a failover scenario. It is very important to note that only two or three copies will be activated on any given disk in the failover scenario where three of four servers are active, and all databases are online.

The test results validate that the Reference Architecture is adequately sized to support 10,512 mailbox users with a 150 message/day profile, with additional performance headroom even in the failover scenario where only three Exchange Servers are online.

All servers were configured identically, except that a processor comparison was designed and delivered. The only difference between the two configurations was that the servers had different processors, as identified below:

- HPE ProLiant DL380 Gen10 Server (Intel® Xeon® Gold 6132 processors, 2.6 GHz, 14 cores) run with 12 cores active per socket (24/28 total)

- HPE ProLiant DL380 Gen10 Server (Intel® Xeon® Gold 6126 processors, 2.6 GHz, 12 cores)

The HPE servers are configured with an HPE Smart Array P816i-a controller that can operate in mixed mode, which combines RAID and host bus adapter (HBA) operations simultaneously. However, the HBA mode configuration does not enable controller write caching and therefore should not be used for Exchange databases. This white paper provides the highlights of installing and configuring the server and storage.

The HPE ProLiant DL380 Server family provides configurations that offer optimal combinations for Exchange Server and large, low-cost mailbox storage, with high-performance, reliability, and ease of deployment and management. The solution presented in this Reference Architecture is based on a building block using HPE ProLiant DL380 Gen10 servers each configured with 21 drives; 19 LFF HDDs, in a RAID-less JBOD configuration and two SFF SSDs for the operating system and Exchange Transport files. The HPE ProLiant DL380 Gen10 server is available in an SFF configuration as well.

DL300 series—Local storage flexibility

Figure 3-5 DL300 series—Local storage flexibility

HPE ProLiant DL380 Gen10 delivers world-class performance with the right balance of expandability and scalability, shown in Figure 3-5. An important feature is the flexibility of local storage configuration, and many chassis types are available:

- 8 SFF with optional Universal Media Bay, and optional SFF or NVMe drive bay options

- 24 SFF bay with additional 6 SFF rear drive bay option to total 30 SFF drives

- 8 LFF with Universal Media Bay

- 12 LFF with optional 4 LFF mid-plane and optional 3 LFF + 2 SFF rear drive bay to total 19 LFF drives + 2 SFF drives

HPE server storage portfolio

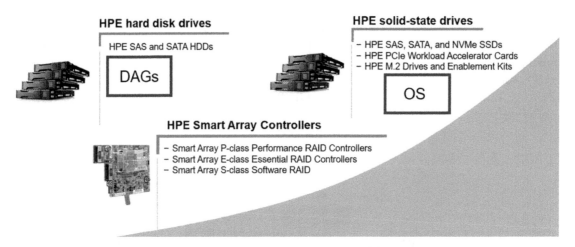

Figure 3-6 HPE server storage portfolio

There are three principal and complementary ways to implement storage solutions, as indicated in Figure 3-6.

- **Direct-attached storage (DAS) storage solutions**—The most straightforward storage solutions are either internal in a single server (usually using the Serial Attached SCSI [SAS] protocol) or directly attached external storage. However, DAS cannot be shared among multiple servers, and the one-to-one connection between device and server can add management complexity.

- **Network-attached storage (NAS) devices**—Primarily used for unstructured data and file sharing, NAS adds increased storage management functionality, increased data protection, performance enhancements, and the ability to share data using industry-standard protocols across an Ethernet network. NAS devices can usually be easily and quickly installed and can be accessed by both servers and nonserver devices.

- **Storage area network (SAN) storage**—SAN is a solution rather than a product, using shared network components. SAN brings a dedicated network of storage systems accessible by multiple servers. In contrast to NAS delivering data using file systems, SAN allows block-level access and delivers even better levels of performance, management, and resilience. SANs offer business continuity with redundant components, automated failover, and centralized management. Common protocols used in SANs are Fibre Channel (FC), internet Small Computer Systems Interface (iSCSI), Fibre Channel over Ethernet (FCoE), and InfiniBand.

Direct-attached storage

Figure 3-7 HPE D3700 enclosure

DAS consists of an open-system server running any application with dedicated internal or external storage subsystems using a SAS protocol. DAS provides dedicated storage for multiple clients with a one-to-one server-to-storage ratio. DAS offers the easiest way to deploy incremental amounts of storage as needed without extensive planning. As RAID inside the server has become less expensive, DAS has grown in popularity. A high percentage of deployed storage is now DAS.

The traditional approach involves DAS solutions that attach RAID arrays or hard drives directly to a server. DAS is familiar, works well, and is less costly than initial SAN investments.

Using a direct-attached strategy, many of the customers today have separate storage systems and storage management software products connected to individual servers.

Advantages of DAS, as illustrated in Figure 3-7, include:

- Ease of deployment
- Scalability
- Relatively inexpensive to acquire, maintain, and expand
- High performance and reliability
- Fast server-to-storage data transfer

DAS disadvantages include:

- **Inefficient resources**—Storage space exists in isolated pools.

- **Unplanned redundancy**—Duplicate copies of the same file might reside on different servers.

- **Increased management**—Server-based management means that islands of data are difficult to bridge and require a significant amount of labor to manage.

- **Decreased access**—If the server becomes unavailable, access to data is disrupted for clients.

Network-attached storage

Figure 3-8 HPE StoreEasy 1660 storage

NAS solutions consist of a specialized server-storage device that connects directly to the network. A file system is located and managed on the NAS device. Data is transferred to servers and other devices through the local area network (LAN) and to clients using industry-standard file-sharing protocols, such as Common Internet File System (CIFS)/Server Message Block (SMB), and Network File System (NFS). The intelligent NAS device enables data sharing among heterogeneous network clients.

NAS devices require storage cabinets providing specialized file access, security, and network connectivity. A network interface controller (NIC) on the server is a requirement to access the storage. NAS provides file-to-disk block mapping and client access at the file level, using network protocols.

NAS technology simplifies manageability and improves data access to clients and applications. A NAS solution generally works with a mix of clients and servers running different operating systems.

The dedicated NAS appliance can provide shared storage between heterogeneous clients. Disk arrays and other storage devices connect to the network through a traditional LAN interface such as Ethernet. Storage devices attach to network hubs similarly to the way servers and other network devices do. All network users have equal access to the stored data and do not have to go through the server. NAS makes storage resources more readily available and helps to alleviate the server bottlenecks commonly associated with accessing storage devices.

Advantages of NAS, as illustrated in Figure 3-8, include:

- Installs easily

- Is affordable

- Incorporates mature technologies

- Offers a scalable solution

- Increases network performance

- Supports remote management

Disadvantages of NAS include:

- Limited performance and storage capacity

- Increased management costs

- Inaccessible data stored on a central server if system shuts down

- Increased network bottlenecks

Storage area network

Figure 3-9 Typical SAN components: Fibre Channel switch, server HBA, and array

The SAN is a separate network that provides a storage repository that is attached to multiple host servers, shown in Figure 3-9. SANs enable external storage to be shared by the servers without impacting system performance or the primary network.

A SAN solution supplies open-system servers running applications on an open operating system. The solution includes shared external storage resources, network infrastructure components (such as Fibre Channel switches), and value-added software for enhanced storage and data management. This technology provides consolidated and virtualized storage with massive scalability and fault tolerance.

Storage interfaces include:

- iSCSI

- FC

- FCoE

The basic purpose of a SAN is to transfer data between computer systems and storage elements and among storage elements.

SAN benefits include:

- Centralized storage management
- Data replication
- Easy expansion and storage reallocation
- Disaster recovery
- Scalability
- Facilitation of backup and disaster recovery

SAN disadvantages include:

- Designing solution can be complex
- Compatibility
- Price level

Drive array basics

Figure 3-10 HPE D3710 enclosure

An array is a set of physical disk drives that can be combined into a single logical drive or subdivided into multiple logical drives that are distributed across all disks in the set.

Having several physical hard drives enables the controller to divide the data across multiple drives. A file is divided into a selected number of sectors, and then the file data is written concurrently across a series of drives in an array, as illustrated in Figure 3-10.

This approach of combining drives brings several advantages:

- **Performance**—Because multiple drives are accessed simultaneously, the process of writing (or reading) a file across multiple drives is much faster than writing to or reading from a single drive.
- **Redundancy**—If configured properly, one or more drives can fail without affecting the data accessibility on the array.

- **Capacity**—Combining multiple drives together allows you to create logical unit numbers (LUNs) that are bigger than individual drives.

- **Management**—Centralized management of all drivers in the system.

RAID levels

Storage solutions usually support a subset from the following different RAID levels.

RAID 0—Disk striping

A file is divided into stripes and then written across multiple disks. Data is striped across all drives.

This greatly decreases disk latency (the amount of time a disk head must wait for the target sector to move under the head).

- All the disk space is available for data.

- RAID 0 is the least costly.

- Overall disk performance is improved, especially the speeding up of operations that retrieve data from disk storage.

- Read and write performance is excellent.

- RAID 0 is not fault tolerant and provides no redundancy (and therefore has no hot-plug capability).

- All data is lost if one of the drives fails.

- By definition, RAID 0 requires two or more drives for a true stripe set. However, with some array controllers, a RAID 0 logical volume can be created with a single drive.

 **Important**

> Data striping is faster than conventional file writing to a single disk; however, there is no fault tolerance if any single drive fails. If one disk should fail, all data on the array would be lost.

RAID 1—Disk mirroring

With disk mirroring, data is written twice to two separate mirrored drives. If one drive fails, the mirrored drive is the backup. A RAID 1 implementation requires an even number of disks, mirrors the entire data structure on different drives, and allows split seeks. The drives with the requested data nearest to the read/write heads are used for the read, which slightly improves read performance. Additionally, drives must be added in pairs to achieve a RAID 1 expansion.

This viable, fault-tolerant solution is considered expensive because it requires twice as much drive storage. Only 50% of the total disk space is available for data storage.

RAID 1+0—Mirroring of stripe sets

RAID 1+0 is mirroring with more than two drives. A stripe set (RAID 0) is created across each half of the mirrored drives (RAID 1), thereby both mirroring and striping the data. RAID 1+0 requires an even number of drives.

Multiple disks can fail without data loss if the disks are not in the same mirror pair. In the example in the preceding graphic, Disks 0 and 1 could fail and all data would be intact on Disks 2 and 3. However, if two disks in the same mirrored pair fail, the data is lost. RAID 1+0 cannot guarantee protection against a two-disk failure.

In a RAID 1+0 configuration, array controllers can:

- Sustain an entire bus failure if the drives are equally distributed across the buses

- Service IO requests to all operational drives in a degraded condition

- Survive n/2 drive failures, where **n** is the number of drives in the array, as long as one member of each mirrored pair survives

This solution is fault tolerant but is considered expensive. It requires double the disk space because only 50% of the total disk space is available for data storage.

RAID 1+0 has good performance and redundancy, but also has write penalties (two physical write requests for one logical write request).

 Note

RAID 1+0 is sometimes referred to as RAID 10 by some manufacturers.

RAID 5—Distributed Data Guarding (data striping and error correction)

Concurrent access and distributed parity are properties of RAID 5. Data is striped across multiple drives and then its parity sum is calculated, which is also striped across multiple drives. Performance increases because parity is spread across all drives, and there is no need to access a single parity drive after every write command.

RAID 5 is best suited for IO-intensive applications and transaction processing, thereby making it an ideal solution for high-performance, fault-tolerant servers. RAID 5 requires four physical IOs from controller to disk per single logical IO from operating system to controller:

- Read old data

- Read old parity

- Write new data

- Write new parity

Any single drive can fail and the information from the lost drive can be recovered from the parity data stored on other drives. A minimum of three drives is required, and n+1 drives are needed, where **n** is the number of drives used for data.

The biggest limitation of RAID 5 is the increased read time in a failure. In RAID 5, regardless of which disk fails, data must be recalculated on each read from the remaining disks.

RAID 6—Advanced Data Guarding

RAID 6, also known as Advanced Data Guarding (ADG), provides high fault tolerance. It distributes two sets of parity data protecting against two drive failures (XOR parity and Reed-Solomon code). Parity (P) is written twice for each piece of data (D). These two sets are different, and each set occupies a capacity equivalent to that of one of the constituent drives.

RAID 6 provides high read performance and high data availability. Any two drives can fail without loss of critical data.

RAID 6 provides:

- Higher fault tolerance than RAID 5

- Lower implementation costs than RAID 1+0

- Greater usable capacity per U than RAID 1

RAID 6 requires a minimum of four hard drives, and n+2 drives, where **n** is the number of drives used for data. Because of the two sets of parity data, RAID 6 provides a relatively low write performance as compared to RAID 5 with its one set of parity data.

RAID 50 (RAID 5+0)

RAID 50 (RAID 5+0) is a nested RAID method that uses RAID 0 block-level striping across RAID 5 arrays with distributed parity. RAID 50 tolerates one drive failure in each spanned array without loss of data. RAID 50 configurations require a minimum of six drives and require less rebuild time than single RAID 5 arrays.

RAID 60 (RAID 6+0)

RAID 60 (RAID 6+0) is a nested RAID method that uses RAID 0 block-level striping across multiple RAID 6 arrays with dual distributed parity. With the inclusion of dual parity, RAID 60 tolerates the failure of two disks in each spanned array without loss of data. RAID 60 configurations require a minimum of eight drives.

HDDs, SDDs, and Smart Array Controllers

Figure 3-11 HPE server storage portfolio includes HDDs, SDDs, and Smart Array Controllers

As data storage and accessibility requirements grow, customers need solutions that can help overcome performance bottlenecks. Storage options for ProLiant Gen10 servers include HDDs, SSDs, NVMe, and Smart Array Controllers, shown in Figure 3-11. These offerings provide customers hassle-free performance, outstanding reliability, and exceptional quality. Backed by more than 2.4 million hours of the industry's most rigorous testing and qualification programs, there is a solution to fit any application workload.

With some storage requirements escalating and others becoming more complex, factors such as flexibility, performance, increased reliability, greater density, security, scalability, and accessibility are more critical than ever. Today's organizations consist of different kinds of environments. Enterprise data centers must be online 24x7, fulfill requests from numerous users simultaneously, and allow for constant growth and expansion while in operation. Other customer environments require high capacity storage and high data availability for low IO environments. The HPE portfolio of drives meets these demands.

All HPE drives pass a rigorous qualification process, which certifies that every HPE drive is proven to perform in a ProLiant server environment.

Internal drive options and selected storage solutions for ProLiant servers include:

- **HDDs**—HPE SAS and Serial Advanced Technology Attachment (SATA) hard drives are available in both 3.5-inch LFF and 2.5-inch SFF and ship with a standard one-year warranty.

  - **SATA HDDs**—HPE SATA hard drives are built for reliability and larger capacity needs for today's non-mission–critical server applications and storage environments. These high-capacity drives provide the lowest cost per GB, and the best price advantage for non-mission–critical applications with low workloads of 40% or less.

  - **SAS HDDs**—HPE SAS drives satisfy the data center requirements of scalability, performance, reliability, and manageability. They also provide a storage infrastructure for both enterprise SAS drives and SATA disk drives. SAS midline drives provide the lowest dollars per gigabyte and economical reliability and performance. The SAS interface is compatible with SATA devices. This compatibility provides users with unprecedented choices for server and storage subsystem deployment.

- **SSDs**—HPE SSDs deliver exceptional performance and endurance and reduce power consumption for customers with applications requiring high random read and write Input/Output Operations Per Second (IOPS) performance. HPE SSDs are categorized as read intensive, mixed use, and write intensive so you can choose the right SSD that tailors to the demands of the workload. Available as SFF and LFF hot-plug devices, non-hot–plug SFF devices, and SFF quick release devices, these drives deliver better performance, better latency, and more power-efficient solutions when compared with traditional rotating media.

  - **Write-intensive SSDs**—HPE write-intensive 12 G SAS and 6 G SATA SSDs provide high write performance and endurance. They are best suited for mission-critical enterprise environments with workloads high in both reads and writes. Workloads best suited for these write-intensive SSDs include online transaction processing (OLTP), VDI, Business Intelligence, and Big Data analytics.

  - **Mixed-use SSDs**—HPE mixed-use 12 G SAS and 6 G SATA SSDs are best suited for high IO applications with workloads balanced between reads and writes. The SAS and SATA SSDs provide the workload-optimized performance required for demanding IO-intensive applications. When paired with ProLiant servers, these SSDs help meet the challenges of Big Data. They achieve twice the performance and endurance of previous HPE SAS and SATA SSDs.

  - **Read-intensive SSDs**—HPE read-intensive 12 G SAS and 6 G SATA SSDs deliver enterprise features for a low price in ProLiant server systems. This entry-level pricing is fueling rapid SSD adoption for read-intensive workloads because the cost per IOPS compares very favorably to HDDs. Read-intensive SSDs deliver great performance for workloads high in reads such as boot/swap, web servers, and read caching, just to name a few.

- **NVMe**—NVMe is an industry standard for using NAND Flash memory in an SSD. NVMe standardizes the interface from the storage driver to the SSD, including command set and features such as power management. The standard enables native OS drivers in Windows, Linux, and VMware to provide a seamless user experience. The standard was defined from the ground up for NVMe, so it is capable of much higher IOPS and lower latency than legacy storage standards, such as SATA and SAS, which were designed for hard drives.

- **M.2**—Storage technology with NAND media is outgrowing the bandwidth limitations of the SATA bus. New high-performance storage solutions connect directly to the PCIe bus for revolutionary performance improvements. These components will be available in a variety of form factors and performance levels, designed specifically for certain market segments, and ultimately the costs will continue to decline as the technology evolves.

- **HPE Smart Array Controllers**—HPE offers a complete portfolio of enterprise-class RAID controllers with fault tolerance for ProLiant-attached storage. Designed to enhance server uptime and maintain flexibility for future growth, Smart Array Controllers blend the reliability of SCSI with the performance advantages of serial architecture. Providing industry-leading performance with unmatched data protection, these controllers are ideal for companies with direct-attached

SAS storage. Smart Array Controllers can help customers meet the requirements of a broad range of applications. Moreover, by providing extensive choices for server and storage deployment, these controllers provide high levels of flexibility and return on investment (ROI).

- **HPE Smart HBAs**—Perfect for environments that require fast access, Smart HBAs provide cost-effective and reliable high-performance SAS connectivity to DAS, shared storage, and tape drives for ProLiant servers running Hadoop, Database Availability Group, and VMware vSAN. Smart HBAs provide a conduit for deploying software-defined storage to manage the IT storage pool. For greater flexibility, Smart HBAs can run in either HBA or simple RAID mode.

- **HPE Dynamic Smart Array**—The Dynamic Smart Array Controller provides an embedded SATA RAID solution for ProLiant Gen9 and Gen10 servers. The common metadata format on the drives allows disks to migrate from Dynamic Smart Array to Smart Array or Smart HBA (when running in RAID mode) if needed. This capability helps to achieve higher performance, capacity, and availability. This controller is ideal for supporting boot device and applications that do not require significant IO workload.

- **Flash media drives**—HPE offers high-performance flash media kits for customers requiring boot-from-flash for integrated hypervisors and first tier operating systems. With high data retention and read write cycles, HPE flash media devices are available in both Secure Digital (SD) and MicroSD form factors.

- **Optical drives**—Optical drives for ProLiant servers feature an industry-standard SATA interface and are supported on most major operating systems.

  - **SATA DVD ROM optical drives**—The DVD ROM drive is designed to read not only CD ROM and CD R/RW discs but also DVD ROM, DVD RAM, DVD +R/RW, and DVD R/RW discs. HPE optical drives are available in half-height, slim, and super slim form factors.

  - **SATA DVD RW optical drives**—The DVD RW drive can read DVD 4.7 GB through 8.5 GB media, as well as standard stamped, CD-R, and CD-RW media. This drive supports writing to CD-R, CD-RW, DVD +R/RW, and DVD-R/RW media via software utilities. For Microsoft operating systems, this is available by installing the included Roxio software disk. For other operating systems, an operating system–specific software utility is required for writing to media.

- **HPE PCIe Workload Accelerators**—PCIe Workload Accelerators for ProLiant servers are PCIe card-based direct-attach solutions. PCIe storage devices provide performance, reliability, and very low latency. With enterprise-class endurance and capacity points up to 3.0 TB, these solutions are ideal for applications and workloads requiring maximized performance.

- **HPE 12 GB SAS Expander Card**—The SAS expander card allows supported ProLiant Gen9 and Gen10 servers to be configured with their maximum number of drives. The expander card is ideal for users who want to configure RAID for more than eight internal HDDs or add an additional internal drive cage and configure RAID across all the internal drives.

- **HPE Smart Storage Battery**—In ProLiant Gen9 and Gen10 servers, a single Smart Storage Battery connected to the system board provides the backup battery power to all the Smart Array Controllers in the system that use flash-backed write cache (FBWC). Each 96-watt Smart Storage Battery in ProLiant ML/DL servers can provide enough power to back up the larger cache sizes (4 GB) found in Smart Array Controllers.

- **HPE Smart Storage Administrator (SSA)**—SSA is the comprehensive management and configuration application for Smart Storage products and solutions. Available as a stand-alone application or as a command-line interface (CLI), this utility provides advanced scripting and diagnostics capability to simplify and streamline array configuration and management.

- **HPE Smart Storage Power Management**—Optimizes controller power consumption based on both array configuration and workload. Smart Storage Power Management can save several watts on storage controller power consumption without greatly impacting overall storage performance.

- **HPE SSD Smart Path**—With SSD Smart Path, the Smart Storage device drivers analyze each IO request to decide whether it can be executed more quickly through the driver itself or whether it should be passed to the Smart Array firmware for execution as normal IO. It is designed specifically to deliver performance gains for logical drives using SSDs on Smart Array Controllers.

- **HPE SmartCache**—In DAS environments, SmartCache uses one or more SSDs as dedicated caching devices for other volumes, increasing storage performance by copying the most frequently accessed data to the low-latency SSDs for quicker access that is completely transparent to host applications.

HPE hard disk drives

Figure 3-12 Proven performance for every workload

HPE hard disk drives, shown in Figure 3-12, are ideal for core compute workloads from SMB to large enterprise—email, CRM, archive, and backup.

HDDs offer lowest $/GB than flash and increased SFF Capacity: 15 K up to 900 GB; 10 K up to 2.4 TB. HPE hard disk drives have rigorous testing/qualification program, backed by 3.35 million test hours (internal HPE Lab Testing).

Note

Verify capacities in latest HPE QuickSpecs.

Key features/benefits:

- All HDDs include Digitally Signed Firmware and Best-in-Class (BIC) firmware security features.

- Support Non-Disruptive Updates (NDUs) firmware updates do not interrupt access to data or system service.

- Prevent unexpected data loss with a "Do Not Remove" button on HPE Smart Carriers.

- Supported on: HPE ProLiant rack and tower servers, HPE BladeSystem, HPE Apollo, HPE Integrity, and HPE Synergy Compute Modules.

HPE solid-state drives

Figure 3-13 Accelerate the performance of data intensive apps

HPE hard disk drives, shown in Figure 3-13, are ideal for demanding workloads requiring fast processing—OLTP, Business Intelligence, Big Data analytics, web servers, boot/swap, virtualization, data warehousing, ERP, and cloud computing.

SSDs offer best IOPS/dollar and low latency: 2.5" NVMe SSDs enable faster data access. An additional benefit is reduced latency and higher performance per server with up to 474,000 IOPS for core enterprise workloads.

 Note

Verify capacities and performance numbers in latest HPE QuickSpecs.

Key features/benefits:

- All SSDs include Digitally Signed Firmware and BIC firmware security features.

- Prevent unexpected data loss with the HPE Smart Carrier featuring a "do not remove" button and intuitive icons that report drive activity at-a-glance.

- Monitor lifespan of SSD with HPE SmartSSD Wear Gauge management tools.

- Rigorous testing/qualification program, backed by 3.35 million test hours.

- Broad support: HPE ProLiant rack and tower servers, HPE BladeSystem, HPE Apollo, HPE Integrity, and HPE Synergy Compute Modules.

HPE Smart Array Controllers

Figure 3-14 Boost storage performance, scalability, and resiliency

HPE Smart Array Controllers, shown in Figure 3-14, are ideal for maximizing performance of enterprise DAS.

Key features/benefits:

- Free up a PCIe slot with Mixed Mode for Smart Array Controllers, offering flexibility to use both HBA and RAID modes simultaneously.

- Increased productivity with New UEFI Configuration Tool, which reduces time to configure simple RAID volumes.

- Save time for newly created RAID 5 or RAID 6 volumes that require parity initialization with Rapid Parity Initialization (RPI).

- Enhanced protection for data at rest on all SAS/SATA drives and data security to comply with regulations for sensitive data (such as HIPPA) using HPE Smart Array SR Secure Encryption that is a FIPS 140-2 Level 1, validated enterprise-class controller-based encryption solution.

Serial attached SCSI

The most common protocol used by Smart Array Controllers is SAS:

- A full-duplex architecture, effectively doubling throughput

- The current SAS standard provides for speeds of 6 Gb/s and 12 Gb/s

- Ability to attach up to 255 devices

- Can address up to 65,535 devices in a single SAS domain by using expanders

- Cabling distance up to 10 m

- Interface backward compatible with SATA disks

- Used with all types of disks:

  - **SSDs**—Single-level cell, multi-level cell, and 3-level cell

  - **10 K/15 K online/enterprise-class disks**—Increased mean time between failures (MTBF) of 1.6+ million hours, higher performance, and lower capacity compared to near line/mid-line (NL/MDL)

  - **7.2 K NL/MDL disks**—SATA drive using a SAS interface provides all the enterprise features that come with SAS, but still has the limitations of SATA for disk performance and MTBF

Solid-state drive technology

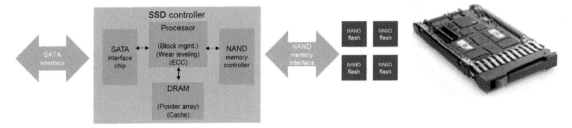

Figure 3-15 NAND flash memory types

NAND flash memory is a type of non-volatile memory that retains data even when power is turned off. The development of NAND flash memory has reduced the cost per bit and increased maximum chip capacity. As a result, flash memory is competitive with HDDs in terms of cost, performance, and reliability and is replacing HDDs in many environments.

NAND flash memory is written and read in 128 KB blocks, which are the smallest erasable units in a NAND device. Several types of NAND flash memory are available, as indicated in Figure 3-15:

- **Single-level cell (SLC)**—Stores one bit per cell and is fast, reliable, and expensive.

- **Multi-level cell (MLC)**—Offers greater storage density than SLC memory, but is slower and less robust.

- **Enterprise multi-level cell (eMLC)**—Stores two bits per cell, has greater endurance than MLC memory, and uses an advanced controller.

- **Consumer-grade multi-level cell (cMLC)**—Stores two bits per cell, is the lowest-cost NAND flash memory type, and is commonly used in cameras, cell phones, and USB drives.

- **Three-level cell (TLC)**—Stores three bits per cell and has more power and better error correction than other types of NAND flash memory.

The newest NAND technology is 3D NAND, in which memory cells are stacked vertically in multiple planes in the chip. This architecture increases the number of bits per chip to offer more storage capacity in a smaller physical space. It also reduces power consumption because the interconnect length between cells is shorter.

Solid-state drives

HPE SSDs are suited to enterprise environments with highly random data under a variety of write-workload applications. SSDs provide significantly better random read and write IOPS compared to HDDs. Although sequential read and write throughput is also improved over HDDs, the greatest benefit is recognized in random data applications. As a result, these high-performance, low-latency, and low-power SSDs provide significant system benefits for applications than previously overprovisioned HDD capacity to achieve better performance.

SSDs use flash memory technology. They have no moving parts and do not experience the latency or synchronization issues that are drawbacks of HDDs. SSD-sustained data transfer rates are much faster than those of HDDs. They also consume much less power.

HPE SSDs are available in categories based on their typical target workloads:

- **Read intensive**—HPE read-intensive 12 G SAS and 6 G SATA SSDs deliver enterprise features for a low price in HPE ProLiant server systems. This entry-level pricing is fueling rapid SSD adoption for read-intensive workloads because the cost per IOPS compares favorably to HDDs. Read-intensive SSDs deliver great performance for workloads high in reads such as boot/swap, web servers, and read caching.

- **Mixed use**—HPE mixed-use 12 G SAS and 6 G SATA SSDs are best suited for high IO applications with workloads balanced between reads and writes. The SAS and SATA SSDs provide the workload-optimized performance required for demanding IO-intensive applications. When paired with ProLiant servers, these SSDs help you meet the challenges of Big Data. They achieve twice the performance and endurance of previous HPE SAS and SATA SSDs. The SATA SSDs ship with a 6 Gb/s SATA hot-plug interface.

- **Write intensive**—HPE write-intensive 12 G SAS SSDs provide high write performance and endurance. They are best suited for mission-critical enterprise environments with workloads high in both reads and writes. Workloads best suited for these SSDs include OLTP, virtual desktop infrastructure, business intelligence, and Big Data analytics.

These categories include both SAS SSDs and SATA SSDs. The categories indicate the number of drive writes per day (DWPD) that you can expect from the drive.

Note

DWPD is the maximum number of 4 K host writes to the entire drive capacity of the SSD per day over a five-year period.

Read-intensive SSDs are typically available at the lowest price with an endurance of less than or equal to one DWPD. Write-intensive SSDs typically have the highest write performance, with a typical endurance of 10 DWPD or more. Mixed-use SSDs are for workloads that need a balance of strong read and write performance, with endurance typically more than one and less than 10 DWPD.

Choosing an HDD or SSD solution for an application

Characteristics	Spinning media/HDDs	Flash media/SSDs	Architectural implications
Typical latencies	In milliseconds	In tens of microseconds	Read/write cache management
IOPS density (IOPS/GB)	0.2 IOPS/GB (for example, ~180 IOPS with 900 GB 10K drive)	100 IOPS/GB (for example, ~40,000 IOPS in 400 GB)	Performance scalability
$/GB	$0.8 to $1/GB	5 to 10X HDDs (raw $/GB)	Storage efficiency
Media write cycle	Virtually unlimited (hundreds of millions)	5000 to 15,000 write cycles	Wear handling
Failure modes	Mechanical/Electronic	Electronic/Flash	Failure handling and reconstruction

Figure 3-16 Solid-state drive technology—HDD vs. SSD

To meet the demands for virtualized and data-intensive workloads, HPE optimized the storage architecture of the latest generation ProLiant servers for SSD performance, energy efficiency, and high density, as shown in Figure 3-16. The criteria for choosing SSD solutions are very strict. For example, consider how well NAND flash manages bad blocks of memory, wear leveling, and write amplification. These characteristics greatly affect SSD endurance.

The HPE SATA SSDs are available in various capacities for ProLiant servers. HPE 100 GB SSD pricing provides a competitive cost alternative with 146 GB 15,000 RPM HDDs and other lower capacity HDDs that are approaching the end of their life span.

Matching storage solutions with application-environment requirements goes beyond looking at specifications. It requires knowledge of current and future business needs.

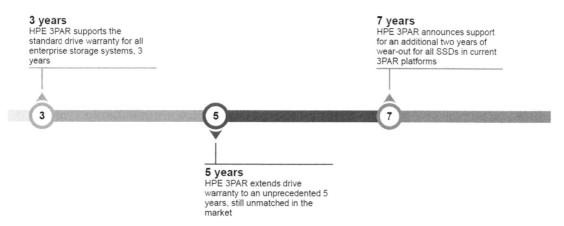

Figure 3-17 Solid-state drive support

The HPE 3PAR seven-year support covers all deployment types, including all-flash and hybrid models, as shown in Figure 3-17.

Comparing drive performance

SSDs provide significant performance advantages over traditional HDDs. The graph shows the relative performance in IOPS and latency for a performance HDD, a mainstream SSD, and an IO accelerator. The HPE IO Accelerator is an interface card containing an SSD, flash memory, and a custom controller that significantly improves data throughput with external storage devices.

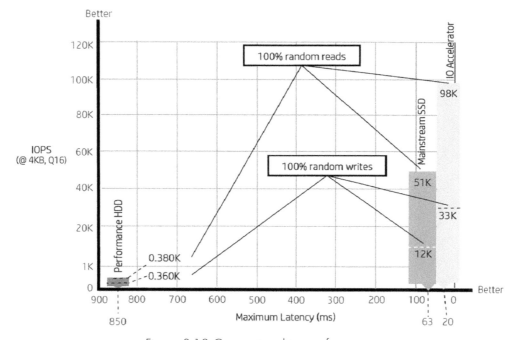

Figure 3-18 Comparing drive performance

SSDs do not have seek or rotational latency time. They address any sector of the NAND flash directly in 0.1 millisecond. SSD latency includes the time for memory access and transfer combined with controller overhead. SSDs excel at random read operations, where their performance can be more than 100 times better than that of spinning media drives. SSDs perform random writes at least 25 times faster than a comparable 15,000 RPM HDD. This means SSDs provide improved application performance, as illustrated in Figure 3-18.

	Enterprise HDD 15K RPM	MDL HDD 7.2K RPM	Enterprise SATA value/ boot (SSD)	Enterprise SATA mainstream (SSD)	Enterprise SAS performance (SSD)
Capacity	300 to 950 GB	500 to 3000 GB	100 GB	400 GB/200 GB	200 GB
IOPS 100% random writes	340	140	7000	10,000	15,000
IOPS 100% random reads	380	130	30,000	32,000	43,000
IOPS random read/write 70/30	370	137	17,000	19,000	26,000

Figure 3-19 High performance SSD vs. HDD technology

Figure 3-19 compares the performance of different storage devices. In this graph, for each vertical bar, the top number indicates IOPS for 100% random reads and the bottom number indicates IOPS for 100% random writes. It shows how the mainstream SSD and IO Accelerator vastly outperform the HDD and are capable of reading and writing data much faster.

Gen10 Smart Array portfolio

Key features	S-class Software RAID	E-class Essential RAID controllers	P-class Performance RAID controllers
ROC (RAID-on-Chip)	✗ (embedded)	✓ (some models)	✓ (some models)
Cache	✗	✗	1 GB / 2 GB / 4 GB
RAID	0 / 1 / 5 / 10	0 / 1 / 5 / 10	0 / 1 / 10 / 5 / 50 / 6 / 60 / 10 ADM
Lanes	14 (Int) (SATA)	8 (Int or Ext) (SAS/SATA)	4, 8, 16, 24 (Int and/or Ext) (SAS/SATA)
Form factor	Embedded	Standard plug-in/Modular	Standard plug-in/Modular/ Mezz.
SmartCache (SR) / CacheCade (MR)	✗	✗	Optional (standard with 800s)
Secure encryption	✗	Optional	Optional (SR only)
FIPS 140-2 Level 1 Certification	✗	✗	✓ (SR only)
Management	SR (Smart Array technology)	SR	SR or MR (MegaRAID)
OS support	Windows only	Windows/Linux/VMware	Windows/Linux/VMware

Figure 3-20 Gen10 comparison of S-Class, E-Class, and P-Class RAIDs

Gen10 Smart Array Controllers are divided into three different classes, as indicated in Figure 3-20:

- S-Class

- E-Class

- P-Class

Most controllers are managed by a traditional Smart Array management, whenever the controller name includes "MR", the MegaRAID, or HPE MR Storage Administrator is used. Not all features are identical when comparing SR and MR line of array controllers.

Security in HPE servers

At HPE, we are resolute to stay one step ahead. We engineer our products based on the belief that infrastructure should be the strongest defense, armed with the latest innovations to prevent, detect, and recover from security attacks. Just as customers expect and deserve high-quality and reliable products, we also believe customers should expect the most secure infrastructure in the industry— which is why we embed security into everything we do. Poor quality and reliability can slow down business, and security vulnerabilities can harm your customer's business and their brand.

We view our supply chain as an essential element of cybersecurity because of the possibility that products could be compromised at their source. We reduce the risk of exposing our supply chain to threats such as counterfeit materials, malicious software embedded in products, and other untrustworthy components by vetting component vendors and sourcing from Trade Agreements Act (TAA) designated countries. Because of the unique and privileged position within the IT infrastructure, we choose to reduce security concerns and threats to BIOS firmware by developing our BIOS firmware and ASICs in-house.

Security technologies and procedures

Security technologies and procedures are a major focus of Gen10. The whole server lifecycle is affected:

- Deploy
    - Connectivity and login procedures
    - Server booting
- Operate
    - Data encryption
    - Secure dispose
- Maintain
    - Updates
    - Digital signatures and verification

A new experience in server security and protection

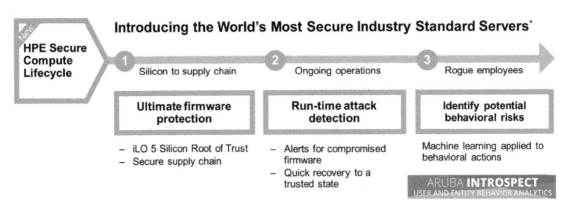

Figure 3-21 Introducing the World's Most Secure Industry-Standard Servers

As a result of our new HPE innovations, we have "The World's Most Secure Industry Standard Servers." The Silicon Root of Trust starts protecting our servers, early in the production process and all the way through the product lifecycle, which we have branded the HPE Secure Compute Lifecycle, shown in Figure 3-21.

Silicon to supply chain

Our customers want HPE to deliver an end-to-end security solution, starting at the very inception of the product with our Silicon Root of Trust. HPE is in a unique position here, because we develop our own custom iLO5 chipset in the fabrication facility, even before the server goes into production. We tie the server essential firmware (iLO5, UEFI, complex programmable logic device [CPLD], innovation engine [IE], and management engine [ME]) into our custom silicon with an unbreakable link. That immutable connection between the silicon and firmware protects the server through the production process, through our supply chain shipping and distribution, right to the customer's final location. From factory to floor, HPE provides protection.

After the server arrives safely to our customer's location, we continue with our HPE Secure Compute Lifecycle, by providing not only protection during operation, but also unparalleled detection and recovery capabilities. From boot to business, our Silicon Root of Trust provides protection because as soon as the server is booted and iLO firmware comes alive, it investigates the silicon for the immutable fingerprint that verifies all the firmware code is valid and uncompromised. Over a million lines of firmware code run before the operating system starts, making it essential to confirm that all server essential firmware is free from malware or compromised code.

Ongoing operations

During operation of the server, HPE has a new technology that conducts run-time firmware validation that checks the firmware stored in the server. At any point, if compromised code or malware is inserted in any of the critical firmware, an iLO audit log alert is created to notify the customer that a compromise has occurred.

Rogue employees

In the unlikely event of a breach into the HPE server firmware, after detection has been completed, the customer may then securely recover the firmware automatically to a previous known good state. HPE provides this function through a new HPE license called HPE iLO Advanced Premium Security Edition. Although a breach is highly unlikely, there may be a case where customers have disgruntled employees who get access to the data center and insert bad code.

This step in the lifecycle process provides security to and through the network. Aruba ClearPass creates a strong networking security clearance protocol for clearing anyone requesting access to the network. ClearPass creates a profile of potential users and clears access of users into our Aruba networks. Our recently acquired company, Niara, is responsible for monitoring the activity of users inside the network. After ClearPass vets and clears users into networks, Niara takes over, and using machine learning, works to predict any nefarious behavior before any serious damage can be done. If Niara identifies abnormal activity resembling potential malicious behavior, it communicates to ClearPass, temporarily terminating the suspected user's access to the network until more thorough vetting can be conducted. In the case of a rogue employee, this predictive capability can block potential bad actors from the network, before any damage is done.

A new experience in accelerating compliance

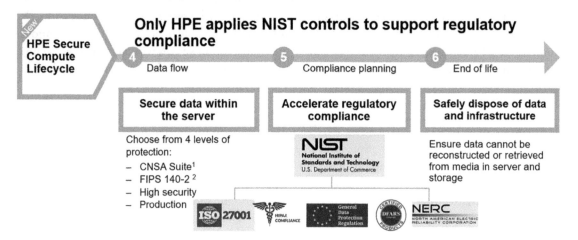

Figure 3-22 A new experience in accelerating compliance

Data flow

Following the lifecycle approach, as illustrated in Figure 3-22, the next step is protecting data and communication to and from the server and inside the server. HPE is the first industry server manufacturer to provide support for the commercial national security algorithms, or CNSA suite. This is the very highest level of security, typically used for the most Top Secret and Confidential information. HPE also has Federal Information Processing Standard (FIPS) validation on firmware and offers that as another level of protection during the operation phase of the server's life.

Scalable encryption is another differentiated offering from HPE that protects data stored in the server. Unlike competitor servers, who use self-encrypting drives that require management of separate keys in each and every drive, HPE offers secure encryption through our Smart Array Controller cards that contain all encryption cards and manage those at scale. Going one step further, the HPE Atalla Enterprise Secure Key Manager (ESKM) is also qualified with our controller cards that takes key management to a higher level. Through this technology, we are saving customers the agony of tracking an unmanageable number of encryption keys—sometimes on spreadsheets.

Compliance planning

Closely related to security are the numerous government regulations with which customers must comply. To aid our customers, HPE applies the National Institute of Standards and Technology (NIST) 800-53 security controls to a solution stack of storage, networking, servers, and software, creating a secure baseline. This secure baseline provides customers with the comfort to issue an authority to operate (ATO) before putting an IT infrastructure into operation.

End of life

The final part of HPE Secure Compute Lifecycle comes after the servers and other equipment have reached their full use and entered end of life. HPE Pointnext security and protection services provide final disposal of the customers' equipment, ensuring the data is properly disposed of according to NIST standards.

Management tools—Compute

HPE ProLiant management innovations target three segments to ensure that customers have complete lifecycle management—for their current environment and in the future as their business grows.

Server management

- **Managing single system ("On System")**—Built-in intelligence and automation for increased server admin productivity. It provides on-system management to provision, monitor, and troubleshoot servers as well as remote and out-of-band management. The on-system management tools available for ProLiant servers include:

    - Intelligence on every HPE server enabling setup, health and alerting, and firmware maintenance

    - UEFI

    - iLO 5

    - RESTful API, HPE RESTful Interface Tool, and other HPE scripting tools

    - Intelligent Provisioning

    - Smart Storage Administrator

    - HPE Smart Update and Service Pack for ProLiant (SPP)

    - HPE BladeSystem management

- **Managing multiple systems**—Installed at customer site ("On Premise")
  - HPE OneView
  - HPE OneView Global Dashboard
  - iLO Amplifier Pack
- **Managing multiple systems**—Cloud-based management for service ticket and warranty tracking, health, and alerting ("On Cloud")
  - Remote Support and Insight Online
  - InfoSight

Activity: ProLiant server management technologies

1. Draft two or three questions about each of these topics:

   - iLO

   _____

   _____

   _____

   - UEFI

   _____

   _____

   _____

   - HPE SUM

   _____

   _____

   _____

   - RESTful API

   _____

   _____

   _____

- Intelligent Provisioning

  _____

  _____

  _____

- Smart Storage Administrator

  _____

  _____

  _____

2. Focus on what you would like to learn about each topic.

3. Be prepared to share your questions with the class.

Activity debrief

1. What questions posed by others in the group do you want to learn the answers to?

   _____

   _____

   _____

   _____

   _____

   _____

   _____

2. Which of these tools do you know the most about?

   _____

   _____

   _____

   _____

   _____

   _____

   _____

3. Which ones are you least familiar with?

_____

_____

_____

_____

_____

_____

_____

UEFI

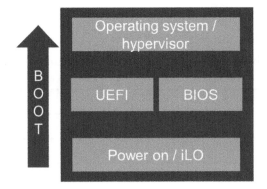

Figure 3-23 Server boot process

UEFI is an industry-standard specification that defines the model for the interface between the operating system and system firmware during the startup process. Developed by a consortium of more than 100 technology companies, including HPE and Microsoft, UEFI is processor architecture-agnostic, supporting x86, x64, ARM, and Itanium processors.

UEFI defines the interface between the operating system and platform firmware during the boot, or startup process, as indicated in Figure 3-23. Compared to BIOS, UEFI supports advanced preboot user interfaces.

UEFI standardizes interfaces within platform initialization firmware and within the preboot UEFI environment/shell. It provides a preboot GUI that standardizes the environment for booting an operating system and preboot applications (boot loaders, diagnostics, setup scripts, and so forth). UEFI also provides a pre-operating system network stack, Secure Boot, and expanded storage.

The UEFI network stack enables implementation on a richer network-based OS deployment environment while still supporting traditional Preboot Execution Environment (PXE) deployments.

UEFI supports both IPv4 and IPv6 networks. In addition, features such as Secure Boot enable platform vendors to implement an OS-agnostic approach to securing systems in the preboot environment. The ROM-Based Setup Utility (RBSU) functionality is available from the UEFI interface, along with additional configuration options.

The goal for implementing UEFI in ProLiant servers is to modernize platform firmware and provide an interface that is not architecture-specific. ProLiant Gen9 servers introduce UEFI as the default BIOS firmware interface, although they continue to support legacy BIOS settings. HPE recommends that the UEFI default be used with all ProLiant Gen9 and Gen10 servers.

 Note

Many option cards are only supported in UEFI mode and need UEFI compliant option ROMs. One example is the HPE Smart Array S100i controller.

UEFI benefits

UEFI benefits for the ProLiant Gen9 and Gen10 server family include the ability to:

- **Use drives larger than 2.2 TB**—Hard drives in UEFI use Global Unique Identifier Partition Table (GPT), which provides far greater boot drive capacities, allowing the use of high-capacity drives for storage and system booting. UEFI offers complete access to the system hardware and resources, allowing UEFI diagnostics and troubleshooting applications to be run before loading an operating system.

- **Configure UEFI with standard boot methods for enhanced flexibility**—UEFI supports PXE boot for IPv6 networks allowing a unified network stack to PXE boot from any network controller while maintaining backward compatibility and continued support for IPv4 PXE. UEFI allows PXE multicast boot support for image deployment to multiple servers at the same time. Servers with an Embedded User Partition (a general-purpose disk partition on non-volatile flash memory, which is embedded on the system board) can be configured using iLO. After the partition is formatted, it can be used for read and write access from the server operating system.

- **Enable Secure Boot to improve security measures**—UEFI protects against unauthorized operating systems and malware rootkit attacks, validating that the system only runs authenticated option ROMs, applications, and operating system boot loaders that have been digitally signed. UEFI uses a public key to verify UEFI drivers loaded from PCIe cards, drivers loaded from mass storage devices, preboot UEFI shell applications including firmware updates, and operating system UEFI boot loaders.

- **Take advantage of the UEFI shell and HPE RESTful API for scalable configuration deployment**—UEFI includes the UEFI shell, a command-line interface (CLI) application that allows scripting, file manipulation, obtaining system information, and running other UEFI applications. The UEFI shell is based on the UEFI Shell Specification 2.0, but it is enhanced with an extended command set for additional functionality. The UEFI shell includes a programming API that can be used to create custom UEFI applications. UEFI supports the HPE RESTful API, an industry-recognized architectural style, for server standardized interactions to configure at scale using an HTTPS Web protocol.

- **Perform industry-standard server configurations with fewer reboots**—Testing in HPE Labs found that configuring BIOS, iLO, and network interface cards (NICs) on a ProLiant DL380 server with UEFI BIOS required two system reboots, compared to a ProLiant DL380 server with legacy BIOS, which required four system reboots.

UEFI in Gen10 supports:

- USB 3.0 stack

- TPM 2.0

- NVMe boot

- iSCSI Software Initiator support

- HTTP/HTTPs boot as a PXE alternative

UEFI System Utilities

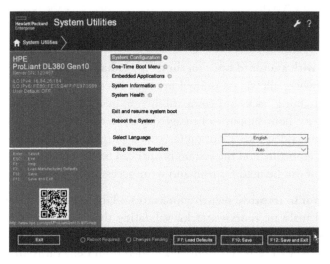

Figure 3-24 UEFI System Utilities

The System Utilities screen, as shown in Figure 3-24, is the main screen in the UEFI menu-driven interface. Press the up or down arrow keys to select a menu option. A selected option changes color from white to yellow. Press **Enter** to display submenus and other configuration options for your selection. The System Utilities screen displays menu options for the following configuration tasks:

- **System Configuration**—Displays options for viewing and configuring the BIOS/Platform Configuration (RBSU) menu and the iLO Configuration Utility.

- **One-Time Boot Menu**—Displays options for selecting a boot override option and running a UEFI application from a file system.

- **Embedded Applications**—Displays options for viewing and configuring embedded applications, including Intelligent Provisioning and firmware updates.

- **System Information**—Displays options for viewing the server name and generation, serial number, product ID, BIOS version and date, power management controller, backup BIOS version and date, system memory, and processors.

- **System Health**—Displays options for viewing the current health status of all devices in the system.

- **Exit and resume system boot**—Exits the system and continues the normal booting process.

- **Reboot the System**—Exits the system and reboots it by going through the UEFI Boot Order list and launching the first bootable option in the system. For example, you can launch the UEFI Shell, if enabled and listed as the first bootable option in the list.

- **Select Language**—Enables you to select a language to use in the user interface. English is the default language.

- **Setup Browser Selection**—Enables administrator to select a graphical or text-based browser for selecting the system utilities.

To access UEFI System Utilities:

1. Reboot the server. The server starts up and the ProLiant POST screen appears.

2. Press **F9** in the ProLiant POST screen. The System Utilities screen appears.

3. Use the up and down arrows to change a selection.

4. Press **Enter** to select an entry.

5. Press **Escape** to go back to the previous screen.

To exit the System Utilities screen and reboot the server, press **Esc** until the main menu is displayed, and then select one of the following options:

- **Exit and resume system boot**—Exits the system and continues the normal boot process. The system continues through the boot order list and launches the first bootable option in the system.

- **Reboot the system**—Exits the system and reboots the system without continuing the normal boot process.

Use **F12** to save settings and exit from System Utilities on Gen10 servers.

Note

For more information, visit:

http://h17007.www1.hpe.com/us/en/enterprise/servers/solutions/info-library

UEFI Shell management environment

Figure 3-25 Embedded UEFI shell

The system BIOS in all ProLiant Gen9 and Gen10 servers includes an embedded UEFI shell in the ROM.

Based on the UEFI shell specification, the shell environment provides an API and CLI that allow scripting, file manipulation, and obtaining system information. The shell also runs other UEFI applications. These features enhance the capabilities of the UEFI System Utilities.

From the System Utilities screen, select **Embedded Applications** → **Embedded UEFI Shell** and the Embedded UEFI Shell screen appears. Press any key to acknowledge that you are physically present.

This step ensures that certain features, such as disabling Secure Boot or managing the Secure Boot certificates using third-party UEFI tools, are not restricted. If an administrator password is set, enter it at the prompt, and press Enter. The Shell> prompt appears. Enter the commands required to complete your task, and enter the exit command to exit the Shell, as illustrated in Figure 3-25.

Built-in commands:

- **Standard commands**—File manipulations, driver management, device access, scripting control, system information, basic network operations.

- **Extensible**—Original equipment manufacturers (OEMs) can provide value-add commands.

Embedded UEFI shell commands

The UEFI shell is a mini operating system and includes many commands to assist in the management of the preboot environment. These commands include:

- `Shell> help –b`—The help command can be used with the –b option to display one page at a time. Press **Enter** to continue or **q** to exit help.

- `alias`—Displays, creates, or deletes UEFI Shell aliases.

- `attrib`—Displays or changes the attributes of files or directories.

- `cd`—Displays or changes the current directory.

- `cls`—Clears standard output and optionally changes background color.

- `comp`—Compares the contents of two files on a byte for byte basis.

- `cp`—Copies one or more files or directories to another location.

- `date`—Displays and sets the current date for the system.

- `devices`—Displays the list of devices managed by UEFI drivers.

- `devtree`—Displays the UEFI Driver Model compliant device tree.

- `dh`—Displays the device handles in the UEFI environment.

- `dmem`—Displays the contents of system or device memory.

- `drivers`—Displays the UEFI driver list.

- `echo`—Controls script file command echoing or displays a message.

- `edit`—Full screen editor for ASCII or UCS-2 files.

- `eficompress`—Compresses a file using UEFI compression algorithm.

- `efidecompress`—Decompresses a file using UEFI decompression algorithm.

- `else`—Identifies the code executed when "if" is false.

- `endfor`—Ends a "for" loop.

- `endif`—Ends the block of a script controlled by an "if" statement.

- `exit`—Exits the UEFI Shell or the current script.

- `for`—Starts a loop based on "for" syntax.

- `fwupdate`—Invokes an HPE UEFI Shell utility to update system BIOS firmware.

- `getmtc`—Gets the monotonic counter (MTC) from Boot Services and displays it.

BIOS/Platform Configuration screen

Figure 3-26 BIOS/Platform Configuration screen

The BIOS/Platform Configuration menu, shown in Figure 3-26, replaces the RBSU on ProLiant Gen9 and Gen10 servers. Use this menu to access and use both UEFI and legacy BIOS options. You can configure system BIOS settings from the BIOS/Platform Configuration screen through the various menus.

Workload Profiles and performance options

Workload Profiles are a configuration option to deploy BIOS settings based on the workload customer intends to run on the server. Workload Profiles are a configuration option to deploy BIOS settings to accommodate the intended application of the server. Workload Profiles is one of the HPE Intelligent System Tuning (IST) features.

Gen10 workload profiles

The system provides these Workload Profiles:

- **General Power Efficient Compute**

  – This profile is the default profile for most ProLiant servers and HPE Synergy compute modules.

  – This profile applies the most common performance settings that benefit most application workloads while also enabling power management settings that have minimal impact to overall performance. The settings that are applied heavily favor a balanced approach between general application performances versus power efficiency.

  – This profile is recommended for customers who do not typically tune their BIOS for their workload.

- **General Peak Frequency Compute**

  – This profile is intended for workloads that generally benefit from processors or memory that must achieve the maximum frequency possible, for any individual core, at any time. Power management settings are applied when they ensure that any component frequency upside can be readily achieved. Processing speed is favored over any latencies that might occur. This profile is a general-purpose profile, so optimizations are done generically to increase processor core and memory speed.

  – This profile benefits workloads that typically benefit from faster compute time.

- **General Throughput Compute**

  – This profile is intended to be used for workloads where the total maximum sustained workload throughput is needed. Increased throughput does not always occur when the processor runs at the highest individual core speed. Increased throughput can occur when the processor is able to perform sustained work across all available cores during maximum utilization. Power management settings are disabled when they are known to have impact on maximum achievable bandwidth.

  – Best throughput is achieved when the workload is also non-uniform memory access (NUMA) aware and optimized so settings that benefit NUMA awareness are applied.

 Note

Non-uniform memory access (NUMA) is a computer memory design used in multiprocessing, where the memory access time depends on the memory location relative to the processor. Under NUMA, a processor can access its own local memory faster than non-local memory (memory local to another processor or memory shared between processors). The benefits of NUMA are limited to particular workloads, notably on servers where the data is often associated strongly with certain tasks or users (Wikipedia.org, April 2019).

- **Virtualization—Power Efficient**—This profile is intended to be used for virtualization environments. The profile ensures that all available virtualization options are enabled. Certain virtualization technologies can have possible performance impacts to nonvirtualized environments and can be disabled in other profiles. Power management settings can have an impact on performance when running virtualization operating systems, and this profile applies power management settings that are virtualization friendly.

- **Virtualization—Max Performance**—This profile is intended to be used for virtualization environments. The profile ensures that all available virtualization options are enabled. Power management settings are disabled in favor of delivering maximum performance.

- **Low Latency**

  - This profile is intended to be used by customers who desire the least amount of computational latency for their workloads. This profile follows the most common best practices that are documented in the "HPE Low Latency" whitepaper. Maximum speed and throughput are often sacrificed to lower overall computational latency. Power management and other management features that might introduce computational latency are also disabled.

  - The profile benefits customers running Real-Time Operating Systems (RTOS) or other transactional latency–sensitive workloads.

- **Mission Critical**—This profile is intended to be used by customers who trade off performance for server reliability above the basic server defaults. The profile enables advanced memory reliability, availability, and serviceability (RAS) features that are known to have more than a measurable impact to computational performance. Enabling this profile will have an impact on maximum memory bandwidth and will increase memory latency.

- **Transactional Application Processing**—This profile is intended to be used for business processing environments, such as OLTP applications that require a database back end. For example, workloads typically comprised of a high number of user-based, transactional applications running on a single server with a cohosted database component. The profile balances the requirement of managing both peak frequency and throughput.

- **High-Performance Compute**—This profile is intended for customers running in a traditional HPC environment. Typically, these environments are clustered environments where each node performs at maximum utilization for extended periods of time to solve large-scale scientific and engineering workloads. The default for our Apollo series servers, power management is typically disabled in favor of sustained available bandwidth and processor compute capacity. This profile is similar to the Low-Latency profile except that some latency is accepted to achieve maximum throughput.

- **Decision Support**—This profile is intended for Enterprise Business Database (Business Intelligence) workloads that are focused on operating and/or accessing data warehouses, such as data mining or online analytical processing (OLAP).

- **Graphic Processing**—This profile is intended for workloads that are run on server configurations which utilize Graphics Processing Units (GPUs). GPUs typically depend on maximum bandwidth between IO and memory. Power management features that have impact on the links between IO and memory are disabled. Peer-to-Peer traffic is also critical, and therefore, virtualization is also disabled.

- **IO Throughput**—This profile is intended to be used for configurations that depend on maximum throughput between IO and memory. Processor utilization-driven power management features that have performance impact to the links between IO and memory are disabled.

- **Custom**

  - This option on the Workload Profiles menu disables Workload Profiles. Use this option if you want to set specific BIOS options for your deployment manually. When you select Custom, all the settings for the previously selected profile are carried forward. You can edit all or some of the options.

  - Custom is not a profile, and settings that you specify are not saved as a template.

Default profiles for servers

Workload Profile options support a variety of power and performance requirements. For most HPE ProLiant Gen10 servers and HPE Synergy compute modules, Workload Profile is set to General Power Efficient Compute by default. This Workload Profile provides common performance and power settings suitable for most application workloads. For ProLiant XL servers in an HPE Apollo system, the Workload Profile is set to HPC by default. Selecting a Workload Profile other than the Custom profile affects other setting options. For example, selecting the General Peak Frequency Compute profile automatically sets the Power Regulator mode to Static High Performance. This setting cannot be changed and is grayed out.

Workload profiles dependencies

There are multiple options that are available for BIOS configuration. Not all profiles set the same options to specific settings. Each profile is designed to obtain specific performance results and sets different options to meet those results. The options that a profile sets are called dependencies. All other options are unaffected by the Workload Profile and are referred to as nondependent settings.

Applying a Workload Profile

You apply a Workload Profile to have the system manage your workload according to predefined settings provided with the system. Dependent options cannot be changed and are grayed out. You can change any nondependent options in a profile.

There may be one or more dependent options that you want to change in your Workload Profile. Dependent options cannot be changed for a predefined profile. You can change the dependent options in Custom mode. When you are in Custom mode, your deployment is no longer in profile mode and you can manually adjust option settings. When you enter Custom mode, all the settings from the previously applied profile are shown. The easiest way to change dependent settings is to modify an applied profile. First, apply a Workload Profile that has most of the settings that you want to use then change to Custom mode. Then change only the settings you want to have new values.

System Options

From the System Options menu, you can configure system settings such as:

- **Serial Port Options**—Assign COM port number and associated resources to the selected physical serial port.

- **USB Options**

  - Configure how USB ports and embedded devices operate at startup (USB Enabled [default], External USB Port Disabled).

  - Configure USB Boot Support to prevent the system from booting any connected USB devices and disable booting the iLO virtual media.

  - Select whether the system should attempt to boot external USB drive keys, internal USB drive keys, or the internal SD card slot first.

  - Control the Virtual Install Disk, which contains server-specific drivers that an operating system can use during installation. If this option is enabled, Windows Server automatically locates required drivers and installs them.

  - Control the Embedded User Partition, which is a general-purpose disk partition on non-volatile flash memory embedded on the system board. After it is enabled, the partition can be formatted using the server operating system or by using the HPE RESTful Interface tool. After the partition is formatted, it can be accessed for read and write access from the server operating system.

  - Set the operating mode of USB 3.0 ports.

- **Processor Options**—Configure processor options such as configuring Intel® Hyperthreading, processor core enablement, and x2APIC support.

- **SATA Controller Options**—Configure options such as selecting the Embedded Serial Advanced Technology Attachment (SATA) configuration and configuring SATA Secure Erase.

- **Virtualization Options**—Configure virtualization options such as Virtualization Technology, Intel® VT-d, and SR-IOV.

- **Boot Time Optimization**—Configure Boot Time Optimizations such as Dynamic Power Capping and Extended Memory Test.

- **Advanced Memory Protection**—Configure Advanced ECC Support (default) or Online Spare with Advanced ECC Support.

HPE rack and power

The HPE Data Center Infrastructure family includes a wide range of small-to-medium business (SMB) to enterprise products for rack and power, as illustrated in Figure 3-27.

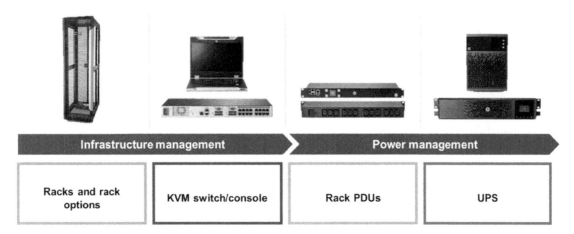

Figure 3-27 HPE rack and power infrastructure—Compatible, flexible, powerful, and trusted

HPE rack and power infrastructure portfolio

HPE rack and power infrastructure portfolio include:

- Racks and rack accessories

- Keyboard, video, mouse (KVM) switch/consoles

- Power distribution units (PDU)

- Uninterruptable power systems (UPS)

Flexible and robust infrastructure solutions

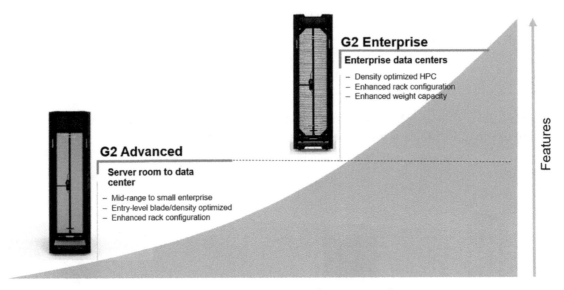

Figure 3-28 Flexible and robust infrastructure solutions

G2 rack portfolio includes two lines, shown in Figure 3-28: Advanced and Enterprise.

G2 Advanced Racks are suitable for any load from a server room to a data center:

- Mid-range to small enterprise

- Entry-level blade/Density optimized

- Enhanced rack configuration

G2 Enterprise Racks are primarily targeted to enterprise data centers:

- Density optimized HPC

- Enhanced rack configuration

- Enhanced weight capacity

HPE G2 Advanced Rack Series

HPE G2 Advanced Rack Series are ideal for mid-range to small enterprise rack environments, entry-level up to blade/density optimized computing, and server rooms to data centers.

HPE G2 Advanced Series Racks are designed for low-to-medium density IT configurations deployed in a diverse set of environments—from the data closet to the data center. Following EIA-310 specifications for 19-inch racks, G2 Advanced Racks are designed specifically to support a wide range of HPE IT equipment (servers, storage, and networking), as well as the entire portfolio HPE Rack and Power Infrastructure solutions (PDU, UPS, and KVM).

All HPE G2 Advanced Series Racks are supported with a 10-year limited warranty that provides either repair or complete replacement of the rack. Offering this industry-leading warranty requires a highly reliable and durable design that includes features such as a fully welded, roll-form rack design, heavy-gauge rails, and heavy-duty castors that can support a static load of up to 3000 lbs. Additionally, select shock pallet models include packaging specifically designed to support the shipment of precon-figured racks with up to 2250 lbs. of IT equipment.

The G2 Advanced Series Rack portfolio includes a wide range of rack models covering a variety of heights, widths, and depths. To simplify purchasing and installation, all rack models include locking side panels and baying kits. Additionally, HPE offers a large portfolio of rack accessories that support airflow management, cable management, and added rack stability.

Key features/benefits of HPE G2 Advanced Rack Series:

- Supports higher density computing using enhanced airflow and thermal management

- Flexible configuration installations with enhanced flexible cable management

- Enhanced security using advanced electronic and biometric lock security solutions

- Put power where you need it in the rack with Flexible PDU mounting options

- Flexible options—22U, 36U, 42U, and 48U options; 600 and 800 mm wide, 1075 and 1200 mm deep

- HPE warranty—10 years

Activity: HPE Reference Architecture for Microsoft Exchange Server 2016 on HPE ProLiant DL380 Gen10 Server

1. Use this document:

   https://h20195.www2.hpe.com/v2/getdocument.aspx?docname=a00048480enw

2. Answer the following questions:

   a. What is the performance difference between Gold 6132 and Gold 6126 in the Reference Architecture?

   _____

   _____

   _____

   _____

   _____

   _____

b. How are the cache settings at the array controller configured?

_____

_____

_____

_____

_____

_____

_____

Activity: HPE Sizer for Exchange Server 2016

1. Download and install the sizer:

    https://h20195.www2.hpe.com/V2/GetDocument.aspx?docname=4AA6-3720ENW

2. Use the inputs from the Reference Architecture document.

3. Prepare to present the BOM.

_____

_____

_____

_____

_____

_____

_____

_____

_____

_____

_____

_____

_____

Solution components

Part numbers are at the time of publication and subject to change. The bill of material (BOM) does not include complete support options or other rack and power requirements.

Qty	Part number	Description
		Rack
2	BW908A	HPE 642 1200mm Shock Intelligent Rack
		Configuration 1 – Servers using Gold 6126 Processor
4	868705-B21	HPE DL380 Gen10 12LFF CTO Server
4	826862-L21	HPE DL380 Gen10 6126 Xeon-G FIO Kit
4	826862-B21	HPE DL380 Gen10 6126 Xeon-G Kit
16	815100-B21	HPE 32GB 2Rx4 PC4-2666V-R Smart Kit
4	826685-B21	HPE DL380 Gen10 3LFF Rear SAS/SATA Kit
4	826686-B21	HPE DL38X Gen10 4LFF MID-plane HDD
8	872376-B21	HPE 800GB SAS 12G MU SFF SC DS SSD
76	857644-B21	HPE 10TB SAS 7.2K LFF SC He 512e DS HDD
4	700751-B21	HPE FlexFabric 10Gb 2-port 534FLR-SFP+ Adapter
4	804338-B21	HPE Smart Array P816i-a SR Gen10 Ctrlr
4	870549-B21	HPE DL38X Gen10 12Gb SAS Expander
4	875241-B21	HPE 96W Smart Storage Battery 145mm Cbl
4	864279-B21	HPE TPM 2.0 Gen10 Kit (Optional)
8	865438-B21	HPE 800W FS Ti Ht Plg LH Pwr Sply Kit
4	Q2F26AAE	HPE Smart Array Secure Encryption E-LTU
4	JG081C	HPE X240 10G SFP+ SFP+ 5m DAC Cable
		Configuration 2 – Servers using Gold 6132 Processor
4	868705-B21	HPE DL380 Gen10 12LFF CTO Server
4	826870-L21	HPE DL380 Gen10 6132 Xeon-G FIO Kit
4	826870-B21	HPE DL380 Gen10 6132 Xeon-G Kit
16	815100-B21	HPE 32GB 2Rx4 PC4-2666V-R Smart Kit
4	826685-B21	HPE DL380 Gen10 3LFF Rear SAS/SATA Kit
4	826686-B21	HPE DL38X Gen10 4LFF MID-plane HDD
8	872376-B21	HPE 800GB SAS 12G MU SFF SC DS SSD
76	857644-B21	HPE 10TB SAS 7.2K LFF SC He 512e DS HDD
4	700751-B21	HPE FlexFabric 10Gb 2-port 534FLR-SFP+ Adapter
4	804338-B21	HPE Smart Array P816i-a SR Gen10 Ctrlr
4	870549-B21	HPE DL38X Gen10 12Gb SAS Expander
4	875241-B21	HPE 96W Smart Storage Battery 145mm Cbl
4	864279-B21	HPE TPM 2.0 Gen10 Kit (Optional)
8	865438-B21	HPE 800W FS Ti Ht Plg LH Pwr Sply Kit
4	Q2F26AAE	HPE Smart Array Secure Encryption E-LTU
4	JG081C	HPE X240 10G SFP+ SFP+ 5m DAC Cable

Learning check

1. You are attending a meeting with a banking customer to discuss their future data center modernization plans. They have been alarmed by reports of firmware-level security breaches, and they tell you that such an event in their infrastructure would cost them millions of dollars in fines. They tell you that they require FIPS-level security or higher, and they ask you if HPE servers can deliver this level of security. They also ask what HPE offers in the Gen10 platform for protecting against firmware-level attack.

   How should you respond?

   _____

   _____

   _____

   _____

   _____

   _____

   _____

   _____

   _____

   _____

   _____

   _____

   _____

2. Match the controller family with available RAID levels and Boot mode support.

P-class	0 / 1 / 10 / 5 and UEFI
E-class	0 / 1 / 10 / 5 and UEFI/Legacy
S-class	0 / 1 / 10 / 5 / 50 / 6 / 60 / 10 ADM and UEFI/Legacy

3. HPE G2 Enterprise Rack Series support up to 3000 lbs. dynamic load.
   - ☐ True
   - ☐ False

4. Name five on-system tools for HPE ProLiant server management.

_____

_____

_____

_____

_____

5. Name the three benefits of using UEFI compared to legacy BIOS?

_____

_____

_____

_____

_____

_____

6. Name three workload profiles configurable in Gen10 RBSU.

_____

_____

_____

_____

_____

Alternative servers for smaller environments

We presented a validated solution for the customer scenario. Some of the solution components, however, can be changed for alternative environments where different performance, capacity, costs, features, and similar requirements can be satisfied with other HPE solutions. Not all the workloads are the same, and a single HPE product cannot match all the requirements.

HPE ProLiant ML30 Gen10 Server

Figure 3-29 ProLiant ML30 Gen10 server

The HPE ProLiant ML30 Gen10 server, as shown in Figure 3-29, is a powerful yet affordable tower server designed for small offices, remote, and branch offices to run on-premises and hybrid cloud solutions, delivering enterprise-class performance, security, reliability, and expandability at a lower cost and standard 3-1-1 warranty.

Ideal use cases:

- Small businesses, remote, and branch offices environment

- Traditional workloads such as IT, web, file, print, and mail servers

- Business applications or an OEM-integrated solution

- Small-medium virtualization or data storage

HPE ProLiant ML110 Gen10 Server

Figure 3-30 HPE ProLiant ML110 Gen10

The HPE ProLiant ML110 Gen10, as shown in Figure 3-30, delivers a performance that meets the growing needs of the SMB. The server is a single processor, 4.5U tower server that is designed to provide enterprise-class features such as redundancy, reliability, and manageability. The server delivers the right size tower with performance and expandability that covers a wide range of applications and workloads and addresses our customers from SMB to enterprise-class server Remote Office/Branch Office (ROBO) environments. Accelerate your customer's business with this right-sized compute.

HPE ProLiant ML350 Gen10 Server

Figure 3-31 HPE ProLiant ML350 Gen10

Driving a wide range of workloads with a flexible, shorter, and rackable chassis design that can fit in different physical environments, the secure 2P HPE ProLiant ML350 Gen10 Server, shown in Figure 3-31, delivers the ideal set of performance and expandability for changing business needs making it the choice for growing SMBs, remote/branch offices of large enterprises and data centers. Choose this 2P tower that grows with your customer in the digital economy.

Key selling points of the ML350 Gen10 include:

- Performance with unmatched capacity and reliability—all in a much smaller form factor

- Availability, expandability, and serviceability—a winning combination

- Agile infrastructure management for essential administration

HPE ProLiant ML350 Gen10 Server is ideal for:

- Workloads and applications such as CRM/ERP, VDI, SAP

- Growing SMBs, remote offices, and branch offices of larger businesses or data centers

- Demanding workloads where storage performance, CPU, and RAM size are at a premium

- Virtualization

HPE ProLiant DL20 Gen10 Server

Figure 3-32 HPE ProLiant DL20 Gen10 server

The dense and compact HPE ProLiant DL20 Gen10 Server powered by the Intel® Xeon® E Processor, Pentium, and Core i3 processors, shown in Figure 3-32, provides a unique blend of enterprise-class capabilities and value. It offers outstanding configuration flexibility to cater to a wide variety of business requirements at an affordable price point. Deploy this dense platform for diverse workloads in space-constrained environments and maintain it with ease by automating the most essential server lifecycle management tasks with HPE iLO 5.

Key selling points include:

- Short-depth chassis of 15.05 inches provides mobility to deploy in a wide variety of environments

- Affordable and versatile, from light workloads to the most demanding workloads

- Offers outstanding configuration flexibility with 6 SFF/2 LFF drives, 290 W, 500 W, or 800 W 48VDC Redundant Power Supply, FlexibleLOM, and PCIe slots

HPE ProLiant DL20 Gen10 Server is ideal for:

- Small and medium businesses and enterprises running general-purpose (IT, web, file, print, email) workloads

- OEM, transport, retail, and hospitality environments deploying custom applications (point of sale (PoS), ERP, billing)

- Service providers who want affordable, edge of network servers for scale-out deployments

HPE ProLiant DL325 Gen10 Server

Figure 3-33 HPE ProLiant DL325 Gen10 server

The HPE ProLiant DL325 Gen10 Server, shown in Figure 3-33, is the secure and versatile single socket server for virtualization and IO-intensive workloads. This 1P, 1U server delivers an exceptional balance of processor, memory, and IO for 2P performance at 1P TCO. Your customers will get the most out of their virtualized environment with this versatile server.

Key selling points include:

● Single-processor HPE ProLiant Gen10 server, based on the AMD EPYC™ processors

● Providing dual-processor performance at single-processor economics

HPE ProLiant DL325 Gen10 Server is ideal for:

● Virtualized environment

● VDI

● vSAN

● Big Data analytics

HPE ProLiant DL360 Gen10 Server

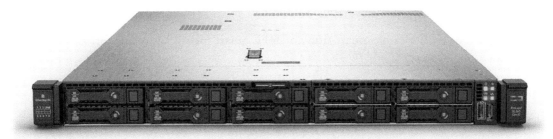

Figure 3-34 HPE ProLiant DL360 Gen10

Does your customer's data center need a secure, performance-driven dense server that they can confidently deploy for virtualization, database, or HPC? The powerful 2P HPE ProLiant DL360 Gen10, shown in Figure 3-34, is redefining dense compute by delivering security, agility, and unmatched expandability businesses want all packed in a dense 1U rack design.

The HPE ProLiant DL360 Gen10 Server supports the Intel® Xeon® Processor Scalable Family with up to 28 cores, plus 2666 MT/s HPE DDR4 SmartMemory supporting up to 3.0 TB max. With the added performance that 12 NVDIMMs and 10 NVMe brings, the HPE ProLiant DL360 Gen10 means business. Customers can deploy this dense platform for diverse workloads in space-constrained environments and maintain it with ease by automating the most essential server lifecycle management tasks with HPE OneView and HPE iLO 5.

HPE ProLiant DL360 Gen10 offers:

- Industry-leading performance

    - Double the capacity of NVDIMMs compared to previous generation

    - Up to 12 NVDIMMs supporting up to 192 GB per system

    - Improved speed with up to two Intel® Xeon® Processor Scalable Family, up to 28 cores

    - Faster memory with 24 HPE Smart Memory DDR4 2666 MHz (3.0 TB max)

    - Intelligent System Tuning (IST) to dynamically tune server performance

    - HPE Dynamic Smart Array to improve performance with a next-generation array controller

- Flexible design

    - Unmatched expandability packed in a dense 1U rack design

    - Ability to mix and match storage within the same chassis

    - Universal backplane supporting SAS/Serial ATA (SATA) or 10 NVMe PCIe SSDs option

    - Choice of storage 8+2 SFF/4 LFF/10 NVMe PCIe SSD plus a new rear drive option and new storage types

    - HPE Dynamic Smart Array S100i

    - Choice of HPE Flexible Smart Array or HPE Smart HBA Controllers for performance or additional features

    - Networking options 4x1 GbE embedded + choice of FlexibleLOM or Standup

    - IO options with 3 PCIe 3.0 slots (for 10 NVMe chassis; only two PCIe slots are available)

- Agile, secure infrastructure

  – Reduced risk of cyber or physical attacks with asset and data protection

  – Up to 1.3x more NVMe storage capacity and M.2 support on riser (compared to previous generation)

  – Enhanced security with HPE Secure Encryption, TPM option, Digitally Signed Firmware, tamper-proof secure preboot environment with SecureStart, Hardware Root of Trust, HTTPS boot, and Intrusion detection

  – Advanced System Management with HPE iLO 5

  – Persistent Memory up to 12 NVDIMM options supporting up to 192 GB per system

  – Boot options supporting UEFI and legacy boot modes

Dense performance for multi-workload compute in the data center

Key selling points of the DL360 Gen10 Server include:

- Leading energy-efficient dense server for better ROI

- Supports improved ambient temperature ASHRAE A3 and A4 standards, helping reduce cooling expenses

- Higher performance with IST, Persistent Memory, and greater NVMe capability

- Increased flexible storage options to support various workloads

- PCIe expansion with HPE FlexLOM and HPE Flexible Smart Array

- Converging management for automation simplicity across servers, storage, and networking with HPE OneView

Ideal workloads include:

- Hypervisor

- Dynamic workloads in dense virtualized environments

- Compute-intensive applications (web caching, data analytics)

- Low-latency and transactional applications (warehouse and database)

- HPC focus on Financial Services Industry (FSI)

Gen10 vs. Gen9 quick comparison

Specifications	Gen9	Gen10
Processor	Intel® Xeon® E5-2600 v3 product family Intel® Xeon® E5-2600 v4 product family	**Intel® Xeon® Processor Scalable family (8100, 6100, 5100, 4100 and 3100 series)**
Processors / cores	1 or 2 processors, 22, 20, 18, 16, 14, 12,10, 8, 6, 4 cores; 3.5 GHz	1 or 2 processors, **28, 26, 24**, 22, 20, 18, 16, 14, 12,10, 8, 6, 4 cores; **3.6 GHz**
Memory (type, max, slots)	Support up to 2400MT/s DDR4 SmartMemory 3 TB Max, 24 DIMM slots	Supports up to **2666** MT/s DDR4 SmartMemory 3 TB Max, 24 DIMM slots
Persistent Memory	Up to (16) 8 GB 2400MT/s NVDIMM option (128 GB max)	Up to (12) **16 GB 2666MT/s** NVDIMMs (**192 GB max**)
Drive Bays	(4) LFF SAS/SATA/SSD, or (8+2) SFF SAS/SATA/SSD or (6) SFF NVMe (optional), m.2 enablement	(4) LFF + (1) SFF SAS/SATA/SSD or (8+2+1) SFF SAS/SATA/SSD or (**10**) SFF NVMe, m.2 enablement
Network controller*	4x1 GbE embedded with optional FlexibleLOM and Standup	4x1 GbE embedded with optional FlexibleLOM and Standup
GPU support	Two single-wide and active 9.5" in length, up to 150W each	Two single-wide and active 9.5" in length, up to 150W each
Infrastructure management	HPE iLO 4 Management (standard), Intelligent Provisioning (standard), iLO Advanced (optional), HP Insight Control (optional)	**HPE iLO 5 Management (standard), Intelligent Provisioning (standard), iLO Advanced (optional), iLO Advanced Premium Security Edition (optional), HPE OneView Advanced (optional)**
Power supply	HPE 500W Flex Slot Platinum; HPE 800W Flex Slot Platinum, HPE 1400W Flex Slot Platinum Plus	HPE 500W Flex Slot Platinum; HPE 800W Flex Slot Platinum, HPE **1600W** Flex Slot Platinum Plus
Storage controller*	Embedded HPE Dynamic Smart Array B140i optional HPE Flexible Smart Array and Smart Array PCIe card	Embedded HPE Dynamic Smart Array **S100i** optional HPE Flexible Smart Array and Smart Array PCIe card
Warranty (parts, labor, onsite support)	3/3/3	3/3/3

* Depending on model
Bold text designates new or improved feature over a previous generation product.

Figure 3-35 HPE ProLiant DL360 Server Gen10 vs. Gen9 quick compare

Figure 3-35 provides a quick comparison between the HPE ProLiant DL360 Gen10 and the Gen9.

HPE ProLiant DL385 Gen10 Server

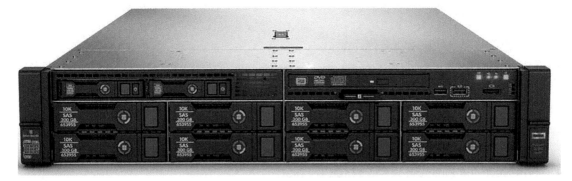

Figure 3-36 HPE ProLiant DL385 Gen10

HPE supports the AMD Secure Root of Trust that is comprised of an AMD secure processor and AMD secure boot. The AMD technology ties with the HPE Silicon Root of Trust at the UEFI or BIOS level as an added validation of the BIOS during the boot process. The HPE Silicon Root of

Trust is more comprehensive and ties into the HPE iLO5 silicon chip, thus substantiating there is no compromised code or malware in the server firmware. The AMD secure processor validates with the BIOS, upon boot up (and only during boot up) that there are no anomalies or compromised code present. After this confirmation, the server boot process can continue. If any compromised code is found, either by the AMD secure processor or the HPE Silicon Root of Trust, the iLO Advanced Premium Security Edition license will initiate an automatic recovery of the server firmware to a known good state.

HPE also supports the AMD Secure Run technology, which consists of the Secure Memory Encryption (SME) and the Secure Encrypted Virtualization (SEV) technologies. The SME technology provides encryption of all data transmitted to and stored on the HPE random-access memory. If those memory modules are ever removed from the HPE server, any information or data on the memory is unusable because it is encrypted. The SEV technology creates encryption of the virtual machines (VMs) on an HPE server and will prevent a user of one VM from tunneling into and viewing or retrieving data from an adjacent VM.

The final AMD security technology is AMD Secure Move, which relies on the establishment of a secure channel between two SEV-enabled platforms, so the hypervisor can implement migration and snapshot functions securely. This capability is only available as the operating system vendors provide support for the SEV technology itself. Currently, no OS vendors support SEV, and therefore, the AMD Secure Move will only be available as such support becomes available.

DL385 Gen10, as shown in Figure 3-36, is using EPYC, the AMD's x86 server processor line, implementing Zen microarchitecture. EPYC large memory capacity delivers excellent performance for applications such as Apache Spark and VoltDB in-memory applications that require high memory bandwidth and/or capacity, are highly parallel, or require extensive IO. Zen is the codename for AMD's computer processor microarchitecture, introduced in 2017.

HPE ProLiant DL385 Gen10 is an ideal server for:

- Virtualized workloads—hosting and VDI

    - EPYC's memory bandwidth, capacity, and massive IO allow for greater VM density

    - VMs can be aligned to specific NUMA domains, providing local access to memory, cores, and IO

- General-purpose compute

- Memory-centric workloads

    - NUMA-aware applications

    - EPYC large memory capacity

- Highly parallel workloads, HPC workloads, GPU compute, machine learning

    - EPYC large memory bandwidth and capacity provide excellent performance for HPC workloads such as weather modeling, seismic analysis, Computational Fluid Dynamics (CFD), Bioinformatics, and so forth

- EPYC delivers a massive number of PCIe lanes allowing multiple GPUs without adding a PCIe switch as well as higher memory bandwidth keeps cores and/or GPUs fed

- Microsoft SharePoint/storage

  - NVMe storage, software-defined storage

  - Up to 24/32 NVMe/SATA devices without the added latency or cost of a PCIe switch or HBA

- Any other enterprise workload

Specifications:

- **CPU**—Up to 64 cores (dual socket system) and 128 threads

- **Memory**—32 DIMMs (up to 4 TB)

- **Storage**

  - Integrated S100i and flexible Smart Array

  - Up to 30 SFF or 19 LFF + 2 SFF or 18 NVMe

  - Embedded M.2, USB, and MicroSD

- **Networking**—4 x 1 GbE, FlexibleLOM, Standup PCIe network cards

- **Management**—iLO 5

- **Power**— Redundant Flex Slot

Scenario 2: HPE Reference Architecture for Microsoft SQL Server 2017 on Red Hat Enterprise Linux with HPE ProLiant DL560 Gen10

The demands of database implementations continue to escalate. Faster transaction processing speeds, scalable capacity, high availability, and increased flexibility are required to meet the needs of today's business. This Reference Architecture is intended to provide customers with the expected performance implications associated with deploying Microsoft SQL Server 2017 on Linux with the HPE ProLiant DL560 Gen10 Server. This will help customers provide the appropriate level of performance and continue to meet service-level agreements (SLAs) that may be a requirement for business enterprises.

Introducing the customer scenario

WRT company will be used as a story line through this scenario. We will introduce the company using an interview:

- What is your primary business?

    - Global automotive supplier

- How many employees do you currently have?

    - 10,000 employees

- What does your selling and delivery channel look like?

    - Long-term contracts with selected car producers, limited marketing, no direct sales

- Where are you currently storing data, and how do you access files?

    - Mix of NAS and SAN devices, mainly HPE

- What does your server and network infrastructure look like?

    - Two data centers, hundreds of devices

- How much data do you currently have on servers and workstations?

    - Unknown

- What is the structure of your IT department?

    - Every location has an IT team and both data center operations team

- What are your current plans?

    - Consolidating the database in the short term and better automation and vendor consolidation in long term

Customer requirements

As a result of multiple interviews and gathering information about customer plans and customer's current infrastructure, the following requirements emerged for the new solution:

- On premise, highly resilient database implementation

    - Faster processing speeds

    - Scalable capacity

    - High availability

    - Increased flexibility

- Improve cost/transaction

- Microsoft SQL Server 2017 as the database platform

- Linux as the operating system

- Scale-up server platform supporting up to 6 TB of memory

- Consistent latency is a top priority (more important than absolute performance)

Activity: Microsoft SQL Server information resources

1. Download these information resources:

   - HPE Reference Architecture for Microsoft SQL Server 2017 on Red Hat Enterprise Linux with HPE ProLiant DL560 Gen10

     http://h20195.www2.hpe.com/v2/GetPDF.aspx/a00036336enw.pdf

   - Microsoft SQL Server 2017 on Linux Quick Start Guide

     http://info.microsoft.com/rs/157-GQE-382/images/EN-US-CNTNT-Whitepaper-DBMC-SQLServerOnLinuxQuickStart_Updated.pdf

   - ProLiant DL560 Gen10 server QuickSpecs

     https://h20195.www2.hpe.com/v2/getdocument.aspx?docname=a00008181enw

   - Workload-based Performance and Tuning Guide for Gen10 servers and HPE Synergy

     https://support.hpe.com/hpsc/doc/public/display?docId=a00016408en_us

   - Operating System Support Matrix

     https://www.hpe.com/us/en/servers/server-operating-systems.html

2. Answer the following questions:

   a. Which Linux distributions are supported by SQL Server 2017?

   _____

   _____

   b. Which of these are supported by DL560 Gen10?

   _____

   _____

   c. What is the recommended configuration of BIOS settings for SQL Server for the HPE ProLiant DL560 Gen10?

   _____

   _____

d. Will the DL560 Gen10 and DL580 Gen10 support the maximum memory configuration required by customers?

_____

_____

e. Which part numbers must be used for maximum memory?

_____

_____

f. What is the recommended configuration of SQL Server in the Reference Configuration?

_____

_____

g. Which settings in the BIOS will "Transactional Application Processing" workload profile configure? For example:

   – Power Regulator?

   – Minimum Processor idle Power Core C-state?

   – Energy Performance Bias?

_____

_____

_____

_____

_____

_____

_____

_____

h. Is a 100 Gb network card supported by the DL560 Gen10 server? What is the part number?

_____

_____

_____

_____

_____

_____

_____

_____

_____

_____

Building blocks of the solution

This Reference Architecture (RA) introduces Microsoft SQL Server 2017 running on a Linux OS using the latest HPE ProLiant DL560 Gen10 server with localized SSD storage. This RA demonstrates an optimized solution for a small to mid-range multi-database, scale-up scenario. Performance testing on this RA configuration demonstrated that the solution scales from a 25 K batch request per second with a two-socket configuration up to 53 K batch requests per second with a four-socket configuration—a 114% increase in performance in the same hardware footprint. This RA also shows the performance characterization of SQL backups and index rebuilds with SQL Server on Linux. The RA highlights and analyzes database performance improvements using specific SQL commands and switches to improve throughput and shorten the maintenance window of these important operational tasks.

This Reference Architecture is ideal for:

- Customers who are looking to improve cost/transaction on general-purpose and entry-/mid-level SQL Server database deployments

- Customers running older versions of SQL Server (for example, SQL 2005) on older infrastructures (x86, Itanium) and seeking better transaction performance

- Oracle customers who wish to stay on Linux and migrate to a lower cost solution

- Customers who are looking to standardize their OS on Linux, coexisting with other database solutions

Portfolio: HPE servers and server systems

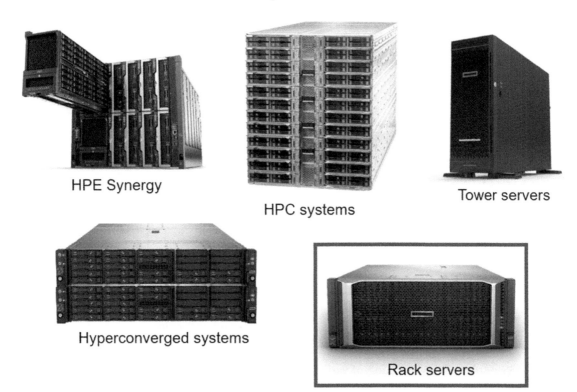

HPE Synergy

HPC systems

Tower servers

Hyperconverged systems

Rack servers

Figure 3-37 Selected HPE server platforms

HPE is offering multiple server platforms for various workloads. The selected reference architecture provides a validated configuration based on HPE rack servers, as illustrated in Figure 3-37.

HPE ProLiant workload-based positioning: Select the series

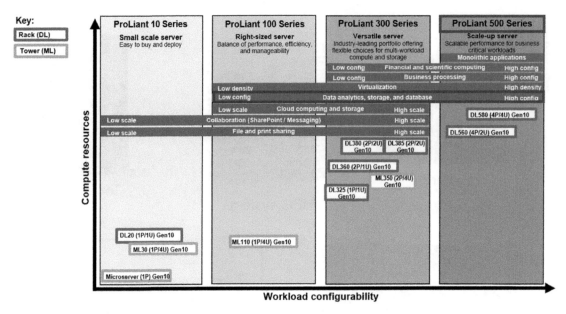

Figure 3-38 HPE ProLiant workload-based positioning

Figure 3-38 displays the positioning of various ProLiant series to workloads. Since the customer is looking for a large-scale database solution, we can select ProLiant 500 series as a preferred hardware platform.

HPE ProLiant DL560 Gen10 Server

Figure 3-39 HPE ProLiant DL560 Gen10

The HPE ProLiant DL560 Gen10 Server, shown in Figure 3-39, is a high-density, four-socket (4S) server with high performance, scalability, and reliability, all in a 2U chassis. Supporting the latest Intel® Xeon® Scalable processors, the HPE ProLiant DL560 Gen10 Server offers greater processing power, up to 6 TB of faster memory, IO of up to eight PCIe 3.0 slots, plus the intelligence and simplicity of automated management with HPE OneView and HPE iLO 5.

The HPE ProLiant DL560 Gen10 Server is the ideal server for:

- Business-critical workloads

- Virtualization and server consolidation

- Database, business processing, and general 4P data-intensive applications where data center space and the right performance are paramount

HPE ProLiant DL560 Gen10 offers:

- Scalable performance

    – Secure compute with up to four processors

    – High-performance options with IST, Persistent Memory, and expanded NVMe capacity

    – Scale from four to 112 cores with up to four Intel® Xeon® Processor Scalable Family

    – Up to 24 NVDIMMs for performance improvement to accelerate data management

    – Faster memory with 48 HPE Smart Memory DDR4 2666 MHz (6.0 TB)

    – Dynamically tune server performance with IST

- Impressive density

    – Unique design enables scale-up performance and IO expandability with large storage and memory footprint in 2U

    – Flex Slot power supplies with slot design to accommodate extra IO

    – 2x more NVMe drives and up to 64 TB delivering direct connect performance compared to previous generation

    – High storage density 24 SFF max, HDD/SSD, M.2 enablement kit, and 12 NVMe PCIe SSD option

    – Support up to two GPUs, eight available IO slots + FlexibleLOM for analytics and HPC applications

    – Up to four 96% efficient Flex Slot power supplies with redundant configurations, efficiency based on certification testing

- Flexibility and security

    – Flexible drive bay supports multiple combinations of SFF drives

    – Silicon Root of Trust powered by iLO 5

    – Modular 2+2 processor design—scale as needed

    – Flexible drive bay supporting multiple combinations of NVMe and SAS SFF drives

- Secure system management with iLO 5 and UEFI to protect assets and data from attack

- Enhanced RAS features for high availability

The HPE ProLiant DL560 Gen10 server is a highly dense scale-up server for compute-intensive workloads. The HPE ProLiant DL560 Gen10 is a great platform with a large memory footprint in a 2U form factor, for in-memory application such as SQL. Customers can start with a two-socket configuration then later add CPUs and memory to scale up as business needs grow without adding another hardware footprint.

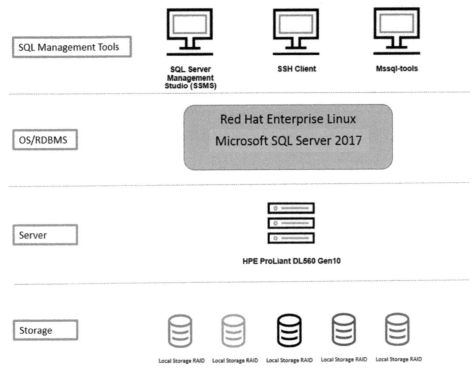

Figure 3-40 Diagram of the components involved

This Reference Architecture, as illustrated in Figure 3-40, explores OLTP use cases with SQL Server 2017 on Red Hat Linux Enterprise with HPE ProLiant DL560 Gen10 server and compares database performances between a two-socket and a scale-up four-socket configuration. The configuration of the HPE ProLiant DL560 Gen10 server in this RA consists of four RAID sets on local SSDs that will be used for the Linux OS and SQL Server database. While Microsoft SQL Server 2017 runs on the Linux platform, it either can be managed by an SQL Server Management Studio v17.3 (SSMS) running on a Windows Server or the mssql-tools package that is available for Linux platform. A Windows Server that hosts SSMS is also used as a remote Secure Shell (SSH) client to access the Red Hat Enterprise Linux (RHEL) machine for configuration and performance metrics purposes.

Processors in HPE servers

HPE ProLiant Gen10 servers are equipped by Intel® Xeon® Processor Scalable Family and EPYC, AMD's x86 server processor line, implementing the Zen microarchitecture.

Unified Intel® Xeon® Scalable Platform

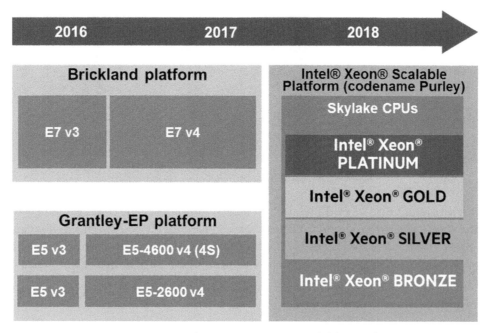

Figure 3-41 Intel® Xeon® Processor Scalable Family

Intel® Xeon® Processor E7 was targeted at mission-critical applications that value a scale-up system with leadership memory capacity and advanced RAS. Intel® Xeon® Processor E5 was targeted at a wide variety of applications that value a balanced system with leadership performance/watt/$.

Five model families are introduced with Intel® Xeon® Processor Scalable Family replacing former Intel® Xeon® E7 (4/8S+) and E5 (2S, 4S) families, as shown in Figure 3-41:

- Platinum
- Gold (6xxx)
- Gold (5xxx)
- Silver
- Bronze

Intel® Tick-Tock development model

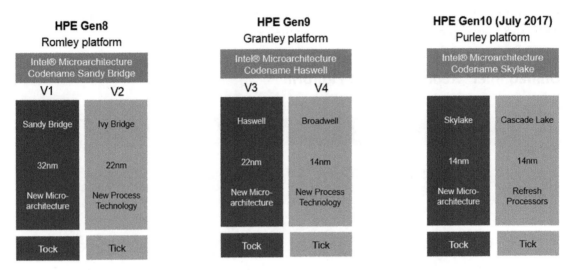

Figure 3-42 Intel® Tick-Tock development model

The new microarchitecture released by Intel® ("Tock"), shown in Figure 3-42, is usually connected to a release of new generation of our ProLiant servers and requires HPE to design a new system board, chassis, risers, and backplanes. Processor refresh ("Tick") usually requires only lighter changes and requires few firmware changes, such as complex programmable logic device (CPLD) and management engine (ME).

 Note

The Tick-Tock development model will be not used in the future.

Intel® Xeon® Processor Scalable Family overview

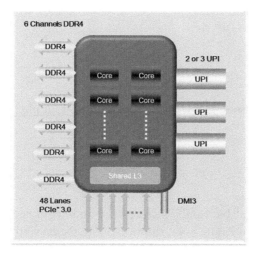

Figure 3-43 Intel® platform (Skylake/Platform Controller Hub)

Features of new Intel® Xeon® Processor Scalable Family (Skylake platform) and its Platform Controller Hub (PCH), as illustrated in Figure 3-43:

Processors:

- **CPU Thermal Design Power (TDP)**—70 to 205 W

- **Socket**—Socket P

- **Scalability**—2 sockets (2S), 4 sockets (4S), 8 sockets (8S)

Memory:

- 6 channels, DDR4

- Registered DIMM (RDIMM), Load-Reduced DIMM (LRDIMM)

- 2133, 2400, 2666

- 2 dual in-line memory modules (DIMMs) per channel

UPI:

- 2 to 3 channels per CPU

- 9.6, 10.4 GT/s

PCIe:

- Bifurcation (splitting the PCIe signal) x16, x8, x4

- 48 lanes per CPU

- PCIe 3.0 (2.5, 5.0, 8.0 GT/s)

PCH:

- Lewisburg (new platform core-logic) DMI3 (chipset-bus)—four physical PCIe 3.0 lanes

- Up to 10x USB3

- 14x SATA3

- 20x PCIe 3.0

The Intel® Xeon® Processor Scalable Family increases the number of cores compared to the Intel® Xeon® E5 series, as illustrated in Figure 3-44, thus increasing the maximum number of threads that can run on a socket. Sockets are connected using an Ultra Path Interconnect (UPI) bus with higher speed and the maximum number of PCIe lanes increased as well.

Features	Intel® Xeon® E5-2600 v4	Intel® Xeon® Processor Scalable Family (Skylake Server)
Cores per socket	Up to 22 cores	Up to 28 cores
Threads per socket	Up to 44 threads	Up to 56 threads
L3 cache	Up to 55 MB	Up to 38.5 MB (non-inclusive)
Socket interconnect speed	2x QPI @ 9.6 GT/s	Up to 3x UPI @ 10.4 GT/s
PCIe* lanes/ controllers/speed(GT/s)	40 / 10 / PCIe* 3.0 (8 GT/s)	48 / 12 / PCIe 3.0 (8 GT/s)
Memory capability	4 channels, 3 DIMMs per channel (RDIMMs, LRDIMMs, or 3DS LRDIMMs)	6 channels, 2 DIMMs per channel (RDIMMs, LRDIMMs, or 3DS LRDIMMs)
Max memory speed (MT/s)	Up to 2400	Up to 2666
TDP (W)	55W to 145W	70W to 205W

Figure 3-44 Comparison of Intel® Xeon® E5 series and Intel Xeon Processor Scalable Family

Intel® Xeon® Processor Scalable Family

Figure 3-45 Intel® Xeon® Processor Scalable Family—Entry processor up to high-performance processor

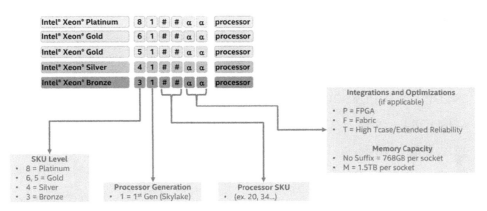

Figure 3-46 Product numbering convention for Intel® Xeon® Processor Scalable Family

As illustrated in Figures 3-45 and 3-46, Skylake platform numbering:

- First number is representing the shelf.

- Second number the generation.

- Third and fourth numbers are representing the SKU.

- The last character is used to distinguish integration:

  - **F**—Fabric

  - **P**— Field Programmable Gate Array (FPGA)

  - **T**—High Tcase/Extended reliability

  - **M**—1.5 TB per socket memory

There are major differentiators between processor families:

- Platinum (81xx)

    - 2S-2UPI, 2S-3UPI, 4S-2UPI, 4S-3UPI, 8S-3UPI capability

    - 6-ch DDR4 @ 2666

    - 3 UPI links @ 10.4GT/s

    - Intel® Turbo Boost Technology

    - Intel® HT Technology

    - Intel® AVX-512 (two 512-bit fused multiply-add [FMA])

    - 48 lanes PCIe Gen3

    - Node Controller Support

    - Advanced RAS

- Gold (61xx)

    - 2S-2UPI, 2S-3UPI, 4S-2UPI, 4S-3UPI capability

    - 6-ch DDR4 @ 2666

    - 3 UPI links @ 10.4GT/s

    - Intel® Turbo Boost Technology

    - Intel® HT Technology

    - Intel® AVX-512 (two 512-bit FMA)

    - 48 lanes PCIe Gen3

    - Node Controller Support

- Gold (51xx)

    - 2S-2UPI, 4S-2UPI capability

    - 6-ch DDR4 @ 2400

    - 2 UPI links @ 10.4GT/s

    - Intel® Turbo Boost Technology

    - Intel® HT Technology

- Intel® AVX-512 (one 512-bit FMA)

- 48 lanes PCIe Gen3

- Advanced RAS

- Silver (41xx)

  - 2S-2UPI

  - 6-ch DDR4 @ 2400

  - 2 UPI links @ 9.6GT/s

  - Intel® Turbo Boost Technology

  - Intel® HT Technology

  - Intel® AVX-512 (one 512-bit FMA)

  - 48 lanes PCIe Gen3

  - Standard RAS

- Advanced RASBronze (31xx)

  - 2S-2UPI

  - 6-ch DDR4 @ 2133

  - 2 UPI links @ 9.6GT/s

  - Intel® AVX-512 (one 512-bit FMA)

  - 48 lanes PCIe Gen3

  - Standard RAS

 Note

The numbers above can change over time, so always verify the latest information.

Intel® Xeon® scalable family processors

HPE offers a wide variety of Intel® Xeon® scalable family processors for ProLiant servers with different SKUs.

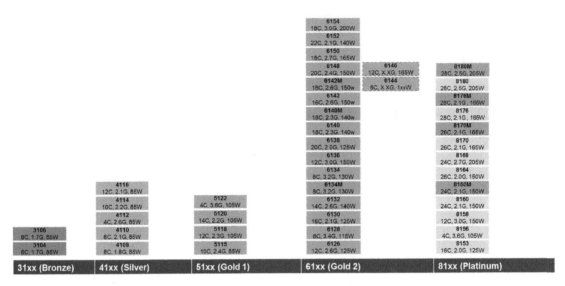

Figure 3-47 Intel® has a wide portfolio of available SKUs

Intel® Processor for the 300/500 series

The new Intel® Xeon® Processor Scalable Family is used in ProLiant Gen10 servers, as shown in Figure 3-47.

- DL300/BL400/SY400 series Gen10:
  - **CPU count**—2
  - **Max wattage**—Up to 205 W (up to 150W for BL servers)
  - **Core counts**—4 to 28 (up to 26 for BL servers)
  - **CPU frequency**—Up to 3.6 GHz
- DL500/BL600/SY600 series Gen10:
  - **CPU count**—4
  - **Max wattage**—Up to 205 W
  - **Core counts**—4 to 28
  - **CPU frequency**—Up to 3.6 GHz

Note
Numbers above can change over time, so always verify latest information in QuickSpecs.

Gen10 new socket design

ProLiant Gen10 servers are using the LGA 3647 socket. The socket supports a six-channel memory controller and an Intel® UltraPath Interconnect (UPI), shown in Figure 3-48.

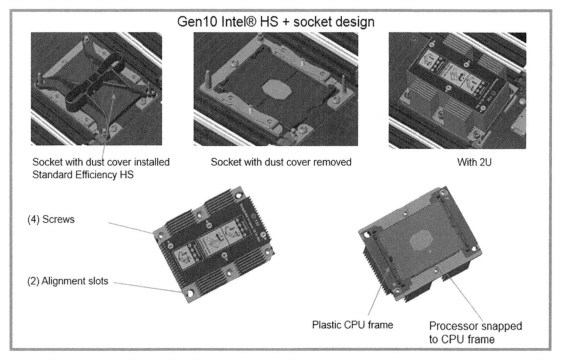

Figure 3-48 Gen10 Intel® socket design

Select the Intel® Xeon® processor

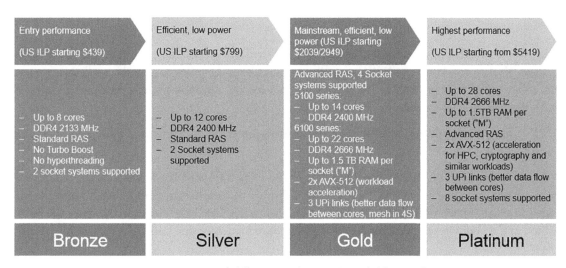

Figure 3-49 Comparison of different Intel® Xeon® Scalable Family processors

The Intel® processor, based on customer and business requirements, can be selected using the information in Figure 3-49.

 Note

Numbers above can change over time, so always verify latest information in QuickSpecs. U.S. ILP are subject to change without notice. Support must be verified for specific model as well. Not all variants are available for all models.

AMD EPYC vs. Intel® Skylake architectures

HPE is using several models in the AMD EPYC architecture, which differs significantly from the Intel® design, as illustrated in Figure 3-50:

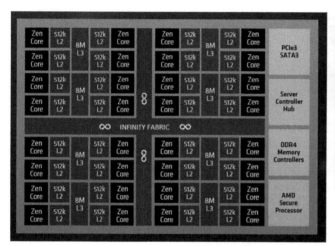 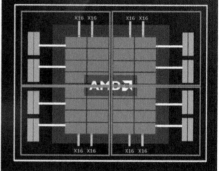

Figure 3-50 AMD EPYC design

AMD has reinvested in core technology and is committed to a consistent execution. They have delivered on Naples, now known as EPYC, as well as talking about the follow-on product called Rome and the follow-on to that product called Milan. All of these are currently under development and will refresh at the cadence that the market refreshes.

HPE is likewise committed to refreshing our existing portfolio to align with those new processor introductions.

A key aspect of the HPE security capability is the HPE Silicon Root of Trust, which creates a hardware root of trust, enabling only known and trusted firmware to run. An encryption key is embedded in the iLO silicon which is used to validate the iLO 5 firmware. The iLO 5 firmware validates the BIOS which in turn validates the options ROMs and OS Boot loader. At any point, if a compromised code is detected, an iLO audit log alert is created to notify the customer that a compromise has occurred. If any compromised firmware is found, the iLO with appropriate license will initiate an automatic recovery of the server firmware to a known good state.

The AMD Secure Processor is a dedicated security processor embedded in the AMD EPYC system on a chip (SoC). The security processor manages secure boot, memory encryption, and secure virtualization:

- **Secure boot**—The HPE Silicon Root of Trust ties to the AMD Secure Processor at the firmware level. The AMD Secure Processor also validates the HPE BIOS during the boot process.

  While data is typically encrypted today when stored on disk, it is stored in dynamic random-access memory (DRAM) in the clear. This can leave the data vulnerable to snooping by unauthorized administrators or software or by hardware probing. The main memory encryption is performed via dedicated hardware in the on-die memory controllers. Each controller includes a high-performance Advanced Encryption Standard (AES) engine that encrypts data when it is written to DRAM and decrypts it when read from DRAM. Control over which pages of memory are encrypted is controlled via the operating system or hypervisor in the software managed page tables.

  There can be full memory encryption or partial memory encryption:

  - With **full memory encryption**, all DRAM contents are encrypted utilizing the random key that provides strong protection against cold boot, DRAM interface snooping, and similar types of attacks.

  - With **partial memory encryption**, the operating system or hypervisor can selectively encrypt a subset of memory. One example of partial memory encryption would be marking memory used by guest VMS as encrypted.

- **Secure Memory Encryption of SME**—You can encrypt all the memory or a portion of memory. With partial memory encryption you can encrypt a subset of memory, for example, marking memory used by guest VMs as encrypted.

- **Secure Encrypted Virtualization (SEV)**—There are encryption keys in the security processor that never leave the processor where they can be exposed to intruders. With SEV, virtual machines have separate encryption keys as does the hypervisor, isolating the VMs from other VMs, and even the hypervisor itself.

  Even though the hypervisor level is traditionally "more privileged" than the guest level, SEV separates these levels through cryptographic isolation. This provides additional security for lower privileged code, without requiring trust in the high privileged code on which the less privileged code is dependent upon for startup and execution.

  SEV uses the same high-performance memory encryption engine as SME. One of the key features of SEV is that guest VMs can choose which data memory pages they would like to be private. Private memory is encrypted with the guest-specific key, while shared memory may be encrypted with the hypervisor key. This allows VMs to mark selected pages of memory data they want to keep confidential or private, and others to be used for communication with other VMs or the hypervisor. This allows the hypervisor to perform its regular functions such as scheduling of the VMs.

As two industry leaders focused on security, together the HPE security technology coupled with the AMD security technology really delivers unprecedented security for server virtualization.

AMD EPYC 7000™ Processors—A new building block

Figure 3-51 ZEN architecture

Characteristics of EPYC 7000™ processors, as shown in Figure 3-51, include:

- 8 to 32 AMD "Zen" x86 cores (32 to 64 threads)
- 512 KB L2 cache per core (16 MB total L2 cache)
- 64 MB shared L3 cache (8 MB per 4 cores)
- TDP range: 120 W to 180 W

Memory architecture:

- 8-channel DDR4 with ECC up to 2667 MHz
- RDIMM, LRDIMM, 3DS, NVDIMM, Flash
- 2 DIMMs/channel capacity of 2 TB/socket

Integrated IO (no chipset):

- 128 lanes PCIe Gen3
- Used for PCIe, SATA, Ethernet, and Coherent Interconnect
- Up to 32 SATA or NVMe devices

- Up to 16 10 GBASE-KR or 1 Gb Ethernet

- Server controller hub (USB, UART, SPI, LPC, I2C, and so on)

EPYC is ideal for memory-bound HPC applications because of its high throughput and floating point (FP) performance:

- Dedicated and efficient FP units

- Maintains clock speed for FP operations

- World record floating point performance on SPEC CPU

- 146% better memory bandwidth on STREAM benchmark (based on SPECrate2017_fb_base benchmark)

 Note

- SPEC CPU benchmark results: **https://www.amd.com/system/files/2018-03/AMD-SoC-Sets-World-Records-SPEC-CPU-2017.pdf**

- The STREAM benchmark is a simple synthetic benchmark program that measures sustainable memory bandwidth (in MB/s). STREAM benchmark results: **https://www.amd.com/system/files/2017-06/AMD-EPYC-SoC-Delivers-Exceptional-Results.pdf**

Select the AMD EPYC 7000 processor

The AMD processor family includes a range of processors with different core counts and frequencies to match specific customer workloads, as shown in Figure 3-52.

Processor	Cores	Freq	Max Boost	Workload Affinity
7601	32	2.20	3.20	DBMS and Analytics, Capacity HPC
7551/7551P	32	2.00	3.00	VM Dense, VDI, DBMS and Analytics, Web Serving
7501	32	2.00	3.00	VM Dense, VDI, DBMS and Analytics, Web Serving
7451	24	2.30	3.20	General Purpose
7401/7401P	24	2.00	3.00	General Purpose, GPU/FPGA Accelerated, Storage
7351/7351P	16	2.40	2.90	General Purpose, GPU/FPGA Accelerated, Storage
7301	16	2.20	2.70	General Purpose, License Cost Optimized
7281	16	2.10	2.70	General Purpose, License Cost Optimized
7261	8	2.50	2.90	General Purpose, License Cost Optimized
7251	8	2.10	2.90	License Cost Optimized

Figure 3-52 Matching of AMD EPYC processor to a workload

 Note

P variant is for single-processor models only (DL325).

HPE Intelligent System Tuning

For the past several years, server-class customers have seen processor-based performance increase generation over generation. This is due in a large part to increases in core counts and more efficient instruction set architectures. Unlike the preceding decades, the base frequency of the CPU has stayed rather stable and only the number of cores has increased. Processor vendors, realizing that not all workloads benefit from increased core counts, introduced features that allow the processor to run opportunistically at higher frequencies when these extra cores or the power to run them is not being utilized.

Although these opportunistic frequency upsides can increase performance, they also introduce an unwanted side effect. Frequency shifting itself introduces computation jitter, or non-determinism, and undesirable latency. Jitter and the latency associated with it create problems for several customer segments. For example, high-frequency traders, who rely on time-sensitive transactions, cannot tolerate the microseconds of delay that can be added randomly to a trade caused by a frequency shift. These delays over time can cost a trader upwards of millions of dollars. Servers running real-time operating systems (RTOS) to control critical functionality also cannot tolerate random latencies that happen when opportunistic frequency features are left enabled.

The current trend for latency-sensitive customers is to disable the features that normally would result in increased application performance. A trade executes faster if the processor runs faster, but if it comes at the cost of random delay, the benefit of increased performance is lost.

Starting with Gen10 servers using Intel® Xeon® Scalable Processors and iLO 5, HPE has introduced a new feature that allows customers to achieve both a frequency upside and low latency. Processor Jitter Control allows the customer to remove or reduce the jitter caused by opportunistic frequency management resulting in better latency response and higher throughput performance.

 Note

Gen10 servers using AMD processors are not supported. An iLO Advanced license is required to use this feature.

Dynamically configure server resources to match specific workloads and achieve higher levels of performance, efficiency, and control in the server environment. IST, a new set of server tuning technologies developed in partnership with Intel®, dynamically tunes servers to align with the unique needs of each workload.

IST leverages exclusive technology developed through close partnership with Intel®. It includes three innovative capabilities—Jitter Smoothing, Workload Matching, and Core Boosting—that together can deliver double digit boosts in performance.

- **Jitter Smoothing**
    - Smooths fluctuations in processor frequency as customers increase performance
    - For multiple segments, particularly financial institutions and live streaming applications

- **Core Boosting**

    - Unique ability to dynamically modulate frequency and performance

    - Reduce application core charges through greater performance with fewer processor cores

- **Workload Matching**—Custom profiles on ProLiant server systems match the more common customer workloads, automatically matching internal resources to those typical needs

---

 Note

For more information on IST, visit: **http://hpe.com/info/ist**

Increased performance delivered through iLO Advanced

Increased performance using IST requires iLO Advanced for some features, such as Jitter Smoothing and Core Boosting. New Gen10 technologies suit customers who need:

- Maximum processor throughput even in workloads sensitive to processor latency

- Ability to easily tune server parameters without needing years of experience or trial and error

Key new features:

- Leverages HPE-developed processor control technology and performance engineering experience.

- Jitter Smoothing mitigates processor frequency fluctuation to improve overall workload throughput above turbo mode.

- Workload Matching allows you to leverage preconfigured profiles that automatically tune internal server resources and deliver up to a 9% performance improvement over server default settings (based on HPE internal benchmarking).

- Core Boosting enables higher performance across fewer processors that can save customers up to $100 K in annual core-based licensing fees or $500 K over five years (based on HPE internal benchmarking).

 Note

Some features may be available only in future releases.

Intelligent System Tuning—Processor Jitter Control

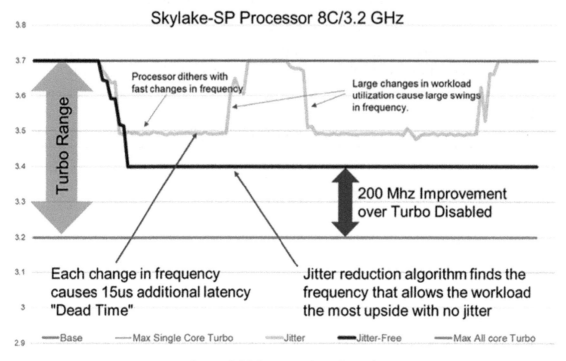

Figure 3-53 Processor Jitter Control

Processor Jitter Control is primarily targeted at the Financial Services Industry (FSI). For this market, the maximum worst case latency is more important than overall bandwidth. Processor frequency changes (including Turbo Mode transitions) introduce latency, and FSI customers typically disable Turbo Mode due to frequency jitter. This HPE unique innovation, as illustrated in Figure 3-53, removes all processor frequency transitions while allowing the processor to run above its base frequency. IST requires an iLO Advanced license.

The processor introduces jitter any time it executes changes in operating frequency. Several possible reasons exist for a processor to dynamically change frequencies during run time. Some of the sources that request frequency changes are driven by software, while others are driven by the processor itself.

Sources of jitter within the processor

Sources of jitter within the processor include:

- P-states and power management
- Turbo Boost
- C-states

- Power and thermal events

- Special instructions (AVX)

P-states and power management

P-states are predefined performance states that are made available by the processor for software to control how much performance the processor can deliver so that it can manage the power-performance efficiency of the platform. Performance states are mapped to a specific frequency at which the processor is capable of operating. Power management software instructs the processor to change P-states (frequency) to save power when processor utilization (demand) is low. A processor often offers several different P-states over a range of operating frequencies.

Turbo Boost

Intel's® Turbo Boost allows the processor to run at higher frequencies than the base frequency guaranteed by its specification, assuming it follows certain conditions. The conditions include the amount of heat being dissipated, the temperature of the part, and the number of cores active (enabled and not idle). When a workload is run on these processors while Turbo Boost is enabled, the processor will opportunistically switch between frequencies to achieve the highest possible performance; however, as the demands of the workload change, so can the frequencies. When frequencies change, we get frequency jitter as well as a small amount of latency that occurs, which is required to electrically change frequencies. The net effect of having Turbo Boost enabled is that while the processor attempts to provide the maximum amount of performance within its limits, it often does so by changing frequency.

C-states

C-states are predefined power-saving states that the processor offers to power management software to use when the operating system idles a processor core. The operating system puts the processor into one of a number of C-states that are made available. The deeper the C-state, the more power that is saved, but at the cost of longer exit latencies to return to the operating state. To save power, C-states on Intel® processors also lower the frequency of the processor. Upon exiting a C-state, the processor, running at the lowest frequency available to the C-state, must perform an additional frequency shift to return to the previously requested P-state by power management software. C-states are useful in saving power when the processor is not being utilized. However, entering and exiting these states introduce a large amount of jitter.

Power and thermal events

The processor, to run within the constraints of its design, employs the use of frequency throttling to protect itself from thermal or overcurrent conditions. Frequency throttling allows the processor to control how much the workload that is running on the host can introduce the stress that results in higher heat and current draw. Several factors can lead to high operating temperature or overcurrent events. Server ambient temperature, air flow, and other factors all play an important role in processor temperature. An overcurrent can occur when the processor executes workloads that can drive very high demand power-hungry resources within the processor itself. An overcurrent can also occur if Turbo Boost is enabled and the processor attempts to maximize the amount of performance when a particularly aggressive workload executes and the power that is available to be consumed is driven very high.

Special instructions (AVX)

Server processors offer special instructions that are capable of performing complex math at the cost of utilizing logic that is capable of driving very high-power usage inside the processor itself. If left unchecked, overcurrent throttling is required when these instructions eventually drive the processor to consume higher power. Instead of reactively throttling, processors typically proactively force cores to run at a lower frequency to limit the chances of extreme power excursions whenever those instructions are executed. On Intel® processors, the use of Advanced Vector Extensions (AVX) instructions cause the processor to limit the processor frequency automatically. Because these instructions cause the processor to automatically limit and potentially lower the frequency, their usage often introduces jitter.

What is Jitter?

Enabling Intel's® Turbo Boost can increase processor frequency dramatically (for example, from 3.2 GHz to 3.7 GHz). At high/turbo frequencies, changes in workloads require the processor to change frequency. Each change in processor frequency requires the processor to stop execution and then execute at the new frequency. Processor downtime during frequency changes can be 10 μs to 20 μs.

Jitter is:

- Frequency fluctuation

- Processor downtime during each frequency change

Jitter is bad, it impacts latency, it impacts overall workload performance, and it is happening even when you are running in Turbo Boost Mode.

Jitter and latency

Jitter and latency are directly related. Jitter induced by processor frequency changes introduces latency observed by a workload. When a processor executes a change in frequency, it goes through a process that causes thread execution to stop entirely before the processor can run at the new chosen frequency. This process occurs regardless of whether the processor will shift to a faster or a slower frequency. The amount of time that the processor is stopped can vary, but it is typically between 10 and 15 microseconds. For a workload that depends on processor execution, a change in frequency will then always introduce an additional 10 to 15 μs of latency. Because frequency shifts are often asynchronous to application tasks running on the server, these latencies are random and thus non-deterministic from an application standpoint. Also, it is important to note that a processor that varies its frequency also creates a non-deterministic level of performance for the running applications. Software will execute slower as the frequency is lowered and vice versa. The difference in frequency itself also means that there is a variable amount of latency involved if an application depends on a certain amount of execution time. Latency introduced by frequency changes can be illustrated by measuring latency when the processor is configured to allow for frequency shifts (that is, Turbo Boost is enabled).

Jitter smoothing—Processor Jitter Control

Processor Jitter Control, as illustrated in Figure 3-54, is a feature that is hosted by platform firmware within HPE ProLiant Gen10 servers. It allows the user to tune servers to reduce or remove processor jitter either automatically or manually. Jitter Control has three modes and can be configured via the ROM Based Setup Utility (RBSU) or via the RESTful interface. Jitter Control can be disabled or configured for auto-tuned or manual-tuned mode.

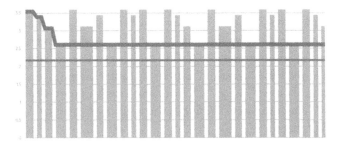

Figure 3-54 Enabling HPE Jitter Smoothing

Auto-tuned mode

When Processor Jitter Control is configured to run in auto-tuned mode, HPE Server firmware disables the impact of power management and dynamically adjusts the processor during run time to eliminate the occurrence of frequency shift induced jitter. The result of running in auto-tuned mode is that the processor will eventually run at the highest frequency that can be achieved where the processor stops making frequency changes to stay within its thermal, power, and core usage constraints.

Auto-tuned mode lowers the frequency upon detection of frequency changes caused by the following sources:

- C-state transitions
- AVX-induced transitions
- Turbo transitions (due to power, thermal, and core usage)
- Thermal throttling

When selecting auto-tuned mode via RBSU, C-state settings are also set to disabled. Most operating systems rely on BIOS reporting of support of C-states via the Advanced Power and Configuration Interface (ACPI). However, certain Linux distributions that load the intel_idle driver will ignore the ACPI reporting of C-state support. For Auto-tuned to function properly, the intel_idle driver must be disabled by adding intel_idle.max_cstate=0 in the kernel line parameters.

Manual-tuned mode

When Processor Jitter Control is configured to run in manual-mode, the processor is configured to run at a user-selectable frequency. In this mode, firmware does not lower the frequency dynamically even if processor frequency changes are detected. This mode is useful for users who desire to manually tune for jitter reduction and for those who wish to set a maximum operational frequency. Unlike in auto-tune mode, if a frequency change occurs below the programmed frequency, the server will not reduce the operating frequency permanently, and the processor is allowed to return to the maximum frequency when the limiting constraints no longer exist.

Configuring Processor Jitter Control via System Utilities

The Processor Jitter Control option has three modes: Disabled, Auto-tuned, or Manual-tuned. Selecting Auto-tuned or Manual-tuned mode allows the user to also edit the Processor Jitter Control Frequency input option, which allows the user to select the desired target frequency for manual-tuned mode or the starting maximum frequency for auto-tuned mode. Frequency is entered in units of megahertz (MHz) and the system firmware rounds up to the nearest frequency interval allowed by the processor. For example, Intel® Xeon® Server processors support frequency programming in intervals of 100 MHz. If a user inputs 2050 MHz, the resulting frequency will be 2100 MHz if supported by the installed processor.

 Note

For more information about configuring and tuning HPE ProLiant Servers for low-latency applications, visit:

https://support.hpe.com/hpsc/doc/public/display?docId=emr_na-c01804533

Workload profiles

Workload Profiles are a configuration option to deploy BIOS settings based on the workload customer intends to run on the server. Workload Profiles are a configuration option to deploy BIOS settings to accommodate the intended application of the server. Workload Profiles is one of the HPE IST features.

There are dozens of server tuning variables to optimize performance and efficiency, such as:

- Intel® Turbo Boost Technology

- Energy Performance Bias

- Adjacent Sector Prefetch

- Sub-NUMA Clustering

- Intel® Hyper Threading

- SR-IOV

- VT-x

- VT-D

- DCU IP Prefetcher

- Channel Interleaving

- DCU Stream Prefetcher

- Intel® DMI Link Frequency

- Collaborative Power Control

- Intel® NIV DMA Channels (IOAT)

- Minimum Processor Idle Power Core C-states

- NUMA Group Size Optimization

- Uncore Frequency Shifting

- Thermal Configuration

- Memory Refresh Rate

- Power Regulator

- A3DC

- x2APIC

- HW Prefetcher

- Energy Efficient Turbo

- Memory Bus Frequency

- Memory Patrol Scrubbing

- UPI Link Power Management

- Minimum Processor Idle Power Package C-states

Intelligent System Tuning—Workload Matching

To leverage the experience of HPE's Performance Engineering Team rather than trial/error method, use workload profiles.

The system provides these Workload Profiles (more details were covered already in this chapter):

- General Power Efficient Compute
- General Peak Frequency Compute
- General Throughput Compute
- Virtualization—Power Efficient
- Virtualization—Max Performance
- Low Latency
- Mission Critical
- Transactional Application Processing
- High-Performance Computing
- Decision Support
- Graphic Processing
- IO Throughput
- Custom
- Default profiles for servers

Workload profiles dependencies

There are multiple options that are available for BIOS configuration. Not all profiles set the same options to specific settings. Each profile is designed to obtain specific performance results and sets different options to meet those results. The options that a profile sets are called dependencies. All other options are unaffected by the Workload Profile and are referred to as nondependent settings.

Applying a Workload Profile

You apply a Workload Profile to have the system manage your workload according to predefined settings provided with the system. Dependent options cannot be changed and are grayed out. You can change any nondependent options in a profile.

There may be one or more dependent options that you want to change in your Workload Profile. Dependent options cannot be changed for a predefined profile. You can change the dependent options in Custom mode. When you are in Custom mode, your deployment is no longer in profile mode, and you can manually adjust option settings. When you enter Custom mode, all the settings from the previously applied profile are shown. The easiest way to change dependent settings is to modify an applied profile. First, apply a Workload Profile that has most of the settings that you want to use, and then change to Custom mode. Then change only the settings you want to have new values.

Core Boosting: Performance and TCO illustration

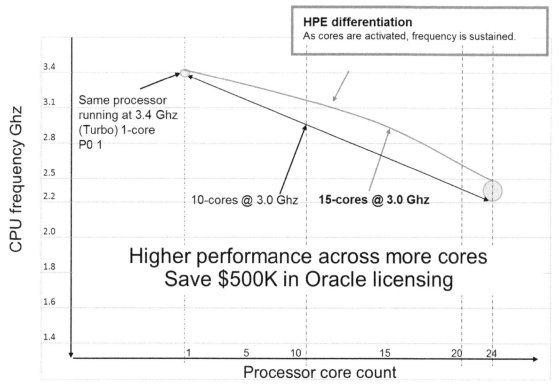

Figure 3-55 Illustration picture only—real numbers may differ

As indicated in Figure 3-55, Core Boosting maximizes the performance of all processor cores while lowering core-based licensing costs—ideal for virtualized environments, HPC, and Big Data—and is available on select ProLiant DL380 Gen10 and Apollo XL230K Gen10 server configurations. Core Boosting is available on select Gen10 server platforms when paired with an Intel® 6143 16-core processor, high-performance heat sinks and fans, and an iLO Advanced License or an iLO Advanced Premium Security Edition License.

HPE Intelligent System Tuning—Requirements

HPE IST requires power supplies based on power needs for processors and options (see Power Advisor) and for specific features:

- **Jitter Smoothing**—HPE Gen10 Platform with iLO 5 and iLO Advanced Premium Security Edition or iLO Advanced license
- **Workload Profiles**—All Gen10 with iLO 5

- **Core Boosting**—HPE Gen10 Platform with iLO 5 and iLO Advanced Premium Security Edition or iLO Advanced license

  – Select Gen10 Platforms

  – One of the following special HPE processor SKUs: 8c/155W, 16c/205W, 24c/205W

  – Standard high-performance processor heat sink

  – Standard high-performance fans

Memory for HPE servers

IT trends such as server virtualization, cloud computing, and high-performance computing are placing significant demands on server memory speed, capacity, and availability. An IT system's reliability, performance, and overall power consumption drive companies toward business outcomes. Choosing the right memory is crucial to ensuring high reliability and delivering a faster return on IT investment.

Many businesses need a faster tier of technology to help them deal with current real-world issues such as Big Data, analytics and search workloads, medical sciences such as human genome mapping, and financial data analysis. Traditional data storage technologies are being augmented by new innovations in the hierarchy of data storage.

Memory/Storage hierarchy

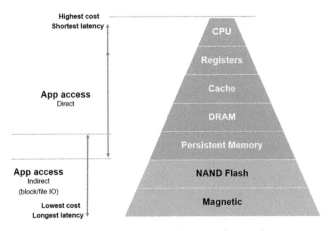

Figure 3-56 Memory/Storage hierarchy

Technologies at the top of the pyramid have the shortest latency (best performance) but come at a higher cost relative to the items at the bottom of the pyramid, as shown in Figure 3-56. These layers are comprised of DRAM (memory), CPU cache(s), and CPU registers. All of these components are accessed directly by the application (CPU)—that is, byte-addressable access. These layers are also volatile in that their contents are lost when power is removed.

Technologies at the bottom of the pyramid—represented by magnetic media (HDDs and tape)—and NAND flash (represented by SSDs and PCIe Workload Accelerators) have longer latency and lower costs relative to the technologies at the top of the pyramid. Data stored on these technologies are non-volatile, even when power is removed. Applications access data on these layers indirectly, typically using Block IO and/or File IO.

The new Persistent Memory technology layer sits between NAND flash and DRAM. It provides faster performance relative to NAND Flash while also providing the non-volatility not typically found in traditional memory. This technology layer provides the performance of memory with the persistence of traditional storage.

Comparing RDIMMs and LRDIMMs

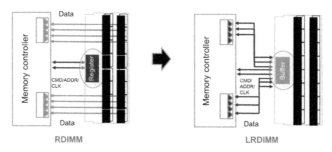

Figure 3-57 Comparison of RDIMM and LRDIMM

RDIMMs improve signal integrity by having a register on the DIMM to buffer the address and command signals between the DRAMs and the memory controller, as illustrated in Figure 3-57. This allows each memory channel to support up to three dual-rank DIMMs, increasing the amount of memory that a server can support. With RDIMMs, the partial buffering slightly increases both power consumption and memory latency.

LRDIMMs use memory buffers to consolidate the electrical loads of the ranks on the LRDIMM to a single electrical load, allowing them to have up to eight ranks on a single DIMM module. The LRDIMM memory buffer reduces the electrical load to the memory controller and allows higher capacity memory to run at three DIMMs per channel. Using LRDIMMs, you can configure systems with the largest possible memory.

LRDIMMs also use more power and have longer latencies compared to the lower capacity RDIMMs. Similar to RDIMMs, LRDIMMs buffer the address and control signals. Unlike RDIMMs, LRDIMMs also buffer the data lines. In RDIMMs, data signals are driven by a controller, limiting performance. Not only do LRDIMMs improve performance, but they also reduce problems associated with heat and power dissipation.

The LRDIMM memory buffer reduces the electrical load to the memory controller and allows higher capacity memory to run at three DIMMs per channel. LRDIMM is ideal for customers who require the maximum memory capacity.

 Note

There is a trade-off between the advantages of Persistent Memory and total RAM size as a result of some of the physical space on the memory module being taken up by SSD rather than RAM.

 Note

Although unbuffered DIMMs (UDIMMs) are defined for the DDR4 standard, they no longer offer any performance advantage (in terms of lower latencies) over RDIMMs and LRDIMMs.

DDR4 SmartMemory

SmartMemory verifies whether DIMMs have passed the HPE qualification and testing processes and determines if the memory has been optimized to run on ProLiant Gen9 and Gen10 servers. Key technology enhancements offered by DDR4 include:

- **Increased bandwidth**—DDR4 SmartMemory provides up to 2666 MT/s better data rate. The DDR4 specification defines eventual data rates of up to 3200 MT/s, more than 70% faster than the 1866 MT/s of DDR3 memory speed.

- **1.2-volt operation**—All DDR4 memory operates at 1.2 volts, compared to 1.35 or 1.5 volts for DDR3 memory. This delivers significant system power savings, particularly in larger memory configurations.

- **16 banks of memory per rank**—Internally, the DRAMs used in DIMMs are organized into arrays of cells defined by banks, rows, and columns. DDR4 memory has 16 banks of memory in a DRAM chip compared to the eight banks in DDR3. This allows an increased number of memory requests that can be queued by the memory controller. It is one of the contributors to the lower latency of DDR4 memory.

- **Encoded Rank Selection**—DDR4 eliminates the work-around known as **rank multiplication** that DDR3 employed to enable four ranks of memory on LRDIMMs using the traditional chip select lines. When there are eight or fewer total ranks installed on a memory channel, DDR4 uses the direct chip select mode to address the correct rank. When more than eight ranks are installed, DDR4 uses a 4-bit encoded chip select value for rank selection. This encoded value is interpreted by the registers on the DIMMs to determine the correct rank to enable for the memory operation.

This new encoded chip select scheme allows DDR4 memory to address up to 24 memory ranks on a memory channel.

- **Retry on error**—DDR4 memory and new memory controllers will retry a memory request whenever a memory error or address parity error occurs. This reduces the number of system halts that may have occurred due to transient errors in previous generations of memory subsystems.

 Note

DDR4 and DDR3 memory are not interchangeable.

HPE Advanced Memory Error Detection

As memory capacities increase, increases in memory errors are unavoidable. Fortunately, most memory errors are both transient and correctable. Current memory subsystems can correct up to a 4-bit memory error in the 64 bits of data that are transferred in each memory cycle.

Instead of simply counting each correctable memory error, HPE Advanced Memory Error Detection analyzes all correctable errors to determine which ones are likely to lead to uncorrectable errors in the future. This approach can better monitor the memory subsystem and increase the effectiveness of the Pre-Failure Alert notification. All ProLiant Gen9 and Gen10 servers feature Advanced Memory Error Detection.

Storage tiering on HPE ProLiant servers—With Persistent Memory

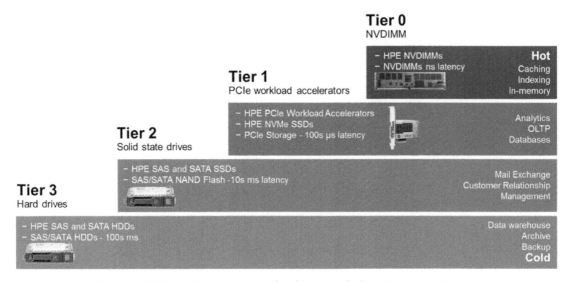

Figure 3-58 Emerging storage technologies including Persistent Memory

NVDIMMs are an example of the type of product in the Persistent Memory product category. The storage tier hierarchy in Figure 3-58 is represented as follows:

- **Tier 0**—NVDIMMs; ns of latency

- **Tier 1**—PCIe SSDs and PCIe workload accelerators (NAND flash on the SAS/SATA or PCIe bus); 100s of μs of latency

- **Tier 2**—SAS HDDs (highest-performing rotational media with lower capacities and greater cost per GB relative to SATA); 10s of ms of latency

- **Tier 3**—SATA HDDs (higher capacity relative to SAS and lower cost per GB but lower performance relative to SAS); 100s of ms of latency

NVDIMMs do not replace NAND flash. NVDIMMs replaced PCIe NAND flash as the fastest storage tier. In addition, although tape dropped off from this example, you could have another tier for archiving data onto tape. NVDIMMs is emerging as the fastest storage tier available in the market and part of an overall tiering strategy that includes HPE PCIe Workload Accelerators, SSDs, HDDs, and tape.

Gen9 vs. Gen10 memory configuration (Intel-based servers)

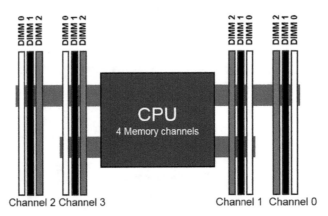

Figure 3-59 Gen9 with four memory channels per CPU

Gen9 servers are using four memory channels per CPU (three slots per channel). This setup, as indicated in Figure 3-59, can be found on DL360/ DL380/ ML350/ DL560, and so forth.

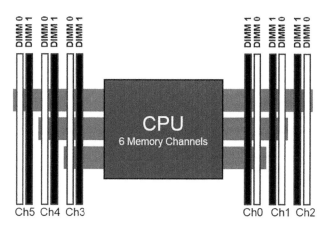

Figure 3-60 Gen10 with six memory channels per CPU

Gen10 servers with Intel® processors are equipped with six memory channels per CPU (two slots per channel), as shown in Figure 3-60. Such architecture can be found on DL360/ DL380/ ML350/ DL560, and so forth.

HPE 16 GB NVDIMM

Figure 3-61 HPE 16 GB NVDIMM

HPE 16 GB NVDIMMs, as show in Figure 3-61, are flash-backed DIMMs designed to eliminate smaller storage bottlenecks while delivering the performance of memory with the persistence of storage. These are ideal for database storage bottlenecks write caching tiers and any workload constrained by storage bottlenecks.

The HPE 8 GB NVDIMM is the first NVDIMM developed for a server platform and was introduced in March 2016. The new 16 GB NVDIMM is the second addition to the NVDIMM product series.

 Note

NVDIMMs can be mixed with RDIMMs only.

HPE Persistent Memory helps enhance your customer's competitive edge, identify areas to cut costs, and uncover new ways to drive revenue. HPE broke ground in the industry with a massive Persistent Memory breakthrough and leads the industry with a server platform offering Persistent Memory in an NVDIMM form factor.

HPE Persistent Memory provides:

- **Breakthrough performance**—Unlocking new levels of performance, HPE Persistent Memory is a game-changer for intensive database and analytic workloads.

- **Resilient technology**—HPE Persistent Memory delivers reliable technology that keeps business data safe.

- **Software ecosystem**—HPE is driving Persistent Memory optimization around performance and fault tolerance domains with operating system and application partners.

Database workloads and preferred solutions:

- HPE NVDIMMs

  - Smaller database, 100s of GB

  - Solves database storage bottlenecks

  - Software licensing reduction

  - Caching

Some use cases for HPE Persistent Memory include:

- **Reducing database storage bottlenecks**. Database performance can be vastly improved using low-latency DRAM to reduce or eliminate storage bottlenecks in lieu of using higher-latency block storage devices.

  Many databases have separate operations for the transactional portion of the database and the analytics portions which uses data tables from the transactional portion.

- **Software-defined storage** implementations can also benefit from HPE Persistent Memory. From commercial applications such as FlashSoft or AutoCache to HPE StoreVirtual VSA and Microsoft Storage Spaces, HPE Persistent Memory can be used to eliminate storage bottlenecks in those implementations as well as be used as a fast caching tier.

- **Restores** using HPE Persistent Memory can also be a source of latency as you restore from HDDs or SSDs. When you restore from HPE Persistent Memory, you are restoring from DRAM with nanoseconds of latency on the memory bus.

Note

These are just a few of the many use cases for HPE Scalable Persistent Memory. Visit the following link for the latest technical papers on emerging use cases:

http://www.hpe.com/info/persistentmemory

Activity: HPE Persistent Memory

Watch the HPE Persistent Memory video and take notes about the types of workloads that Persistent Memory is designed to benefit: **https://www.hpe.com/us/en/servers/persistent-memory.html**

You will need to scroll to the bottom of the page to find the video. Take notes about the types of workloads that Persistent Memory is designed to benefit.

Activity debrief

Answer the following questions:

1. In addition to databases and analytics, can you think of other workloads that would benefit from Persistent Memory?

    _____

    _____

    _____

    _____

2. Do you have any customers with these types of workloads? How would you explain to these customers how Persistent Memory would benefit them?

    _____

    _____

    _____

    _____

3. Which workload types mentioned by others in the group did you not consider?

    _____

    _____

    _____

    _____

4. Can you see how Persistent Memory would benefit any of your customers who have these or similar requirements?

_____

_____

_____

_____

Management tools — Compute

Provision
Rapid Discovery &
Remote access

Monitor
Server health, power
& thermal usage

Optimize
Remote
management

Support
Diagnosis &
alerting

Figure 3-62 HPE iLO functions

The HPE Integrated Lights-Out (iLO) subsystem is a standard component of ProLiant servers that simplifies initial server setup, server health monitoring, power and thermal optimization, and remote server administration, shown in Figure 3-62. The iLO subsystem includes an intelligent microprocessor, secure memory, and a dedicated network interface. This design makes iLO independent of the host server and its operating system.

iLO enables you to monitor and manage servers and other network equipment remotely even when the server is off and regardless of whether the operating system is installed or functional. It allows access to BIOS settings and the reinstallation of the operating system.

iLO enables you to:

- **Provision**—Inventory and deploy servers using virtual media and iLO Federation remotely with the iLO web interface, Remote Console, CLI, or mobile app.

- **Monitor**—iLO provides health and performance protection with advanced power and thermal control for maximum power efficiency. Agentless Management monitors core hardware and related alerts without installation of agents or providers on the host operating system.

- **Optimize**—iLO provides an Integrated Remote Console for remote administration so your customers can control their server from any location through the iLO web interface, Remote Console, CLI, or mobile app. Integrated Remote Console capabilities include Keyboard, Virtual Media, Global Team Collaboration, and Video Record/Playback. To remotely manage groups of servers at scale, iLO Federation offers built-in rapid discovery of all iLOs, group configurations, group health status, and the ability to determine which servers have iLO licenses. With an iLO Advanced license, you can enable the full implementation of iLO Federation management for features such as Group Firmware Updates, Group Virtual Media, Group Power Control, Group Power Capping, and Group License Activation.

- **Support**—iLO provides core instrumentation that operates whether the operating system is up or down. Should something go wrong, you can view the Integrated Management Log through the iLO web interface or download Active Health System logs, and send them to HPE Support for faster problem identification.

HPE iLO management technologies

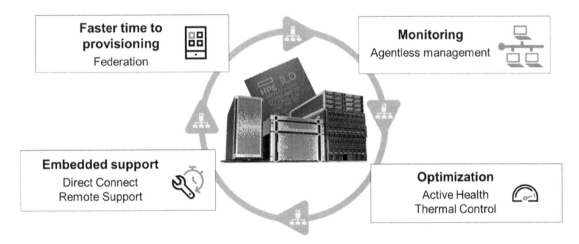

Figure 3-63 iLO has built-in features for instant availability

HPE iLO provides the core foundation and intelligence for all ProLiant servers, as shown in Figure 3-63. iLO is ready to run and does not require additional software installation. iLO management technologies simplify server setup, enable health monitoring, provide power and thermal control, and promote remote administration. iLO management technologies support the complete lifecycle of all ProLiant servers, from initial deployment through ongoing management and service alerting. The iLO capabilities that ship standard on all ProLiant Gen8/Gen9/Gen10 servers include:

- **Server health monitoring**—iLO monitors temperatures in the server and sends corrective signals to the fans to maintain proper server cooling. iLO also monitors installed firmware and software versions and the status of fans, memory, the network, processors, power supplies, storage, and devices installed on the system board.

- **Agentless Management**—With Agentless Management, the management software (Simple Network Management Protocol, or SNMP, operates within the iLO firmware instead of the host

OS. This configuration frees memory and processor resources on the host OS for use by server applications. iLO monitors all key internal subsystems and can send SNMP alerts directly to a central management server, even with no host OS installed.

- **Integrated Management Log**—View server events and configure notifications through SNMP alerts, remote syslogs, and email alerts.

- **Learn more links**—Troubleshooting information for supported events is available on the Integrated Management Log page.

- **Active Health System Log**—Download the Active Health System log. Your customers can send the log file to HPE when they have an open support case or upload the log to the Active Health System Viewer.

- **iLO Federation management**—Use the iLO Federation features to discover and manage multiple servers at a time.

- **Integrated Remote Console**—If your customers have a network connection to the server, they can access a secure high-performance console to manage the server from any location.

- **Virtual Media**—Remotely mount high-performance Virtual Media devices to the server.

- **Power management**—Securely and remotely control the power state of the managed server.

- **Deployment and provisioning**—Use Virtual Power and Virtual Media for tasks such as the automation of deployment and provisioning.

- **Power consumption and power settings**—Monitor the server power consumption, configure server power settings, and configure power capping on supported servers.

- **Embedded remote support**—Register a supported server for HPE remote support.

- **User access**—Use local or directory-based user accounts to log in to iLO. Your customers can use **Common Access Card (CAC)** smartcard authentication with local or directory-based accounts.

- **Two-factor authentication**—Two-factor authentication is supported with Kerberos and CAC smartcard authentication.

- **Secure Recovery**—Validates the iLO firmware when power is applied. If the firmware is invalid, the iLO firmware is flashed automatically (iLO Standard license). It validates the system ROM during server startup. If a valid system ROM is not detected, the server is prevented from booting. Recovery options include swapping the active and redundant ROM and initiating a firmware verification scan and recovery action (the iLO Advanced Premium Security Edition license is required for scheduling and automated recovery).

- **Firmware verification and recovery**—Run scheduled or on-demand firmware verification scans and configure recovery actions to implement when an issue is detected.

- **iLO security states**—Configure a security state that fits your environment. iLO supports the Production security state (default) and high security states such as HighSecurity, FIPS, and SuiteB.

- **iLO interface controls**—For enhanced security, enable or disable selected iLO interfaces and features.

- **Firmware management**—Save components to the iLO Repository and use Smart Update Manager (SUM) to configure install sets and manage the installation queue.

- **iLO Service Port**—Use a supported USB Ethernet adapter to connect a client to the iLO Service Port to access the server directly. HPE recommends the HPE USB to Ethernet Adapter (part number Q7Y55A). You can also connect a USB key to download the Active Health System Log.

- **Intelligent Platform Management Interface (IPMI)**—The iLO firmware provides server management based on the IPMI version 2.0 specification.

- **iLO RESTful API and RESTful Interface Tool (iLOrest)**—iLO 5 includes the iLO RESTful API, which is Redfish API conformant.

iLO 5 focus

The most important changes in iLO 5 are:

- **Security**—Raising our industry-leading bar even higher

- **Firmware update technology**—Update everything through iLO network

- **Agentless management**—Retiring OS-based agents

- **RESTful everything**—Redfish

- **At Server Management**—New innovation

- **Performance**—Everything faster

Connecting to iLO

Figure 3-64 iLO 5 overview

iLO can be accessed through several user interfaces, as illustrated in Figure 3-64:

- **Web-based interface**—The iLO web interface groups similar tasks for easy navigation and work-flow. The interface is organized in a navigational tree view located on the left side of the page. To access the iLO web interface, use local user accounts or domain user accounts. Local user accounts are stored inside iLO memory when the default user administrator is enabled.

- **Secure Shell**—With the SSH interface, your customers can use the most important iLO features from a text-based console.

- **ROM-based configuration utility**—Initial setup from UEFI System Utilities.

- **iLO scripting and command line**—You can use the iLO scripting tools to configure multiple iLO systems to incorporate a standard configuration into the deployment process and to control servers and subsystems.

- **HPE RESTful API**—iLO 4 2.00 on Gen9 and later includes the HPE RESTful API, which is a management interface that server management tools can use to perform configuration, inventory, and monitoring of a ProLiant server via iLO. A REST client such as the HPE RESTful Interface Tool sends HTTPS operations to the iLO web server to GET and PATCH JSON-formatted data, and to configure supported iLO and server settings, such as the UEFI BIOS settings. iLO 4 2.30 and iLO 5 are Redfish-conformant and remain backward compatible with the existing HPE RESTful API.

- **iLO mobile app**—The HPE iLO mobile app provides access to the remote console of a ProLiant server from an iOS or Android device. The mobile app interacts directly with the iLO processor on ProLiant servers, providing total control of the server at all times as long as the server is plugged in. For example, you can access the server when it is in a healthy state or when it is powered off with a blank hard drive. IT administrators can troubleshoot problems and perform software deployments from almost anywhere.

 Note

HPE iLO mobile is the name of the application in the HPE app store; iLO Console is the name of the icon.

iLO 5 allows high granularity to control the possibility to use user interfaces.

Controlling and monitoring power

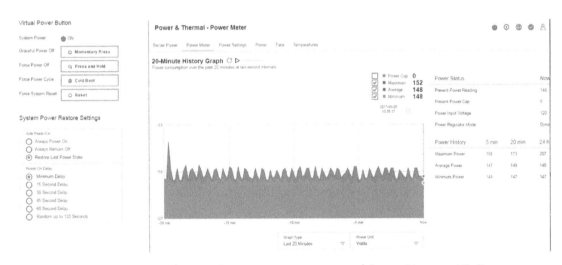

Figure 3-65 Virtual Power Button, power settings, and Power Meter in iLO 5

Power meter graphs display recent server power usage, as shown in Figure 3-65. Power history information is not collected when the server is powered off. When you view a graph that includes periods in which the server was powered off, the graph displays a gap to indicate that data was not collected.

The graph data is cleared when iLO is reset or the server is power cycled. For example, the data is cleared when you use the Virtual Power Button Reset or Cold Boot actions, but it is not cleared when you use the Momentary Press or Press and Hold actions.

The Power Settings page enables administrators to view and control the power management features of the server. The power management features on this page vary, based on the server configuration.

The Virtual Power Button section on the Server Power page displays the current power state of the server, as well as options for remotely controlling server power. System Power indicates the state of the server power when the page is first opened. The server power state can be ON, OFF, or Reset. Use the browser refresh feature to view the current server power state. The server is rarely in the Reset state.

Virtual Power Button options:

- **Momentary Press**—The same as pressing the physical power button. If the server is powered off, a momentary press will turn on the server power. Some operating systems might be configured to initiate a graceful shutdown after a momentary press or to ignore this event. HPE recommends using system commands to complete a graceful operating system shutdown before you attempt to shut down by using the Virtual Power button.

- **Press and Hold**—The same as pressing the physical power button for five seconds and then releasing it. The server is powered off as a result of this operation. Using this option might circumvent the graceful shutdown features of the operating system. This option provides the Advanced Configuration and Power Interface (ACPI) functionality that some operating systems implement. These operating systems behave differently depending on a short press or long press.

- **Reset**—Forces the server to warm-boot, and CPUs and IO resources are reset. Using this option circumvents the graceful shutdown features of the operating system.

- **Cold Boot**—Immediately removes power from the server. Processors, memory, and IO resources lose main power. The server will restart after approximately six seconds. Using this option circumvents the graceful shutdown features of the operating system.

The System Power Restore Settings section enables you to control system behavior after power is lost. You can also configure these settings by using the UEFI System Utilities during POST.

Using the Integrated Remote Console

The iLO Integrated Remote Console is a graphical remote console that turns a supported browser into a virtual desktop, allowing full control over the display, keyboard, and mouse of the host server. Using the Remote Console also provides access to the remote file system and network drives.

With Integrated Remote Console access, you can observe POST boot messages as the remote host server restarts and initiate ROM-based setup routines to configure the remote host server hardware. When you are installing operating systems remotely, the Integrated Remote Console (if licensed) enables you to view and control the host server monitor throughout the installation process.

iLO provides the following Integrated Remote Console access options:

- **.NET Internet Relay Chat (IRC)**—Provides access to the system Kernel-based Virtual Machine (KVM), allowing control of Virtual Power and Virtual Media from a single console through a supported browser on a Windows client. In addition to the standard features, the .NET IRC supports Console Capture, Shared Console, Virtual Folder, and Scripted Media.

- **Java IRC and Java Web Start**—Provides access to the system KVM, allowing control of Virtual Power and Virtual Media from a Java-based console. In addition to the standard features, the Java IRC includes the iLO disk image tool and Scripted Media.

- **Stand-alone IRC (HPLOCONS)**—Provides full iLO Integrated Remote Console functionality directly from a Windows desktop, without going through the iLO web interface. The HPE Lights-Out Console (HPLOCONS) has the same functionality and requirements as the .NET IRC application that is launched from the iLO web interface.

- **iLO Mobile Application for iOS and Android devices**—Provides Integrated Remote Console access from a supported mobile phone or tablet.

- **SSH console**—Offers `textcons` command to display the remote console in the terminal as far as the server is in text video mode.

Email alerting

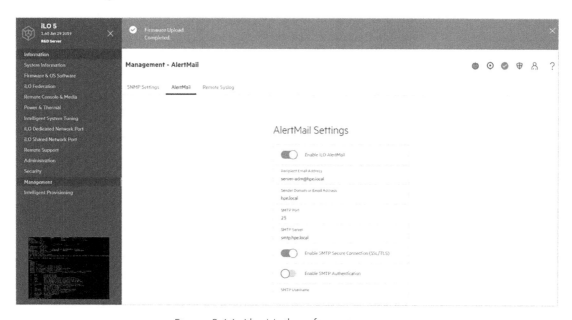

Figure 3-66 AlertMail configuration screen

iLO AlertMail enables you to configure iLO to send alert conditions detected independently of the host operating system to a specified email address, as shown in Figure 3-66. iLO mail alerts include major host system events. Some email service providers establish filters and rules to block problem emails such as spam, commercial content, and unwanted volume. These tools might block the receipt of messages generated by iLO. These email services are not suitable for receiving iLO AlertMail messages.

Using iLO Federation

Today's enterprise IT administrators face management problems directly related to scale-out environments that continue to be managed with existing tools not designed for these environments. These problems include how to communicate with thousands of servers to discover and manage these systems in a timely manner, using server data that is current and relevant. Traditional management environments are based on outdated hierarchical models and present a single point of failure.

Monitoring and managing server status in large data center environments with traditional methods, such as the use of host files or ping sweeps (using direct interrogation), are time-consuming. Server status information can be inaccurate by the time it is reported. Ping sweep approaches to iLO discovery and software updates take between one and two minutes per server. This means that in large server farms, essential management tasks can take days. In addition, direct interrogation is used to discover additional devices, which might not be on the same subnet. These conditions allow many existing solutions to cross network boundaries. This IT infrastructure discovery solution does not scale well.

Administrators have typically managed large infrastructures by using scripts and DHCP. Current approaches also use trust systems that typically employ back doors or impose the burden of a public key infrastructure (PKI) to configure secure communication.

iLO Federation eliminates the need for adjusting scripts during server migration and data center re-architecture efforts. It also removes reliance on tools for external communication. iLO Federation standardizes several fields within the protocol so that a ping sweep approach is still possible and adds extra information to support direct interrogation of responders.

In the past, iLO operated on a one-to-one approach, meaning that administrators could only look at one iLO at a time. iLO Federation is a fully distributed method for performing discovery of multiple systems, self-organizing those systems into groups, establishing trust, and securely communicating between systems.

iLO Federation uses the industry-standard multicast approach and provides multicast methods, allowing other systems to discover iLOs. iLO uses a peer-to-peer management system, in which the iLOs communicate with each other and share the workload of managing all the systems. The closest iLO neighbor is identified as a peer. The local iLO identifies its peers through multicast discovery.

iLO Federation also standardizes several fields within the protocol, so that a ping sweep approach is still possible, and adds extra information to support direct interrogation of responders. These core technologies provide reliability and interoperability, and include the following capabilities:

- **On-system intelligence**—Robust scalability, self-healing, with no single points of failure.

- **Real-time self-discovery**—With multicast discovery of any bare metal server, iLOs can be discovered after the server receives auxiliary power.

Important

iLO Federation discovery is a standard feature that allows for queries of data and viewing of iLO information without a license. However, iLO Federation management requires an iLO Advanced or iLO Scale-Out license to push data and define security groups. Licensing provides additional iLO functionality, such as graphical remote console, multi-user collaboration, and video record/playback along with many more advanced features. There are multiple levels of licensing depending on business needs.

- **Group membership**—iLOs can be configured with Federation settings and configured to be a member of a group. iLOs that are members of the same group will discover each other on the network and begin reporting data/distributing commands.

- **Security**—iLO Federation uses shared key encryption to implement trust requirements and ensure high levels of security.

 Note

Any user can view information on iLO Federation pages, but some features require a license. Visit the following site for more information:

https://www.hpe.com/us/en/servers/integrated-lights-out-ilo.html

iLO Federation operations

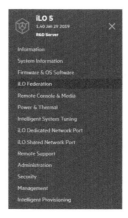

Figure 3-67 Selecting iLO Federation

iLOs can be grouped, and then activities can be directed to the group of iLOs. When iLO systems are in the same iLO Federation management group, the iLO web interface on one system can be used to manage all the iLO systems in the group, as illustrated in Figure 3-67.

iLO Federation provides the following functionality in the GUI:

- **Multi-System View**—Get a summary of the status of multiple systems at one time.

- **Multi-System Map**—Display information about the iLO systems in a selected group.

- **Group Virtual Media**—Provide an ISO image to the systems in the group.

- **Group Power**—Power the systems up and down and display power status.

- **Group Power Settings**—Configure Automatic Group Power Capping for multiple servers.

- **Group Firmware Update**—Update the firmware of multiple servers.

- **Group Configuration**—Add, delete, and modify federation group membership.

 Note

HPE recommends that iLO systems in the same iLO Federation group have the same version of iLO firmware.

Group Health Status

Figure 3-68 Viewing Group Health status

With iLO Federation, using the Multi-System View enables you to drill into various displays, as indicated in Figure 3-68. Clicking a server name filters by that server. Clicking the iLO hostname or IP address launches the iLO web interface.

Group Health Status provides an overview that shows system summary information. To view the status for a configured group of servers:

- Navigate to the **iLO Federation → Multi-System View** page.

- From the Selected Group menu, select a group.

The page displays the following information for the servers in the selected group:

- **Health information**—The number of servers in each listed health status (OK, Degraded, Critical). The percentage of the total number of servers that is in the listed health status also displays. The health status value can be clicked to select a subset of systems matching that health status.

- **Model information**—The list of servers, grouped by ProLiant model number. The percentage of the total number of servers for each model number also displays. The model number can be clicked to select a subset of systems matching that model.

- **Critical and degraded systems**—The list of servers with a Critical or Degraded status.

Filtering and target selecting available on most iLO Federation subpages:

- Click links in Health, Model, Firmware, and so forth, sections.

- Use Group for filtering.

Group Health Status—Critical and Degraded Systems

Figure 3-69 Group Health Status—Critical and Degraded Systems

The Critical and Degraded Systems view displays additional details, as shown in Figure 3-69, for systems that are not OK, including:

- System Name, System Health, System ROM version

- Server Power and Unit Identification (UID) indicator

- iLO Hostname and IP Address

From the Critical and Degraded Systems view, you can determine the severity of the issue:

- A status of Degraded means that a system component has changed to a less robust state (single fan failure, single points of failure, and so forth).

- A status of Critical indicates that a condition has occurred that might cause a system to fail (over-heating, all fans fail, and so forth).

Group Virtual Media

Setup	Multi-System View	Multi-System Map	Group Virtual Media	Group Power	Group Power Settings	Group Firmware Update	Group Licensing	Group Configuration

Insert Media

Virtual CD/DVD-ROM Status on 2 Systems

Media Inserted	Scripted Media
Connected	☑
Image URL	esx65.iso - 1 System
Image URL	litecoin_mining_unattended.iso - 1 System

Eject Media

Figure 3-70 Viewing Group Virtual Media in iLO Federation

The Group Virtual Media feature enables you to connect scripted media that can be accessed by the servers in an iLO Federation group, shown in Figure 3-70. Scripted media refers to connecting images hosted on a web server by using a URL. iLO will accept URLs in HTTP or HTTPS format. File Transfer Protocol (FTP) is not supported.

When there is a requirement for mass deployment of an operating system, the traditional one-to-one media installation consumes a tremendous amount of time and manual effort. Using Group Virtual Media, a single operating system image can be deployed over thousands of servers.

When using Group Virtual Media, note the following:

- Scripted media can be connected to the iLO systems in an iLO Federation Management group. Scripted media supports only 1.44 MB floppy images (.img) and CD/DVD-ROM images (.iso). The image must be located on a web server on the same network as iLO.

- To use the Group Virtual Media feature with an iLO Federation group, ensure that each member of the group has the Virtual Media privilege.

- Only one of each type of media can be connected to a group at the same time.

- You can view, connect, eject, or boot from scripted media.

The Group Virtual Media screens provide fields for entering a URL representing an ISO image or a CD/DVD-ROM image. iLO also supports mounting a .img file of a USB key; it does not need to be a floppy .img image.

Group Power Control

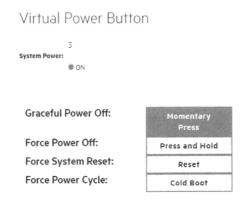

Figure 3-71 Viewing Group Power Control in iLO Federation

iLO Federation provides a way to control the power on all systems in a group or in multiple groups. It is possible to control power to individual systems as well.

The Group Power feature, as shown in Figure 3-71, enables you to manage the power of multiple servers from a system running the iLO web interface. You can:

● Power off, reset, or power cycle a group of servers that are in the On or Reset state.

● Power on a group of servers that are Off.

Group Power Control — Affected systems

The Group Power Control within iLO Federation provides a view of the systems that will be affected by pushing the Virtual Power Button. This provides a bail-out mechanism before the actions are taken.

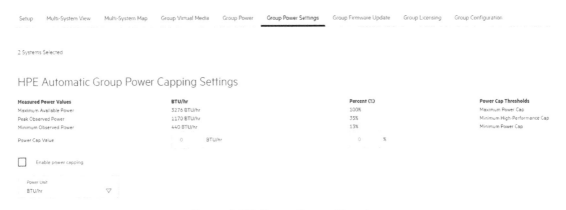

Figure 3-72 Group Power Capping

With iLO Federation, you can set dynamic power caps for grouped servers. Group Power Capping, as illustrated in Figure 3-72, enables you to conserve energy costs by controlling power to idling systems.

A separate power cap can be set for every group. With Group Power Capping, the power caps that are set for a group operate concurrently with the power caps that can be set on the Power Settings page for an individual server.

To configure power capping settings for an iLO Federation Management group, ensure that each member of the group has granted the Configure iLO Settings privilege to the group. When a group power cap is set, the grouped systems share power to stay below the power cap. More power is allocated to busy servers and less power is allocated to servers that are idle. When a power cap is set, the average power reading of the grouped servers must be at or below the power cap value.

Group Power Capping Settings

The Automatic Group Power Capping Settings section enables you to view measured power values, set a power cap, and disable power capping.

The Measured Power Values section lists the following:

- **Maximum Available Power**—The total power supply capacity for all servers in a group.

- **Peak Observed Power**—The maximum observed power for the servers in a group.

- **Minimum Observed Power**—The minimum observed power for the servers in a group.

- **Power Cap Value**—The value of the power cap that has been set for the servers in a group.

During POST, the ROM runs two power tests that determine the peak and minimum observed power values.

The Power Capping Settings section allows you to configure the power capping settings. The Current State section shows the current power consumption.

- **Present Power Reading**—The current power reading for all servers in a group

- **Present Power Cap**—The configured power cap for all servers in a group. This value is 0 if the power cap is not configured.

Group Firmware Update

This feature adds value to the task of upgrading the firmware on multiple systems. Rather than having to spend several days upgrading individual systems, you can use the Group Firmware Update feature to update the firmware of multiple servers from a system running the iLO web interface.

Firmware types supported for update are:

- iLO firmware

- System ROM (BIOS)

- Chassis firmware (Power Management)

- Power Management Controller

- System Complex Programmable Logic Device (CPLD)

- NVMe Backplane Firmware

- Language packs

 Note

The firmware images (raw .bin or .flash files) must be hosted on a web server on the same network as the iLO, similar to virtual media, and entered as a URL on the Group Firmware Update page.

Group Firmware Update views

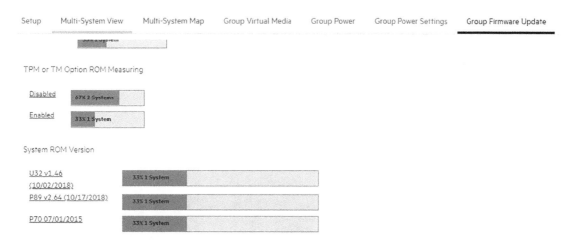

Firmware Update

Figure 3-73 Viewing Group Firmware Update in iLO Federation

When the firmware is being updated, the iLO Federation Group Firmware Update screen reports on the progress in real-time, as shown in Figure 3-73.

The Group Firmware Update feature enables you to:

- View the number of severs with each firmware version. The percentage of the total number of servers with the listed firmware version also displays.

- View the flash status for the grouped servers. The percentage of the total number of servers with the listed flash status also displays.

- View the TPM status for the grouped servers. The percentage of total servers with the listed TPM status also displays.

A TPM is a computer chip that securely stores artifacts used to authenticate the platform. These artifacts can include passwords, certificates, or encryption keys. TPM can also be used to store platform measurements to ensure that the platform remains trustworthy. On a supported system, iLO decodes the TPM record and passes the configuration status to iLO. The iLO Overview page displays the following TPM status information:

- **Not Supported**—A TPM is not supported.

- **Not Present**—A TPM is not installed.

- **Present**—This indicates one of the following statuses:

    - A TPM is installed but is disabled.

    - A TPM is installed and enabled.

A TPM is installed and enabled, and Expansion ROM measuring is enabled.

Accessing Intelligent Provisioning

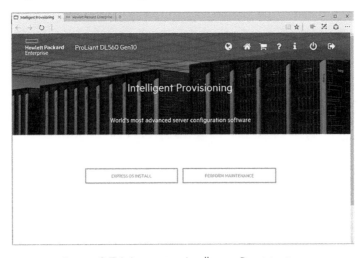

Figure 3-74 Accessing Intelligent Provisioning

To access Intelligent Provisioning, as illustrated in 3-75, power on or reboot the server and press **F10** when prompted during the server POST. When you access Intelligent Provisioning, one of the following happens:

- If this is the first time you are using Intelligent Provisioning, on-screen prompts provide guidance through initial configuration and registration tasks.

- If Intelligent Provisioning was previously accessed and the initial configuration and registration tasks are complete, the Intelligent Provisioning home page displays. In the home screen, select one of the following menus to use Intelligent Provisioning:

  - Express OS install

  - Perform maintenance

To exit Intelligent Provisioning, reboot the server by clicking the power icon at the top right of the page.

Figure 3-75 Always On Intelligent Provisioning

Intelligent Provisioning with limited features can be also accessed directly from iLO 5.

Intelligent Provisioning setup

The Set Preferences screen appears automatically the first time Intelligent Provisioning runs on a server. To set up the software, you must perform the following steps:

1. Choose the interface language and keyboard language.

2. Confirm that the system date and time are accurate. To change the date or time, click the displayed date or time, and use the displayed calendar or clock to select the new values.

3. Read and accept the end-user license agreement (EULA).

4. Enter network settings.

5. Select the active NIC from the list, and then choose from one of the following IP addressing schemes:

   – **DHCP Auto-Configuration**—HPE recommends selecting DHCP to have IP addresses assigned automatically to servers.

   – **IPv4 Static**—Selecting IPv4 adds four new fields: the static IPv4 address, network mask, gateway address, and DNS address.

   – **IPv6 Static**—Selecting IPv6 adds two fields: the static IP address and the gateway address.

6. Specify whether a proxy is being used. If there is a proxy on the network, it might need to be configured for use with features that communicate across the network. If **Use Proxy** is chosen, enter a proxy address and port.

⚠ Important

When entering the proxy address, make sure to include the appropriate protocol (FTP, HTTP, or HTTPS). If the protocol is not included, the installation of VSA may fail.

---

7. Enter the iLO network settings. Select one of the following iLO network IP addressing schemes:

   – **DHCP Auto-Configuration**—HPE recommends selecting DHCP to have IP addresses assigned automatically to servers.

   – **Off**—Selecting Off makes this server unavailable through iLO.

8. Select a delivery option for System Software Updates for Intelligent Provisioning.

   – **HPE website**—HPE recommends selecting this option to be prompted when updates are available and download all software updates for the server from the HPE website.

   – **HTTP/FTP**—When prompted, enter an address in the URL field.

   – **Disable**—Select this to disable automatic updates if it is planned to update system software manually.

Intelligent Provisioning—Installing the operating system

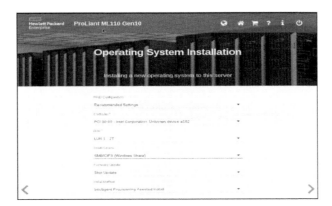

Figure 3-76 Express OS Install

To use Intelligent Provisioning to configure the hardware and install an operating system on a ProLiant server, follow the on-screen prompts in the Express OS Install menu, shown in Figure 3-76:

1. Configure RAID:

   – Recommended settings

   – Keep current settings

2. Select Controller and Disk.

3. Select Installation source:

   – DVD-ROM

   – File on a USB drive

   – CMB/CIFS

   – FTP server

4. Update Firmware:

   – Skip

   – Update

5. Select install method:

   – Assisted (only option when accessing from iLO web page—Always on)

   – Manual

6. Select the OS.

7. Review the settings.

8. Start the installation.

Perform maintenance

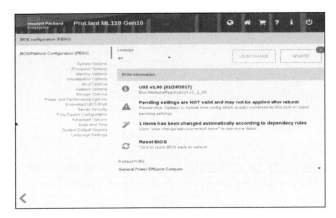

Figure 3-77 Performing maintenance

The Intelligent Provisioning Perform Maintenance screen provides access to numerous maintenance-related tasks, shown in Figure 3-77:

- **Active Health System download**—Download Active Health System telemetry data from the server onto a USB key in the form of an Active Health System log file. After you download the Active Health System log, the log file can be sent to HPE when support cases are opened to assist with troubleshooting. HPE support uses the log file for problem resolution.

- **Firmware Update**—ProLiant servers and their installed hardware options are preloaded with the latest firmware, but updated firmware might be available. Use the Firmware Update utility to find and apply the latest firmware for ProLiant server and installed options.

- **Intelligent Provisioning Preferences**—Change basic preferences, including the interface and keyboard languages, network and share setting, system date and time, and software update settings. In addition, the EULA is accessible from this screen.

- **Deployment Settings**—Create a server configuration package that can be deployed to one or more ProLiant Gen9 servers and server blades using a USB key and iLO scripting. Using the deployment settings is an alternative to using the HPE Scripting Toolkit.

- **Smart Storage Administrator**—These utilities provide high-availability configuration, management, and diagnostic capabilities for all HPE Smart Array products.

- **BIOS Configuration (RBSU) utility**—Access BIOS Configuration utility directly from Intelligent Provisioning without the need to reboot.

- **iLO Configuration**—View and change iLO settings through Intelligent Provisioning, instead of through the iLO web interface.

- **Erase Utility**—Clear hard drives and the Active Health System logs, and reset the RBSU settings in the UEFI System Utilities.

Post-installation tasks

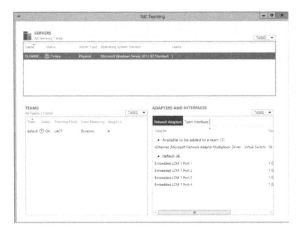

Figure 3-78 NIC teaming configuration

After the installation completes, as illustrated in Figure 3-78, perform post-installation tasks, such as:

- Update drivers and management components from Service Pack for ProLiant.

- Configure additional storage.

- Configure teaming/bonding.

- Set up update procedures.

- Verify logs.

SSA home page

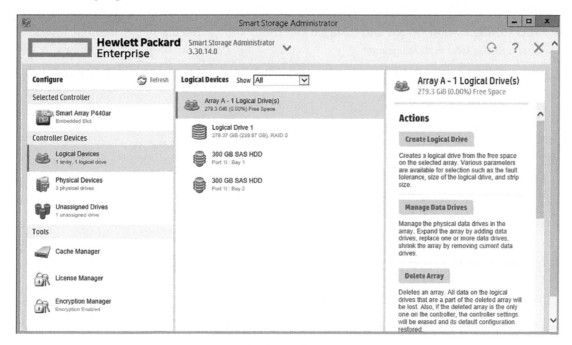

Figure 3-79 SSA home page

The Smart Storage Administrator (SSA) is a web-based application that helps you configure, manage, diagnose, and monitor Smart Array Controllers and HBAs, as shown in Figure 3-79.

Additional features of SSA include:

- GUI, CLI, and scripting interfaces

- English, French, German, Italian, Japanese, Simplified Chinese, and Spanish languages

- The ability to run on any machine that uses a supported browser

All formats provide support for standard configuration tasks. SSA also supports advanced configuration tasks, but some of its advanced tasks are available in only one format. The diagnostic features in SSA are also available in the stand-alone software, HPE Smart Storage Administrator Diagnostics Utility CLI.

Additional SSA features and functions include:

- **Support for HPE Secure Encryption**—Is a data encryption solution for ProLiant Gen8 and Gen9 servers that protects data at rest on any bulk storage attached to a Smart Array Controller.

- **SSD Over Provisioning Optimization**—Optimizes SSDs by deallocating all used blocks before data is written to the drive. The optimization process is performed when the first logical drive in an array is created and when a failed drive is replaced with a physical drive.

- **Rapid Rebuild Priority**—Determines the urgency with which a controller treats an internal command to rebuild a failed logical drive. SSA offers four settings: low, medium, medium high, and high.

- **Auto RAID 0**—Creates a single RAID 0 volume on each physical drive specified, enabling the user to select multiple drives and configure as RAID 0 simultaneously.

The SSA quick navigation menu is in the top, left-hand corner of the screen. Clicking the down arrow displays the available devices, and clicking one of the available devices displays additional information and options for the device. Return to a server home screen, or choose **Configuration** or **Diagnostics** for a device listed.

Available devices are listed on the left-hand side of the screen. Clicking a server or array controller displays the available actions, alerts, and summary for that device. Point to the status alerts to see details on an alert. The "What's New?" section summarizes the changes previous versions.

The Refresh button is near the top right of the screen. After adding or removing devices, click **Refresh** to update the list of available devices. The Help button is near the top right of the screen.

SSA Controller actions screen

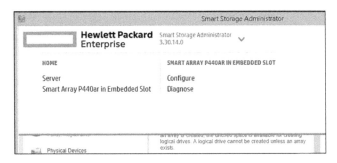

Figure 3-80 SSA Controller actions screen

Selecting a controller from the left-hand pane displays the actions page for that controller, as shown in Figure 3-80. Available actions include:

- **Configure**—Modify Controller Settings, Advanced Controller Settings, Modify Spare Activation Mode, Clear Configuration, and so on

- **Diagnose**—Array diagnostic report and SmartSSD Wear Gauge Report

SSA Configure screen

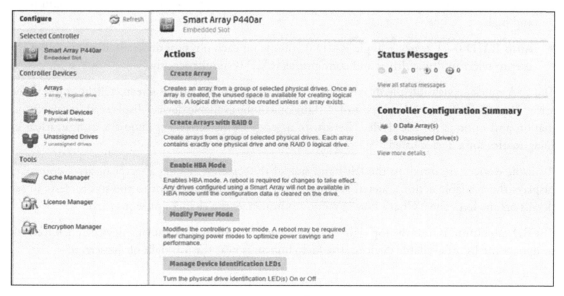

Figure 3-81 SSA Configure screen

To access this screen, as shown in Figure 3-81, either click a device under Configuration in the quick navigation menu, or select an available device from the Home screen, and then click **Configure** under the available options.

The Configure screen displays the GUI elements from the Welcome screen and lists available actions, status messages, more detailed information, and a controller configuration summary for a selected controller. When a controller is selected, the following elements appear:

- **Selected Controller, Controller Devices, and Tools**—This panel, at the left, displays systems, controllers, arrays, physical drives, logical drives, cache, and license manager.

- **Actions**—This panel, in the middle, provides the following information:

  – Tasks that are available for the selected device, based on its current status and configuration

  – Options and information pertinent to the task, after a task is selected

- **Status Messages**—This panel provides:

  – Status icons with the number of individual alerts for each category

  – A view all status messages link that displays device-specific alerts

- **Controller Configuration Summary**—This panel provides a summary of the following elements:

  - Data arrays

  - Data drives and logical drives

  - Unassigned drives

SSA Diagnostics screen

Figure 3-82 SSA Diagnostics screen

When you select either the Array Diagnostic Report or the SmartSSD Wear Gauge Report on the SSA Diagnostics page, as shown in Figure 3-82, the available actions on the Actions panel include viewing the report or saving the report.

 Note

The SSA Diagnostics feature replaces the Array Diagnostic Utility supported by SmartStart v8.20 and earlier.

SSA generates the following reports and logs:

- **Array diagnostic report**—This report contains information about all devices, such as array controllers, storage enclosures, drive cages, as well as logical, physical, and tape drives. For supported SSDs, this report also contains SmartSSD Wear Gauge information.

- **SmartSSD Wear Gauge report**—This report contains information about the current usage level and remaining expected lifetime of SSDs attached to the system.

- **Serial output logs**—This log details the serial output for the selected controller.

For each controller, or for all of them, the following tasks can be selected:

- View Diagnostic Report

- Save Diagnostic Report

- View SmartSSD Wear Gauge Report

- Save SmartSSD Wear Gauge Report

For the view tasks, SSA generates and displays the report or log. For the save tasks, SSA generates a report without the graphical display.

For either task, the report can be saved. In online and offline environments, SSA saves the diagnostic report to a compressed folder, which contains an XML report, a plain text report, and a viewer file so the report can be displayed and navigated using a web browser.

Each SSA Diagnostics report contains a consolidated view of any error or warning conditions encountered. It also provides detailed information for every storage device, including the following:

- Device status
- Configuration flags
- Firmware version numbers
- Physical drive error logs

SSA Diagnostics never collects information about the data content of logical drives. The diagnostic report does not collect or include the following:

- File system types, contents, or status
- Partition types, sizes, or layout
- Software RAID information
- Operating system device names or mount points

SSA Array Details screen

Figure 3-83 SSA Array Details screen

The array details page, shown in Figure 3-83, displays logical drives and their member physical drives. Actions include:

- Manage data drives

- Manage spare drives

- Split mirrored array

- Delete array

- Create split mirror backup

Creating a logical drive

Figure 3-84 Selecting a physical drive for the new array

To create a new logical drive (array), as illustrated in Figure 3-84:

1. Select a controller, and click **Create Array.**

2. Select the physical drives for the new logical drive.

3. Make selections for RAID Level, Strip Size/Full Stripe Size, Sectors/Track, and Size.

4. Click **Create Logical Drive.**

Activity: HPE Reference Architecture for Microsoft SQL Server 2017 on Red Hat Enterprise Linux with HPE ProLiant DL560 Gen10

1. Use this document: **http://h20195.www2.hpe.com/v2/GetPDF.aspx/a00036336enw.pdf**

2. Answer the following questions:

    – What is the recommended RAID level for SQL log files? _____

    – What is the recommended RAID level for SQL backup repository? _____

    – What is the difference in batch request/sec between 2S and 4S configurations?

    _____

    _____

    _____

    – Was NUMA used for performance testing?

    _____

    _____

    _____

Solution components

Part numbers are at time of publication and subject to change. The BOM does not include complete support options or other rack and power requirements.

Variant with two sockets:

Qty	Part number	Description
		HPE ProLiant DL560 Gen10 server
1	841730-B21	HPE DL560 Gen10 CTO Server
1	840379-L21	HPE DL560 Gen10 Intel Xeon-Platinum 8176 (2.1GHz/28-core/165W) FIO Processor Kit
1	840379-B21	HPE DL560 Gen10 Intel Xeon-Platinum 8176 (2.1GHz/28-core/165W) Processor Kit
12	815101-B21	HPE 64GB (1x64GB) Quad Rank x4 DDR4-2666 CAS-19-19-19 Load Reduced Memory Kit
1	873444-B21	HPE DL5x0 Gen10 12Gb SAS Expander Kit / Cables
1	872233-B21	HPE DL560 Gen10 8SFF Bay1 Kit
1	872235-B21	HPE DL560 Gen10 8SFF Bay2 Kit
2	873359-B21	HPE 400GB SAS 12G MU SFF SSD
6	872359-B21	HPE 800GB SATA 6G WI SFF SSD
4	873365-B21	HPE 1.6TB SAS 12G MU SFF SSD
1	789006-B21	HPE Ethernet 10Gb 2-port 562FLR-SFP+ Adapter
1	869079-B21	HPE Smart Array E208i-a SR Gen10 12G SAS Controller
1	875675-B21	HPE DL560 Gen10 4xPSU Enablement Kit
4	865414-B21	HPE 800W Flex Slot Platinum Hot Plug Low Halogen Power Supply Kit
1	733662-B21	HPE 2U LFF Easy install Rail Kit
1	BD505A	HPE iLO Adv incl 3yr TSU 1-Svr Lic

Variant with four sockets:

Qty	Part number	Description
		HPE ProLiant DL560 Gen10 server
1	841730-B21	HPE DL560 Gen10 CTO Server
1	840379-L21	HPE DL560 Gen10 Intel Xeon-Platinum 8176 (2.1GHz/28-core/165W) FIO Processor Kit
3	840379-B21	HPE DL560 Gen10 Intel Xeon-Platinum 8176 (2.1GHz/28-core/165W) Processor Kit
1	872222-B21	HPE DL5x0 Gen10 CPU mezzanine Board kit
24	815101-B21	HPE 64GB (1x64GB) Quad Rank x4 DDR4-2666 CAS-19-19-19 Load Reduced Memory Kit
1	872225-B21	HPE DL560 Premium Gen10 6SSF and 2 NVMe or 8SFF Bay1 Kit
1	872227-B21	HPE DL560 Premium Gen10 6SSF and 2 NVMe or 8SFF Bay2 Kit
2	873359-B21	HPE 400GB SAS 12G MU SFF SSD
10	872359-B21	HPE 800GB SATA 6G WI SFF SSD
4	873365-B21	HPE 1.6TB SAS 12G MU SFF SSD
1	789006-B21	HPE Ethernet 10Gb 2-port 562FLR-SFP+ Adapter
1	873444-B21	HPE DL5x0 Gen10 12Gb SAS Expanded Card Kit with Cables
1	804394-B21	HPE Smart Array E208i-a SR Gen10 12G SAS Controller
1	875675-B21	HPE DL560 Gen10 4xPSU Enablement Kit
4	865414-B21	HPE 800W Flex Slot Platinum Hot Plug Low Halogen Power Supply Kit
1	733662-B21	HPE 2U LFF Easy install Rail Kit
1	BD505A	HPE iLO Adv incl 3yr TSU 1-Svr Lic

Learning check

7. Match the processor family with its benefits.

Bronze	Up to 22 cores, 4 socket system support
Silver	Up to 8 cores, standard RAS features
Gold	2x AVX-512, 8 socket system support
Platinum	DDR4 2400 MHz, standard RAS features

8. Name three components of HPE Intelligent System Tuning.

_____

_____

_____

9. Memory controllers in HPE Gen10 ProLiant servers support up to four memory channels per CPU.

   ☐ True

   ☐ False

10. What are three possibilities for connecting to iLO?

_____

_____

_____

11. Which HPE tool can be used to configure Smart Array Controller?

_____

_____

_____

12. Intelligent Provisioning allows administrators to perform an assisted installation of an HPE ProLiant server.

   ☐   True

   ☐   False

13. You are in a meeting with a customer, and they challenge you with a question: "Is it possible to select the type of a local storage? Amount of drives, type of drive and physical size?"

   How should you respond?

   _____

   _____

   _____

   _____

   _____

   _____

   _____

   _____

   _____

   _____

   _____

   _____

Alternative server for smaller environments

We presented a validated solution for customer scenario. Some of the solution components, however, can be changed for alternative environments, where different performance, capacity, costs, feature, and similar requirements can be satisfied with other HPE solutions. Not all the workloads are the same and a single HPE product cannot match all the requirements.

HPE ProLiant DL580 Gen10 Server

Figure 3-85 HPE ProLiant DL580 Gen10

The HPE ProLiant DL580 Gen10 Server, as shown in Figure 3-85, is a high-density, four-socket server with high performance, scalability and reliability, all in a 4U chassis. Supporting the latest Intel® Xeon® Scalable processors, the HPE ProLiant DL580 Gen10 Server offers greater processing power, up to 6 TB of faster memory, IO of up to sixteen PCIe 3.0 slots, plus the intelligence and simplicity of automated management with HPE OneView and HPE iLO 5.

The HPE ProLiant DL580 Gen10 Server is the ideal server for business-critical workloads, virtualization, server consolidation, database, business processing, graphics-intensive, and general 4P data-intensive applications where the right performance is paramount.

Key benefits

- Scalable performance: compute, memory, storage, and IO expandability in a 4U design

- Enhanced drive (including NVMe) capacity with 4.8x more drives

- Increased performance with IST, Persistent Memory, and greater NVMe capability

Ideal use cases

- Server consolidation, virtualization environments

- Structured data management (Oracle, SQL)

- Business-critical workloads (ERP, CRM)

Positioning

- The secure and highly dense 4P 4U HPE ProLiant DL580 Gen10 Server delivers a mix of high performance and reliability making it the ideal choice for business-critical computing

- Enterprise-class warranty (3-3-3)

Learning check

14. Write a summary of the key concepts presented in this chapter.

_____

_____

_____

_____

_____

_____

_____

_____

_____

_____

_____

_____

_____

_____

_____

_____

_____

_____

_____

_____

_____

_____

_____

_____

Summary

- HPE provides wide portfolio of rack and tower-based servers. Servers can be selected based on:
  - Target workload
  - Performance and memory requirements
  - Internal storage and PCIe requirements
- Configurable internal components of HPE server include processors, memory modules, array controllers, hard drives, solid-state drives.
- HPE ProLiant Gen10 servers are addressing known and unknown security risks. Most internal components of HPE ProLiant Gen10 are tuned to bring higher level of security.
- HPE provides various tools for managing a single device, including UEFI, iLO, and SSA.

Prelearning check

Before proceeding with this section, answer the following question to assess your existing knowledge of the topics covered in this chapter. Record your answer in the space provided here.

1. You are in a meeting with a customer, and they challenge you with a statement: "I heard that HPE data center networking devices only support a traditional core/aggregation/access layered architecture. This approach does not match my current modernization plans."

   How should you respond?

   _____

   _____

   _____

   _____

   _____

   _____

   _____

   _____

   _____

4 Recommending HPE data center networking solutions for customer use cases

LEARNING OBJECTIVES

After completing this chapter, and given a customer scenario, you should be able to:

✓ Recommend and position HPE networking products, solutions, tools, and appropriate services for customer use cases.

✓ Describe, differentiate, and apply industry-standard networking architectures and technologies.

✓ Explain the HPE approach to converged management for the infrastructure lifecycle of networking devices.

Scenario 3: Optimize data center networking with Cloud-First approach

The wide HPE portfolio of data center products can be introduced using customer scenarios and recommended, validated configurations, based on HPE Reference Architecture or HPE Reference configuration.

Introducing the customer scenario

AREWMOS company will be used as a story line through this scenario. We will introduce the company using an interview:

- What is your primary business?

  - Regional service provider for accounting software "as a service." Including government institution (bound to various regulations such as GDPR and mandatory IPv6)

- How many employees do you currently have?

  - 100+ employees

- What does your selling and delivery channel look like?

  - Private e-shop (no resellers), reference program, marketing in regional media

- Where are you currently storing data, and how do you access files?

  - Block access: HPE 3PAR StoreServ

  - File access: storage file controller (NFS)

- What does your server and network infrastructure look like?

  - Single data center, mix of vendors (both servers and networking), 2000 servers

- What are your current plans?

  - Consolidation of data center networking

Customer requirements

As a result of multiple interviews and gathering information about customer plans and customer's current infrastructure, the following requirements emerged for the new solution:

- Provide a modern data center networking

  - Modern architecture, no Spanning Tree Protocol (STP)/Rapid Spanning Tree Protocol (RSTP)

  - Spine/Leaf

- 10 Gb server connectivity

- 2000 physical servers, private data center

  - Hypervisor with 30 to 50 virtual machines (VMs) on each server

- High availability and resiliency

- Exceptional performance and high bandwidth

- Flexibility

- Ability to scale past 2000 servers

- Support for IPv6 transition and Virtual Extensible LAN (VXLAN)

Activity: Information resources

1. Download these information resources:

   – HPE Cloud-First Reference Architecture Guide—2000 servers
     https://h20195.www2.hpe.com/v2/getdocument.aspx?docname=4aa5-7340enw

   – HPE FlexFabric 12900E QuickSpecs
     https://h20195.www2.hpe.com/v2/getdocument.aspx?docname=c04111378

   – HPE FlexFabric 5940 QuickSpecs
     https://h20195.www2.hpe.com/v2/getdocument.aspx?docname=c05158726

2. Answer the following questions:

   a. What are the two fundamental architectures described by the Reference Architecture?

   _____

   _____

   _____

   _____

   _____

   b. What is the name of the technology that allows two 12900E switches to look like a single switch?

   _____

   _____

   c. Which orchestration technologies are supported for daily everyday management functions?

   _____

   _____

   _____

   _____

   d. What are the key benefits of the leaf/spine design?

   _____

   _____

   _____

   _____

e. What is the speed of ports that the 12900E series support?

_____

_____

_____

_____

f. What is the meaning of the acronym DCB?

_____

_____

_____

_____

g. Does the HPE FlexFabric 5940 Switch support VXLAN?

_____

_____

_____

_____

h. What are the most important IPv6-related technologies that the 5940 supports?

_____

_____

_____

i. What is the model number of the HPE FlexFabric 12900E series that supports 16 IO modules?

 — What is the PN?

 — What is the maximum amount of 100 GbE ports?

_____

_____

_____

_____

Building blocks of the solution

We live and work in the Idea Economy. It has never been easier to turn ideas into new products, services, applications, and industries. To compete in this Idea Economy, today's enterprises need to be able to create and deliver new value instantly and continuously from all their applications. This requires a hybrid infrastructure that can maximize performance and cost.

Businesses must change along four axes to survive and thrive in the Idea Economy. They must transform to a hybrid infrastructure, protect the digital enterprise, empower the data-driven organization, and enable workplace productivity.

This reference architecture focuses on optimizing a ground up data center deployment which consists of 2000 physical servers supporting 30 to 50 VMs on each server. These architectures include critical features such as agility and flexibility, high bandwidth, high availability, resiliency, exceptional performance, and the ability to scale well past 2000 servers.

Whether you are building a one-tier solution or a spine and leaf solution, the objectives in each case can be summed up as follows:

- **Public, private, hybrid cloud support:**

    – It is critical when building out a new hybrid infrastructure data center that the infrastructure chosen provides developers with the on-demand infrastructure they require to go from idea to revenue.

    – Enable DevOps orchestration infrastructure that can accelerate IT operations, app delivery, and quality

- **Create flexibility:** Open and standard-based systems and environments reduce risk and increase flexibility for applications, infrastructure, and data needs.

- **Flatter network with increased frame forwarding and packet forwarding:**

    – Traditional legacy three-tier data centers were not able to keep providing the performance needed in the modern virtualized data centers that now see immense amounts of east-west traffic flows. Data center networks can see great benefits from eliminating these unnecessary hops needed to get from rack to rack.

    – One-tier networks can truly optimize the traffic flows between racks by ensuring each rack can reach another rack with just one hop.

    – Two-tier spine and leaf deployments have become the most common data center network architectures used by the industry today. These types or designs offer greater flexibility and scalability than one-tier solutions while still providing for exceptional performance, predictably, efficiency, and resiliency with a maximum of two hops from rack to rack.

    – HPE Intelligent Resilient Fabric (IRF) can be used as a switch virtualization feature, helping to create larger scalable devices that provide many benefits, including adding redundancy, but also allowing extra layers like aggregation layers to be eliminated thus helping to reduce the number of hops and increasing performance.

- **L2 vMotion flexibility:** L2 connectivity always needs to be considered. Data centers can deploy a single L2 domain, leveraging Transparent Interconnection of Lots of Links (TRILL) or Shortest Path Bridging (SPB), or by using L3 VXLAN overlay technology.

- **Reduced management complexity:** Flattening the network with large core switches and the elimination of aggregation switches combined with leveraging IRF in the various layers of the network simplifies what was typically a complex management scheme.

- **Zero need for STP/RSTP:** HPE IRF and an L3 fabric provides better performance and faster fail-over with redundant server connectivity and a loop-free, multi-pathed fabric ensuring multiple equal cost paths exist between each Top of Rack (ToR) switch.

High-level selection considerations

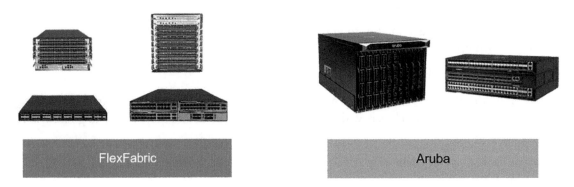

Figure 4-1 High-level selection considerations

HPE unifies wired and wireless networking to create superior, high-performance campus, branch, and data center solutions. Multiple HPE networking platforms are available for data center networking, including FlexFabric and Aruba, as illustrated in Figure 4-1.

- **FlexFabric**—HPE data center networking solutions support a broad range of 1 to 100 GbE ToR and core Ethernet switches to help accelerate applications and business outcomes.

  FlexFabric switches are suitable where traditional requirements prevail, or software feature depth and unique requirements and integrations are needed.

- **Aruba**—The Aruba Mobile First Platform is the intelligent software layer that turns connectivity into a rich experience for mobile users and actionable insights for business and IT. It is designed to accelerate the adoption of mobile and IoT initiatives and separate your customer's business from the crowd.

  Aruba components are preferred when consistency with campus devices is needed, or the customer is looking for analytics, automation, simplicity, and is interested in customer experience (CX) innovations.

HPE FlexFabric portfolio

Figure 4-2 Top of Rack/Leaf switches

To meet all the new data center networking requirements, HPE FlexFabric switches can be deployed, as illustrated in Figure 4-2. This portfolio has been deployed by HPE to date and is well known by customers.

This portfolio covers the traditional data center use cases with a great selection of ToR within the 5710, 5940, 5945, 5950, and 5980 series. ToRs accommodate diverse requirements for server link speed, fixed or modular configurations, deep buffers, and uplink bandwidth.

Figure 4-3 Spine switches

The spine switch model can also be selected among fixed configurations such as 5950 and 5980, limited in scale, or modular 12900E systems that exist in a different form factor, from one to a highly scalable 16 chassis, as illustrated in Figure 4-3.

These advanced switches meet today's requirements for higher-performance networking for more powerful compute and faster storage. With FlexFabric, customers benefit from:

- Greater agility, flexibility, and efficiency

- Increased speed for meeting service-level agreements (SLAs)

- Quicker time to service delivery

- Enhanced availability for reducing risk and costs

- Simplified, right-sized network infrastructure

Pick the switches that meet your customer's needs

HPE FlexFabric ToR switches address a wide range of customer requirements, with superior economics, performance, and reliability, as shown in 4-6.

HPE FlexFabric 5710

Figure 4-4 HPE FlexFabric 5710

- Budget-friendly solution
- For applications with less stringent capacity/performance requirements with 1/10 GbE downlinks and 40/100 G uplinks
- Perfect for out-of-band management (Integrated Lights-Out, or iLO) connectivity

HPE FlexFabric 5940/5945

Figure 4-5 HPE FlexFabric 5940/5945

- For high-capacity, high-performance applications with 10/25 GbE downlinks and 40/100 G uplinks
- VXLAN support for network virtualization
- Enhanced support for telemetry
- Fixed and modular options

HPE FlexFabric 5980

Figure 4-6 HPE FlexFabric 5980

- For high-capacity, high-performance applications with 1/10 downlinks and 50/100 G uplinks
- Available in fixed or modular configurations for ultimate flexibility
- Delivers up to 3.2 Tbps switching capacity
- Provides a best-in-class IP feature set and low-latency, high-availability connectivity

HPE FlexFabric 12900E family

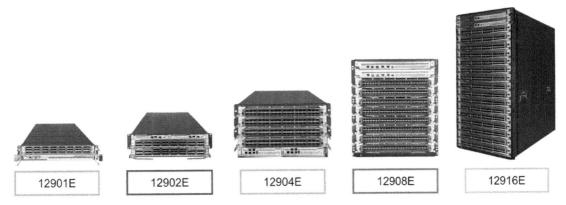

Figure 4-7 HPE FlexFabric 12900E family

The HPE FlexFabric 12900E Switch Series, as illustrated in Figure 4-7, is a next-generation modular data center core switch designed to support virtualized data centers and the evolving needs of private and public cloud deployments.

The FlexFabric 12900E switch delivers unprecedented levels of performance, buffering, scale, and availability with high-density GbE, 10 GbE, 40 GbE, and 100 GbE. The HPE FlexFabric 12900 Switch Series includes 16-, 10-, 8-, 4-, 2-, and 1-slot chassis.

Software-defined networking (SDN) enabled with OpenFlow 1.3, the switch supports full Layer 2 and 3 features, including advanced features such as VXLAN, TRILL, and IRF, which provide the ability to build large, resilient switching fabrics. The HPE FlexFabric 12900 Switch Series also supports fully redundant and hot-swappable components to complement its other enterprise-class capabilities.

Available chassis:

- HPE FlexFabric 12916E Switch Chassis
- HPE FlexFabric 12908E Switch Chassis
- HPE FlexFabric 12904E Switch Chassis
- HPE FlexFabric 12902E Switch Chassis
- HPE FlexFabric 12901E Switch Chassis

Benefits of the 12900E family include:

- Up to 120 Tbps switching capacity
- Up to 768 concurrent Ethernet virtual private network (EVPN) sessions
- Up to 3072 25 GbE ports

- Mix and match switches to meet local needs

- Ideal for east-west traffic and reducing the number of tiers

- Leaf-spine increases resiliency and reduces complexity for traffic policies

- Upgrade to 10/25 GbE at the edge

- Future-proof with 100 GbE in the core today and 400 GbE in the future

- Automate network operations to keep up with the demand

- Future-proof network capacity and ensure high availability

- Consolidate networking for servers and storage

- Enable cost-effective, disruption-free data center migration

- Give developers the platforms they need for rapid innovation

Networking technologies and architectures: ProLiant servers and FlexFabric switches

FlexFabric devices and networking products for servers differ in various parameters, such as port count, connectors, speed of the ports, and additional features.

Secure networking flexibility at the speed of compute

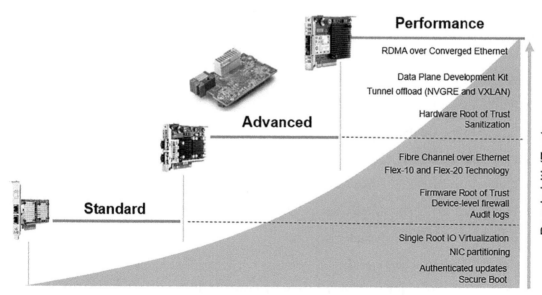

Figure 4-8 HPE network adapters

NICs, or network adapters for HPE server options, are divided into three product series, as shown in Figure 4-8:

- **Standard**—Enables a cost-effective Ethernet solution for your customer's everyday applications. The economic scalability of these adapters feature functionality like Single Root IO Virtualization (SR-IOV) for increased performance via direct access to hardware from a virtual environment. Network Partitioning (NPAR) enables users to "right size" data paths.

  The series offers two- and four-port choices and a broad selection of features at the lowest power and cost per port. The SR-IOV feature enables basic virtualization for expanding the network fabric and increasing performance.

- **Advanced**—Simplifies network and storage topology to build the new hybrid server infrastructure using the converged network adapter (CNA) FlexFabric technology. The configurable flexibility of these adapters reduces the number of network interface cards (NICs) required to connect disparate storage and IP networks, the number of cables and switches, and power and cooling costs.

  One of the Advanced Series features is Fibre Channel over Ethernet (FCoE), which reduces the hardware complexity required connect to disparate storage and IP networks by 50% or more. It also eliminates network sprawl at the server edge and saves up to 47% on upstream ToR switch cable connection.

- **Performance**—Delivers higher bandwidth at a lower latency. Expressly Fast adapters can maximize packet throughput and workload performance with the Data Plane Development Kit (DPDK).

HPE is only vendor with a 25/100 GbE end-end branded solution (ToR switch, transceiver, cable, and NIC). Based on an HPE TCO analysis done in May 2016, a 25 GbE enabled server in 25/100 GbE solution gives you 27% lower TCO, 31% power reduction, and 30% less cabling, when compared to a 10/40 GbE System.

Advanced networking technologies and use cases

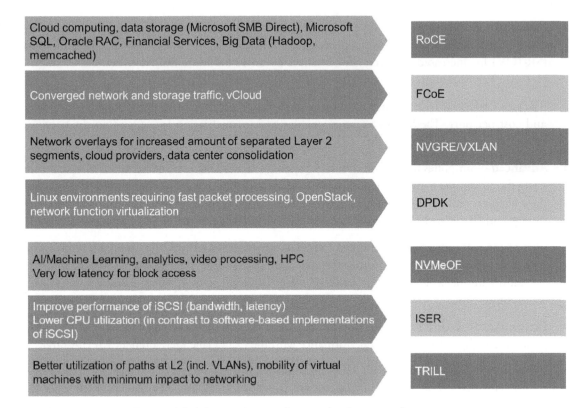

Cloud computing, data storage (Microsoft SMB Direct), Microsoft SQL, Oracle RAC, Financial Services, Big Data (Hadoop, memcached) — RoCE

Converged network and storage traffic, vCloud — FCoE

Network overlays for increased amount of separated Layer 2 segments, cloud providers, data center consolidation — NVGRE/VXLAN

Linux environments requiring fast packet processing, OpenStack, network function virtualization — DPDK

AI/Machine Learning, analytics, video processing, HPC Very low latency for block access — NVMeOF

Improve performance of iSCSI (bandwidth, latency) Lower CPU utilization (in contrast to software-based implementations of iSCSI) — ISER

Better utilization of paths at L2 (incl. VLANs), mobility of virtual machines with minimum impact to networking — TRILL

Figure 4-9 Advanced networking technologies and use cases

Figure 4-9 shows several use cases for advanced networking technologies.

What is Remote Direct Memory Access?

The latest networking technologies can help businesses boost reliability and productivity, eliminate silos and complexity, and provide better services faster. HPE advancements in networking technologies can address typical data center and server challenges.

Windows Server 2012 R2 and later versions include SMB Direct and support the use of network adapters that have Remote Direct Memory Access (RDMA) capability. RDMA network adapters can function at full speed with very low latency and use very little CPU. For workloads such as Microsoft Hyper-V or SQL Server, this enables a remote file server to resemble local storage. SMB Direct provides:

- **Increased throughput**—Leverages the full throughput of high-speed networks where the network adapters coordinate the transfer of large amounts of data at line speed

- **Low latency**—Provides extremely fast responses to network requests and, as a result, makes remote file storage assume that it is directly attached to block storage
- **Low CPU utilization**—Uses fewer CPU cycles when transferring data over the network, which leaves more power available to server applications

RDMA and RoCE

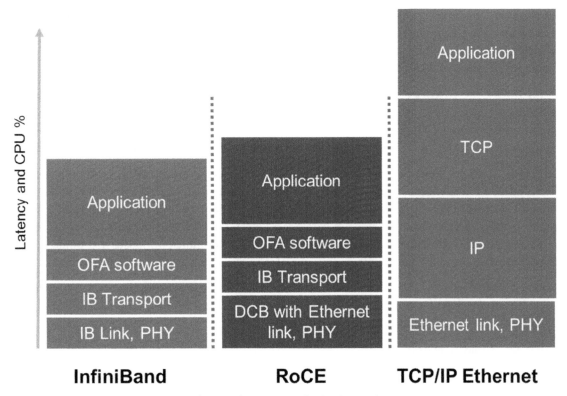

Figure 4-10 InfiniBand, RoCE, and TCP/IP stacks comparison

RDMA allows data to move between application memory in different servers without any CPU involvement. RoCE (RDMA over Converged Ethernet) provides this data transfer with very low latencies on lossless Ethernet networks and is ideal for live migration and Microsoft SMB Direct environments. RoCE is an accelerated IO delivery mechanism that allows data to be transferred directly from the memory of the source server to the memory of the destination server, bypassing the operating system kernel. RoCE benefits from improved IO performance and improved application CPU efficiency when compared to Transmission Control Protocol/Internet Protocol (TCP/IP), as illustrated in Figure 4-10.

Data center bridging (DCB) is a set of IEEE standards that create a lossless fabric on top of Ethernet. RDMA works best when the underlying wires implement a lossless fabric. DCB requires switches and NICs to implement important IEEE specs.

Application and user growth are impacting network traffic and driving increased VM deployment, straining system IO and CPU resources. Customers need an agile and efficient infrastructure to maximize the use of virtualized workloads throughout their lifecycle.

Converged local area network (LAN) and storage area network (SAN) can provide cost savings in infrastructure and simplified management. However, low latency and higher efficiency are extremely important and need further improvement in clustered, grid, and utility computing. Every microsecond delay in data transfer, algorithmic execution, or transaction derivation can result in millions of dollars in losses. RoCE reduces CPU utilization and helps maximize host VM density and server efficiency.

With RoCE, the RDMA data transfer is performed by the direct memory access engine on the adapter's network processor. This means the CPU is not used for the data movement, freeing it to perform other tasks such as hosting more virtual workloads (increased VM density). Workloads that would benefit from more CPU processing power include data mining and computational databases.

RDMA also bypasses the host TCP/IP stack in favor of upper layer InfiniBand protocols implemented in the adapter's network processor. Bypassing the TCP/IP stack and removing a data copy step reduce overall latency to deliver accelerated performance for applications such as Hyper-V Live Migration, Microsoft SQL, and Microsoft SharePoint with SMB Direct. For example, Hyper-V Live Migration is much faster using SMB Direct with RoCE than using TCP/IP. Additional workloads that would benefit from low latency include clusters with app-to-app RDMA transfers from one node to another.

RoCE is a key feature of some server network cards and converted network adapters. The adapters provide tunnel offload for efficient overlay networking to increase VM migration flexibility and network scale with minimal impact to server performance.

What are overlay networks?

The evolution to cloud data centers requires deployment at scale of tens of thousands of secure, private networks for tenants. Traditional technologies limit these data centers in the areas of speed, scalability, and manageability of application deployments. Current virtual LAN (VLAN) technology is limited to 4096 VLAN IDs, allowing for a small number of isolated private networks.

Two overlay networking technologies address these challenges: Network Virtualization using Generic Routing Encapsulation (NVGRE) (which is supported by Microsoft) and VXLAN (which is supported by VMware). A network overlay is a virtual network that runs independently on top of another one. Interconnected nodes share an underlying physical network, allowing applications that require specific network topologies to be deployed without needing to modify the underlying network.

In both NVGRE and VXLAN, a virtual Layer 2 overlay network (tunnel) is automatically created on top of a Layer 3 network. VM-to-VM communications traffic traverses this virtual network, and a VM can now be freely migrated across the data center over an overlay network without reconfiguration, thereby saving time.

Overlay networks can be used in data centers to support the following use cases:

- **Multi-tenancy at scale**—Provide scalable Layer 2 networks for a multi-tenant cloud that extends beyond current limitations. VXLAN uses an identifier that is 24 bits long, compared to the 12-bit VLAN ID that provides for only 4094 usable segments. As a result, potentially more than 16 million VXLAN segments can be used to support network segmentation at the scale required by cloud builders with large numbers of tenants.

- **Simplified traffic management**—Shift the network complexity from the physical network to the overlay network with software, and provide network resources from a single management point without changing the physical network.

- **Hybrid cloud capabilities**—Incorporate bare-metal servers anywhere and move the workload as needed, with public and private clouds working in sync.

Overlay network tunneling technologies (VXLAN and NVGRE) help address the issues of traditional Layer 2 networks. However, these technologies can significantly impact performance of data center compute resources. More specifically, they cause significant increases of CPU utilization, reduction in network throughput, and more power consumption.

 Note

Inserting the VXLAN/NVGRE header on an Ethernet frame, as well as calculating the new checksum value, creates a tremendous burden on throughput, host CPU utilization, and power consumption. This limits the number of VMs per physical server platform.

Many HPE CNA and network card adapters minimize the impact of overlay networking on host performance with tunnel offload support for VXLAN and NVGRE. By offloading packet processing to adapters, customers can use overlay networking to increase VM migration flexibility and network scale with minimal impact to performance. Tunnel offloading increases IO throughput up to 129%, reduces CPU utilization up to 46%, and lowers power consumption up to 122%. These adapters are the first in the industry to support VXLAN, NVGRE, and RoCE.

Data Plane Development Kit

DPDK is a set of libraries and drivers designed to run on any processor to enable fast packet processing. It is an open source Berkeley Software Distribution (BSD) licensed project that allows software-based customization and optimization of network performance by using polling instead of traditional interrupt-driven network processing. It is used in network functions virtualization (NFV) deployments.

NVMe over fabrics

NVMe over fabrics (NVMeOF) is a network protocol similar to internet Small Computer System Interface (iSCSI). This protocol can be used to communicate between a host and a storage system over a network. NVMeOF requires the use of RDMA and can utilize RoCE or other technologies such as iWARP or InfiniBand. In contrast to iSCSI, NVMeOF provides much lower latency.

iSER

iSCSI Extensions for RDMA (iSER) is an extension of the data transfer model of iSCSI, a storage networking standard for TCP/IP. It uses the iSCSI components while taking advantage of the RDMA protocol suite. The link protocol below iSER can be Ethernet or InfiniBand. It provides both high bandwidth and low latency to block storage traffic as it eliminates the TCP/IP processing inside the operating system. Deployment of iSER requires RDMA at the adapter card and utilizes iWARP, InfiniBand (IB), or RoCE transport layers over Ethernet.

TRILL

TRILL is an Internet Engineering Task Force (IETF) standard. The goal of the TRILL protocol is to provide large-scale Layer 2 fabric services. The intent is to maintain the simplicity of traditional Layer 2 systems while adding the scalability and convergence of a Layer 3 routed network.

From the perspective of an endpoint device, a standard frame continues to transport data from source-to-destination MAC address. However, traditional STP between switches is replaced with the routing-like functionality of TRILL. STP uses a single path in the network, which may not actually be the best path for a specific source-to-destination traffic flow. With TRILL, Layer 2 forwarding is based on best path selection, very much like that of Open Shortest Path First (OSPF) or Intermediate System to Intermediate System (IS-IS). This provides actual best path selection while supporting a redundant, active-active topology.

The TRILL protocol is documented in a set of IETF RFCs, or Request for Comments. TRILL frames use a hop count or Time-To-Live (TTL) mechanism, which must be processed by switch hardware. For this reason, TRILL will typically only be supported on newer generation data center switches that have been designed with application-specific integrated circuits (ASICs) that support this TTL processing. Fine Grain Labels (FGLs) enable TRILL to handle more than 4094 VLANs by using labels instead of VLAN IDs. FGL support requires appropriate ASIC support as well, and support in a specific device needs to be verified.

A switch that runs TRILL is called a Routing Bridge, or RBridge. This is because it is a Layer 2 bridging device that uses routing functionality to determine optimal data flow.

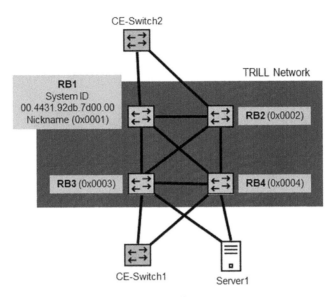

Figure 4-11 Trill concepts

Figure 4-11 shows four RBridges that form the TRILL network. This network supports connectivity for standard endpoints and Classic Ethernet (CE) switches. The CE is used to indicate a traditional Ethernet switch that does not run the TRILL protocol. Two such switches are indicated in the figure, as CE-Switch1 and CE-Switch2. Each RBridge is identified by a unique system ID, which is automatically generated by the TRILL protocol. The ID is based on the device MAC address by default. A system ID can be manually configured, but automatic generation works well.

The system ID is not used to forward frames. It is used to uniquely identify each RBridge inside the Link State Database (LSDB) of the TRILL network. This can be compared to how each OSPF router is identified by its router ID in OSPF's LSDB, often derived from the IP address of a loopback interface.

An RBridge forwards frames through a TRILL network based on source and destination nicknames. Each RBridge in the figure has a unique hexadecimal value for this purpose. RB1 has been assigned a nickname of 0x0001, RB2 has 0x0002, and so on. When RB1 sends a frame to RB2, TRILL adds source and destination nicknames to the frame. In this scenario, RB1's nickname of 0x0001 is the source, and RB2's nickname of 0x0002 is the destination. Each RBridge in the path processes these frames based on the destination nickname address. Again, this can be compared with how a routing protocol like OSPF routes frames based on the destination IP address.

Nicknames can be automatically generated by the system. Unlike IP addressing, nicknames do not have a hierarchical structure. There is no network and host portion for nicknames neither is there any sort of mask. Nicknames create a simple, flat address space.

Nicknames are 16-bit values, so the theoretical number of available addresses is 65,536. They can be randomly chosen from this space. However, an administrator can manually assign nicknames, making network documentation and diagnostics more intuitive. Instead of random hexadecimal numbers, a schema can be used to distinguish between distribution and access switches, or perhaps to indicate rack locations inside a data center. TRILL is based on the IS-IS link-state routing protocol. IS-IS operates between all RBridges, exchanging link-state information and building an LSDB. The SPF algorithm is run on this database to determine optimal paths through the TRILL network.

Selecting the data center networking architecture

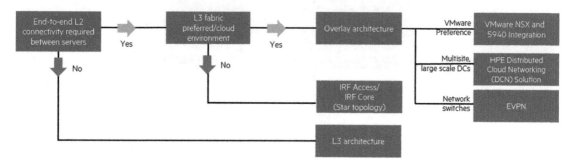

Figure 4-12 Selecting the data center architecture

The preceding graphic, shown in Figure 4-12, and the table below, shown in Figure 4-13, simplify the decision process, and they break down the overall solution into two recommended options. Of course, not all data centers may fall fully in line with one of the provided options, but these options can be used as a starting point. HPE data centers are very flexible so that the solution can be modified in a way that meets the specific needs of the environment.

DC Network Design	Option 1 (Recommended)	Option 2
Traditional 3-Tier	IRF	MSTP
Spine & Leaf—Layer 2	IRF	MSTP
Spine & Leaf—Layer 3	BGP	OSPF
L3 Overlay	EVPN	EVPN
LAN/SAN Convergence	FC/FCoE	iSCSI
DC Interconnect	EVPN DCI	EVPN DCI

Figure 4-13 Selecting protocols for specific data center network designs

Many data centers use a combination of L2 and L3 solutions, but how much and at what layer each solution is deployed varies widely. Administrators should have a thorough understanding of why and when L2 or L3 should be used.

L2 networks were widely used in the early days of networking when networks were small. As networks grew, they shifted toward L3 designs so they could scale and reduce broadcast domains. However, the rapid growth and deployment of virtualization saw the resurgence of L2 architectures and the deployment of new large-scale L2 architectures. Server virtualization solutions and cloud orchestration solutions such as HPE Helion OpenStack are two examples of frameworks that leverage L2 and VLAN technologies for VM communications and migration. These deployments are designed so that VLANs can extend from rack to rack and even across data center boundaries, creating a large L2 environment optimized for the growing use of VM migration and disaster recovery.

L3 architectures that route packets at each device were widely deployed before the proliferation of virtualization. Virtualization drove the deployment of L2 architectures to satisfy the requirements of VM migration. However, within many environments L2 extension is still not a priority. These types of environments can benefit from the scaling and efficiency advantages that L3 architectures provide.

Typical spine/leaf topology

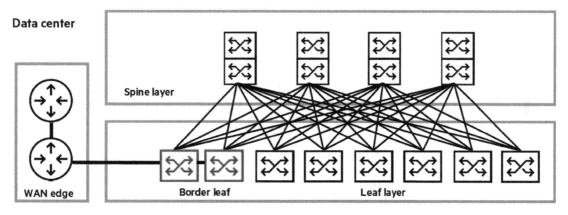

Figure 4-14 Typical spine/leaf topology

The spine/leaf topology is a topology design that has only two layers—the leaf layer and spine layer. The leaf layer consists of access switches that connect to servers, and the spine layer is the backbone of the network. Every leaf switch is interconnected with each and every spine switch, as illustrated in Figure 4-14.

Leaf-spine networking fabrics have become the preferred, best-of-breed data center network architecture.

Benefits of a leaf-spine architecture

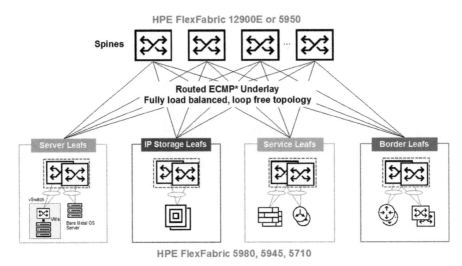

Figure 4-15 Benefits of a leaf-spine architecture

With leaf-spine configurations, all devices connected to the network have an identical number of hops to any other device, as illustrated in Figure 4-15. This design provides a predictable and consistent amount of delay or latency for the traffic.

HPE FlexFabric delivers following benefits for leaf/spine architectures:

- Agility, flexibility, efficiency
- Right sizing of spine with 1/2/4/8/16-slot chassis options
- Speed, moving faster, meeting SLAs
- Time to service delivery
- Availability, reducing risk and costs
- Orchestration network with the rest of the software-defined infrastructure (SDI), such as servers, storage, cloud automation, and so forth
- Software-defined fabrics, open source tools automation, multi-tenant, analytics, and telemetry
- Integration with Nuage and other third-party controllers

Extending the 25/50/100 GbE value across the data center

The 25 GbE networking is less expensive to use. It provides 2.5x more bandwidth over the same number of wires and switch ports than 10 GbE, but it costs about 1.5x more per NIC port than 10 GbE. This gives 25 GbE a 40% lower cost/bandwidth than 10 GbE.

Compared to 40 GbE solutions, the 25 GbE technology provides superior switch port density by requiring just one lane (vs. four with 40 GbE) along with lower costs and power requirements.

A 25 GbE (and 50 GbE) solution will be backward and forward compatible with 10, 40/100, and 400 GbE products, since they use the same IEEE 802.3 frame format. IT engineers started adding four, six, eight, or even 10 lanes of 1 Gb or 10 Gb Ethernet to the server infrastructure to address performance bottlenecks. However, these additions conveyed major costs with more cables, transceivers, and overall data center complexity.

An Ethernet at 25/50/100/200 Gbps will be the preferred network for non-block–based access. Compatibility with the installed base, cost, and operational skill sets will ensure the Ethernet remains unchallenged for this use case. Link speed increases do not just support increased capacity; they provide increased bandwidth, as bit insertion delays at 100 Gbps is one-fourth as long as at 25 Gbps.

Extending the 25/40/100 GbE across the data center:

- **Compute**—Move from 10 GbE to 25 GbE

    - 25 GbE uses the same number of copper or fiber lanes as 10 GbE

    - Higher server bandwidth

    - Same number cabling elements

- **Storage**—Move from 40 GbE to 50 GbE

    - 50 GbE uses half the number lanes as 40 GbE

    - 2X storage node connectivity

    - 25% more bandwidth per node

- **Fabric**—Move from 40 GbE to 100 GbE

    - 2.5X performance increase for every link in a three-tier leaf-spine

    - Better load distribution

    - Lower application latency

Management tools

HPE network management tools span across products and bring innovations to complete lifecycle management, as illustrated in Figure 4-16. As network management becomes more complex, the risks associated with a compromised data flow have also increased.

HPE management tools deliver comprehensive management across data center networks. HPE management tools convert meaningless network data into actionable information to keep the network and business moving.

HPE networking software

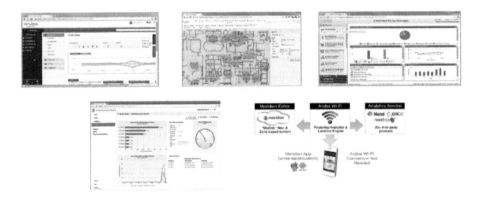

Figure 4-16 Network management tools

HPE network management tools include:

- **Aruba Central**—Aruba Central offers a simple, secure, and cost-effective way to manage and monitor Aruba Instant APs, switches, and branch gateways. It also has advanced capabilities like customizable guest Wi-Fi and presence analytics for smarter decision making. With Aruba Central, you can get your network up and running in minutes with intelligent Zero Touch Provisioning (ZTP). The intuitive dashboards along with reporting, maintenance, and firmware management make monitoring and troubleshooting easy—no technical expertise is required.

- **Airwave**—Aruba AirWave is a scalable, full featured management solution for multi-vendor wired and wireless networks. Organizations gain the visibility, control, and troubleshooting tools required to fully manage today's distributed enterprise environments. AirWave integrates configuration, deployment, real-time visibility, and control for comprehensive management and troubleshooting. This provides a flexible platform for maintaining the reliability and performance of Aruba access points, controllers, switches, and selected multi-vendor devices.

- **ClearPass**—Aruba's ClearPass Policy Manager, part of the Aruba 360 Secure Fabric, provides role- and device-based secure network access control for:

  - Internet of Things (IoT)

  - bring your own device (BYOD)

  - Corporate devices

  - Employees, contractors, and guests

ClearPass Policy Manager works across any multi-vendor wired, wireless, and VPN infrastructure that use them. With a built-in context-based policy engine, RADIUS, TACACS+, non-RADIUS enforcement using OnConnect, device profiling, posture assessment, onboarding, and guest access options, ClearPass is unrivaled as a foundation for network security for organizations of any size.

Unified network management with HPE Intelligent Management Center

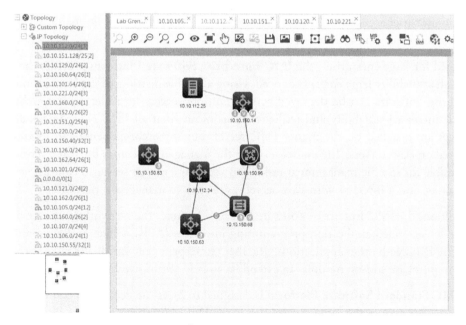

Figure 4-17 Intelligent Management Center (IMC)

IMC consolidate the management functions needed to manage today's networks while providing the tools needed to address emerging networking trends and applications, as indicated in Figure 4-17. IMC allows your customers to manage both their physical and virtual networks. Because IMC automates the configuration of virtual and physical network infrastructures, it eliminates service interruptions caused by virtual/physical network configuration errors. It also accelerates the delivery of new applications.

Specifically, IMC provides the following support for virtual environments:

- Virtual and physical topology views and status indicators for network resources

- VM and virtual switch resource management, including the creation of virtual switches and port groups

- Automatic reconfiguration of network policies that "move" with virtual applications and workloads

- Discovery of VMs and virtual switches and their relationship to the physical network

IMC also provides a single pane-of-glass network management for multi-vendor environments. From a single interface, you can monitor and manage network traffic and devices, including HPE and third-party network infrastructure devices. IMC can manage thousands of devices from more than 200 manufacturers.

IMC is designed to provide greater visibility of the entire network, allowing your customers to control and monitor user access. IMC meets the needs of any organization—no matter what its size or network requirements. It is available in three packages:

- Designed for large enterprises, the **IMC Enterprise Software Platform** provides the scalability and high availability large enterprises need. Using a flexible distributed deployment model, IMC Enterprise Software can be deployed across multiple servers in a hierarchical architecture to provide increased scalability and resilience. This means that all IMC components and add-on modules are installed on the master IMC server, but some components and modules can be deployed on slave servers. The master server is the management center for IMC; slave servers are responsible for specific management tasks. You access the master server to complete all management tasks, and it interacts with slave servers as needed to manage the network.

  In addition, the IMC Enterprise Software Platform includes the Network Traffic Analyzer and a license for extended application programming interfaces (APIs), which enable organizations to integrate IMC with other applications. The IMC Enterprise Software Platform is also extensible. You can purchase add-on modules to extend its already impressive capabilities.

- The **IMC Standard Software Platform** is designed to meet the needs of medium to large organizations. It provides the same capabilities as the IMC Enterprise Software Platform with one exception: The Standard Software Platform does not support the distributed deployment model.

- Created specifically for small- to medium-sized businesses, the **IMC Basic Software Platform** provides a simple-to-use interface. Limited to 50 nodes, the IMC Basic Software Platform provides sFlow traffic analysis, centralized reports, performance monitoring, network monitoring, and device management (including discovery, baseline configurations, software management, version tracking, and alerts). Designed for companies that need basic management functionality, it does not support the IMC add-on modules.

sFlow

Many HPE devices support sFlow is an industry-standard technology that uses statistical sampling to enable network monitoring. sFlow relies on two components:

- sFlow agents

- sFlow collector (which is also sometimes called a receiver)

sFlow agents run on network devices—such as switches, routers, and access points—gathering information about the packets transmitted on these devices and sending that information to the sFlow collector for analysis. Specifically, agents can send traffic samples and polling counters.

For traffic samples, the sFlow standard defines all the packets that a network device receives on one interface and are forwarded to another interface as a "flow." Using a statistically accurate algorithm, the sFlow agent examines on average one of every nth packets, where **n** is the number of packets. The samples are taken "on average" because sFlow employs some randomness to avoid sampling packets at precise intervals that might coincide with certain traffic patterns.

An sFlow agent packages sampled information into small datagrams, which include Layer 2 through 7 information, such as:

- Source and destination interface

- Sampled packet header

- Length of sampled packet

- Forwarding the decision the switch made for this packet

An sFlow agent can also use counter polling to gather traffic statistics. It polls data sources at specified intervals, adds this information to the sFlow datagrams, and sends them to a specified sFlow collector.

The agents can include information from several packets into a single datagram. Because traffic samples are compact and agents sample only a small percentage of traffic, sFlow does not require a large amount of network bandwidth or processing power on network devices.

 Note

sFlow® is an industry-standard technology for monitoring high-speed switched networks. It gives complete visibility into the use of networks enabling performance optimization, accounting/billing for usage, and defense against security threats (sflow.org, April 2019).

IMC for the data center

IMC orchestrates network fabrics:

- VXLAN manageability

- Unified SPB, TRILL, IRF fabric management

- Manages across geographically dispersed locations Data Center Interconnect/Ethernet Virtual Interconnect, or DCI/EVI

- VMware vMotion playback

- Unified DCB, FCoE management

Complete the SDN architecture with management:

- Configuration, monitoring, and policy management for all SDN layers

- OpenFlow switch management

- SDN controller performance management

- One application for managing SDN and traditional environments

Accelerates deployment of services and applications:

- "Just right" network services tuned to business requirements

- Simplifies provisioning, monitoring, and troubleshooting of applications

- Eliminates manual provisioning of network service parameters

- Easy to use service modeling tool with drag and drop user interface (UI)

HPE IMC base platform options

- **IMC Basic**—Fixed-device limit of 50 nodes

- **IMC Standard:**
  - Base license for 50
  - Up to 15,000 devices

- **IMC Enterprise:**
  - Large network systems that scale to tens of thousands
  - Base license for 50 managed devices
  - Fifty APs for the included Wireless Services Module
  - Five nodes of Network Traffic Analyzer Software
  - Additional licenses for purchase

Activity: HPE Cloud-First Reference Architecture Guide—2000 Servers

1. Use this document: **https://h20195.www2.hpe.com/v2/getdocument. aspx?docname=4aa5-7340enw**

2. Answer the following questions:

   a. What is the recommended leaf switch for the scenario?

   _____

   _____

   _____

   _____

   b. How many leaf switches are recommended?

      – What is the rationale behind the number?

   _____

   _____

   _____

   c. What is the recommended spine switch for the scenario?

   _____

   _____

   _____

   d. What is the speed of the uplink interface of the leaf switch?

   _____

   _____

   _____

   e. What are the scalability limits of the spine switch:

      – Maximum MAC addresses

      – Maximum amount of ingress/egress ACLs

   _____

   _____

   _____

Solution components

Part numbers below are at the time of publication and subject to change. The bill of material (BOM) does not include complete support options or other rack and power requirements.

Part number	Description	Quantity	Comments
JH255A	HP FF 12908E Switch Chassis	2	
JH108A	HP FF 12900E 2400W AC PSU	16	
JH424A	HPE 12908E High Speed Fan Tray Assembly	4	
JC665A	HPE X421 Chassis Universal 4-post RM Kit	2	
JH362A	HPE 12908E 14.4Tbps Type H Fabric Module	12	
JH669A	HPE 12900E v2 Main Processing Unit	4	
JH357A	HPE 12900E 36p 100GbE QSFP28 HB Module	12	
JL275A	HPE X150 100G QSFP28 LC LR4 10km SM Transceiver	400	Used for leaf switch connectivity

Part Number	Description	Quantity	Comments
JH391A	HPE FF 5940 48XGT 6QSFP28 Switch	100	
JC680A	HPE 58x0AF 650W AC Power Supply	200	
JG552A	HPE X711 Frt(prt) Bck(pwr) HV Fan Tray	200	
JL272A	HPE X240 100G QSFP28 3m DAC Cable	200	Used for IRF connections and BFD MAD
JL275A	HPE X150 100G QSFP28 LC LR4 10km SM Transceiver	400	Used for spine switch connectivity

Learning check

1. Match the switch family with the description.

HPE FlexFabric 5710 series	Cost effective ToR switch for 1/10 Gb
HPE FlexFabric 5945	Compact, cost effective, 100 GbE
12901E	Fixed/modular, 10/25 GbE downlinks, 40/100 GbE uplinks

2. What is the typical speed of uplink ports on the HPE FlexFabric 5710/594x/5980 series?

_____

_____

_____

_____

_____

_____

3. Your customer is interested in network management software for a mixed environment with 30 devices. Which software will you recommend?

_____

_____

_____

_____

_____

Alternative servers for different environments

We presented a validated solution for customer scenario. Some of the solution components, however, can be changed for alternative environments where different performance, capacity, costs, features, and similar requirements can be satisfied with other HPE solutions. Not all the workloads are the same and a single HPE product cannot match all the requirements.

FlexFabric 5710 Switch Series — Overview

FlexFabric 5710 Switches are purpose-built ToR data center switches that address the growth of web, cloud, and dense virtualized environments that require high-performance 1/10 GbE server connectivity, direct-attached IP storage networking, and GbE out-of-band server management.

They provide choices that fit the customer's budget and IT environment by offering different port density and speeds (1/10 G) SFP+ or 10 Base-T with 40 and 100 GbE high-speed uplinks options.

FlexFabric 5710 Switch Series, as illustrated in Figure 4-18, are affordably priced, contain a comprehensive set of data center features, including full support for Layer 2, Layer 3, IPv4, and IPv6 networking protocols at no additional cost.

HPE FlexFabric 5710 Switch Series

Figure 4-18 FlexFabric 5710 Switch Series

Technical specifications:

	HPE 5710 48SFP+ 6QS+/2QS28 Switch (JL585A)	HPE 5710 48XGT 6QS+/2QS28 Switch (JL586A)	HPE 5710 24SFP+ 6QS+/2QS28 Switch (JL587A)
IO ports and slots	48 x 1/10 GB SFP+ ports	48 x 1/10 GBASE-T ports	24 x 1/10 GB SFP+ ports
	6 x QSFP+ ports (or a maximum of 2 x QSFP28 ports)	6 x QSFP+ ports (or a maximum of 2 x QSFP28 ports)	6 x QSFP+ ports (or a maximum of 2 x QSFP28 ports)
Additional ports and slots	Management ports	Management ports	Management ports
	1 x 10 M/100 M/1000 MBASE-T copper port	1 x 10 M/100 M/1000 MBASE-T copper port	1 x 10 M/100 M/1000 MBASE-T copper port
	1 x SFP port	1 x SFP port	1 x SFP port
	Console ports	Console ports	Console ports
	1 x mini USB console port	1 x mini USB console port	1 x mini USB console port
	1 x serial console port	1 x serial console port	1 x serial console port

HPE FlexFabric 5945 Switch Series—Overview

Figure 4-19 HPE FlexFabric 5945 48SFP28 8QSFP28 and HPE 5945 four-slot switches

HPE FlexFabric 5945 Switch Series are high-density, ultra-low–latency ToR switches ideally suited for deployment at the aggregation or server access layer of large enterprise data centers. The 5945 series supports modern spine and leaf data center solutions that require demanding throughput and modern feature support needed for today's virtual environments. It provides support for 10/25/100 GbE interfaces, allowing for high-performance server connectivity as well as high bandwidth 100 GbE uplinks.

The 5945 series, as illustrated in Figure 4-19, provides choices that fit the customer's IT budget via unique modular options and allow for cut-through for ultra-low–latency solutions.

The 5945 series supports fan trays with back to front airflow (power-to-port, different models for different versions of the switch) or front to back airflow (port-to-power). Different fan trays cannot be mixed in the same switch enclosure.

HPE FlexFabric 5945 Switch Series—Technical specifications

HPE FlexFabric 5945 48SFP28 8QSFP28	HPE FlexFabric 5945 4-slot Switch
48 x 25 Gb SFP28 ports	4 module slots
8 x 100 Gb QSFP28 ports	8x QSF28 or 24x SFP28/2x QSFP28
2 x 1 Gb SFP ports (IEEE 802.3ae Type 10 GBASE-ER); IEEE 802.3ae Type 10 GBASE-LR, IEEE 802.3ae Type 10 GBASE-SR, IEEE 802.3z Type 1000 BASE-SX, IEEE 802.3z Type 1000BASE-LX	2 x 1 Gb SFP ports (IEEE 802.3ae Type 10 GBASE-ER); IEEE 802.3ae Type 10 GBASE-LR, IEEE 802.3ae Type 10 GBASE-SR, IEEE 802.3z Type 1000 BASE-SX, IEEE 802.3z Type 1000 BASE-LX
Supports 48 x 10/25 GbE and 8 x 100 GbE fixed ports, or up to 80 x 10 GbE ports when using splitter cables	Supports up to a maximum of 96 x 10/25 GbE and 8 x 100 GbE ports, or up to 32 x 100 GbE ports

HPE FlexFabric 7900 Switch Series

Figure 4-20 HPE FlexFabric 7904 and 7910 Switches

HPE FlexFabric 7900 Switch Series offers, as shown in Figure 4-20:

- Compact modular data center core switch

- Performance, buffering, scale, and availability

- High-density 10 GbE, 40 GbE, and 100 GbE interfaces

- Up to ten IO module slots

- Maximum of (120) 40 GbE ports, (480) 10 GbE ports, (240) 1/10 GbE ports, or a combination

- Throughput 5.8 Bpps

- Switching capacity 9.6 Tbps

Aruba core and data center switching

FlexFabric portfolio meets the majority of the traditional use cases, but we also have alternative platforms: Aruba data center switches, as illustrated in Figure 4-21. These are ideal choice for:

- Spine/Leaf

- Mobile First Campus Networking Core

- Future-proof wired infrastructure, wireless LAN (WLAN), and IoT enabling

- Highly scalable, programmable automated data center solution

- User, device, server aware—ZTP, ease of deployment

Aruba 8320 Switch Series

Figure 4-21 Aruba 8320 Switch Series

Aruba 8320 is a high-performance switch with 2.3 Tbps switching capacity, and has 48 ports of 10 Gig and 6 ports of 40 Gbe—so plenty of capacity for campus core and aggregation. This switch supports two hot swappable, redundant power supplies that help to ensure high availability that is needed at the aggregation and core layers of a campus network.

It supports the same advanced Layer 3 software features as the 8400: OSPF, Border Gateway Protocol (BGP), virtual routing and forwarding (VRF), Multi-Chassis Link Aggregation (M-LAG) for switch virtualization and is designed for usability with easy to replace fans and five fan modules. 8320 provides a five-year hardware warranty with no software licensing required.

There are three models with high-speed connectivity:

- 48p 10 G SFP/SFP+ and 6p 40 G QSFP+ Switch (JL479A)

- 32p 40 G QSFP+ (JL579A)

- 48p 1 G/10 GBASE-T and 6p 40 G QSFP+ (JL581A)

Aruba 8325 Switch Series

Figure 4-22 Aruba 8325-32C and 8325-48Y8C

The Aruba 8325 Switch Series, as illustrated in Figure 4-22, offers a flexible and innovative approach to addressing the application, security, and scalability demands of the mobile, cloud, and IoT era. These switches serve the needs of the next-generation core and aggregation layer, as well as emerging data center requirements at the ToR and End of Row (EoR). They provide over 6.4 Tbps of capacity, with line-rate Gigabit Ethernet interfaces including 10 Gbps, 25 Gbps, 40 Gbps, and 100 Gbps.

The 8325 series includes industry-leading line rate ports 1/10/25 GbE (SFP/SFP+/SFP28) and 40/100 GbE (QSFP+/QSFP28) with connectivity in a compact 1U form factor. These switches offer a fantastic investment for customers wanting to migrate from older 1 GbE/10 GbE to faster 25 GbE, or 10 GbE/40 GbE to 100 GbE ports.

Features of Aruba 8325 include:

- 6.4 Tbps switching capacity in compact 1U form factor

- VSX for high availability

- Advanced Layer 3 including OSPF and BGP

- High hardware scale, including full internet routing

- N+1 redundant, hot swappable power supplies

- All bundles include hot-swappable, removable fan and power supplies

- REST for distributed or centralized orchestration

- Database-driven ArubaOS-CX architecture for HA and fault tolerance

- 48 ports of 10/25 G with 8 ports of 40/100 G, and 32 ports of 40/100 G

Aruba 8400 Switch Series

Figure 4-23 Aruba 8400 Switch

The Aruba 8400 campus core and aggregation switch series, shown in Figure 4-23, provides a game-changing solution, offering a flexible and innovative approach to dealing with the new application, security, and scalability demands of the mobile-cloud and IoT era.

It combines a modern, fully programmable OS with carrier-grade hardware, leading performance, and incorporates the industry-first Network Analytics Engine to monitor and troubleshoot network, system, application, and security-related issues easily.

By enabling faster automation and network insights, the operating system reduces the time spent on manual tasks and addresses current and future demands driven by Mobility and IoT.

The 8400 contains a high-speed fully distributed architecture and provides up to 19.2 Tbps switching capacity with up to 8571 billion packets per second (BPPS) for throughput. All switching and routing is performed in the IO modules and meets the demands of bandwidth-intensive applications today and in the future.

Features of Aruba 8400 include:

● High-speed 32-port 10 GbE module, 8-port 40 GbE module, or 6-port 40/100 G module

● Convenient bundles simplify ordering

● Redundant management, fabric, and power supplies

● Energy efficient, hot swappable, power supplies with N+N redundancy with 80 Plus Gold certification

Management features include:

● Out-of-Band management (OOBM)

● Console management ports

● Status LEDs for fans, power

● supplies, and modules

Network topology innovation

Figure 4-24 From static client-server to dynamic, software-defined cloud architecture

Today's business and government organizations are focused on digital transformation. As a result, DevOps and business agility are at the forefront of most current strategic IT discussions. To deliver both, enterprise organizations have increasingly leveraged public cloud service providers and are now building on-premises clouds with infrastructure that delivers on three basic requirements, shown in Figure 4-24:

- Friction-free agility of physical resources

- Control systems that maximize physical resource utilization and provide maximum ROI

- Integration of the various infrastructure components for automated provisioning and resource management

While these requirements exist across the spectrum of infrastructure components (compute, storage, and network), the network plays a foundational role. The network fabric acts as the glue between compute and storage, so the agility, control, and integrity of the network (or lack thereof) directly impacts an organization's ability to maximize their compute and storage resources. Any bottlenecks in the data center fabric will negatively impact the organization's ability to run applications efficiently and optimally distribute data. The more the network is in your way, the less business/mission agility can be attained.

Traditional networks resource utilization

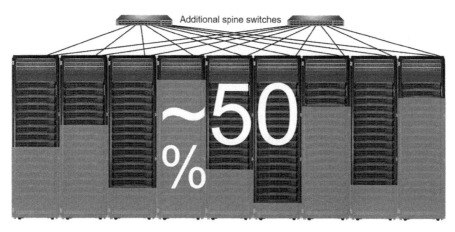

Figure 4-25 From poor and fragmented resource utilization...

Traditional networks have many obstacles including, but not limited to, full resource agility, network control, and utilization, as indicated in Figure 4-25. Many enterprises are forced to impose network-specified boundaries that do not correspond to business or workload needs. They also leverage tightly coupled control planes that cannot easily be overridden to achieve specific objectives. In addition, the network contains no inherent, simple mechanism to manipulate the overall state or specific aspects of the fabric. Instead, these enterprises rely on a port/box configuration paradigm that, at best, can only provide scripted automation. Let's look at these in more detail.

Traditional data center networks are typically wired in traditional multi-tier architecture or in a leaf-and-spine configuration, whereby a set of ToR leaf nodes (switches) aggregate rack-based servers and storage. This ToR leaf switch is then connected to a cross-rack spine layer to provide broader connectivity to other hosts. The rack-to-rack bandwidth available in the leaf-and-spine architecture depends on the number of fabric-dedicated ports in each ToR switch and their bandwidth. The remaining ports on the switch can be used for host connectivity. For example, if a given ToR switch has 32 ports with the same link rate, but only four of these are dedicated to the fabric, 28 ports are available for node connectivity. When all 28-node ports are in use and the traffic pattern from the attached nodes desires to leave the ToR switch, such a port economy has a contention ratio of 28:4 or 7:1.

This rate of oversubscription favors workloads that can be contained locally in the rack with traffic patterns only traversing the ToR switch. When rack-to-rack traffic is encountered at full-node bandwidth, the first four nodes have ample bandwidth, but the fifth node has no choice but to wait for the available bandwidth. The result of such bandwidth crowding increases transfer times, higher latency, and potential link timeouts. In fact, at this point, the network has stopped functioning as the network and applications begin to suffer.

Less contention at the ToR enables a more agile data center fabric. It is, therefore, highly desirable to design balanced networks that have just as many ports dedicated to nodes as is dedicated to the fabric itself. Again, using a 32-port switch as the example, it would mean using 16 ports for nodes and 16 ports for the fabric. This ToR configuration is considered non-blocking.

Within limitations, it is possible to build a non-blocking leaf-and-spine fabric by dedicating half the bandwidth in the ToR switch to the fabric, but in many cases this strategy is deemed too expensive. This is especially true for modern data center fabrics where the same 32-port switch is intended for both the leaf-and-spine duty. The challenge with building high-bandwidth leaf-and-spine fabrics is the cost of the optical transceivers. Using a modern fully configured 32-port 100 GbE switch, the cost of the optics can easily constitute two-thirds of the overall cost. It is, therefore, easy to understand why network designers are willing to live with some ToR contention, even when the decision to do so impedes the goal of maximum business agility.

HPE Composable Fabric

Figure 4-26 ...to maximum and even resource utilization

HPE has created a composable data center fabric operating environment that leverages commodity off-the-shelf Ethernet hardware and innovative software that forms a single distributed network without the limitations of traditional approaches—HPE Composable Fabric, as illustrated in Figure 4-26. Within the HPE Composable Fabric solution, the physical Ethernet devices that make up the fabric are referred to as rack connectivity modules.

For enterprise customers as well as cloud providers, this modern cloud fabric can be leveraged as a fully integrated data center networking solution (switches, controllers, and such) for ease of deployment. For larger cloud providers, the constituent technologies are designed to be leveraged as a set of tools woven into the overall cloud orchestration strategy.

HPE Composable Fabric architecture

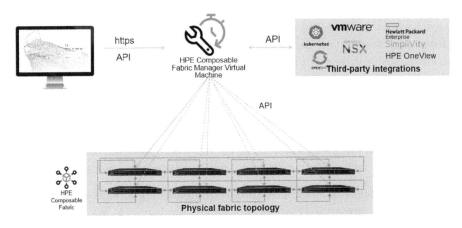

Figure 4-27 HPE Composable Fabric architecture

HPE has built a comprehensive, composable data center fabric that addresses these issues at the data plane, the control plane, and the integration plane, as illustrated in Figure 4-27. Each of these planes is meant to evolve independently. In some large cloud environments, the individual technologies within each plane can be leveraged and mated to technologies that the cloud operator might already be implementing in the other planes. However, the goals of the three planes are very clear and represent what HPE believes to be required capabilities for cloud builders.

The data plane

The HPE Composable Fabric's rack connectivity modules form a composable network fabric or data plane that provides physical connectivity, topology, and data/packet forwarding. Central to the HPE Composable Fabric is the collapsing of connectivity and routing into a single building block. Due to advanced distributed software, there is no longer a need for dedicated spine switches. HPE Composable Fabric Manager performs distributed intelligent routing between rack connectivity modules. This enables a variety of new, more efficient, and highly diverse data center fabric topologies.

By serving as a high-diversity fabric, the HPE Composable Fabric data plane provides many ways for workloads to interconnect (between member resources as well as other workloads). In contrast to aggregation-based (or low-diversity fabrics) such as traditional multi-tier, leaf-spine, Clos, and such, a high-diversity fabric allows intelligent software algorithms. These selectively place workload traffic on the corresponding fabric paths that meet specific SLA or security parameters for that workload.

These advanced fabrics have been used successfully in closed systems such as high-performance computing clusters with proprietary interconnects such as Torus, Hypercube, and more. However, they have not been generally available until now for Ethernet/IP-based networks due to the limitations of a traditional legacy protocol-based control plane. The HPE Composable Fabric solution allows these advanced topologies to be used with Ethernet/IP traffic by supplementing the embedded protocol-based control plane with a highly advanced algorithm-based control plane.

Control and management plane

The control and management plane, which is part of the HPE Composable Fabric Manager, supplements the embedded protocols used in the data plane and provides a single point of management for the network. It also provides APIs to directly manipulate the network state and objects from external systems.

Integration plane

The integration plane creates an easy-to-use, event-based automation platform that allows the user to define very simple conditions (trigger events) that result in specific actions. This type of event-based automation is powerful as it allows users to make the network fully dynamic in the face of network-intensive events (such as data ingest or movement, time-of-day events, and more).

Additionally, HPE supports a number of built-in integrations into popular cloud orchestration and software-defined storage systems (SDSS). HPE Composable Fabric Manager is built on top of a popular open source project called StackStorm that has a vibrant community that also builds integrations into popular DevOps and ChatOps automation tools.

HPE Composable Fabric Manager

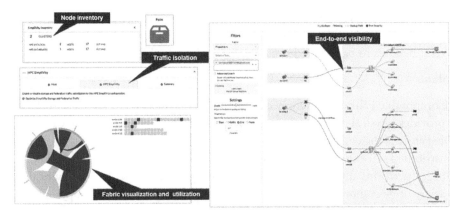

Figure 4-28 HPE Composable Fabric Manager

What makes HPE Composable Fabric Manager different from a basic SDN controller, as illustrated in Figure 4-28, is the ability to define workloads through the affinity data model and associated APIs that are used to define workload and their relationships. This is done with the algorithms that are used to manipulate how and what type of connectivity these workloads receive from the data plane (a process called fitting). Fitting allows users to add new workloads that have specific performance (bandwidth, latency, isolation) or security/fate sharing (keep apart/keep together) requirements explicitly.

Learning check

4. You are in a meeting with a customer and they challenge you with a statement: "I heard that HPE data center networking devices only support a traditional core/aggregation/access layered architecture. This approach does not match my current modernization plans."

   How should you respond?

   _____

   _____

   _____

   _____

   _____

   _____

   _____

   _____

Summary

- HPE is providing future-proof network switch technology. HPE network switches can handle the massive amounts of network traffic businesses have right now, as well as the increase in network data that will come in the future.

- HPE networking devices support modern network architectures, such as leaf-spine and latest technologies including 40/100 GbE.

- Models include both modular and fix-port devices, allowing customers to select appropriate device for the environment.

- HPE Intelligent Management Center is next-generation network management software with unified resource and device management, designed for simplicity and ease of use.

Prelearning check

Before proceeding with this section, answer the following question to assess your existing knowledge of the topics covered in this chapter. Record your answers in the space provided here.

1. You are in a meeting with a customer, and they challenge you with a statement: "Data security and availability is my top concern. I was reviewing Nimble specifications, and I like the deduplication and compression capabilities, but I heard that HPE Nimble storage can survive only a single drive failure per enclosure. This technology is not compatible with my views on enterprise-class storage."

   How should you respond?

   _____

   _____

   _____

   _____

   _____

   _____

   _____

5 Recommending Hybrid IT storage solutions for customer use cases

LEARNING OBJECTIVES

After completing this chapter, and given a customer scenario, you should be able to:

✓ Recommend and position HPE storage products, solutions, tools, and appropriate services for customer use cases.

✓ Identify and position key HPE storage solutions and workloads offerings with the key alliance partner ecosystem components to the appropriate customer use case.

✓ Differentiate and position HPE products and services products for the appropriate customer use case.

✓ Describe, differentiate, and apply industry-standard architectures and technologies.

✓ Explain the HPE approach to converged management for the infrastructure lifecycle.

Scenario 4: Red Hat OpenShift on HPE Synergy and HPE Nimble Storage

The wide HPE portfolio of data center products can be introduced using customer scenarios and recommended, validated configurations based on HPE Reference Architecture or HPE Reference configuration.

Introducing the customer scenario

aZLa company will be used as a story line through this scenario. We will introduce the company using an interview:

- What is your primary business?

    - Regional consumer electronics retailer

- How many employees do you currently have?

  - 1500+ employees

- What does your selling and delivery channel look like?

  - Electronic stores, show rooms, delivery boxes around the country

- Where are you currently storing data, and how do you access files?

  - Shared array, non-HPE, for critical data required onsite; temporary/cached data in a hosted environment

- What does your server and network infrastructure look like?

  - Single data center, mix of vendors (both servers and networking)

- What is the structure of your IT department?

  - E-shop development, operations team

- What are your current plans?

  - Consolidation of front-end applications, faster, easier development of front-end applications, and more flexibility when handling peaks

Customer requirements

As a result of multiple interviews and gathering information about customer plans and customer's current infrastructure, the following requirements emerged for the new solution:

- Faster development of applications

- Both compute and storage resources need to stay on site

- Selected container solution: Red Hat OpenShift Container Platform

  - Common 16-core processor for both management and worker nodes

  - Support for 1500 pods

- Storage:

  - Local server storage (solid-state disk, or SSD)

  - Shared, future-proof, storage for Docker containers and management platform

  - 15 TB of storage for pods

- Reducing management and deployment costs

  - Pre-integration of networking and rack components

- Software-defined approach to infrastructure management

Activity: Information resources

1. Download these information resources:

   – HPE Reference Configuration for Red Hat OpenShift on HPE Synergy and HPE Nimble Storage

      http://h20195.www2.hpe.com/V2/GetDocument.aspx?docname=a00056101enw

   – HPE Deployment Guide for Red Hat OpenShift Container Platform on HPE Synergy with HPE Nimble Storage

      https://github.com/HewlettPackard/hpe-solutions-openshift/tree/master/synergy/ scalable/nimble

   – RHEL OpenShift Container Platform: Sizing Considerations

      https://access.redhat.com/documentation/en-us/openshift_container_platform/3.7/ html/installation_and_configuration/installing-a-cluster#sizing

2. Answer the following questions:

   a. What type of data will be stored on HPE Nimble Storage?

      _____

      _____

   b. Does HPE Nimble Storage support ephemeral volumes for containers?

      _____

      _____

   c. What additional licenses are needed by HPE Nimble Storage to support the solution?

      _____

      _____

   d. Which storage protocol is used to access the Nimble Storage?

      _____

      _____

Building blocks of the solution

In today's digital world, organizations are under increasing pressure to deliver applications faster while reducing costs. As these applications grow more complex, this puts stress on the IT infrastructure, IT teams, and processes. To remain competitive, organizations must adapt quickly, and developers need to be more effective, efficient, and agile. Container technology provides the right application platform to help organizations become more responsive and iterate across multiple IT environments as well as develop, deploy, and manage applications faster. However, implementing a containerized environment across an existing infrastructure is a complex undertaking that can require weeks or months to mobilize, particularly for enterprises. To help accelerate container application delivery, HPE and Red Hat have collaborated to optimize Red Hat OpenShift Container Platform on HPE platforms, including HPE Synergy, the industry's first composable infrastructure, and HPE Nimble Storage.

Red Hat OpenShift Container Platform on HPE Synergy provides an end-to-end fully integrated container solution that, once assembled, can be configured within hours. This eliminates the complexities associated with implementing a container platform across an enterprise data center and provides the automation of a hardware and software configuration to quickly provision and deploy a containerized environment at scale. The Red Hat OpenShift Container Platform provides organizations with a reliable platform for deploying and scaling container-based applications, and HPE Synergy provides the flexible infrastructure your customers need to run that container platform to dynamically provision and scale applications, whether they run in VMs or containers or are hosted on-premises, in the cloud, or somewhere in between.

This Reference Configuration provides architectural guidance for deploying, scaling, and managing a Red Hat OpenShift environment on HPE Synergy Composable Infrastructure along with HPE Nimble Storage.

This Reference Configuration describes how to:

- Leverage HPE Synergy strengths in rapid provisioning, along with the automation capabilities of Red Hat Ansible Tower, to provide a one-click deployment of a Red Hat OpenShift Container Platform on HPE Synergy.

- Efficiently layout an OpenShift configuration using a mix of virtualized and bare metal technologies.

- Configure container persistent storage using HPE Nimble Storage.

This Reference Configuration demonstrates the following benefits of utilizing HPE Synergy for Red Hat OpenShift Container Platform:

- Automated initial installation of a highly available Red Hat OpenShift Container Platform on HPE Synergy reduces the initial solution deployment from several days, as provided by a services organization, to less than two hours

- Deployed management and infrastructure nodes on VMs to optimize resource usage while keeping the worker nodes on bare metal to optimize for performance

Building blocks of the solution

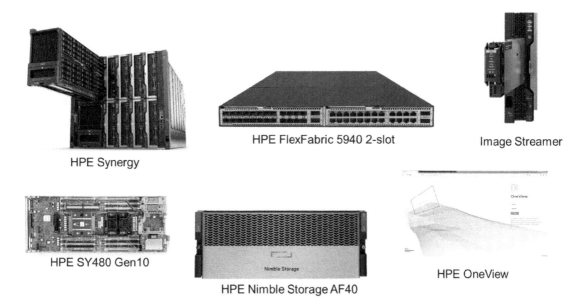

HPE Synergy

HPE FlexFabric 5940 2-slot

Image Streamer

HPE SY480 Gen10

HPE Nimble Storage AF40

HPE OneView

Figure 5-1 Building blocks of the solution

The solution in Reference Configuration deploys Red Hat OpenShift 3.10 as a combination of virtual and physical resources. The OpenShift Master, Infrastructure, etcd daemon, and load balancers are deployed as virtual machines (VMs) running on three HPE Synergy 480 Gen10 Compute Modules running Red Hat Virtualization Host 4.2 and managed by Red Hat Virtualization Manager and HPE OneView.

Red Hat OpenShift worker nodes are deployed on bare metal on six HPE Synergy 480 Gen10 Compute Modules running Red Hat Enterprise Linux 7.5. The hypervisor is installed via a Kickstart file over Preboot Execution Environment (PXE), and post-installation configuration steps are performed using Ansible. Worker nodes are deployed using HPE Synergy Image Streamer, and post-installation configuration steps are performed using Ansible. HPE Nimble Storage provides support for both ephemeral and persistent container volumes.

Reference Configuration recommends, shown in Figure 5-1:

- HPE Synergy
- Image Streamer
- HPE SY480 Gen10
- HPE FlexFabric 5940 two-slot
- HPE Nimble Storage AF40
- HPE OneView

The industry's broadest and deepest flash portfolio

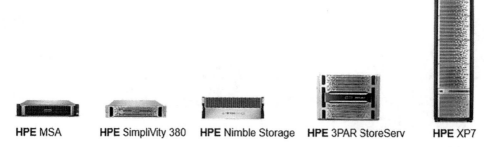

| HPE MSA | HPE SimpliVity 380 | HPE Nimble Storage | HPE 3PAR StoreServ | HPE XP7 |

Figure 5-2 Flash solutions for our smallest to our most extreme customers

To succeed in business today, your customer's #1 priority must be speeding time to value. The new generation of apps and data—the world of "Hybrid IT"—requires a technology foundation that is different from those of the past, as illustrated in Figure 5-2. It must meet **two** important criteria:

- It must be **fast, flexible, scalable, and "composable"** to meet the realities of today's **Hybrid IT** environments. Whether your customer's apps and data are in their data center, private and/or public clouds, multiple clouds, or at the edge of the network, their technology platform must have the flexibility to operate seamlessly across these different environments.

- It must be able to **take advantage of intelligence gathered at the edge**—the "intelligent edge"— by taking advantage of information gathered from apps and data gathered from customers, employees, users, and transactions. These connections must be reliable and secure; however, data collection and analytics must also be built in. This provides context and insights that generate value from data.

HPE believes enterprises must excel in both areas—across all apps (old and new) and data (wherever that data lives).

The HPE Storage portfolio includes converged storage and traditional storage. HPE supports a range of Fibre Channel (FC)- and Internet Protocol (IP)-attached (storage attached over an IP network) primary storage arrays including the latest addition, the Nimble Storage family. Entry-level storage supports both block and file provisioning for network-attached storage (NAS) and storage area network (SAN) environments.

Virtual Storage Appliance (VSA) compliments the portfolio with software-defined storage (SDS) for converged and composable solutions.

 Note

> Software-Defined Storage (SDS) marks a departure from the traditional use of Network-Attached Storage (NAS) and Storage Area Networks (SANs). In contrast to the hardware-centric NAS and SAN, SDS uses storage virtualization to control storage through a software layer abstracted from physical storage devices. This approach allows storage pooling and automated storage management. The SDS software may manage policies for data deduplication, replication, thin provisioning, snapshots, and backup.

StoreOnce and StoreEver make up the portfolio providing the backup and archiving capabilities required in today's SAN.

In addition to StoreOnce and StoreEver portfolio, HPE is adding state-of-the-art storage networking products and accessories for entry-level, midrange, and high-end environments, including FC switches, converged protocol switches and directors, as well as routers, host bus adapters (HBAs), converged network adapters (CNAs), transceivers, and cables.

HPE has flash solutions for our smallest to our most demanding customers, as indicated in Figure 5-3:

- **MSA**—It is an affordable solution, but with fewer data services than our other products. For smaller deployments or customers who need to consolidate just a few applications and for whom price performance is paramount.

- **SimpliVity**—SimpliVity is a hyperconverged offering with built-in data protection.

- **3PAR and Nimble**—The most advanced flash portfolio to provide a foundation for Hybrid IT. Integration with VMware, Microsoft, OpenStack, Docker, Mesosphere, Ansible, Chef, Puppet, and Jenkins. They have a proven 99.9999% availability.

- **XP7**—For customers who need extreme availability providing 14 nines of availability and including mainframe connectivity.

	MSA	Nimble	3PAR StoreServ (midrange)	SimpliVity
Positioning statement	Most affordable storage for the performance needs of small sites	Simplest, predictive storage with analytics-driven support	Most flexible Unified Storage for tier-1 all-flash enterprise datacenter	Hyperconverged offering with built-in data protection
Starting Street Price	$8K and up	$20K and up	$35K and up	$40K (2-nodes)
Controllers Configuration	2 node dual-controller	2 node dual-controller. 6-nines	2 to 4 node Mesh-Active with zero RPO/RTO (midrange). 6-nines	N node. Active –Active.
Connectivity	SAS, FC and iSCSI (strongest in SAS and FC)	iSCSI or FC (strongest in iSCSI)	Mixed FC, FCoE, iSCSI, SMB/CIFS and NFS (strongest in FC; complex topologies)	NFS (vSphere), SMB (with HyperV)
Scalability (per array)	Up to 220K read IOPS, 5.3GB/s sequential read 1PiB raw capacity	Up to 350K read IOPS 4.3GB/s sequential read 1.3PiB raw capacity	Up to 2M read IOPS 34GB/s sequential read 6PiB raw capacity	Up to 32 nodes. 16TB raw per node Avg. 55K IOPS per node 1.5GB/s random reads
Replication and data protection	Async; local and remote snapshots	Async; built-in app-aware snapshots and integrated data protection	Sync and async; stretch clusters; app-aware snapshots and data protection	Built-in Data Protection. 10 min RPO via GUI. 1min through CLI. Stretch clusters
Analytics	–	Best – Predictive (InfoSight) with full infrastructure visibility (VM Vision)	Good – Telemetry for capacity/perf planning and system health (StoreFront)	Good - vCenter monitoring @ VM/cluster level. OmniView – For deeper monitoring
Support	Telephone and onsite support Customer self install and upgrade	Automated, remote and onsite support Customer installable upgrades	Remote and onsite support	Customer self install and upgrade

Figure 5-3 Comparison of HPE Storage products

HPE Nimble Storage

Nimble Storage Arrays are available from HPE and HPE partners. Nimble arrays are ideal for organizations seeking a new approach to storage that combines affordable flash performance with simplicity for mixed, mainstream workloads, as illustrated in Figure 5-4.

HPE Nimble Storage portfolio overview

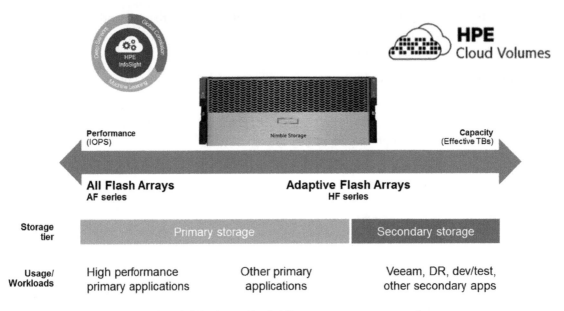

Figure 5-4 HPE Nimble Storage

Nimble secondary storage arrays enable your customers to put their backup data to work with flash performance to support development, test, and analytics on copy data.

A Nimble array tolerates three simultaneous drive failures and provides additional protection from intra-drive parity. Application-consistent snapshots and replication as well as integration with leading backup software solutions provide an ideal foundation for comprehensive data protection. Backed by the Timeless Storage guarantee that ships with all Nimble Storage Arrays, there is no need to pay for optional software, and upgrades are easy.

All-Flash Array family

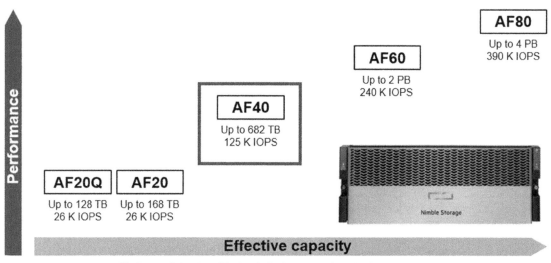

- Effective capacity based on a 5X data reduction from compression and dedupe on a single node.
- Note: The maximum capacity numbers reflect what each model is capable of handling.
- Performance based on random mixed 50/50 R/W on 4 KB blocks, 2X dedupe.

Figure 5-5 Nimble All-Flash storage family

Figure 5-5 shows the Nimble All-Flash storage family.

- The AF20Q and AF20 are the perfect entry points for all IT organizations that require speed and economy for performance-sensitive workloads.

- The AF40 and AF60 offer high performance and attractive economics for performance-sensitive workloads that need the best blend of price, performance, and scalability.

- The AF80 is designed for consolidating multiple large-scale performance-sensitive applications with aggressive performance and high scalability demands.

 Note

HPE recommends HPE racks with a depth of 1200 mm to best accommodate the length of the Nimble Storage chassis; the HPE 1200 mm rack provides ample room for cabling and ease of serviceability.

Drive layout—AF-Series

- 4U Chassis
- 48 SSD capacity
- 2 Banks of 24 x 3.5" SSDs
- Bank A – SSDs 1 – 24
- Bank B – SSDs 25 – 48

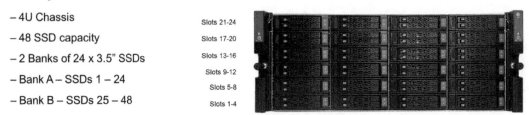

Figure 5-6 AF-Series slot numbering

The AF chassis has two banks of 24 small form factor (SFF) SSDs for a total of 48 SSDs. Bank A consists of SSD slots 1 to 24, and Bank B consists of SSD slots 25 to 48, as indicated in Figure 5-6.

- Bank A Drive slot 1 is located in the lower left Dual Flash Carrier lower SSD slot, and SSD slot 24 is located in the Upper Right Dual Flash Carrier lower SSD slot.

- Bank B Drive slot 25 is located in the Lower Left Dual Flash Carrier upper SSD slot and SSD slot 24 is located in the Upper Right Dual Flash Carrier Upper SSD slot.

What is in AF and HF Arrays?

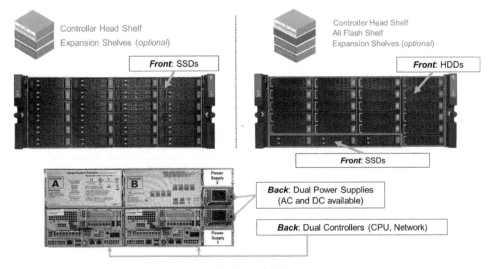

Figure 5-7 AF and HF Arrays

Figure 5-7 shows a high-level overview of what is in a Nimble Storage AF (on the left side of the graphic) and HF-Series array (on the right side of the graphic) and what can be connected to a controller shelf. There are three primary components in each Controller Head Shelf:

- SSDs (and hard disk drives [HDDs] in the HF), located in the front of the chassis

- Dual power supplies, located in the back of the chassis

- Dual controllers, located in the back of the chassis

The Controller Head Shelf can then have the All-Flash Shelf and the Disk Expansion Shelves connected to it. Both the All-Flash Shelf and the Disk Expansion Shelves are optional.

Scale out with clustered arrays

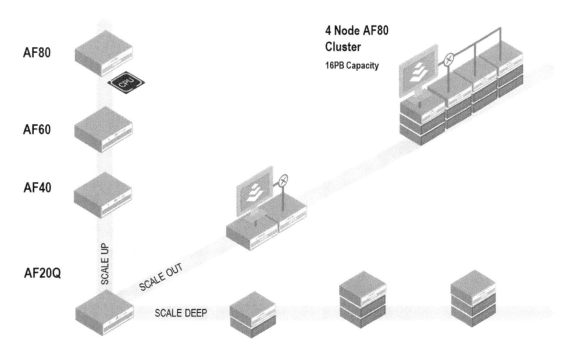

Figure 5-8 Cluster of Nimble Storage Arrays

You can cluster up to four of any Nimble Storage Arrays, as illustrated in Figure 5-8. Features include:

- Simple configuration

- Automated host connection management

- Dynamic load-balancing and automated capacity rebalancing

- Linear performance scaling

- Automatic data migrations

- Add what you need, **when** you need it, avoid storage silos

- Maintain a single, unified storage platform

- Easier on the storage budget

- Avoid overspending to achieve storage service-level agreements (SLAs)

- Extend storage return on investment (ROI)

HPE NimbleOS is the operating system (firmware) that runs on all Nimble Arrays. The exact same versions of NimbleOS can run on all arrays.

AF-Series triple+ parity and integrated spare

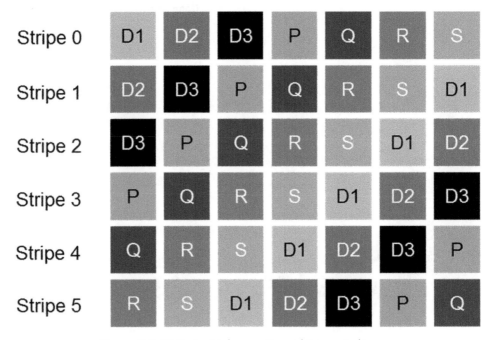

Figure 5-9 AF-Series triple+ parity and integrated spare

Nimble unique parity mechanism is writing three drives worth of parity information. Every chunk in a stripe consists of data, metadata (checksums, sequence number, and so forth), and parity (XOR of data), as illustrated in Figure 5-9. Built-in availability tolerates simultaneous failure of any three SSDs, and built-in virtual spare allows a fourth failure. Besides the RAID, intra-drive parity fixes sector loss in a single read.

SCM/NVMe ready HPE Nimble Storage All-Flash platform

HPE is committed to future-proofed technologies and storage platforms. All Nimble AFAs are Storage Class Memory (SCM)/Non-Volatile Memory Express (NVMe) ready and have a technology roadmap that unlocks the full potential of NVMe. Non-disruptive, seamless upgrades to next-generation technology will be facilitated.

 Note

For more information, visit: **http://hpe.com/storage/MemoryDrivenFlash**

HPE FlexFabric

Multiple HPE networking platforms, as shown in Figures 5-10 and 5-11, are available for data center networking, including FlexFabric and Aruba. For this scenario, the Reference Architecture/Reference Configuration (RA/RC) recommends the FlexFabric platform.

High-level selection considerations

Figure 5-10 High-level selection considerations

FlexFabric switches are suitable where traditional requirements prevail or when software feature depth and unique requirements and integrations are needed.

Aruba components are preferred when consistency with campus devices is needed or customer is looking for analytics, automation, simplicity, and is interested in customer experience (CX) innovations.

HPE FlexFabric portfolio

To meet all the new data center networking requirements, HPE FlexFabric switches can be deployed. This portfolio has been deployed by HPE to date and is well known by customers.

Figure 5-11 Top of Rack/Leaf switches

This portfolio covers the traditional data center use cases with a great selection of Top of Rack (ToR) within the 5710, 5940, 5945, 5950, and 5980 series. ToR accommodates diverse requirements for server link speed, fixed or modular configurations, deep buffer, and uplink bandwidth. For this scenario, the RA/RC recommends the 5940 series.

HPE FlexFabric 5940/5945

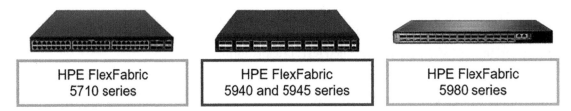

Figure 5-12 Pick the switches that meet your customer's needs

HPE FlexFabric 5940/5945, as shown in Figure 5-12, provides:

- High-capacity, high-performance applications with 10/25 GbE downlinks and 40/100 G uplinks
- Virtual Extensible LAN (VXLAN) support for network virtualization
- Enhanced support for telemetry
- Fixed and modular options

Storage technologies

The data center is undergoing its most dramatic shift since the move to client/server computing 20 years ago. The changes impacting customers include explosive growth, new workloads, virtualization, automation, cloud computing, and infrastructure and technology shifts such as in-memory databases.

There are two major storage trends—All-Flash systems and SDS.

Both have different deployment models:

- All Flash optimized Tier 1 Storage with assured quality of service (QoS) that comes from a shared storage system.

- SDS as processing power and server density has reached new levels.

  Offering lower costs, leveraging industry-standard server hardware and the ability to collocate applications, storage servers, and hypervisors on the same CPU and disks.

The deployment and consumption models discussion has turned to the use of converged and hyper-converged systems as "easy-to-deploy-and-manage" building blocks for IT. Use of these integrated systems is on the rise to accelerate time to value and free up data center resources.

However, most workloads do not scale with perfect ratios of compute and storage over time, so there is still a need to grow the compute, networking, and storage resources flexibly to maintain efficiency.

Your customers need both approaches as they approach their business transformation. The real key is to embrace these changing vectors and make decision points that do not incrementally bring more complexity into what is already a very complex data center environment.

This converged and hybrid infrastructure requires instant mobility of data and application logic to assign the right resource to the right workload at the right time, enabling real-time data services and on-demand business agility.

The HPE Composable Infrastructure architecture addresses business demands by combining HPE Converged Infrastructure, software-defined management, and hyperconverged systems. This approach reduces costs, eliminates silos, and frees available compute, storage, and networking resources.

NVMe and SCM

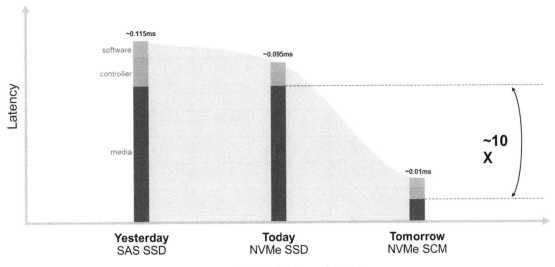

Figure 5-13 NVMe and SCM

There are several emerging technologies that are being implemented at the product level these days, as indicated in Figure 5-13:

- **NVM Express**

  - Is a high-performance, scalable host controller interface

  - Designed for enterprise, data center, and client systems that use Peripheral Component Interconnect express (PCIe) SSDs

  - Can be adopted across multiple platforms

  - Improves random and sequential performance

  - Reduces latency

- **SCM**

  - Hybrid storage and memory access

  - Typically used as a cache/tier layer

  - Performance between dynamic random-access memory (DRAM) and SSD

Activity: SCM and NVMe for HPE 3PAR and Nimble Storage

1. Watch this video: **https://www.youtube.com/watch?v=hKDcNWpipes**.

2. Take notes about SCM performance and typical workloads.

_____

_____

_____

_____

_____

_____

_____

_____

_____

_____

_____

_____

Activity debrief

Answer the following questions:

1. What is an example of a workload that may benefit from SCM?

   _____

   _____

2. Is the latency typically consistent over different workloads (IOPS) with current storage technologies?

   _____

   _____

   _____

3. What is the latency difference between SSDs using NVMe and SAS protocols?

   _____

   _____

4. What is the latency difference between NVMe SSD and NVMe SCM technologies?

   – What is the expected latency reduction when used in an array?

   _____

   _____

   _____

5. Name three customer benefits of SCM.

   _____

   _____

   _____

   _____

   _____

   _____

Storage array—Spare disk implementation

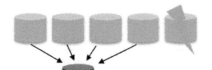

Dedicated spare disk drives

Spare drive

Few-to-one rebuild

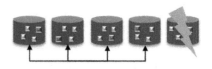

Distributed sparing

Many-to-many rebuild

Figure 5-14 Spare disk implementation

Although RAID does provide a degree of resiliency, it should always be considered "plan for the unexpected." Utilizing spare disks capacity for disks failure should be incorporated into the storage design. This could be a dedicated spare disk, as illustrated in Figure 5-14, known as a hot spare, a global group of disks shared across multiple RAID sets, or a dedicated area spread across all disks within a storage array.

Any disk failures should be replaced as quickly as possible to keep the integrity of the storage array and data intact.

Thin virtual volumes or fully provisioned

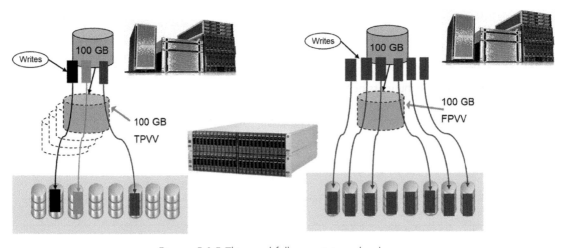

Figure 5-15 Thin and fully provisioned volumes

Thin provisioning can improve storage utilization when compared to fully (thick) provisioned volumes because thin provisioning allocates disk storage space based on the minimum space required by a volume at any given time. Fully provisioned volumes consume all the storage space that was specified when the volume was created, as indicated in Figure 5-15.

To the end user, whether a volume is full or thin is irrelevant. All the end user sees is that a volume has been assigned, and it is this size. However, to the storage administrator, whether a volume is full or thin is relevant because it dictates how much capacity is consumed. For example, when creating a fully provisioned virtual volume, the size is allocated and consumed at the time of provisioning. Giving a user a 1 TB virtual volume would consume 1 TB of storage from the array.

Thin provisioning involves using virtualization technology to give the appearance that a virtual volume is larger than the resources that have been provided. For example, a user could see that a drive on their system appears to be 2 TB in size, but the storage initially consumed is a fraction of that size. Over time, as data is written to the thin provisioned volume, it grows to the maximum size which was defined when it was created.

Care must be taken when using thin provisioned storage as administrators can over-provision. This means that a virtual volume can be created that is greater than the physical storage available in the array. For this reason, thin provisioned storage must be managed to ensure that all unnecessary data is deleted correctly. This ensures that the storage array can reclaim capacity from the thin provisioned volume and reuse it for other virtual volumes, if required. This process is known as thin persistence.

Management tools

HPE network management tools span across products and bring innovations to complete lifecycle management. As network management becomes more complex, the risks associated with compromised data flow have also increased, as illustrated in Figure 5-16.

NimbleOS WebUI

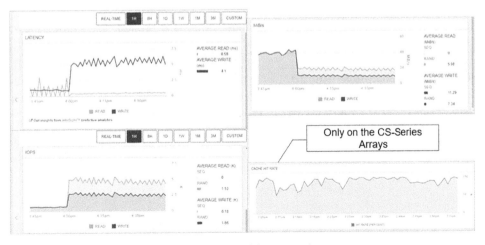

Figure 5-16 NimbleOS WebUI

The Nimble Array provides a simple-to-use, intuitive WebUI from which you manage the array. To access the WebUI, open any supported browser, and enter the array's management IP address, shown in Figure 5-17. You are presented with the login page. Enter the password that you set during the array creation and log in.

Figure 5-17 NimbleOS WebUI login screen

The home page gives you system-wide information at a glance. It lets you track performance, capacity, traffic load, and events for the entire system. Other sections include:

- **Performance**—Data throughput and input/output operations per second (IOPS) are the pulse of the array—changes in either of these may mean that system use has changed or that there is a problem somewhere in the array or from an application. The center section of the home page gives you an at-a-glance status of data movement activity.

- **Capacity**—The Space section lets you see the overall space usage. Immediately beneath the disk space is the space savings panel, which displays the compression factor, aggregated for the entire array. By understanding the total space use, you can manage the overall array more efficiently. Individual space usage appears on the Volumes details page for each volume. The details on the efficiency of the inline compression engine let you track actual space usage. This gives you better information when tracking usage trends and making decisions about future growth.

 Note

If the volume displayed on the Volumes detail page is a replica, the WebUI shows the information relevant to the replication space.

- **Protection and Hardware**—Another key data point that administrators want at a glance is the ability to quickly see that their data is protected and that the hardware is healthy. This section provides a summary of both those data points.

- **Events**—The Event Summary and Recent Events sections, displayed on the right side of the page, shows you the system health. You can then move to the Events details page to view event details.

The upper portion of the Home page displays the main menu. Use the menu items to move to any location of interest. Menus include:

- **Home**—The home page is where you land when you first login or when you click the Nimble logo.

- **Manage**—Submenus let you manage volumes, arrays, volume collections, protection, replication partners, and Access Control List (ACL) setup. Each submenu selection opens a more detailed area for the selection. For example, selecting Volumes displays a list of existing volumes and how many snapshots and replicas those volumes retain. New volumes are created from this page. All submenus (such as Storage Pools, Arrays, Replication partners, and CHAP users) have similar information.

- **Hardware**—This menu provides a means of viewing a graphical representation of the system hardware, including all attached shelves.

- **Monitor**—This menu shows all aspects of the array, grouped into intuitive selections. See Monitoring your array and its components for details.

- **Events**—Events can be filtered by severity and time frame. Patterns within events can improve your ability to predict problems and correct them before they become critical.

- **Administration**—Administer the system configuration such as alerts, software, autosupport, time zones, and general management in this menu. See Administering the array for details.

- **Help**—This selection provides access to technical support, array/group software version, and another means to access InfoSight.

The upper right corner of the screen displays login information, array name, and a link to InfoSight.

Each submenu provides links for drilling down and right-click commands for most actions. For example, to see detailed information at the volume level, you would move from Volume Summary to Volume Details.

Wherever you see the Information icon, hovering the pointer over it gives you more information about that item. For charts and graphs, hovering the pointer gives you details based on the area on which the pointer hovers.

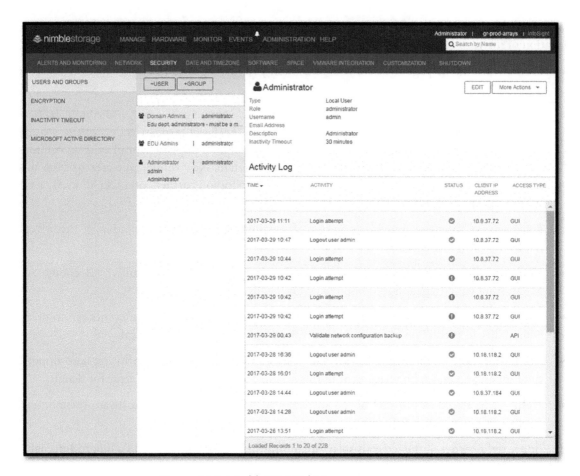

Figure 5-18 NimbleOS WebUI user management

NimbleOS supports role-based access control (RBAC). This allows administrators to create multiple users with predefined roles, as shown in Figure 5-18. By default, new arrays have a user called "admin," and its password is set during the initial array configuration. It supports Microsoft Active Directory (AD).

To make changes, navigate to: **ADMINISTRATION → SECURITY → USERS AND GROUPS**.

Unified network management with HPE Intelligent Management Center

Proactive management that spans the network

HPE Intelligent Management Center

– End-to-end multivendor management—1000s of devices, including Cisco!

– Single-pane-of-glass visibility

– Proactive health, performance, and fault monitoring

– Advanced network analytics

Data center	Campus
– Automation and orchestration	– Unified infrastructure
– Visualization of virtualized networks	– Traffic and application visibility
– Consistency across data center	– Zero touch deployment

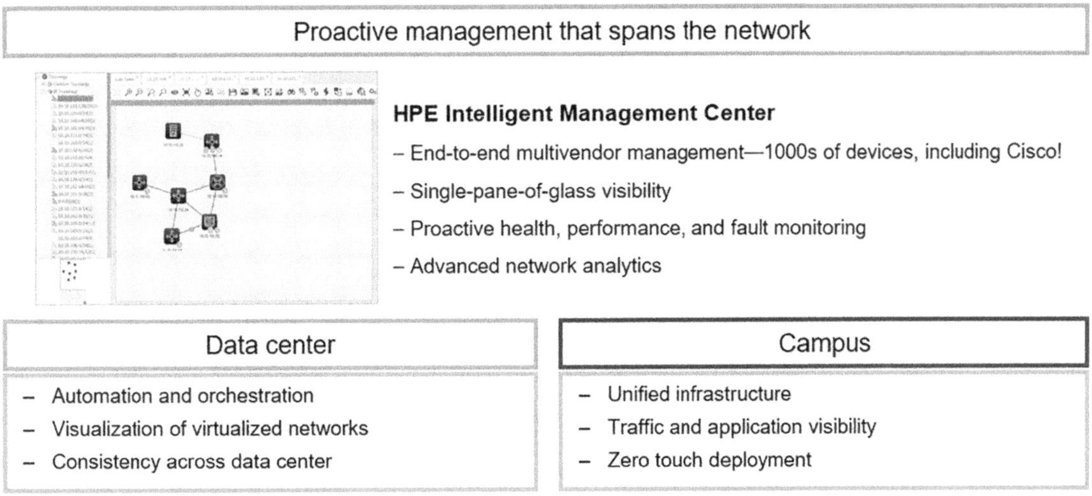

Figure 5-19 Unified network management with HPE IMC

Intelligent Management Center (IMC) consolidates the management functions needed to manage today's networks while providing the tools needed to address emerging networking trends and applications, as indicated in Figure 5-19. IMC allows your customers to manage both their physical and virtual networks. Because IMC automates the configuration of virtual and physical network infrastructures, it eliminates service interruptions caused by virtual/physical network configuration errors. It also accelerates the delivery of new applications.

Activity: HPE Reference Configuration for Red Hat OpenShift on HPE Synergy and HPE Nimble Storage

1. Use this document: http://h20195.www2.hpe.com/V2/GetDocument.aspx?docname=a00056101enw

2. Answer the following questions:

   a. What is the recommended size of shared storage for management hosts?

   _____

   _____

   b. What is the recommended size of shared storage for OpenShift container registry?

   _____

   _____

Solution components

Part numbers are at the time of publication and subject to change. The bill of material (BOM) does not include complete support options or other rack and power requirements.

Qty	Part number	Description
		Rack and Network Infrastructure
2	P9K10A	HPE 42U 600mmx1200mm G2 Kitted Advanced Shock Rack with Side Panels and Baying
2	P9K10A 001	HPE Factory Express Base Racking Service
2	H6J85A	HPE Rack Hardware Kit
2	BW932A	HPE 600mm Rack Stabilizer Kit
2	BW932A B01	HPE 600mm Rack include with Complete System Stabilizer Kit
6	AF533A	HPE Intelligent Modular 3Ph 14.4kVA/CS8365C 40A/208V Outlets (6) C19/Horizontal NA/JP PDU
		HPE Synergy Composable Infrastructure
3	797740-B21	HPE Synergy 12000 Configure-to-order Frame with 1x Frame Link Module 10x Fans
4	779218-B21	HPE Synergy 20Gb Interconnect Link Module
2	794502-B23	HPE Virtual Connect SE 40Gb F8 Module for Synergy
2	804937-B21	HPE Synergy Image Streamer
3	798096-B21	HPE 6x 2650W Performance Hot Plug Titanium Plus FIO Power Supply Kit
2	804353-B21	HPE Synergy Composer
3	804938-B21	HPE Synergy Frame Rack Rail Kit

Qty	Part number	Description
3	804942-B21	HPE Synergy Frame Link Module
1	804943-B21	HPE Synergy Frame 4x Lift Handles
1	859493-B21	Synergy Multi Frame Master1 FIO
1	859494-B22	Synergy Multi Frame Master2 FIO
8	804101-B21	HPE Synergy Interconnect Link 3m Active Optical Cable
2	720199-B21	HPE BladeSystem c-Class 40G QSFP+ to QSFP+ 3m Direct Attach Copper Cable
2	861412-B21	HPE Synergy Frame Link Module CAT6A 1.2m Cable
1	861413-B21	HPE Synergy Frame Link Module CAT6A 3m Cable
		Virtualized Hosts
3	871940-B21	HPE Synergy 480 Gen10 Configure-to-order Compute Module
3	873381-L21	HPE Synergy 480/660 Gen10 Intel Xeon-Gold 6130 (2.1GHz/16-core/125W) FIO Processor Kit
3	873381-B21	HPE Synergy 480/660 Gen10 Intel Xeon-Gold 6130 (2.1GHz/16-core/125W) Processor Kit
54	815097-B21	HPE 8GB (1x8GB) Single Rank x8 DDR4-2666 CAS-19-19-19 Registered Smart Memory Kit
18	815098-B21	HPE 16GB (1x16GB) Single Rank x4 DDR4-2666 CAS-19-19-19 Registered Smart Memory Kit
6	875478-B21	HPE 1.92TB SATA 6G Mixed Use SFF (2.5in) SC 3yr Wty Digitally Signed Firmware SSD
3	P01367-B1	HPE 96W Smart Storage Battery (up to 20 Devices) with 260mm Cable Kit
3	804424-B21	HPE Smart Array P204i-c SR Gen10 (4 Internal Lanes/1GB Cache) 12G SAS Modular Controller
3	777430-B21	HPE Synergy 3820C 10/20Gb Converged Network Adapter

		Worker Nodes
6	871943-B21	HPE Synergy 480 Gen10 6130 2P 64GB-R P204i-c SAS Performance Compute Module
3	873381-L21	HPE Synergy 480/660 Gen10 Intel Xeon-Gold 6130 (2.1GHz/16-core/125W) FIO Processor Kit
3	873381-B21	HPE Synergy 480/660 Gen10 Intel Xeon-Gold 6130 (2.1GHz/16-core/125W) Processor Kit
108	815097-B21	HPE 8GB (1x8GB) Single Rank x8 DDR4-2666 CAS-19-19-19 Registered Smart Memory Kit
36	815098-B21	HPE 16GB (1x16GB) Single Rank x4 DDR4-2666 CAS-19-19-19 Registered Smart Memory Kit
6	P01367-B1	HPE 96W Smart Storage Battery (up to 20 Devices) with 260mm Cable Kit
6	804424-B21	HPE Smart Array P204i-c SR Gen10 (4 Internal Lanes/1GB Cache) 12G SAS Modular Controller
6	777430-B21	HPE Synergy 3820C 10/20Gb Converged Network Adapter
		HPE Nimble Storage
1	Q8H41A	HPE Nimble Storage AF40 All Flash Dual Controller 10GBASE-T 2-port Configure-to-order Base Array
1	Q8B88B	HPE Nimble Storage 2x10GbE 2-port FIO Adapter Kit
1	Q8G27B	HPE Nimble Storage NOS Default FIO Software
1	Q8H47A	HPE Nimble Storage AF40 All Flash Array R2 11.52TB (24x480GB) FIO Flash Bundle
2	R0P84A	HPE Nimble Storage NEMA IEC 60320 C14 to C19 250V 15 Amp 1.8m FIO Power Cord
1	Q8F56A	HPE Nimble Storage 10GbE 2-port Spare Adapter
2	P9Q66A	HPE G2 IEC C20 Input/(8) C13 Expansion Outlets/PDU Extension Bar Kit
		HPE 5940 FlexFabric Switching
2	JH397A	HPE FF 5940 2-Slot Switch
2	JH180A	HPE 5930 24p SFP+ and 2p QSFP+ Module

Learning check

1. What is the default type of RAID at Nimble AF-Series?

_____

_____

_____

_____

2. When will you offer Nimble HF-Series over AF-Series?

_____

_____

_____

_____

3. Match the Nimble model with its max capacity.

AF20	Up to 2 PB
AF60	Up to 4 PB
AF80	Up to 168 TB

Alternative components for different environments

We presented a validated solution for customer scenario. Some of the solution components, however, can be changed for alternative environments, where different performance, capacity, costs, features, and similar requirements can be satisfied with other HPE solutions. Not all the workloads are the same and a single HPE product cannot match all the requirements.

Adaptive Flash Array family

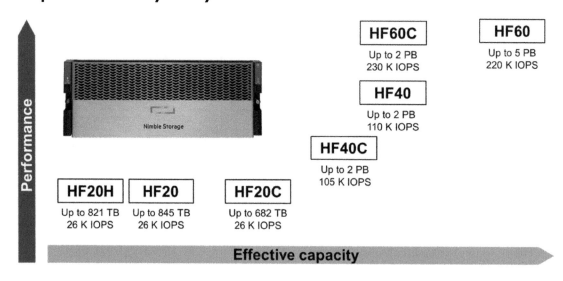

Figure 5-20 Adaptive Flash Array family

HPE Nimble Storage Adaptive-Flash Platform is engineered to meet the needs of the small- and mid-sized business (SMB) and smaller enterprise customers. Each consecutive member of the HF-Series family provides more performance along with a large effective capacity, as illustrated in Figure 5-20.

Variants with H are only half-populated; variants with C are not using deduplication.

AFxx series chassis front view/Dual-Flash Carrier

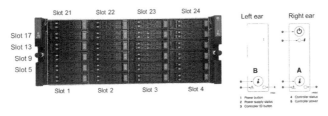

Figure 5-21 AFxx series chassis front view

The Dual Flash Carrier (DFC) is the same carrier found in the all-flash array. Each carrier has a Bank "A" and a Bank "B" supporting up to two SSDs. Each bank has its own release latch, allowing users to remove a single SSD, while the DFC that contains both banks has a single latch that removes both bank slots (A and B), as shown in Figures 5-21 and 5-22.

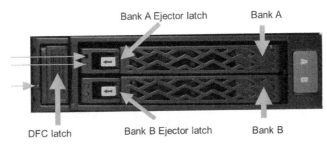

Figure 5-22 DFC details

The LED panels display the same LEDs that are found on all Nimble Storage Arrays.

Drive layout—HF20C, HF20, HF40, HF60

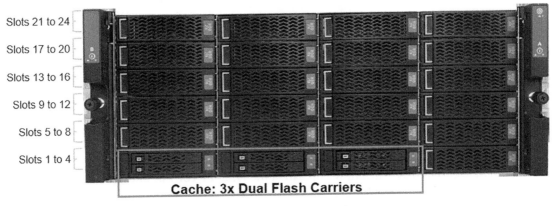

Figure 5-23 HF-Series slot numbering

The HF-Series chassis are 4U in height and support twenty-four 3.5" slots, which can be populated with 21 HDDs and three DFCs for a total potential of six SSDs. The minimum number of SSDs that can be configured with these arrays is three, which populates Bank A in the DFC.

The chassis slots are numbered from left to right and top to bottom, as illustrated in Figure 5-23. Slots 1 through 3 contain the DFCs, and slots 4 through 24 are populated with disk carriers.

For workloads that require peak performance, Nimble HF storage systems allow a pinning of the entire volume in the cache. When a volume is pinned in cache the HF-Series arrays will write data to the hard disk drives and maintain a copy of the full volume in cache.

Specifications include:

- 4U 24 chassis

- 24 x 3.5" slots carry 21x HDDs + 3x DFCs

- HDDs: 18 + three RAID (new Nimble-branded HDD carriers)

- DFCs: A minimum of three SSDs in Bank A (Bank B is available for cache upgrades)

Drive layout—HF20H: A half-populated HF20

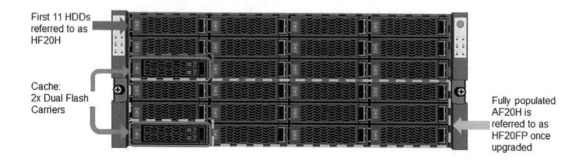

Figure 5-24 HF20H drive layout

The HF20H is an HF20 that is half-populated, as indicated in Figure 5-24. This configuration introduces a few differences from the other HF-Series chassis. The first difference is in the number of hard disk drives and SSDs supported. When half populated, it supports 11 hard disk drives and two DFCs with only slot A of the DFCs populated. These are located in the top half of the chassis. Later, customers can upgrade an HF20H to an HF20FP (HF20 fully populated). After it is upgraded, the HF20FP supports 22 hard disk drives and two fully populated DFCs.

The second difference is that, when fully populated, the HF20FP consists of two RAID stripes—one in the top half of the chassis consisting of 11 HDDs and the other in the bottom half of the chassis. This means that the capacities of an HF20H and HF20FP will be different than an HF20.

Note

The WebUI will display only HF20. To identify an HF20H or HF20FP, look at the system capacity or navigate to **Manage** → **Array** → [select array], and view the visual representation.

The first 11 HDDs are used to create a single RAID group. When the HF-20 is expanded, the second set of 11 drives creates a second RAID group that is added to the storage pool.

Nimble Storage HFx0 scale to fit

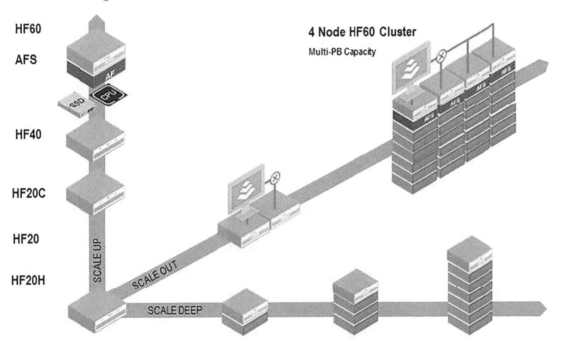

Add expansion shelves to meet storage growth

Figure 5-25 HF-Series scaling options

Just like the AF-Series arrays, the HF-Series arrays can scale in many ways, as illustrated in Figure 5-25. You can:

- Upgrade the amount of available cache or upgrade your controllers.
- Add expansion shelves or an All-Flash Shelf.
- Cluster four arrays together and expand/upgrade them as needed.

HFx0 controller upgrades

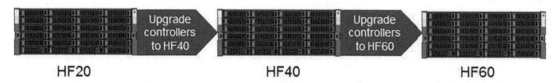

Figure 5-26 HF-Series controller upgrade path

In addition to upgrading cache, users can also upgrade HF-Series arrays to a higher model, as indicated in Figure 5-26. This is done by replacing the controllers using the same procedure as with the AF-Series arrays. This upgrade is non-disruptive within the HFx0 controller family. Be aware that cache upgrades might be required to meet the proper Memory to Flash Ratio (MFR).

Features include:

- Non-disruptive controller upgrades are within the HFx0 controller family.

- Cache upgrades might be required to meet MFR.

- Timeless Storage supported at launch.

HF-Series triple+ parity

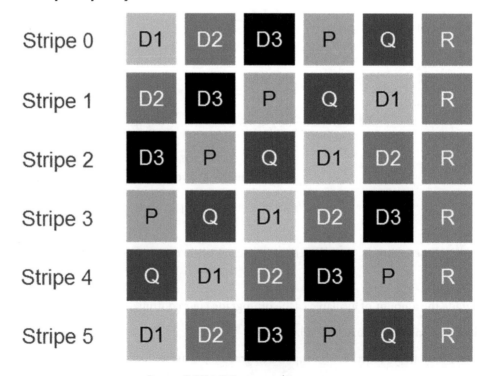

Figure 5-27 HF-Series triple+ parity

The Adaptive Flash Platform utilizes triple parity RAID to concatenate all hard disk drives in each shelf. HPE Nimble Storage uses left synchronous rotation in our implementation. When writing parity, the first two parity blocks (P and Q) are rotational as seen in Figure 5-27. The third parity block is not rotational and is written to the disk in slot one, though it should be noted that if that disk fails, the R block may be written to another disk. To see which disks are holding the R block obtain and run the "iostat.sh" script during a heavy read workload. The disks containing the R block should stick out with significantly less read activity.

HPE Nimble Storage's triple parity design supports the loss of three hard disk drives in a single shelf before it reaches zero disk redundancy. This means that three disk drives within a single shelf can fail without the system losing data. Failed drives are only counted if they are actively marked as failed by the controllers.

Should a single shelf reach a point where there is zero redundancy within the RAID group, the system will stop data services.

Drive layout—ES3 Expansion Shelf

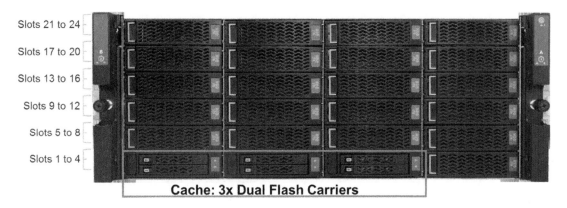

Figure 5-28 ES3 drive layout

From the front, the ES3 chassis looks identical to an HF-Series controller shelf and includes 21 HDDs and up to six SSDs, as shown in Figure 5-28.

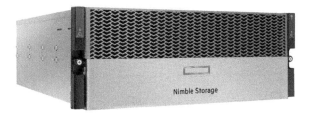

Figure 5-29 ES3 Expansion shelf

Capacity of the HF-Series arrays can be scaled with the addition of one to six Gen2 expansion shelves, as shown in Figure 5-29.

Specifications include:

- 4U 24 chassis

- 24 x 3.5" slots carry 21x HDDs + 3x DFCs

- HDDs: 18 + three RAID

- New Nimble-branded HDD carriers

- DFCs: Bank A preconfigured with three SSDs

- Bank B available for cache upgrades

AFS3—AF All-Flash Expansion Shelf

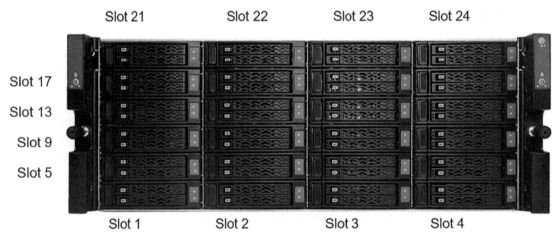

Figure 5-30 AFS3—AF All-Flash Expansion Shelf

AFS3 has a same layout as AFxx arrays. AFS3 is used to expand a capacity of the AF-Series arrays, as shown in Figure 5-30. Various stock keeping units (SKUs) are available with different SSDs (11.52 TB, 23 TB, 46 TB, 92 TB) and 24 x 3.5" slots carry 24 DFCs.

Scenario 5: Oracle RAC 12c best practices and scaling on HPE Synergy Gen10 platforms and HPE 3PAR StoreServ 9450 Storage

The wide HPE portfolio of data center products can be introduced using customer scenarios and recommended, validated configurations, based on HPE Reference Architecture or HPE Reference Configuration.

Introducing the customer scenario

aZLa company will be used as a story line through this scenario. We will introduce the company using an interview:

- What is your primary business?
    - Regional consumer electronics retailer
- How many employees do you currently have?
    - 1500+ employees
- What does your selling and delivery channel look like?
    - Electronic stores, show rooms, delivery boxes around the country
- Where are you currently storing data, and how do you access files?
    - Shared array, non-HPE, for critical data required onsite; temporary/cached data in a hosted environment
- What does your server and network infrastructure look like?
    - Single data center, mix of vendors (both servers and networking)
- What is the structure of your IT department?
    - E-shop development, operations team
- What are your current plans?
    - Consolidation of Oracle database

Customer requirements

As a result of multiple interviews and gathering information about customer plans and customer's current infrastructure, the following requirements emerged for the new solution:

- Deploying an Oracle Real Application Cluster
- Software-defined approach to infrastructure management
- Latest technology and security
- Both compute and storage resources need to stay on site
- Enterprise class all-flash array
    - Utmost performance of storage subsystem
- Array designed for 99.9999% availability
    - Full hardware redundancy

- Reducing management and deployment costs
  - Ability to predict and prevent infrastructure problems
- Data protection solution
  - Integrated with the storage array
- Compute requirements:
  - 4x 2S server, 512 GB of memory each
  - 1x 4S server, 512 GB of memory each
- Storage requirements:
  - 32 TB of raw capacity
  - Serial-attached SCSI (SAS) SSD
  - 16 Gb FC connectivity
  - FC switch ready for 32 Gb
- Networking requirements:
  - 20 Gb Ethernet connectivity
- Data protection:
  - Four weeks of retention

 Note

Data protection and the FC switch are not part of the Reference Architecture.

Activity: Information resources

1. Download these information resources:

   - HPE Reference Architecture for Oracle RAC 12c best practices and scaling on HPE Synergy Gen10 platforms and HPE 3PAR StoreServ 9450 Storage
     https://h20195.www2.hpe.com/v2/getdocument.aspx?docname=a00049200enw

     HPE 3PAR StoreServ Storage: A reference and best practices guide
     https://h20195.www2.hpe.com/v2/GetPDF.aspx/4AA4-4524ENW.pdf

   - Best Practices for Oracle Database on HPE 3PAR StoreServ Storage
     https://support.hpe.com/hpsc/doc/public/display?docId=emr_na-a00038978en_us

2. Answer the following questions:

   a. Which management tool is recommended by RA for creating volumes?

   _____

   _____

   b. Which Synergy server was selected?

   _____

   _____

   c. What are the recommended RAID levels?

      – Database, tablespaces, indexes _____

      – Redo logs _____

      – RAC voting disk and database recovery file destination _____

   d. How did RAC throughput change between single-node and four-node clusters at 600 connections?

   _____

   _____

   e. What is the difference in GiB between 1 TB and 1 TiB? _____

   f. What is a chunklet, and what is the size?

   _____

   _____

   g. What is the best practice when connecting ports 0:2:3, 1:2:3, 0:2:4, and 1:2:4 to two fabrics?

   _____

   _____

   h. How will data-at-rest encryption influence the solution design?

   _____

   _____

i.   How do Oracle redo logs benefit from thin provisioning?

_____

_____

_____

j.   How do you verify that device mapper multipathing is installed and running on an Oracle host?

_____

_____

Building blocks of the solution

HPE Synergy

StoreFabric SN6600B
Fibre Channel Switch

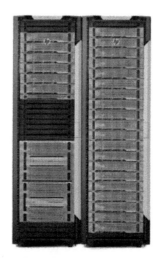

HPE 3PAR StoreServ 9450

HPE OneView

HPE StoreOnce 3640

Figure 5-31 Building blocks of the solution

IT departments are under constant pressure to reduce costs without sacrificing quality or functionality. When implementing and operating huge data repositories with Oracle databases, the amount of compute and storage resources required is significant. One common approach to reducing costs is to standardize on a specific hardware and software stack. This reduces the complexity of the environment and reduces total operating expenses. However, standardizing on a platform that does not offer a full feature set and the latest technology and security defeats the purpose. HPE Synergy and HPE 3PAR storage provide the benefit of standardizing on systems that offer the latest technology and security with Gen10 platforms and provide the ability to scale up and out as needed.

In today's business, the demands of rapid Oracle database implementations continue to escalate. Faster transaction processing speeds, capacity-based scaling, increased flexibility, high availability, and business continuity are required to meet the needs of the 24x7 business. In the day-to-day management of Oracle database environments, administrators need to be able to quickly deploy new servers, easily update existing systems, and upgrade processing capabilities for scale-out performance. With a traditional infrastructure, these activities are disruptive and time consuming.

HPE Synergy Gen10 platforms and HPE 3PAR StoreServ All-Flash storage provide an ideal environment for deploying Oracle Real Application Clusters (RACs). HPE Synergy offers fluid resource pools which can be customized for specific database needs. Oracle resources can be deployed rapidly through the software-defined intelligence embedded in the HPE Synergy Composer and HPE Synergy Image Streamer. An administrator can utilize HPE Synergy Image Streamer to develop a deployment plan to install and configure both the operating system and the application software. A server profile defined in the HPE Synergy Composer can use that deployment plan to configure a new server in a matter of minutes, compared to hours or days utilizing traditional infrastructure.

Figure 5-31 shows key components of this solution are HPE Synergy Composer, HPE Synergy Image Streamer, HPE Synergy Gen10 Compute Modules, HPE 3PAR StoreServ 9450 All-Flash Storage, HPE Application Tuner Express, and Oracle RAC.

HPE 3PAR StoreServ

HPE 3PAR StoreServ Storage allows your customers to break down the silos that stand between them and the efficiency and agility required to succeed in the Idea Economy. HPE 3PAR StoreServ delivers rapid and automated provisioning, hardware-accelerated deduplication, and flash-optimized performance with sub-1 ms latency within a single storage architecture, as illustrated in Figure 5-32. Combining all-flash capabilities and a multiprotocol workload support with a converged management framework, HPE 3PAR StoreServ offers the industry's most efficient storage engineered for the true convergence of block, file, and object access.

Compared with the competition, HPE 3PAR StoreServ Storage systems are twice as easy to provision and twice as easy to monitor in one-third of the data center space. When customers apply space-efficient snapshot features such as those in StoreServ to the multiple full data copies used for developers and data warehouses, they can reduce capacity needs by six times, reducing cost per gigabyte.

All models support unified block and file workloads as well as object access for cloud-developed application consolidation. This density and workload flexibility assure customers can prevent flash-array sprawl caused by introducing separate, capacity-limited flash architectures into the data center. Flash arrays and all-flash data centers must include built-in data availability and business continuity to reduce risk without performance penalty.

3PAR leadership

Rapid provisioning
Maintain service levels
Replication, recovery, and federation
ASIC
QoS
Virtual Copy
Remote Copy
Federate
(Peer Motion)
RMC
15 seconds to provision a LUN, and 3PAR Smart SAN reduces SAN setup steps by up to 90%
High performance thanks to the 3PAR ASIC, adaptive IO handling, wide striping, and QoS
Replicate, snap, move, backup, and restore valuable data

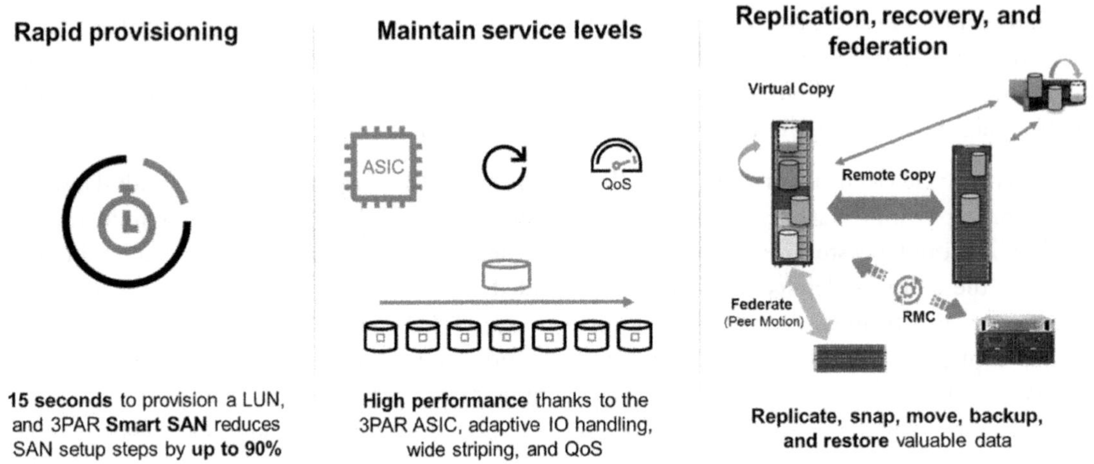

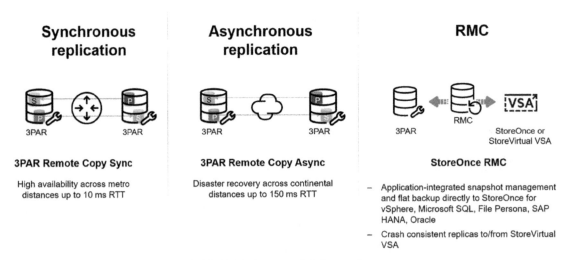

Figure 5-32 HPE 3PAR StoreServ

HPE provides leadership in automation for 3PAR StoreServ customers by reducing the storage management burden by up to 90%.

3PAR leadership—Data availability and protection

Synchronous replication
Asynchronous replication
RMC
3PAR
3PAR
3PAR
3PAR
3PAR
RMC
VSA
StoreOnce or StoreVirtual VSA
3PAR Remote Copy Sync
High availability across metro distances up to 10 ms RTT
3PAR Remote Copy Async
Disaster recovery across continental distances up to 150 ms RTT
StoreOnce RMC
– Application-integrated snapshot management and flat backup directly to StoreOnce for vSphere, Microsoft SQL, File Persona, SAP HANA, Oracle
– Crash consistent replicas to/from StoreVirtual VSA

Figure 5-33 3PAR data availability and protection

HPE provides leadership in data availability for 3PAR StoreServ customers by providing high availability, disaster recovery, and backup and restore solutions, as shown in Figures 5-33 and 5-34.

3PAR leadership—Efficient

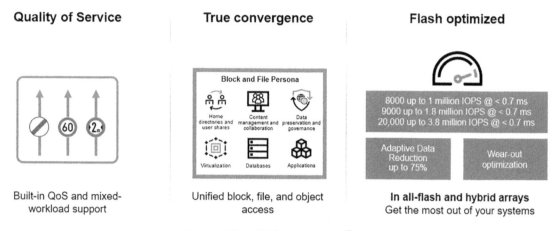

Quality of Service

True convergence

Flash optimized

Built-in QoS and mixed-workload support

Unified block, file, and object access

In all-flash and hybrid arrays
Get the most out of your systems

Figure 5-34 3PAR storage is efficient

HPE provides leadership in efficiency for 3PAR StoreServ customers by reducing TCO by more than 50%.

Converged block, file, and object access

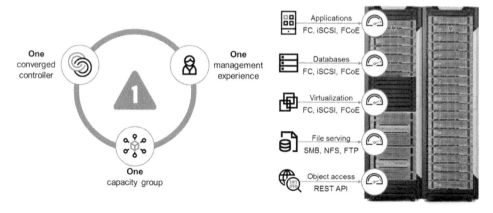

Figure 5-35 Converged block, file, and object access

3PAR began life as a block device, and block is still the recommended mode for most applications, including databases and virtualized environments, as illustrated in Figure 5-35. HPE included file capabilities starting with the 7000c models, and we call this File Persona. File Persona is integrated right onto the 3PAR controllers, and file and block are managed from a single pane of glass. All the current models can provide not only FC, internet Small Computer System (iSCSI), and Fibre Channel over Ethernet (FCoE) block access but also Network File System (NFS), Small Message

Block, File Transfer Protocol (FTP), and REpresentational State Transfer Application Programming Interface (REST API) access. The initial use case for file-oriented sharing was home directories and corporate shares. Those are still core use cases; however, HPE is continually qualifying additional use cases for File Persona.

HPE 3PAR StoreServ family

	← Same OS, management console, and software features →								
	Hybrid arrays					**All-Flash arrays**			
	8200	**8400**	**8440**	**20800**	**20840**	**8450**	**9450**	**20450**	**20850**
Controller nodes	2	2 to 4	2 to 4	2 to 8	2 to 8	2 to 4	2 to 4	2 to 4	2 to 8
16 Gb FC ports (Host, RCFC, Peer Ports)	4 to 12	4 to 24	4 to 24	0 to 160	0 to 160	4 to 24	0 to 80	0 to 80	0 to 160
10 Gb Ethernet host ports	0 to 4	0 to 8	0 to 8	0 to 80	0 to 80	0 to 8	0 to 40	0 to 40	0 to 80
10 Gb Ethernet IP ports (File Persona, RCIP)	0 to 4	0 to 8	0 to 8	0 to 48	0 to 48	0 to 16	0 to 48	0 to 48	0 to 48
1 Gb Ethernet IP ports	0 to 8	0 to 16	0 to 16	NA	NA	0 to 8	NA	NA	NA
Built-in Remote Copy IP ports (Speed)	2 (1 Gb)	2 to 4 (1 Gb)	2 to 4 (1 Gb)	2 to 8 (10 Gb)	2 to 8 (10 Gb)	2 to 4 (1 Gb)	2 to 4 (10 Gb)	2 to 4 (10 Gb)	(10 Gb)
Cache per node-pair / per system GiB	64 / 64	64 / 128	192 / 384	448 / 1792	900 / 3600	192 / 384	448 / 896	896 / 1792	896 / 3584
Flash cache per node-pair / system GiB	768 / 768	768 / 1536	4000 / 8000	8192 / 32768	12288/ 49152	NA	NA	NA	NA
Max drives per StoreServ array	8 to 240	8 to 576	8 to 960	8 to 2304	8 to 2304	8 to 480	8 to 576	8 to 576	8 to 1152
Max SSD per StoreServ array	120	240	480	1152	1152	480	576	576	1152
Max raw capacities (TiB) (SSD only)	1000 (838)	2400 (1676)	4000 (3351)	9600 (8043)	9600 (8043)	3351	6000	4021	8043
Max presentable file capacities	128 TiB	256 TiB	256 TiB	512 TiB	512 TiB	256 TiB	256 TiB	256 TiB	512 TiB
Max random IOPS RAID 6 - 60/40 r/w [1]	46'200	90'500	151'000	438'000	485'000	151'000	276'000	198'000	485'000
Front-end performance RAID 1 - 100% read [2]	400'000	800'000	1'000'000	3'200'000	3'800'000	1'000'000	1'800'000	1'800'000	3'800'000
Max sequential GB/s RAID 6 - 100% DECO	2.9	5.8	7.0	16.1	18.8	7.0	12.6	11.1	18.8
Front-end read performance [3] RAID 6 - no DECO	6.4	12.7	12.7	26.4	27.2	12.7	14.8	12.4	27.2

[1] Distributed layout, 8 kiB, 60/40 r/w, no cache hits, with 2:1 data reduction using DECO (deduplication + compression)
[2] Local Node layout, 8 kiB, 100% read, no cache hits, no DECO
[3] 100% sequential reads, 256 kB

Figure 5-36 HPE 3PAR StoreServ family

Description and usage	When value matters most.			When scale matters most.			When performance matters most.		
Model	8200	8400	8440	20800	20840	8450	9450	20450	20850
Storage controllers	2	2 or 4	2 or 4	2, 4, 6, or 8	2, 4, 6 or 8	2 or 4	2 or 4	2 or 4	2, 4, 6, or 8
Maximum host ports	12	24	24	160	160	24	-	80	160
16 Gb/s Fibre Channel	4–12	8–24	8–24	0–160	0–160	8–24	0–80	0–80	0–160
10 Gb Ethernet	0–4	0–8	0–8	0–48	0–48	0–8	0–24	0–24	0–48
10 Gb iSCSI/FCoE	0–4	0–8	0–8	0–80	0–80	0–8	0–40	0–40	0–80
Maximum initiators per system	2,048	4,096	4,096	8,192	8,192	4,096	-	8,192	8,192
Drive types (mixable)	SAS (performance, nearline, SSDs)	SAS (performance, nearline, SSDs)	SAS (performance, nearline, SSDs)	SAS (performance, nearline, SSDs)	SAS (performance, nearline, SSDs)	SAS SSDs	SAS SSDs	SAS SSDs	SAS SSDs
Max Drives (all types)	240	576	960	1920	2304	480	-	576	1152
Max Solid State Drives (SSDs)	120	240	480	1024	1152	480	576	576	1152
Maximum capacity raw	750 TiB	2400 TiB	3000 TiB	6000 TiB	9600 TiB[11]	1843 TiB (SSD-only)	6000 TiB	1966 TiB	8043 TiB[12] (SSD-only)

Figure 5-37 HPE 3PAR StoreServ family

HPE 3PAR StoreServ product families, as illustrated in Figures 5-33 and 5-37, include:

- **HPE 3PAR StoreServ 8000**—It delivers the performance advantages of a purpose-built, flash-optimized architecture without compromising resiliency, efficiency, or data mobility. HPE 3PAR StoreServ 8000 storage offers a range of options that support true convergence of block and file protocols, all-flash array performance, and the use of spinning media to further optimize costs. HPE 3PAR StoreServ 8000 storage offers rich Tier 1 data services, quad-node resiliency, seamless data mobility between systems, high availability through a complete set of persistent technologies, and simple and efficient data protection with a flat backup to HPE StoreOnce backup appliances. The HPE 3PAR Gen5 Thin Express Application-Specific Integrated Circuit (ASIC) provides silicon-based hardware acceleration of thin technologies, including inline deduplication, to reduce acquisition and operational costs by up to 75% without compromising performance.

- **HPE 3PAR StoreServ 9000**—This is an enterprise-class flash array that helps you consolidate primary storage workloads—for file, block, and object—without compromising performance, scalability, data services, or resiliency. This newest 3PAR model, based on the proven 3PAR architecture, is purpose built for all-flash consolidation, delivering the performance, simplicity, and agility needed to support the Hybrid IT environment. HPE 3PAR StoreServ 9450 Storage is available as an all-flash model with quad-node resiliency. Raw capacity of 6 tebibytes (TiB) with up to 576 SSF SSDs. Options include up to eighty 16 G FC ports or forty 10 GbE iSCSI/FCoE ports or twelve 10 Gb/s Ethernet ports.

- **HPE 3PAR StoreServ 20000**—The HPE 3PAR StoreServ 20000 family offers enterprise flash arrays for demanding workloads with over 3.2 million IOPS at sub-millisecond latency and consumes 85% less space than traditional high-end arrays for a massive footprint reduction. The StoreServ 20000 family scales out to eight nodes and is ideal for customers consolidating multiple racks of legacy, high-end storage. The StoreServ 20850 all-flash array can deliver over 75 GB/s of sustained throughput for maximum application performance. It also includes the StoreServ 20800 Converged Flash Array, which scales up to 15 PB of usable capacity. This product family also features the HPE 3PAR Gen5 Thin Express ASIC.

HPE 3PAR StoreServ—All-flash 8450 and 9450

	9450	8450
Max. IOPS estimate* (4k random 100% Read)	>1.8M IOPS @ sub ms latency	>1M IOPS @ sub ms latency
On-node cache per node pair	448 GiB	192GiB
SSDs supported	400 GB, 1.92 TB, 3.84 TB, 7.68 TB, and 15.36 TB SSDs	
Max SSDs	6 to 576 SSDs	6 to 480 SSDs
Number of HDDs	N/A	N/A
Raw capacity	6000 TiB	3351 TiB

Price is driving factor. Capacity up to 1000 TB is adequate	Upgradeable with up to 4 controller nodes	Flash with HDD backing	All-flash with >1 million IOPs with sub millisecond latency	All-flash with >1.8 million IOPs with sub millisecond latency	Scalability up to 8 PB
8200	8400	8440	8450	9450	20000

Figure 5-38 HPE 3PAR StoreServ—Converged flash 8450 and all-flash 9450

Figure 5-38 compares 8450 and 9450 and possible based on customer requirements. Figure 5-39 compares performance improvement of 9450 array over 8450.

Specs per node pair	8450	9450	Improvement
CPU cores (Ivy Bridge—2.4 GHz)	20	40	100%
Gen5 ASICs	2	4	100%
Cache in GiB	192	448	130%

Workload	RAID	Volume	8450	9450	Improvement
256 KiB sequential reads (local)	RAID 1	Full	23 GB/s	38 GB/s	65%
8 KiB OLTP 60/40 (distributed)	RAID 5	Full	382K IOPS	571K IOPS	49%
16 KiB random reads (distributed)	RAID 5	DECO	376K IOPS	569K IOPS	51%
16 KiB OLTP 60% read (distributed)	RAID 5	DECO	144K IOPS	243K IOPS	69%

Figure 5-39 HPE 3PAR StoreServ 9450 performance

Figure 5-39 shows performance numbers coming from empirical measurements and estimates as of June 2017; final numbers for specific configuration are available in NinjaSTARS.

HPE 3PAR StoreServ 8000

HPE 3PAR StoreServ 8000 is the ideal solution for customers who:

- Need an affordably priced, non-disruptive solution that is scalable to four nodes.

- Are looking for true convergence of file, block, and object.

- Require a single architecture to take advantage of common data services, including integrated file services, and common management across their data center.

- Deploy some or all applications and data types in physical or virtual environments and the cloud.

- Need to upgrade their SAN, especially in virtualized environments or to address unpredictable workloads with a modern architecture.

- Require low latency and higher speed support for higher VM density.

- Are large customers/enterprise customers needing departmental storage.

Thanks to all-inclusive software licensing, 3PAR is the only array with included software that optimizes the entire IO path for flash at no additional cost:

- File Persona increases capacity requirements by opening new file-based workloads for consolidation.

- Smart SAN simplifies StoreFabric attach with SAN zoning automation of 16/32 Gb switches.

- RMC drives StoreOnce attach with flash-integrated data protection.

HPE 3PAR StoreServ delivers one architecture from midrange to enterprise, including an all-flash array with integrated file, block, and object access, as well as common data services and common management across the portfolio.

HPE 3PAR StoreServ 8440—Converged flash array

HPE 3PAR StoreServ 8440 offers the performance of flash, the affordability of a hybrid storage with converged file, block, and object access, and the scalability and resiliency of high-end storage. With up to four controllers and replication between any 3PAR StoreServ models, compromising between application availability and affordability is now a thing of the past.

HPE 3PAR StoreServ 8450 Storage—All-flash array

StoreServ 8450 removes bottlenecks with a flash-optimized, scale-out architecture delivering over 1 million IOPS. The HPE 3PAR StoreServ 8450 delivers industry-leading affordability with all-flash performance.

HPE 3PAR StoreServ 9450 Storage—All-flash array

StoreServ 9450 delivers close to twice the all-flash performance of the HPE 3PAR 8450 with 1.8 million IOPS at sub-millisecond latency.

Target customers include:

- Large-scale enterprise deployments where data center transformation is a priority

- Customers wanting to move to an all-flash data center who want to consume storage in a secure on-premises model at cloud prices

- Customers looking at the consolidation of multiple workloads, along with the best all-flash performance

- Dell EMC, Pure, or IBM customers who are looking to modernize and consolidate their flash storage

- Segments: Global, Commercial, and Enterprise accounts

- Verticals: Financial, Healthcare, Manufacturing, and Service providers

HPE 3PAR StoreServ 9450 and 20000 provide highest resiliency

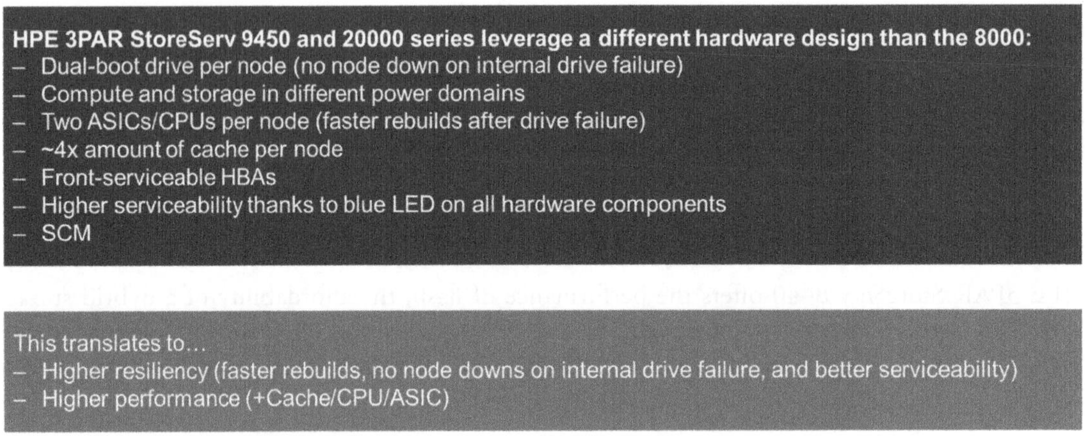

HPE 3PAR StoreServ 9450 and 20000 series leverage a different hardware design than the 8000:
- Dual-boot drive per node (no node down on internal drive failure)
- Compute and storage in different power domains
- Two ASICs/CPUs per node (faster rebuilds after drive failure)
- ~4x amount of cache per node
- Front-serviceable HBAs
- Higher serviceability thanks to blue LED on all hardware components
- SCM

This translates to…
- Higher resiliency (faster rebuilds, no node downs on internal drive failure, and better serviceability)
- Higher performance (+Cache/CPU/ASIC)

Figure 5-40 HPE 3PAR StoreServ 9450 and 20000 resiliency

How is the hardware on HPE 3PAR StoreServ 9450 and 20000 different from 8000, as indicated in Figure 5-40?

- The 20000 has an average of about 26% faster rebuilds after a drive fails (based on 1.92 TB SSD).

- Power domains for compute and storage elements isolate failure domains, which provides greater resiliency.

- There are two ASICs and CPUs per node.

- You can service all participating HBAs from the front so you can service more easily, and there are no built-in ports.

- The blue LED notification on the front of the enclosure aids in serviceability on the 9450/20000.

- There is a point-to-point SAS connection on the 20000 with directly connected drive enclosures that have a shorter pause in IO if the backend path or the enclosure fails, as compared to a loop connection with daisy-chained enclosures.

HPE 3PAR StoreServ 20000

HPE 3PAR StoreServ 20000 is the ideal solution for customers who:

- Need massive consolidation with workloads that require up to three million IOPS and/or scalability up to 9 PB raw.

- Have large mission-critical projects like enterprise resource planning (ERP) roll-out on a private cloud.

- Have next-gen data center requirements that require the latest infrastructure, density, power, and cooling.

- Require a complex disaster recovery and need to fan in or fan out multiple systems.

- Need to reduce the number of storage systems and consolidate/upgrade their legacy SANs.

	20450	20800	20850	20840
Controller nodes	2 or 4	2, 4 , 6, or 8	2, 4 , 6, or 8	2, 4 , 6, or 8
Max. total cache	1.8 TiB	33.8 TiB	3.6 TiB	51.3 TiB
Max. on-node cache	1792 GiB	1792 GiB	3584 GiB	3584 GiB
Total flash cache	N/A	32 TiB	N/A	48 TiB
Max # of HDDs / SDDs	N/A / 576	2304 / 1152	N/A / 1152	2304 / 1152
Max raw capacity	4021 TiB all-flash	9600 TiB	8043 TiB all-flash	9600 TiB
16 Gb/s FC host ports **10 Gb/s iSCSI/FCoE ports** **10 Gb/s FBO NIC ports** **Built-in 10 Gb RC ports**	0 to 80 0 to 40 0 to 24 2 to 4	0 to 160 0 to 80 0 to 48 2 to 8	0 to 160 0 to 80 0 to 48 2 to 8	0 to 160 0 to 80 0 to 48 2 to 8

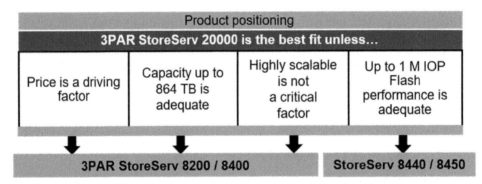

Figure 5-41 HPE 3PAR StoreServ 20000 product positioning

HPE 3PAR StoreServ 20000 Storage is a new class of enterprise flash arrays for massive consolidation of your customer's most demanding workloads. As illustrated in Figure 5-41, StoreServ 20000 is:

- **Hyper-scalable**—Massive scalability with up to eight Mesh-Active Clustered Nodes for up to 8 PB raw and 24 PB usable, to meet growing enterprise requirements.

- **Flexible**—Meet unpredictable business demands. Flash-optimized with greater than three million IOPS at less than 1 millisecond of latency and 40 GB/s bandwidth.

- **Resilient**—Consolidate with confidence, assure service levels with enterprise-class business continuity/disaster recovery using Async Streaming replication, and assure end-to-end data integrity with Persistent Checksum.

3PAR StoreServ 9450 hardware building blocks

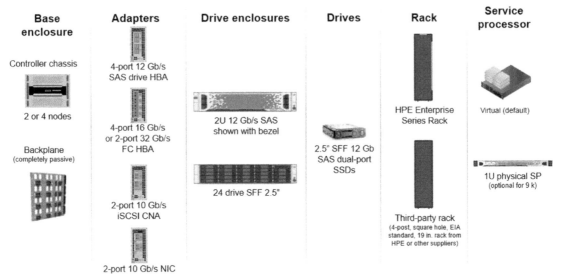

Figure 5-42 HPE 3PAR StoreServ 9450 hardware building blocks

The HPE 3PAR StoreServ 9000 Storage is an enterprise-class flash array that helps you consolidate primary storage workloads—for file, block, and object—without compromising performance, scalability, data services, or resiliency, as illustrated in Figure 5-42.

This newest 3PAR model based on the proven 3PAR architecture is purpose built for all-flash consolidation, delivering the performance, simplicity, and agility needed to support the Hybrid IT environment. HPE 3PAR StoreServ 9000 Storage is available in a single all-flash model, the 9450, that offers rich Tier-1 data services and quad-node resiliency.

Customers have the option of self-installing the HPE 3PAR StoreServ 9000 Storage array. The customer self-installation option is available for HPE 3PAR StoreServ 9000 Storage arrays that meet the following criteria:

- Two-node or four-node configurations

- Configure-to-order (CTO) configurations (factory integrated)

- Single rack (the physical SP can be in a separate rack)

When performing an initial configuration of a StoreServ 9000 storage system, there are a few specifications to keep in mind:

The building blocks of the 9450 are very similar to the other 3PAR models. The backplane of the 9450 can contain either two or four controller nodes, so in HPE's configuration tools, you would select the base model, and then add the other two nodes if necessary. Next, you need to choose which host-facing HBAs should be added to each node pair. The controllers on the 9450 do not contain any drives, and so you must add drives in the drive-only enclosures.

Since the 9450 can have only SSDs, we only need to have SFF enclosures. The 9450 might be racked either in the factory in an HPE rack or onsite in a customer supplied or HPE rack. For the HPE racks that contain the controllers, you can choose either the 1075 mm or 1200 mm racks. The last component is the Service Processor (SP), which is used only for remote maintenance and connectivity to HPE Customer Support. The 9450 supports either a dedicated physical SP or a virtual service processor (VSP). The SP is also needed for HPE InfoSight support.

HPE 3PAR StoreServ 9450 controller

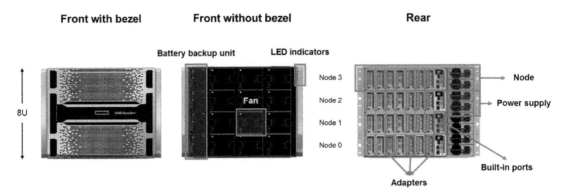

Figure 5-43 HPE 3PAR StoreServ 9450 controller

The LED on the front of the enclosure is used when servicing the 9450—blue means safe to remove and doubles up as a locate indicator; green is status OK; and amber indicates a fault.

HPE 3PAR StoreServ 9000 configuration considerations

HPE 3PAR StoreServ 9000 configurations start with the selection of the base. The base includes the controller node chassis and two controller nodes. Each controller node consists of CPUs, ASICs, cache banks, and connectivity options for the storage array, as indicated in Figure 5-43.

 IOPS **might** be more limited with iSCSI than with Fibre Channel, depending on the size of the configuration

iSCSI port can do 45,000 IOPS and 675 MB/sec*

 Response time with iSCSI will be longer

iSCSI provides ~1.6 x Fibre Channel response

*Measured with HPE 3PAR OS 3.2.2 on the 8000 and 20000

Figure 5-44 iSCSI performance

The following are performance numbers you can use for guidance on the new models. However, because the HBAs are different, they do not apply to the older 3PAR model arrays:

- One dual-port iSCSI card can do 90,000 8 K IOPS.

- One dual-port iSCSI card can do 1350 MB per second.

From a response time stand point, iSCSI has some additional overhead vs. FC, so you can expect the iSCSI response time to be about 1.6 times the equivalent FC response time, as indicated in Figure 5-44.

HPE 3PAR StoreServ architecture

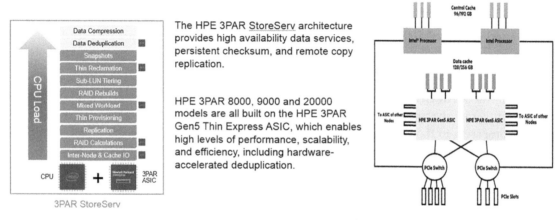

The HPE 3PAR StoreServ architecture provides high availability data services, persistent checksum, and remote copy replication.

HPE 3PAR 8000, 9000 and 20000 models are all built on the HPE 3PAR Gen5 Thin Express ASIC, which enables high levels of performance, scalability, and efficiency, including hardware-accelerated deduplication.

Figure 5-45 HPE 3PAR StoreServ 20000 architectural diagram

Compared to traditional arrays where all advanced features must be handled by the CPU in software, the 3PAR ASIC offloads the CPU in a way to allow much more advanced features to be used without sacrificing system performance, as indicated in Figure 5-45.

HPE 3PAR StoreServ Storage is a family of storage systems with Tier 1 models that provide autonomic provisioning, tiering, and management capabilities. HPE offers a full range of services including multiple care levels and data migration, integration, and consulting services. This proactive approach leverages products, tools, and technologies to avoid problems and optimize performance.

- **Multitenant and federated**—These storage systems manage unpredictable workloads and VM density. They support huge numbers of applications and mixed workloads without performance or resiliency impact. HPE Peer Motion software provides non-disruptive data mobility between federated systems.

- **Efficient**—HPE 3PAR StoreServ Storage reduces upfront capacity requirements and technology refresh costs and eliminates stranded capacity using thin technologies.

- **Autonomic**—Customers can save up to 90% of administrator time. These systems simplify, automate, and expedite storage management intelligently and without administrator intervention. The system is self-managing, self-healing, and self-configuring.

HPE 3PAR ASIC

HPE 3PAR StoreServ employs purpose-built HPE 3PAR ASICs at the center of each controller node. The ASICs feature efficient, silicon-based mechanisms to drive in-line deduplication. This implementation relies on the HPE 3PAR ASICs to generate and assign signatures to each unique incoming write request.

HPE 3PAR 8000, 9000, and 20000 models are all built on the HPE 3PAR Gen5 Thin Express ASIC, which enables high levels of performance, scalability, and efficiency, including hardware-accelerated deduplication. The 3PAR Gen5 Thin Express ASIC provides silicon-based hardware acceleration of thin technologies, including in-line deduplication, to reduce acquisition and operational costs by up to 75% without compromising performance.

Powered by the 3PAR Gen5 Thin Express ASIC, HPE 3PAR Persistent Checksum ensures end-to-end data integrity from the application server through the storage array for any workload. It remains completely transparent to those servers and applications. This data validation capability protects against flash media and transmission errors as data moves from the ProLiant servers through the fabric and to the HPE 3PAR StoreServ Storage array.

Features of StoreServ architecture

Key features of the StoreServ architecture include:

- HPE 3PAR provisioning technologies offer efficiency features for primary storage that can significantly reduce both capital and operational costs. Thin provisioning has achieved widespread adoption because it dramatically increases capacity efficiencies. Deduplication is also an essential consideration when looking into deploying workloads onto a flash tier or an all-flash array. Thin technologies can vary widely in how they are implemented.

- HPE 3PAR Adaptive Flash Cache (AFC) is a functionality of StoreServ that allows SSDs to act as Level 2 read cache holding random read data for spinning media that has aged out of DRAM read cache. AFC reduces application response time for read-intensive IO workloads and can improve write throughput in mixed-workload environment. AFC effectively increases the amount of random read data cached on high-speed media on a node.

- The HPE 3PAR File Persona Software Suite can be enabled on a StoreServ node pair with an optional license. It requires either a two-port 10 GbE or a four-port 1 GbE network interface card (NIC) installed in the system or the onboard 1 GbE RCIP port enabled for File Persona.

- The HPE 3PAR Data Optimization Software Suite v2 combines capabilities that provide autonomic storage tiering and dynamic data mobility with assured QoS. Adaptive Optimization provides highly reliable, non-disruptive, cost-optimized storage tiering at the subvolume level to deliver the right QoS to the right data at the right time on a large scale, and Dynamic Optimization delivers it at the volume level.

- Peer Motion software enables seamless technology refresh and cost-optimized asset lifecycle management and lowers the technology refresh capital expenditure. Priority Optimization software allows customers to ensure QoS on HPE 3PAR StoreServ Storage systems. With Priority Optimization, customers can protect their tenants and environments from an unpredictable burst of IO and maintain a predictable SLA for multiple tenants.

No single point of failure with StoreServ components

StoreServ storage components such as storage nodes, cache cards, disk- and host-facing HBAs, power supplies, batteries, and disks feature N + 1 and in some cases N + 2 resilience. As a result, system interruption does not occur if any of these components fail.

The system's power domains are designed to prevent power loss to back-end disk devices by tolerating up to two disk chassis power supply failures. StoreServ storage systems offer up to four current load-balanced power distribution units (PDUs) per rack, providing a minimum of two and support for up to four separate data center power feeds to offer even more power redundancy and protection against events.

All storage nodes run a separate copy of HPE 3PAR OS software. The software is both statefully managed and self-healing in the case of a failure or restart of a process, across all cache-coherent, active-active storage controller nodes. Each controller node supports one Ethernet connection to a switch or hub. Separate connections from the Ethernet switch or hub to at least two controller nodes are required to support redundancy. With redundancy, one IP address is shared between the two connections, and only one network connection is active at a time. If the active network connection fails, the IP address is automatically moved to the surviving network connection.

 Notice

> At a minimum, the storage system requires one FC (or iSCSI) connection from a host computer to a controller node. HPE recommends separate connections from each host computer to each of the controller nodes in the storage system, with connections distributed evenly across all nodes.

HPE 3PAR StoreServ—Embracing new technologies

New technology

Reduced costs

Increased density

Rapid adoption

Figure 5-46 HPE 3PAR StoreServ benefits

3D NAND technology enables SSDs to be cheaper, denser, and faster. The reason is that memory chips are stacked in layers to pack in more data, unlike single-plane chips. This is cutting-edge technology, and 3PAR's architecture enables customers to smoothly transition to 3D NAND, as illustrated in Figure 5-46. 3PAR arrays are built for IO, not a particular drive type. That is why 3PAR continues to be on the leading edge of new drive types that bring down the cost of flash without passing on any of the risks, thanks to our five-year unconditional warranty.

 Note

NAND flash uses floating-gate transistors. These are connected in a way that resembles a NAND gate: several transistors are connected in series, and the bit line is pulled low only if all the word lines are pulled high. In digital electronics, a NAND gate (negative-AND) is a logic gate that produces an output which is false only if all its inputs are true (May 2018, Wikipedia.org).

Adopting new flash

Most architectures are designed for a single type of flash media and struggle to adopt new types of flash as they are released, resulting in a lag before support.

The 3PAR architecture

HPE 3PAR StoreServ's unique architecture allows HPE 3PAR arrays to adopt new flash technologies as soon as they become available.

3D NAND

For 3PAR, 3D NAND introduces new capabilities, including higher-performing writes, faster erase cycles, higher capacity, and improved endurance.

HPE 3PAR gets you ready for what is next

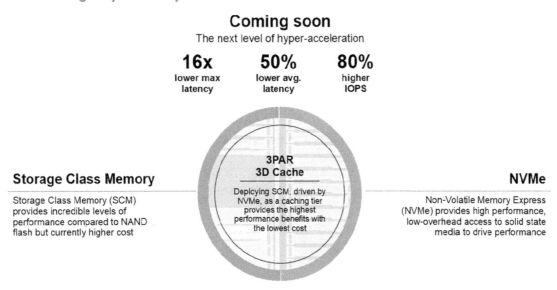

Figure 5-47 The next level of acceleration

There are two new technologies: SCM and NVMe, shown in Figure 5-47. When you combine these with 3PAR's intelligent caching, you get the next level of hyper-acceleration, called 3PAR 3D Cache.

Architected for efficiency today and for what comes next

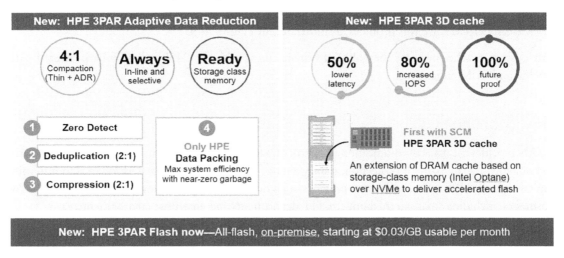

Figure 5-48 HPE 3PAR efficiency

Flash is all about consolidating racks and racks of storage. You need density to do that, and HPE has been pushing the boundaries by being first to market with larger and larger SSDs. Right now, you can find a single SSD with over 15 TB on it. However, if you want to continue to grow this density, eventually you would sacrifice performance for more capacity. 3PAR 3D Cache with SCM and NVMe solves this problem and ensures that we never have to make those tradeoffs, as illustrated in Figure 5-48.

Fifty percent lower average latencies and 80% higher IOPS

Figure 5-49 3D cache performance

Flash is all about consolidating racks and racks of storage. You need density to do that, and we are already pushing the boundaries, thereby being first to market with larger and larger SSDs.

Right now, you can do over 15 TB on a single SSD, but if you want to continue to grow this density, eventually you would sacrifice performance for more capacity. 3PAR 3D Cache with SCM and NVMe can help to solve this problem, as illustrated in Figure 5-49.

Any customers who purchase these 20000 systems along with the 9450 will be fully protected with NVMe and SCM support.

HPE StoreFabric

A SAN provides the data communication infrastructure for advanced, cost-efficient storage systems. SAN technology offers investment protection, management features, and IO price:performance to minimize capital expense. HPE SAN architecture provides open network storage solutions for all sizes and types of businesses, including small- to medium-sized IT departments and enterprise environments.

Fibre Channel currently supports a maximum of 239 switches in a single fabric. HPE specifies support based on rules for the maximum number of switches and ports in a single fabric or multi-fabric SAN. Using many switches to obtain a high number of ports is unacceptable if the fabric exceeds the total switch count limit. Similarly, using large-capacity switches can create a network that exceeds the maximum number of ports.

Features of Fibre Channel

Fibre Channel Technology allows for up to 16 million devices, which include host computers, disk drives, drive arrays, and tape storage to be combined into a single network connected to interconnect devices such as a switch.

FC is scalable, and it not only exceeds the parallel limits defined within SCSI of 16 devices (15 devices plus a controller), but it also allows for the addition of ports, or links, which can increase performance.

Distances of 10 Km between devices can be achieved using single-mode fiber optic cables. With the use of Extended Long-Wavelength Laser (ELWL), distances far greater than this can be achieved.

Other FC features include:

- Data transfer rates in the original implementation were 1.0625 Gb/sec, and these rates are now up to 32 Gb/sec.

- Data reliability is assured with a bit error rate of 10^{-12}.

- FC supports multiple topologies, providing for more flexibility in achieving higher availability and performance.

Fibre Channel distance cabling

Multimode 50 μm transceivers provide short-wave transmission maximum lengths using 50/125 micron (OM4 4700 MHz-km at 850 nm).

- 100 m for 32 Gbps FC

- 125 m for 16 Gbps FC

- 550 m for 10 Gbps FC

- 190 m for 8 Gbps FC

- 400 m for 4 Gbps FC

Single-mode 9 μm transceivers provide long-wave transmission in the 1310 nm or 1550 nm range. Extended distances are:

- 10 KM for 32 Gb/s FC Inter-Switch Links (ISLs)

- 10 KM for 16 Gb/s FC ISLs

- 10 KM for 10 Gb/s FC ISLs

- 10 KM for 8 Gb/s FC ISLs

- 10 KM for 4 Gb/s FC ISLs

- 10 KM for 2 Gb/s FC ISLs

- 10KM for 1 Gb/s FC ISLs

All 32 Gb/s, 16 Gb/s, 8 Gb/s, 4 Gb/s, and 2 Gb/s FC components use industry-standard LC connectors for fiber optic cable connections; all 1 Gb/s FC components use industry-standard SC connectors. Cables and adapters are available with SC connectors on one end and LC connectors on the other end.

Some fiber optic cable installations require SC or LC duplex couplers to couple the cable connector ends (for example, if you use wall jacks or connect to existing installed cables). HPE supports the use of duplex couplers, if you do not exceed the overall cable loss budget for that cable segment.

HPE recommends the use of HPE PremierFlex OM4 and OM3+ fiber optic cables for 50 micron cable installations. HPE PremierFlex OM3+ fiber optic cables provide higher bend performance and improved signal-transmission integrity, providing significant improvements in signal quality over industry-standard OM3 fiber optic cable technologies.

The HPE StoreFabric portfolio

The HPE StoreFabric portfolio includes:

- HPE FC switches

  - Gen6 FC (32 Gb FC)

  - Protocol support: 4/8/16/32 Gb/s FC

  - Ports: 24 to 64; active ports vary by model

- Brocade FC switches

  - Gen5 FC 16 Gb FC, embedded FC switches for HPE Synergy, or BladeSystem (c-class)

  - 12 to 16 downlinks

  - Internal ports and 12 uplinks; active ports vary by model

- HPE SAN Director

  - Gen6 B-series and Gen5 C-series

  - Ports: 48 to 511 ports

  - 32/16 Gb models available

  - Supports "six nines" availability

  - Redundant hot-swappable components

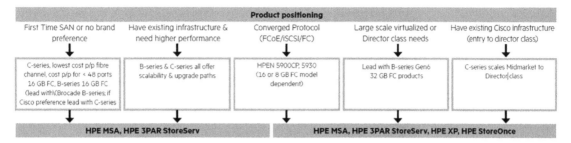

Figure 5-50 HPE StoreFabric product positioning

HPE StoreFabric storage networking advantage

From small- and mid-sized operations to data centers and the cloud, HPE StoreFabric, as shown in Figure 5-50, has dynamic end-to-end solutions that solve even your customer's most frustrating storage networking challenges.

HPE StoreFabric offers Gen6 and Gen5 (32/16 Gb) FC Storage Networking solutions that ensure that your customer's SAN does not suffer from an outdated infrastructure that was not designed to meet the needs of server virtualization or flash-based storage.

Include storage networking in all your storage discussions with your customer. Virtualization, flash, and Big Data are requiring faster networks; 4 Gb FC is in its End of Service Life (EOSL); and 8 Gb FC is starting to End of Life (EOL) too.

Gen6 Fibre Channel

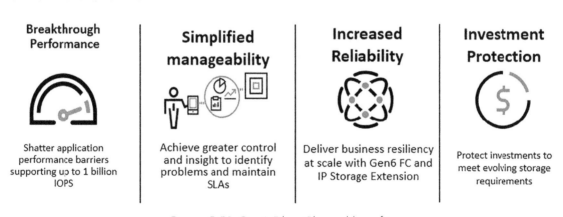

Figure 5-51 Gen6 Fibre Channel benefits

Today's mission-critical storage environments require greater consistency, predictability, and performance. Brocade Gen6 FC solutions meet those requirements by accelerating data access, adapting to evolving requirements, and driving always-on business operations. The HPE Gen6 SN8600B

Director combines innovative hardware, software, and built-in instrumentation to ensure the industry's highest level of operational stability while redefining application performance for hyperscale, mission-critical storage, as illustrated in Figure 5-51.

HPE StoreFabric FC switches

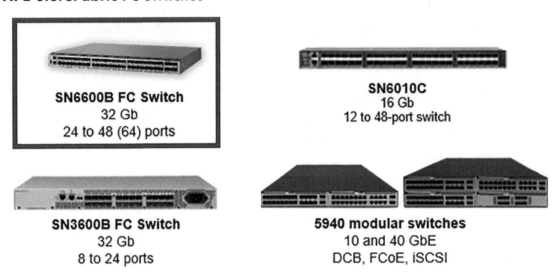

Figure 5-52 HPE StoreFabric FC switches

HPE StoreFabric FC switches product lines, as shown in Figure 5-52:

- HPE FlexFabric
- B-Series
- C-Series
- BladeSystem and Synergy switches

Differentiators include:

- **Hardware vendor**—H-Series (HPE), B-Series (Brocade), C-Series (Cisco)
- **Form factor**—BladeSystem, Synergy, rack
- **Protocol support**—FC, Fibre Channel over IP (FCIP), FCoE, Ethernet, Converged Enhanced Ethernet (CEE), ISL, SAS
- **Maximum number of ports**—16, 20, 22, 24, 48, over 80
- **Extra features**—SAN extension, stackable, encryption

HPE B-Series SAN portfolio

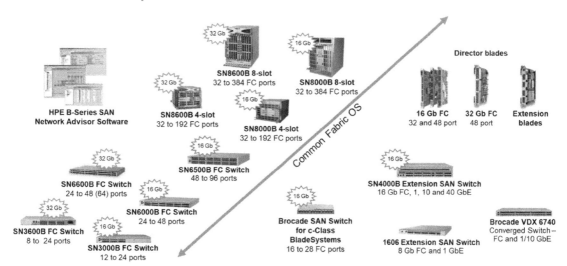

Figure 5-53 HPE B-Series

HPE B-Series switches are available from entry level up to director, providing connectivity from 8 G to 32 G. Ports are made available by the use of Ports on Demand (POD) licenses.

The HPE B-series portfolio, shown in Figure 5-53, offers HPE SAN Network Advisor Software for the management of B-series directors, routers, switches, HBAs, and FCoE devices. The HPE B-series SAN Network Advisor includes the same level of support for management of FC SANs as its predecessor, HPE B-series Data Center Fabric Manager (DCFM) and introduces management support of 16 Gb FC SANs.

The SAN Network Advisor offers management of data center fabrics including configuration, monitoring, and diagnostics. HPE B-series SAN Network Advisor provides comprehensive management of data center fabrics, including configuration, monitoring, and management of all B-series directors, switches, and HBAs. It provides support for FC SANs with configuration, zoning, and visualization capabilities, including HBA, storage, SAN fabric, and Layer 2 switch topology views.

SAN diagnostics help meet SLAs via proactive alerting and advanced SAN diagnostic capabilities, including SAN port diagnostics, bottleneck detection, and best-practices validation of SAN configurations.

HPE C-Series SAN portfolio

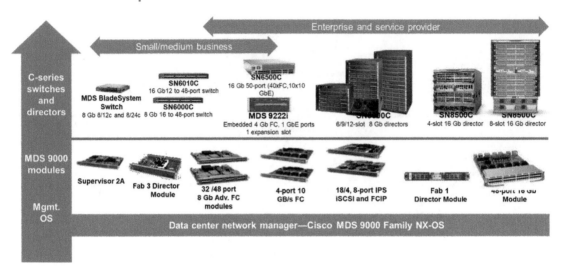

Figure 5-54 HPE C-Series

HPE partner, Cisco, delivers a comprehensive portfolio of switching solutions for enterprise networks, data centers, and smaller businesses, as illustrated in Figure 5-54. These solutions are optimized for a wide range of industries, including service providers, financial services, and the public sector.

HPE StoreFabric SN6600B Fibre Channel Switch

Figure 5-55 Midrange 32 GB SAN switch

HPE StoreFabric SN6600B Fibre Channel Switch, shown in Figure 5-55, is a high-performance, ultra-dense, highly scalable, easy-to-use enterprise-class storage networking switch delivering market-leading Gen6 FC capabilities. It is designed to support data growth, demanding workloads, and data center consolidation in small- to large-scale enterprise infrastructures. Delivering 32/128 Gb performance, industry-leading port density, and integrated network sensors, it accelerates data access, adapts to evolving requirements, and drives always-on businesses. It can scale from 24 to 64-ports with 48 SFP+ and four QSFP+ ports, all in an efficient 1U package. The SN6600B has a 3-3-3 warranty.

The HPE StoreFabric SN6600B Fibre Channel Switch scales up to 64 FC ports in an efficiently designed 1U form factor, delivering increased port density and space utilization for simplified scalability.

Each of the 48 SFP+ ports supports 4, 8, 10, 16, and 32 Gb FC speeds, while each of the four Quad Small Form-factor Pluggable (QSFP) ports can support 128 Gb.

 Note

SFPs are tri-speed. For example, a 32 GB SFP can operate at 32, 16, and 8 Gb speeds.

This midrange switch supports E, EX, F, diagnostic, and mirror ports.

Optional Power Pack+ software includes:

- 12-port upgrade

- Integrated routing

- ISL trunking

- SAN Network Advisor Professional+ or Enterprise

HPE StoreOnce

HPE StoreOnce is a stand-alone, disk-based data protection appliance that can be implemented as hardware or deployed as a software virtual storage appliance on VMware vSphere or Microsoft Hyper-V. The key features of StoreOnce are deduplication, compression, encryption, remote replication, and direct application-managed integration. Backup applications use StoreOnce backup systems as targets or can be unified with HPE 3PAR by using HPE Recovery Manager Central (RMC). The StoreOnce portfolio spans from entry to enterprise and can expand into the cloud with HPE Cloud Bank Storage—tripling usable capacity.

HPE StoreOnce—What is it?

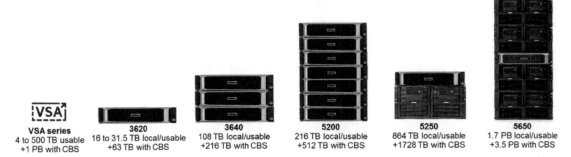

Figure 5-56 HPE StoreOnce systems portfolio

HPE StoreOnce, as shown in Figure 5-56, is a single deduplication engine to drive the movement of data across the entire organization. HPE provides a unified solution for low-cost, lights-out backup of remote offices. For environments that are too small for dedicated hardware-based backup solutions, HPE offers software-based deduplication and replication.

The StoreOnce deduplication engine means that data can be efficiently replicated or copied between remote data centers and regional offices and headquarters. The goal is to deliver these capabilities using a backup application to manage the entire data protection process.

HPE StoreOnce Catalyst

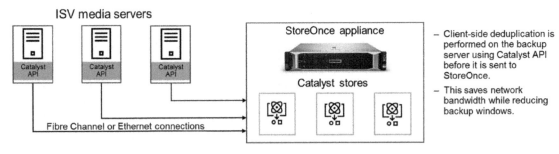

Figure 5-57 StoreOnce Catalyst

HPE StoreOnce Catalyst software, as illustrated in Figure 5-57, provides a simple, consistent, high-performing architecture that spans the organization. It delivers high backup speeds to meet shrinking backup windows. It also provides federated deduplication across the enterprise, including the consolidation of backup and disaster recovery (DR) from multiple remote offices to the data center. Multiple StoreOnce appliances and VMs can replicate to the central StoreOnce appliance. Your customers can protect data from unauthorized access through data-at-rest encryption and secure erase functionality for disks that are lost, stolen, or discarded.

Benefits for independent software vendor (ISV) software:

- Is a device that ISVs can use with none of restrictions of tape emulation and NAS shares. No unnecessary "geometry" limitations (library slots, cartridge sizes, and so on).

- Allows ISV software to be aware of the StoreOnce Backup system and its capabilities.

- Allows the backup server to support node failover in multinode systems without complex restart scripts (some ISV still have scripts) and restart from checkpoints.

- Use bandwidth efficient methods to move (copy) data without rehydration. This enables backup over wide area network (WAN) or local area network (LAN), with increased performance.

- Enables deduplication in different locations (federated deduplication).

- Enables ISV applications control copies of backups. Copy to multiple locations and to set different expiration dates. ISV is fully aware of all copies and jobs.

Catalyst provides tight integration with Micro Focus Data Protector and fully supports Symantec OST or Veeam. StoreOnce Cloud Bank leverages object storage for long-term retention of backup data copies. Features include:

- Control of copy to object storage using existing backup application

- Ability to take advantage of StoreOnce deduplication-optimized copy to the cloud

- Multi-threaded upload to cloud to minimize effects of latency

- Metadata for externally stored backup copies is cached locally

- Support for multiple object storage vendors

- Ability to leverage public cloud services for DR

HPE StoreOnce Cloud Bank Storage use cases

Use Case 1—Long-term backup retention:

- Wants to retain data for a long time as cheaply as possible

- Plans to seldom read the data, if ever

Use Case 2—Offsite DR protection:

- Wants to regularly send backups offsite for the purposes of DR protection

- No secondary site to replicate to

- Only plans to read the data for DR

Use Case 3—StoreOnce VSA in the cloud backed by Object Storage:

- Using StoreOnce VSA as a backup/replication target within Cloud Compute
- Would like to reduce running costs by hosting data on cheaper object storage

HPE StoreOnce Catalyst ISV integration

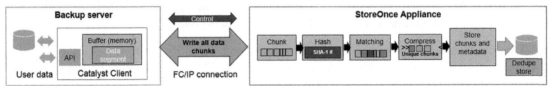

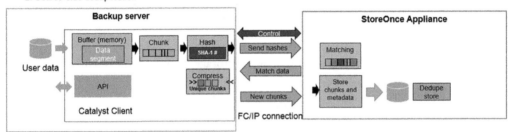

Figure 5-58 Target and source-side deduplication

Without Catalyst, there are only target-based deduplication for virtual tape library (VTL)/NAS. This dedupe architect is also being called high-bandwidth backup because during a full backup, the complete data capacity travels over a LAN/SAN.

Also, deduplication uses unidirectional communication, so the server has to use its own CPU/memory to do data replications and synthetic full backups, as shown in Figure 5-58.

With Catalyst, low-bandwidth backup, server-side/source-side deduplication are possible, so even in a full backup, only the unique blocks are sent by servers to StoreOnce.

As it is a bidirectional communication, the backup server can now offload jobs like data replication and generating a virtual synthetic full backup job to StoreOnce, and StoreOnce will inform the backup ISV after these jobs are finished.

Catalyst Stores allow backup applications to use:

- Low-bandwidth deduplication, server-side deduplication on
- High-bandwidth deduplication, server-side deduplication off

You can manage backup and DR operations from a single console with StoreOnce Catalyst. Catalyst over FC provides all the ISV control and source-side deduplication benefits of StoreOnce Catalyst but via an FC fabric. Automated, efficient backup and DR operations with StoreOnce Catalyst include:

- DR plans that were not previously feasible because of the lack of multi-site capabilities, cost of bandwidth, and time.

- One-to-many DR moves data simultaneously from one site to many sites.

- Cascaded DR moves data sequentially from one site to any number of other sites.

HPE StoreOnce 3640

Base unit

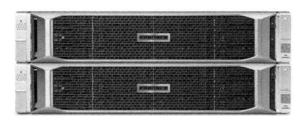

Expansion shelves

Figure 5-59 HPE StoreOnce 3640

HPE StoreOnce 3640, shown in Figure 5-59, delivers scalable backup and restore for small- to mid-sized data centers, and it provides an ideal replication target device for up to 36 remote and branch offices. This scalable 2U appliance offers from 36 to 108 TB of usable local capacity, using upgrade kits and up to 324 TB with Cloud Bank Storage and provides a solution to shrinking backup windows with speeds of up to 18 TB/hour using HPE StoreOnce Catalyst.

Actual performance depends on multiple factors including configuration, data type, data deduplication, data compression, the number of data streams, the number backup targets and concurrent tasks such as housekeeping, or replication. Actual capacity depends on multiple factors including data deduplication, data compression, storage formatting, log file size, metadata size, and the housekeeping backlog.

Actual usable capacity for customer data storage is dependent upon drive formatting, log file size, metadata size, and the housekeeping backlog.

StoreOnce 3640 (minimum configuration 36 TB usable) is based on HPE ProLiant Gen10 platform and contains two Intel® Xeon® 4110 Skylake CPUs (eight core). The front cage can accept 12 large form factor (LFF) disks. The maximum height with maximum expansion is 6U.

Other components include:

- Four 1 GbE NIC ports

- iLO 5

- Optional 10 GbaseT, 10/25 GbE, 16/32 Gb FC

- HPE p1224 SAS RAID controller

- HPE P408i Smart Array (for boot disks)

- Two 600 GB SFF operating system disks (at rear)

- SAS expander

- Dual redundant power supplies

What is HPE Recovery Manager Central?

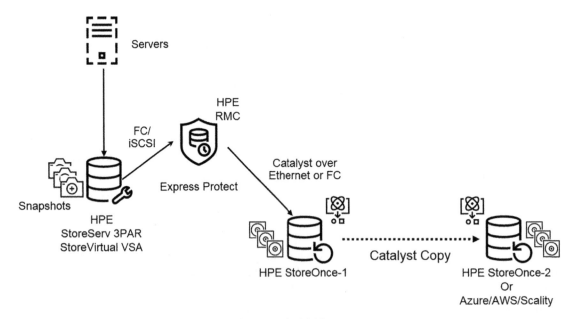

Figure 5-60 Example RMC environment

RMC integrates HPE 3PAR StoreServ and StoreVirtual storage with HPE StoreOnce Backup systems to provide a converged availability and backup service that offers an alternative to traditional backup software, as indicated in Figure 5-60.

Combining the performance of snapshots with the protection of backups, RMC enables fast, efficient, reliable, and simple protection for business-critical applications.

RMC leverages HPE 3PAR StoreServ and StoreVirtual snapshot technology and HPE StoreOnce Catalyst to provide a scalable backup system. This backup feature facilitates direct backup of HPE 3PAR StoreServ snapshots to HPE StoreOnce Backup Systems without the need for third-party backup software.

The RMC appliance is the data mover and runs in a VM. A Catalyst client "moves" the snapshot data to the StoreOnce Systems which deduplicates the data. RMC is a CentOS-based virtual appliance. It is deployed in the form of the VM on the supported hypervisor.

HPE RMC Express Protect Backup allows users to create application-consistent snapshots on an array and back them up directly to a StoreOnce physical or virtual appliance. Incremental changes are used to create and maintain an up-to-date, synthetic, full backup.

RMC:

- Is software that integrates HPE 3PAR StoreServ and StoreVirtual storage with HPE StoreOnce backup systems

- Offers an alternative to traditional backup software (supports flat backup of **any** data in these arrays)

- Provides fast and affordable end-to-end protection for SAP HANA, Oracle, Microsoft SQL databases, and VMware on 3PAR

- Combines the performance of snapshots with the protection of backups

- Offers direct backup of HPE 3PAR StoreServ snapshots to HPE StoreOnce backup systems (Express Protect)

- Provides a feature-rich REST API and could be used for scripting

HPE Recovery Manager Central ecosystem

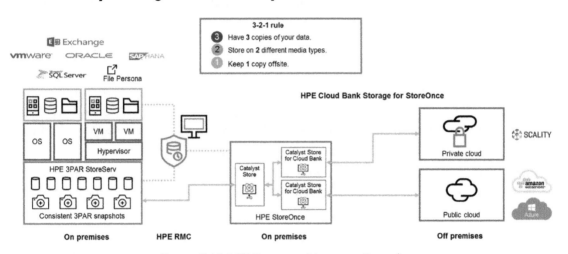

Figure 5-61 HPE Recovery Manager Central

An RMC solution is based on different components that work together, as illustrated in Figure 5-61. The result of this collaboration is that the snapshots that are created on the HPE 3PAR StoreServ get backed up in the Catalyst Store on HPE StoreOnce.

To get an idea about what Catalyst Store represents, you must know that each backup job requires a destination. Traditionally, the destination could be the tape device, a virtual tape library, or a shared folder. The backup engine capable of using the Catalyst Store as the backup destination benefits from its deduplication function, known as Federated Deduplication, which might be deployed across a storage infrastructure. The use of a common deduplication engine enables the native communication and movement of data across the various systems without rehydrating the data. Therefore, the subsequent snapshots moved to the Catalyst Store would be automatically deduplicated.

Virtual volumes are created on the HPE StoreServ and StoreVirtual, and they can belong the VMs or to the individual servers within the data center environment. Snapshots of these virtual volumes are created on the 3PAR using the 3PAR snapshot technology.

The VMware ESXi host is used to support the customer's VMs and a special virtual appliance executing the RMC engine.

The RMC graphical user interface (GUI) could be accessed over the network and is used for monitoring and initiating the Express Backup procedure.

Another important component is the vCenter plug-in. This plug-in will not work with the vCenter Appliance. It requires the vCenter running on the discrete server and only works with the vCenter web client.

Through the vCenter console, the administrator can initiate snapshots that will be crash consistent. The legacy version of the Recovery Manager requires the backup software to handle the creation of the snapshots and move that snapshot to the StoreOnce System. With RMC, there is no need for backup software, and the snapshot is moved directly from 3PAR to the StoreOnce System.

RMC and RMC-V

HPE RMC is a virtual appliance hosted on the VMware ESXi or Microsoft Hyper-V hypervisor. Its function is to move data between HPE 3PAR StoreServ and HPE StoreOnce and provide functionality to perform crash-consistent backups of virtual volumes.

HPE RMC-V is the vCenter plug-in used to integrate the RMC functionality into the VMware management GUI. RMC-V depends on the RMC appliance to move the data, but it orchestrates VMware operations to provide application-consistent backups of virtual volumes containing the VMware datastores.

Peer Copy

Peer Copy is a data movement technology to move data between HPE StoreVirtual to/from HPE StoreServ.

RMC data protection has many advantages compared to traditional data protection deployment:

- Snapshot based

- Utilizes 3PAR StoreServ thin provisioning technologies

- (Near) instantaneous snaps

- Block-level differentiation from ancestor to current snap

- Utilize Catalyst to deduplicate plus derive synthetic full backups (block modify for changed blocks in streams) (Express Protect)

- Restore as virtual volumes

RMC catalog maps snapshots to Catalyst objects; it is not the same as an ISV catalog.

The following is an RMC terminology list:

- Recovery set is a group of base volumes on which your application is hosted.

- Snapshot sets are group-consistent (created simultaneously) copies of the volumes in the recovery sets. RMC allows you to create snapshot sets for local recovery sets and remote recovery sets.

- Backup policies specify the target backup stores and backup-related attributes such as transport type, expiration time, and number of streams. You can use a backup policy to create multiple Express Protects.

- Copy policies (Catalyst Copy Policies) are the policies required for Catalyst Copy operations. To define a copy policy, select an existing backup policy.

- A replication set is used for bidirectional data replication between the primary storage systems, HPE 3PAR StoreServ and HPE StoreVirtual.

- Express Protect provides a second-tier of data protection with backup from HPE 3PAR StoreServ to HPE StoreOnce. Backups to HPE StoreOnce are block-level copies of volumes, deduplicated to save space, and can be used to recover back to the original or a different HPE 3PAR StoreServ or HPE StoreVirtual, even if the original base volume is lost.

- Catalyst Copy creates a copy of an Express Protect, snapshot, database on another HPE StoreOnce Catalyst Store, or on a different Catalyst Store of the same HPE StoreOnce.

HPE RMC Express Protect Backup

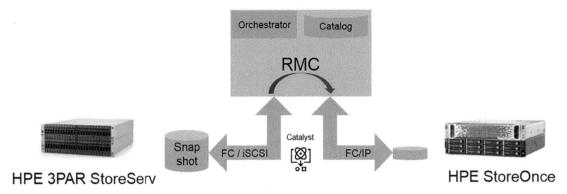

Figure 5-62 Simplified Express Protect Backup

RMC VM uses the Express Backup to move the data between HPE StoreServ or HPE StoreVirtual and StoreOnce, as shown in Figure 5-62. The Express Backup is initiated from the RMC console, and it orchestrates the end-to-end process:

- Creating the application-consistent snapshot

- Mounting the snapshot

- Moving the data to the HPE StoreOnce Appliance

Backup metadata is collected and stored in the internal catalog.

Management tools

HPE network management tools span across products and bring innovations to complete lifecycle management. As network management becomes more complex, the risks associated with compromised data flow have also increased.

HPE 3PAR StoreServ Management Console

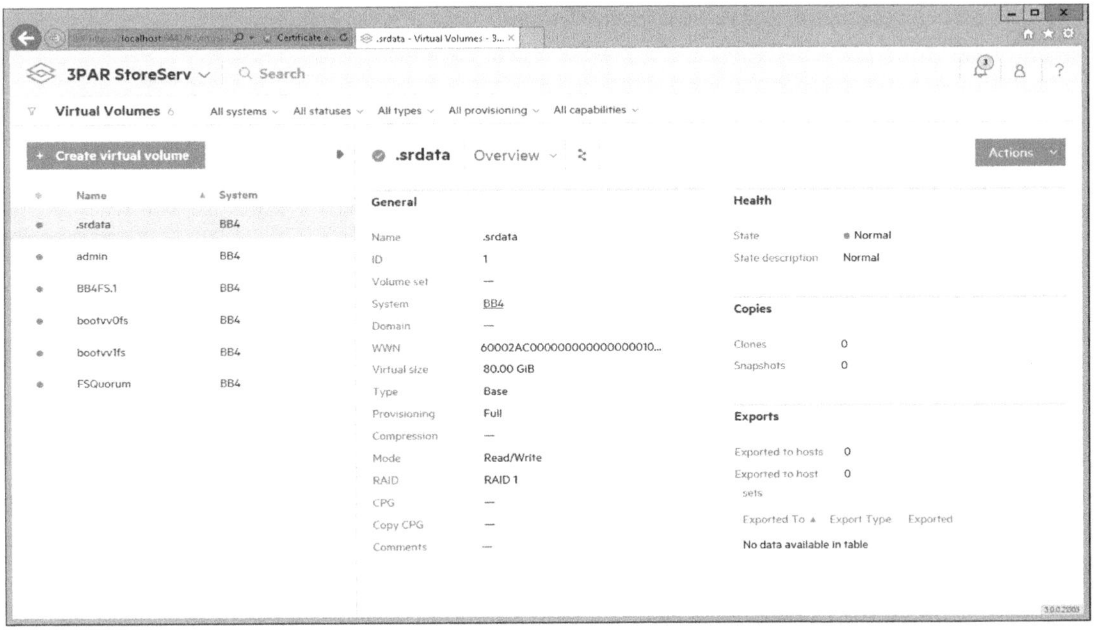

Figure 5-63 HPE 3PAR StoreServ Management Console

HPE 3PAR StoreServ Management Console (SSMC), as indicated in Figure 5-63, offers a modern look, a consistent feel, and a common interface and language with HPE Management tools such as HPE OneView. Designed to use the latest application program interface (API) and user interface (UI) technologies, HPE 3PAR SSMC centralizes all HPE 3PAR StoreServ Management under a single pane of glass and offers converged management and reporting for both file and block.

Accessible through a web-based UI, you can run your operations as HPE 3PAR SSMC tasks with an improved user experience and better responsiveness. All the information you need from HPE 3PAR StoreServ is available at a glance with customizable reporting capabilities, eliminating the need for add-on software tools or diagnostics and troubleshooting.

3PAR Service Console

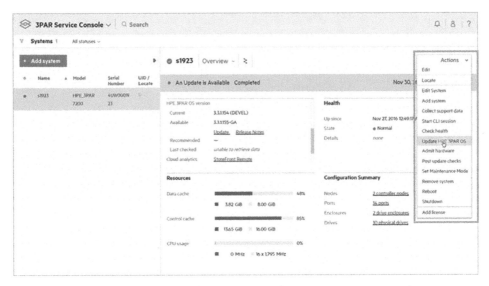

Figure 5-64 Checking for updates on the 3PAR Service Console

The 3PAR Service Console (SC), as indicated in Figure 5-64, also allows service functions to be per-formed by a company admin, HPE support, or an authorized service provider. SC replaces Service Processor Onsite Customer Care (SPOCC), the GUI for SP versions 4.4 and earlier. SC functionality is similar to SPOCC. The HPE 3PAR SC is an appliance that collects data from an attached 3PAR StoreServ Storage system in predefined intervals as well as an on-demand basis and sends the data to the call home infrastructure, if configured. The Service Processor (SP) is the platform on which the SC runs. It sends support data back to HPE and provides a way for HPE Technical Support Engineers to remotely log in to resolve problems. The SP is also needed for HPE InfoSight support. The SC is the GUI for the SP. It provides a streamlined, more usable interface with a layout that closely resem-bles the HPE 3PAR SSMC.

From Actions, you can check updates for your System OS or the SP.

- **Main menu and banner**—Clicking the menu area opens the main menu of screens. Selecting a screen from the menu displays a summary of configuration settings for the selected screen and provides Actions menus. Depending on the screen selected, system resources such as CPU usage, throughput, physical memory, and so on might be displayed.

- **Screens**—The Screens area displays tabular and graphical information and provides action dia-logs for managing storage systems.

- **Detail pane**—This displays the detailed information that can be seen and allows you to select further views.

- **List pane**—When you select an item in the List pane, additional information about it is displayed in the Detail pane. When an item is selected, you can perform actions on it. Many lists can be sorted and filtered and include multiple views that you can select.

- **Actions**—The Actions menu allows you to perform actions on one or more resources that you have selected, in the list pane. If you do not have permission to perform an action, the action does not display in the menu. Also, some actions might not display because of system configurations, user roles, or properties of the selected resource.

Remote benefits of the SP include:

- **Remote diagnostics**—Key diagnostic information maintained centrally on a historical basis. System health statistics, configuration data, performance data, and system events can be transferred frequently and maintained centrally. As a result, proactive fault detection and analysis are maximized, and manual intervention is minimized.

- **Remote serviceability**—SP provides fast predictive response and remediation. HPE 3PAR technical support delivers rapid responses with 24x7 remote monitoring and analysis to identify issues and proactively communicate them back to the customer. As an integrated support model, HPE 3PAR technical support can remotely connect to a customer's HPE 3PAR StoreServ system through a secure IP connection to resolve issues quickly and reduce onsite visits.

- **Remote online software upgrade**—Upgrade software with no application disruption. Changes to the HPE 3PAR OS software are released for new functionality, maintenance updates, and software patches. The ability to apply these updates can be serviced as an online upgrade, where the arrays' capability to process customer data does not need to be disrupted during the software upgrade.

Additional features of the HPE 3PAR SP include:

- Collects periodic data from HPE 3PAR StoreServ (alerts, configuration, events, performance, status, and so on)

- Performs hourly health checks on the HPE 3PAR StoreServ system

- Provides remote support capabilities over Ethernet

- Serves as a local maintenance terminal for onsite support

- Serves as a remote maintenance terminal for remote support

- Contains guided maintenance scripts used for guided parts replacement activities

VSP infrastructure planning and deployment best practices

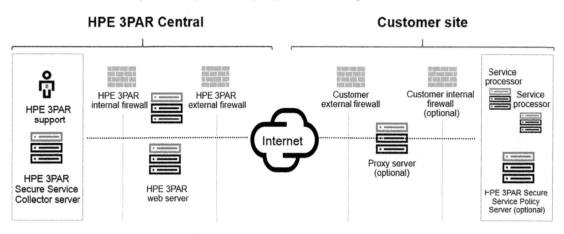

Figure 5-65 VSP infrastructure planning and deployment best practices

The SP can be deployed in two modes: SP mode or Secure Network mode (which is recommended). SP mode enables communication between an SP (version 4.3 and below) and the HPE 3PAR connection portal server located at HPE, as illustrated in Figure 5-65.

In Secure Network mode, the SP communicates with the HPE 3PAR Collector Server using the HPE 3PAR Secure Service Agent (SSA). The Collector Server provides software updates, access to service tool applications, and access to resources such as the HPE Support Center. Rather than using a connection portal to connect to HPE 3PAR Central, an SP in Secure Network mode requires SSA for the connection. The SSA facilitates communication between the SP and Collector Server. Communications are performed using HTTPS.

Secure Network mode is the preferred method of transfer because it is secure and offers the most access control options. This mode is easy for users to implement in the firewall. When using HPE 3PAR VSP in Secure Network mode, use Port 443 for the bidirectional communication. When deploying the HPE 3PAR VSP, using the Secure Network mode is recommended.

Local notification service

The SP local notification features enable users to request notifications for important storage system events and alerts on a subscription basis. Notifications are sent through email to all subscribers, with each subscriber specifying up to three email addresses. When Real-time Alert Processing (RAP) forwarding is enabled, copies of all notification messages sent to subscribers are automatically forwarded to HPE 3PAR Central as well.

There are two types of local notification messages that users might receive:

- **Standard notification messages**—Standard notification is a text-based email message that alerts users to an important event or an alert generated by a storage system.

- **Grouped, low-urgency notification messages**—A grouped, low-urgency notification is a text-based email message that informs users of noncritical events generated by a storage system.

Low-urgency notification messages are informational and do not typically require any corrective action. When a situation or event reported in a low-urgency notification message becomes urgent, a standard notification message is issued to alert subscribers.

System support information

It is critical that the VSP contains the correct system support information. The installation site information and customer contact information are critical to support delivery. Having the latest information helps ensure that service calls are completed without any issues because of incorrect or outdated contact information.

Remote support

All HPE 3PAR customers are required to run SP. This enables HPE to provide customers with the best possible remote support for their HPE 3PAR storage systems, including:

- Timely remote service

- Remote online software updates

- Accelerated troubleshooting and issue resolution

Remote support sends diagnostic information (for example, system health statistics, configuration data, performance data, and system events) to HPE 3PAR Central. These diagnostics are required for HPE to perform fault detection and analysis on HPE 3PAR StoreServ systems, which helps maximize storage availability.

All remote communications are encrypted and transferred securely to HPE 3PAR Central, and no customer application data is ever transferred. No other business information is collected, and the data is managed according to the HPE Data Privacy policy.

Remote support can be configured during the initial setup of the HPE 3PAR StoreServ system using the HPE 3PAR SmartStart process in the SP setup wizard. You can validate and test the connectivity using SPOCC. HPE highly recommends having remote support deployed and configured for your system.

VSP networking configuration

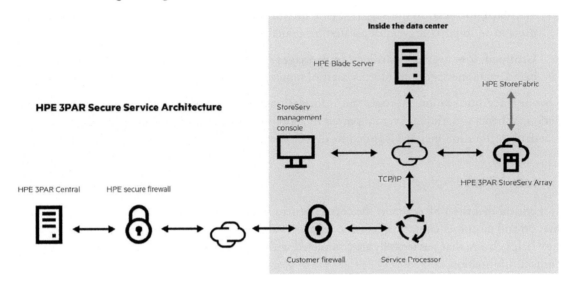

Figure 5-66 VSP networking configuration

HPE recommends that the VSP be configured with a static IP address, as indicated in Figure 5-66. Providing network redundancy to the virtual network cards of the VSP enables availability in case of different failure scenarios. Users should consider using network card teaming in the hypervisor when supported. They can also consider using multiple network cards and physical network switches to avoid a single point of failure on the hypervisor, which might affect the VSP network connectivity.

Each VSP manages one HPE 3PAR StoreServ system. Users should consider separating each VSP from the HPE 3PAR StoreServ system that it is managing. This helps ensure that the VSP is available to troubleshoot any issues with the array. Users can deploy the VSP on the local disk of the hypervisor or put it on another array that the VSP is not managing.

Putting the VSP on shared storage allows users to leverage hypervisor high-availability options or mobility features. VMotion is the vSphere technology used to move VMs across datastores. If VSP runs from an internal local drive, you can migrate it with the latest vSphere enhancements. HPE recommends running it on a different shared storage. It is also recommended that thin provisioning be used when deploying the disk for the VSP. It reduces the amount of disk space that the VSP consumes.

STaTS

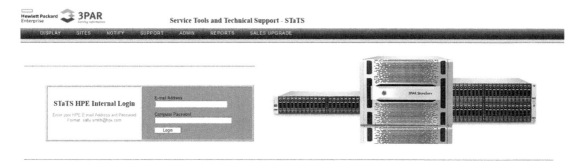

Figure 5-67 STaTS

Data collected from the HPE 3PAR Secure Service Architecture is stored at HPE in a central repository known as Service Tools and Technical Service (STaTS), as indicated in Figure 5-67. STaTS allows authorized HPE personnel to access historical performance, event, and configuration data from customers of HPE 3PAR StoreServ arrays. STaTS data is guarded and always treated as HPE Confidential data. In some cases, customer site-specific data may be retained in HPE service records as a service to customers. The data retention allows for quick analysis of a customer's storage and access to event data from previous data captures. Data stored within the STaTS database can only be accessed by securely authenticated and authorized HPE employees associated with the users account.

You can review specific information about a customer's solutions, including:

- Configuration date

- Model and version numbers

- Number of nodes, cages, magazines, or drives

- Capacity

 Note

You can access the tool using an HPE Passport login through the HPE Partner Portal at:
https://partner.hpe.com/

StoreOnce Management Console

Figure 5-68 StoreOnce Management Console

The StoreOnce Management Console, shown in Figure 5-68, is the primary interface to configure and manage all backup targets and Catalyst copy functions. To access the console, browse to the IP address or Fully Qualified Domain Name (FQDN) of the StoreOnce System.

Management federation

Management federation allows administrators to manage multiple StoreOnce systems from a single appliance. The managing system in a federation is called the lead system and the other systems in the federation are called member systems. When logged into a lead system, administrators can manage not only that system but also any of the member systems in the federation. For example, from the lead system you can create StoreOnce Catalyst Stores on any member systems in the federation. The Federation Dashboard screen on a lead system displays aggregated information. When logged into a member system, you can manage the system as usual, however, you cannot manage other systems in the federation from a member system.

Figure 5-69 Federation Dashboard

The Federation Dashboard on a member system indicates that the system is part of a federation. Multiple federations can be configured where StoreOnce systems can be leads, members, or both within overlapping federation domains. The Federation Dashboard, shown in Figure 5-69, provides a single view for management and reporting for up to 20 VSA and physical systems (up to 100 by request).

HPE StoreOnce Recovery Manager Central

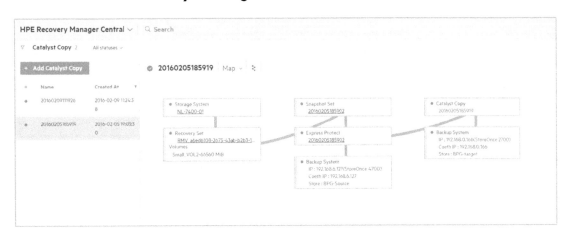

Figure 5-70 HPE StoreOnce Recovery Manager Central

The RMC GUI is used to manage and monitor tasks in RMC appliance (VM deployed from the template).

Using the RMC GUI, as indicated in Figure 5-70, you can perform the following:

- View all the tasks performed in RMC appliance using dashboard.

- Add storage systems and backup systems.

- Create snapshots, Express Protect backups, and Catalyst Copies.

- Add users and assign roles.

- Schedule snapshots and Express Protect backups.

- Schedule and configure Catalog Protection of the RMC appliance to the network share or Catalyst Store.

- Access all the features of RMC-S, RMC-O, RMC-SH, and RMC-E.

- Restart or shut down the appliance.

- Replicate data between source storage system and target storage system. You can also schedule data replication.

- Generate a support ticket.

- Diagnose RMC issues by checking the status of subsystems.

InfoSight—Leading AI for hybrid cloud

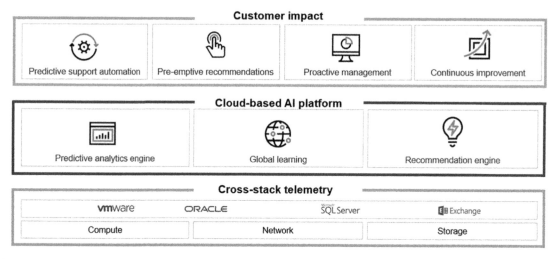

Figure 5-71 InfoSight summary

HPE InfoSight is built on a unique approach to data collection and analysis, as indicated in Figure 5-71. It starts with having the right data. Data from the infrastructure has always been limited to log files and graphs on obvious metrics and stuck on-prem. InfoSight takes a much more comprehensive approach. Every second, InfoSight is collecting thousands of embedded sensors built into every array and pulling in data from across the infrastructure stack

And we are not just analyzing individual systems, but we are also analyzing all the systems in our installed base in our cloud-based AI platform, where we use machine learning to generate predictive analytics, continuously learn from every system, and automate recommendations that improve every environment.

InfoSight takes a comprehensive approach to data collection and analysis. Data is the key to InfoSight's global learning. Every second, millions of sensor measurements capturing the state of the systems, subsystems, and surrounding IT infrastructure in our global installed base are collected and analyzed. InfoSight continuously learns from the telemetry and develops an understanding of the ideal operating environment for every system, workload, and application.

Advanced machine learning then drives InfoSight's predictive analytics and recommendation engines, where problematic behavior is predicted through recognition of the underlining patterns and configurations in each system.

InfoSight features:

- Predictive support automation

    - Predicts and prevents issues

    - Solves problems across infrastructure

    - Transforms the support experience

- AI-driven management

    - Makes managing effortless

    - Optimizes resource allocation

    - Sees what others cannot

- Unique product experience

    - Makes the infrastructure smarter

    - Enables the infrastructure to self-improve

    - Simulates work-load changes

- Provides access to various documents, such as HPE Nimble Storage Integration Guide

This platform drives predictive support automation (predicting and automating resolution to problems before they can impact customers), preemptive recommendations (decisions that are automatically made for IT that prevent issues and improve every environment), proactive management through advanced analytics in our cloud portal, and continuous improvement of our systems (making them smarter and more reliable).

The benefits have been game-changing. As demonstrated with Nimble Storage:

- Predictive support enables us to deliver a radically better support experience. Eighty-six percent of problems are predicted and automatically resolved before customers even realize there is an issue, where 54% are even beyond storage. This automation has enabled Nimble Storage to completely automate Level 1 and 2 support.

- AI-driven management has made managing infrastructure effortless and brings 79% lower storage OpEx.

- Infrastructure is no longer sitting idle and unconscious. It is self-improving. This is realized in the fact that Nimble Storage has over 99.9999% of measured, proven, and guaranteed availability across its installed base, going back to the first array that ever shipped and across all OS, models, and configurations. Historically, infrastructure gets less reliable as it ages, but Nimble has flipped that paradigm with InfoSight.

InfoSight has fundamentally transformed how infrastructure is managed and supported. Traditional infrastructures were not designed with the intelligence to effectively harness the data across a hybrid cloud world. More specifically, IT departments are constantly reacting to problems, with considerable time spent on troubleshooting/doing nonvalue-added activities. These factors dictate that a new level of intelligent resources needs to be applied to tackle the data challenge and effectively bridge from discovery to insight to action.

HPE InfoSight brings simplified, AI-driven operations to your customer's hybrid cloud world that transforms how infrastructure is managed and supported. It uses cloud-based artificial intelligence to provide global insights into the status and health of infrastructure, all in one location. As it analyzes and correlates millions of sensors every minute, all customers benefit as their systems get smarter and more reliable. InfoSight watches over your customer's infrastructure 24x7, so they do not have to spend their days, nights, and weekends dealing with infrastructure issues anymore.

Analytics are only as good as the data available to analyze. Data has always been limited to one-off log files on obvious metrics or bolted on to collect data after an event—and it has always been analyzed one array at a time. We consciously architected for predictive analytics when we started. This required taking a fundamentally different approach to data collection. When we started, we began embedding sensors into every module of code in our operating system to understand all the factors that can impact the IO path.

The plan for HPE is to extend InfoSight and its AI and predictive capabilities across the portfolio. InfoSight supports many platforms, such as Nimble, 3PAR StoreServ, and ProLiant, Synergy, and Apollo servers with iLO5 and iLO4.

The self-healing, self-managing, and self-optimizing data center is all about taking advantage of all the rich telemetry that is available across the installed base and doing something with that telemetry to make intelligent decisions.

HPE InfoSight: Improving efficiency through AI

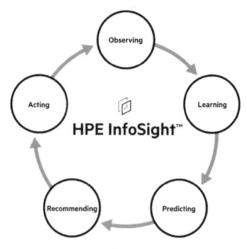

Figure 5-72 HPE InfoSight

There are five key steps in the machine learning and predictive analytics process of InfoSight that are built on top of each other, as illustrated in Figure 5-72:

- **Observing**—The 1000s of data points and sensors built into the HPE server and storage products

- **Learning**—Applying advanced pattern recognition to the sensor data collected across all devices globally

- **Predicting**—Anticipating problems based on the observations and learnings

- **Recommending**—Intelligent decisions that prevent issues, improve performance, and optimize resources

- **Acting**—Automation resulting in game-changing benefits and outcomes

By performing the five keys steps iteratively over time, InfoSight gets smarter every second and sees beyond the limits of other tools because of its unique approach to data collection and analysis.

InfoSight—A cloud-based management and support system

Figure 5-73 InfoSight

HPE InfoSight, shown in Figure 5-73, is a cloud-based management and support system that:

- Integrates, automates, and substantially simplifies administrative storage tasks

- Automatically opens 90% of all support cases and generates resolutions for more than 80%

- Provides actionable recommendations on how to scale storage resources

- Enables you to:

  - Easily and quickly meet changing SLAs with expert guidance on storage resource planning

  - Obtain detailed planning data for more informed decision making

  - Maintain peak storage health with accurate, real-time performance analytics

  - Simplify storage management with a single cloud-connected portal

HPE InfoSight for Servers

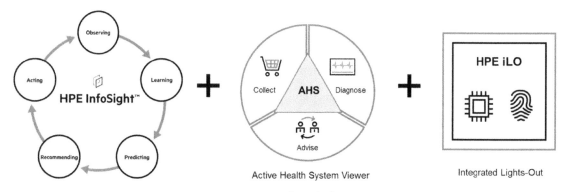

Figure 5-74 HPE InfoSight for Servers

InfoSight for Servers is the extension of InfoSight for ProLiant, Synergy, and Apollo Gen10, Gen9, and Gen8 servers with iLO 5 and iLO 4, as indicated in Figure 5-74.

The initial release of InfoSight for Servers will include:

- Predictive analytics to predict and prevent problems

    - Data analytics for server security

    - Predictive data analytics for parts failure

- Global learning that provides wellness and performance dashboards for your customer's global inventory of servers

- A recommendation engine to eliminate performance bottlenecks on servers

HPE InfoSight for Servers has three major components:

- **InfoSight for Servers**—With InfoSight for Servers, HPE combines the cloud-based machine learning of InfoSight with the health and performance monitoring of Active Health System (AHS) and Integrated Lights-Out (iLO) to optimize performance and predict and prevent problems on Gen10, Gen9, and Gen8 ProLiant, Synergy, and Apollo servers.

- **AHS:**

    - AHS is like a "flight recorder" for the server that provides continuous, proactive health monitoring, and recording 1000s of system parameters and diagnostic telemetry data 24x7 on the server.

    - AHS is available on Gen10, Gen9, and Gen8 servers with iLO 5 and iLO 4.

- **iLO:**

    - iLO is HPE's management processor that is embedded on the ProLiant, Apollo, and Synergy servers.

    - iLO and AHS are tightly integrated and work together to gather and record the 1000s of system parameters and diagnostic telemetry data.

    - Access to AHS is through iLO (customers access the AHS data through iLO).

It is important to note that although InfoSight for Servers is new, the capturing and recording of health, configuration, and performance sensor and telemetry data at the individual server level has been around since AHS was introduced in Gen8 with iLO 4. What's new with InfoSight for Servers is the automatic collection of this data into InfoSight.

Cross-stack analytics for VMware environments

Figure 5-75 Cross-Stack Analytics for VMware Environments

A difficult and common problem for customers is identifying and resolving performance bottlenecks in virtualized environment. InfoSight cross-stack analytics save customers tremendous time. The solution correlates storage with VMware to quickly diagnose the root cause to performance problems—identify if it is coming from the host, VMs, network, or array, as illustrated in Figure 5-75.

Cross-Stack Analytics for VMware Environments include following features:

- **Noisy neighbor**—Determine if VMs are hogging resources from another VM. Feature is accessible via VM I/O Contention Treemap view.

- **Host and memory analytics**—Visibility into host CPU and memory metrics

- **Latency attribution**—Identify root cause across host, storage, or SAN

- **Inactive VMs**—Visibility into inactive VMs to repurpose/reclaim resources

- **Top performing VMs**—Visibility into Top 10 VMs by IOPS and latency

Activity: HPE Reference Architecture for Oracle RAC 12c best practices and scaling on HPE Synergy Gen10 platforms and HPE 3PAR StoreServ 9450 Storage

1. Use this document:
   https://h20195.www2.hpe.com/v2/getdocument.aspx?docname=a00049200enw

2. Answer the following questions:

   a. Which file on the Linux server contains configuration of multipathing?

   _____

   _____

   b. Which utility can fix the discrepancy between free space reported by 3PAR StoreServ system and Oracle Automatic Storage Management?

   _____

   _____

   c. What is the best-practice for enabling compression—at the array level or Oracle level?

      – What is the benefit of best-practice approach?

   _____

   _____

   _____

   _____

   _____

   _____

   _____

   _____

   _____

Solution components

Part numbers are at the time of publication and subject to change. The BOM does not include complete support options or other rack and power requirements.

		Storage
1	BW904A	HPE 42U 600X1075mm Enterprise Shock Rack
1	Q0E92A	HPE 3PAR StoreServ 9450 2N+SW Storage Base
2	Q7F41A	HPE 3PAR 9450+SW Storage Node
4	Q0E96A	HPE 3PAR 9000 4pt 12Gb SAS HBA
8	Q0E97A	HPE 3PAR 9000 4-pt 16Gb FC Adapter
80	Q0F40A	HPE 3PAR 9000 400GB+SW SFF SSD
2	QK753B	HPE SN6000B 16Gb 48/24 FC Switch
48	QK724A	HPE B-series 16Gb SFP+SW XCVR
48	QK735A	HPE Premier Flex LC/LC OM4 2f 15m Cbl
8	QK734A	HPE Premier Flex LC/LC OC4 2f 5m Cbl
1	P9M30A	HPE 3PAR Direct Connect Cabling Option
1	Q1H95A	HPE 3PAR 1U Rack Accessories Kit
16	716197-B21	HPE Ext 2.0m MiniSAS HD to MiniSAS HD Cbl
8	Q0E95A	HPE 3PAR 9000 2U SFF SAS Drive Encl
1	Q0F86A	HPE 3PAR StoreServ RPS Service Processor
1	TK808A	HPE Rack Front Door Cover Kit
4	P9Q39A	HPE G2 Basic Mdlr 4.9kVA/C19 NA/JP PDU
1	BW932A	HPE 600mm Rack Stabilizer Kit
1	BW906A	HPE 42U 1075mm Side Panel Kit
1	L7F19A	HPE 3PAR All-inclusive Single-system Latest Media

The Reference Architecture and customer scenario do not match completely, the backup solution, StoreOnce is missing and the FC switch needs to support 32 Gb.

Learning check

4. Match the data protection product/technology with its description.

HPE StoreOnce	Software that integrates array with backup systems
Catalyst	Stand-alone, disk-based data protection appliance
HPE Recovery Manager Central	Backup protocol developed by HPE

5. Name three features that are part of HPE 3PAR StoreServ.

_____

_____

_____

_____

6. Match the HPE 3PAR StoreServ array with maximum front-end performance characteristics (IOPS) when RAID1 is used and 100% random read.

20800	3'200'000
9450	1'000'000
20850	1'800'000
8440	3'800'000

7. Select the management tool you will use for daily management tasks on 3PAR array, such as creating volumes. (Select A, B, or C.)

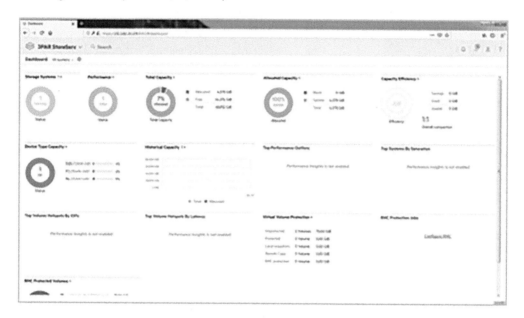

A

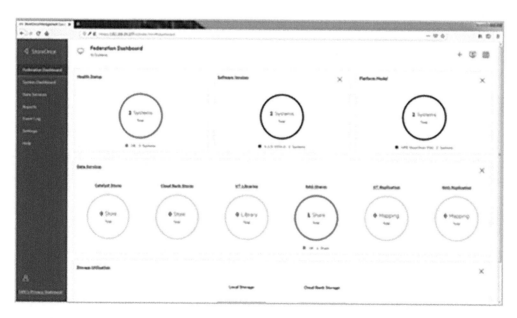

B

C

8. Which ports can be used to connect HPE 3PAR StoreServ 8000 to servers?

Alternative components for different environments

We presented a validated solution for customer scenario. Some of the solution components, however, can be changed for alternative environments, where different performance, capacity, costs, features, and similar requirements can be satisfied with other HPE solutions. Not all the workloads are the same and a single HPE product cannot match all the requirements.

HPE 3PAR StoreServ 8000

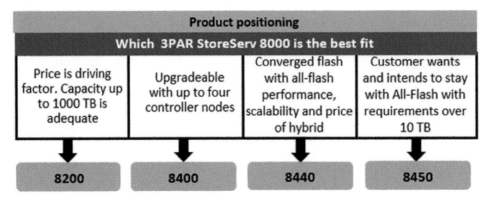

Figure 5-76 HPE 3PAR StoreServ 8000 product positioning

HPE 3PAR StoreServ 8000, shown in Figure 5-76, is the ideal solution for customers who:

- Need an affordably priced, non-disruptive solution that is scalable to four nodes

- Are looking for true convergence of file, block, and object

- Require a single architecture to take advantage of common data services, including integrated file services, and common management across their data center

- Deploy some or all applications and data types in physical or virtual environments and the cloud

- Need to upgrade their SAN, especially in virtualized environments, or to address unpredictable workloads with a modern architecture

- Require low latency and higher speed support for higher VM density

- Are large customers/enterprise customers needing departmental storage

Thanks to the all-inclusive software licensing, 3PAR is the only array with included software that optimizes the entire IO path for flash at no additional cost:

- File Persona increases capacity requirements by opening up new file-based workloads for consolidation.

- Smart SAN simplifies StoreFabric attach with SAN zoning automation of 16/32 Gb switches.

- RMC drives StoreOnce attach with flash-integrated data protection.

HPE 3PAR StoreServ delivers one architecture from midrange to enterprise, including an all-flash array with integrated file, block, and object access, as well as common data services and common management across the portfolio.

Additional features of HPE 3PAR StoreServ 8000:

- Multi-tenant with support for multiple applications and workload in secure virtual domains

- Efficient with adaptive data reduction technologies (including deduplication and compression) that reduce capacity by over 75%

- Autonomic and self-configuring to improve administration efficiency

- Federated Peer-to-Peer transparency, non-disruptive data mobility

- QoS to assure service level for most critical business applications

HPE 3PAR StoreServ 8400 node pair

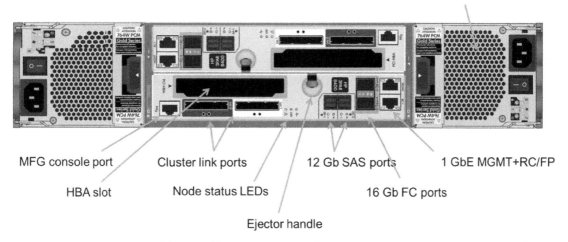

Figure 5-77 A pictorial layout of key components of an HPE 3PAR StoreServ controller shelf

The port numbering convention is Node:Slot:Port (N:S:P) and is used in the creation of the 3PAR World Wide Name (WWN).

The example in Figure 5-77 graphic assumes Node 0, so the port number referenced is the onboard FC port slot (slot 1), and the port referenced is port 2 (0:1:2).

The management (MGMT) port is used to connect to the network for storage array management.

 Note

The 8000 series uses Gen3 PCIe versus Gen2 PCIe in the 7000 series models.

Each 8000 series controller contains:

- One built-in 1 GbE Remote Copy

- One built-in 1 GbE management port

- Two built-in 16 Gb FC ports

- Two four-lane 12 Gb/s SAS drive chassis connections

- Two four-node cluster interconnects

- An optional PCI-e card slot

 Note

Slot 3 contains the RCIP data replication port (used for Remote Copy), but can also be configured and used with the File Persona feature.

 Note

Visit the Customer Self Repair Services Media Library—Media Selection site at:

https://sml-csr.ext.hpe.com/.

HPE 3PAR StoreServ 8000 controller nodes

Per node configuration

1 Intel® Ivy Bridge Processor
- – 8200   6-core 2.2 GHz
- – 8400   6-core 2.2 GHz
- – 8440   10-core 2.4 GHz
- – 8450   10-core 2.4 GHz

Data cache
- – 8200   16 GB
- – 8400   16 GB
- – 8440   32 GB
- – 8450   32 GB

Control cache
- – 8200   16 GB
- – 8400   16 GB
- – 8440   64 GB
- – 8450   64 GB

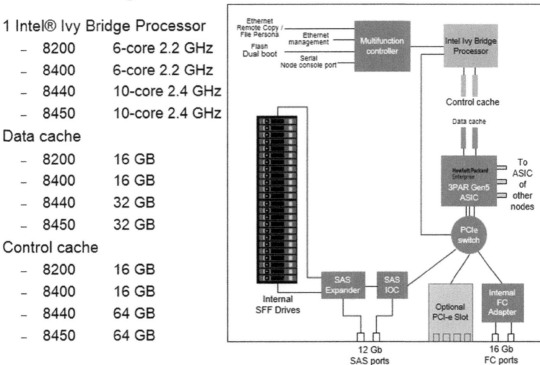

Figure 5-78 The core components of the HPE 3PAR StoreServ controllers

The HPE 3PAR StoreServ 8000 Storage requires one storage base (controller node enclosure), as illustrated in Figure 5-78. These are the available options:

- **HPE 3PAR StoreServ 8000 Storage 2-node Storage Base**—2U controller node enclosure with 24 SFF 6.4 cm (2.5 in) drive bays at the front and two controller nodes at the rear.

- **HPE 3PAR StoreServ 8000 Storage 4-node Storage Base**—Two 2U controller node enclosures totaling 48 SFF 6.4 cm (2.5 in) drive bays at the front and four controller nodes at the rear.

Important

An upgrade from a two-node to a four-node storage system applies only to the following models with a limit of four-nodes per storage system:

- HPE 3PAR StoreServ 8400 Storage
- HPE 3PAR StoreServ 8440 Storage
- HPE 3PAR StoreServ 8450 Storage

HPE 3PAR StoreServ 8000 12 Gb SAS drive enclosures

Figure 5-79 HPE 3PAR StoreServ small and large form factor

The 8000 Series supports two types of expansion cages: a 2U 24-drive 2.5" SFF cage and a 4U 24-drive 3.5" LFF, both with a 12 Gb SAS interface, as indicated in Figure 5-79.

The 8000 series expansion cages support both 6 Gb and 12 Gb SAS drives.

 Note

The SFF cages (including the base enclosure) only support a 2 TB 7.2k near line (NL) disks. The LFF expansion cage supports 2, 4, and 6 TB NL disks.

 Note

The LFF expansion cage does not support any 10 k or 15 k FC (fast class) disks and only supports a cMLC 480 GB SSD. No data encryption can be done on the cMLC SSD disks (including the 8450 model) in the LFF expansion cage.

The 8000 series array uses a C:M:D addressing convention where C = cage, M = magazine, and D = disk. This is a legacy issue where the T and 10000 series used a cage with magazines. None of the current 3PARs use magazines, but the C:M:D addressing convention is still used to identify a disk.

The D = Disk value will always be zero (0). For example, if a disk had failed in disk bay 12 in cage 2, the number of the drive would be 2.11.0. The reason it is 11 and not 12 is because HPE 3PAR drives are numbered from 0 to 23 in a 24-drive cage.

HPE 3PAR StoreServ 8000 hardware architecture

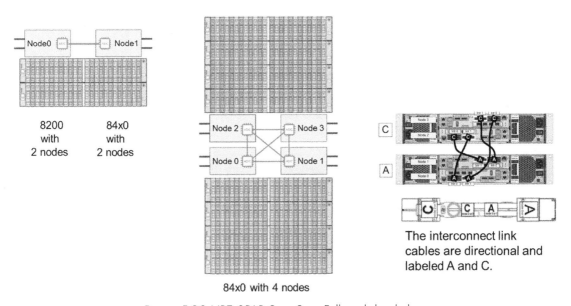

Figure 5-80 HPE 3PAR StoreServ Full-mesh backplane

Backplane interconnects within servers have evolved dramatically over the years. Most, if not all, server and storage array architectures have traditionally employed simple bus-based backplanes for high-speed processor, memory, and IO communication. Parallel to the growth of Symmetric multi-processing (SMP)-based servers, significant investments were also made to switch architectures, which have been applied to one or two enterprise storage arrays.

The move from buses to switches was intended to address latency issues across the growing number of devices on the backplane (more processors, larger memory, and IO systems). Third-generation full-mesh interconnects first appeared in the late 1990s in enterprise servers.

The HPE 3PAR StoreServ full-mesh backplane, as illustrated in Figure 5-80, is a passive circuit board that contains slots for up to four or eight controller nodes, depending on the model. As noted earlier, each controller node slot is connected to every other controller node slot by a high-speed link (4 GB/s in each direction, or 8 GB/s total), forming a full-mesh interconnect between all controller nodes in the cluster—something that HPE refers to as a "Mesh-Active" design. These interconnects deliver low-latency, high-bandwidth communication and data movement between controller nodes through dedicated point-to-point links and a low overhead protocol that features rapid internode messaging and acknowledgment. It is important to note that, while the value of these interconnects is high, the cost of providing them is relatively low. In addition, a completely separate full-mesh network of serial links provides a redundant low-speed channel of communication for exchanging control information between the nodes.

The HPE 3PAR StoreServ 20000 features an eight-node-capable backplane that supports two to eight controller nodes. HPE 3PAR StoreServ 8000 systems feature either a dual-node- or quad-node-capable system that is essentially an equivalent of what was used in former enterprise-class arrays that offer the same high-speed links between nodes.

HPE 3PAR StoreServ 8000 hardware building blocks

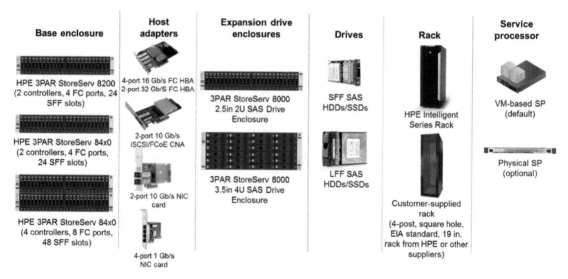

Figure 5-81 The basic building blocks of an HPE 3PAR StoreServ array

Each HPE 3PAR StoreServ 8000 requires its own service processor. The SP functions as the communication interface between a customer's IP network and HPE 3PAR Central by managing all service-related communications, as indicated in Figure 5-81. The SP leverages the industry-standard HTTP over Secure Sockets Layer (HTTPS) protocol to secure and encrypt data communication. The SP can be deployed either as a VSP or a physical SP.

A VSP is included free with the base HPE 3PAR Operating System. The VSP can be installed on a customer-provided VMware or Microsoft Hyper-V system.

The physical SP is a dedicated storage appliance located within the storage rack, providing close proximity to the HPE 3PAR StoreServ 8000 Storage. The physical SP is fully supported and maintained by HPE Services. The physical SP has serial port connectivity that provides maintenance access for troubleshooting capabilities.

If a VMware server is not available to run the VSP, the physical SP is the alternative for remote monitoring and remote service. The physical SP is available in two versions: with a Single Power Supply and with a Redundant Power Supply.

HPE 3PAR StoreServ 8000 host adapters

Host adapters can be ordered separately to be installed in the field, or they can be factory configured into controller nodes. Host adapter cards provide the array with additional FC ports, with 10 Gb/s iSCSI/FCoE ports, or with 1 GbE/s and 10 Gb/s Ethernet ports. The additional FC ports can be used for connection to hosts or used to connect to other HPE 3PAR StoreServ Storage systems in a Remote Copy relationship. The iSCSI/FCoE ports permit host connection in iSCSI and FCoE environments. The Ethernet ports can be used only with the HPE 3PAR File Persona Software for file services connectivity.

HPE 3PAR StoreServ 8000 HBAs include:

- HPE 3PAR StoreServ 8000 2-port 32 Gb FC Adapter

- HPE 3PAR StoreServ 8000 4-port 16 Gb FC Adapter

- HPE 3PAR StoreServ 8000 2-port 10 Gb iSCSI/FCoE Adapter

- HPE 3PAR StoreServ 8000 4-port 1 Gb Ethernet Adapter

- HPE 3PAR StoreServ 8000 2-port 10 Gb Ethernet Adapter

- HPE 3PAR StoreServ 8000 4-port 16 Gb FC/10 Gb NIC Combo Adapter

- HPE 3PAR StoreServ 8000 4-port 10 Gb iSCSI/10 Gb NIC Combo Adapter

HPE 3PAR StoreServ 20000

	20450	20800	20850	20840
Controller nodes	2 or 4	2, 4 , 6, or 8	2, 4 , 6, or 8	2, 4 , 6, or 8
Max. total cache	1.8 TiB	33.8 TiB	3.6 TiB	51.3 TiB
Max. on-node cache	1792 GiB	1792 GiB	3584 GiB	3584 GiB
Total flash cache	N/A	32 TiB	N/A	48 TiB
Max # of HDDs / SDDs	N/A / 576	2304 / 1152	N/A / 1152	2304 / 1152
Max raw capacity	4021 TiB all-flash	9600 TiB	8043 TiB all-flash	9600 TiB
16 Gb/s FC host ports 10 Gb/s iSCSI/FCoE ports 10 Gb/s FBO NIC ports Built-in 10 Gb RC ports	0 to 80 0 to 40 0 to 24 2 to 4	0 to 160 0 to 80 0 to 48 2 to 8	0 to 160 0 to 80 0 to 48 2 to 8	0 to 160 0 to 80 0 to 48 2 to 8

Figure 5-82 Overview of HPE 3PAR StoreServ 20000 models

HPE 3PAR StoreServ 20000, as indicated in Figures 5-82 and 5-83, is the ideal solution for customers who:

- Need massive consolidation with workloads that require up to 3 million IOPS and/or scalability up to 9 PB raw

- Have large mission-critical projects like enterprise resource planning (ERP) roll-out and private cloud

- Have next-gen data center requirements for the latest infrastructure, density, and power and cooling

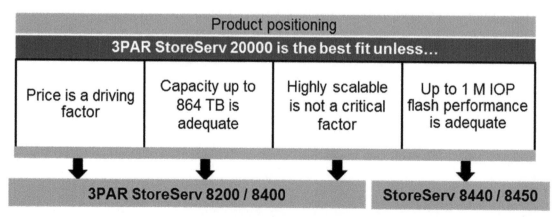

Figure 5-83 HPE 3PAR StoreServ positioning

HPE StoreFabric Gen6 Director Switch

Figure 5-84 StoreFabric SN8600B 8-slot Director switch

The HPE SAN Director portfolio contains the existing HPE StoreFabric SN8000B Switch 16 Gb Switch and the recently introduced HPE StoreFabric SN8600B 32 Gb FC Switch. The HPE StoreFabric SAN Director consists of an eight-slot 14U chassis and a four-slot 8U chassis providing up to 384 Gen6 32 Gb FC ports and up to 32 QSFP-based ICLs (inter-chassis link) that are equivalent to 128 FC ports.

The StoreFabric B-series Gen6, shown in Figure 5-84, eliminates performance bottlenecks and provides performance at 32 Gbps in the SAN.

Enhanced diagnostics tools like Fabric Vision and Gen6 with IO Insight provide real-time monitoring and simplified management to optimize application performance and accelerate problem resolution, reducing operational costs and improving business agility. Protect customers' investments with the Gen7 FC-ready storage networking platform.

HPE StoreOnce VSA

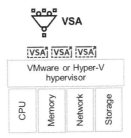

Figure 5-85 StoreOnce VSA

HPE StoreOnce VSA, as illustrated in Figure 5-85, is a virtual backup and deduplication appliance, excellent for backing up a smaller sites or moving data from remote sites to a centralized data center. With HPE StoreOnce Catalyst, deduplicated data can be moved seamlessly across the enterprise without the need to rehydrate, and all data movement is controlled by your customer's backup application from a single console.

SDS is a storage functionality delivered as software. Instead of deploying dedicated storage hardware, your customers can consolidate shared storage onto the same servers as their applications. This easy-to-deploy storage solution converges applications and data on the same platform to reduce your customer's hardware footprint by half without losing any required storage functionality.

Virtual storage appliance:

- **Maximum write performance:** 36 TB/hour (Catalyst)

- **Maximum number of concurrent data streams:** 256

- **Maximum number of backup targets:** 32 stores

- **Fan-in ratio:** 8 sources

- **License:** 90-day demo license

Resource minimums and maximums:

- **vRAM:** 24 GB/320 GB

- **vCPU:** 2/36

- **IOPS:** 600/10,800

- **Dedicated hard drives:** 4/72

Capacity

- **Minimum configuration:** 4 TB

- **Maximum configuration (with expansion):** 500 TB (attain maximum storage capacity by adding licenses)

- **Cloud Bank Storage (licensed) maximum capacity:** 1 PB

HPE StoreOnce 3620

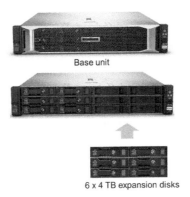

Base unit

6 x 4 TB expansion disks

Figure 5-86 HPE StoreOnce 3620

HPE StoreOnce 3620 delivers entry-level, disk-based backup and disaster recovery that is ideal for smaller remote or branch offices and data centers. This 2U Backup System offers 16 to 31.5 TB of usable local capacity, up to 94.5 TB with Cloud Bank Storage, and speeds of up to 14 TB/hour with StoreOnce Catalyst (depending on the configuration, data set type, compression levels, number of data streams, number of devices emulated, and number of concurrent tasks such as housekeeping or replication and storage configuration).

StoreOnce 3620, shown in Figure 5-86, is very similar to 3640, except of expansion shelves. The minimum configuration is 16 TB with an optional size 4 TB disk expansion kit (max useable 31.5 TB)

HPE StoreOnce 5200

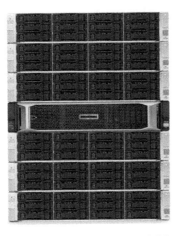

Figure 5-87 StoreOnce 5200

StoreOnce 5200, shown in Figure 5-87, is based on ProLiant DL380 LFF Disk Gen10 Server and contains two Intel® Xeon® 5118 Skylake CPUs.

Performance and capacity numbers include:

- Storage system with minimum configuration: 36 TB

- Can scale to maximum configuration (with expansion): 216 TB

- Maximum write performance: 33 TB/hour (Catalyst)

- Maximum number of concurrent data streams: 512

- Maximum number of data stores: 64

- Maximum fan-in or backup targets: 32

- Redundant 800 W power supply units (PSUs) standard

- Dedicated, redundant operating system drives (front drive bays)

- Flexible IO configurations

- Supports one to four IO HBAs in any combination

- Four types available:

  - 10 base-T

  - 10 Gb or 25 Gb Ethernet

  - 16 Gb FC (there is no 8 Gb HBA)

  - 32 Gb FC

- Attain maximum storage capacity by adding up to five disk enclosures

- Shelf data disk RAID 6 (9+2) plus hot spare

- Cloud Bank Storage (licensed) maximum capacity: 432 TB

HPE StoreOnce 5250

Figure 5-88 StoreOnce 5250

HPE StoreOnce 5250, shown in Figure 5-88, is very similar to 5200. Using different expansion shelves, some performance and capacity numbers differ:

- Minimum configuration: 36 TB

- Maximum configuration (with expansion): 864 TB

- Attain maximum storage capacity by adding up to one additional (fully populated) storage enclosure (BB976A)

- Cloud Bank Storage (licensed) maximum capacity: 1728 TB

- Maximum write performance: 41 TB/hour (Catalyst)

Learning check

9. You are in a meeting with a customer, and they challenge you with a statement: "Data security and availability is my top concern. I was reviewing Nimble specifications, and I like the deduplication and compression capabilities, but I heard that HPE Nimble Storage can survive only a single drive failure per enclosure. This technology is not compatible with my views on enterprise-class storage."

    How should you respond?

    _____

    _____

    _____

    _____

    _____

    _____

    _____

    _____

    _____

    _____

    _____

Summary

- HPE has multiple storage solutions. Each has a target market and overlap between the products is normal. Aligning them to the customers' requirements is important, to cover growth, performance, and cost.

- HPE storage products arrays differ in supported capacity, performance, features set, and type of used storage.

- HPE 3PAR StoreServ arrays support up to 8 PB of primary storage and include advanced enterprise features.

- HPE StoreOnce is the disk-based data protection appliance that can be implemented as hardware or deployed as a software virtual storage appliance.

Prelearning check

Before proceeding with this section, answer the following questions to assess your existing knowledge of the topics covered in this chapter. Record your answers in the space provided here.

1. You are in a meeting with a customer, and they challenge you with a statement: "I heard that HPE specializes in traditional data center components and does not offer a software-defined platform, where hardware provisioning can be done from the management application."

   How should you respond?

   _____

   _____

   _____

   _____

   _____

   _____

   _____

   _____

   _____

   _____

   _____

6 Recommending HPE software-defined and cloud solutions

LEARNING OBJECTIVES

After completing this chapter, and given a customer scenario, you should be able to:

✓ Recommend and position HPE software-defined and cloud solutions, tools, and appropriate services for customer use cases.

✓ Identify and position key HPE software-defined and cloud solutions and workload offerings with the key alliance partner ecosystem components to the appropriate customer use case.

✓ Differentiate and position HPE products and services products for the appropriate customer use case.

✓ Describe, differentiate, and apply industry-standard architectures and technologies.

✓ Explain the HPE approach to converged management for the infrastructure lifecycle.

Scenario 6: Red Hat OpenShift on HPE Synergy and HPE Nimble Storage

The wide HPE portfolio of data center products can be introduced using customer scenarios and recommended, validated configurations based on the HPE Reference Architecture or HPE Reference Configuration.

The customer scenario is almost identical to the one in previous chapters; however, we will not deep dive to storage components and networking now, but we will present the software-defined computing part of the solution.

Introducing the customer scenario

aZLa company will be used as a storyline through this scenario. We will introduce the company using an interview:

- What is your primary business?

  – Regional consumer electronics retailer

- How many employees do you currently have?

  – 1500+ employees

- What does your selling and delivery channel look like?

  – Electronic stores, show rooms, delivery boxes around the country

- Where are you currently storing data, and how do you access files?

  – Shared array, non-HPE, for critical data required onsite; temporary/cached data in a hosted environment

- What does your server and network infrastructure look like?

  – Single data center, mix of vendors (both servers and networking)

- What is the structure of your IT department?

  – E-shop development, operations team

- What are your current plans?

  – Consolidation of front-end applications, faster, easier development of front-end applications and more flexibility when handling peaks

Customer requirements

As a result of multiple interviews and gathering information about customer plans and the customer's current infrastructure, the following requirements emerged for the new solution:

- Faster development of applications

- Both compute and storage resources need to stay on site

- Selected container solution: Red Hat OpenShift Container Platform

  – Common 16-core processor for both management and worker nodes

  – Support for 1500 pods

- Storage:
  - Local server storage (SSD)
  - Shared, future-proof, storage for Docker containers and management platform
  - 15 TB of storage for pods
- Reducing management and deployment costs
  - Pre-integration of networking and rack components
- Software-defined approach to infrastructure management

Activity: Container Platform information resources

1. Download these information resources:
   - HPE Reference Configuration for Red Hat OpenShift on HPE Synergy and HPE Nimble Storage

     http://h20195.www2.hpe.com/V2/GetDocument.aspx?docname=a00056101enw

   - HPE Deployment Guide for Red Hat OpenShift Container Platform on HPE Synergy with HPE Nimble Storage

     https://github.com/HewlettPackard/hpe-solutions-openshift/tree/master/synergy/scalable/nimble

   - RHEL OpenShift Container Platform: Sizing Considerations

     https://access.redhat.com/documentation/en-us/openshift_container_platform/3.7/html/installation_and_configuration/installing-a-cluster#sizing

2. Answer the following questions:

   a. How many application nodes can we recommended for a solution where 5000 pods are planned to be deployed?

   _____

   _____

   _____

   b. How many nodes are needed for 1500 pods, as required by the customer?

   _____

   _____

   _____

c. What is the maximum recommended number of pods per core?

_____

_____

_____

d. How many management hosts are recommended for OpenShift Container Platform?

_____

_____

_____

e. Which technology is recommended to be configured at FlexFabric switches for high availability and redundancy?

_____

_____

_____

f. What is the management and orchestration platform used in the HPE Deployment Guide?

_____

_____

_____

g. What is the required Docker version for the OpenShift Container Platform 3.7?

_____

_____

_____

h. How many network and storage connections are needed per each compute chapter?

_____

_____

_____

_____

Building blocks of the solution

HPE Synergy

HPE FlexFabric 5940 2-slot

Image Streamer

HPE SY480 Gen10

HPE Nimble Storage AF40

HPE OneView

Figure 6-1 Building blocks of the solution

This Reference Configuration provides architectural guidance for deploying, scaling, and managing a Red Hat OpenShift environment on HPE Synergy Composable Infrastructure along with HPE Nimble storage.

This Reference Configuration, as shown in Figure 6-1, describes how to:

- Leverage HPE Synergy strengths in rapid provisioning along with the automation capabilities of Red Hat Ansible Tower to provide a one-click deployment of a Red Hat OpenShift Container Platform on HPE Synergy.

- Efficiently layout an OpenShift configuration using a mix of virtualized and bare-metal technology.

- Configure container-persistent storage using HPE Nimble Storage.

HPE Synergy

HPE introduced the concept of a converged infrastructure because businesses that were trying to compete in the applications-driven economy found their traditional business infrastructure struggling. Traditional infrastructure is stable and allows organizations to slowly (over longer, planned periods of time) roll out applications that support the business, such as online transaction processing (OLTP) applications, and databases. However, maintaining a traditional infrastructure in an application-driven economy is a challenge for which there is a solution.

Why is Composable Infrastructure important?

Many CIOs and data center system administrators feel challenged to deliver traditional business applications while at the same time standing up new applications such as mobile and cloud native apps that drive revenue. Operations-driven and cost-focused, traditional IT environments make it difficult to deliver value to the business—IT cannot move fast enough for today's application delivery goals.

Traditional applications are designed to support and automate existing business processes such as collaboration, data processing and analytics, supply chain, and web infrastructure. They include applications such as enterprise resource planning (ERP) and other large databases that have been prepackaged and pretested. These applications and services typically go through one or two release cycles per year. IT has been built around these for the last 20 to 30 years.

New apps-driven and agility-focused IT environments deliver apps and services that drive revenue and enhanced customer experiences through mobility, Big Data, and cloud native technologies. These apps challenge IT to maintain a digital enterprise in a digital economy alongside traditional applications. However, maintaining two different sets of infrastructures, one designed for traditional apps and another designed for cloud native apps, increases costs and complexity. This approach is not sustainable.

Gartner gives the name "bi-modal computing" to the strategy of maintaining an existing infrastructure for traditional applications while transitioning to infrastructure and tools for emerging applications. The HPE vision is to pull both together with one infrastructure that provides the agility of an on-premise cloud infrastructure, as illustrated in Figure 6-2.

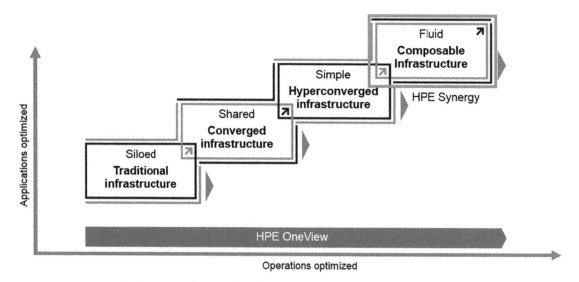

Figure 6-2 A Composable Infrastructure meets traditional and Idea Economy demands

In addition to its focus on stability, reliability, and scalability, the traditional infrastructure is often siloed and burdened with complex processes. It can take IT months to stand up environments for traditional applications—regardless of whether these environments are meant to support physical, virtual, or containerized workloads.

HPE followed its converged infrastructure with hyper-converged solutions that only require minutes to deploy. These workload-specific offerings deliver fluid virtual IT and software-defined storage (SDS) in a single appliance.

HPE converged infrastructure and hyper-converged appliances help organizations succeed in the Idea Economy. Doing business in the Idea Economy—which is also called the digital, application, or mobile economy—means turning an idea into a new product, capability, business, or industry. To stay competitive, organizations need to develop new IT capabilities, create new outcomes, proactively manage risk, be predictive, and create a hyper-connected workplace. HPE converged infrastructure, software-defined management, and hyper-converged systems reduce costs and increase operational efficiency by eliminating silos and freeing available compute, storage, and networking resources.

However, most organizations must still maintain their traditional infrastructure, which can involve using a different set of tools and application programming interfaces (APIs). Businesses need a single, fluid infrastructure that is optimized to deliver infrastructure for both traditional and new applications in seconds. This infrastructure must be agile and flexible enough to change personalities dynamically so that it can meet traditional and Idea Economy workload demands without overprovisioning resources for either. This architectural approach is a Composable Infrastructure.

Moving to a Composable Infrastructure

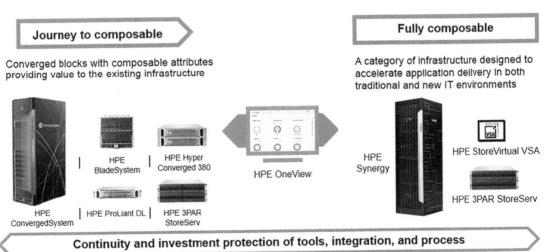

Figure 6-3 HPE offers several solutions that provide customers with a bridge to Composable Infrastructure

Building on a converged infrastructure, HPE has designed the Composable Infrastructure around three core principles:

- Fluid resource pools meet each application's changing needs by allowing for the composition and recomposition of single blocks of disaggregated compute, storage, and fabric resources needed to run applications in sizes at the appropriate scale. This allows new applications to be quickly provisioned.

- Software-defined intelligence provides a single management interface to integrate operational silos and eliminate complexity. Workload templates speed deployment, and frictionless change eliminates unnecessary downtime.

- The unified API provides a single interface to discover, search, inventory, configure, provision, update, and diagnose the Composable Infrastructure. A single line of code enables full infrastructure programmability and can provision the infrastructure required for an application.

A Composable Infrastructure, as illustrated in Figure 6-3, facilitates the move to a continuous services and application delivery model and enables applications to be updated as needed, rather than just once or twice a year. IT operates in a manner similar to how a cloud provider handles lines of business and the extended enterprise. This type of framework consistently meets service-level agreements (SLAs) and provides the predictable performance needed to support core workloads.

HPE offers several solutions that provide customers with a bridge to Composable Infrastructure. For example, HPE developed ConvergedSystem and hyper-converged solutions to help customers respond more quickly to their demands.

With the release of Synergy, customers can move to a fully Composable Infrastructure. Synergy greatly reduces the operational complexity of managing infrastructure and enables customers to accelerate application deployment. It is designed for today and architected to anticipate the evolution of technologies in the future.

Synergy—The first platform architected for composability

HPE Synergy combines hardware infrastructure, software, and services to deliver a single Composable Infrastructure platform that enables customers to be well positioned for the cloud. The Synergy platform reduces operational complexity for traditional workloads and increases operational speed for emerging applications and services. Using a single interface, Synergy composes physical and virtual compute, storage, and fabric pools into any configuration for any application. The extensible platform easily enables a broad range of applications and operational models such as virtualization, hybrid cloud, and DevOps.

 Note

DevOps is a set of software development practices that combines software development (Dev) and information technology operations (Ops) to shorten the systems development lifecycle while delivering features, fixes, and updates frequently in close alignment with business objectives (Wikipedia.org, April 2018).

Synergy offers the following benefits of a Composable Infrastructure:

- Composable compute provides performance, scalability, density optimization, storage simplicity, and configuration flexibility.

- HPE Synergy Composer uses integrated, software-defined intelligence to self-discover, auto-integrate, provision, and scale from racks to rows.

- Its composable frame provides everything needed to run applications and allows IT to be quickly set up and consumed.

- Rack-scale, multi-fabric connectivity eliminates stand-alone Top-of-Rack (ToR) switches.

- High-density, integrated storage can be used to compose any compute with any storage pool (SDS, direct-attached storage [DAS], and storage area network [SAN]).

With the emergence of cloud and other technologies, customers need faster operations to drive more profitability. HPE customers want to be relevant to and succeed on both ends of the applications spectrum. IT needs a more efficient approach that can create and deliver new value instantly and continuously.

With Synergy, IT can become not only the internal service provider, but also the business partner needed to rapidly launch new applications. The platform allows IT to continuously:

- **Run anything**—Optimize any application and store all data on a single infrastructure with fluid pools of physical and virtual compute, storage, and fabric.

- **Move faster**—Accelerate application and service delivery through a single interface that precisely composes logical infrastructures at near-instant speeds.

- **Work efficiently**—Reduce operational effort and cost through internal software-defined intelligence with template-driven, frictionless operations.

- **Unlock value**—Increase productivity and control across the data center by integrating and automating infrastructure operations and applications through a unified API.

Synergy allows customers to:

- Dramatically reduce overprovisioning, CapEx, and stranded resources.

    - Compose any compute with any storage pool (including non-SAN simplicity).

    - Quickly recompose within a frame, across racks and rows in seconds.

    - Optimize SDS, DAS, and SAN.

- Deploy at cloud-like speed.

    - Stand up the infrastructure in minutes, not months.

    - Auto-assemble all resources.

    - Quickly deploy the configuration, drivers, firmware, and operating system through workload-based templates (catalog of images).

- Develop apps and program infrastructure based on their preferences.

  - Program all resources using a single line of code.

  - Program infrastructure at near run-time.

  - Store images for fast iteration and repeatable scale.

Software-defined architecture

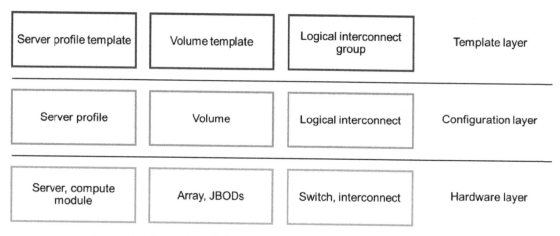

Figure 6-4 Examples of abstraction of configuration from the hardware

Software-defined architecture is an approach to data center computing, when abstraction of configuration from the hardware is used, as indicated in Figure 6-6. Low-level, hardware configuration tools are no longer needed to perform most configuration tasks and a centralized management application is used instead. The most important benefits include:

- Faster provisioning of new resources with less errors

- Easier and faster change management

- Compliance management

 Note

> Sometimes called "virtual data centers," software-defined data centers consist of fully virtualized computing infrastructure that can be easily managed by software in an automated fashion. The abstraction of CPU, networking, storage, and security allow flexible pools of resources to be seamlessly allocated across workloads as needed, which in turn allows IT to become highly elastic and scalable with highly simplified operations.

HPE Synergy: Powering your customer's hybrid cloud transformation

Figure 6-5 HPE Synergy components

A Synergy solution allows customers to select the right ratios of fabric, storage, and compute to compose the infrastructure necessary for their particular workloads.

HPE Synergy solution components, as illustrated in Figure 6-5, include:

- **Composable frame**—Everything needed to run applications, so IT can be quickly set up and consumed. Auto-integrating makes scaling simple and automated at rack/row scale.

- **Composer**—Integrated software-defined intelligence to self-discover, auto-integrate, provision, and scale from racks to rows.

- **Composable compute**—Provides the performance, scalability, density optimization, storage simplicity, and configuration flexibility.

- **Composable fabric**—Rack-scale multi-fabric connectivity eliminates stand-alone ToR switches.

- **Composable storage**—High-density integrated storage to compose any compute with any storage (SDS, DAS, SAN).

The process you follow to building a Synergy solution for a customer involves four loosely defined main steps:

1. First, configure the infrastructure by determining the number of frames the customer requires and the associated Composers, Frame Link Modules (FLMs), and compute modules.

2. Determine how the Composers and FLMs will be connected in a management ring. The Synergy system via the Synergy Composer will automatically discover all the compute, fabric, and storage resources that have been added to the management ring.

3. Consider how to configure fabric elements (the data network) as part of a Composable Infrastructure. Determine whether the Image Streamer is appropriate for the customer's configuration. If you are adding an Image Streamer to the customer's configuration, determine how it fits into the fabric and the management ring.

4. Lastly, build out storage modules based on the customer's requirements.

HPE Synergy 12000 frames

1. Frame sized to fit in existing infrastructure (10U rack space)
2. Double-wide storage node
3. Half-height compute node
4. Full-height compute node
5. Redundant management appliance modules
6. Front panel of Synergy console

Figure 6-6 HPE Synergy 12000 front view

The Synergy frame reduces complexity through an intelligent autodiscovery infrastructure and delivers performance to accelerate workload deployment. As the building block for a Synergy infrastructure, a Synergy frame offers substantial expansion and scalability.

Every frame offers dual hot-plug integrated appliance bays for redundancy. They have 10 GB network direct connected to FLM for inter- or intra-frame management communications.

A Synergy frame's unique design, shown in Figure 6-6, physically embeds Synergy Composer with HPE OneView management software to compose compute, storage, and fabric resources in any configuration. HPE Synergy frames may be linked into larger groups or domains of frames to form a dedicated management network, increasing resources available to the business and IT efficiency as the size of the infrastructure grows—achieving both CapEx and OpEx economies of scale.

The HPE Synergy 12000 frame accommodates compute, storage, fabric, and management in a single infrastructure to significantly reduce cost and complexity while delivering significant performance gains to accelerate workload deployment. It provides the base for an intelligent infrastructure with embedded management and scalable links for expansion as business demand requires.

The HPE Synergy 12000 frame physically embeds management as code into an intelligent infrastructure to offer management and composability of integrated compute, storage, and fabric resources. Whether resources are in a single frame or multiple linked frames, the system offers composability of all resources.

The Synergy frame takes the same 10U of rack space as a BladeSystem c7000 enclosure. Synergy is slightly deeper, and there are some significant considerations in placing a Synergy frame in a 1-m deep rack.

(1) Three primary interconnect bays

(2) Three redundant interconnect bays

(3) Two frame link module slots

(4) Ten system fan bays

(5) Six Titanium 2650 W power supplies

Figure 6-7 HPE Synergy 12000 rear view

The Synergy 12000 frame eases installation by using the standard power feeds of BladeSystems. Synergy supports up to six 96% Titanium Efficient, 2650 Watt power supplies that offer redundant N+N, N+1 power setup. The Synergy frame provides an efficient cooling system and has 10 built-in fans in every frame, as indicated in Figure 6-7. It delivers the frame link topology (the ring architecture) through 10 Gbase-T RJ-45 jacks and CAT6 cables, providing resource discovery and status, management commands, and inventory reporting.

The Synergy 12000 frame provides a walk up diagnostic and configuration link through a display port and USB connections, either at the rear or at the front panel of the frame.

Synergy management subsystem

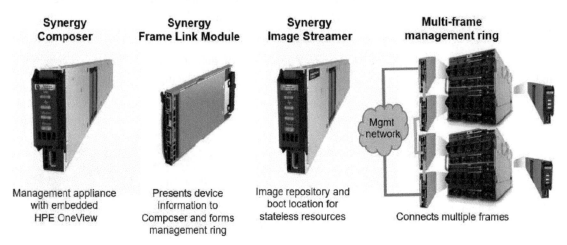

Figure 6-8 Synergy management subsystem components

The Synergy management subsystem, as illustrated in Figure 6-8, comprises the following components:

- **Composer**—A management appliance that directly integrates into the frame of the system and provides a single interface for assembling and reassembling flexible compute, storage, and fabric resources in any configuration. Its infrastructure-as-code capability accelerates transformation to a hybrid infrastructure and provides on-demand delivery and support of applications and services with consistent governance, compliance, and integration.

- **Image Streamer**—A new approach to deployment and updates for a Composable Infrastructure. This management appliance works with Composer for fast software-defined control over physical compute modules with operating system provisioning. Image Streamer enables true stateless computing combined with instant-on capability for deployment and updates. This management appliance deploys and updates infrastructure at extreme speed.

- **Frame Link Modules**—The integrated resource information control point. FLMs report asset and inventory information about all the devices in the frame. As resource controllers, they provide functions such as inventory and configuration checking. They also provide the management uplinks to the customer's network.

 Note

An uplink port (or link aggregation group) is used to expand a network by connecting to another network or a device such as a router, switch, or server. A downlink port is used to receive data from another (often larger) network.

A single Synergy Composer manages one frame or multiple racks of frames linked through the FLMs. The Synergy Composer option that you select determines the number of frames linked and managed. HPE recommends using two Synergy Composer modules for redundancy and high availability.

HPE Synergy Composer

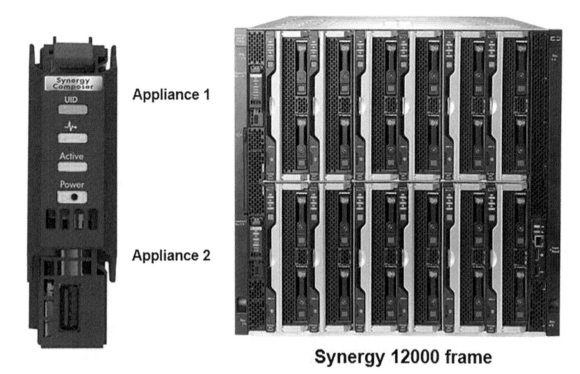

Appliance 1

Appliance 2

Synergy 12000 frame

Figure 6-9 Synergy embedded management appliance

Composer is a physical appliance integrated within the Synergy frame. It plugs into an appliance bay in the side of the Synergy frame, as indicated in Figure 6-9.

 Note

Composer does not use a compute module slot.

Composer embeds the HPE OneView management solution to manage compute modules, fabrics, and storage, which is the essence of software-defined intelligence in Synergy.

Composer deploys, monitors, and updates the infrastructure from one interface and one unified API. It allows IT departments to deploy infrastructure for traditional, virtualized, and cloud environments in a single step, in just a few minutes. Resources can be updated, flexed, and redeployed without service interruptions. This allows infrastructure to be deployed and consistently updated with the right configuration parameters and firmware versions, streamlining the delivery of IT services and the transition to a hybrid cloud. Its reduced complexity and faster service delivery times ultimately enable IT to better respond to changing business needs.

Server templates are a powerful new way to quickly and reliably update and maintain an existing infrastructure. Composer uses templates to simplify one-to-many updates and manage compute module profiles. This feature adds inheritance to the process, meaning updates can be made once, in the template, and then propagated out to the profiles created from that template. Elements that can be updated via a template include firmware, BIOS settings, local RAID settings, boot order, network configuration, shared storage configuration, and many others.

Composer templates also provide **monitor and flag** capabilities with remediation. Profiles created from the template are monitored for configuration compliance. When inconsistencies are detected, an alert is generated indicating that the profile is out of compliance with its template. When a new update is made at the template level, all profiles derived from that template will be flagged as inconsistent. From there, the user has complete control over the remediation process for bringing individual modules or multiple systems back into compliance.

HPE Synergy Frame Link Modules

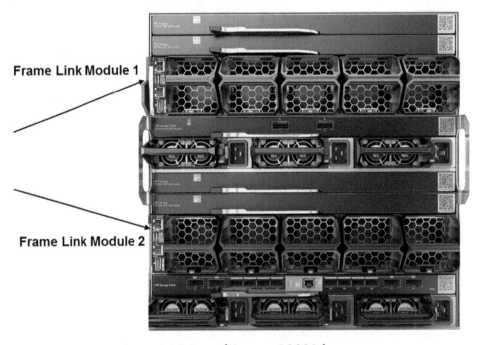

Figure 6-10 Rear of Synergy 12000 frame

The FLM is the intelligence behind the frame and the management architecture. It provides shared frame services such as power, cooling, auto-discovery, and inventory of all installed components on the management interface. For example, they report, in real-time, the power each module uses and the total power used per frame.

An FLM, as shown in Figure 6-10, enables you to take one composable element or frame and connect multiples of them together to allow them to automatically scale together. You can start off with one element and add more infrastructure as needed. As you add elements, they auto-assemble together into one larger infrastructure that can still be managed as a single infrastructure. You can start up to a rack or even a row scale deployment and have it all managed as a single element. Appliance bays link directly to the FLMs in the rear of the frame to provide detailed information of compute, storage, and fabric resources for management of the Composer with HPE OneView.

FLMs have a plug-and-play system assembly, which means the installation technician can cable the modules and then automatically assemble the system. Two FLMs per frame are used to provide fault tolerance.

FLMs link to the management appliances and provide control points for providing resource and health information of the frame to the management appliances. A management port on each FLM provides access to the management appliance and link ports for linking modules for multi-frame linking and setup.

HPE Synergy Image Streamer

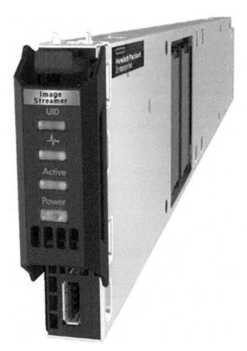

Figure 6-11 Image Streamer can be streamed across multiple compute modules in a matter of seconds

To accelerate workload deployment, Synergy uses the Image Streamer, a physical appliance repository of bootable (golden) images that can be streamed across multiple compute modules in a matter of seconds. This unique capability enables Synergy to set up and update infrastructure quickly and consistently. This is significantly faster than the traditional, sequential process of building compute modules—physical provisioning followed by operating system or hypervisor installation. It is ideal for situations such as web scale deployments where IT needs to provision an operating environment across a large number of infrastructure blocks.

Traditional server deployment is a sequential process of provisioning the physical hardware, followed by provisioning an operating system, and then by provisioning a hypervisor installation. Traditional memory-based server deployments use general deployment/provisioning tools for service operating system deployment, which uses a RAM-based operating system, and is also known as a **preboot (pre-install) environment**.

Image Streamer enables true stateless operation by integrating server profiles with golden images (operating environment and IO driver) and personalities (operating system and application) for rapid implementation onto available hardware. The fast deployment and compliance management capabilities leverage software-defined intelligence and are accessible via the unified API. These capabilities set HPE Image Streamer apart from traditional approaches.

Updates to highly replicated physical compute nodes with their operating environments at extreme speeds enables Image Streamer to deliver fast virtualized image changeovers (for use in Test and Dev, DevOps, multiple Platform as a Service [PaaS]) or secure boot and image compliance (for use in defense, government, or financial services institutions). These capabilities are ideal for web scale deployments where IT needs to provision an operating environment across a large number of infrastructure blocks.

Image Streamer, as shown in Figure 6-11, ensures high availability by providing redundant repositories of bootable images, which are used in a secure manner. These golden images can be rapidly cloned to create unique bootable images for compute nodes. It enables HPE Synergy to quickly deploy a new compute module or update an existing one. This is far faster than the traditional, sequential process of building servers—physical provisioning followed by operating system, hypervisor installation, IO drivers, and application stacks.

Administrators using Image Streamer can design bootable images for compute nodes, with the operating system and application stacks included, for ready-to-run environments.

 Important

> Image Streamer requires a minimum of three Synergy frames with redundant Composers for operation and must be implemented as redundant pairs. This minimal system requires four cables, two transceivers, and one interconnect module (ICM) for complete operation.

Synergy scaling: Management and production networks

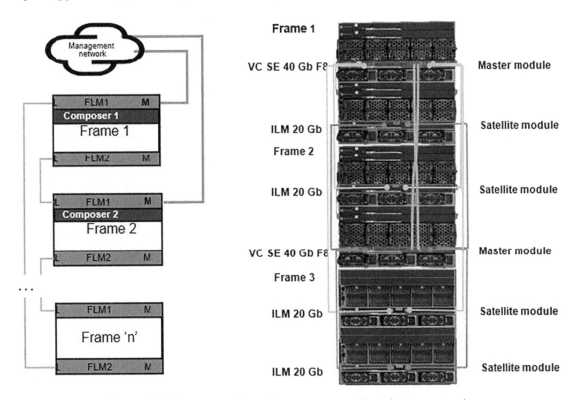

Figure 6-12 Synergy scaling: Management and production networks

A Synergy solution can be flexibly configured from one frame to a multi-frame solution, as illustrated in Figure 6-12. One or multiple management rings can be used to create a management domain manageable by single Composer or redundant pair of Composers. One HPE Synergy Composer can manage up to 21 frames in a single management ring. An HPE Synergy frame is automatically added during the hardware setup procedure (executed only once for one HPE Synergy system). If that Synergy frame is connected to a group of linked Synergy frames (the management ring), each Synergy frame in the group is discovered.

The management ring is highly available—disconnecting one cable does not cause a failure. After the initial hardware setup is completed, adding any new frames to the management ring is easy—just reinsert the cables between the LINK ports of the FLMs to include the new frames into the management ring, and they will be recognized automatically without starting hardware setup again.

HPE Synergy management ring—Single frame

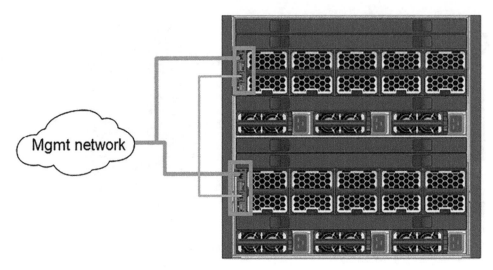

Figure 6-13 FLMs are critical to auto-discovery and growth

Even in a single-frame configuration, as a best practice, you should design a redundant solution with two Composers and two FLMs. Although there is a 10 GbE connection between the two FLMs across the midplane of the Synergy 12000 frame, you must cable the two modules together using the link port to complete the full management ring. In addition to being connected to each other, the FLMs are also connected to the management network using the uplink port as shown in the preceding graphic.

This redundant design ensures that you maintain operational use of the Synergy management network, eliminating a single point of failure. This design, shown in Figure 6-13, also allows you to update the FLM firmware without disrupting the entire system.

Connection locations in a single-frame management ring are:

- Frame link connection location

  – Frame 1 FLM 1 Link Port to Frame 1 FLM 2 Link Port

- Management network connection locations

  – Frame 1 FLM 1 management port to management network

  – Frame 1 FLM 2 management port to management network

Synergy management ring—Two frames

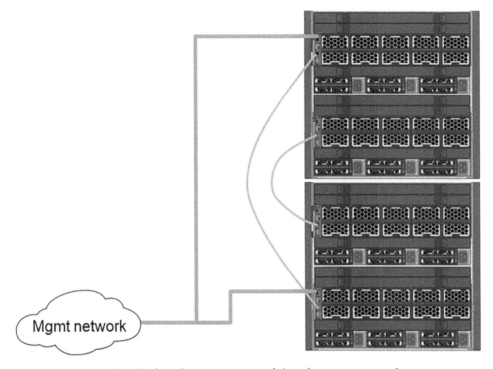

Figure 6-14 Scaling the management fabric from one to two frames

To scale this one-frame configuration to a two-frame configuration, you must disconnect the existing management ring and then cable the FLM in the first frame to the FLMs in the second frame, creating a management ring across frames, as indicated in Figure 6-14. The FLMs then auto-discover all the devices within the additional frame.

As a best practice, you should move one of the Composers to the second frame. You should also move one of uplinks to an FLM in the second frame. This creates a highly redundant management ring, which spans the physical architecture and creates one logical unit, from which the IT staff can compose resources.

A benefit to the newly configured ring is that new frames are automatically discovered and inventoried.

Synergy management ring—Three frames

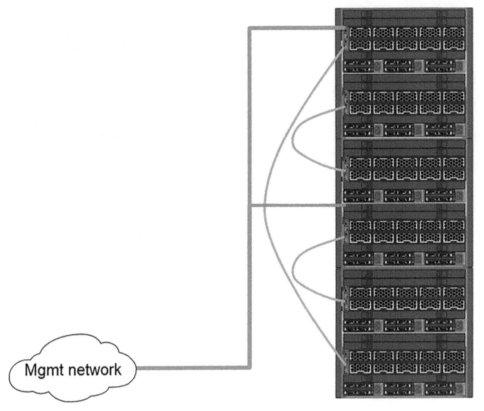

Figure 6-15 Scaling the management fabric from two to three frames

To move to a three-frame configuration, you need to change the cabling that connects the FLMs so that you can add the additional frame, as indicated in Figure 6-15. The FLMs are connected as follows.

- Frame 1 FLM 2 Link Port to Frame 2 FLM 1 Link Port

- Frame 2 FLM 2 Link Port to Frame 3 FLM 1 Link Port

- Frame 3 FLM 2 Link Port to Frame 1 FLM 1 Link Port

The FLMs auto-discover components in the third frame, dynamically adding resources into the same pool. This configuration is highly available because Composers are spread across the Composable Infrastructure and multiple uplinks are connected to the management data center.

Whether the environment is configured with two frames per rack or three, customers can expand their infrastructure without adding management complexity. They can simply move frame link cables to provide a single, redundant management ring across enclosures and then manage the solution through a single pair of Composers.

A pair of redundant Composers can manage up to 21 frames.

Rack-scale fabric architecture

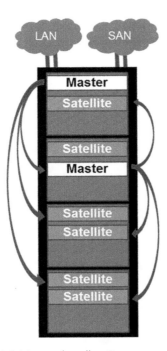

Figure 6-16 Master/satellite Synergy architecture

The disaggregated, rack-scale Synergy design uses a master/satellite architecture to consolidate data center network connections, reduce hardware and management complexity, and scale network bandwidth across multiple frames, as illustrated in Figure 6-16. This architecture enables several Synergy frames to establish a single logical fabric, interconnecting compute modules at high speeds, and low latency. Satellite modules—either HPE Synergy 10 GB Interconnect Link Modules or HPE Synergy 20 GB Interconnect Link Modules—connect to one of two master modules, which also connect to each other over ICM cluster links. The combined modules form a logical fabric. The master vs. satellites modules in the logical fabric connect over links with 1:1 subscription and ultra-low latency. This one-hop design for traffic across the aggregated frames maximizes data throughput and minimizes latency for large domains of VMs or compute modules.

The master modules provide the uplinks for the complete logical fabric, consolidating the connections to the data center network. They contain intelligent networking capabilities that extend connectivity to satellite frames through the ILM, eliminating the need for a ToR switch and substantially reducing cost. The reduction in components simplifies fabric management at scale while consuming fewer ports at the data center aggregation layer.

A satellite module extends the composable fabric to additional satellite frames and replaces fixed ratios of interconnects in each frame by extending the fluid pool of network resources from the master module.

The master/satellite stacking domain using 20 Gb Interconnect Link Modules is limited to three frames (10 Gb ICMs to five frames), which means that only up to 36 compute modules or 60 respectively can be connected to a master module. Advantages of a master/satellite architecture include:

- 40% or more lower fabric hardware costs

- 10 GB and 20 GB bandwidth with a future path to 40 GB/100 GB to compute modules

- Flexible bandwidth allocation in 100 MB increments

- Ethernet, Fibre Channel (FC), Fibre Channel over Ethernet (FCoE), and internet Small Computer System Interface (iSCSI)

- Zero touch change management

- Upgrade with minimum downtime

Synergy compute modules: Run any workload better

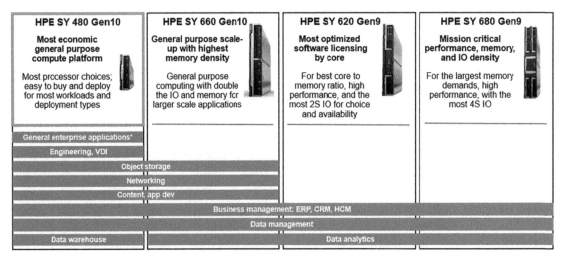

Figure 6-17 HPE Synergy Gen9 and Gen10 compute module portfolio

The Synergy Gen9 and Gen10 compute modules deliver general-purpose to mission-critical x86 levels of availability with real-time performance enabled by Intel® Xeon® EP and EX class processors

(Gen9) or Intel® Xeon® Scalable Family processors and a variety of memory, storage, and fabric choices. Synergy supports both two-socket and four-socket x86 compute modules, which provide the performance, scalability, density optimization, and storage simplicity.

As illustrated in Figure 6-17, available Synergy compute modules are:

- **HPE Synergy 480 Gen10 Compute Module**—Has increased memory capacity (up to 3 TB) and 24 dual in-line memory module (DIMM) slots. It supports the entire Xeon® Scalable Family processors without any DIMM slot restrictions. Greater consolidation and efficiency are achieved through an increase in virtual machine (VM) density per compute module.

- **HPE Synergy 660 Gen10 Compute Module**—Handles data-intensive workloads with uncompromised performance and exceptional value. The HPE Synergy 660 Gen10 Compute Module is a full-height, high-performance module with Intel® Xeon® Scalable Family processors, 48 DIMM slots providing up to 6 TB of available memory, flexible IO fabric connectivity, and right-sized storage options. Its HPE DDR4 SmartMemory offers up to a 30% performance increase over the previous generation.

- **HPE Synergy 620 Gen9 Compute Module**—Delivers mission-critical availability and performance, as well as flexible memory, storage, and fabric options in a full-height, two-socket form factor. With 48 DIMM slots, it supports up to 6 TB of HPE DDR4 memory and has five IO Peripheral Component Interconnect Express (PCIe) 3.0 connectors (two x16 and three x8).

- **HPE Synergy 680 Gen9 Compute Modules**—Is a four-socket, full-height, double-wide compute module with 96 DIMM slots for up to 12 TB of HPE DDR4 memory. It features 10 PCIe 3.0 IO connectors (four x16 and six x8).

Ideal workloads for Synergy composable computing

	Synergy 480 Gen10	Synergy 660 Gen10	Synergy 620 Gen9	Synergy 680 Gen9

Types of workloads	– Mainstream workloads and business applications:
	  – Collaborative
	  – Content mgmt
	  – IT/Web Infrastructure
	– Workload consolidation
	– Composable compute
	– Optimum performance for mainstream applications with headroom to grow
		Mainstream compute with greater CPU and memory requirements:
		  – Enterprise IT consolidation
		  – Virtualization
		  – Business processing
		  – Decision support
			Enterprise class reliability, availability, and serviceability
			  – Enterprise IT consolidation
			  – Virtualization
			  – Structured database
			  – High memory-intensive workloads
				– Enterprise class performance, scalability, and RAS
				– Maximum memory-intensive workloads
				  – Scale up applications
				  – Enterprise IT consolidation
				  – Large in-memory database

Figure 6-18 Types of workloads suitable for Synergy compute modules

Synergy compute modules have the configuration flexibility to power a variety of workloads, including business processing, IT infrastructure, web infrastructure, collaborative, and high-performance computing, as illustrated in Figure 6-18. Ideal workloads include:

- **HPE Synergy 480 Gen10 Compute Module**—Delivers superior capacity, efficiency, and flexibility to power more demanding workloads and increase VM density by providing a full range of processor choices, right-sized storage options, and a simplified IO architecture. It is designed to optimize general-purpose enterprise workload performance, including business processing, IT and web infrastructures, collaborative applications, and High-Performance Computing (HPC) in physical and virtualized environments while lowering costs within a Composable Infrastructure.

- **HPE Synergy 660 Gen10 Compute Module**—Supports demanding workloads such as in-memory and structured databases. It is also ideal for enterprise IT consolidation and virtualization.

- **HPE Synergy 620 and HPE Synergy 680 Gen9 Compute Modules**—Are designed to meet the needs of almost any enterprise IT tier and workload. These two-socket and four-socket x86 compute modules are ideal for financial, insurance, healthcare, manufacturing, and retail enterprises that require mission-critical levels of availability, extended versatility, and real-time performance. They are also designed for HPC applications with large memory demands.

 Note

For more information about HPE Synergy compute modules, visit:

https://www.hpe.com/us/en/product-catalog/synergy/synergy-compute.hits-12.html

HPE Synergy 480 Gen10 Compute modules

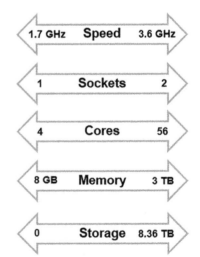

IT demands:
- Flexible and scalable environment
- Infrastructure and workload consolidation
- Structured database
- Web infrastructure

Composable compute **optimized for any workload** including engineering and VDI with graphics enhancements

Scale economically with choice of 1 or 2 processors

Full range of scalable processor choice up to 205 watts and 28 cores with no restrictions

Rapid and simple provision and reprovision composable resources

Different backplane options: standard, premium (NVMe support), and w/o backplane for stateless computing

1.7 GHz	Speed	3.6 GHz
1	Sockets	2
4	Cores	56
8 GB	Memory	3 TB
0	Storage	8.36 TB

Figure 6-19 HPE Synergy 480 Gen10 Compute modules

HPE Synergy 480 Gen10 is a composable solution optimized for any workload with a single, software-defined management. Built-in intelligence for auto-discovery and frictionless scaling helps customers with rapid infrastructure and applications provision.

HPE Synergy 460 Gen 10 features, as indicated in Figure 6-19:

- Customer priorities:

    – Consolidate workloads

    – Flexible, composable compute architecture

    – Optimum performance for mainstream applications with headroom for future upgrades

- Compute requirements:

    – Full availability of processor stack with no limitations

    – Optimum memory availability for most mainstream applications

    – Enterprise-class performance, scalability, and reliability

The following table provides detailed information about the HPE Synergy 480 Gen10:

	Synergy 480 Gen10
Compute	1 or 2 Intel® Xeon® Scalable Family processors
Memory	3 TB max: HPE Smart Memory (24) DDR4, up to 2666 MT/s
Persistent Memory	16 GB NVDIMM, (12 total DIMMs are NVDIMM enabled)
Local storage	– Diskless – 0 to 2 SFF SAS/SATA/HDDs or NVMe SSDs (6 TB max) – Up to 4 uFF drives; – 1 internal USB 3.0 and 1 microSD for boot – Up to 2 internal M.2 drives for more boot-store options (up to 680 GB max)— requires optional adapter – Different backplane options: standard, premium (NVMe support), and w/o backplane for stateless computing
DAS	760 TB max: Up to 200 drives per controller, in frame
Mezzanine slots	3x 16 PCIe 3.0 (slot number 2 requires second CPU)
Storage controllers	– Software RAID: S100i, 6 GB SATA / 14 int lanes – Essential RAID: E208i-c HBA, 12G SAS / 8 int lanes – Performance RAID: P204i-c, 12G SAS / 4 int lanes / 1 GB cache; and P416ie-m Mezzanine, 12 G SAS / 8 int 8 ext lanes / 2 GB cache

Networking	– CNAs: Synergy 3820C 10/20 GbE Converged Network Adapter 2 Ports per controller; Synergy 2820C 10 GbE Converged Network Adapter 2 ports per controller
	– HBAs: HPE Synergy 3530C 16G Fiber Channel Host Bus Adapter 2 ports per controller; Synergy 3830C 16G Fiber Channel Host Bus Adapter 2 ports per controller
	– Ethernet: Synergy 6810C 25/50 GbE Ethernet Adapter 2 ports per controller
GPU support	Mezzanine MXM: NVIDIA M6, M3000SE and AMD S7100X MXM; Multi-MXM Expansion Module with NVIDIA or AMD MXM options; or PCIe Expansion Module with NVIDIA TESLA M60 and M10, or Quadro P6000 GPUs
Management	HPE OneView, HPE iLO 5, Insight Control (EOL)

HPE Synergy 480 Gen10 Compute Module internal view

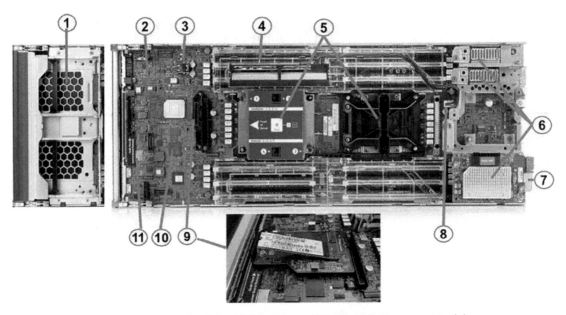

Figure 6-20 Details of the HPE Synergy 480 Gen10 Compute Module

HPE Synergy 480 Gen10 Compute Module, as shown in Figure 6-20, is half-height form factor (5U high) server with physical dimensions:

- Width 8.39"
- Length 22.5"
- Height 2.5"

The compute module contains following components:

- Removable drive cage with two hot-plug drive bays

- Trusted Platform Module (TPM) connector (under drive cage)

- USB 3.0 (under drive cage)

- 24 DDR4 DIMM memory slots (12 per processor, up to 2666 MT/s)

- Up to two Intel® Xeon® processors

- Three Mezzanine connectors (x16 PCIe 3.0)

- Power/management combo connector

- HPE Smart Storage Battery connector

- Storage controller connector and Dual M.2 Adapter (under drive cage)

- iLO5 application-specific integrated circuit (ASIC) (under drive cage)

- Micro SD Slot (under drive cage)

HPE Synergy 480 Gen10 Compute CTO Module

Different CTO configurations can be ordered: the CTO Standard Compute Module, CTO without Drives Compute Module, and the CTO Premium Compute Module.

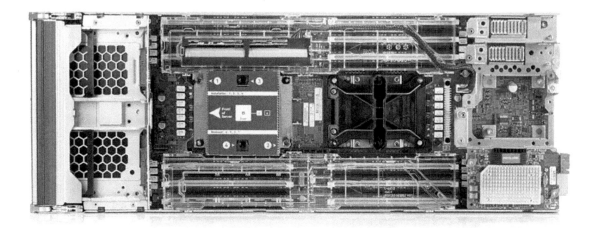

Figure 6-21 CTO Standard Compute Module

The CTO Standard Compute Module, shown in Figure 6-21, contains:

- Local Storage on standard backplane to support Serial AT Attachment (SATA)/SAS HPE controllers

    - S100i, E208i-c, P204ie-c

- M.2 SATA Storage with optional adapter

- D3940 Storage Module support with P416ie-c

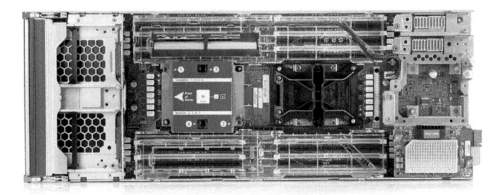

Figure 6-22 CTO without Drives Compute Module

The CTO without Drives Compute Module, shown in Figure 6-22, contains:

- No local storage (no backplane/controller)

- M.2 SATA storage with optional adapter

- D3940 Storage Module support with P416ie-c

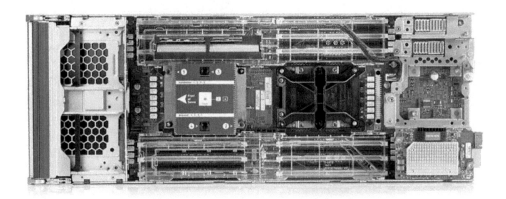

Figure 6-23 CTO Premium Compute Module

The CTO Premium Compute Module, shown in Figure 6-23, contains:

- Local storage on premium backplane for small form factor (SFF) Non-Volatile Memory Express (NVMe) storage

- M.2 SATA storage with optional adapter

- D3940 Storage Module support with P416ie-c

    - Support SATA/SAS local storage with SAS cable options

Synergy fabric portfolio

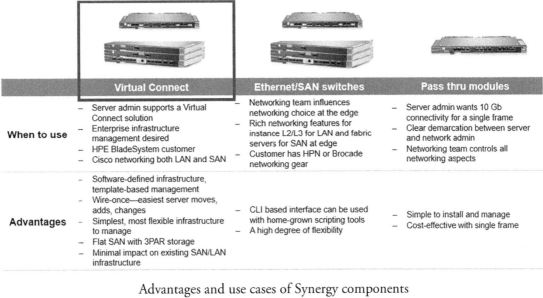

	Virtual Connect	Ethernet/SAN switches	Pass thru modules
When to use	– Server admin supports a Virtual Connect solution – Enterprise infrastructure management desired – HPE BladeSystem customer – Cisco networking both LAN and SAN	– Networking team influences networking choice at the edge – Rich networking features for instance L2/L3 for LAN and fabric servers for SAN at edge – Customer has HPN or Brocade networking gear	– Server admin wants 10 Gb connectivity for a single frame – Clear demarcation between server and network admin – Networking team controls all networking aspects
Advantages	– Software-defined infrastructure, template-based management – Wire-once—easiest server moves, adds, changes – Simplest, most flexible infrastructure to manage – Flat SAN with 3PAR storage – Minimal impact on existing SAN/LAN infrastructure	– CLI based interface can be used with home-grown scripting tools – A high degree of flexibility	– Simple to install and manage – Cost-effective with single frame

Advantages and use cases of Synergy components

	Virtual Connect SE 40 GB F8	20 GB Interconnect Link Module	10 GB Interconnect Link Module	10/40 GB Pass Thru Module	40 GB F8 Switch Module	Virtual Connect SE 16 GB FC	Brocade 16 GB/24 FC Switch	Brocade 16 GB/12 FC Switch	12 GB SAS Connection Module	Mellanox SH2200
Management and config	OneView managed	OneView managed	OneView managed	Zero Config	CLI configured	OneView managed	CLI configured	CLI configured	OneView managed	CLI/Web UI
Downlink ports (to compute)	12x 10/20 GB Ethernet/ FCoE	12x 20 GB Ethernet/ FCoE	12x 10 GB Ethernet/ FCoE	12x 10/40 GB Ethernet/ FCoE	12x 20 GB Ethernet	12x 16 GB FC	12x 16 GB FC	12x 16 GB FC	12 GB SAS	12x25/50 GB Ethernet
Uplink ports (to data net)	8x 40 GB Ethernet	N/A	N/A	12x 10/40 GB Ethernet	8x 40 GB Ethernet	12x 4/8/16 GB FC	24x 4/8/16 GB FC	12x 4/8/16 GB FC	N/A	8x QSFP28 Ethernet
Interconnect link ports	4x 120 GB ports to satellite	2x 120 GB ports to master	1x 120 GB port to master	N/A	4x 120 GB ports to satellite	N/A	N/A	N/A	N/A	N/A

Figure 6-24 Choice of fabrics to match workload and customer network requirements

Synergy offers a choice of fabrics to match workload and customer network requirements, as shown in Figure 6-24.

 Note

For more information about the HPE Synergy fabric portfolio, visit:

https://www.hpe.com/us/en/product-catalog/synergy/synergy-fabric.html

Composable fabric architecture

Synergy composable fabric delivers high performance and composability for the delivery of applications and services. It simplifies network connectivity using disaggregation in a cost-effective, highly available, and scalable architecture. Composable fabric creates a pool of flexible fabric capacity that can be configured almost instantly to rapidly provision infrastructure for a broad range of applications.

A composable fabric architecture has three key elements:

- A Composable Infrastructure starts with fluid resource pools, which is essentially a single structure that boots up, ready for any workload with fluid pools of compute, storage, and fabric that can be instantly turned on and flexed.

- Software-defined intelligence means embedding intelligence into the infrastructure and using workload templates to tell it how to compose, recompose, and update quickly, in a very repeatable, frictionless manner.

- The third element uses all of these capabilities and exposes them through a unified API, which allows the infrastructure to be programmed like code so it can become infrastructure as a service.

By delivering a highly flexible, high-performance pool of composable resources centered around a unified API to simplify and speed up deployment and management, Synergy offers value and flexibility. This is useful for businesses who just want to write existing apps or code new apps and be able to derive infrastructure directly as code.

Switch or Virtual Connect: What is the difference?

Figure 6-25 Comparison of traditional switches and Virtual Connect

What is the difference between a switch and a Virtual Connect (VC) module, as indicated in Figure 6-25? In part, it depends on where the interconnect device sits in the data center architecture and who manages it.

Switch

A switch is part of the Ethernet network or storage network. It is directly connected to a server network interface card (NIC) or host bus adapter (HBA), it communicates with other switches that make up the data center fabrics, and it is managed as part of those fabrics.

In most enterprises, by definition, a switch is owned and managed by the network operations group or the storage operations group. In whatever way the device works, if it is a switch, it must be managed by the local area network (LAN) or SAN administrator because they must have total control over their network fabrics to make sure they can operate securely and efficiently.

Virtual Connect

Virtual Connect is part of the server system. It forms a Layer 2 bridge between the servers and the Ethernet and storage networks. Because it is part of the server system, it requires less effort to manage VC because it is not as complicated as a switch.

It is ideal for virtualization environments because it pools and shares the network connections for the servers so that server changes are transparent to the LAN and SAN networks, and the networks cannot see any changes in the servers.

The VC does not enable any-to-any communication. Ingress and Egress ports are by "design."

HPE Virtual Connect SE 40 Gb F8 module

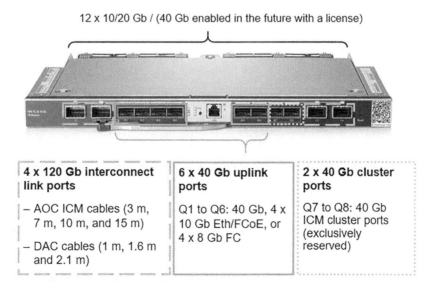

12 x 10/20 Gb / (40 Gb enabled in the future with a license)

4 x 120 Gb interconnect link ports	6 x 40 Gb uplink ports	2 x 40 Gb cluster ports
– AOC ICM cables (3 m, 7 m, 10 m, and 15 m) – DAC cables (1 m, 1.6 m and 2.1 m)	Q1 to Q6: 40 Gb, 4 x 10 Gb Eth/FCoE, or 4 x 8 Gb FC	Q7 to Q8: 40 Gb ICM cluster ports (exclusively reserved)

Figure 6-26 HPE Virtual Connect SE 40 GB F8 module

The HPE Virtual Connect SE 40 GB F8 Module, as illustrated in Figure 6-26, operates as the master module. It has 8xQSFP+ uplinks; six are unified (FC and Ethernet) and dedicated for the upstream switches. The last two are reserved exclusively for ICM cluster ports that enable multi-chassis link aggregation groups (M-LAGs) between two VC modules and cannot be used as Ethernet uplink ports.

An FC license is needed to leverage the FC interface on the uplinks. After the FC uplinks are activated, they can be used for either N_Port ID virtualization (NPIV) or Flat SAN.

The four link ports each with 120 GB bandwidth are reserved for connecting to ICLMs. In the case of 10 GB satellite modules, up to four ICLMs can be connected to a single VC master module. In case of 20 GB ICLMs, only two modules can be connected.

The Virtual Connect SE 40 GB F8 Module has 12 downlinks ports. Each downlink port can operate at 10/20 GB with support planned for 40 GB. The 40 GB downlinks will be enabled with 40 GB adapters availability in the future, and a 40 GB license will be needed to activate 40 GB downlinks on VC.

Because this module is a VC module, it is compatible with VC features such as edge-safe, profiles, support for Flex-10/20, Flat SAN, and so forth. In addition, it supports M-LAG on uplinks and has better firmware upgrade with minimal traffic disruption. When combined with satellite modules, it offers itself as composable fabric for Synergy. VC capabilities can be extended to satellite frames.

HPE Synergy 20 Gb Interconnect Link Module

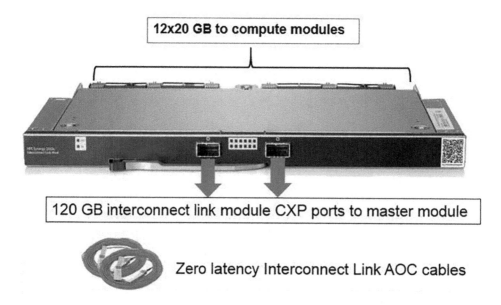

Figure 6-27 Simplest way to extend fabric resources pool to satellite frames for 20 GB

The HPE Synergy 20 GB Interconnect Link Module is a 20 GB satellite module. It connects only to the master module, which in this case is Synergy VC. It has two 120 GB uplinks and 12x20 GB downlinks to the compute module.

The uplink is connected to a master module with zero latency Active Optical Cable (AOC) or Direct Attach Copper (DAC) interconnect link cables, as indicated in Figure 6-27. After a satellite module is connected to a master module, it automatically extends SerDes of the respective compute modules in that satellite frame to the master module. In essence, all the compute modules in the satellite frame become extended ports of the master module.

Like the 10 GB Interconnect Link Module, the Synergy 20 GB Interconnect Link Module has no intelligence other than a silicon timer to amplify the signal. Because there is no processing of any signal with any silicon logic, the latency of 20 GB satellite modules is almost negligible. The satellite module can be thought of as a link extender from compute modules to the master module. All the to-and-from traffic from compute modules in a satellite frame is processed within the master module.

Synergy Converged Network Adapters

Figure 6-28 HPE Synergy 3820C 10 Gb/20 Gb CNA

IO adapters for network connectivity can be selected for each Synergy compute module. Network adapters, as shown in Figure 6-28, can be installed in any mezzanine connector, but the best practice is to install the first network adapter in mezzanine connector 3 to facilitate the installation of Type C and D mezzanines in connectors 1 or 2.

HPE's high-performance adapters support:

- 10 G or 20 Gb for HPE Synergy compute modules

- Converged traffic (FCoE or iSCSI and Ethernet)

- Orchestrates reliable adapter firmware updates with an entire Synergy infrastructure from a single tool—Synergy Composer

You can select from many Converged Network Adapters (CNAs), including:

- HPE Synergy 3820C 10 Gb/20 Gb CNA

  – Three FlexNICs and one FlexHBA/FlexNIC per port

  – Flex-10 and Flex-20 technologies for simplified IO hardware and reduced costs

  – NPAR, SR-IOV, RSS, jumbo frames, and PXE boot

- HPE Synergy 2820C 10 Gb CNA

  – Converged 10 Gb Ethernet connectivity

  – NPAR, SR-IOV, RSS, jumbo frames, and PXE boot

We also have the option to use the NVIDIA Tesla cards, a GPU mezzanine card designed to accelerate enterprise applications. This option occupies mezzanine slot 1 when implemented.

HPE Flex-10/Flex-20 and FlexHBA overview

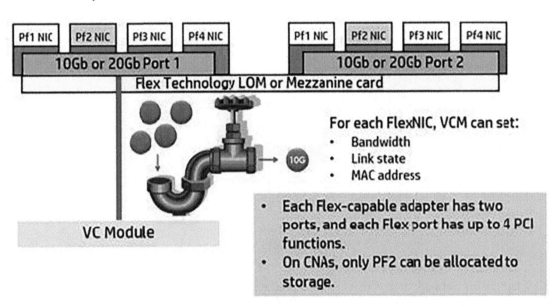

Figure 6-29 HPE Flex-10/Flex-20 and FlexHBA technology

Synergy CNAs support the Flex-10/Flex-20/FlexHBA technology. This HPE technology, as illustrated in Figure 6-29, is the simplest, most converged, and most flexible way to connect virtualized compute modules to any data or storage networks. Using Flex-10/Flex-20 technology with FCoE, the VC interconnects converge traffic over high-speed 10 Gb (with Flex-10 technology) or 20 Gb (with Flex-20 technology) connections to servers with HPE CNA adapters. This pipe (10/20 Gb) can be subdivided into up to four (or more, depending on the card) pipes. On the server NIC port, each of these is referred to as a Flex-NIC. So, each interconnect provides four adjustable connections (three data and one storage, or all data) to each 10/20 Gb server port. You can take the second Flex-NIC (PF2) and use it as a NIC, HBA (FCoE), or iSCSI.

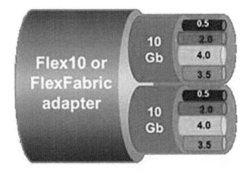

Figure 6-30 Example of two 10 Gb Flex ports

The HPE Flex-10/Flex-20 and HPE CNA technology consist of two HPE components, as illustrated in Figure 6-30:

- HPE dual-port CNA server adapters
- HPE VC interconnect (using Flex-10 or Flex-20 technology)

HPE OneView recognizes and manage each FlexNIC or FlexHBA within a server profile.

 Note

Flex server adapters can also be deployed with other interconnects, but they operate only as standard dual-port NICs.

Management tools

HPE network management tools span across products and bring innovations to complete lifecycle management. As network management becomes more complex, the risks associated with compromised data flow have also increased.

HPE OneView

Figure 6-31 HPE OneView benefits

HPE OneView is the foundation solution for the SDDC that helps drive the business and enable innovation, as indicated in Figure 6-31. HPE OneView:

- Helps deploy the infrastructure faster by leveraging template-based provisioning
- Simplifies lifecycle operations with advanced self-monitoring and maintenance tools
- Performs frictionless updates for important lifecycle ops like firmware and driver updates
- Helps with increasing the productivity by making integrating third-party tools a programmatic task through our unified API.

HPE OneView and HPE Synergy Composer

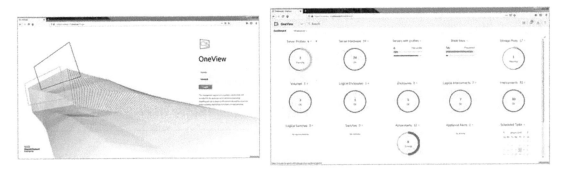

Figure 6-32 HPE OneView and HPE Synergy Composer: two different OneView implementations

HPE OneView exists in two different implementations, as illustrated in Figure 6-32. First HPE OneView implementation is a standalone appliance for VMware, Hyper-V, or Kernel-based Virtual Machine (KVM) virtualization environment. This VM manages and/or monitors traditional environment, such as the c-class BladeSystem, DL servers, Apollo, Superdome Flex, and so on. The second implementation is inside the HPE Synergy Composer, the management appliance built into HPE Synergy Frame that hosts HPE OneView and manages groups of Synergy frames (enclosures).

HPE OneView: Ramp up to Composable Infrastructure

Figure 6-33 Manageable and monitored resources in HPE OneView

HPE OneView is a ramp up to composable Infrastructure, implementing its three basic pillars: a converged management, a software-defined approach, and a common API. HPE OneView provides converged management that provides simplified and consistent management across server, storage, and networking, as indicated in Figure 6-33. Devices that can be managed and/or monitored from the user interface (UI) include HPE ProLiant, HPE Synergy, HPE StoreVirtual VSA, HPE BladeSystem, HPE 3PAR, HPE SimpliVity, HPE Converged System, HPE Nimble, and more.

Deploy the infrastructure at cloud-like speed

Through software-defined intelligence, HPE OneView takes a template-driven approach to provisioning, updating, and integrating compute, storage, firmware/device drivers, and networking infrastructure. This approach not only reduces the risk of human error by enabling administrators to develop a template once and then replicate as needed, but it also helps boost the productivity of administrators and software developers. In addition, change operations can be implemented by using templates so that tasks such as adding more storage to a service, modifying network connectivity, or updating firmware are implemented automatically.

Continuous, automated lifecycle operations reduce cost, save time, and increase time to value for businesses. With templates, you can simplify system updates and enforce compliance to ensure infrastructure stability. You can also manage deployment plans and create bootable images from capturing, cloning, or customizing golden images. Furthermore, customers can enforce compliance by using templates to quickly provision, update, or roll back images to minimize maintenance windows.

For customers with HPE BladeSystems, HPE OneView automates the creation of FC and Ethernet connections, reducing setup time from hours to minutes. Integration with HPE networking's Intelligent Management Center (IMC) and HPE VC advances this process further. IMC listens for newly provisioned BladeSystem enclosures and then automatically connects them to the production network.

Develop more apps faster

The HPE OneView unified API, together with the growing ecosystem of partner integrations, enables you to accelerate application and service delivery; developers, IT administrators, and independent software vendors (ISVs) can automate infrastructure with a single line of code.

A substantial portion of the work of operations consists of routine tasks related to infrastructure life-cycle management, including designing, provisioning, monitoring, and updating. HPE OneView is designed to automate day-to-day responsibilities by simplifying time-consuming tasks leading to increased productivity and reduced operational costs. It is an automated infrastructure provider under any environment that supports traditional, virtualized, and cloud workloads, including VMware, Microsoft, and OpenStack.

HPE OneView addresses two approaches to IT management

HPE OneView makes daily IT operations more efficient and effective by enabling large and small enterprises to manage their environments from a single, centralized console. HPE OneView also enables programmatic instantiation and management of the infrastructure though a standards-based API. When software-defined processes are combined with automation, less IT staff time is needed to deploy, manage, and support core infrastructure, saving much-needed IT resources and simplifying management.

For example, when you add a device to an environment, HPE OneView automatically detects the hardware and prepares it for monitoring and management. If it already has a server profile, it is allocated and fully configured. If it does not yet have a server profile, the hardware is available in a global pool awaiting a new configuration. This supports dynamic hardware reconfiguration and makes it easy to provision a new server profile just like the last one. It guarantees that the server profile will successfully deploy to the allocated hardware, based on knowledge of the server hardware type and enclosure group.

In addition to facilitating daily IT operations, HPE OneView benefits enterprise DevOps, where the rate of IT infrastructure provisioning, configuration, and deployment activity is dramatically increasing. New code is often deployed monthly, weekly, or even more frequently. The HPE OneView unified infrastructure management platform is designed to enable customers to streamline complex lifecycle operations and application delivery activities across data center resources. HPE OneView combines software-defined resources with template-driven provisioning and management to provide the right resource at the right time for each workload in the data center.

 Note

To watch a video about using the integration between HPE OneView and the ServiceNow cloud portal to increase IT operational efficiencies, visit:

https://youtu.be/W1MrCdQ-9KE

Two methods for an enhanced user experience

The HPE OneView UI approach is designed to enhance the interaction among IT staff and match work practices in the data center. It is simple, efficient, and consistent, and it is inspired by commonly used web technology. It works on desktops, tablets, and mobile devices. You can right-click the HPE OneView UI to open up a new tab, copy and paste browser bookmarks, email links to colleagues, and print diagrams and data. Search capabilities, newsfeeds, and other functions work as expected in a web experience.

The HPE OneView UI builds functionality around an administrator's work practices and puts resources in the menu. The combination of Java compatibility checks and security updates creates an operational burden, so HPE OneView uses HTML5 as well as CSS3, JavaScript, and AJAX.

You also have the choice of programmatic interfaces based on Representational State Transfer (REST) APIs. REST APIs involve the use of relatively basic create, read, update, and delete (CRUD) operations that are applied to resources (objects) by using standardized HTTP POST, GET, PUT, and DELETE commands. Using the REST API support available in HPE OneView, you can manipulate resources in a way that is consistent with the equivalent actions you perform using the HPE OneView UI. The REST APIs integrate with a broad ecosystem of management partners. This includes service desk, orchestration, monitoring tools, configuration management database (CMDB), and more.

The HPE OneView UI and REST APIs are organized by resource. The online help for each screen in the UI describes the resources and their configuration rules, as needed.

HPE OneView default Dashboard

Figure 6-34 Dashboard for a single HPE OneView instance

The default Dashboard provides a unified IT management console that serves as a single point of view across the entire data center. This centralized console eases management and deployment by enabling you to manage resources from a single location.

The default Dashboard screen, as shown in Figure 6-34, displays a graphical representation of the general health and capacity of the resources in the data center. From the Dashboard screen you can immediately see the areas that need attention. The screen displays the status of the most relevant resources that are associated with assigned user roles. If you are assigned multiple roles, such as Network and Storage roles, it displays the combination of resources that each role would see on the dashboard. You can customize the display by adding, deleting, and moving resource panels.

The Dashboard presents information about the general health and status of the appliance and managed resources in the data center. For direct access to resources needing your attention, click the resource name.

- **Status**—Summarizes health status. The number displayed next to the resource name indicates the total number of resource instances known to the appliance. To learn more, click the resource name to display the resource's main screen and view detailed health and status information. A dark-gray chart slice indicates the number of resources that are not reporting information because they are either disabled or not being managed by the appliance.

- **Servers with profiles**—Reports the number of server hardware instances with server profiles assigned to them. If the circle is not solid blue, hover your cursor over the light-gray slice to see the number of servers without server profile assignments.

- **Blade/compute modules bays**—Reports the count of server hardware instances in all managed enclosure bays. If the circle is not solid blue, hover your cursor over the light-gray chart slice to see the count of empty enclosure bays.

REST APIs: Designed for automation

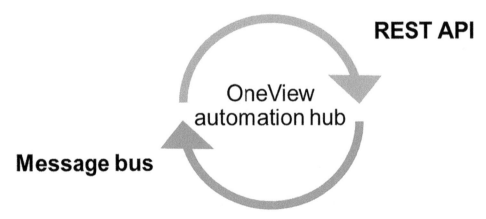

Figure 6-35 Message buses and REST API provide a closed-loop automation system

A complimentary relationship exists between the REST API and the HPE OneView message bus, which is a messaging broker or intermediary for exchanging messages. It is well suited for large-scale management of virtualized and cloud environments. HPE OneView provides two message buses:

- The state change message bus (SCMB) contains messages about any change in the resources managed by HPE OneView.

- The metric streaming message bus (MSMB) contains metrics such as temperature and power or CPU utilization for managed resources.

HPE pairs the message buses with an industry-standard REST API. Together, they form a symbiotic relationship that allows HPE OneView to serve as a closed-loop automation hub. HPE OneView "listens" to changes in the environment and publishes messages about the changes to all the consumers on the bus. Message bus consumers can then leverage the REST API to carry out CRUD operations or integrate with other systems. This powerful combination of the REST API and the message buses, as indicated in Figure 6-35, provides the foundation for building higher-level IT automation.

Health monitoring

Figure 6-36 Managing the health of ProLiant servers

Efficient data views and effective control enable your customer to respond to issues when managing the health of ProLiant servers, as indicated in Figure 6-36. When managed resources are added to the appliance, they are automatically set up for monitoring, including the automatic registration of

Simple Network Management Protocol (SNMP) traps and scheduling of health data collection. ProLiant Gen8, Gen9, and Gen10 servers are monitored immediately without requiring your customer to invoke additional configuration or discovery steps.

All monitoring and management of data center devices is agentless and out-of-band for increased security and reliability. Operating system software is not required, open SNMP ports on the host operating system are not required (for Gen8, Gen9, and Gen10), and Zero Downtime updates can be performed for these embedded agents. ProLiant Gen8, Gen9, and Gen10 servers support agentless monitoring by Integrated Lights-Out (ILO). HPE OneView uses SNMP in read-only mode to the iLO only, not to the host operating system. ProLiant G6 and G7 servers require host operating system SNMP agents. Read-only mode means SNMP uses gets and traps, but not sets.

HPE OneView provides proactive alert notifications by email (instead of using SNMP trap forwarding) and automated alert forwarding. Your customer can view, filter, and search their alerts using Smart Search. Alerts can be assigned to specific users and annotated with notes from administrators. Notifications or traps can be automatically forwarded to enterprise monitoring consoles or centralized SNMP trap collectors. The customized dashboard capability allows you to select and display important inventory, health, or configuration information and to define custom queries for new dashboard displays. The single user interface provides additional summary views of firmware revisions of the hardware inventory for servers, storage, and networks. Other data and inventory elements are visible through the user interface, and REST API and can be found using Smart Search.

HPE OneView has the capability to perform automatic creation and follow-up of support cases in case of failures.

Using HPE 3PAR StoreServ storage within HPE OneView is as simple as selecting a storage template and a server profile. HPE OneView automation carves out the storage volume, zones the FC SAN, and attaches the storage to the server profile. After they are rolled out, the SAN resources are immediately exposed in the topology map. This includes multi-hop FC and FCoE architectures. In HPE OneView, proactive alerts are provided when the expected and actual connectivity and states differ or when SAN health issues are immediately visible in the topology map. HPE OneView provides SAN configuration reports, which include guidance for SAN efficiency and help in resolving potential SAN issues before there is a business impact.

The HPE OneView appliance monitors the health status of storage systems and issues alerts when there is a change in status. The appliance also monitors the connectivity status of storage systems. If the appliance loses connectivity with a storage system, an alert is displayed until connectivity is restored. The appliance attempts to resolve connectivity issues and clear the alert. If it cannot, you must use the Storage Systems screen to refresh the storage system manually and synchronize it with the appliance. The appliance also monitors storage systems to ensure that they are synchronized with changes to hardware and configuration settings. However, changes to storage systems made outside the appliance (such as changing credentials) might cause the storage system to lose synchronization with the appliance, in which case you must manually refresh the storage system.

Server profile

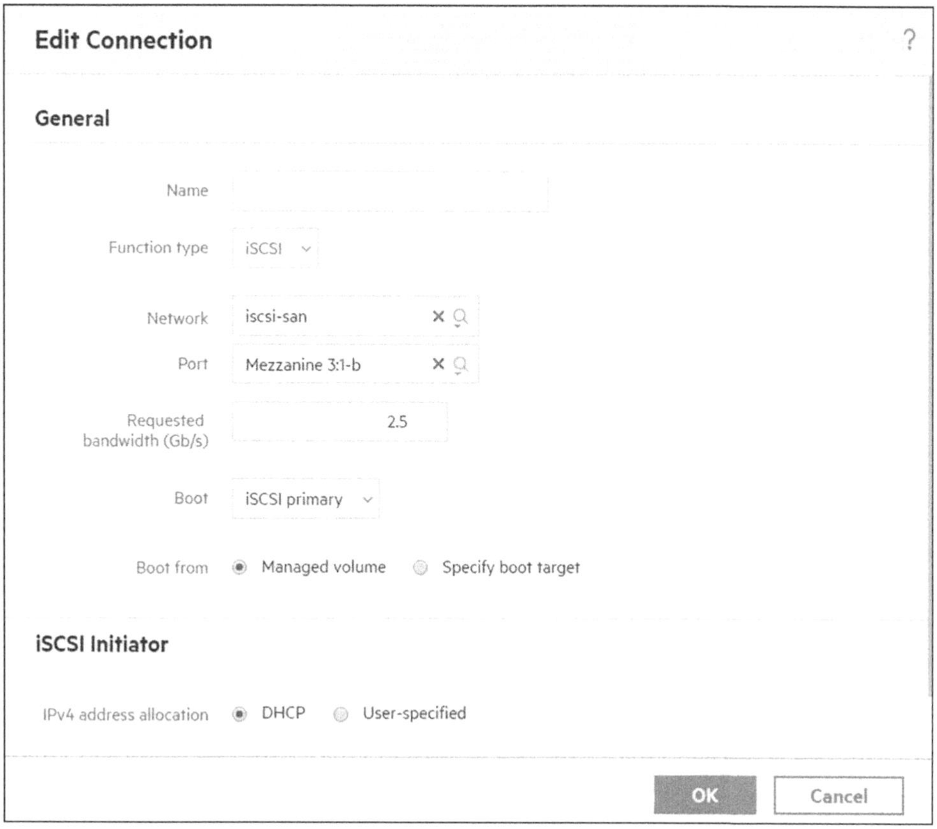

Figure 6-37 Connection settings in the HPE OneView server profile

Server profiles and server profile templates enable you to provision hardware quickly and consistently according to your best practices. Store your best practice configuration in a server profile template and then use the server profile template, shown in Figure 6-37, to create and deploy server profiles.

A server profile captures key aspects of a server configuration in one place, including:

- Firmware update selection and scheduling (optionally including drivers/software)

  - Method of updating

- BIOS settings

- Local RAID configuration and DAS configuration on Synergy (D3940)

- Network connectivity

  - Leveraging VC

  - Selecting FlexNIC and FlexHBA assignments

- Boot order configuration

- SAN storage

  - 3PAR StoreServ

  - StoreVirtual

  - Nimble

- Unique IDs

  - MAC

  - WWN

  - Serial number

- OS Deployment Settings for Synergy compute modules

- iLO configuration

If similar hardware has been discovered, server profiles enable your customer's experts to specify a server configuration before the server arrives. When the server hardware is installed, their administrators can quickly bring the new server under management. For example, they can create an unassigned server profile from a template that specifies all the configuration aspects—such as BIOS settings, network connections, and boot order—to use for a type of server hardware.

Before the server is installed in an enclosure bay, they can do one of the following:

- Assign the server profile at the time of creation to an empty bay in an enclosure where the server will eventually reside.

- Create an unassigned profile, and assign it after the hardware arrives.

Your customer can move a server profile that has been assigned to hardware in an enclosure bay. They can copy server profiles to multiple servers with or without using server profile templates. They can control the server profile behavior. For example, they can assign a server profile to an empty bay and when an appropriate server is inserted into that bay, the server profile is automatically applied to the server hardware. The server profile can also be associated with a specific server to ensure that the profile is not applied if the wrong type of server is accidentally inserted into the bay.

The ability to edit existing server profiles and change the server hardware type and enclosure group allows them to perform tasks such as:

- Add or remove a mezzanine card to or from a server.

- Move server hardware from one enclosure to another enclosure with a different configuration.

- Move server profiles to servers with different adapters, generations of hardware, or hardware models.

- Move workloads to different servers or enclosure configurations.

In an existing server profile, click the **Change** link adjacent to the Server hardware type or Enclosure group settings to make changes to these values. Your customer can edit a server profile or a server profile template any time after it has been created. When you edit a server profile, the state of the server changes. The appliance analyzes the changes and determines the actions needed to update the server. For example, if they change the BIOS settings but not the firmware baseline, the firmware is not updated. Only the requested changes are applied.

When they edit a server profile template, the appliance analyzes the changes and updates the template configuration. Then all the server profiles created from the template are evaluated for compliance and a notification indicates the number of profiles that will be affected by the change. The profiles are marked as non-compliant. Your customer can use the Update from template option in Server Profiles to accept all the changes from the template.

If they change the server hardware type or enclosure group, other settings within a server profile can be affected. For most of the following attributes, settings remain unchanged so long as the selected server hardware type or enclosure group supports the existing settings. If the settings are not supported by the selected server hardware type or enclosure group, the settings are removed.

Server profile templates

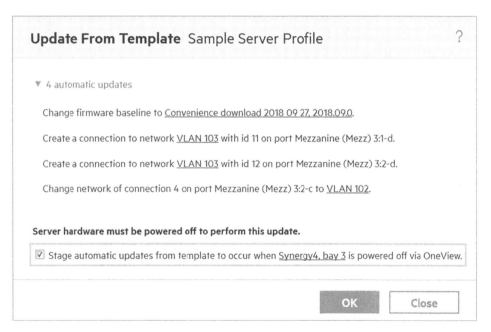

Figure 6-38 Server profile templates

Server profile templates, as shown in Figure 6-38, allow users to define configurations once, and then provision or update the configuration many times—consistently and reliably with no repetitive tasks—across compute, storage, and networking resources. This way, profile mobility is not limited to migrations across the same server hardware type and enclosure groups. HPE OneView provides profile mobility across different:

- Adapters

- Generations

- Server blade models

The HPE OneView appliance monitors both the server profile and server profile template. It compares both elements and ensures the server profile matches the configuration of its parent server profile template.

The profile mobility feature enables you to modify enclosure groups and server hardware templates. However, the resources must be detached from the server profile template before changes are made or you will receive an error. Instead of detaching the server profile template, you can change the server profile template itself, but all servers attached to that template will be affected.

Server profile templates provide automated change management across multiple systems and are at the center of software-defined policies and solutions. Templates enable administrators to drill down into dashboard panels to identify issues or troubleshoot problems connected to inconsistencies.

Editing templates is very similar to editing profiles in that templates do not have identifiers and cannot be assigned to the hardware. Easily move from the high-level status down to the connections summary and individual connections can be expanded to reveal complete connection configuration details.

Consistency checking is validating a server profile to ensure that it matches the configuration of its parent server profile template. The appliance monitors both the server profile and server profile template, compares the two, and checks them for consistency.

HPE OneView storage management

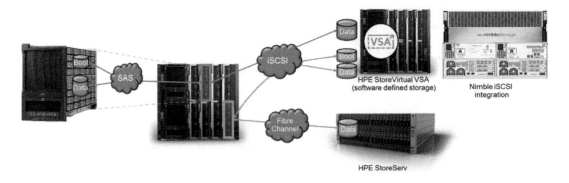

Figure 6-39 HPE OneView storage management

HPE OneView provides automated, policy-driven provisioning of supported storage resources. It is fully integrated with server profiles so that your customer can manage their new or existing storage infrastructure, as indicated in Figure 6-39. With HPE OneView, they can view and manage their storage system and storage pools. They can add existing volumes and create new volumes, and then they can create volume templates to provision multiple volumes with the same configuration.

Switched fabric, direct-attached, virtual SAN (vSAN) storage area network topologies, and iSCSI connections are supported. Storage system and storage pools are added to the appliance followed by volumes, which are associated with networks.

The volumes can then be attached to server profiles. Your customer can also add SAN managers to make their managed SANs available to the appliance. Managed SANs can be associated with FC or FCoE networks on the appliance to enable automated zoning and automatic detection of connectivity.

HPE OneView allows administrators to:

- Automate HPE 3PAR StoreServ volume creation and SAN zoning.

- Automate StoreVirtual and Nimble volume provisioning.

- Attach the storage volumes to server profiles.

For example, a 32-server cluster can be automatically created in hours rather than manually configured in days. After deployment, storage and servers are monitored in HPE OneView, and the storage topology is visible in Map View.

HPE OneView discovers the SAN paths and provides connectivity services for the following infrastructures:

- HPE 3PAR StoreServ storage systems connected directly to an enclosure using FC

- HPE 3PAR StoreServ storage systems connected to an HPE B-series FC SAN configuration (SANs managed through the HPE B-series SAN Network Advisor software)

- HPE 3PAR StoreServ storage systems connected to a Brocade FC SAN configuration (SANs managed through Brocade Network Advisor software)

- HPE FlexFabric 5900 AF/CP switches, Cisco MDS series switches, Cisco Nexus 5000 and 6000 series switches, and Brocade switches

With HPE OneView, advanced automation enables an IT generalist to define and provision storage volumes, automatically zone the SAN as part of the provisioning process, and attach the volumes to server profiles.

HPE OneView storage automation makes businesses more responsive, secure, and efficient. HPE 3PAR StoreServ storage is fully integrated with HPE OneView server profiles for automated, policy-driven rollout of enterprise-class storage resources. After the storage has been rolled out, your customer can select an HPE 3PAR StoreServ volume in HPE OneView and create a snapshot from that volume. Snapshots in OneView allow copy and provisioning access to non-storage professionals such as database administrators, software developers, and test engineers working with systems. Users can restore their own copies of test data safely and quickly without relying on a storage administrator. They can easily replace and restore copies of their volumes by copying, promoting, and attaching their volumes to server profiles. This enables users to update specific snapshots with more recent snapshots, resulting in faster turnaround times for developers who need refreshed snapshots. This also alleviates the workload for storage administrators.

Using HPE 3PAR StoreServ storage within HPE OneView is as simple as selecting a storage template and a server profile. HPE OneView automation carves out the storage volume, zones the FC SAN, and attaches the storage to the server profile.

After they are rolled out, the SAN resources are immediately exposed in the topology map. This includes multi-hop FC and FCoE architectures. In HPE OneView, proactive alerts are provided when the expected and actual connectivity and states differ or when SAN health issues are immediately visible in the topology map. HPE OneView provides SAN configuration reports, which include guidance for SAN efficiency and help in resolving potential SAN issues before there is a business impact.

The HPE OneView appliance monitors the health status of storage systems and issues alerts when there is a change in status. The appliance also monitors the connectivity status of storage systems. If the appliance loses connectivity with a storage system, an alert is displayed until connectivity is restored. The appliance attempts to resolve connectivity issues and clear the alert. If it cannot, you must use the Storage Systems screen to refresh the storage system manually and synchronize it with the appliance. The appliance also monitors storage systems to ensure that they are synchronized with changes to hardware and configuration settings. However, changes to storage systems made outside the appliance (such as changing credentials) might cause the storage system to lose synchronization with the appliance, in which case you must manually refresh the storage system.

HPE OneView network management with HPE Virtual Connect

Figure 6-40 HPE OneView network management

HPE OneView manages connectivity of composable interconnects on Synergy and VC management interconnects on some older environments, as illustrated in Figure 6-40.

HPE OneView provides several networking features to streamline the provisioning of networking resources for server hardware and to manage configuration changes, including firmware updates, to VC ICMs.

Supported networks

The VC ICMs in enclosures support the following types of data center networks:

- Ethernet for data networks, including tagged, untagged, or tunnel networks
- FC for storage networks, including FC fabric attach (SAN switch) connections
- FC direct attach (Flat SAN) connections to supported 3PAR storage systems
- FCoE for storage networks where storage traffic is carried over a dedicated
- Ethernet virtual LAN (VLAN)

VC features in HPE OneView:

- Configures uplinks and VLANs

- Configures downlinks via profiles (allows multiple networks per single server port)

- VC dual-hop FCoE support

- VC Quality of Service (QoS) priority queuing

- Supports master/satellite architecture on Synergy

- Per port statistics

Enclosure and frame management

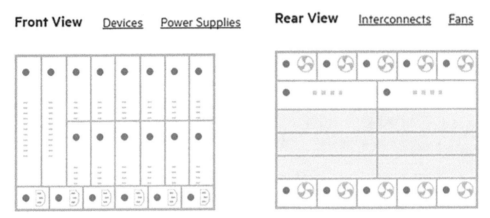

Figure 6-41 BladeSystem enclosure in HPE OneView

HPE OneView, as indicated in Figure 6-41, provides:

- Health monitoring at the enclosure and frame level (including power supplies)

- Automatically adds all components under HPE OneView management

  - Compute modules/server blades

  - ICMs

  - Management infrastructure components

- Configures according to template/group settings

  - **c-Class**—Runs Secure Shell (SSH) script on Onboard Administrator (OA)

  - **Synergy**—Configures iLO and ICM IP addresses

Change management with driver and firmware updates

Figure 6-42 Firmware and software maintenance in HPE OneView

HPE OneView provides fast, reliable, and simple firmware management across the appliance. When you add a resource to the appliance to be managed, the appliance automatically updates the resource firmware to the minimum version required by the appliance, as indicated in Figure 6-42. A firmware bundle must be uploaded to the appliance for the automation to occur. Various firmware-related reports are available in the Reports section of the main menu.

HPE OneView manages updates for:

- Infrastructure components:
  - Onboard Administrator
  - FLMs
  - VC modules
- Server hardware:
  - Using Intelligent Provisioning
  - Using HPE Smart Update Tools (SUT)/integrated SUT (iSUT): Firmware and drives support

Scheduled firmware and OS driver updates are supported as well as an external firmware repository that provides unlimited storage space for Service Pack for ProLiant (SPPs) and supports multi-appliance environments with a single external appliance.

Inventorying power and physical infrastructure

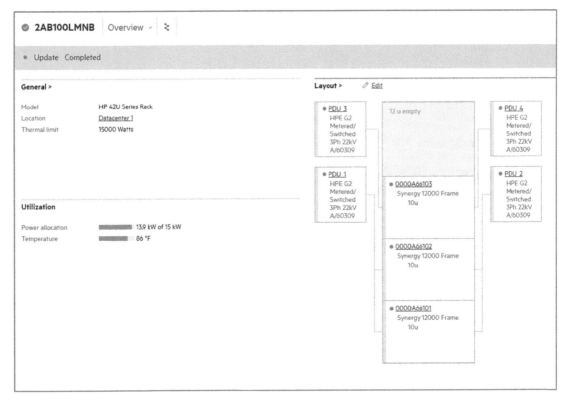

Figure 6-43 Inventory feature of HPE OneView

In HPE OneView, a data center represents a physically contiguous area in which racks containing IT equipment—such as servers, enclosures, and devices—are located. Your customer creates a data center to describe a portion of a computer room, summarizing their environment and its power and thermal requirements. A data center resource is often a subset of their entire data center and can include equipment that is not managed by HPE OneView. By representing the physical layout of their data center equipment, including unmanaged devices, they can use detailed monitoring information for space planning, and determining power and cooling requirements.

In HPE OneView, as Figure 6-43 shows, customers can:

- View a 3D model of the data center layout that includes a color-coding scheme to help them identify areas that are too hot or too cold.

- View temperature history data.

- More easily locate specific devices for hands-on servicing.

HPE OneView collects and reports processor utilization and power and temperature history for your customer's data center hardware. The appliance monitors power, automatically detects and reports power delivery errors, and provides precise power requirement information for HPE ProLiant Gen8 (or later) servers and HPE Blade System enclosures that the customer can use for planning rack and power usage. Power Discovery Services enable automatic discovery and visualization of the power delivery topology for the data center. HPE Intelligent Power Distribution Units (iPDUs) enable the appliance to map the rack power topology automatically. The appliance detects wiring errors—such as lack of redundancy—and updates the electrical inventory automatically when new servers are installed. The appliance also supports per-outlet power control for remote power cycling of each iPDU outlet. Your customer can manually define the power requirements and power topology for devices that do not support Power Discovery Services.

A rack is a physical structure that contains IT equipment such as enclosures, servers, power delivery devices, and unmanaged devices in a data center. By describing the physical location, size, and thermal limit of equipment in the racks, your customer enables space and power planning and power analysis features for their data center.

An unmanaged device is a physical resource that is located in a rack or consumes power, but it is not currently managed by HPE OneView. Some unmanaged devices are unsupported devices that cannot be managed by HPE OneView.

All devices connected to an iPDU using an Intelligent Power Discovery (IPD) connection are added to HPE OneView as unmanaged devices. Other devices that do not support IPD—such as KVM switches, routers, in-rack monitors, and keyboards—are not added to the list of unmanaged devices automatically. To include these devices in HPE OneView, customers can add them manually and describe their names, rack positions, and power requirements.

Summary: HPE OneView

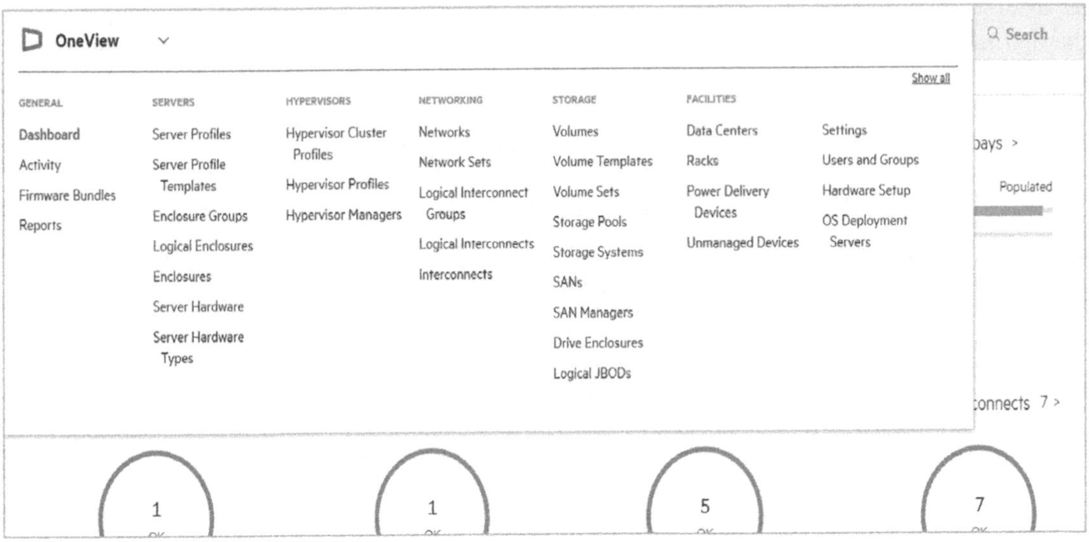

Figure 6-44 HPE OneView—main menu

To summarize, HPE OneView, as illustrated in Figure 6-44:

- Is an API-driven infrastructure management platform

- Is optimized for software-defined and hybrid cloud environments that experience frequent changes to infrastructure configurations and resource assignments

- Offers a platform to uniformly define and maintain firmware and system configurations while maintaining consistent availability and control across virtualized, containerized, and bare-metal resources

Activity: HPE Reference Configuration for Red Hat OpenShift on HPE Synergy and HPE Nimble Storage

1. Use this document:
    http://h20195.www2.hpe.com/V2/GetDocument.aspx?docname=a00056101enw

2. Answer the following questions:

    a. When configuring connections at the server profile template level, what is the difference between worker nodes and management virtualized hosts?

b. What is the recommended size of local disks for management hypervisors?

Solution components

Qty	Part number	Description
		Rack and Network Infrastructure
2	P9K10A	HPE 42U 600mmx1200mm G2 Kitted Advanced Shock Rack with Side Panels and Baying
2	P9K10A 001	HPE Factory Express Base Racking Service
2	H6J85A	HPE Rack Hardware Kit
2	BW932A	HPE 600mm Rack Stabilizer Kit
2	BW932A B01	HPE 600mm Rack include with Complete System Stabilizer Kit
6	AF533A	HPE Intelligent Modular 3Ph 14.4kVA/CS8365C 40A/208V Outlets (6) C19/Horizontal NA/JP PDU
		HPE Synergy Composable Infrastructure
3	797740-B21	HPE Synergy 12000 Configure-to-order Frame with 1x Frame Link Module 10x Fans
4	779218-B21	HPE Synergy 20Gb Interconnect Link Module
2	794502-B23	HPE Virtual Connect SE 40Gb F8 Module for Synergy
2	804937-B21	HPE Synergy Image Streamer
3	798096-B21	HPE 6x 2650W Performance Hot Plug Titanium Plus FIO Power Supply Kit
2	804353-B21	HPE Synergy Composer
3	804938-B21	HPE Synergy Frame Rack Rail Kit

Qty	Part number	Description
3	804942-B21	HPE Synergy Frame Link Module
1	804943-B21	HPE Synergy Frame 4x Lift Handles
1	859493-B21	Synergy Multi Frame Master1 FIO
1	859494-B22	Synergy Multi Frame Master2 FIO
8	804101-B21	HPE Synergy Interconnect Link 3m Active Optical Cable
2	720199-B21	HPE BladeSystem c-Class 40G QSFP+ to QSFP+ 3m Direct Attach Copper Cable
2	861412-B21	HPE Synergy Frame Link Module CAT6A 1.2m Cable
1	861413-B21	HPE Synergy Frame Link Module CAT6A 3m Cable
		Virtualized Hosts
3	871940-B21	HPE Synergy 480 Gen10 Configure-to-order Compute Module
3	873381-L21	HPE Synergy 480/660 Gen10 Intel Xeon-Gold 6130 (2.1GHz/16-core/125W) FIO Processor Kit
3	873381-B21	HPE Synergy 480/660 Gen10 Intel Xeon-Gold 6130 (2.1GHz/16-core/125W) Processor Kit
54	815097-B21	HPE 8GB (1x8GB) Single Rank x8 DDR4-2666 CAS-19-19-19 Registered Smart Memory Kit
18	815098-B21	HPE 16GB (1x16GB) Single Rank x4 DDR4-2666 CAS-19-19-19 Registered Smart Memory Kit
6	875478-B21	HPE 1.92TB SATA 6G Mixed Use SFF (2.5in) SC 3yr Wty Digitally Signed Firmware SSD
3	P01367-B1	HPE 96W Smart Storage Battery (up to 20 Devices) with 260mm Cable Kit
3	804424-B21	HPE Smart Array P204i-c SR Gen10 (4 Internal Lanes/1GB Cache) 12G SAS Modular Controller
3	777430-B21	HPE Synergy 3820C 10/20Gb Converged Network Adapter
		Worker Nodes
6	871943-B21	HPE Synergy 480 Gen10 6130 2P 64GB-R P204i-c SAS Performance Compute Module
3	873381-L21	HPE Synergy 480/660 Gen10 Intel Xeon-Gold 6130 (2.1GHz/16-core/125W) FIO Processor Kit
3	873381-B21	HPE Synergy 480/660 Gen10 Intel Xeon-Gold 6130 (2.1GHz/16-core/125W) Processor Kit
108	815097-B21	HPE 8GB (1x8GB) Single Rank x8 DDR4-2666 CAS-19-19-19 Registered Smart Memory Kit
36	815098-B21	HPE 16GB (1x16GB) Single Rank x4 DDR4-2666 CAS-19-19-19 Registered Smart Memory Kit
6	P01367-B1	HPE 96W Smart Storage Battery (up to 20 Devices) with 260mm Cable Kit
6	804424-B21	HPE Smart Array P204i-c SR Gen10 (4 Internal Lanes/1GB Cache) 12G SAS Modular Controller
6	777430-B21	HPE Synergy 3820C 10/20Gb Converged Network Adapter
		HPE Nimble Storage
1	Q8H41A	HPE Nimble Storage AF40 All Flash Dual Controller 10GBASE-T 2-port Configure-to-order Base Array
1	Q8B88B	HPE Nimble Storage 2x10GbE 2-port FIO Adapter Kit
1	Q8G27B	HPE Nimble Storage NOS Default FIO Software
1	Q8H47A	HPE Nimble Storage AF40 All Flash Array R2 11.52TB (24x480GB) FIO Flash Bundle
2	R0P84A	HPE Nimble Storage NEMA IEC 60320 C14 to C19 250V 15 Amp 1.8m FIO Power Cord
1	Q8F56A	HPE Nimble Storage 10GbE 2-port Spare Adapter
2	P9Q66A	HPE G2 IEC C20 Input/(8) C13 Expansion Outlets/PDU Extension Bar Kit
		HPE 5940 FlexFabric Switching
2	JH397A	HPE FF 5940 2-Slot Switch
2	JH180A	HPE 5930 24p SFP+ and 2p QSFP+ Module

Part numbers are at time of publication and subject to change. The bill of material (BOM) does not include complete support options or other rack and power requirements.

Learning check

1. Name the components of the HPE Synergy management subsystem.

_____

_____

_____

_____

2. What is the total Ethernet throughput on uplinks on a single Synergy Virtual Connect master module (HPE VC SE 40 Gb F8)?

   A. 80 Gb/s

   B. 120 Gb/s

   C. 240 Gb/s

   D. 2.56 Tb/s

3. What is the name of the configuration object inside HPE OneView that can be used to define server configurations?

_____

_____

_____

_____

4. Which HPE storage products are supported by HPE OneView for automating volume provisioning?

   A. HPE 3PAR StoreServ

   B. HPE Nimble Storage

   C. HPE StoreVirtual

   D. HPE StoreEasy

5. Select the Synergy CNA.

Alternative components for different environments

We presented a validated solution for the customer scenario. Some of the solution components, however, can be changed for alternative environments where different performance, capacity, costs, features, and similar requirements can be satisfied with other HPE solutions. Not all the workloads are the same and a single HPE product cannot match all the requirements.

HPE Synergy 660 Gen10 Compute Module

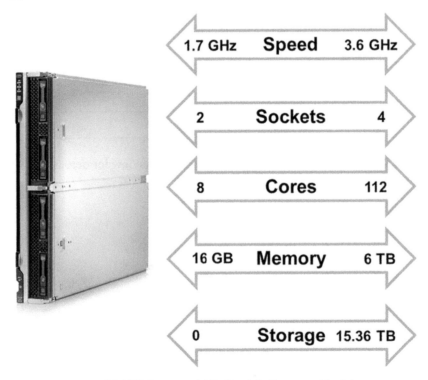

Figure 6-45 HPE Synergy 660 Gen10 Compute Module

HPE Synergy 660 Gen10 Compute Module, as indicated in Figure 6-45, solves the following IT demands:

- Scale-up composable environment

- Infrastructure and workload consolidation

- Dense virtualization solutions

- Core software licensing optimization

Benefits:

- High-performance scalable compute and virtualization density with reduced Oracle licensing and memory costs

- Composable and software-defined choice of two to four processors

- Ideal performance for scale-up workloads with up to 3.6 GHz, 205 Watts, and 28 cores

- Flexible and secure with twice the DIMMs, local storage, and persistent memory options

Customer priorities for using the HPE Synergy 660 Gen10 Compute Module:

- Consolidate workloads

- Flexible, composable compute architecture

- Optimum performance for mainstream applications with headroom for future upgrades

Compute requirements:

- Full availability of processor stack with no limitations

- Optimum memory availability for most mainstream applications

- Enterprise-class performance, scalability, and reliability

HPE Synergy 660 Compute technical description

The following table provides detailed information about the HPE Synergy 660 Compute:

	Synergy 660 Gen10
Compute	2 or 4 Intel® Xeon® Scalable Family processors
Memory	3 TB max (6 TB with 128 GB DIMMs in 2H17): HPE Smart Memory (24) DDR4, up to 2666 MT/s
Persistent Memory	16 GB NVDIMM (2H17), 12 total DIMMs are NVDIMM enabled

Local storage	– Diskless
	– 0 to 4 SFF SAS/SATA/HDDs or NVMe SSDs (15 TB max)
	– Up to 8 uFF drives
	– 1 external USB 3.0 and 1 USB iLO port; 1 internal USB 3.0 and uSD
	– Up to four internal M.2 drives for more boot options (up to 1.36 TB max)
DAS	608 TB max: Up to 160 drives per frame (4x D3940 Storage Modules)
Mezzanine slots	6 x16 PCIe 3.0
Storage controllers	– Software RAID: S100i, 6 GB SATA / 14 int lanes
	– Essential RAID: E208i-c HBA, 12G SAS / 8 int lanes
	– Performance RAID: P408i-c, 12G SAS / 8 int lanes / 2 GB cache; and P416ie-m Mezzanine, 12G SAS / 8 int 8 ext lanes / 2 GB cache
Networking	– CNAs: Synergy 3820C 10/20 GbE Converged Network Adapter 2 ports per controller; Synergy 2820C 10 GbE Converged Network Adapter 2 ports per controller
	– HBAs: HPE Synergy 3530C 16G Fiber Channel Host Bus Adapter 2 ports per controller; Synergy 3830C 16G Fiber Channel Host Bus Adapter 2 ports per controller
	– Ethernet: Synergy 6810C 25/50 GbE Ethernet Adapter 2 ports per controller
Management	HPE OneView, HPE iLO 5, Insight Control (EOL)
Power and cooling	Frame-based (96% Platinum), ASHRAE A3, Energy Star
Warranty	3/3/3

HPE Synergy 660 Gen10 Compute Module internal view

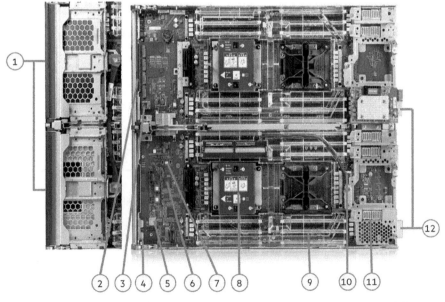

Figure 6-46 Details of the HPE Synergy 660 Gen10 Compute Module

HPE Synergy 660 Gen10 Compute Module, as indicated in Figure 6-46, is a full height form factor (10U high) server and contains the following components:

- Removable drive cages (four SFF or eight M.2 uFF drives)

- Four M.2 connectors (under drive cage)

- Internal USB 3.0 connector (under drive cage)

- External USB 3.0 connector

- Micro SD slot (under drive cage)

- iLO 5 ASIC (under drive cage)

- TPM connector (under drive cage)

- Up to four Intel® Xeon® processors

- 48 DDR4 DIMM slots (12 per processor)

- HPE Smart Storage Battery connector

- Six mezzanine connectors (x16 PCIe 3.0)

- Two power/management combo connector

Run any workload—HPE SY 620 / 680 Gen 9 EX Compute Modules

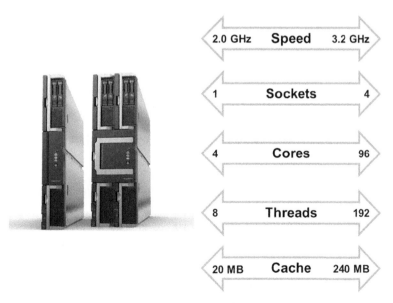

Figure 6-47 HPE SY 620/680 Gen 9

HPE Synergy 620 and HPE Synergy 680 Gen9 Compute Modules, as illustrated in Figure 6-47, are designed to meet the needs of almost any enterprise IT tier and workload. These two-socket and four-socket x86 compute modules are ideal for financial, insurance, healthcare, manufacturing, and retail enterprises that require mission-critical levels of availability, extended versatility, and real-time performance. They are also designed for HPC applications with large memory demands.

- **HPE Synergy 620 Gen9 Compute Module**—Delivers mission-critical availability and performance, as well as flexible memory, storage, and fabric options in a full-height, two-socket form factor. With 48 DIMM slots, it supports up to 6 TB of HPE DDR4 memory and has five IO PCIe 3.0connectors (2 x16 and 3 x8).

- **HPE Synergy 680 Gen9 Compute Modules**—Is a four-socket, full-height, double-wide compute module with 96 DIMM slots for up to 12 TB of HPE DDR4 memory. It features 10 PCIe 3.0 IO connectors (4 x16 and 6 x8).

HPE Synergy 10 GB Interconnect Link Module

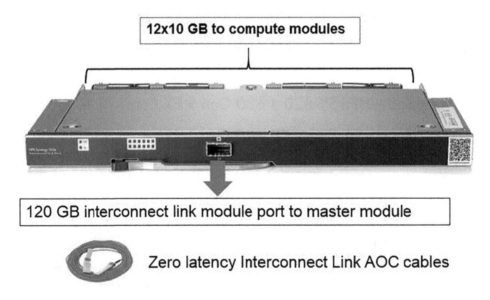

Figure 6-48 Simplest way to extend fabric resources pool to satellite frames for 10 GB

The Synergy 10 GB Interconnect Link Module is a 10 GB satellite module, as shown in Figure 6-48. It connects only to the master module, which in this case is a Synergy VC module. It has one 120 GB uplink and 12x10 GB downlinks to the compute module. The uplink is connected to a master module with zero latency Active Optical Cable (AOC) or Direct Attach Copper (DAC) Interconnect link cables. After a satellite module is connected to a master module, it automatically extends SerDes of the respective compute modules in that satellite frame to the master module. All the compute modules in the satellite frame become extended ports of the master module.

The Synergy 10 GB Interconnect Link Module has no intelligence other than a timer silicon to amplify the signal. Because there is no processing of any signal with any silicon logic, the latency of satellite modules is almost negligible. The satellite module can be thought of as a link extender from compute modules to the master module.

HPE Synergy 40 GB F8 Switch Module

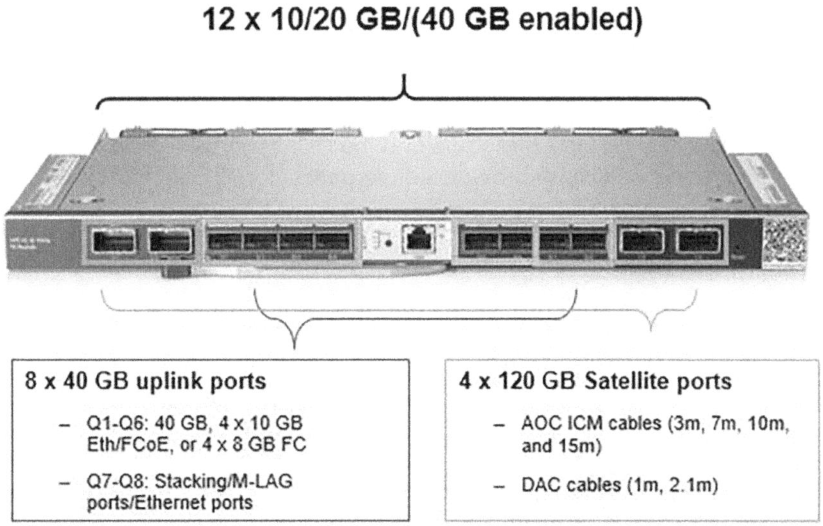

Figure 6-49 HPE Synergy 40 GB F8 Switch Module

The HPE Synergy 40 GB F8 Switch Module, as illustrated in Figure 6-49, is a network switch element of Synergy providing resilient fabric functionality. It offers network switching to data or storage networks. This module eliminates up to 95% of network sprawl at the compute module edge. It converges traffic from within Synergy 12000 frames and directly connects to external networks.

Each redundant pair of Synergy 40 GB F8 Switch Modules provides Ethernet downlink connections to dual-port 10/20 GB CNAs on each compute module. There are six QSFP+ uplink multifunction ports available for connection to upstream 40 GB Ethernet switches. These six ports can be configured as four 10 GB Ethernet ports per QSFP+ connector. A QSFP+ 40 GB/4x10 GB/4x8 GB transceiver provides four uplinks per QSFP+ port for connection to upstream 4x10 GB Ethernet connections.

In addition to the six multi-use QSFP+ uplinks, there are two additional QSFP+ ports that can be used for stacking links between Synergy 40 GB F8 Switch Modules or for additional Ethernet uplinks. The master/satellite architecture removes traditional fixed ratios of ports in a single frame and allows a high-speed, near-zero latency connection of network resources directly to other frames through interconnect link modules.

This module provides an industry-standard Layer 2 interface to upstream network switch environments and offers a full range of Ethernet switch features including data center bridging exchange

(DCBX) for FCoE support. The Synergy 40 GB F8 Switch Module provides both industry-standard FCoE capabilities as well as native FC port capability. When configured with native FC support, HPE 3PAR StoreServ storage systems can be supported in a flat SAN configuration. Additional features of this module include 12 MB shared buffer and support for 288,000 MAC tables.

Like VC for Synergy products, the Synergy 40 GB F8 Switch Module can be combined with satellite modules to extend composable fabric capabilities to satellite frames. The Synergy 40 GB F8 Switch Module is managed by industry-standard management resources that allow network functions to be managed by network administrators.

 Note

The Virtual Connect SE 40 GB F8 Module and the HPE Synergy 40 GB F8 Switch Module (and their connected satellites) provide convergence for iSCSI, FCoE, and traditional Ethernet traffic.

Mellanox SH2200 Switch Module for HPE Synergy

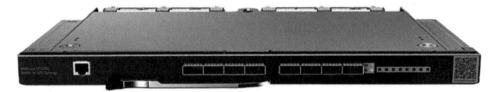

Figure 6-50 Mellanox SH2200 Switch Module for HPE Synergy

Mellanox SH2200 Switch Module for HPE Synergy, as shown in Figure 6-50, delivers high-performance, high-speed 25 Gb and 50 Gb Ethernet connectivity to the Synergy compute modules, and 40/100 Gb Ethernet to the upstream network switches. Designed for hybrid IT data centers requiring advanced feature sets such as deterministic low-latency network fabric, hardware-based virtualization support, or storage offloading. Based on the Mellanox Spectrum ASIC, the module delivers up to 2.8 Tbps switching capacity, 8.4 Billion Packets per Second (BPPS) throughput and ultra-low latency for the most demanding data center workloads such as Network Function Virtualization (NFV), financial services, high-frequency trading, or virtualized enterprise data centers.

HPE Synergy is a single infrastructure of physical and virtual pools of compute, storage, and fabric resources, and a management interface that allows configuration of server resources in any configuration. The Mellanox SH2200 Switch Module is managed by industry-standard management resources that allow network functions to be managed by network administrators. As the foundation for the composable infrastructure, HPE Synergy eliminates hardware and operational complexity so IT organizations can precisely deliver infrastructure resources to applications faster and with greater flexibility.

HPE Synergy Brocade 16 GB Fibre Channel SAN Switch Module

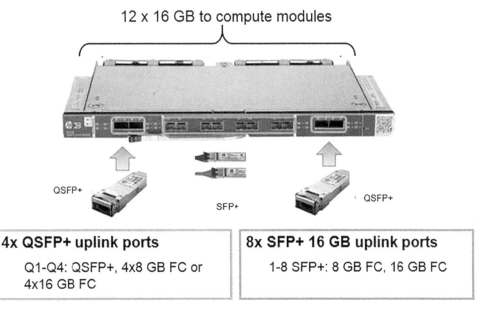

12 x 16 GB to compute modules

QSFP+   SFP+   QSFP+

4x QSFP+ uplink ports	**8x SFP+ 16 GB uplink ports**
Q1-Q4: QSFP+, 4x8 GB FC or 4x16 GB FC	1-8 SFP+: 8 GB FC, 16 GB FC

Figure 6-51 Brocade 16 GB Fibre Channel SAN Switch Module for HPE Synergy

The Brocade 16 GB Fibre Channel SAN Switch Module for Synergy Frame 12000, as shown in Figure 6-51, is a high-performance, scalable, 48-port capable, embedded traditional switch module with 16 GB Fibre Channel technology. It hot plugs into the back of the Synergy Frame 12000. Enhanced trunking support with external switches provides higher bandwidth up to 128 Gb/s Fibre Channel per trunk group to support demanding applications and high-density server virtualization.

 Note

A maximum of 36 ports is currently supported, and there are 12 FC internal ports with dual mezzanine cards. Expandable FC ports are planned for future use.

The Brocade 16 GB FC SAN Switch Module is capable of supporting 48 FC ports—up to 24 uplink FC ports and up to 24 downlink FC ports. However, with dual-port 16 GB FC mezzanine cards, only a maximum of 12 downlinks are supported. This allows each Brocade module to support a maximum of 36 FC ports.

An optional license to use (LTU) provides up to 12 additional usable ports. This LTU adds ports in increments of 12, up to a total of 36 usable ports. For example, the 16 GB 12-port base model allows customers to add up to two 12-port upgrade LTUs. With the 16 GB 24-port model, customers can add one 12-port upgrade LTU. Both options allow for a total of 36 ports.

Additional features of this SAN switch module include:

- Custom designed for the Synergy frame

- Powered by the same Brocade enterprise ASIC that powers director-class switches (Condor 3)

- Twelve downlink internal server ports, including up to eight uplink (SFP+) external ports and four uplink (QSFP) external ports

    - 4 Gb/s, 8 Gb/s, or 16 Gb/s for external SFP+ ports

- Zero footprint hot-pluggable modular design

- Powered and cooled by shared infrastructure

- Monitored by HPE OneView

- Manageable using WebTools or Brocade Network Advisor 12.4.2 or later

- Brocade Fabric OS v7.3.0b running on Gen6 processor complex

- Up to 576 Gb/s aggregate device bandwidth

- Inflight compression and encryption through an Inter-Switch Link (ISL)

- Up to six switches per Synergy frame

- Extensive SAN management with Power Pack+ software and optional SAN management software

HPE Synergy 10 GB Pass-Thru Modules

Figure 6-52 HPE Synergy 10 GB Pass-Thru Modules

HPE Synergy 10 GB Pass-Thru Modules are designed for the Synergy 12000 frame, as indicated in Figure 6-52. They are ideal for customers requiring a non-blocking, one-to-one connection between each Synergy compute module and the network. The Synergy 10 GB Pass-Thru Module provides:

- Twelve uplink ports that can accept QSFP+ connectors and SFP+ connectors using a QSFP+ to SFP+ adapter

- Support for 10 GB connections on a port-by-port basis

- Optical and DAC cables

 Note

Currently, Synergy pass-thru modules only support 10 GB connections to the network adapter on the server. This is a pass-thru connection, so both the server side and the network connection are 10 GB.

 **Important**

One QSFP+ to SFP+ adapter is required for each port to be connected on the Synergy 10 GB Pass-Thru Module. Standard 10 GB cables and SFP+ modules can then be added for a range of 10 GB connection choices.

The following adapters are supported with Synergy 10 GB Pass-Thru Modules:

- HPE Synergy 2820C 10 GB Converged Network Adapter (Emulex)

- HPE Synergy 3820C 10/20 GB Converged Network Adapter (Emulex)

Cable options

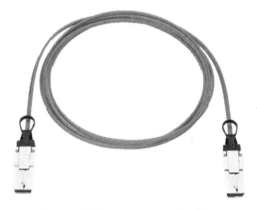

Figure 6-53 Active optical cable

Architects need to consider cable options when designing a Synergy solution, as illustrated in Figure 6-53:

- Management ring (FLM LINK)
    - CAT6A (10 GBASE-T)
- Management network (FLM MGMT)
    - CAT6A (10 GBASE-T)
- Interconnect link modules (Master/Satellite)
    - Active optical cables or direct-attached copper (120 Gbps)
- Cluster ports (Master/Master)
    - QSFP+ AOC/DAC cables or transceivers (40 Gbps)
- VC master module uplinks
    - QSFP+ AOC/DAC cables (40 Gbps)
    - QSFP/SFP+ AOC/DAC splitter cable (4x10 Gbps)
    - QSFP+ transceivers and cables (40 Gbps SR4,LC; breakout cables 4x10 Gbps/4x8 Gbps)
    - QSFP/SFP+ adapter (1x 10 Gbps)

Not all protocols are supported on all cables and transceivers:

- Ethernet only:
    - HPE FlexNetwork X240 40G QSFP+ to 4x10G SFP+ 1m Direct Attach Copper Splitter Cable
    - HPE B-series SFP+ to SFP+ Active Copper 3.0m Direct Attach Cable
- Ethernet of FC:
    - HPE Synergy 40 GbE/4x10 GbE/4x8 Gb FC QSFP+ Transceiver
    - HPE Multi Fiber Push On to 4 x Lucent Connector 5m Cable
    - HPE BladeSystem c-Class QSFP+ to SFP+ Adapter
- FC only:
    - HPE B-series 16 Gb SFP+ Short Wave Transceiver
    - HPE B-series 4x16 Short Wave QSFP Transceiver

Scenario 7: HPE Reference Architecture on VMware Cloud Foundation on HPE Synergy Reference Architecture

The wide HPE portfolio of data center products can be introduced using customer scenarios and recommended, validated configurations based on the HPE Reference Architecture or HPE Reference Configuration.

Introducing the customer scenario

WRT company will be used as a storyline through this scenario. We will introduce the company using an interview:

- What is your primary business?
  - Global automotive supplier
- How many employees do you currently have?
  - 10,000+ employees
- What does your selling and delivery channel look like?
  - Long-term contracts with selected car producers, limited marketing, no direct sales
- Where are you currently storing data, and how do you access files?
  - Mix of NAS and SAN devices, mainly HPE
- What does your server and network infrastructure look like?
  - Two data centers, hundreds of devices (networking brand is Aruba)
- What is the structure of your IT department?
  - E-shop development, operations team
- What are your current plans?
  - Hybrid cloud solution for selected multi-tier applications, better automation

Customer requirements

As a result of multiple interviews and gathering information about customer plans and the customer's current infrastructure, the following requirements emerged for the new solution:

- Private cloud solution
  - Supporting migration of workloads to public cloud environment
  - Both containerized and VM-based applications

- 20 compute hosts for first phase of deployment
  - 16-core CPU
  - 512 GB per server
- Distributed shared storage
  - Two tiers
  - 230 TB of raw capacity tier storage
  - 32 TB of cache tier storage
- Networking devices aligned with current infrastructure
  - 2x 20 Gb connectivity required per server
  - Maximum bandwidth for east-west traffic
- Four weeks of retention
- Software-defined control of hardware resources
- Aggregated management of cloud resources
- VMware Cloud Foundation 3.0 as the private cloud platform

 Note

The number of nodes and networking do not match the Reference Architecture (six nodes only and Arista instead of Aruba).

Activity: Private cloud information resources

1. Download these information resources:
   - HPE Reference Architecture on VMware Cloud Foundation on HPE Synergy

     http://h20195.www2.hpe.com/V2/GetDocument.aspx?docname=a00064661enw

   - Download HPE Converged Infrastructure Solution Sizer Suite installation files from:

     https://sizersllb.itcs.hpe.com/sb/installs/Converged_Infrastructure_Solution_Sizer_Suite.zip

2. Answer the following questions:

   a. Which virtualization products are integrated in the selected virtualization platform?

   _____

   _____

   _____

   _____

   _____

   b. What is the recommended server platform by HPE in Reference Architecture?

      – How many servers are part of the reference configuration?

   _____

   _____

   _____

   c. What is the recommended storage platform by HPE in Reference Architecture?

   _____

   _____

   _____

   d. Which devices will provide networking to the solution?

   _____

   _____

   _____

   e. What is the ratio of capacity and cache tier in the vSAN?

   _____

   _____

   _____

   f. Which components of the reference architecture need to be changed to match the customer requirements?

   _____

   _____

   _____

   _____

Software-defined infrastructure

What does the data center need to be able to deliver this kind of service to the business? What the data center needs is to redefine itself at its core, to transform its existing infrastructure into a software-defined, intelligent infrastructure that can automate and streamline tasks, self-monitor and maintain, be manageable at scale, and can integrate with a vast number of third-party tools quickly and easily so that IT can deliver infrastructure as a service to the developers who are driving innovation for the business.

Software-defined intelligence

Software-defined intelligence for infrastructure that:

- Utilizes software-defined intelligence to automate and streamline every task

- Seamlessly maintains, monitors, and manages across multiple platforms at scale

- Easily integrates with tools that enable IT to better deliver services to developers

HPE OneView: The foundation for a software-defined data center

HPE OneView has been designed to eliminate management complexity through convergence. HPE OneView is designed to deliver management that spans server, storage, and networking using the same interface, the template process, and the REST API.

HPE OneView is software defined. This means that the infrastructure elements are defined by experts using templates. This enables new infrastructure to be rolled out and updated consistently every time with the right configuration parameters and the right firmware version.

VMware vSAN

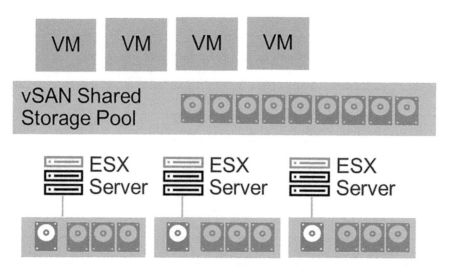

Figure 6-54 Example of software-defined storage offering in the HPE pricelist

VMware vSAN is built into the hypervisor kernel, making it very simple and seamless with a zero-step installation process, as illustrated in Figure 6-54.

Product features:

- Deduplication, compression, and erasure coding on All-Flash systems

- Data at rest encryption (software based)

- Smart Drive support—degraded device handling

- One-click firmware and driver upgrades

- iSCSI target service for block storage

- Two-node cluster with a witness at a third site

- Min. 100 Mbps bandwidth, <300 ms RTT for witness

Architecture:

- Minimum of three VMware vSphere ESX servers up to 64 nodes

- One to five disk groups per host:

  - One solid-state drive (SSD) per disk group

  - One to seven hard disk drives (HDDs) per disk group

- Software mirroring

- Up to four copies of data can be stored in the VSAN pool

Building blocks of the solution

In today's world, businesses need to turn ideas into services faster, respond quickly to new customer demands, and innovate by building new services with technology to stay competitive. To meet these business demands, IT is increasingly adopting new cloud technologies, moving away from expensive purpose-built hardware to a software-defined model, and running VMs in the public cloud, while keeping most of their workloads on premises. Enterprises need an ideal Hybrid IT model that supports both a traditional and a new breed of cloud-native applications. Therefore, businesses are embracing a journey to digital transformation and the software-defined data center (SDDC) to balance the needs of the business and the needs of IT to support this change.

To address this challenge, HPE and VMware have collaborated to help customers accelerate the journey to hybrid cloud, bringing the promise of the SDDC to life. The combination of HPE's Composable Infrastructure with VMware's SDDC solution dramatically improves both the value and business outcomes our customers experience. HPE Synergy, combined with VMware Cloud Foundation (VCF), delivers a simplified and secure, private cloud, based on the VMware SDDC stack on a Composable Infrastructure that is flexible, easy to deploy, seamless to manage, and simple to operate. For enterprise customers looking to accelerate their journey to hybrid cloud, HPE Synergy, combined with VCF, is the right solution to deliver a simplified and secure private cloud for your customers to run all their enterprise apps—both traditional and containerized—in cloud environments.

This Reference Architecture provides architectural guidance for deploying and managing VCF on HPE Synergy for traditional application and a modern, containerized-based application, both automated by vRealize Automation and secured by NSX within a single VCF workload domain. The traditional application showcased in this Reference Architecture is WordPress, and the containerized application is Yelb. There are three use cases demonstrated in the RA on VMware Cloud Foundation:

- **Use case 1**—Demonstrate a traditional multi-tier application and a containerized application deployment

- **Use case 2**—Demonstrate auto-provisioning of the network uplink and downlink ports, using Ansible scripts

- **Use case 3**—Demonstrate ease of monitoring and reporting of the VCF infrastructure using HPE OneView for vRealize Operations

This Reference Architecture demonstrates the following benefits:

- The value of combining HPE Synergy with VMware VCF from a deployment and lifecycle perspective in a cost-effective and simplified management for a faster time to value.

- A tested and tuned solution architecture that offers optimal performance and security to deploy VMware VCF 3.0 running multi-tier apps and containerized apps. Both applications are delivered through vRealize Automation blueprints that include security tied in with NSX including micro-segmentation to provide dynamic isolation between different tiers of the application and edge-services, such as load balancing of the web tier.

- Automation of the Arista end of row switch operations, by adding uplinks trunk group ports for bringing up VMware VCF deployment with Ansible Playbooks.

- Ability to efficiently scale storage and compute independently, to deploy SDDC environments. Grow-as-you-go and support both traditional VMs and cloud-native applications.

- To expand and contract the physical and virtual infrastructures on-demand, to quickly meet changing business requirements with HPE OneView.

- An efficient monitoring for VCF environment using HPE OneView for VMware vRealize Operation's custom dashboards.

This Reference Architecture demonstrates design best practices for customers building a private cloud solution in an enterprise data center and deploying business-critical applications in a fully secure and automated manner. The solution design is based on VCF on HPE Synergy. VCF provides a unified SDDC platform integrating the VMware vSphere platform, VMware Virtual SAN Storage, and VMware NSX networking as well as fully automating and providing lifecycle management with SDDC Manager. In addition, VCF delivers the VMware vRealize suite, which includes vRealize Automation, vRealize Orchestration, and vRealize Operations to provide cloud management and automation capabilities.

The VCF software is deployed over HPE Synergy's composable, software-defined infrastructure platform, which provides a fluid pool of physical and virtual compute, storage, and fabric resources, ready for any configuration for any application.

The solution provides architectural details for deploying a traditional multi-tier application and a modern VMware vSphere Integrated Container (VIC)-based application, both automated by vRealize Automation and secured by NSX within a single VCF Workload domain. The traditional multi-tier application showcased in this Reference Architecture is WordPress and the containerized application shown is Yelb. Both these applications are delivered through vRealize Automation blueprints, which include security tied in with NSX, including micro-segmentation to provide dynamic isolation between different tiers of the application and edge-services such as load balancing of the web tier.

 Note

"The cloud" is not a place, but a method of managing IT resources that replaces local machines and private data centers with virtual infrastructure. In this model, users access virtual compute, network, and storage resources made available online by a remote provider. These resources can be provisioned instantly, which is particularly useful for companies that need to scale their infrastructure up or down quickly in response to fluctuating demand.

Portfolio: HPE servers and server systems—Select the platform

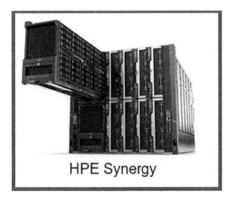

HPE Synergy

HPC systems

Tower servers

Hyperconverged systems

Rack servers

Figure 6-55 Select the platform for the Reference Architecture

The solution involves two Synergy 12000 frames, each equipped with four HPE Synergy 480 Gen10 Servers and an HPE Synergy D3940 Module, as indicated in Figure 6-55.

HPE Synergy

Each HPE Synergy 12000 frame uses an HPE VC SE 40 Gb F8 Module as a fabric module to provide an uplink to the data center network. The eight HPE Synergy 480 Gen10 servers are used to configure one management workload domain and one compute workload domain for the virtual infrastructure. The compute workload domain is used to host the WordPress application which is VM based and the Yelb application which is vSphere Integrated Container (VIC) based. Using the HPE D3940 direct-attached storage module, VMware vSAN provides software-based distributed storage for the entire solution.

HPE Synergy components for the selected solution

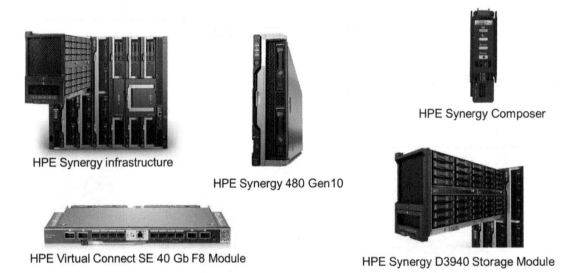

HPE Synergy infrastructure

HPE Synergy 480 Gen10

HPE Synergy Composer

HPE Virtual Connect SE 40 Gb F8 Module

HPE Synergy D3940 Storage Module

Figure 6-56 HPE Synergy components for the selected solution

HPE Synergy components required to solve customer requirements, as illustrated in Figure 6-56, include:

- HPE Synergy infrastructure (frame, power supplies, fans, FLMs, and more)
- HPE Synergy 480 Gen10 compute module
- HPE Virtual Connect SE 40 Gb F8 module
- HPE Synergy D3940 Storage Module
- HPE Synergy Composer

HPE Synergy D3940 Storage Module

Figure 6-57 HPE Synergy D3940 Storage Module

When configuring storage for a Synergy system, shown in Figure 6-57, consider the number of drives that can be included in each frame, as shown in Figure 6-58. The graphic below shows sample storage configurations. There is no fixed ratio of compute to storage, so the numbers are average drive calculations per compute.

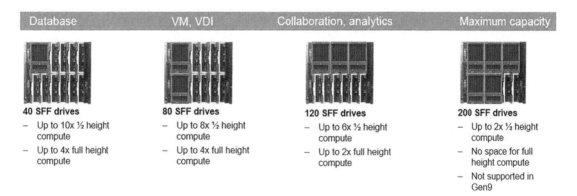

Figure 6-58 Flexible capacity for a wide range of uses and workloads

Direct-attached, composable storage can be configured for a wide range of uses and workloads. VM or Virtual Desktop Infrastructure (VDI) use cases:

- The first example shows 40 SFF drives, which would require up to 10 half-height compute modules or four full-height compute modules.

- The next example includes 80 SFF drives. This configuration would use up to eight half-height compute modules and four full-height compute modules.

- For 120 SFF drives, you would need six half-height compute modules or two full-height compute modules.

- For 200 SFF drives or five D3940 storage modules, there would be no room for full-height modules in the frame. Because the frame needs compute modules, you could have up to two of the half-height compute modules. This configuration is not supported with Gen9 modules.

The D3940 Storage Module can provide DAS for compute modules in the same frame. It provides up to 40 SFF HDDs or SSDs. You should choose SAS HDDs, which provide a maximum capacity of 2 TB each, if the customer values a lower TCO and can tolerate the tradeoff in performance. Choose SAS SSDs, which support capacities up to 3.86 TB each, if the customer is willing to pay more to receive the best performance.

All storage modules are fully connected to all the compute blades through the SAS ICMs. You can map any number of the drives—from one to 200—to a compute module. For example, you can install one storage module and 10 compute blades. You can evenly distribute the 40 drives across the compute blades, with four drives assigned to each. Alternatively, you could map all 40 drives to a single server. Any combination in between is valid as well. The D3940 Storage Module uses a one-to-one initiator to target model; compute modules cannot share drives. Each server that attaches to the drives directly controls the drives via an integrated Smart Array controller.

 Note

For more information about the Synergy storage module, visit:

https://www.hpe.com/us/en/product-catalog/synergy/synergy-storage.html

HPE Synergy in-frame storage solution

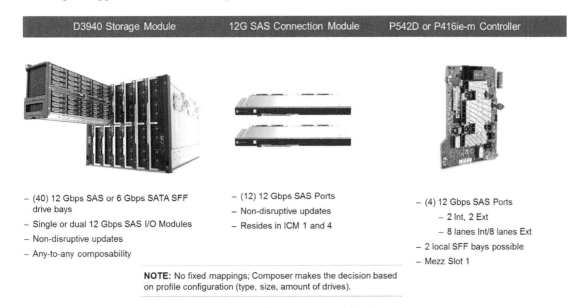

D3940 Storage Module	12G SAS Connection Module	P542D or P416ie-m Controller

- (40) 12 Gbps SAS or 6 Gbps SATA SFF drive bays
- Single or dual 12 Gbps SAS I/O Modules
- Non-disruptive updates
- Any-to-any composability

- (12) 12 Gbps SAS Ports
- Non-disruptive updates
- Resides in ICM 1 and 4

- (4) 12 Gbps SAS Ports
  - 2 Int, 2 Ext
  - 8 lanes Int/8 lanes Ext
- 2 local SFF bays possible
- Mezz Slot 1

NOTE: No fixed mappings; Composer makes the decision based on profile configuration (type, size, amount of drives).

Figure 6-59 The required Synergy modules for DAS storage

Synergy requires the following three components, as illustrated in Figure 6-59:

- **HPE Synergy D3940 Storage Module**—A 40 SFF drive bay that enables you to create logical drives for any compute module in the Synergy frame. Each D3940 module supports between eight and 40 hot-plug SFF SSDs via SAS and SATA. Each Synergy frame supports up to five such modules, thus enabling a single frame to deliver up to 200 disk drives total. D3940 Storage Modules feature a simple configuration and setup via HPE Synergy Composer. They are easy to maintain and troubleshoot with industry-standard tools. These modules use a high-performance SAS connection with sixteen 12 Gbps SAS lanes. With this design, Synergy storage can deliver up to eight times the bandwidth of other just a bunch of disk (JBOD) options. It supports single or dual 12 GB IO modules, with dual modules providing non-disruptive updates.

- **HPE Synergy 12 GB SAS Connection Module (single or dual)**—HPE Synergy D3940 Storage Modules connect to compute modules within the Synergy frame via Synergy 12 GB SAS Connection Modules. These modules reside in ICM Bays 1 and 4, where they create a non-blocking fabric for storage traffic routed from storage controllers inside compute modules through 12 Gbps SAS ports, each of which has four 12 Gbps second channels for an aggregated total of 48 Gbps per port. With the Synergy D3940 Storage Module, the Synergy 12 GB SAS Connection Module connects composable DAS for up to 10 compute modules in a single frame.

- **HPE Smart Array P542D or P416ie-m Controller Module**—A PCIe 3.0 mezzanine, four-port, 12 Gbps SAS RAID controller that connects HPE Synergy compute modules to local and zoned DAS. Its advanced RAID capabilities provide enterprise-level reliability. The latest Small Computer System Interface (SCSI) technology delivers enterprise-level connectivity and performance. The controller supports flash-backed write cache (FBWC) to maximize data retention in case of power failure. It provides a consistent set of tools and works across multiple applications to deliver a lower total cost of ownership (TCO). In addition to RAID mode, the controller supports HBA mode, which allows the controller to present drives to operating systems and applications as JBOD—a requirement for some solutions.

Together, these three components enable you to assign storage module drives to any Synergy compute module as JBOD, which can be configured as RAID volumes by the module's P542D/P416ie-m controller or not, as you choose.

Synergy storage configurations

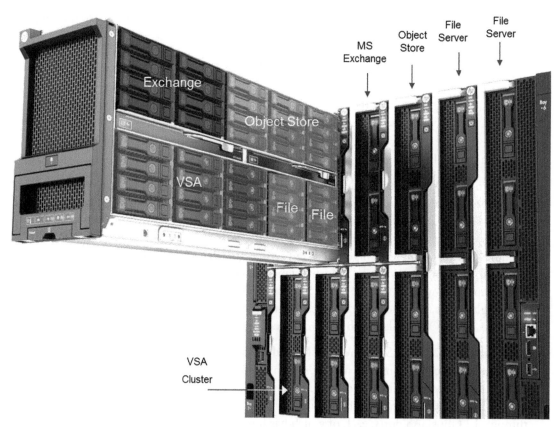

Figure 6-60 Example of a Synergy storage configuration

Currently, the storage modules cannot span multiple frames; they provide DAS only for compute modules in the same frame. However, customers can set up multi-frame clusters of compute modules that act as block, file, or object servers by connecting the servers on a backend network, as required by the particular application, as illustrated in Figure 6-60. For example, object servers can connect over an Ethernet network.

DAS environments can be built up dynamically with the optimal number of drives assigned per server as needed. The preceding graphic illustrates an example of this. A Synergy frame includes compute modules that host a Microsoft Exchange server, an object storage server, two file servers, and a cluster of six virtual storage appliance (VSA) servers. The architect has created a plan for assigning the appropriate number of drives in the storage module to each of these compute modules.

Many newer applications, including Hadoop, object stores, file servers, and data analytics applications, such as Vertica, expect compute resources to operate on data in DAS. This architecture enables all of these applications. Additionally, HPE VSA software can be loaded on two or more compute blades and represent the DAS as SAN-based block storage. This allows any compute node or server that can reach the VSA cluster over Ethernet to connect to the same storage.

HPE Networking

Part of the configuration in Reference Architecture is the networking subsystem.

Aruba core and data center switching: Powered by CX innovations

Aruba 8400

Aruba 8320

Aruba 8325

Figure 6-61 Aruba data center switches

The FlexFabric portfolio meets the majority of traditional use cases, but we also have an alternative platform: Aruba data center switches, as indicated in Figure 6-61. These are an ideal choice for many scenarios.

Aruba 8320 Switch Series

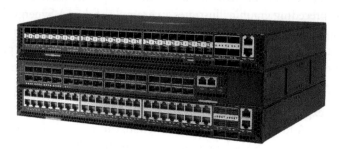

Figure 6-62 Aruba 8320 Switch Series

Aruba 8320 is a high-performance switch with 2.3 Tbps switching capacity. As illustrated in Figure 6-62, it has 48 ports of 10 Gig and six ports of 40 Gbe—so plenty of capacity for campus core and aggregation. This switch supports two hot swappable, redundant power supplies that help ensure high availability when needed at the aggregation and core layers of a campus network.

It supports the same advanced Layer 3 software features as the 8400—OSPF, BGP, VRF, M-LAG for switch virtualization and is designed for usability with easy-to-replace fans and five fan modules. Aruba 8320 contains a five-year hardware warranty with no software licensing required.

There are three models with high-speed connectivity:

- 48p 10 G SFP/SFP+ and 6p 40 G QSFP+ Switch (JL479A)

- 32p 40 G QSFP+ (JL579A)

- 48p 1 G/10 GBASE-T and 6p 40 G QSFP+ (JL581A)

Management tools

HPE network management tools span across products and bring innovations to complete lifecycle management. As network management becomes more complex, the risks associated with compromised data flow have also increased.

HPE OneView for VMware vRealize Operations

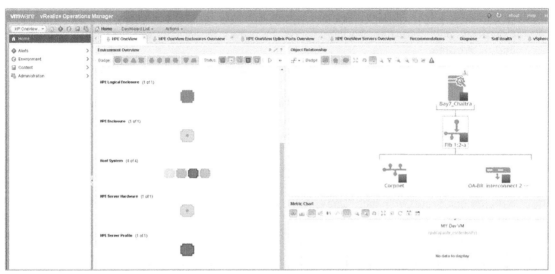

Figure 6-63 HPE OneView Adapter for VMware vRealize Operations

Typically, shifting from one management tool to another, each with a partial view of available data, is both time-consuming and complex. HPE OneView includes integrations that reduce the time needed to make important administrative changes. These integrations provide additional support for partner management platforms.

HPE OneView integrations deliver comprehensive system health and alerting, driver and firmware updates, operating system deployment, detailed inventory, and HPE VC fabric visualization, as indicated in Figure 6-63. System administrators can gain insight and control of virtualized environments while reducing the time it takes to make important changes, increase capacity, or manage planned and unplanned downtime.

HPE OneView offers the following plug-ins for virtualization management products:

- **HPE OneView for VMware vCenter**—Delivers useful HPE hardware management capabilities to virtualization administrators, enabling comprehensive deployment, provisioning, monitoring, remote control, and power optimization directly from the vCenter console. Integration includes an end-to-end connectivity diagram available in vCenter.

- **HPE OneView for Microsoft System Center**—Supports health monitoring and alerting with server profile provisioning to create or grow a Hyper-V cluster.

HPE OneView for VMware vCenter brings the native manageability of the HPE infrastructure to VMware environments.

Note

> HPE OneView for VMware vCenter supports Synergy Gen10 compute modules, Synergy Composer, HPE Storage products (3PAR StoreServ, MSA, StoreVirtual), and Synergy Image Streamer.

HPE OneView for VMware vCenter 9.0 seamlessly integrates the manageability features of ProLiant, BladeSystem, VC, and storage with VMware solutions. It reduces the time needed to make changes, increase capacity, or manage planned and unplanned downtime.

 Note

> HPE OneView for VMware vCenter 9.0 is compatible with BladeSystem c7000 and Synergy enclosures with HPE OneView 3.10 and 4.0.

By leveraging HPE OneView software-defined templates and the HPE OneView REST API, HPE OneView for VMware vCenter simplifies the process of deploying a complete vSphere cluster. Users can deploy ESX/ESXi hosts on bare-metal ProLiant servers directly from vCenter by right-clicking on a cluster or deploying a VMware hypervisor on a bare-metal server. When completed, the new hypervisor is added to the appropriate cluster.

Other functions include:

- Simplify administration with VMware console access to HPE infrastructure management for health, inventory, and configuration monitoring.

- Reduce planned and unplanned downtime by automating responses to hardware events and access to detailed resolution information for health alerts.

- Proactively manage changes with detailed relationship dashboards that provide insight into the relationship between the physical and virtual infrastructure, from the VM to the network edge.

- Maintain stability and reliability with online firmware inventory and deployment.

- Consistently and repeatedly deploy bare-metal servers.

The OneView for VMware portfolio provides comprehensive lifecycle management of HPE converged infrastructure directly from the VMware vCenter consoles. These plug-ins are ideal for customers who have standardized on VMware tools as their management platform. In addition, they:

- Integrate directly into VMware consoles.

- Leverage the HPE OneView infrastructure automation engine.

- Reduce complexity by using the same VMware tools for HPE management tasks.

- Simplify the admin learning curve by using the VMware tools with which they are already familiar.

The following VMware extensions are available as part of each HPE OneView Advanced license:

- **HPE OneView for VMware vRealize Operations** is a development and process automation tool. It provides a predefined set of libraries and workflows that can be used to access and control third-party applications, technologies, and infrastructure. This plug-in provides health, utilization, and performance metrics in the context of the HPE hardware hierarchy, so administrators can monitor critical trend changes. Its dashboards facilitate the identification of root cause problems and impacted resources across the converged infrastructure.

- **HPE OneView for VMware vCenter Log Insight** allows deep troubleshooting of an environment by analyzing unstructured data contained in iLO and Onboard Administrator (OA) logs. Information is displayed in the dashboards of VMware vCenter and vRealize Log Insight, allowing counts of critical events to be quickly identified and investigated for optimal resource utilization and rapid problem resolution.

- **HPE OneView for VMware Operations Manager** reveals critical trend changes. It includes dashboards that facilitate the identification of root cause problems and impacted resources across the data center. The HPE OneView for VMware vRealize Operations Manager provides HPE OneView server and infrastructure topology, status, and alerts to the vRealize Operations Manager environment.

HPE OneView for VMware supports enhanced integration with VMware vCenter Operations Manager and vRealize Log Insight with HPE unique entitlement to use vCenter Operations Manager integration with the standard edition.

Extensions for vCenter are licensed for use with both HPE OneView and HPE Insight Control. Although only one of these two licenses is required on any given host, the advanced provisioning features are only available with HPE OneView licensed hosts. VMware Operations Manager and Log Insight integrations are licensed with HPE OneView only.

 Note

These integrations can be downloaded online. For more information, visit the Hewlett Packard Enterprise Information Library at:

http://www.hpe.com/info/oneview/docs

 Note

You can use the HPE OneView for VMware vRealize Operations integration with an existing vRealize Operations Manager Standard version by incorporating the limited usage vRealize Operations Manager Advanced entitlement, which is provided with the purchase of HPE OneView Advanced. If you are using a version of vCenter Operations Manager earlier than 5.2.x, you need a specific license key. This license key can be obtained by registering the Partner Activation Code (PAC) from the HPE OneView license at the VMware portal.

HPE OneView for Microsoft System Center

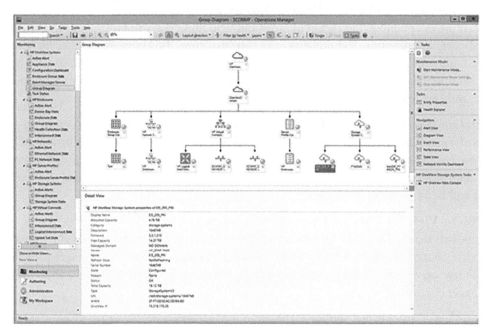

Figure 6-64 HPE OneView for Microsoft System Center

HPE OneView for Microsoft System Center, as illustrated in Figure 6-64, integrates ProLiant, BladeSystem, and Synergy manageability features into Microsoft System Center. This integration provides comprehensive system health and alerting, driver and firmware updates, and operating system deployment. Using this plug-in for Microsoft System Center, you can provision hosts using HPE OneView server profiles to create or grow a Hyper-V cluster consistently and reliably. In addition, the health monitoring and alerting information from an HPE OneView infrastructure perspective shows relationships clearly.

HPE OneView for Microsoft System Center integrates with Synergy Gen10 compute nodes and Synergy Composer to provide:

- Comprehensive health monitoring and alerting for Synergy frames, compute nodes, storage modules, and interconnects via the HPE OneView Management Pack for System Center Operations Manager (SCOM).

- Fabric visualization and automated Hyper-V deployment and updates (using Synergy Composer server profile templates) occur via the HPE Fabric Management Add-in for System Center Virtual Machine Manager (SCVMM).

- Compute module firmware and Windows driver updates occur via the HPE ProLiant Updates Catalog for SCCM and SCVMM.

This integration delivers server profile–based deployment and automated HPE StoreVirtual or StoreOnce deployment for secure backup and recovery. In addition, Microsoft System Center displays the network mapping, storage connections, and hardware status. HPE OneView for Microsoft System Center includes the following components to provide a single repository of Microsoft System Center suite of products:

- **HPE OneView Storage System Management Pack**—Part of the HPE OneView SCOM Integration Kit, it integrates an HPE 3PAR Storage Management Pack and BladeSystems/VC Management Pack. It provides a unified view to alerts/events and topological view of HPE hardware managed under HPE OneView, enabling quick response to hardware events on HPE storage and servers running Windows and Linux, as well as BladeSystem enclosures and VC.

- **HPE Storage Management Pack for System Center**—Also part of the SCOM Integration Kit, it provides seamless integration with Microsoft System Center Operations Manager (SCOM) to enable predefined discovery and monitoring policies, event processing rules, and topology views for HPE Storage.

System Center consoles

SCVMM	OpsMgr	ConfigMgr
• Automates HPE storage management • Provides an integrated view of virtual machines and storage • Provides enhanced provisioning that uses profiles to grow clusters • Offers HPE fabric visualization	• Manages hardware health on servers running Windows and Linux, BladeSystem enclosures, and VC • Monitors the health of servers that do not have an operating system loaded	• Uses ICsp for deployment to bare metal HPE servers • Provides component-level inventory of every managed server

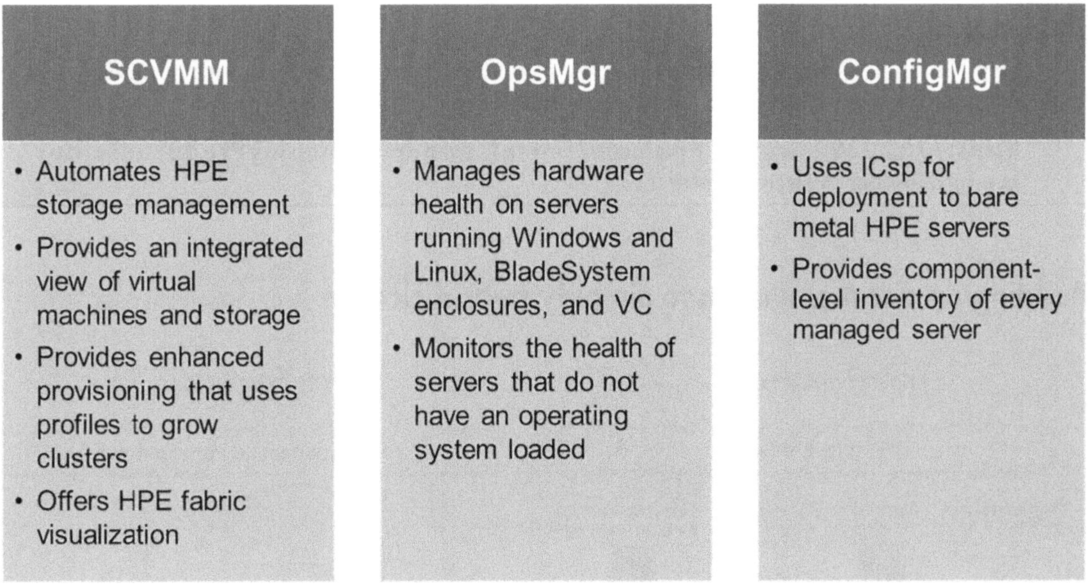

Figure 6-65 System Center consoles

Microsoft System Center is a collection of extensions that expose HPE management features within the context of the System Center consoles, as indicated in Figure 6-65:

- **System Center Virtual Machine Manager (SCVMM):**

  - Automates HPE storage management and provides an integrated view of VMs and associated storage resources

  - Provides enhanced provisioning that uses HPE OneView profiles to create or grow Microsoft Hyper-V clusters

  - Offers HPE fabric visualization using the HPE ProLiant Updates Catalog

- **System Center Operations Manager (OpsMgr):**

  - Manages hardware health on servers running Windows and Linux, as well as BladeSystem enclosures and VC

  - Monitors the health of servers that do not have an operating system loaded, as well as ProLiant Gen8 and Gen9 servers running any operating system that has a supported Agentless Monitoring Service (such as ESXi)

- **System Center Configuration Manager (ConfigMgr):** Provides a component-level inventory of every managed server using the HPE ProLiant Inventory Tool

---

⚑ Note

HPE OneView Advanced licensing allows you to download and use HPE OneView for Microsoft System Center. For more information, visit:

**https://h20392.www2.hpe.com/portal/swdepot/displayProductInfo.do?
productNumber=System_Center**

Building on our momentum to simplify hybrid cloud

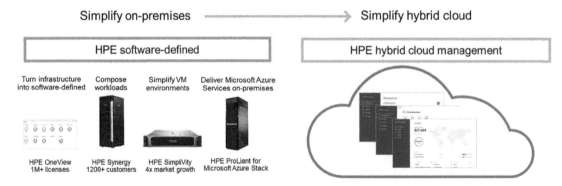

Figure 6-66 Building on our momentum to simplify hybrid cloud

Hybrid infrastructure use is pervasive—and it is resulting in complexity. Multi-cloud is being driven by developer preferences across cloud providers. The orchestration tools are maturing, yet we are still challenged without consolidated management. Moreover, apps are being developed differently—they are cloud-native or being optimized for the cloud and span multiple clouds and sites.

Customers have complex, highly distributed environments, each operating as a silo with no way to manage it all in aggregate. IT Ops wants to spend less time operating infrastructure and more time devoted to enabling application development, and they want to eliminate operational friction. Developers want fast app deployment. The typical wait time for the handshaking between developers and IT just does not cut it. Developers want access to what they want, where and when they want it—and IT wants to provide them that agility and the business wants insights in real time, not at the end of a consumption or billing cycle. We need intelligence and insights to optimize workload deployments and placement, rather than getting notified at the end of the month of their investment.

HPE OneView helps our customers transform their infrastructure into a software-defined infrastructure. It takes a software-defined, programmatic approach to managing an infrastructure with efficient workflow automation, a modern dashboard, and a comprehensive partner ecosystem. With HPE OneView, infrastructure can be configured, monitored, updated, and repurposed with a single line of code, allowing IT teams to more effectively meet changing application needs, as illustrated in Figure 6-66.

HPE Synergy is a single software-defined infrastructure that combines compute, storage, and fabric so all resources are available to run any application. HPE Synergy composer leverages integrated software-defined intelligence to accelerate operations through a single interface. This allows IT to precisely compose and recompose logical infrastructures very rapidly. HPE Synergy offers a dynamic, flexible, cost-effective infrastructure that introduces efficient operations and staff productivity.

HPE SimpliVity is our hyper-converged infrastructure solution that organizations use to simplify virtualized environments. This all-flash, pre-integrated, hyper-converged building block dramatically simplifies IT by combining all hyper-converged infrastructures and advanced data services for virtualized workloads—including VM-centric management and mobility, data protection, and guaranteed data efficiency—delivered on HPE ProLiant DL380 Servers. HPE SimpliVity hyperconvergence consolidates discrete software and hardware devices and functionality in a single building block. This reduces the cost and complexity of IT environments

We introduced our ProLiant-based Microsoft Azure Stack appliance to enable Azure cloud on premises. The API-compatible services running on premises allow workloads to be deployed in either an Azure Stack private cloud or an Azure Stack public cloud without modification.

HPE ProLiant for Microsoft Azure Stack:

- Brings integrated solution for delivering on-premises Azure-consistent services

- Offers 50% greater VM computing capacity and more configuration flexibility than competing solutions

- Optimized for Azure Stack and built to scale

HPE also recently introduced HPE OneSphere, our offering to simplify management of customers' hybrid cloud environments.

HPE OneSphere simplifies hybrid cloud environments

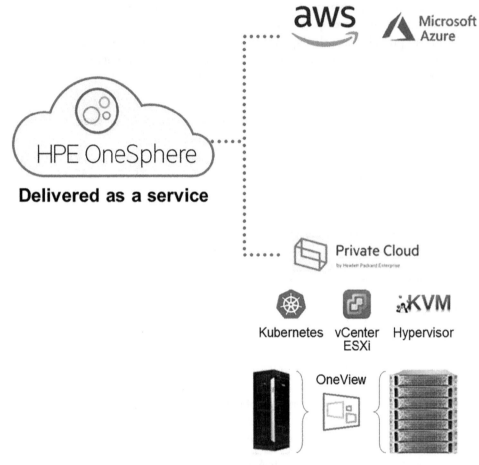

Figure 6-67 HPE OneSphere

HPE OneSphere simplifies **public cloud,** as illustrated in Figure 6-67:

- **Start up instantly via Software as a Service (SaaS)** management and access to public cloud services

- **Build on-premises clouds and connect** to public clouds in a few clicks

- **Get real-time insights** on cost and utilization across clouds

- **Optimize** workload deployment

- **Streamline DevOps** workflow

- **Guardrails** for the enterprise with governance and compliance

HPE OneSphere simplifies **private cloud**:

- Speed resource vending

- Automate infrastructure lifecycle management

- Automate everything through APIs

- Optimize on-premises utilization

- Choose from consumption models to optimize costs

HPE OneSphere is designed for IT, business execs, and developers to work together faster. Developers want to work unencumbered. They want to be self-sufficient and work with the tools and clouds with which they are familiar and comfortable. They also want access to services, tools, and templates that will save them time. They do not want to trip over IT when it is time to deploy. They want to consume everything as a service, so they can move faster. HPE OneSphere eliminates the need to submit tickets and wait for infrastructure. HPE OneSphere enables one or more developers to access project workspaces that have a quota of resources and a hybrid catalog, so everyone can self-service.

IT Ops wants to be more strategic to the business. They want to seamlessly enable IT services to their organization—be an IT service broker. No other solution makes it this simple to transform virtual clusters, containers, and bare-metal servers into a true private cloud with multi-tenancy, self-service portal, and a catalog.

We not only eliminate silos across on-premises and public clouds, but we also enable IT to move faster, from weeks or months to minutes. Business executives, typically the force behind digital transformation, want is to know what is happening with their investments—and not the end of a billing cycle.

Getting accurate costs, usage, and utilization across on-premises and public clouds is complex and often a manual process—and it is even harder to accurately allocate costs to workgroups or projects.

OneSphere shows a near-real-time view of consumption insights across public and on-premises clouds, which enables business leaders to drive resource utilization up and costs down to make everything more efficient.

 Note

Verify the support for HPE OneSphere in your country.

Key features

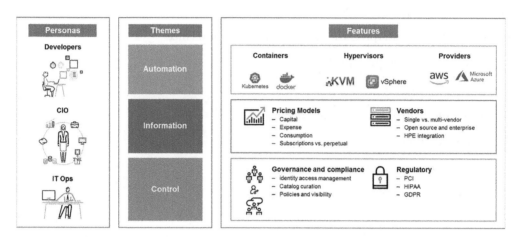

Figure 6-68 HPE OneSphere features

HPE OneSphere provides features for all the members of IT team, as shown in Figure 6-68:

- Developers

- Management / CIO

- IT Ops

Automation features of HPE OneSphere include:

- Offered as SaaS Solution

- Automated vCenter and KVM provisioning of on-premise virtual resources

- Import services and applications into a curated catalog

- Deploy workloads from the self-service catalog and APIs

- Provides KVM provisioning on private preconfigured infrastructure

- Uses HPE OneView appliance and reports metrics for server resources

- Discovers and deploys HPE OneView Server Profiles

- OneSphere provisions production grade Kubernetes clusters on AWS and on-premises VMware environments with a few clicks

- OneSphere admin can import public and private Docker images and Helm Charts into the Catalog

- Enable customers to import AWS/Azure public or private template definitions into the OneSphere catalog

- Deploy consistent and approved templates on a per project basis for CloudFormation (AWS) and ARM (Azure)

HPE OneSphere is working with various pricing models: Capital, Expense, Consumption, Subscriptions vs Perpetual. Environments with multiple vendors are also supported.

HPE OneSphere Insights

The initial release of HPE OneSphere Insights provided a limited set of fixed reports and drilldowns for both private and public cloud providers. The next release of Insights will feature an updated user interface that is focused more on enabling users with the ability to define and create custom data views and reports from a large set of 60 different data fields. The ability to download report data with two different options will also be available in this release to provide integration with other analytics, graphic, and reporting applications as well as other systems like a billing application.

HPE will follow up with additional report functions such as the ability to define a budget value to specific data fields and configure threshold-based reports such as when a specific budget is exceeded, or other user-defined thresholds are met.

Additional cost reporting features will continue to be added in future releases including the ability to share report results, customize the dashboard, define different monetary values, apply custom discount rates, automatically send threshold-based report notifications, and support additional public and private cloud providers. HPE also plans to extend our current private cloud cost and rate table support with additional cost values and complementary services offerings.

We plan to offer our initial cost analytics–focused features that will help customers better plan current and future deployments via what-if modelers, trend and forecasting via historical use, and workload deployment recommendations tied back to governance policy settings.

HPE OneSphere allows admins to curate the service catalog to govern access of approved services. Approved services can be grouped and applied to a project, and multiple users are assigned to projects.

HPE OneSphere provides a control mechanism to policies regarding which internal compliance regulations must be followed per provider, line of business, project, user, and so forth.

HPE RESTful API and PowerShell cmdlets

While a graphical user interface (GUI) is available for the vast majority of Hybrid IT components in the data center, these tools are usually not usable for integration and automation.

REST communication

The HPE RESTful API is a management interface that server management tools can use to configure, inventory, and monitor many components of the data server. It is an architectural style consisting of a coordinated set of architectural constraints applied to components, connectors, and data elements within a distributed hypermedia system.

The open, industry-standard HPE RESTful API provides a programmable interface and lightweight data model specification that is simple, remote, secure, and extensible. REST has become a popular communication protocol on service-oriented architecture styles. It enables IT staff to quickly and securely customize configurations and provisioning, and at the same time, provide a common interface for integration to many ecosystems.

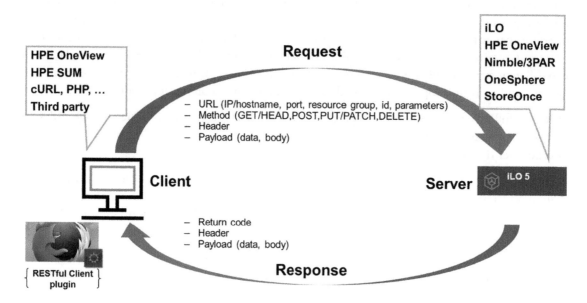

Figure 6-69 REST communication architecture

REST is a web service that uses basic CRUD operations performed on resources using HTTP Post, Get, Put, Delete, and Patch. REST is an alternative to more complex programming mechanisms such as SOAP, CORBA, and RPC. Simply put, a REST call is an HTTP request to the server.

A REST client sends HTTPS operations to the server (such as iLO, HPE OneView, Nimble array, and so forth) to GET and PATCH JSON-formatted data, and to configure supported settings, such as Unified Extensible Firmware Interface (UEFI) BIOS settings.

The REST architecture generally runs over HTTP, although other transports can be used. What the HPE OneView user interface allows you to do graphically, the RESTful API enables you to do programmatically, as indicated in Figure 6-69. For example, you can use a scripting language such as Microsoft PowerShell to perform tasks by using RESTful API calls that you might otherwise complete through the web-based UI.

Today, many available tools for server management via scripting bring with them limitations around automation, orchestration, and management. Because scripting interfaces are not common across HPE management tools, HPE is using the HPE RESTful API as a standardized scripting solution to address key challenges around:

- **Unsecure remote capabilities**—Remote scripting is often not secure, triggering the need for another mechanism to transport scripts to target nodes.

- **Learning and deployment**—This can be time-consuming because a single command utility does not work across server components with existing scripting tools. The learning curve increases because administrators are required to learn different types of interfaces across the data center.

- **Scripting efficiency**—Using different tools creates complexity. Running the server through PXE for updates also delays scripting. Running scripts on too many servers is not readily scalable.

Designed for ProLiant Gen9 and Gen10 servers, the HPE RESTful API directly addresses scripting challenges in a way that is:

- **Simple**—Easier access to information eliminating multiple tools to run scripts and provision server

- **Remote and secure**—Capabilities leveraging an industry-proven HTTPS protocol

- **Extensible**—Ability to script and expose new functionalities with few or no firmware upgrade dependencies

Example of HPE RESTful API implementation—iLO

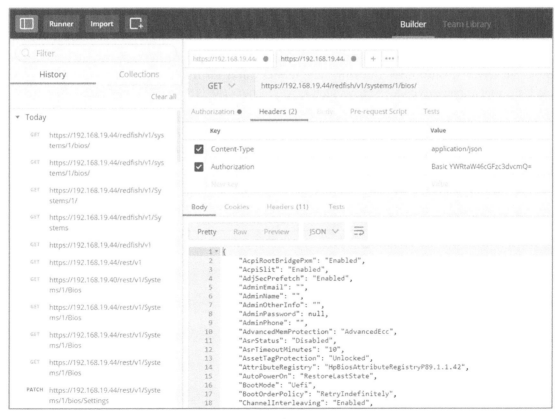

Figure 6-70 HPE RESTful API implementation

The HPE RESTful API for iLO is designed using the Hypermedia as the Engine of Application State (HATEOAS) REST architecture. This architecture allows the client to interact with iLO through a simple fixed URL—rest/v1. This has the advantage of the client not needing to know a set of fixed URLs. When creating a script to automate tasks using the HPE RESTful API for iLO, you only need to hardcode this simple URL, and design the script to discover the RESTful API URLs that are needed to complete a task.

 Note

For more information about HATEOAS, visit:

http://en.wikipedia.org/wiki/HATEOAS

The HPE RESTful API for iLO is the main management API for iLO-based HPE servers. Using this API, it is possible to take a full inventory of the server, control power and reset, configure BIOS and iLO settings, and fetch event logs, in addition to performing many other functions, as indicated in Figure 6-70.

This API follows the internet trend in moving to a common pattern for new software interfaces. Many web services in a variety of industries use RESTful APIs because they are easy to implement and easy to consume, and they offer scalability advantages over previous technologies. HPE OneView, OpenStack, and many other server management APIs are now RESTful APIs. Most HPE management software offerings, as well as the entire SDDC architecture, are built upon RESTful APIs.

The HPE RESTful API for iLO has the additional advantage of consistency across all present and projected server architectures. The same data model works for traditional rack-mount servers and blades as well as newer types of systems such as Moonshot. The HPE RESTful API for iLO provides this advantage because the data model is designed to self-describe the service's capabilities to the client and has room for flexibility designed in from the start.

 Note

Open the hyperlink for more information on the HPE RESTful API.

https://hewlettpackard.github.io/ilo-rest-api-docs/ilo5/

HPE RESTful Interface Tool

```
Administrator: Command Prompt - ilorest                                    _ □ X

C:\Program Files\Hewlett Packard Enterprise\RESTful Interface Tool>ilorest
iLOrest : RESTful Interface Tool version 2.0
Copyright (c) 2014, 2017 Hewlett Packard Enterprise Development Company
---------------------------------------------------------------------
iLOrest > login 192.168.19.44 -u admin
Password:
Discovering data...Done
WARNING: Cache is activated. Session keys are stored in plaintext.
iLOrest > bootorder

Current Persistent Boot Order:
1. HD.Emb.1.4 (Windows Boot Manager)
2. HD.Emb.1.3 (Assisted_Installation)
3. CD.Emb.10.1 (Embedded SATA Port 10 CD/DVD ROM : hp DVDRAM GU90N )
4. Generic.USB.1.1 (Generic USB Boot)
5. HD.Emb.1.2 (Embedded RAID 1 : Smart Array P440ar Controller - 279.37 GiB, RAID 1 Logical Drive(Target:0, Lu
n:0))
6. NIC.LOM.1.1.IPv4 (Embedded LOM 1 Port 1 : HPE Ethernet 1Gb 4-port 331i Adapter - NIC (PXE IPv4) )
7. NIC.LOM.1.1.IPv6 (Embedded LOM 1 Port 1 : HPE Ethernet 1Gb 4-port 331i Adapter - NIC (PXE IPv6) )

Continuous and one time boot options:
1. None
2. Cd
3. Hdd
4. Usb
5. Utilities
6. Diags
7. BiosSetup
8. Pxe
9. UefiShell
10. UefiTarget

Continuous and one time boot uefi options:
1. HD.Emb.1.4 (Windows Boot Manager)
2. HD.Emb.1.3 (Assisted_Installation)
```

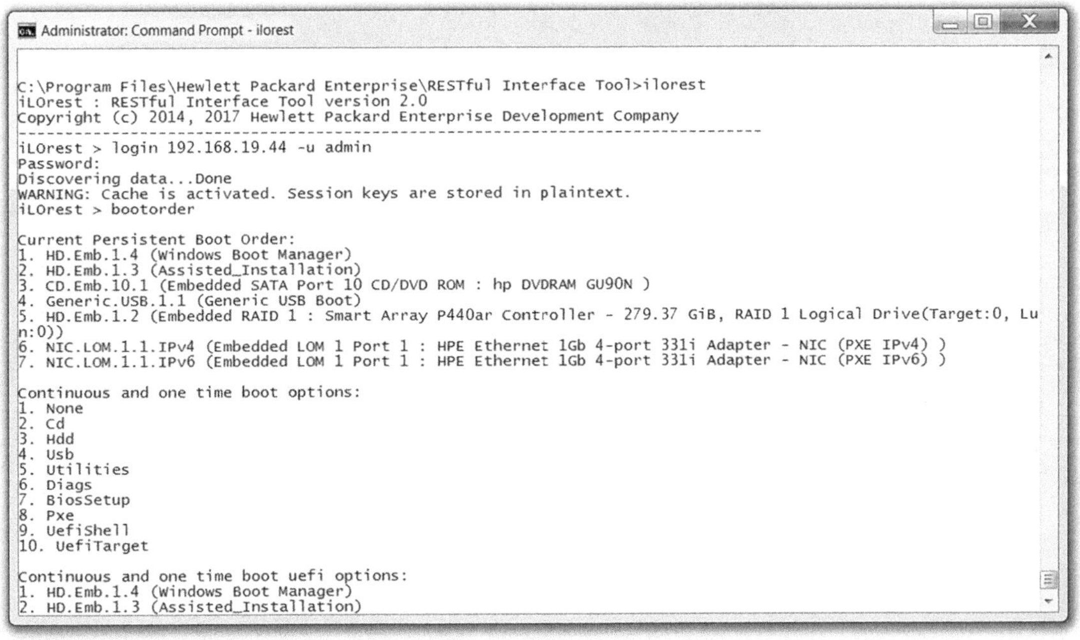

Figure 6-71 HPE RESTful Interface Tool version 2.0

The HPE RESTful Interface Tool simplifies server configuration by using industry-recognized RESTful APIs, enabling you to script provisioning on ProLiant Gen9 and Gen10 servers. The RESTful Interface Tool, as shown in Figure 6-71, offers a single command-line interface (CLI) to configure various server components, plus document-allowed server configurations and dependencies. The HPE RESTful API for UEFI can be used to configure settings through this CLI.

The RESTful Interface Tool is key to enabling software-defined computing for the Idea Economy. Benefits include:

- **Easy customization**—A single command line to simplify customizing workflows and scripts by standardizing a set of commands that interacts with all server components

- **Reduced travel costs**—Capability to remotely manage servers

- **Reduced deployment complexity**—Enablement of any of the three modes—interactive, scriptable, or file-based—to program and execute scripts easily

- **Simplified scripting**—Self-descriptive tool to reduce the learning curve adoption

iLO RESTful API Explorer

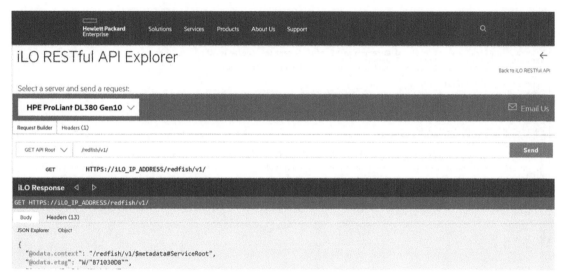

Figure 6-72 iLO RESTful API Explorer

iLO RESTful API Explorer can be used to explore the iLO API even without accessing the server. Various Gen9 and Gen10 servers are demonstrated in the tool. The application allows simulated calls to be sent to iLO, and replies can be reviewed in the web browser, as indicated in Figure 6-72.

 Note

For testing the iLO RESTful API Explorer, visit:

https://ilorestfulapiexplorer.ext.hpe.com/

Using PowerShell to manage HPE devices

Windows PowerShell provides a powerful set of utilities that you can use to perform various configuration tasks on Hybrid IT data center components. Windows PowerShell cmdlets for managing HPE devices are designed for customers familiar with Windows PowerShell. It is the Microsoft task automation framework, consisting of a command-line shell and associated scripting language built on Microsoft .NET Framework. It follows the standard PowerShell syntax and scripting model, making it easy for customers to incorporate these functions into their administrative scripts.

The HPE Scripting Tools for Windows PowerShell uses lightweight commands (cmdlets) that better enable integration with the current IT ecosystem, allowing retrieval of firmware versions from multiple enclosures and servers. PowerShell Onboard Administrator cmdlets enable retrieval of firmware versions from multiple BladeSystem enclosures and servers, and pipe information to cmdlets that update enclosures, blade, and enclosure options.

PowerShell is standard environment in Windows and uses simple syntax: VERB-NOUN or ACTION-ResourceName. It is also available for Linux and as a container. PowerShell allows you to extend the language by importing custom modules and adding more CmdLets, as illustrated in Figure 6-73.

 Note

Many modules are available at the Microsoft PowerShell Gallery: **https://www.powershellgallery.com/**. HPE is shipping several modules, including HPE OneView, iLO, Storage, OneSphere, BIOS, and Smart Array.

Example of PowerShell cmdlets—HPE OneSphere with PowerShell

```
PS C:\Users\LALLI\github\OneSphere\ns-api-ps> get-command -module hpeonesphere

CommandType     Name                           Version      Source
-----------     ----                           -------      ------
Function        Add-HPEOSCatalog               1.0.0.0      hpeonesphere
Function        Add-HPEOSDeployment            1.0.0.0      hpeonesphere
Function        Add-HPEOSMembership            1.0.0.0      hpeonesphere
Function        Add-HPEOSProject               1.0.0.0      hpeonesphere
Function        Add-HPEOSProvider              1.0.0.0      hpeonesphere
Function        Add-HPEOSRegion                1.0.0.0      hpeonesphere
Function        Add-HPEOSTag                   1.0.0.0      hpeonesphere
Function        Add-HPEOSTagKey                1.0.0.0      hpeonesphere
Function        Add-HPEOSUser                  1.0.0.0      hpeonesphere
Function        Add-HPEOSVolume                1.0.0.0      hpeonesphere
Function        Add-HPEOSZone                  1.0.0.0      hpeonesphere
Function        Compress-HPEOSZoneCompute      1.0.0.0      hpeonesphere
Function        Compress-HPEOSZoneStorage      1.0.0.0      hpeonesphere
Function        Connect-HPEOS                  1.0.0.0      hpeonesphere
Function        Disconnect-HPEOS               1.0.0.0      hpeonesphere
Function        Expand-HPEOSZoneCompute        1.0.0.0      hpeonesphere
Function        Expand-HPEOSZoneStorage        1.0.0.0      hpeonesphere
Function        Get-HPEOSappliance             1.0.0.0      hpeonesphere
Function        Get-HPEOSCatalog               1.0.0.0      hpeonesphere
Function        Get-HPEOSCatalogType           1.0.0.0      hpeonesphere
Function        Get-HPEOSConnectApp            1.0.0.0      hpeonesphere
Function        Get-HPEOSDeployment            1.0.0.0      hpeonesphere
Function        GET-HPEOSDeploymentConsole     1.0.0.0      hpeonesphere
Function        Get-HPEOSKeyPair               1.0.0.0      hpeonesphere
Function        Get-HPEOSMembership            1.0.0.0      hpeonesphere
Function        Get-HPEOSMembershipRole        1.0.0.0      hpeonesphere
Function        Get-HPEOSMetric                1.0.0.0      hpeonesphere
Function        Get-HPEOSNetwork               1.0.0.0      hpeonesphere
Function        Get-HPEOSProject               1.0.0.0      hpeonesphere
Function        Get-HPEOSProvider              1.0.0.0      hpeonesphere
Function        Get-HPEOSProviderType          1.0.0.0      hpeonesphere
Function        Get-HPEOSrate                  1.0.0.0      hpeonesphere
Function        Get-HPEOSRegion                1.0.0.0      hpeonesphere
Function        Get-HPEOSRole                  1.0.0.0      hpeonesphere
```

Figure 6-73 Output from cmdlet: `get-command -module hpeonesphere`

Activity: HPE Reference Architecture on VMware Cloud Foundation on HPE Synergy

1. Use this document:

    http://h20195.www2.hpe.com/V2/GetDocument.aspx?docname=a00064661enw

2. Answer the following questions:

    a. Compare the scenario requirements and RA. How many Synergy frames need to be part of the solution, and why?

    _____

    _____

    _____

    _____

    _____

    b. Do HPE OneView profiles contain RAID or HBA configuration options for local storage?

    _____

    _____

    _____

    _____

    _____

Solution components

Part numbers are at time of publication and subject to change. The BOM does not include complete support options or other rack and power requirements.

Qty	Product		product
			Rack and power
1	P9K10A		HPE 42U 600mmx1200mm G2 Kitted Advanced Shock Rack with Side Panels and Baying
1	P9K10A	001	HP Factory Express Base Racking Service
1	804938-B21		HPE Synergy Frame Rack Rail Kit
1	H6J85A		HPE Rack Hardware Kit
1	BW932A		HPE 600mm Rack Stabilizer Kit
1	BW932A	B01	HPE 600mm Rack include with Complete System Stabilizer Kit
			Synergy Frames
2	797740-B21		HPE Synergy 12000 Configure-to-order Frame with 1x Frame Link Module 10x Fans
2	779218-B21		HPE Synergy 20Gb Interconnect Link Module
2	794502-B23		HPE Virtual Connect SE 40Gb F8 Module for Synergy
1	798096-B21		HPE 6x 2650W Performance Hot Plug Titanium Plus FIO Power Supply Kit
1	798096-B21		HPE 6x 2650W Performance Hot Plug Titanium Plus FIO Power Supply Kit
2	804353-B21		HPE Synergy Composer
2	804942-B21		HPE Synergy Frame Link Module
1	804943-B21		HPE Synergy Frame 4x Lift Handles
1	859493-B21		Synergy Multi Frame Master1 FIO
4	804101-B21		HPE Synergy Interconnect Link 3m Active Optical Cable
2	720199-B21		HPE BladeSystem c-Class 40G QSFP+ to QSFP+ 3m Direct Attach Copper Cable
2	861412-B21		HPE Synergy Frame Link Module CAT6A 1.2m Cable
8	871940-B21		HPE Synergy 480 Gen10 Configure-to-order Compute Module

The Reference Architecture and customer scenario do not match completely. The missing components include:

- Aruba switches

- HPE OneSphere licenses

- More servers and their components and infrastructure

The networking subsystem also needs to be redesigned (10 Gb modules or two more VC SE 40 Gb F8 modules).

Learning check

6. What are the three required components for composable, local, in-frame storage in HPE Synergy solution?

    _____

    _____

    _____

    _____

    _____

7. Select the Synergy local disk module.

8. Which HPE products or subsystems can be managed from PowerShell?

    _____

    _____

    _____

    _____

9. Which HPE solution can simplify private and hybrid cloud management?

    _____

    _____

    _____

    _____

10. You are in a meeting with a customer, and they challenge you with a statement: "I heard that HPE specializes in traditional data center components and does not offer a software-defined platform, where hardware provisioning can be done from the management application."

How should you respond?

_____

_____

_____

_____

_____

_____

_____

_____

_____

_____

_____

_____

_____

_____

Alternative components for different environments

We presented a validated solution for customer scenario. Some of the solution components, however, can be changed for alternative environments, where different performance, capacity, costs, feature, and similar requirements can be satisfied with other HPE solutions. Not all the workloads are the same and single HPE product cannot match all the requirements.

HPE Composable Cloud for ProLiant DL: Business value

IT Ops
- Compose clouds and workloads in minutes
- Scale like the cloud, without needing to be a networking expert
- AI-driven saves time, increases uptime and performance
- Built-in compliance and security to protect and build digital brands

Developer
- Develop apps faster; access to all clouds and tools
- Curated catalogs and self-service provides guardrails to move fast with compliance

App owners
- Visibility to cost, usage, and performance
- Pay for only what is used
- Financial levers to unlock capacity
- Access to expertise to accelerate transformation

Figure 6-74 Business value of HPE Composable Cloud for ProLiant DL

HPE is extending the vision of composability to rack servers. With HPE Composable Cloud for ProLiant, IT professionals can:

- Scale the infrastructure in real-time without needing specialized networking skills

- Compose clouds and workloads in minutes

- Manage on-premises and public cloud resource utilization and costs in a uniform way

The solution is optimized for cloud-native workloads and composable rack-scale environments with template-driven automation, which streamlines the deployment of cloud stacks and automates the lifecycle, initially supporting Red Hat OpenShift and VMware workload deployments.

HPE Composable Cloud for ProLiant DL, as illustrated in Figure 6-74, is ideal for:

- Companies that have standardized on rack

- Cloud-native apps

- Storage flexibility (IP-based, SDS)

- Large enterprise deployments with up to 40 nodes

HPE Composable Cloud for ProLiant DL: Overview

HPE Composable Cloud for ProLiant DL provides the following benefits:

- Built on industry-leading HPE ProLiant DL servers

  - HPE ProLiant DL Gen10

  - Rack scale for VMs, containers, and cloud native

- Scaling composability across the data center with HPE Composable Fabric

  - Purpose-built for workload-driven performance and scale

  - Real-time incremental scale within a rack, between racks, and across data centers

  - Self-optimizing for improved performance

- Automate your customer's private cloud with HPE OneView for Composable Cloud

  - Template-based provisioning, firmware, and driver updates

  - Single interface monitoring

  - Unified API for open integration with third-party tools

  - Integration with HPE Composable Fabric Manager

- Platform for all your customer's software stacks and tools with ecosystem partners

  - Broad software partner ecosystem supporting DevOps, automation, and IT management initiatives

  - Enable organizations to easily integrate applications, containers, hypervisors, cloud stacks, and tools

- Built-in AI ops with HPE InfoSight

  - Artificial intelligence-driven operations

  - Predict and prevent problems before they can impact business

  - Continuously learns as it analyzes data, making systems smarter and more reliable

- Innovate across clouds

  - Multi-cloud management

  - Self-service infrastructure provisioning

  - Control utilization and cost

HPE ProLiant for Microsoft Azure Stack

Figure 6-75 HPE ProLiant for Microsoft Azure Stack

The HPE ProLiant for Microsoft Azure Stack, shown in Figure 6-75, brings a strong set of flexibility and services. Let's start with a factory integrated, validated solution that offers multiple configuration options that allow customers to customize a solution that meets their workload requirements. Customers can customize CPU, RAM, storage, pick any number of nodes between four and 12, and even have it installed in their choice of rack.

HPE is the only vendor to offer RAM memory configurations that operate at full speed all the time with our high-performance memory option. We provide integrated system management with HPE OneView and HPE Insight Remote. With Microsoft Azure Stack, as illustrated in Figure 6-76, we can now provide the common developer experience, based on a consistent API that allows deployment to Azure Stack or Azure Public.

Common developer experience for Azure and Azure Stack simplifies app development

 Consistent API allows deployment to Azure Stack or Azure public

 Integrated system management simplifies operations
(HPE OneView)

 Multiple configuration options
(processors, memory, storage, nodes, networking switches, rack and power supplies)

 Multiple packaging options
(factory integration or virtual rack)

 Multiple financing options
(capital purchase, pay as you go and leasing)

 Multiple sourcing options
(HPE, HPE and Microsoft, direct CSP and indirect CSP)

Figure 6-76 Deliver Azure-consistent services from the data center

The HPE ProLiant for Microsoft Azure Stack allows organizations to run Azure-consistent cloud services in their data center. The key features of this solution include:

- **Common developer experience**—Applications can be deployed to either an Azure Stack private cloud or an Azure public cloud without modification. This is a powerful benefit to developers that makes it easier and faster to develop applications.

- **Workload portability**—Since Azure public cloud and Azure Stack services are API-compatible, applications can be deployed in Azure Stack and in Azure public cloud.

- **Integrated systems management**—Managing and maintaining a rack of servers, storage, and switching can be complex. HPE ProLiant for Microsoft Azure Stack includes integrated system management that makes is easier to perform software and firmware updates as well as monitor system status. HPE includes HPE OneView and HPE Insight Remote support running on a separate management server.

- **Single vendor support**—Solving problems for services running on multiple servers, network switches, and software products can be complex and frustrating. HPE offers single vendor support, so regardless of what component causes a problem, HPE manages the resolution with no finger pointing.

- **Multiple configuration options**—We know your customer's workload requirements are dependent on their specific needs. That is why we offer more configuration options. You can choose the number of nodes (from four to 12), the processor type, memory, and storage. We support larger memory configurations, up to 768 GB/node, than most competing systems.

- **Multiple packaging options**—For most of our customers, we build the systems in our factory and ship them to the customer site. However, some of our customers would rather we use their own racks. In those cases, we can build the systems **in our factories**, using your customer's racks, or we can build the systems **in their data** center using their rack. The choice is theirs.

- **Multiple financing options**—We provide you with multiple ways to purchase HPE ProLiant for Microsoft Azure Stack. We have pay-as-you-go, leasing, and capital purchase options.

- **Multiple sourcing options**—We provide your customers with multiple ways to source the solution. They can purchase the entire solution from HPE, hardware and software; you can purchase the hardware from us and the software from Microsoft; or HPE can be an indirect Cloud Solution Provider (CSP) or distributor. Whatever fits your needs the best.

HPE ProLiant for Microsoft Azure Stack delivers the largest capacity and highest performance, at full speed, giving the ability to run even more workloads, faster.

Microsoft Storage Spaces Direct (S2D)

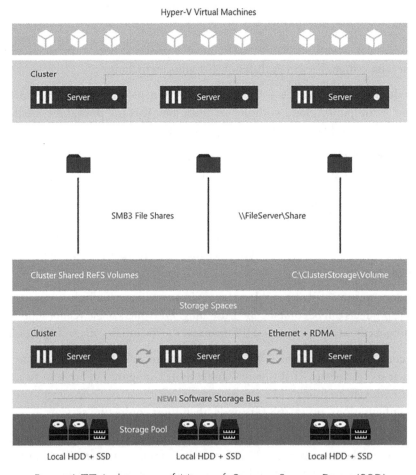

Figure 6-77 Architecture of Microsoft Storage Spaces Direct (S2D)

Storage Spaces Direct uses industry-standard servers with local-attached drives to create a highly available, highly scalable software-defined storage (SDS) at a fraction of the cost of traditional SAN or network-attached storage (NAS) arrays. Its converged or hyper-converged architecture radically simplifies procurement and deployment, while features such as caching, storage tiers, and erasure coding, together with the latest hardware innovations (such as RDMA networking and NVMe drives), deliver unrivaled efficiency and performance, as indicated in Figure 6-77.

Storage Spaces Direct is included in Windows Server 2019 Datacenter **and** Windows Server 2016 Datacenter.

Product overview:

- Scalability from two to 16 servers (all servers should be the same make and model)

- Windows 2016/2019 Datacenter required

- Software Storage Bus spans the cluster (all the servers can see all of each other's local drives)

- A combination of NVMe, SSD, and HDDs are supported

    – No tiering

    – Fastest drives are used for caching

- Software RAID

    – Three-way mirroring or dual parity recommended

    – Mirror-accelerated parity (optional)

- Storage made available via SMB3

- 10 GbE network (RDMA capable) recommended

Scality RING

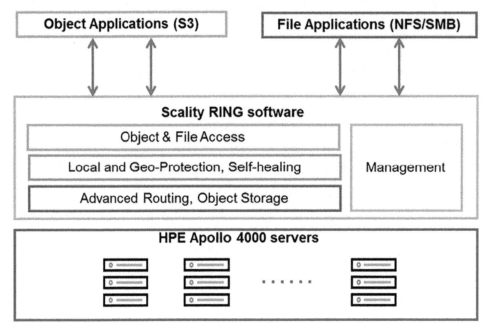

Figure 6-78 Scality RING

Scality RING, as illustrated in Figure 6-78, provides scalable SDS for object and file access with efficient data storage utilizing both erasure coding and replicas. Scality RING includes native data protection in a shared-nothing, distributed architecture with no single point of failure and is scalable from 100s of terabytes to exabytes. Extreme data durability is available with native multi-node, multi-site, multi-geo data distribution.

Connectors for multiple file and cloud access protocols can easily support your customer's favorite business applications.

Scality RING features:

- Scale

    - Even scale-out filers can maybe do a few PBs, while object can do 100s of PBs and looking to Exabytes.

    - Connected/autonomous vehicles and other Internet of Things (IoT) use cases are pushing toward Exabyte capacities over the next few years.

- Data security

    - Nobody connects their NAS to the internet; additional cost and complexity to put a front-end process and internet access security in front of a filer

– AWS S3, Google Cloud, Azure is always on the internet; object storage is not going away

– Scality gives you the same data access security as AWS with S3 and IAM functions

HPE Apollo 4200 with Qumulo File Fabric

Qumulo Core is a modern scale-out storage system designed from the ground up for the new era of multi-petabyte data scale on premises and in the cloud.

Available on density-optimized HPE Apollo 4200 servers, the solution can:

- **Seamlessly scale to billions of files with flash-first design**—It scales to billions of files with Qumulo File Fabric's (QF2's) advanced file-system technology that handles small files as efficiently as large ones. Available today on density-optimized HPE Apollo 4200 servers, there is no practical limit to scale. A flash-first hybrid software and hardware architecture optimizes cost and performance. You can simultaneously get the speed benefits of SSD and the economic advantages of HDD. User files can occupy 100% of provisioned capacity, not just 70% or 80%. QF2 on HPE Apollo 4200 Servers is more economical than legacy storage appliances on a capacity basis. Sophisticated data protection techniques enable the fastest reprotect times in the industry. Rebuild times for even 10 TB Nearline HDDs are measured in hours, not days, regardless of cluster size and without degrading performance. In addition, snapshots can be taken instantly, or scheduled, with no limit to the number.

- **Control at scale with up to the minute analytics**—Up-to-the-minute analytics allow administrators to pinpoint problems and effectively control how storage is used. Storage administrators can instantly see usage, activity, and throughput at any level of the unified directory structure, no matter how many files in the file system. All of the information is available from a central web GUI. Directory-based capacity quotas give administrators instant control over storage allocation. Capacity quotas can be applied to any directory, even nested ones. Moving a directory with a quota is easy. HPE Active Health System (a component of the HPE iLO) is an industry-first technology that provides continuous, proactive health monitoring of over 1600 system parameters, and 100% of configuration changes are logged. Cloud-based monitoring proactively detects potential problems, such as disk failures, and you can access historical trend data about how your system is being used. HPE Secure Encryption is a controller-based, data-at-rest encryption solution on Apollo 4200 with QF2 that can help comply with data privacy requirements and meet compliance regulations.

- **Provide a new experience defined by customer success rather than support**—The customer success program offered by Qumulo provides responsive, personal customer care, with one of the highest Net Promoter Scores (NPS) in the industry. Included as part of the Qumulo Core subscription, it offers a direct path to true subject matter experts (Customer Success Managers [CSMs]), a dedicated slack channel for instant access to CSMs, and cloud monitoring across the entire fleet (on-premises and cloud). Simple subscription pricing covers everything—all features, updates, and software support. A hardware-transferable licensing model eliminates the need to purchase new licenses with each platform refresh, and your customers can purchase additional licenses as-you-grow. Qumulo uses modern development practices with frequent, easy-to-consume releases that steadily advance the product and keep it on the leading edge of what is possible. In addition, out-of-the-box simplicity means that from the moment Apollo 4200 with QF2 is unboxed to when it can start serving data is a matter of hours, not days. Together with HPE, the industry-leading server vendor, your customers can expect an enterprise quality product and service.

- **Provide your customer's data where they want it, on premise or public cloud**—Your customers can store their data anywhere and get multiple GB/s of performance for their workloads both on and off premises. They get scalable performance regardless of number of files or file sizes. Continuous replication moves the data where it is needed, when it is needed. Continuous replication operates across storage clusters, whether on premises or in the cloud. After a replication relationship between a source cluster and a target cluster is established, QF2 automatically keeps data consistent. Use the QF2 REST API to build and manage a modern application stack. It is the future of infrastructure, and it is available today.

11. Write a summary of the key concepts presented in this module.

_____

_____

_____

_____

_____

_____

_____

_____

_____

_____

_____

_____

_____

_____

_____

_____

_____

_____

_____

_____

Summary

- HPE Synergy is the example of HPE Composable Infrastructure empowering hybrid cloud transformation.

- Virtual Connect provides a virtualization layer between Synergy compute modules and the corporate LAN and SAN environment.

- HPE OneView is the foundation for an SDDC that helps drive the business and enable innovation. HPE OneView helps to deploy infrastructure faster, simplify lifecycle operations, and increase productivity using a unified API.

- HPE OneSphere, delivered as a service, is an HPE offering to simplify management of customers' hybrid cloud environments.

Prelearning check

Before proceeding with this section, answer the following questions to assess your existing knowledge of the topics covered in this module. Record your answers in the space provided here.

1. You are in a meeting with a customer, and they challenge you with a question: "I'm interested in a modern virtualization solution that will include all the resources needed for running virtual machines in a single building block. Is there anything HPE can offer in this space?"

   How should you respond?

   _____

   _____

   _____

   _____

   _____

   _____

   _____

   _____

   _____

   _____

7 Recommending Hybrid IT hyperconverged solutions for customer use cases

LEARNING OBJECTIVES

After completing this chapter, and given a customer scenario, you should be able to:

✓ Recommend and position HPE hyperconverged solutions, tools, and appropriate services for customer use cases.

✓ Describe, differentiate, and apply industry-standard architectures and technologies.

✓ Explain the HPE approach to converged management for the infrastructure lifecycle.

Scenario 8: VMware Horizon on HPE SimpliVity 380 Gen10

The wide HPE portfolio of data center products can be introduced using customer scenarios and recommended, validated configurations, based on HPE Reference Architecture or HPE Reference Configuration.

Introducing the customer scenario

EDASH company will be used as a story line through this scenario. We will introduce the company using an interview:

- What is your primary business?
  - Car producer, part of global holding
- How many employees do you currently have?
  - 10,000 employees with access to IT services
- Where are you currently storing data, and how do you access files?
  - Mix of NAS and SAN devices, mainly HPE

- What does your server and network infrastructure look like?

  – Two data centers, hundreds of devices

- How much data do you currently have on servers and workstations?

  – Unknown

- What are your current plans?

  – VDI initiative, want to virtualize desktops and application access, probably in batches, start with first group from quality management and project management teams; to provide better business continuance and disaster recovery strategy

Customer requirements

As a result of multiple interviews and gathering information about customer plans and the customer's current infrastructure, the following requirements emerged for the new solution:

- On premises, highly resilient VDI solution

- 1500 users in phase 1

- Windows 10 desktops with Microsoft Office 2016

- Best-in-class user density

- Simplified deployment

- Ability to scale out

- Enterprise-class data protection and resiliency

- VMware Horizon 7 as the virtual desktop infrastructure

  – Simplify desktop and application management

  – Consistent user experience

Activity: Information resources

1. Download these information resources:

   – HPE Reference Architecture for VMware Horizon on HPE SimpliVity 380 Gen10

     https://h20195.www2.hpe.com/v2/getdocument.aspx?docname=a00053300enw

   – HPE SimpliVity 380 Gen10 QuickSpecs

     https://h20195.www2.hpe.com/v2/getdocument.aspx?docname=a00021989enw

      –   HPE SimpliVity 2600 Gen10 QuickSpecs

      https://h20195.www2.hpe.com/v2/getdocument.aspx?docname=a00043499enw

2. Answer the following questions:

    a.   What is the functionality of OmniStack Accelerator Card?

3. What is the functionality of HPE OmniStack Virtual Controller?

    a.   What is the recommended hardware configuration of nodes for VDI management?

_____

_____

_____

_____

b. What is the recommended hardware configuration of nodes for desktop workloads?

_____

_____

_____

_____

_____

c. Where does the HPE SimpliVity arbiter need to be deployed?

_____

_____

_____

_____

_____

d. What is the OmniStack Software license based on?

_____

_____

_____

_____

_____

_____

e. How many different types of nodes are available for SimpliVity 2600?

    – What is the difference between individual nodes?

_____

_____

_____

_____

_____

_____

_____

_____

_____

Activity: HPE SimpliVity efficiency

1. Access the SimpliVity overview at HPE.com:

   https://www.hpe.com/us/en/integrated-systems/simplivity.html

2. Watch this game-changing data efficiency video. You will need to scroll down at the page to find the video.

3. Take notes of the key points from the presentation.

_____

_____

_____

_____

_____

_____

_____

_____

_____

_____

_____

Answer the following questions:

1. What is the technology used for accessing the datastore?

_____

_____

_____

_____

2. At what level does the deduplication occur?

_____

_____

_____

_____

3. What is the minimum number of nodes to provide resiliency?

_____

_____

_____

_____

4. What is the typical deduplication ratio based on Forrester Research?

_____

_____

_____

_____

_____

Industry-standard architectures and drivers

Virtualization is one of the most important infrastructure drivers. Virtualization improves the utilization of server, storage, and networking hardware utilization.

Fundamentals of virtualization

Virtualization is the pooling of multiple resources into what appears to be a single device that is managed from a central console. Virtualization:

- Aggregates physical resources into a unified structure or pool

- Presents those resources as capabilities that can be consumed by applications or other types of storage clients

- Abstracts storage at the block level

Virtualization improves server utilization, but it also depends on shared storage to meet application requirements more effectively. Virtual environments require high levels of data availability and storage utilization as well as the ability to scale nondisruptively as business needs expand. This gives clear insight into the real costs of storage. At the same time, virtual environments:

- Reduce costs for multi-site, high availability storage by approximately 50%.

- Increase capacity utilization by approximately 33% to improve storage investments.

- Deploy shared storage without disrupting business operations.

Virtualization exposes storage challenges in the areas of efficiency, availability, and management.

Journey of virtualization

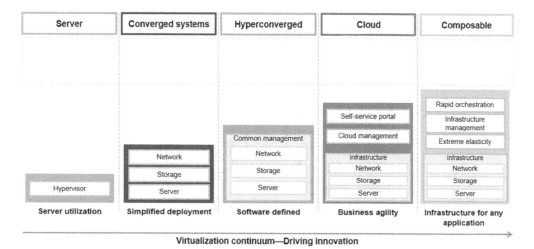

Figure 7-1 Journey of virtualization

The flexibility of server utilization vastly improved with the introduction of hypervisors and converged systems. Virtualization adds faster time to value, where factory racking and stacking greatly improves the time to value, as indicated in Figure 7-1. As the industry moves into hyperconverged and software-defined architectures, virtualization solutions in a single platform are simplifying management again with factory-integrated systems.

The cloud increases business agility, improving the speed of provisioning with new governance controls and self-service portals. Composable Infrastructure is able to support the Idea Economy for both virtualized and legacy workloads from a single platform, offering extreme elasticity, improved infrastructure management, and providing rapid orchestration.

 Note

> Hyperconvergence, like convergence, eliminates traditional IT management issues by packaging data center services such as server, storage, and network and allowing them to be managed in a single application. But unlike convergence, hyperconvergence is a software-defined infrastructure that decouples infrastructure operations from the system hardware and converges them at the hypervisor level into a single building block (thus hyperconverged). Hyperconverged systems leverage software-defined intelligence to break down the silos of storage and compute, and allow them to run and be managed on the same server platform, which eliminates inefficiencies and accelerates compute.

Storage integration into hypervisors

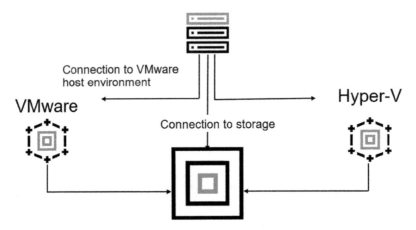

Figure 7-2 Storage integration into hypervisors

A hypervisor virtualizes hardware to provide an environment in which you can run multiple operating systems at the same time on one physical server, as illustrated in Figure 7-2. The hypervisor enables you to create and manage virtual machines (VMs) and their resources.

Each VM is an isolated, virtualized computer system that can run its own operating system. The operating system that runs within a VM is called a **guest operating system**.

VM storage is virtualized in a data center that implements server virtualization because all VMs store at least one virtual disk file and a configuration file. A storage hypervisor extends that basic virtualization by managing different types of infrastructures.

A storage hypervisor aggregates unused capacity from various physical storage devices into one resource pool. Because it is software-based, a storage hypervisor can run on dedicated storage in a VM or inside a server hypervisor. When used with server virtualization, a storage hypervisor provides better storage performance.

Storage systems designed for VMs can enhance data migration, performance, and integration with virtual server environments.

HPE provides management integration for VMware vCenter and Microsoft System Center to allow typical management operations to be performed directly from the hypervisor management software.

Storage capacity monitoring and storage provisioning are accessible for the virtualization administrators through HPE OneView for vCenter and HPE OneView for System Center. These components connect the hypervisor management software and the storage systems (all primary storage array families in the HPE portfolio).

HPE OneView for vCenter is provided as a virtual appliance, and HPE OneView for System Center is software that is installed on the System Center server(s). HPE recommends these management integrations for all HPE StoreVirtual virtual storage appliance (VSA) installations.

Desktop virtualization

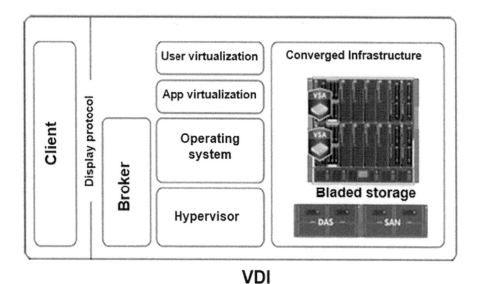

Figure 7-3 Desktop virtualization

Desktop virtualization is the concept of separating the logical desktop from the physical machine. A **virtual desktop infrastructure** (VDI) is a form of desktop virtualization that involves more advanced hardware virtualization, as illustrated in Figure 7-3. Rather than interacting with a host computer directly using a keyboard, mouse, and monitor, the user interacts with the host computer using another desktop computer or a mobile device by means of a network connection, such as a LAN, wireless LAN, or even the internet. The host computer in this scenario becomes a server capable of hosting multiple VMs at the same time for multiple users.

As organizations continue to virtualize and converge their data center environments, client architectures such as VDI also continue to evolve to take advantage of the predictability, continuity, and quality of the service delivered by their converged infrastructure. For example, HPE and IBM provide a hybrid VDI model with a range of virtualization software and delivery models to address the limitations of a distributed client computing.

VDI deployments are great candidates for data deduplication because the virtual hard disks that drive the remote desktops for users are essentially identical. Additionally, data deduplication can help with the so-called **VDI boot storm**, which is the drop-in storage performance when many users simultaneously sign in to their desktops to start the day.

 Note

VDI is a prime application for both Hyper-V Server and deduplication because the server component does not need licensing, and VDI can often achieve significant savings from deduplication. VDI is also the primary solution to use when updating deduplication for virtualization loads. When implementing VDI and Microsoft deduplication, consider using a file server on Windows Server 2016 to store them.

Another form of desktop virtualization is called **session virtualization**. This allows multiple users to connect and log in to a shared but powerful computer over the network and use it simultaneously. Each user is given a desktop and personal folder to store their files. With multi-seat configuration, session virtualization can be accomplished using a single PC with multiple monitors, keyboards, and mice connected.

Certain client environments move workloads from PCs and other devices to data center servers, creating well-managed virtual clients, with applications and operating environments hosted on servers and storage in the data center. This means that users can access their desktops from any location without being tied to a single client device. Client virtualization enables IT administrators to provide a consistent, seamless desktop experience for users who conduct business transactions on multiple device types, including mobile devices, tablets, laptops, and desktops. IT administrators can use a more centralized, efficient client environment that is easier to maintain and can quickly respond to the changing needs of users and the business.

HPE offers all the components needed for a client virtualization implementation: software, hardware, and services, along with a proven methodology to enable faster installation of the right solution the first time. An HPE Converged Infrastructure solution views server, storage, and network resources as pools that are allocated as needed to optimize the delivery of business services while simplifying IT operations.

With an HPE Converged Infrastructure, IT organizations can overcome many of the common challenges associated with operating a virtualized client environment. The standardized infrastructure in an HPE Converged Infrastructure offers application mobility, IT simplicity, and lower costs. The ability to migrate applications and workloads efficiently across tightly integrated network, storage, and compute resources can greatly enhance both IT and business operations continuity.

Who uses VDI?

Full graphics acceleration

11%

those who need access
to dedicated graphics
resources like CAD
applications

Single applications

46%

call centers that require
access to 1 or 2
applications at a time

General desktops

70%

Companies that need to
access on-demand
applications (for example,
Microsoft Office)

Figure 7-4 Use cases of VDI

There are numerous benefits from using VDI; the percentage of users depend often on the applications, as indicated in Figure 7-4.

VDI allows users to access a device based on a Windows operating system, leave for the evening, and come back the next workday to find all data and customized desktop and applications settings intact.

A standard VDI configuration might use rack-based servers distributed across the data center with Top of Rack (ToR) switches at the network edge or HPE BladeSystem deployment.

Building blocks of the solution

Client virtualization is a top initiative for many IT organizations, driven in part by the promise of a flexible, mobile computing experience for end users and consolidated management for IT. Organizations are looking to client virtualization solutions, like VMware Horizon 7, to reduce application distribution and administration expenses, to minimize the expenses associated with the operation of their desktop environment, and to improve data security and ensure compliance.

Too often, client virtualization deployments are plagued by sluggish and unpredictable desktop performance and higher than expected up-front capital expenses. As a result, organizations that adopt client virtualization solutions need to compromise between the competing needs of a strong solution performance, resiliency, and cost reduction.

The HPE SimpliVity 380 Gen10 is a market-leading hyperconverged infrastructure platform, ideally suited for addressing the challenges of client virtualization. It fulfills the primary requirement of many organizations—performance—without sacrificing economics or resilience. The HPE SimpliVity 380 Gen10 provides:

- Simplified deployment with hyperconverged building blocks

- Ability to start small and scale out in affordable increments—from pilot to production

- Highest density of desktops, per node, in the hyperconverged infrastructure category

- Independently validated, unmatched client virtualization performance for a superb end user experience

- Deployment of full-clone desktops with the same data efficiency as linked clones

- Enterprise-class data protection and resiliency

This Reference Architecture (RA) provides a roadmap for architecting these capabilities and showcases a third-party validated Login Virtual Session Indexer (Login VSI) performance testing. It provides an enterprise-scale architecture for implementing VMware Horizon 7 on HPE SimpliVity 380 Gen10 hyperconverged infrastructure and describes the tests performed by HPE to validate the efficiency of the recommended solution.

The performance testing illustrates the ability of the HPE SimpliVity 380 Gen10 to deliver an excellent end user experience on VMware Horizon 7.

Highlights include:

- **Performance at scale:** In Login VSI testing, consistently low latency was observed for both hosted desktops running Microsoft Windows 10 with Microsoft Office 2016, even as additional nodes were added to the solution.

- **Best-in-class user density:** 1500 knowledge worker users hosted on only 8x HPE SimpliVity 380 Gen10 nodes, including resilient N+1 design.

Many businesses are constrained by a legacy IT infrastructure that is not well suited for client virtualization initiatives. Siloed data centers composed of independent compute, storage, network, and data protection platforms with distinct administrative interfaces are inherently inefficient, cumbersome, and costly. Each platform requires support, maintenance, licensing, and power and cooling—not to mention a set of dedicated resources capable of managing and maintaining each component.

Rolling out a new complex solution, such as client virtualization, becomes a time-consuming effort involving many different technology platforms, management interfaces, and operational teams. Expanding system capacity can take days or even weeks due to the cumbersome processes and administration. Troubleshooting problems and performing routine data backup, replication, and recovery tasks can be just as inefficient.

Portfolio: HPE servers and server systems

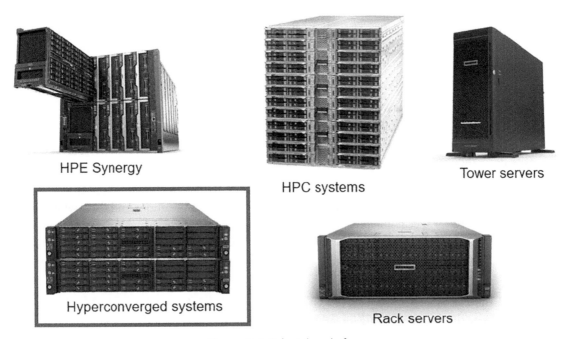

Figure 7-5 Select the platform

While grappling with this complexity, organizations also need to address challenges that are unique to virtualization, as illustrated in Figure 7-5, including:

- Difficulty sizing client virtualization workloads upfront, due to random and unpredictable user behaviors

- Periodic spikes in demand, such as "login storms" and "boot storms" that may significantly degrade performance, if not properly handled

- High cost of downtime in the event of an outage, either unexpected or due to system maintenance

The HPE SimpliVity 380 Gen10 addresses each of these challenges by providing a scalable, building block style approach to deploying an infrastructure for virtualization. This solution offers the enterprise predictable cost and delivers a high-performing desktop experience to end users.

HPE SimpliVity—Ideal environments

The HPE SimpliVity hyperconverged infrastructure solution is designed from the ground up to meet the increased performance, scalability, and agility demands of today's data-intensive, highly virtualized IT environments. HPE SimpliVity technology transforms IT by virtualizing data and incorporating all IT infrastructure and services below the hypervisor into compact building blocks. With 3x total cost of ownership (TCO) reduction, HPE SimpliVity delivers the best of both worlds: the enterprise-class performance, protection, and resiliency that today's organizations require, with the cloud economics businesses demand.

As a solution, HPE SimpliVity provides a single, shared resource pool across the entire IT stack, eliminating point products and inefficient siloed IT architectures. The solution is differentiated from other converged infrastructure solutions by three unique attributes: accelerated data efficiency, built-in data protection functionality, and global unified management capabilities:

- **Accelerated data efficiency**—HPE SimpliVity performs inline data deduplication, compression, and optimization on all data at inception across all phases of the data lifecycle, all handled with fine data granularity of just 4 KB to 8 KB. On average, HPE SimpliVity customers achieve 40:1 data efficiency, while simultaneously increasing application performance.

- **Built-in data protection**—HPE SimpliVity includes native data protection functionality, enabling business continuity and disaster recovery for critical applications and data, while eliminating the need for special-purpose backup and recovery hardware or software. The inherent data efficiencies of the HPE SimpliVity platform minimize IO and wide-area network (WAN) traffic, reducing backup and restore times from hours to minutes, while avoiding the need for special-purpose WAN optimization products.

- **Global unified management**—The VM-centric approach of the HPE SimpliVity platform to management eliminates manually intensive, error-prone administrative tasks. System administrators are no longer required to manage logical unit numbers (LUNs) and volumes; instead, they can manage all resources and workloads centrally, using familiar interfaces such as VMware vCenter Server.

The target market for the HPE SimpliVity hyperconverged infrastructure solution is:

- Mid-market/virtualized environments: ~2000 VMs or less

- Customers who require data services—backup and disaster recovery (DR)

- Storage opportunities that need integrated backup

- DL deals that include virtual SAN (VSAN) ready node requests

- VMware environments (6.0 and 6.5)

- Hyper-V 2016 environments (test/dev and small-scale Remote Office/Branch Office [ROBO]—two nodes/cluster, four clusters/federation)

- Customers who value a single VM-centric management interface

Alternative solutions to HPE SimpliVity

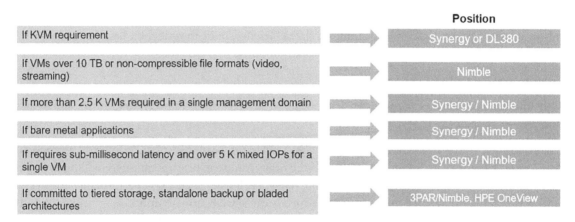

	Position
If KVM requirement	Synergy or DL380
If VMs over 10 TB or non-compressible file formats (video, streaming)	Nimble
If more than 2.5 K VMs required in a single management domain	Synergy / Nimble
If bare metal applications	Synergy / Nimble
If requires sub-millisecond latency and over 5 K mixed IOPs for a single VM	Synergy / Nimble
If committed to tiered storage, standalone backup or bladed architectures	3PAR/Nimble, HPE OneView

Figure 7-6 Alternative solutions to HPE SimpliVity

In case SimpliVity is not the correct answer, HPE has a complete portfolio to meet your customer's needs. Figure 7-6 offers an alternative solution:

HPE SimpliVity Data Virtualization Platform

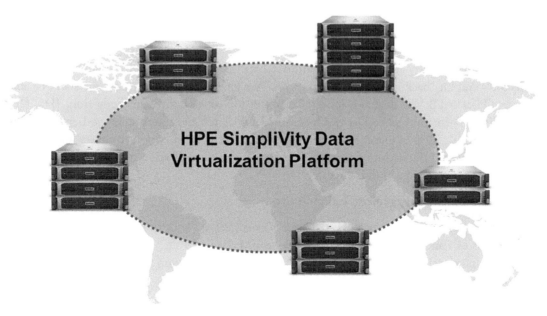

Figure 7-7 HPE SimpliVity Data Virtualization Platform

HPE SimpliVity infrastructure's core technology is the HPE SimpliVity Data Virtualization Platform, a globally aware file system and object store that facilitates globally shared resource pools across multiple sites. The Data Virtualization Platform, as indicated in Figure 7-7, is characterized by the advanced data services it delivers: guaranteed data efficiency, built-in resiliency, backup, and disaster recovery, and global VM-centric management and mobility.

Guaranteed data efficiency

Our solution deduplicates, compresses, and optimizes **all** data inline at inception, in real-time, once and forever across all tiers of data.

The real power comes from the HPE OmniStack Accelerator Card (OAC), a Peripheral Component Interconnect Express (PCIe) card that offloads the heavy infrastructure operations, enabling the Intel x86 resources to do what they do best: running VMs. HPE does it all a 0% performance impact to production VMs. In fact, we increase performance because we eliminate unnecessary Input/Output Operations Per Second (IOPS). That is revolutionary and differentiated—no one else can do it—and it is all possible because of the Accelerator Card. HPE SimpliVity customers experience, on average, 40:1 data efficiency, with many seeing over 100:1 data efficiency. HPE guarantees 10:1 data efficiency as part of our standard warranty.

Built-in resiliency, backup, and disaster recovery

Only HPE SimpliVity hyperconverged systems deliver the resilience, built-in backup, and bandwidth-efficient replication needed to ensure the highest levels of data integrity and availability, eliminating the need for legacy data protection.

All data protection is built-in, all at the VM level. Your customers can easily back up, restore, and move VMs, and they do not have to worry about the underlying storage infrastructure. They can just right click in vCenter—or use orchestration tools like VMware vRealize Automation or UCS Director—and hit "backup," "restore," or "move." We guarantee that your customers will be able to restore a local 1 TB VM in one minute or less. On top of that, a recent study from IDC ("HPE SimpliVity Hyperconvergence Drives Operational Efficiency and Customers are Benefiting," June 2017) found that 70% of our customers reported improvement in backup/recovery and DR, and a majority eliminated the use of existing third-party backup or replication tools after deploying HPE SimpliVity hyperconverged infrastructure.

Global VM-centric management and mobility

Given our approach to data efficiency, the Data Virtualization Platform makes VMs lightweight and mobile. It is extremely easy to move and/or clone VMs between sites to support global "follow the sun" development efforts or to move VMs to the appropriate location based on the requirements of the application.

Our approach to management is also unique. With global VM-centric management, gone are the days of managing LUNs, shares, and volumes. Instead, all management is done at the VM level with a single view across all of data centers and remote sites. Our unique file system abstracts the VMs, policies, and management from the underlying hardware. Managing the system is designed to be simple and easy, which is why IDC ("Datacenters Leverage HPE SimpliVity to Drive Operational Simplicity, Improved Performance, and Other Critical Datacenter Benefits," August 2018) found that our customers reported a 91% increase in time spent supporting new projects.

HPE SimpliVity: The powerhouse in hyperconvergence

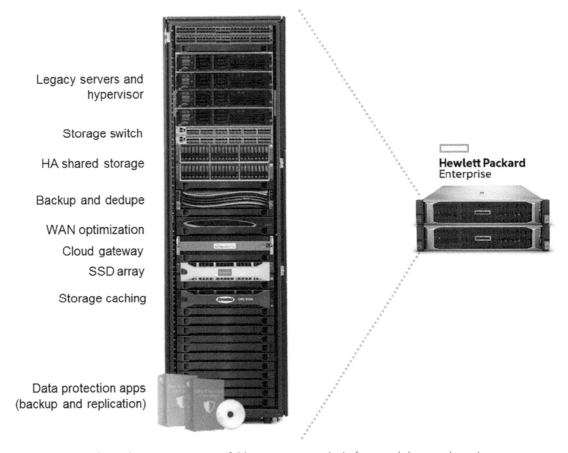

Legacy servers and hypervisor

Storage switch

HA shared storage

Backup and dedupe

WAN optimization
Cloud gateway
SSD array

Storage caching

Data protection apps
(backup and replication)

Hewlett Packard
Enterprise

Figure 7-8 The industry's most powerful hyperconverged platform with best-in-class data services

Here is another view of what we can specifically do to simplify Hybrid IT. For legacy environments that have older servers, hypervisors, storage, and other components, we collapse the stack by leveraging hyperconvergence. We can dramatically simplify the environment and lower costs compared to legacy IT.

By consolidating the entire stack, HPE SimpliVity can provide all IT and data services for virtualized workloads on a powerful HPE ProLiant server. This is all enabled by the HPE SimpliVity Data Virtualization Platform, as illustrated in Figure 7-8.

HPE SimpliVity collapses the stack with advanced data services in a single building block:

- Integrated with hypervisor to run virtualized workloads on x86 resource pools

- All functionality managed via an existing native hypervisor tool (vCenter, System Center Virtual Machine Manager [SCVMM])

- High resiliency, with integrated backup and DR functionality to rapidly recover

- Performance improved with data locality, all-flash, and inline deduplication and compression

- Reduced costs compared to legacy IT

- Designed for simplicity, easy deployment, and scale, and both hypervisor and hardware independence

Deduplication with HPE SimpliVity

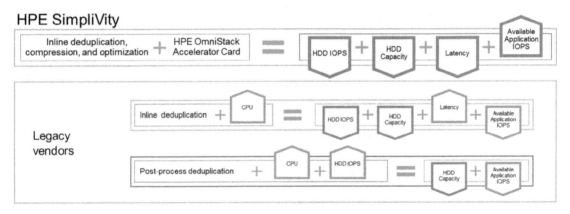

Figure 7-9 Deduplication with HPE SimpliVity

The HPE SimpliVity Data Virtualization Platform, as indicated in Figure 7-9, delivers inline deduplication, but without a performance penalty. That is because the HPE OmniStack Accelerator Card allows offloads deduplication and compression from the host CPUs. This leaves as much CPU as possible available to run the business applications. The HPE OAC also delivers extremely predictable performance, which allows an HPE SimpliVity hyperconverged infrastructure to deliver predictable performance to business applications.

By deduplicating and compressing all data inline with a hardware accelerator/offload engine, HPE SimpliVity can provide significant advantages in terms of performance without compromising the performance of the application VMs running on the same hardware platform.

Top use cases for HPE SimpliVity and hyperconverged

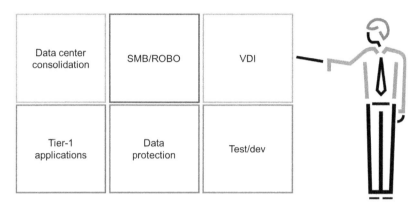

Figure 7-10 Top use cases for SimpliVity

HPE SimpliVity is not designed for any single use case, and the core use case is simplification and data mobility, as indicated in Figure 7-10. HPE SimpliVity opportunities usually center on data center consolidation, ROBO, VDI, or private cloud infrastructures, but customers gain large secondary benefits when tier-1 applications, data protection, or test/dev use cases are pain points.

With SimpliVity, in many situations, typical use cases include:

- **Data center consolidation**—Data center consolidation is the most common use case for hyperconverged solutions. SimpliVity platform is an ideal choice to consolidate a current virtualization environment and transform it from traditional server, storage, and networking silos to a real hyperconverged solution.

- **SMB/ROBO**—HPE SimpliVity 380 Gen10 now comes in extra small and small entry-level, all-flash solutions in single- and dual-socket configurations, priced right for small- and mid-sized businesses (SMBs) and ROBOs. HPE SimpliVity provides data protection and improves application performance, Recovery Time Objectives (RTOs), and Recovery Point Objectives (RPOs). Hyperconverged infrastructure makes better use of bandwidth-constrained WAN links and cuts TCO. Centralized management means it reduces the need for IT expertise—onsite or otherwise.

- **VDI**—HPE SimpliVity delivers more virtual desktops on less hardware. It offers high desktop density, without sacrificing performance or resiliency. HPE SimpliVity for VMware Horizon demonstrates enterprise scale in a single VDI building block, and unmatched performance, independently validated by Login VSI, the industry-standard benchmarking tool for virtualized workloads. HPE SimpliVity 2600 is a highly dense solution with Login VSI validation and supports NVIDIA graphics processing units (GPUs), up to two GPUs per 2U enclosure. HPE SimpliVity 380 Gen10 supports NVIDIA M10 GPUs for high-performance graphics. We work with several VDI platforms including Horizon view, Citrix, and Workspot.

- **Cloud computing**—HPE SimpliVity is the ideal choice if you are pursuing a cloud strategy that delivers the best of both worlds: cost savings and the agility of cloud—with enterprise performance and reliability. With a highly scalable, flexible, and cost-effective foundation for implementing private clouds, as well as on-demand services and hybrid cloud offerings available through a broad network of HPE SimpliVity powered service providers, HPE SimpliVity helps your customers deliver a cloud model that fits any requirement—private, public, or hybrid.

- **Tier-1 applications**–HPE SimpliVity 380 Gen10 frees up staff time to focus on projects that support and grow the business. Virtualized tier-1 applications run faster and become easier to manage, so you can significantly reduce the need for dedicated server, storage, and data protection specialists. IT generalists and the application team can now back up, restore, clone, or move VMs in just seconds.

- **Data protection**—Only HPE SimpliVity delivers a hyperconverged solution with full-featured, built-in backup and recovery at no additional cost. HPE SimpliVity RapidDR—an integrated disaster recovery automation solution—simplifies and accelerates off-site DR and provides VM protection across primary and secondary sites to minimize service disruption and manual errors. With HPE SimpliVity, RPOs and RTOs shrink dramatically because virtualized workloads can be backed up or restored in seconds or minutes, instead of hours or days.

- **Test/dev**—HPE SimpliVity provides a highly efficient, agile infrastructure that meets the rapidly changing demands of test/dev environments. Inherent data efficiencies and VM-centric management capabilities, plus seamless integration with key orchestration tools, dramatically simplify operations and accelerate IT service agility. Software developers and test engineers can initiate services without any IT involvement.

Hyperconverged use cases

Hyperconverged infrastructure solves problems and addresses the needs of various use cases without pigeonholing your customers into a single area. A majority of our midmarket customers use HPE SimpliVity infrastructure for over 75% of their virtualized workloads, including their tier-1 applications like SQL, Oracle, SAP, and industry-specific applications like Epic Hyperspace.

Remote locations

Businesses with remote locations benefit from standardized systems that are easy to deploy, manage, and scale, with the work handled by IT generalists. To keep pace with growing and sometimes unpredictable workloads, remote sites need systems that can scale quickly and seamlessly. To maintain business continuity, they need systems that provide centralized backup, recovery, and replication of data, following standard configurations and corporate processes.

Hyperconverged systems meet all these needs. For example, if a company has offices located around the world, a common solution is ideal. It allows the company to standardize processes for deploying, managing, and supporting its systems in remote locations. The company can also standardize its backup and recovery processes and leverage the existing resources in the corporate data center.

Developers in different locations also benefit from the capabilities of the hyperconverged system, since each development team can have its own dedicated VM for projects. As their projects grow, developers can quickly add infrastructure resources to maintain excellent response times. The simplicity of hyperconverged systems allows IT generalists to handle the day-to-day systems maintenance and management work in the remote locations. That helps the company reduce operating costs and meet the full range of computing and storage needs at the remote sites.

Lines of business

In many large organizations, lines of business or internal departments need a simple way to handle application services without a lot of IT overhead and without reducing performance expectations.

For example, your customer's finance department might routinely deal with quarter-end report generation. As the data grows, the reports take longer and longer to process. This finance department also has new projects in the planning stage, including an advanced accounting system that may need to be rolled out within the quarter. A hyperconverged system is a perfect solution to support new applications or services because it can be easily ordered and set up quickly with prescribed configuration tools. The ability to quickly roll out a fully functioning IT environment could allow the company to deploy its new accounting system before the end of the quarter, generate reports in a timely manner, and avoid the end-of quarter chaos.

Midsize businesses

Hyperconverged systems can also support midsize businesses. For example, your customer is a midsize business that needs to expand its server and storage capacity and wants to avoid taking on a lengthy, costly IT project. Hyperconverged systems are essentially turnkey data centers in a box that can be easily procured and deployed in minutes.

Another example is a hospital that wants to provide its clinical staff members with access to applications and data in a secure manner, whether they are on the hospital floor or working from a remote location. The hospital can deploy hyperconverged systems to run a VDI environment. The VDI solution gives hospital staff access to applications and data that reside on a centralized system. This allows the hospital to meet the access and performance requirements of clinical staff in an efficient manner and maintain patient confidentiality.

As the volume of stored data grows over time, the hospital can easily expand its VDI environment by adding additional hyperconverged systems, which seamlessly expand a common pool of resources in a virtualized, software-defined environment. The hospital also benefits from the small footprint of the systems, which makes it easier to scale out infrastructure in a space-constrained data center.

HPE SimpliVity HyperGuarantee

Features of the HPE SimpliVity HyperGuarantee include:

- **HyperEfficient**—Save 90% capacity across storage and backup combined

- **HyperProtected**—Under one minute to complete a local backup or local restore of a 1 TB VM

- **HyperSimple**—Three clicks to back up, restore, move, or clone a VM from a single console

- **HyperManageable**—Under one minute to create or update backup policies for 1000s of VMs across dozens of sites

- **HyperAvailable**—Add or replace HPE SimpliVity systems with zero downtime for local or remote sites

    - Zero disruption to local or remote SimpliVity backups

    - Zero reconfiguration of SimpliVity backup policies for local or remote sites

    - Zero re-entry of IP addresses in remote sites

 Note

HPE SimpliVity HyperGuarantee applies to current HPE SimpliVity and HPE OmniStack products and the new HPE SimpliVity 380 product.

The HPE HyperGuarantee is supported for multiple hypervisors, VMware, and Microsoft Hyper-V.

HPE SimpliVity 380 Gen10

Figure 7-11 HPE SimpliVity 380 Gen10

HPE SimpliVity 380 (available on HPE ProLiant DL380 Gen10 servers) is a compact, scalable 2U rack-mounted building block that delivers server, storage, and storage networking services. Adaptable for diverse virtualized workloads, the secure 2U HPE ProLiant DL380 Gen10, as illustrated in Figure 7-11, delivers world-class performance with the right balance of expandability and scalability. It also provides a complete set of advanced functionalities that enables dramatic improvements to the efficiency, management, protection, and performance—at a fraction of the cost and complexity of today's traditional infrastructure stack.

HPE SimpliVity 380 Gen10 is scalable, configurable, and expandable in one-node increments to up to 32 total nodes.

 Note

It is strongly recommended that an HPE SimpliVity 380 Gen10 cluster have a minimum of two nodes to realize the full benefit of the high availability hyperconverged solution. A single cluster supports up to eight nodes, while a single Federation supports up to 32 nodes.

HPE SimpliVity 380 Gen10 offers:

- A choice of Intel® Xeon® Scalable Processors

- From 144 GB to 1536 GB of memory (per node)

- 10 Gb or 1 Gb network

- Redundant power

- Virtualization software and licensing

- A compact 2U form factor

The HPE SimpliVity 380 Gen10 software features include:

- VMware vSphere

- HPE SimpliVity management plugin for VMware vCenter

- Cluster expansion without downtime

- Hot-pluggable solid-state drive (SSD)

- Integrated storage controller with battery-backed cache

- HPE ProLiant iLO Advanced Remote Management

HPE SimpliVity 380 model specifications

	Extra small	Small	Medium	Large/Extra large
	SMB remote offices	Small environments and remote offices	Wide range of use cases, optimized for core applications	Variety of use cases and large capacity requirements
CPU	Latest Intel® Xeon® Scalable Processor Family spanning single, dual socket, and multi-cores			
Memory	HPE Smart Memory DDR4 spanning various configurations up to 1436 GB			
Effective capacity	3 to 6 TB	6 to 12 TB	12 to 25 TB	Large: 20 to 40 TB Extra large: 40 to 80 TB
Storage configurations	5 x 960 GB SSD RAID-5	5 x 1.92 TB SSD RAID-5	9 x 1.92 TB SSD RAID-6	Large: 12 x 1.92 TB SSD Extra large: 12 x 3.84 TB RAID-6
New common options	GPU accelerator for VDI, end-user computing Data at rest encryption for data privacy RapidDR for DR automation FlexCapacity consumption options			
Common features	Accelerated inline dedupe/compression, high availability, redundant power, VM-centric policy-based backup/recovery/DR, replication, VM mobility, integrated management via hypervisor (VMware, MSFT SCVMM)			

Size

Figure 7-12 HPE SimpliVity 380 models

Storage configurations for VMware are available in two versions: 6000-series and 4000-series, except for Extra Large 4000-series. GPU and RapidDR options are only for VMware variants.

Storage Configurations for Microsoft Hyper-V **are** available for 4000-series in extra small, small, medium, and large configurations, as illustrated in Figure 7-12. The 6000-series is best for high-performance, IO-intensive mixed workloads and 4000-series is best for typical workloads (heavy reads/lower ratio of writes) at a lower cost than the 6000-series.

The 4000-series utilizes mixed-use SSDs with a lower write endurance and are targeted for less write-intensive workloads and not 24-hour workloads. The 6000-series utilizes IO-intensive SSDs that have about three times higher write endurance. Both platforms provide the same capacity and burst performance, but a feature called Media Lifecycle Manager can throttle write performance to ensure a full three years of life on the SSDs in the 4000-series nodes. HPE SimpliVity 380 Gen9 nodes are not offered in multiple series, and all nodes are equivalent to the Gen10 6000-series.

The HPE SimpliVity 380 4000-series utilizes SSDs that have a lower average Drive Writes Per Day (DWPD). To guarantee a three-year life on the 4000-series SSDs, a new feature called Media Lifecycle Manager was introduced in v3.7.3. This feature is always running and observes the rate of write IO on the disks. If Media Lifecycle Manager detects a DWPD trend that will result in a lifespan of less than three years, it will incrementally throttle VM and backup write throughput to ensure the lifetime writes will not be exhausted prior to the three-year warranty period. Utilizing this approach, there is less risk of disk failure from inadequately sized infrastructures or implementations that are used more heavily than designed. Alerts will be raised within the vSphere client whenever Media Lifecycle Manager is actively throttling write throughput. Read IO does not affect the life of SSDs, and therefore will never be throttled by Media Lifecycle Manager, nor will write activities associated with maintaining data high availability.

HPE OmniStack Virtual Controller

The OmniStack Virtual Controller (OVC) is a VM-based controller running on a hypervisor. It is the foundational software of the HPE SimpliVity HyperConverged infrastructure. Each OmniStack node has a single OVC. The OVC has direct hardware access to the two PCIe cards through VM direct path IO. In terms of resources, the OVC leverages four vCPUs within the host and works in conjunction with the HPE OmniStack Accelerator Card to deliver efficient data movement, high throughput, and high IOPS.

In normal operations, each OVC provides its hypervisor access to a network file system (NFS) datastore where the hypervisor stores the workload VMs. The OVC has three network connections for three different purposes:

- The storage network is where the NFS datastore is available. Usually this access happens inside each OmniStack node without touching the physical network, but there are few times when the NFS datastore is accessed over the physical network.

- The federation network is used for OVC-to-OVC communications.

- The management network is used by the HPE SimpliVity plugin to the vSphere client. This network is used to manage the HPE OmniStack–based environment.

Those networks are used to connect all virtual controllers in a cluster and allow this system to scale horizontally across the cluster, to act as a single share—a single datastore within the environment. Multiple datastores are also supported, but that single datastore allows a single image to create a shared resource pool across a cluster.

HPE OmniStack Accelerator Card

Figure 7-13 HPE OmniStack Accelerator Card

The OmniStack Accelerator Card (OAC) is a purpose-built PCIe-based accelerator card designed by the HPE SimpliVity team, shown in Figure 7-13. The OAC performs inline data efficiency processing, deduplication, compression, optimization, and write acceleration, as VMs write to their virtual disks.

The HPE OAC handles the heavy lifting, delivering the required processing power without the high costs. With the OAC, only a minimum amount of CPU is required to manage data efficiently. This leaves most of the CPU resources in the OmniStack node available to run customers' business applications.

The OAC contains a Field Programmable Gate Array (FPGA) programmed with the HPE SimpliVity deduplication, compression, and optimization algorithms. The card contains flash, and it is also protected by super-capacitors to allow dynamic random-access memory (DRAM) to be saved in the event of a power loss, making it extremely reliable. This design enables very low write latency given the high-speed and non-volatile capabilities of the card.

The port on the external section of the card is not a network port, but it is used as a diagnostic port by Support and Engineering. The card is inserted into a commodity server, and it provides ultra-fast write processing and caching services that do not rely on commodity CPUs.

When a write is issued by a VM to the NFS datastore, HPE OVC receives the write and sends it to a local and remote HPE OAC. This protects the data from any single point-of-failure and allows the HPE OVC to acknowledge the write back to the VM. The write is then serialized and coalesced with other random IO into a sequential write by the HPE OAC before being written to disk, which solves the IO blender issue (when many VMs are all hitting the disk in a random manner). Another advantage of using a PCIe flash device is that there is a very long-life expectancy when compared to an SSD.

Within a given HPE SimpliVity system, deduplication makes each storage media tier—DRAM, flash, SSD, and hard disk drive (HDD)—more efficient, thereby dramatically lowering the cost of the system compared to traditional offerings.

HPE SimpliVity RapidDR

Figure 7-14 Integrated, automated, simplified off-site disaster recovery

RapidDR provides a streamlined process for developing an automated DR plan that can then be later executed to recover VMs at a DR site in an automated fashion with minimal user interaction, as indicated in Figure 7-14. This also can specify which VMs to fail over to a DR site, in what order, and with which configuration.

RapidDR v2.1 adds support for automated failover and failback of VMs across primary and secondary sites for improved orchestration and reduced complexity. Users can execute or test a RapidDR failback with a single disaster recovery plan.

When executed, the DR plan will handle a majority of the tasks needed to recover their environment at the DR site, such as restoring VMs from backups, attaching them to new networks, and configuring appropriate network settings within the VM.

For VMware environments, HPE RapidDR enables DR orchestration for site-to-site recovery to improve application availability during planned or unplanned DR events. For example, one customer uses RapidDR to failover all 50 of their mission-critical VMs across two cities 500 miles apart. Before this, failover/failback DR event would have taken them days to accomplish, and now they orchestrate and automate the failover and failback in hours.

 Note

See details in the public customer story here:
https://upshotstories.com/stories/running-multiple-apps-on-san-it-might-be-time-for-an-upgrade

---

This is a perfect data protection and DR solution for many midmarket customers who have highly virtualized workloads.

It is available as an optional software-licensed product in 25 VM or 100 VM license packs.

For enhanced automation/orchestration in virtualized DR environments and to reduce complexity, RapidDR 2.1 also improves scalability to support 600 VMs in recovery plans for failover and failback. The limit increased to 600 VMs from 150 VMs. RapidDR client can now run on Windows 10 and Windows Server 2016 machines.

 Note

HPE SimpliVity RapidDR, an optional component, is not part of the selected Reference Architecture and customer scenario.

HPE Composable Fabric and SimpliVity

HPE Composable Fabric and SimpliVity integration empowers VM admin to control the full virtual environment:

- **Hyperconverge everything**—Industry-leading hyperconverged solution that fully integrates software-defined compute, storage, and composable fabric into a single system

- **Rack-scale automation**—VM administrator enjoys end-to-end automation of storage and networking tasks

- **Unified management**—Intuitive global management of VMs, storage, and networking using a familiar vCenter interface

Composable Fabric allows automatic deployment of network fabric for SimpliVity in minutes and nondisruptively scale out additional switches with zero downtime and zero touch configuration. New network-related features and functionalities can be added through software. Integration of server, storage, and networking hyperconvergence reduces CapEx network costs by 50% and can be managed by IT generalists through a single unified management.

HPE Composable Fabric and HPE SimpliVity—Example

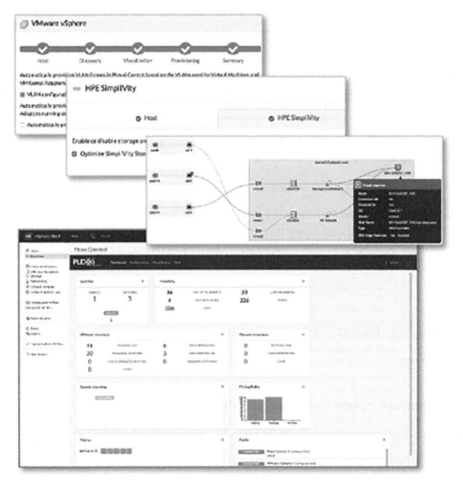

Figure 7-15 Converged management tools

HPE Composable Fabric and HPE SimpliVity management tools, as illustrated in Figure 7-15, include:

- vSphere web client
- Host fabric analyzer
- Fabric and host visualization

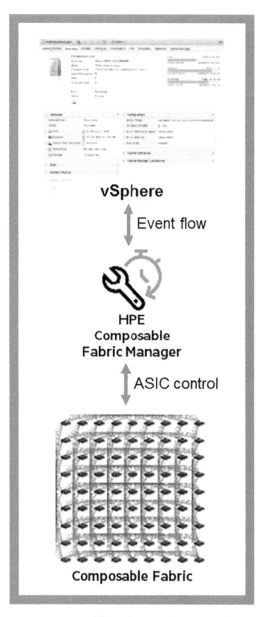

Figure 7-16 HPE Composable Fabric and HPE SimpliVity Integration

Available features in a VMware environment, as illustrated in Figure 7-16:

- Compute lifecycle
  - Host auto discovery
  - VM/switches/adapters/interfaces/Link Aggregation Groups (LAGs)
  - Auto configure Link Layer Discovery Protocol (LLDP) and Cisco Discovery Protocol (CDP)
  - VLAN auto-configuration
  - On VM adds/moves/deletes
  - NSX (VMware network virtualization) discovery and visualization
- Storage lifecycle
  - Detect HPE SimpliVity storage elements
  - Dynamically allocate fabric capacity
  - Automated storage traffic isolation
- Compute dynamic fabric
  - Detect and visualize vMotion events, and provide optimized path resources via pre-allocated bandwidth
- Storage dynamic fabric
  - Automatically isolated storage and federation networks
  - Detect switch or cluster member add/remove

HPE SimpliVity—Configuration workflow

Use the following steps to order a new SimpliVity 380 Gen10 system:

- **Step 1:** Start with the base node.
  - HPE SimpliVity 380 Gen10 Node
  - Hypervisor (VMware or Hyper-V)
  - HPE SimpliVity 2600 (VMware only)
  - HPE SimpliVity 170 Gen10
  - HPE SimpliVity 190 Gen10

- **Step 2:** Select the hardware options to add to the base node: processors, memory, storage, net-working, power, hardware options.

  – Processors

  – Memory

  – Storage (4000-series: mixed-use SSDs, Media Lifecycle Manager [write throttling]; 6000-series: write-intensive SSDs)

  – Networking

  – Power and rack

  – Additional hardware options, such as Trusted Platform Module (TPM) or bezel lock kit

- **Step 3:** Auto add software that correlates to node configuration.

  – HPE OmniStack

  – iLO Advanced

  – VMware vSphere

  – RapidDR

- **Step 4:** Select service and support.

  – Technology Services for increased uptime, productivity, and return on investment (ROI)

  – Installation and Startup Services

Management tools: HyperConverged solutions

HPE network management tools span across products and bring innovations to complete lifecycle management. As network management becomes more complex, the risks associated with compromised data flow have also increased.

HPE SimpliVity vSphere user interface

Figure 7-17 HPE SimpliVity vSphere user interface

HPE SimpliVity management is provided primarily by plugins to virtualization management tools, such as HPE SimpliVity management plugin for VMware vCenter and HPE SimpliVity management plugin for Microsoft System Center, as illustrated in Figure 7-17.

HPE SimpliVity Federation Home tab

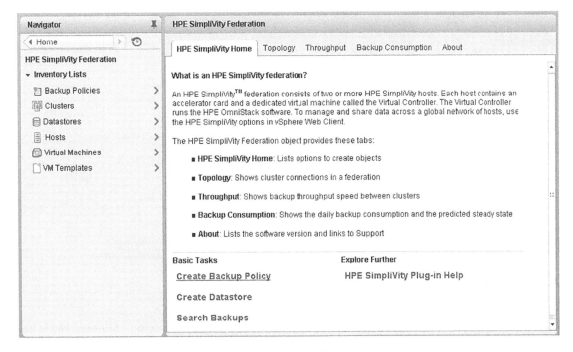

Figure 7-18 HPE SimpliVity Federation Home tab

The HPE SimpliVity Home tab, as shown in Figure 7-18, provides an overview of the HPE SimpliVity software and virtual objects. The tab provides you with an HPE SimpliVity Federation Inventory List (on the left of the screen), which offers a filtered display of all the objects in the HPE SimpliVity inventory.

The center of the page displays the information about an HPE SimpliVity Federation, as well as a brief description of the HPE SimpliVity tabs on the top of the screen. The HPE SimpliVity–specific tabs are:

- Topology
- Throughput
- Backup Consumption
- About

At the bottom of the screen following Basic Tasks links are available:

- Create Backup Policy
- Create Datastore
- Search Backups

There is also a link to open the HPE SimpliVity Plug-in Help.

HPE SimpliVity actions

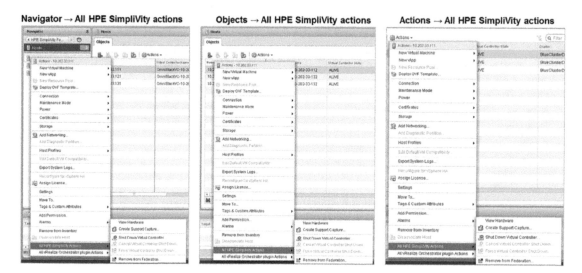

Figure 7-19 HPE SimpliVity actions

HPE SimpliVity is fully integrated into the vCenter Web Client. Leveraging vSphere's Navigator pane at the left, Administrators can quickly access all typical VMware resources as well as those with unique HPE SimpliVity significance. As indicated in Figure 7-19, the menu options to launch a dialog for HPE SimpliVity actions are located under All HPE SimpliVity Actions and sub-menu options.

Go into an object, right-click it, and select **All HPE SimpliVity Actions** to view a list of all HPE SimpliVity functionalities.

Click on the **Actions gear** icon dropdown from the top of the panel to gain access to the All HPE SimpliVity Actions option as well.

Note

The available actions under the All HPE SimpliVity Actions option change, based on the inventory item you select.

HPE SimpliVity Federation screen—Topology tab

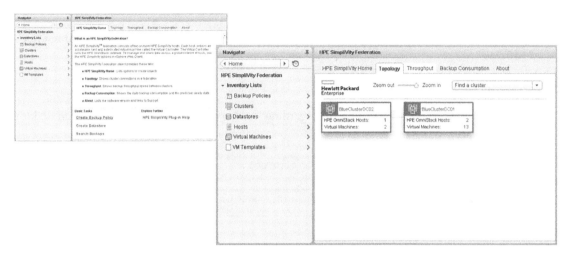

Figure 7-20 HPE SimpliVity Federation screen—Topology tab

When you open the Topology tab, as illustrated in Figure 7-20, you can see all the clusters in your Federation, including those in a ROBO configuration.

From vSphere Web Client Home, click **HPE SimpliVity Federation**.

Click **Topology** to open the Topology tab. All clusters in the Federation are displayed as containers. Each container has a building icon representing the VMware cluster.

The icon includes the following information:

- Cluster name

- Number of VMs

- Number of hosts

Do any of the following, depending on how you want to navigate the screen:

- To see a cluster's performance, click the name of the cluster, and you will be taken to the Monitor tab on the HPE SimpliVity Performance screen.

- To zoom in, slide the zoom bar to the right.

- To zoom out, slide the zoom bar to the left.

To find a cluster, select the cluster from the Find a cluster dropdown list.

Activity: HPE Reference Architecture for VMware Horizon on HPE SimpliVity 380 Gen10

1. Use this document: **https://h20195.www2.hpe.com/v2/getdocument.aspx?docname=4aa5-7340enw**

2. Answer the following questions:

   a. What is the recommendation in RA regarding sharing of memory resources between desktop workloads?

   _____

   _____

   _____

   _____

   _____

   b. Does HPE SimpliVity use vStorage API for Array Integration?

   _____

   _____

   _____

   _____

   c. Which benchmarking tool was used to verify performance of recommended solution?

   _____

   _____

   _____

   _____

Solution components

Part numbers are at time of publication and subject to change. The bill of material (BOM) does not include complete support options or other rack and power requirements.

Qty	Product #	Product Description
1	Q8D81A	HPE SimpliVity 380 Gen10 Node
1	Q8D81A 001	HPE SimpliVity 380 Gen10 VMware Solution
1	826884-L21	HPE DL380 Gen10 Intel Xeon-Gold 6150 (2.7GHz/18-core/165W) FIO Processor Kit
1	826884-B21	HPE DL380 Gen10 Intel Xeon-Gold 6150 (2.7GHz/18-core/165W) Processor Kit
1	826884-B21 0D1	Factory Integrated
2	Q8D88A	HPE SimpliVity 384G 6 DIMM FIO Kit
1	Q5V86A	HPE SimpliVity 380 for 6000 Series Small Storage Kit
1	873209-B21	HPE DL38X Gen10 x8/x16/x8 PCIe NEBS Riser Kit
1	873209-B21 0D1	Factory Integrated
1	P01366-B21	HPE 96W Smart Storage Battery (up to 20 Devices) with 145mm Cable Kit
1	P01366-B21 0D1	Factory Integrated
1	804331-B21	HPE Smart Array P408i-a SR Gen10 (8 Internal Lanes/2GB Cache) 12G SAS Modular Controller

Learning check

1. Which typical data center components is HPE SimpliVity replacing?

    _____

    _____

    _____

    _____

    _____

2. What is the maximum recommended amount of VMs for the SimpliVity platform?

    _____

    _____

3. What does the HyperProtected part of HPE SimpliVity HyperGuarantee stand for?

    a. Save 90% capacity across storage and backup combined

    b. Add or replace HPE SimpliVity systems with zero downtime for local or remote sites

    c. Under one minute to complete a local backup or local restore of a 1 TB VM

    d. Three clicks to back up, restore, move, or clone a VM from a single console

4. How is the SimpliVity management implemented?

_____

_____

_____

_____

_____

_____

5. At which level does the data optimization happen in the HPE SimpliVity platform?

    a. CPU and memory

    b. Hypervisor (VMware vSphere or Hyper-V)

    c. HPE OmniStack Accelerator Card

    d. HPE OmniStack Virtual Controller

6. You are in a meeting with a customer, and they challenge you with a question: "I'm interested in a modern virtualization solution that will include all the resources needed for running virtual machines in a single building block. Is there anything HPE can offer in this space?"

    How should you respond?

_____

_____

_____

_____

Alternative servers for other environments

We presented a validated solution for customer scenario. Some of the solution components, however, can be changed for alternative environments, where different performance, capacity, costs, features, and similar requirements can be satisfied with other HPE solutions. Not all the workloads are the same, and a single HPE product cannot match all the requirements.

HPE SimpliVity 2600

Figure 7-21 HPE SimpliVity 2600

Figure 7-22 Rear view of HPE SimpliVity 170 and HPE SimpliVity 190

HPE SimpliVity 2600 is based on Apollo 2600 and provides a different HPE SimpliVity platform choice for dense solutions for compute centric workloads, as illustrated in Figures 7-21 and 7-22.

The solution does not use the HPE OAC; it is 100% software optimized with always-on dedupe and compression. HPE is the first vendor to deliver consistent performance with always-on dedupe and compression enabled by software—tested by HPE Labs and Login VSI.

VDI use case includes:

- Architected and optimized for best VDI configuration performance
- HPE SimpliVity makes VDI simple to implement and manage
- VMware offering

HPE SimpliVity 2600 offers:

- Four times denser for space-constrained environments
- 100% software-defined (dedup/compression)
- Optimized for compute-intensive workloads
- Use cases: general virtualization, VDI, ROBO, retail locations, Internet of Things (IoT) systems, and other edge computing environments
- Global, unified scalability
- Enhanced operational efficiency for HPE SimpliVity

Two compute modules are available—HPE SimpliVity 170 and HPE SimpliVity 190. Figure 7-23 shows a comparison of their features.

Server node models	CPU configuration	Memory	Storage configuration	Effective storage capacity	RAID configuration
HPE SimpliVity 170	1 to 2P Intel Xeon **8** to **22** cores per socket	**256** to 768 GB	6 x 1.92 TB SSD	**7 to 15 TB**	Multi-tier (RAID 1+0 + RAID 5)
	– Minimum **2** nodes per chassis – Maximum **4** nodes per chassis				
HPE SimpliVity 190	2P Intel Xeon **8** to **22** cores per socket	**256** to 768 GB	6 x 1.92 TB SSD	**7 to 15 TB**	Multi-tier (RAID 1+0 + RAID 5)
	– 2 nodes per chassis – Two optional PCIe GPU or NIC supported with HPE SimpliVity 190 models				

Figure 7-23 HPE SimpliVity 170 and HPE SimpliVity 190

Mixed federations: SimpliVity 380 with SimpliVity 2600

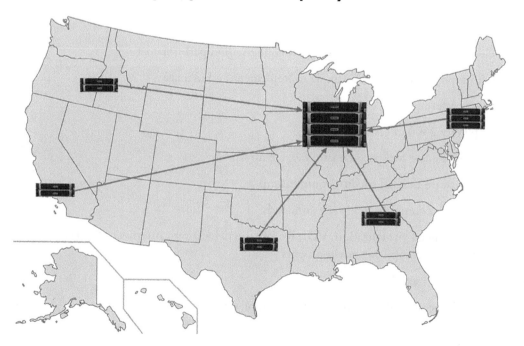

Figure 7-24 Mixed federations: SimpliVity 380 with SimpliVity 2600

Clusters of SimpliVity 380 can be mixed with clusters of SimpliVity 2600 in the same federation, as indicated in Figure 7-24, but SimpliVity 380 and SimpliVity 2600 nodes cannot be mixed in the same cluster. The maximum scalability is up to 96 nodes total per federation.

Benefits

- Deploy SimpliVity 2600 at ROBO and edge sites where space is constrained or storage requirements are low

- Deploy SimpliVity 380 at headquarters or core data centers

- Backup and replicate data from the edge to the core

HPE SimpliVity 380 Gen10 Expansion

HPE SimpliVity 380 Gen10 single-CPU servers can be upgraded to dual-CPU servers. The second CPU must match the existing CPU, and the expansion must be completed by HPE Pointnext. The CPU Expansion Kit contains CPU, memory, software license, and HPE Pointnext service.

Storage expansion must be completed by HPE Pointnext and requires all servers within a cluster to be the same storage size. Two paths are available: small to medium and medium to large. Cables and Smart Array cards are part of the order kit. Customer data migration and redeployment is required.

The expansion process includes:

- **Step 1:** Start with the expansion stock keeping unit (SKU).

- **Step 2:** Add the software license that correlates to either a storage expansion or a CPU add-on configuration.

- **Step 3:** Select the hardware options to add—either the storage drive kits or additional CPU and memory.

- **Step 4:** Select the service and support to perform (CPU upgrade, storage upgrade, data migration, component install, and redeployment).

These expansions are available only for DL380 Gen10 and are not supported for the HPE SimpliVity 170, 380 Gen9, or legacy nodes.

Learning check

7. Write a summary of the key concepts presented in this chapter.

_____

_____

_____

_____

_____

_____

_____

_____

_____

_____

_____

_____

_____

_____

_____

_____

_____

_____

_____

_____

Summary

- HPE SimpliVity is the hyperconverged solution with built-in data protection and automated disaster recovery.

- The hyperconverged infrastructure solves problems and addresses the needs of various use cases, such as data center consolidation, SMB/ROBO, VDI, cloud computing, Tier-1 applications, data protection, test/development environments.

- Two different types of nodes are available: HPE SimpliVity 380 Gen10 and HPE SimpliVity 2600.

- SimpliVity management is integrated with a virtualization platform (VMware vCenter or Microsoft System Center).

Prelearning check

Before proceeding with this section, answer the following question to assess your existing knowledge of the topics covered in this chapter. Record your answers in the space provided here.

1. You are in a meeting with a customer and they challenge you with a question: "I'm interested in a state of the art, mission-critical, scale-up hardware with multi-terabyte capacity for RAM. I heard that the maximum number of processors for HPE ProLiant servers is four, and the memory scalability goes all the way to 6 or 12 TB of RAM. Is there any other platform that is more suitable to my needs?"

   How should you respond?

   _____

   _____

   _____

   _____

   _____

   _____

   _____

   _____

   _____

8 Recommending HPE density and mission-critical solutions for customer use cases

LEARNING OBJECTIVES

After completing this chapter, and given a customer scenario, you should be able to:

✓ Recommend and position HPE mission-critical and high-density solutions, tools, and appropriate services for customer use cases.

✓ Describe, differentiate, and apply industry-standard architectures and technologies.

✓ Explain the HPE approach to converged management for the infrastructure lifecycle.

Scenario 9: Artificial Intelligence on HPE Elastic Platform for Analytics

The wide HPE portfolio of data center products can be introduced using customer scenarios and recommended, validated configurations based on HPE Reference Architecture (RA) or HPE Reference Configuration.

Introducing the customer scenario

ZAIL company will be used as a story line through this scenario. We will introduce the company using an interview:

- What is your primary business?

  – Large-scale, state-of-the-art drones for industrial purposes

- How many employees do you currently have?

  – Small high-tech company with 40 employees

- What does your selling and delivery channel look like?

  – Several government customer and large construction companies, no marketing, no sales force other than the owner

- Where are you currently storing data, and how do you access files?

  – Several network-attached storage (NAS)devices

- What does your server and network infrastructure look like?

  – Small computer room, 20 rack-based servers, open source shared block storage, two Top-of-Rack (ToR) switches, router

- What are your current plans?

  – Expansion to non-European markets

  – Considering storing and analyzing data generated by drones, such as operational statistics from engines and gyro stabilization decisions, potentially cameras

Customer requirements

As a result of multiple interviews and gathering information about customer plans and the customer's current infrastructure, the following requirements emerged for the new solution:

- On-premise hardware platform for machine learning (ML) and deep learning (DL) workloads

- Modular platform providing both compute and storage resources

- Possibility to use flexible, on-demand consumption of high-performance computing services

- Selected software platform: Spark, YARN, and TensorFlow

- Three years support: Hardware, Hortonworks Data Platform (HDP), and SUSE Linux Enterprise Server (SLES)

- Hardware requirements for the first phase of the project:

  – 512 TB of RAW storage capacity

  – 2P compute nodes

  – Adequate amount of management nodes

  – Three replicas

  – 25 Gb Ethernet connectivity

HPE Elastic Platform for Analytics

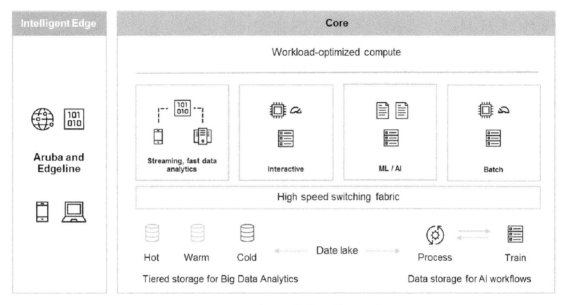

Figure 8-1 HPE Elastic Platform for Analytics

HPE's Elastic Platform for Analytics (EPA) offers an asymmetric architecture and a different approach to building a data pipeline optimized for Big Data Analytics, as illustrated in Figure 8-1. Asymmetric architecture consists of separately definable and scalable compute and storage resources, connected via HPE high-speed network components (25 Gb, 40 Gb, or 100 Gb), along with integrated management software and bundle support.

HPE's asymmetric architecture allows customers to build an initial configuration with HPE compute and storage servers, including heterogeneous compute/storage in the same cluster, purpose-matched for the planned workload, with the ability to add the right node profile as needs change.

What are the benefits of an elastic platform?

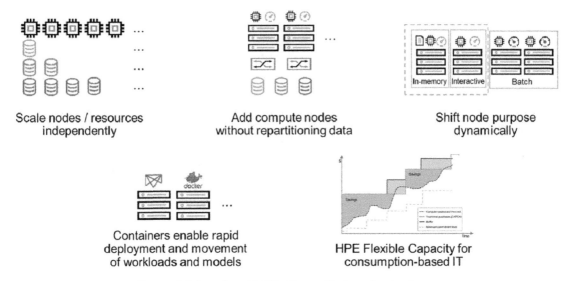

Figure 8-2 Benefits of HPE's Elastic Platform for Analytics

What makes the EPA Platform "elastic", as indicated in Figure 8-2?

- It allows us to scale node types independently. We could simply add new compute nodes with additional solid-state drives (SSDs) in those compute nodes to better handle the storage workload.

- It can add compute nodes without repartitioning data. Since none of the data persists locally on the compute node, we can do workload consolidation or scale the compute environment and do so quickly and elastically without having to repartition data.

- It can shift the purpose of nodes dynamically. Tools like YARN Node Labels, or resource managers like Mesosphere and Kubernetes, identify pools of resources that are focused on a particular workload task.

  Example: Financial Services customers typically have certain services they want to perform during the business day, but then have a maintenance window when they need to execute rollups and aggregations and want the flexibility to shift those resources to support a very different set of workloads at night, for example, for supporting certain analytic queries they want to run on a certain data pool.

- It enables the use of new technology like containers; containers are playing a bigger role—not just with DevOps, but across the entire data pipeline—to be able deploy models anywhere along that data pipeline and to perform analytics at that digital thread.

- It supports Flexible Capacity consumption models. For example, we have a customer in the automotive industry that is looking to deploy Big Data as a Service from their own internal service provider, which HPE offers through our HPE GreenLake offering (on premises), through HPE Pointnext, also an ala carte services approach.

Activity: EPA information resources

1. Download these information resources:

   – HPE Reference Architecture for AI on HPE Elastic Platform for Analytics (EPA) with TensorFlow and Spark

   https://h20195.www2.hpe.com/v2/getdocument.aspx?docname=a00060456enw

   – HPE Reference Configuration for Elastic Platform for Analytics (EPA)

   http://h20195.www2.hpe.com/V2/GetDocument.aspx?docname=4AA6-8931ENW

   – HPE EPA Sizing Tool

   https://sizersllb.itcs.hpe.com/sb/installs/EPA_Sizer.zip

2. Answer the following questions:

   a. What is the hardware platform recommended by RA for storage, compute, and management blocks?

   _____

   _____

   _____

   _____

   b. Which HPE Networking platform was selected in Reference Architecture for providing high-performance and redundant networking connectivity?

   _____

   _____

   _____

   _____

   c. Which CPU is recommended for Spark?

   _____

   _____

   _____

   _____

d. What is the recommended shared file system for distribute TensorFlow?

_____

_____

_____

_____

e. How many 2S nodes will fit the chassis selected for the compute block?

_____

_____

_____

_____

f. Which HPE service provides customer with the on-demand capacity and agility on "pay-as-you-go" basis?

_____

_____

_____

_____

g. What is the typical replication factor used to calculate usable capacity of shared storage?

_____

_____

_____

_____

Building blocks of the solution

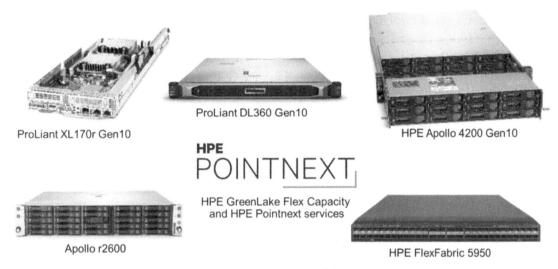

Figure 8-3 Building blocks of the solution

As organizations strive to identify and realize the value in Big Data, many now seek more agile and capable analytic systems to deliver on that value. Enterprises are looking to accelerate their analytics workloads to drive real-time use cases such as fraud detection, recommendation engines, and advertising analytics. The separation of processing from resource management with YARN has driven new architecture frameworks for Big Data processing, such as Lambda, Kappa, and SMACK (Spark, Mesos, Akka, Cassandra, and Kafka). These frameworks are designed to extend Hadoop beyond the often IO-intensive, high-latency MapReduce batch analytics workloads, to also address real-time and interactive analytics. Technologies like Spark, NoSQL, and Kafka are critical components of these new frameworks to unify batch, interactive, and real-time Big Data processing. These technologies typically have different capacity and performance requirements to scale-out processing, and they need a variety of options for compute, storage, memory, and networking. This presents a significant challenge to the traditional framework in Hadoop, where collocated compute and storage inhibit scale of either resource independently, and multi-tenancy of workloads creates scheduling and performance challenges.

With the increase in data generated outside of the data center, or at the edge, businesses are looking at how to capture, analyze, and grow new services from that data. The challenge lies in harnessing the data and processing it, while streaming for real-time or near-real-time analysis and response. An end-to-end data pipeline that extends from the edge to the data center needs to exist to accomplish this.

The HPE EPA is designed as a modular infrastructure foundation to address the need for a scalable multi-tenant platform, by enabling independent scaling of compute and storage through infrastructure building blocks that are workload optimized, as indicated in Figure 8-3.

Artificial Intelligence (AI) is increasingly being used to accelerate innovation and drive competitive advantage across a number of industries and applications. Organizations are now utilizing ML and

DL techniques to explore a new breed of analytics, to use predictive tools, and to speed to time to insight. Deep learning, a branch of ML, is about enabling computers to learn new concepts from raw data—much like the human mind—using Deep Neural Networks. The key enablers for the AI revolution are recent ground-breaking advances in DL research, making use of vast computing power of multi-core Graphical Processing Units (GPUs), and the availability of Big Data to train the Deep Neural Networks. The age of Big Data has made ML and DL much easier as the availability of huge amounts of data eliminates the need to rely on statistical estimations used in the past. The accuracy of the ML models had been plateauing prior to the use of DL techniques, and the recent Deep Neural Network innovations in the last decade have improved the accuracy by a huge margin as evidenced by the results of the ImageNet challenge.

TensorFlow, originally developed by researchers and engineers from the Google Brain team within Google's AI organization, has become a popular choice for AI practitioners who are implementing ML and DL algorithms. Its flexible architecture allows easy deployment of computation across a variety of platforms, and its support for distributed training allows multiple machines to train a model faster and to improve the productivity of AI teams.

However, the challenge aspect of AI is not necessarily the development AI code. The AI code represents a very small fraction of a real-world AI system. The rest is the ecosystem surrounding it that enables the AI data pipeline. Most of the AI effort is spent in configuring the ecosystem, collecting and cleansing the data, verifying the data, extracting the features from the raw data to feed to the AI algorithms, managing the model serving infrastructure, and monitoring it.

Spark provides a well-understood and effective solution to the ecosystem needs surrounding AI, as it can connect to all the AI ecosystem components and has become the de facto processing framework for Big Data, due to its ability to speed up batch, interactive, and streaming analytics and its ability to scale out to Big Data sets. It also offers the flexibility to run analytics on data stored not just in the Hadoop Distributed File System (HDFS), but also across object stores and traditional databases, making Spark the ideal platform for accelerating cross-platform analytics on-premises and in the cloud.

While distributed AI training with TensorFlow improves the productivity through faster training turnaround times, it is also difficult to configure and does not come with a resource manager to manage the cluster resources. This problem can be solved effectively by running Spark on Hadoop YARN and integrating Spark and TensorFlow together to make ML/DL drastically easier to use and scale.

While enterprises utilizing AI already have systems in place for Big Data ecosystems with ML/DL, they are frequently siloed, resulting in operational complexities tied to copying, duplicating, and maintaining the freshness of data. Integrating AI and Big Data ecosystem components into a consolidated platform can help organizations avoid these costly missteps.

The HPE EPA is designed as a modular infrastructure foundation to address the need for a scalable, multi-tenant platform, enabling independent scaling of compute and storage through infrastructure building blocks that are optimized for different workloads. HPE EPA can accommodate AI workloads by using AI compute blocks. These blocks are based on platforms that support GPUs (for example, HPE Apollo 6500) and can be added independently to the cluster from the storage tier.

The solutions highlighted here are geared toward most organizations that already have deployed Hadoop and Spark and are looking to integrate AI into their existing ecosystem. One of the benefits of the HPE EPA platform is that newer workloads like DL can be easily integrated into the existing infrastructure by adding additional EPA building blocks optimized for those workloads. The solution for this RA uses and validates this approach by adding an AI compute block to a previously released RA solution for Spark, available at HPE Reference Architecture for Apache Spark 2.1 on HPE Elastic Platform for Big Data Analytics (https://h20195.www2.hpe.com/v2/GetDocument.aspx?docname=a00041363enw). HPE has performed extensive testing with multiple workloads including Spark (for example, MapReduce, Hive, and HBase) to determine the optimal building block configurations to balance the compute power, storage capacity, and network bandwidth.

Based on this testing for the Spark RA, HPE recommends a "balanced" single rack elastic cluster design with three memory accelerated compute blocks of HPE Apollo 2000 chassis with XL170r servers and four standard storage blocks of HPE Apollo 4200 Gen9 servers. To extend this solution to include AI workloads, an AI compute block of HPE Apollo 2000 chassis with XL190r servers is added to the solution for entry-level DL workloads. Note that this a starter configuration example. HPE has developed the HPE Sizer for the HPE EPA to assist customers with proper sizing of EPA environments. Based on design requirements, the sizer will provide a suggested bill of materials (BOM) and metrics data for an HPE EPA cluster that can be modified further to meet customer requirements

HPE Apollo 2000 compute block delivers a scalable, high-density layer for compute tasks and includes four HPE ProLiant XL170r Gen10 nodes in a single 2U chassis. Each XL170r node harnesses the performance of dual Intel® Xeon® Gold 6130 processors each with 16 cores and 768 GB of memory, expandable to 1.5 TB for memory-rich Spark workloads. The local SSDs on the ProLiant XL170r servers provide ideal speed and flexibility for shuffle operations during a Spark job. Local storage can scale up to 6 small form factor (SFF) disks on each node.

HPE Apollo 2000 AI compute block includes two HPE ProLiant XL190r Gen10 nodes in a single 2U chassis. The ProLiant XL190r Gen10 Server is a 2U half-width, 2P server with the same configuration options as the XL170r for CPU and memory, but it has additional Peripheral Component Interconnect Express (PCIe) slots in multiple configurations providing support for additional expansion cards and support for two GPU accelerators per server. For the entry-level DL workloads, NVIDIA Tesla P100 (PCIe based) with 16 GB of memory is the recommended option. Tesla P100 includes 3584 CUDA cores and offers 4.7 teraFLOPS of peak double-precision performance and 9.3 teraFLOPS of peak single-precision performance.

HPE Apollo 4200 Gen9 servers make up the HDFS storage layer, providing a single repository for Big Data. The HPE Apollo 4200 saves valuable data center space through its unique density-optimized 2U form factor which holds up to 28 large form factor (LFF) disks with a capacity of 112 TB per server using 4 TB disks.

The single rack RA example provides a core-to-disk ratio of approximately 2:1 that can easily accommodate interactive Spark workloads and more than the canonical 1:1 ratio recommended for batch workloads using MapReduce, and so forth. In addition, as the HPE EPA architecture provides great flexibility in deploying disparate workloads and managing data growth, by decoupling storage growth from compute through high-speed networking, it enables a wide range of compute-to-storage ratios by adding more compute or storage as needed without having to add both in lockstep. Thus, a "hot" single rack elastic RA for compute-intensive ML Spark workloads could have a higher compute-to-storage ratio with more compute blocks; and a "cold" single rack elastic RA for Spark ETL workloads on storage-demanding use cases could have a lower compute-to-storage ratio with more storage blocks.

This logic also applies as the solution scales beyond a single rack. Similarly, the Apollo 2000 AI compute block could be replaced with a higher performing Apollo 6500 AI compute block for demanding DL workloads. From a GPU perspective, the NVIDIA Tesla P100 could be replaced by NVIDIA Tesla V100, which has 640 Tensor cores and 5120 CUDA cores, and offers 7.8 teraFLOPS of peak double-precision performance and 15.7 teraFLOPS of peak single-precision performance. This level of flexibility provides a wide range of configuration options to address varying analytics requirements.

High-Performance Computing

High-performance computing (HPC) accelerates digital transformation. In the case of weather forecasting, HPC systems provide accurate weather and climate projection. The Energy sector can utilize HPC systems to achieve higher efficiency and productivity in both reservoir simulation and seismic exploration. Modeling and simulation insights powered by HPC accelerates innovation in a variety of industries.

Financial Services are achieving competitive advantages leveraging HPC solutions in the areas of stochastic modeling (financial modeling), high-frequency trading, risk, and compliance. The Oil and Gas industry is seeing an increase in efficiency and productivity in reservoir simulation, seismic exploration, or Internet of Things (IoT).

HPC is assisting Life Sciences in improving healthcare while lowering costs through next generation sequencing, drug discovery, and predictive medicine. In Manufacturing, HPC is helping to speed time to market and increase product quality by leveraging HPC apps like computer-aided design (CAD)/computer-aided engineering (CAE) or parametric modeling (product design).

Results are showing up in competitiveness, product and service quality, and rapid time to market as well as another big one: return on investment (ROI).

HPC is key to continued business success

HPC customers use IT differently from corporate IT organizations. An HPC customer's expenditure on IT often approaches 90% of the total cost of the business, 10 times that of a corporate IT organization. Additionally, the IT growth rates for a service provider can be many times the IT growth rate of a corporation. For service providers, IT is the business.

HPC customers are focused on how to get the best performance possible with limited resources. HPC is firmly linked to economic competitiveness as well as scientific advances. Governments, academia, and enterprises use HPC to drive advances in their respective fields:

- Governments and academia leverage IT to solve the world's greatest problems (such as curing genetic illnesses, solving climate change, or determining the origin of the universe).

- Researchers are continually trying to solve more and increasingly complex problems in the life and materials science industries. HPC solutions increase research agility, lower costs, and allow researchers to process, store, and interpret petabytes of data. HPC enables simulation and analytical solutions to some of the most vexing problems in areas such as nanotechnology, climate change, renewable energy, neuroscience, bioinformatics, computational biology, and astrophysics.

- HPC solutions for upstream oil and gas exploration and production enable the industry to meet the increasing global demand for petroleum products.

- Financial Services companies face the most challenging analytics and trading environments in the industry. From risk management to high-frequency trading, IT solutions need to deliver the performance, efficiency, and agility to maximize the ability to add or adapt services quickly as market conditions change.

At one time, HPC was regarded as a specialist area. Today, it is becoming essential to the continued success of businesses requiring optimal computational performance, unprecedented reliability, memory, and storage scalability. Examples of such applications include:

- Computer-aided engineering (CAE)

- Electronic design automation (EDA)

- Research and development

- Life sciences

- Pharmaceutical

- Geophysical sciences

- Energy research and production

- Meteorological sciences

- Entertainment

- Media production

- Visualization and rendering

- Government

- Academia

- Financial Services

- Automotive and aerospace design

HPE purpose-built portfolio for HPC

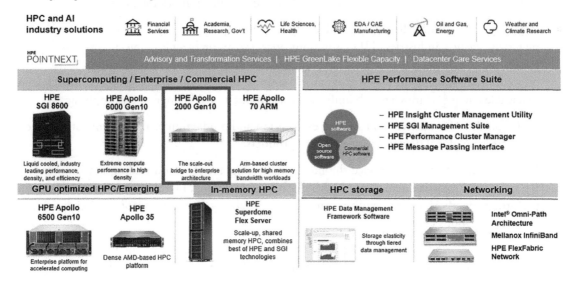

Figure 8-4 HPE industry solutions for HPC

The HPE Apollo family, as illustrated in Figure 8-4, is a set of purpose-built Compute offerings designed to address the needs of HPC workloads as well as Big Data Analytics, object storage, AI, and enterprise service provider needs. The emerging scale-out type of architectures driven by the cloud for Big Data Analytics and object storage requires simple storage at massive scale, substantial configuration flexibility, and a high degree of density optimization. The HPC type of workloads require significant parallel processing performance in combination with increased data center infrastructure efficiency to maximize the performance per unit of data center resource consumption (power/cooling/space/admins). As the need for HPC moves beyond the traditional domain of academia and research institutions to mainstream enterprise applications to drive business innovation, customers need the capability to shift from traditional platforms to scale-out solutions and HPC solutions in a nondisruptive manner to become enterprise service providers.

The common IT requirement for HPC is the need for extreme compute solutions that deliver massively parallel processing of large, unstructured data sets. This requirement exceeds the capabilities of typical industry-standard servers that are suboptimized for this activity. HPE has many choices to address all types of scenarios. For Petaflop scale, HPE has the HPE SGI 8600. This liquid-cooled platform delivers leading performance, density, and efficiency and is used for extremely large, training modeling and complex HPC.

HPE Apollo 6500 Gen10 System is a reliable enterprise DL and HPC platform with industry-leading accelerators that delivers exceptional performance for faster intelligence. The Apollo 6000 delivers HPC capabilities for the next level of processing requirements in midsize and large enterprise with rack scale efficiencies in terms of power, cooling, and space together with targeted workload optimization to enhance performance.

The Apollo 2000 is the ideal enterprise bridge for customers who are embarking on the scale-out journey for the enterprise and need a solution for small deployments of HPC as well as general-purpose workloads. These compute platforms are enhanced by a wide array of fabric choices (Ethernet, InfiniBand, or Intel® Omni-Path Architecture [OPA]), and HPC storage, software, in-memory platforms, and HPE Pointnext Services.

HPE Apollo 10 Systems offers mixed workload HPC for even the smallest departments, running on industry-standard accelerated compute servers.

Deliver automated intelligence in real-time for deep learning

Deep learning use cases include:

- Video, image, text, audio, time series pattern recognition

- Large, highly complex, unstructured simulation and modeling

- Real-time, near real-time analytics

Customer benefits when using unprecedented performance and scale with HPE high-density GPU solutions:

- HPE Apollo 6500 and SGI C1102-GP8 are ideal HPC and DL platforms, providing unprecedented performance with up to eight GPUs, high-bandwidth fabric, and GPU topologies designed to match DL workloads

- Up to eight high-powered GPUs per tray (node) configurable system topologies

- Choice of high-speed, low-latency fabrics

- Enterprise management: HPE Integrated Lights Out (iLO), HPE OneView, HPE Apollo Platform Manager (APM), or the SGI Management Suite

---

 Note

> In deep learning, large artificial neural networks are fed learning algorithms and ever-increasing amounts of data, continuously improving their ability to "think" and "learn" the more data they process. "Deep" refers to the many layers the neural network accumulates over time, and performance improves the deeper the network gets. While most deep learning is currently done with human supervision, the aim is to create neural networks that are able to train themselves and "learn" independently.

HPE Apollo 2000 Gen10 System

Figure 8-5 HPE Apollo 2000 Gen10 System

The HPE Apollo 2000 offers all the features of traditional enterprise servers and provides twice the amount of density than standard 1U rack servers. This system increases available data center floor space, improves performance while lowering energy consumption, and provides flexible configurations that fit into industry-standard racks, as illustrated in Figures 8-5 and 8-6.

Apollo 2000 systems offer a dense solution with up to four HPE ProLiant XL170r Gen10 Server nodes or up to two HPE ProLiant XL190r Gen10 Server nodes in a standard 2U chassis. Each server node can be serviced individually without impacting the operation of other nodes sharing the same chassis, providing increased server uptime. The ability to combine ProLiant XL170r servers and ProLiant XL190r servers in the same chassis and the unique drive-mapping flexibility lends itself to optimizing server configurations for many applications. Chassis, or groups of chassis, can be custom-configured to act as affordable, modular, 2U building blocks for specific implementations at scale—and for future growth.

Figure 8-6 ProLiant XL170r Gen10 and ProLiant XL190r Gen10

The Apollo 2000 is also compatible with the HPE APM, which enables an aggregate and detailed level of power measurement and control of groups of servers. It also provides static and dynamic capping of power across the nodes.

HPE Apollo 2000 features and benefits

Features of the Apollo 2000 include:

- Redundant fans and power infrastructure with up to two 1400 W power supplies

- Increased storage flexibility with options that support serial-attached SCSI (SAS)/serial advanced technology attachment (SATA)/SSDs

- Up to four independent, hot-pluggable server nodes in one chassis, delivering twice the compute density than 1U rack-mount servers

- Front hot-pluggable drives and rear serviceable nodes

- Cost-effective configurations for various workloads

- 1U and 2U servers that can be mixed and matched for workload optimization, allowing customers to partially populate the chassis and scale out as they grow

- HPC performance with accelerators, top bin processors, and a broad range of IO options

- 12 LFF or 24 SFF drive cage options, including an option for an SAS expander to enable flexible allocation of drives per server node

HPE Apollo 2000 Gen10 System features and sample use cases

The following table, as illustrated in Table 8-1, provides valued features and sample use cases for various segments:

Segment	**HPC** Workload and departmental	**Service providers** Enterprise, T2/3	**General purpose** Mid market, enterprise, and remote site
Valued features	– High performance processors – Accelerators – IO expansion – Storage flexibility	– Flexible configurations – Low cost options – Shared infrastructure efficiency – Density	– Flexible configurations – Single node service domain – Redundant power and fans – Traditional rear cabling and front hot plug drives
Sample use cases	– Manufacturing simulation – Seismic analysis – Life sciences	– Virtualized cloud – Web serving – Hosting – MemCache	– VDI/Remote workstation – Virtualized storage – File/Email Server

Table 8-1 HPE Apollo 2000 Gen10 System features and sample use cases

Big Data

The data landscape is radically changing. In yesterday's data-driven world, analytics and insights (and the technologies used to store/manage/analyze) were limited to (and for) traditional business data—the data generated from business-process applications like customer relationship management (CRM), enterprise resource planning (ERP) human resource management (HRM), and supply chain. However, as we have all seen, the data landscape has been radically changing over the past few years—90% of the data available today was created in the last two years—and the landscape will continue to change due to the fastest growing segments of human data and machine data.

Human data includes all the content we create—some of which is highly regulated for compliance purposes (contracts, legal docs) and social media, emails, call logs, and other images, audio, and video.

Machine data is the complete opposite of human data. It is the high-velocity information generated by the computers, networks, and sensors embedded in just about everything—the IoT.

Together, human data and machine data are growing 10x faster than traditional business data, and organizations that are data-driven are not only able to leverage this data to create new value, but they are also able to bridge the interconnection of data across the silos and repositories for integrated intelligence.

For example, in retail, retailers can maximize customer loyalty across multiple channels by integrating data from real-time inventory, in-store location positioning sensors, radio-frequency identification (RFID), and social media.

Big Data: Data-driven in the Idea Economy

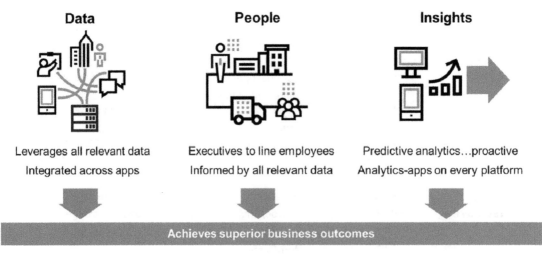

Figure 8-7 Data-driven in the Idea Economy

Now, the term data-driven is not actually new, it has been around for 20+ years since Business Intelligence (BI). However, the concept of being data-driven has changed—from what it can and could not do yesterday to what it can do for your customer's business today

If you look across three dimensions, as indicated in Figure 8-7—data, people, and insights—yesterday, being data-driven meant:

- Utilizing limited business data in siloed departments and applications

- Empowering a few people, typically business analysts, often from a tops-down approach, who do not even know the right questions to ask of the data to extract the value

- Delivering insights via monolithic BI reports to the limited few without regard to time sensitivity

- Reviewing analytics that were only available to the analysts reactively about what happened (in hindsight), with limited actionable value

Infrastructure was not designed to monetize the value of data and create insights, but rather designed around supporting application workloads. In yesterday's architecture, analytics was an afterthought and was separated from the compute resources, making it difficult to analyze and complex to manage.

Although it was the right intent, the business benefit had marginal impact with a ton of room for improvement.

Today, being data-driven is about:

- Harnessing all the relevant data (business/human/machine) available today and in the future

- Empowering and delivering insights for all stakeholders (collaboratively) in the organization (from line of business (LOB) leadership, operations, line workers, and so forth) irrespective of level or function—in-real time, at the moments that matter

- Operationalizing analytics through many apps, resulting in better results across the entire business/operations

- Achieving greater value through insight and foresight analytics—answering why did something happen or what will happen instead of just answering reactively what happened, so you can take action and be proactive

At the end of the day, it is about quickly and iteratively turning ideas to insights to better outcomes.

HPE's platform for Big Data and Scalable Object Storage

Figure 8-8 HPE's platform for Big Data and Scalable Object Storage—HPE Apollo 4000 Family

Big Data is growing at an exponential rate, and enterprises are seeking to translate Big Data Analytics into a competitive business advantage. Today's general-purpose infrastructure runs into problems when Big Data workloads move to petabyte scale. The data center can experience capacity constraints, spiraling energy costs, infrastructure complexity, and inefficiencies. To maximize the value of Big Data, businesses require systems that are purpose-built for Big Data workloads.

HPE Apollo 4000 systems are designed specifically for Hadoop and other Big Data Analytics and object storage systems. These systems allow customers to manage, monitor, and maintain increasing data volumes at petabyte scale. Businesses can use Apollo 4000, shown in Figure 8-8, to address data center challenges of space, energy, and time to results.

HPE Apollo 4200 Gen10

- Up to 384 TB of bulk storage in just 2U
- All front-accessible hot-plug LFF/SFF
- Ideal for many-node geo-deployments with small fault zones

HPE Apollo 4510 Gen10

- Next-generation 4U density-optimized
- Up to 720 TB of bulk storage
- One node in 4U rackmount
- Improved design puts 4U density into standard depth 1075 mm racks
- Easier to service—twin front-accessible disk drawers

HPE Apollo 4200 Gen10 Server

Figure 8-9 Apollo 4200 Gen10

The HPE Apollo 4200 Gen10 server, shown in Figure 8-9, is a density-optimized server storage solution designed for traditional enterprise and rack-server data centers. This versatile 2U Big Data server integrates seamlessly into traditional data centers with the same rack dimensions, cabling, and serviceability, as well as the same administration procedures and tools. It is the ideal bridge system for implementing a purpose-built Big Data server infrastructure, with the capability to scale in affordable increments in the future.

Typical workoads include:

- Workload-optimized architecture
- Big Data and Analytics
- Scale-out software-defined storage
- Backup and archive
- Other data storage–intensive applications

HPE Services

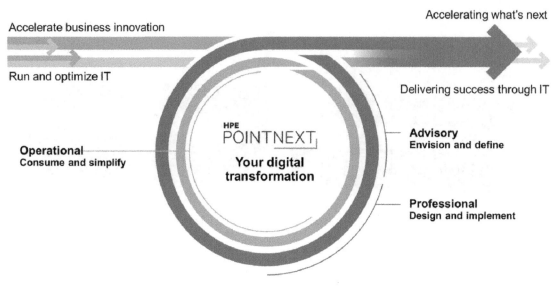

Figure 8-10 HPE Services portfolio

Success in today's mobile, connected, interactive, and immediate world requires that technology helps businesses create growth. Success demands transformative IT and business strategies and a highly flexible and responsive technology infrastructure. Leading organizations use technology to respond to business requirements and market opportunities quickly by overcoming aging, inflexible infrastructures.

HPE Pointnext services, as indicated in Figure 8-10, make it easy to accelerate digital transformation. HPE Pointnext uses professionals around the globe to help customers design, deploy, and optimize Hybrid IT infrastructure. These professionals collaborate on thousands of projects per year, and the experience they have gained, coupled with an extensive library of infrastructure blueprints and design tools, helps to reduce risk for customers undergoing transformation. Working with a large cross-section of businesses and a rich ecosystem of partners, HPE Pointnext professionals can help with advisory, professional, and operational services to find, implement, and support the optimal solution for customers' business needs.

Digital transformation requires continuous innovation, adoption, and evolution. HPE Pointnext can help simplify the experience. We have thousands of global IT operational services and experts who work with your customers on a daily basis. We will help them create new experiences for the business, from the core to the edge, offering new ways of delivering IT support services by automating and optimizing workloads, resources, and capacity, on-premises, and in the cloud.

HPE Pointnext Services include:

- **Platform Consulting Services**—HPE assists in developing IT strategies to modernize and migrate to an on-premises automated, digital platform.

- **Data Center Facilities Consulting Services**—HPE helps determine the best data center strategy to provide the right-sized requirements and provide the right mix of Hybrid IT.

- **Cloud Services**—HPE provides an extensive catalog of cloud services to help customers define their strategy and roadmap for the journey to the cloud.

- **Storage Services**—HPE Pointnext storage consultants analyze and design storage systems to improve efficiency, reduce costs, and apply scalability to meet business needs, while keeping it all safe.

- **Network Services**—HPE helps businesses plan and manage the lifecycle of services. This could be in deploying complex, business-critical solutions and helping to mitigate costly installation and configuration errors. Onsite services provide an end-to-end program that includes project management, implementation, and multivendor integration.

Make IT happen with HPE

Figure 8-11 Make IT happen with HPE

This is who we are and why HPE exists—to enable enterprises to accelerate innovation and time to value with the new apps and data, as well as to help your customers optimize their current environments, as indicated in Figure 8-11, by:

- **Making Hybrid IT simple**—To power your customer's right mix to accelerate innovations for their unique enterprise

- **Powering the Intelligent Edge**—To create the next gen of digital experiences and services

- **Providing the expertise to make IT happen**—To advise, integration and accelerate the outcomes for your customer's enterprise

Advisory & Transformation Services

Hybrid IT	Data & Analytics	Intelligent Edge
– Optimize your customer's applications and IT operations	– Modernize your customer's data infrastructure	– Redefine the workplace experience
– Accelerate DevOps to build and deliver new apps and services	– Operationalize next gen analytics	– Transform the guest experience
– Deliver IT-as-a-service for speed and agility	– Generate insights from Big Data	– Modernize Edge IT and enable IoT platforms
– Protect your customer's digital enterprise and ensure resilience	– Protect and archive digital assets	– Protect your users, networks, and devices

Figure 8-12 Accelerating what's next for your customer's enterprise

The Advisory & Transformation Services group is at the forefront, where we focus on business outcomes and goals. It focuses on three key practices: Hybrid IT, Big Data, and Intelligent Edge.

Our **Hybrid IT** practice defines the right-mix strategy and roadmap for Hybrid IT delivery, covering the Hybrid IT platform, operations, and brokering. We hear again and again the need to harness the right mix of hybrid, including dedicated, workload-optimized solutions as well as building foundations to develop and deliver a new generation of apps and workloads, and managing the complexity of multiple cloud. We bring the benefit of our substantial expertise, purpose-built intellectual property (IP), and deep technical knowledge to your Hybrid IT digital transformation, as illustrated in Figure 8-12.

A key growth area within our Hybrid IT practice addresses new challenges for DevOps and AppDev. Our Hybrid IT Applications Modernization practice focuses on cutting edge transformations to modernize application infrastructures and development through application migration, cloud-native development, and DevOps/Agile development. In every industry today, customers face a significant challenge to rapidly support the modernization, migration, and development of modern-day apps and AppDev methodologies, truly transforming the apps of today and tomorrow.

Our **Big Data** practice works to monetize the value of data through Big Data framework data management and actionable analytics. We see an increasing need to build optimized platforms for the most demanding data and analytics, to drive real-time decision making, accelerate predictive insights, and the data sets of tomorrow.

Our **Intelligent Edge** practice helps build out the Intelligent Edge to enhance user experiences, drive business value from mobility and IoT, and transform work spaces through Intelligent Spaces and Intelligent Venues. Compute at the edge is exploding today, and we increasingly hear from our customers the desire to capture opportunities they see around harnessing the data, connectivity, and real-time engaging going on at the edge.

Finally, the need for security and risk mitigation is integrated into each of these practices and applied to IT, data, apps, and the mobile edge network. Protection is built-in and interwoven as part of the solution to each use case.

Professional Services

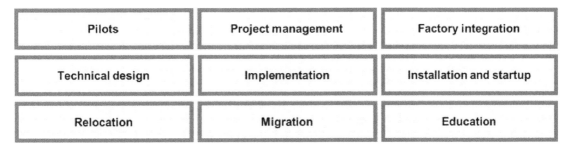

Pilots	Project management	Factory integration
Technical design	Implementation	Installation and startup
Relocation	Migration	Education

Figure 8-13 Converting ideas into reality at the speed of business

The Professional Services team specializes in flawless and on-time implementation, on-budget execution, and creative configurations that get the most out of software and hardware alike. Since we are top-stack agnostic, we work with your customer's preferred technologies, and they get the right solution for their needs, and not a one-size-fits-all model. We bring the IP and experience of thousands of implementations and deployments around the global to derisk your customer's transformation and get it done on time, on budget, and on target.

Professional Services takes a strategic plan and functional design and moves it into production, with a focus on Hybrid IT and Intelligent Edge, through a series of tactical transitions, the developed roadmap, functional requirements, and a functional design. We work in tandem with your customer's teams from technical design to implementation, build to migration, distribution, and finally to operational consulting and service.

HPE Pointnext provides a wide range of professional services from deployment to implementation and on-going education, as illustrated in Figure 8-13.

Operational Services

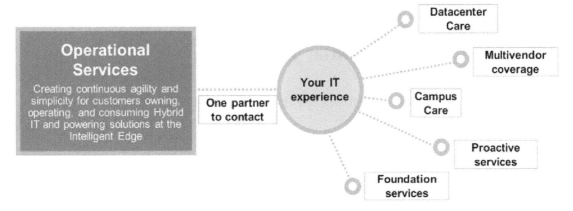

Figure 8-14 Simplifying IT experiences to power your customer's digital business

Digital transformation is not an event in time, but rather a continuous evolution and adaptation for any global organization. IT needs to adapt continuously to remain relevant in a changing market and defining the best way to enable business to deliver its products, services, and solutions to its customers.

The Operational Services team understands that success means being accountable for the whole solution—accountable across your customer's ecosystem and accountable across their old and new infrastructure and aps.

We have redefined the concept of "operational efficiency." We aim to create new IT experiences for your customer's business, from the core to the edge. Our innovative services, such as Datacenter Care and Campus Care, offer new ways of delivering IT by managing and optimizing workloads, resources, and capacity, on-prem and in the cloud, to simplify the experience and offer choice in where to land your customer's workloads and what they can self-manage or out-task. They benefit by being able to move to a consumption-based IT model, leveraging an agile, developer-centric architecture, and making IT easier to free up resources, as illustrated in Figure 8-14.

We have thousands of operational experts working closely with your customers on a daily basis to make sure your customers get the most out of their digital transformation, as well as support services specialists to keep their business operating at peak performance.

HPE GreenLake Flex Capacity: Consume infrastructure

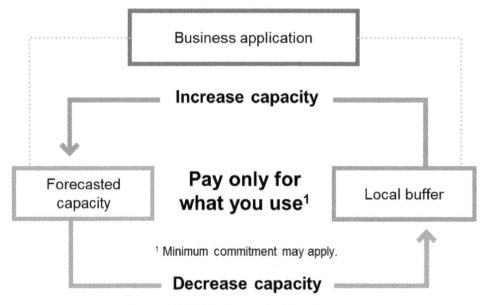

Figure 8-15 HPE GreenLake Flex Capacity

HPE GreenLake Flex Capacity, as illustrated in Figure 8-15, is a service delivered by HPE Pointnext that brings on-premises infrastructure consumption to customers today. With variable payments based on actual metered usage, rapid scalability using an onsite buffer of extra capacity, and enterprise-grade support, it brings a cloud-like experience for infrastructure on premises. Your customers can:

- First, choose the technology they want. They can select from a wide range of HPE and partner technologies, either customized or pre-packaged for faster deployment.

- Align services with their business needs. We support, meter, and manage the capacity of their installed hardware. Your customers can add additional services as needed to operate any or all of their IT stack. There is opportunity to tailor the experience to meet their needs—from mission-critical to least cost.

- Then they are off and running, paying only for what they consume. We meter their usage and they pay monthly for what they use, above a minimum commitment.

- Always have capacity ahead of demand as we install a buffer of capacity and actively monitor, manage, and deploy capacity ahead of business demand.

Management tools: Apollo Platform

In addition to iLO, HPE offers additional management options that are ideal for managing Apollo solutions at scale.

HPE Insight Cluster Management Utility

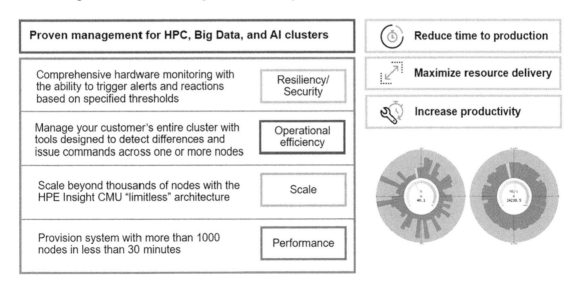

Figure 8-16 HPE Insight Cluster Management Utility

The Insight Cluster Management Utility (CMU), as illustrated in Figure 8-16, is a hyperscale-optimized management framework that includes software for the provisioning, control, performance, and monitoring of groups of nodes and infrastructure. This collection of tools helps customers manage, install, and monitor a large group of compute nodes, specifically HPC and large Linux clusters. This framework is optional for Apollo 4000 systems. Businesses can use Insight CMU to lower the total cost of ownership (TCO) of this architecture. Insight CMU is scalable and can be used for any size cluster. Users can access this utility through a graphical user interface (GUI) or a command-line interface (CLI).

- The Insight CMU GUI:

  - Monitors all the nodes of the cluster at a glance

  - Configures Insight CMU according to the actual cluster

  - Manages the cluster by sending commands to any number of compute nodes

  - Replicates the disk of a compute node on any number of compute nodes

- The Insight CMU CLI:

  - Manages the cluster by sending commands to any number of compute nodes

  - Replicates the disk of a compute node on any number of compute nodes

  - Saves and restores the Insight CMU database

HPE Apollo Platform Manager

Rack management	Power management	Server management
- Automatic chassis and shared device discovery with topographic views - Time stamped rack-level event logging - Rack and chassis shared power and thermal component management - Integrated Gb Ethernet switch for server iLO consolidation	- Power control and measurement at the server, chassis, and rack - PDU level power outlet control and current measurement - Rack level static or Dynamic Power Capping - DC power shelf management - Integration with HPE UPS subsystem	- Server health monitoring - iLO single sign on access - Server inventory

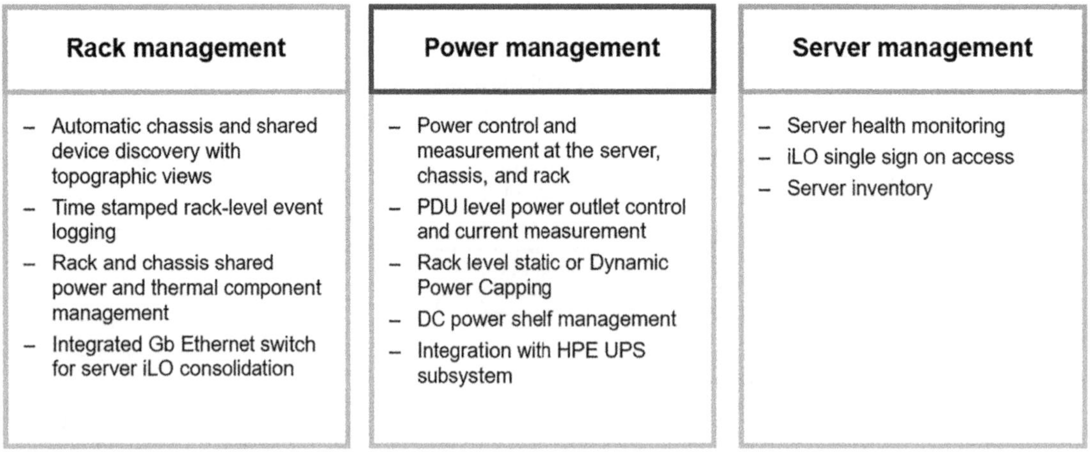

Figure 8-17 HPE Apollo Platform Manager

The Apollo Platform Manager (APM), as illustrated in Figure 8-17, is an optional rack-level solution for Apollo system*s*. HPE APM automatically discovers hardware components and enables bay-level power on and off, server metering, aggregate dynamic power capping, configurable power-up depen-dencies and sequencing, consolidated Ethernet access to all resident iLOs, and asset management capabilities.

The APM does not replace rack power distribution units (PDUs), but it is designed to enable the utilization of basic, low-cost rack PDUs while providing the functionality of switched PDUs. Switched PDUs provide hardware power on and off of individual servers by turning off the AC power to the power supplies of a given server. Because the servers share power supplies to optimize power efficiency, using switched PDUs to turn off all the power supplies in the chassis results in the loss of all server nodes in that chassis. The APM solves this by allowing server node-level hardware power on and off of the DC power to the individual server node motherboards.

Additional features include:

- Rack-level event logging

- Remote Authentication Dial-In User Service (RADIUS) authentication

- Integrated serial concentrator

- Up to 11 local user accounts

- Read-only service port

- Supports Simple Network Management Protocol (SNMP), Secure Shell (SSH), Syslogd, and Telnet

Activity: HPE Sizer for the Elastic Platform for Analytics

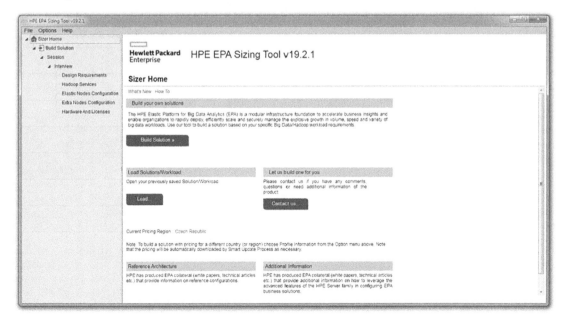

Figure 8-18 HPE Sizer for the Elastic Platform for Analytics

1. Download and install the sizer, shown in Figure 8-18:

   https://sizersllb.itcs.hpe.com/sb/installs/EPA_Sizer.zip

2. Use the inputs from the beginning of the presentation:

   - Hardware platforms

   - Software services

   - RAW storage capacity

   - Network interface card (NIC) speed

   - Replication factor of three

   - 25% overhead for logs and metadata

   - 24 x 7 three-year support

3. Prepare to present the BOM.

   - Maximum MAC addresses

   - Maximum amount of ingress/egress ACLs

_____

_____

_____

_____

_____

_____

_____

_____

_____

_____

_____

_____

_____

The additional requirements are:

- 512 TB of RAW storage

- YARN and Spark services

- Hardware platforms: XL170r, DL360 Gen10

- Support: 24 x 7 for hardware, SLES, and HDP

- Keep other values default

Solution components

Quantity	Part Number	Description	Status	List Price(EC)	Cost at Quantity(EC)
8	867055-B21	HPE ProLiant XL170r Gen10 CTO Svr	Active	1,765	14,120
2	874308-B21	HPE r2600 Gen10 Redundant Fan Module Kit	Active	140	280
4	830272-B21	HPE 1600W FS Plat Ht Plg LH Pwr Sply Kit	Active	460	1,840
8	874286-L21	HPE XL170r Gen10 Xeon-G 6130 FIO Kit	Active	2,840	22,720
2	867158-B21	HPE Apollo r2600 24SFF-Prem CTO Chassis	Active	1,625	3,250
2	880186-B21	HPE r2600 Gen10 PSU Enbl Kit	Active	25	50
8	874286-B21	HPE XL170r Gen10 Xeon-G 6130 Kit	Active	2,840	22,720
96	835955-B21	HPE 16GB 2Rx8 PC4-2666V-R Smart Kit	Active	432	41,472
8	817749-B21	HPE Eth 10/25Gb 2P 640FLR-SFP28 Adptr	Active	720	5,760
16	872344-B21	480GB SATA 6G MU 2.5in SC DS SSD	Active	780	12,480
8	874300-B21	HPE XL170r Gen10 P1 LP Riser Kit	Active	120	960
8	874305-B21	HPE XL170r Gen10 S100i SATA Cbl Kit	Active	35	280
8	866464-B21	HPE Eth 1Gb 2P 368FLR-MMT Adptr	Active	70	560
2	740713-B21	HP t2500 Strap Shipping Bracket	Active	20	40
2	822731-B21	HP 2U Shelf-Mount Adjustable Rail Kit	Active	110	220
32	AF595A	HP 3.0M,Blue,CAT6 STP,Cable Data	Active	28	896
16	JL295A	HPE X240 25G SFP28 to SFP28 3m DAC	Active	290	4,640
2	H7J34A3#ZBJ	HPE 3Y FC 24x7 Apollo 2000 Gen10 Support	Active	817	1,634
				Total Price(EC)	133,922

Quantity	Part Number	Description	Status	List Price(EC)	Cost at Quantity(EC)
3	867959-B21	HPE DL360 Gen10 8SFF CTO Server	Active	2,010	6,030
6	830272-B21	HPE 1600W FS Plat Ht Plg LH Pwr Sply Kit	Active	460	2,760
3	874449-L21	HPE DL360 Gen10 4116 Xeon-S FIO Kit	Active	1,505	4,515
3	871246-B21	HPE DL360 Gen10 High Perf Heat Sink Kit	Active	190	570
3	874449-B21	HPE DL360 Gen10 4116 Xeon-S Kit	Active	1,505	4,515
24	835955-B21	HPE 16GB 2Rx8 PC4-2666V-R Smart Kit	Active	432	10,368
3	817749-B21	HPE Eth 10/25Gb 2P 640FLR-SFP28 Adptr	Active	720	2,160
3	804331-B21	HPE Smart Array P408i-a SR Gen10 Ctrlr	Active	545	1,635
24	872479-B21	1.2TB SAS 10K 2.5in SC DS HDD	Active	600	14,400
3	P01366-B21	HPE 96W Smart Storage Battery 145mm Cbl	Active	95	285
3	874543-B21	HPE 1U Gen10 SFF Easy Install Rail Kit	Active	100	300
6	AF595A	HP 3.0M,Blue,CAT6 STP,Cable Data	Active	28	168
3	873770-B21	HPE DL3xx Gen10 Rear Serial Cable Kit	Active	30	90
3	867996-B21	HPE DL360 Gen10 SFF SID Pwr Module Kit	Active	140	420
6	JL295A	HPE X240 25G SFP28 to SFP28 3m DAC	Active	290	1,740
3	H7J34A3#WAG	HPE 3Y FC 24x7 DL360 Gen10 Support	Active	1,747	5,241
				Total Price(EC)	55,197

Quantity	Part Number	Description	Status	List Price(EC)	Cost at Quantity(EC)
3	P07244-B21	HP Apollo 4200 Gen10 24LFF CTO Svr	Active	3,645	10,935
6	830272-B21	HPE 1600W FS Plat Ht Plg LH Pwr Sply Kit	Active	460	2,760
3	P08048-L21	HPE XL420 Gen10 Xeon-G 5118 FIO Kit	Active	1,887	5,661
3	807878-B21	HPE LFF HDD Spade Blank Gen9 Kit	Active	20	60
3	P08048-B21	HPE XL420 Gen10 Xeon-G 5118 Kit	Active	1,887	5,661
24	835955-B21	HPE 16GB 2Rx8 PC4-2666V-R Smart Kit	Active	432	10,368
3	817753-B21	HPE Eth 10/25Gb 2P 640SFP28 Adptr	Active	750	2,250
45	881787-B21	12TB SATA 7.2K 3.5in LP He 512e DS HDD	Active	1,550	69,750
3	822731-B21	HP 2U Shelf-Mount Adjustable Rail Kit	Active	110	330
6	AF595A	HP 3.0M,Blue,CAT6 STP,Cable Data	Active	28	168
3	813546-B21	HP SAS Controller Mode for Rear Storage	Active	1	3
3	822640-B21	HPE Apollo 4200 Gen9 FIO Strap Ship Brkt	Active	10	30
6	JL295A	HPE X240 25G SFP28 to SFP28 3m DAC	Active	290	1,740
3	H7J34A3#YSN	HPE 3Y FC 24x7 Apollo 4200 SVC	Active	3,306	9,918
				Total Price(EC)	119,634

Quantity	Part Number	Description	Status	List Price(EC)	Cost at Quantity(EC)
3	P07244-B21	HP Apollo 4200 Gen10 24LFF CTO Svr	Active	3,645	10,935
6	830272-B21	HPE 1600W FS Plat Ht Plg LH Pwr Sply Kit	Active	460	2,760
3	P08048-L21	HPE XL420 Gen10 Xeon-G 5118 FIO Kit	Active	1,887	5,661
3	807878-B21	HPE LFF HDD Spade Blank Gen9 Kit	Active	20	60
3	P08048-B21	HPE XL420 Gen10 Xeon-G 5118 Kit	Active	1,887	5,661
24	835955-B21	HPE 16GB 2Rx8 PC4-2666V-R Smart Kit	Active	432	10,368
3	817753-B21	HPE Eth 10/25Gb 2P 640SFP28 Adptr	Active	750	2,250
45	881787-B21	12TB SATA 7.2K 3.5in LP He 512e DS HDD	Active	1,550	69,750
3	822731-B21	HP 2U Shelf-Mount Adjustable Rail Kit	Active	110	330
6	AF595A	HP 3.0M,Blue,CAT6 STP,Cable Data	Active	28	168
3	813546-B21	HP SAS Controller Mode for Rear Storage	Active	1	3
3	822640-B21	HPE Apollo 4200 Gen9 FIO Strap Ship Brkt	Active	10	30
6	JL295A	HPE X240 25G SFP28 to SFP28 3m DAC	Active	290	1,740
3	H7J34A3#YSN	HPE 3Y FC 24x7 Apollo 4200 SVC	Active	3,306	9,918
				Total Price(EC)	119,634

Learning check

1. Which HPE platforms are part of the HPE Elastic Platform for Analytics?

   _____

   _____

   _____

2. How many two-socket servers will fit in the HPE Apollo r2000 Gen10 chassis, if no GPU support is required for a specific workload?

   A. 1

   B. 2

   C. 3

   D. 4

3. Match the HPE platform for HPC with the description.

HPE SGI 8600	Extreme compute performance in high density
HPE Apollo 6000 Gen10	Liquid cooled, industry-leading performance, density, and efficiency
HPE Apollo 35	Scale-up, shared memory HPC
HPE Superdome Flex Server	Dense AMD-based HPC platform

4. How many 2.5" (SFF) SSDs will fit into the Apollo 4200 Gen10 Server?

_____

_____

_____

5. Which HPE solution will you recommend or add to the quote for configuring and installing cluster environments, monitoring cluster and node metrics, and remotely managing resources?

_____

_____

_____

Alternative servers for different environments

We presented a validated solution for customer scenario. Some of the solution components, however, can be changed for alternative environments, where different performance, capacity, costs, feature, and similar requirements can be satisfied with other HPE solutions. Not all the workloads are the same and single HPE product cannot match all the requirements.

HPE Apollo kl20 Server with Intel® Xeon® Phi Processors

Figure 8-19 HPE Apollo kl20 Server

Specifications of HPE Apollo kl20 Server with Intel® Xeon® Phi Processors, as indicated in Figure 8-19:

- **Processor**—Four Intel® Xeon® Phi Processor (one per server) (up to 230 watts), supports up to two integrated Omni Path with –F processor

- **Memory**—24 DDR4 dual in-line memory modules (DIMMs), 2400 MHz (six per server)

- **Network**—Dual-port GigE controller (Intel® I350)

- **Storage**—12 x LFF drives (three per server)

- **IO options**—Eight PCIe 3.0 x16 low-profile (two per server)

- **Management**—Integrated Intelligent Platform Management Interface (IPMI) 2.0

HPE Apollo 40—Flexibility, expertise, lower costs

HPE Apollo 40 family brings optimized industry-standard servers supporting latest technology for DL and HPC Workloads. HPE Apollo 40 family consists of two products:

- **HPE Apollo sx40**—A 1U rackmount dual socket Intel® Xeon® server with support for four NVIDIA Tesla SXM2 GPUs with NVLink. This configuration allows for up to 14,336 NVIDIA CUDA cores and 42.4 TFLOPS single precision floating point performance.

- **HPE Apollo pc40**—A cost-effective 1U dual socket Intel® Xeon® server that is optimal for mixed workload GPI-accelerated HPC. With support for up to four PCIe GPU cards, Apollo pc40 provides up to 37.2 TFLOPS of single precision performance per server.

HPE Apollo 40 family provides:

- Flexibility

  - Choice of CPU, memory, drives, GPU form factor

  - Multiple network topologies: Fat Tree, Hypercube, and Enhanced Hypercube

  - Comprehensive factory integration

  - Readily integrated into a standard cluster environment

- Expertise

  - Expertise in HPC, data management, visualization, systems management, and HPDA

  - Responsive and flexible support

  - Custom solutions—one size does not fit all

  - Committed account and technical resource teams

- Lower entry costs

  – Air cooling for standard server environments

  – Energy efficiency—dual high-efficiency power supplies

  – Select the right-sized network topology for cost model

  – Integrated IPMI 2.0 Management

  – Choice of GPU form factor

HPE Apollo pc40 Server

Figure 8-20 HPE Apollo pc40 Server

The HPE Apollo pc40 system's use of the latest GPU technologies enables breakthrough density, scale, and efficiency. Using NVIDIA GPUs with PCIe enables your customer to choose the best GPU for their workload, whether that is Tesla P100 or Tesla M40.

The HPE Apollo pc40 Server, as shown in Figure 8-20, is a 1U dual socket server featuring up to four NVIDIA Tesla GPUs and is based on the Intel® Xeon® Processor Scalable Family. The HPE Apollo pc40 Server is an optimized, industry-standard server for DL and HPC workloads that uses the PCIe form factor for greater choice in GPU selection. Your customers can enjoy quicker and easier deployments with their systems configured, integrated, and tested by HPE. Using industry-standard IPMI 2.0 system management and the HPE Performance Software Suite, the server is easy to use and manage. The HPE Apollo pc40 Server delivers cost-effective DL and HPC performance with high-compute density (up to four GPUs per 1U rack space), helping to turn data into insights and insights into actions.

Your customers can optimize the server for required workloads by choosing from the available CPUs in the Intel® Xeon® Processor Scalable Family, up to twelve 2666 MHz DDR4 DIMMs, optional network adapters, and up to two SFF hard drives or SSDs.

Fully integrated and factory-tested clusters are delivered with a complete cluster management software stack to simplify deployment and management and can be custom configured for perfect right-sizing.

Multiple network topologies are supported in cluster builds: Fat Tree, Hypercube, and Enhanced Hypercube for increased flexibility. The server is readily integrated into a standard cluster environment.

Specifications of HPE Apollo pc40 Server:

- **Chassis profile:** 1U standard-depth

- **Servers/System:** One dual socket

- **Max. processors:** Two Intel® XPSF processors

- **Max. CPU TDP:** 165 W

- **Memory slots:** 12 DIMM slots

- **Memory type:** 2666 MHz DDR4 ECC reg.

- **Max. hard disk drives:** 2 x 2.5" drives. 1 x M.2

- **Expansion slot: Includes five PCIe slots:**

  - 1 x PCIe 3.0 x16, Low Profile

  - 1 x PCIe 3.0 x16, FH/FL

  - 3 x PCIe 3.0 x16, FH/FL, Internal Only

- **Networking (Onboard):** Dual-port GigE controller (Intel® I350)

- **IPMI Remote Management**: Integrated IPMI 2.0

- **Power supply:** 2000 W Redundant Platinum Level

- **Max. GPUs:** 4x Tesla

- **GPU support:**

  - HPE NVIDIA Tesla P100 PCIe 12 GB Module

  - HPE NVIDIA Tesla P100 PCIe 16 GB Module

  - HPE NVIDIA Tesla P40 PCIe 24 GB Module

HPE Apollo sx40 Server

Figure 8-21 HPE Apollo sx40 Server

The HPE Apollo sx40 is a purpose-built, dense, and flexible 1U GPU server for the most demanding HPC and DL workloads. This server brings cost-effective, industry-standard GPU-accelerated computing into even the smallest HPC department.

The HPE Apollo sx40 Server, as shown in Figure 8-21, is a 1U dual socket server featuring up to four NVIDIA Tesla GPUs in SXM2 form factor and based on the Intel® Xeon® Processor Scalable Family. The HPE Apollo sx40 Server is an optimized industry-standard server supporting DL and HPC workloads, using the SXM2 form factor to provide increased available GPU memory bandwidth and performance. Your customers can enjoy quicker and easier deployments with systems configured, integrated, and tested by HPE. Using industry-standard IPMI 2.0 system management and the HPE

Performance Software Suite, the server is easy to use and manage. The HPE Apollo sx40 Server delivers cost-effective DL and HPC performance with high-compute density (four GPUs per 1U rack space), helping to turn data into insights and insights into actions.

The HPE Apollo sx40 Server features up to four NVIDIA Tesla GPUs with the high-bandwidth, energy-efficient interconnect NVIDIA NVLink to accelerate mixed-application HPC computing as well as DL workloads. NVLink enables increased GPU performance for DL workloads.

Your customers can optimize the server for required workloads by choosing from the available CPUs in the Intel® Xeon® Processor Scalable Family, up to twelve 2666 MHz DDR4 DIMMs, optional network adapters, and up to two SFF hard drives or SSDs.

Fully integrated and factory-tested clusters are delivered with a complete cluster management software stack to simplify deployment and management, and it can be custom configured for perfect right-sizing. Multiple network topologies are supported in cluster builds: Fat Tree, Hypercube, and Enhanced Hypercube.

Specifications of HPE Apollo sx40 Server:

- **Chassis profile:** 1U standard-depth

- **Servers/System:** One dual socket

- **Max. processors:** Two Intel® XPSF processors

- **Max. CPU TDP:** 165 W

- **Memory slots:** 12 DIMM slots

- **Memory type:** 2666 MHz DDR4 ECC reg.

- **Max. hard disk drives:** 2 x 2.5" drives

- **Expansion slot:**

  – Includes 3 PCIe 3.0 x16, Low-Profile slots

  – Includes 4 SXM 2.0 slots (two slots are already occupied by two SXM GPUs)

- **Networking (Onboard):** Dual-port GigE controller (Intel® I350)

- **IPMI Remote Management:** Integrated IPMI 2.0

- **Power supply:** 2000 W Redundant Power Supplies Titanium Level (96%)

- **Max. GPUs:** Four Tesla P100 SXM2

HPE Apollo 35 System

Figure 8-22 HPE Apollo 35 System

The Apollo 35 System was created to provide a dense, high-performance AMD Epyc HPC solution. Building on the strengths of the AMD Epyc processor, the Apollo 35 provides high-efficiency, high throughput performance, and scalable performance, as illustrated in Figures 8-22 and 8-23.

Figure 8-23 HPE Apollo 35 System

Ideal HPC workloads include:

- Computational Fluid Dynamics (Ansys Fluent, Star-CCM+, OpenFOAM)

- Weather simulation (WRF)

- Seismic modeling (Navier Stokes, Wave, Heat-Mass transfer, RTM, FWI, and so on)
- Biology, genomics (NAMD)
- Crash simulation (LS-DYNA)

HPE Apollo 70 System

Figure 8-24 HPE Apollo 70 System

The HPE Apollo 70 is a density-optimized, 2U-shared infrastructure chassis for up to four independent, hot-plug servers with all the traditional data center attributes—standard racks and cabling and rear-aisle serviceability access, as shown in Figure 8-24.

The platform includes a 2U chassis with two modular power supplies. Eight new generation single-rotor fans are included per chassis for redundancy.

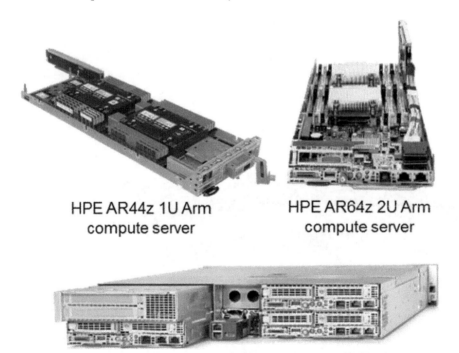

HPE AR44z 1U Arm
compute server

HPE AR64z 2U Arm
compute server

Rear View with AR64z and two AR44z

Figure 8-25 HPE Apollo 70 System

The chassis can support four half-width 1U server trays or two half-width 2U server trays. There are two server tray options, as indicated in Figure 8-25:

- **Up to four 1U Server/Chassis**—Eight LFF hot-plug SATA HDDs or SSDs (two per node)

- **Up to two 2U Server/Chassis**—Four LFF hot-plug SATA HDDs or SSDs (two per node)

HPE Apollo 6000 Gen10 System

Figure 8-26 HPE Apollo 6000 Gen10 System (k6000 Chassis)

The HPE Apollo k6000 Chassis, as illustrated in Figure 8-26, is designed with density optimization and HPC solution integration in mind to help your customers manage and scale to their HPC computing demands. The new modular HPE Apollo k6000 Chassis is designed to hold the next generation of compute servers to fit your customer's specific HPC workloads.

The new modular, fully integrated, and highly flexible HPE Apollo k6000 Chassis accommodates up to 24 XL230k server trays, redundant power and cooling, Ethernet, and high-speed fabric switches to address various HPC workload needs. The Apollo k6000 System is a performance-optimized, air-cooled solution that fits in your customer's space limitations. This solution offers outstanding configuration flexibility, simplified administration, and rack-scale efficiency that lowers the TCO needed for mass scale HPC deployments.

Cooling concerns are reduced by 12 hot-pluggable dual rotor fans while the chassis power can be managed by either an HPE Chassis Controller or enhanced (simplified) with an optional HPE APM that allows granular power control at rack level.

Features:

- Performance-optimized, air-cooled solution

- Outstanding configuration flexibility

- Fully redundant power system

- Simplified administration efficiencies

- Ideal for highly parallel applications

- Leading edge technology and performance

  - 206 TFLOPS per rack with next-generation processors

  - Single or dual plane fabric

  - Integrated, purpose-build HPC system

  - Up to 205 W 28c 2.8 GHz processor

  - 100 Gbps node to node connectivity

  - Lower latency and higher input/output operations per second (IOPS) with NVMe storage

  - Increased performance and future proofing with 3D Xpoint storage on memory bus

- Rack scale efficiency

  - Improved rack-level reliability, availability, serviceability, and manageability (RASM) features through integration

  - Fast and simpler deployment

  - Quickly deploy, service, and manage with cold aisle front accessible nodes

  - Improved reliability with choice of Ethernet, Omni-Path Architecture, and EDR InfiniBand switches

  - Enhanced security with Trusted Platform Module (TPM), secure firmware updates, iLO, secure encryption

- Optimized for best TCO

  - Optimized architectural integrated design

  - Purpose-built solution aligned to fabric radix without stranded ports (for example, architecture uses all the switch ports)

- Reduce IT deployment, maintenance time, and support costs through minimized cabling

- Rapidly install and deploy using consolidated iLO port

- Minimize power consumption and reduce cooling costs when nodes are not fully utilized using advanced thermal technology

HPE Apollo 6000 Gen10 System is purpose-built for large-scale HPC deployments, and it has fast, secure, and resilient compute, storage, and fabric technologies built with rack-level efficiencies to deliver exceptional price per performance.

HPE Apollo k6000 — Quieter, lower power, more efficient chassis

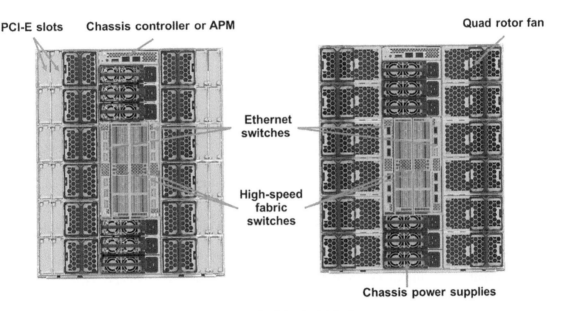

Figure 8-27 Back of the k6000 chassis

HPE Apollo k6000 chassis, as illustrated in Figure 8-27, brings the flexibility to use PCIe slots or quad-rotor fans. Let us look at the back of the chassis. On the left-hand side, we have 12 dual rotor fans at 100% at duty cycle that will generate 1500 cubic feet per minute (CFM). The advantage on the left side is the flexibility to support a PCIe card. The IO option can be workload accelerator, network card such as 25 GbE Ethernet if the bandwidth of the integrated is insufficient, or a Smart Array card that allows external storage connectivity.

On the right-hand side, we have the efficient quad-rotor fans that consumes lower power and has lower acoustics. These powerful fans can generate more CFM than the dual rotor fans.

HPE Apollo 6500 Gen10 System

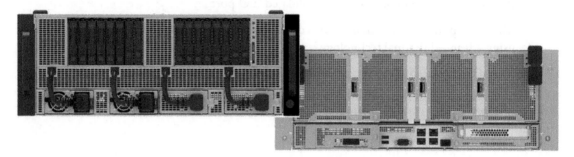

Figure 8-28 HPE Apollo 6500 Gen10 System

HPE has created Apollo 6500 Gen10 System as the industry-leading enterprise platform for accelerated computing. HPE Apollo 6500 Gen10 System, as indicated in Figure 8-28, delivers:

● Unprecedented performance

● Economical AI and DL capabilities

● Rock-solid enterprise-level reliability, availability, serviceability (RAS) features

● Easier system management

● Flexibility to support a wide range of workloads, including DL and complex simulations and modeling that is typical of HPC workloads

For Gen10, we focused upon simplifying the solution, based on extensive customer feedback:

● Enterprise Standard Design

  – Compared to the Gen9 solution which required three core components, Gen10 is a traditional 4U rack server designed to fit comfortably within a standard 1 m deep rack

  – iLO experience you have today

  – Standard air-cooled design for enterprise racks

  – Broad choice of options and operating system (besides Ubuntu, choose from Enterprise OS like Red Hat, SLES, or CentOS)

  – The design leverages the DL380 Gen10 heavily

  – Modular design throughout for ease of access and simplified serviceability

  – Standard rack-mounted server design

● Maximum performance and TCO

  – Up to eight accelerators from NVIDIA, AMD, or others

  – Our best TCO for accelerated workloads

- Customers can maximize their spend on accelerators rather than the CPU, RAM, fabric, and other infrastructure

- Flexible to match your customers' workloads

  - Get NVLink 2.0 with the SXM-2 GPU Module

  - Traditional GPU support with our PCIe Module

HPE SGI 8600 Gen10 System

Leading performance
- >1/2 petaflop of pure x86 compute TFLOPS per rack with Intel® Xeon® Processor Scalable family
- Clustered solution supports most powerful processors and interconnect technology

Ease of use
- Robust system and cluster management tools
- Off-the-shelf OS and applications for quick time to solution

Density/Scale/Efficiency
- Designed to scale to meet any customer's requirements
- Liquid cooling for maximum density and power efficiency

Figure 8-29 Addressing key requirements for large-scale distributed computing

The HPE SGI 8600 is a liquid-cooled, tray-based, high-density clustered computer system designed from the ground up to deliver the utmost in performance, scale, and density, as indicated in Figure 8-29. The basic building block of the HPE SGI 8600 system is the E-cell. The E-cell consists of two 42U high E-racks that are separated by a cooling rack. The E-cell is a sealed unit, uses closed-loop cooling technology, and does not exhaust heated air into the data center. A direct-attached liquid-cooled "cold sink" provides for efficient heat removal from high-power devices including processors, GPUs, and switches via an auxiliary cooling distribution unit (CDU).

A single E-rack can accommodate up to 36 compute tray slots within four compute enclosures. The E-rack is not configured with any cooling fans. All the cooling needs for the E-rack are provided by the cooling rack. This approach to cooling provides greater efficiency for the rack-level cooling, decreases power costs associated with cooling (fewer blowers), and utilizes a single water source for two racks. The custom-designed 42U-high E-rack supports both indirect and direct cooling methods. The indirect method is where the conditioned air supplied by the cooling rack provides the cooling to the components in the E-rack. This method can be used for configurations that require a lower level of heat removal. The direct method is the addition of liquid-cooled cold sinks to the processors in the compute trays. This method is used in parallel with the indirect cooling when the indirect cooling method is not sufficient to remove all of the heat from the E-rack.

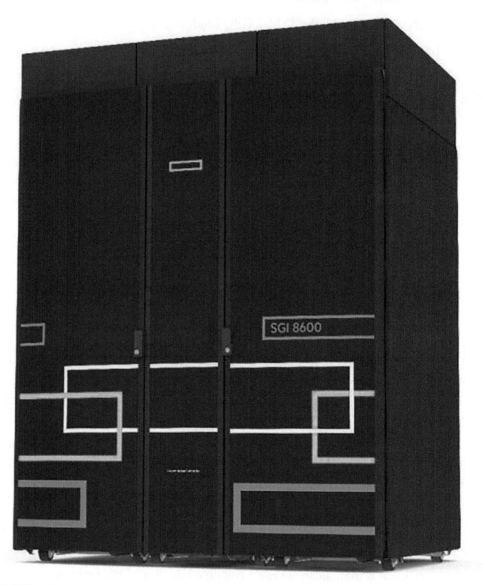

Figure 8-30 HPE SGI 8600 Gen10 System—Addressing key requirements for large-scale distributed computing

One 42U high, 60 cm wide E-rack supports the following:

- Maximum of four 10.5U compute enclosures
- Maximum of 36 quad-node compute trays (up to 288 sockets)

- Maximum of 16 InfiniBand switch blades

- Maximum of nine power supplies per compute enclosure—36 total 3000 W power supplies

- One AC input power raceway

- Maximum of two PDUs

- Maximum 221.184 TB of memory (36 trays x 4 nodes/tray x 2 sockets x 6 channels x 128 GB)

Designed to solve the world's most complex problems in areas ranging from life, earth, and space sciences to engineering and manufacturing to national security, as illustrated in Figure 8-30, the HPE SGI 8600 offers leading performance, density, scale, and efficiency coupled with robust system tools for the quickest times to solutions.

Features of the SGI 8600 Gen10:

- Leading performance

  - Intel® Xeon® Processor Scalable Family

  - Clustered solution supports most powerful processors and interconnect technology

  - World record performance for major message passing benchmarks using the latest, most performant interconnect technologies coupled with leading HPE Message Passing Interface (MPI) software

- More compute options—choice of three server trays

  - Four dual socket next-generation node tray—up to 288 nodes/512 CPUS per E-cell

  - One dual socket next-generation node supports up to 165 W and up to four NVIDIA Tesla P100 with NVLink tray (SXM2)

  - Four single sockets with Intel® Xeon® Phi node tray

- Ease of use

  - Robust system and cluster management tools

  - Off-the-shelf OS and applications for quick time to solution

- Density/Scale/Efficiency

  - Designed to scale to meet any customer's requirements

  - Liquid cooling for maximum density and power efficiency

  - Runs complex HPC workloads at petaflop speed with a liquid-cooled, tray-based, scalable, high-density clustered computer system

  - Designed to efficiently scale to thousands of nodes through superior power and cooling efficiency coupled with advanced power management

HPE Apollo 4510 Gen10 System

Figure 8-31 Workload-optimized storage server for Big Data solutions

The HPE Apollo 4510 Gen10 System, as illustrated in Figure 8-31, offers revolutionary storage density in a 4U form factor fitting in HPE standard 1075 mm racks, with one of the highest storage capacities in any 4U server with standard server depth. When your customers are running Big Data solutions, such as object storage, data analytics, content delivery, or other data-intensive workloads, the HPE Apollo 4510 Gen10 System allows them to save valuable data center space. Its unique, density-optimized 4U form factor holds up to 60 LFF and additional two SFF or M.2 drives. For configurability, the drives can be NVMe, SAS, or SATA disk drives or SSDs.

This table highlights some of the details of the Apollo 4510 Gen10:

Feature	Apollo 4510 Gen10 details
Processors	Up to two Intel® Xeon® Scalable Family Processors, up to 150 W per socket
Memory	16 DIMM slots, up to two NVDIMMs per processor (Type-N)
Drive support	Apollo 4510: 60 LFF, side loaded
	PMC Belmont SAS expander
	Dual PCIe M.2 drives on node PCA for boot
	2x SFF HDD/SSD/NVMe for node or 2x UFF Dual SATA M.2 Kit
	Micro SD Flash Media
Network	Dual-Port 1 GbE from PCH
Expansion	Up to one FlexibleLOM (x8), 1 x16 LP and 2 x16 FHHL PCIe slots with two processors
Display	SUV port, Video, Power/Health/UID buttons, and LEDs

(Continued)

Feature	Apollo 4510 Gen10 details
Management	iLO 5 + dedicated iLO NIC port + iLO USB port
	HPE OneView support
	HPE Advanced Power Management support
Other features	4U chassis height; fits in HPE Standard 1075 mm rack
	Hot-plug rear serviceable N+1 redundant fans
	HPE Gen10 Flex Slot power supplies (AC and DC versions) up to 1600 W

HPE Edgeline Converged Edge Systems

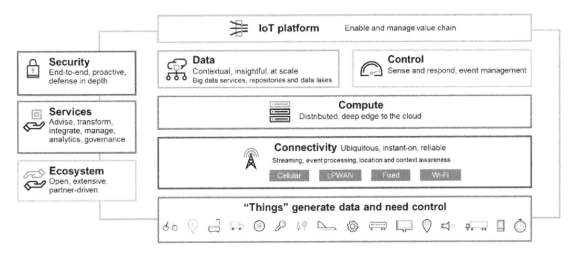

Figure 8-32 Providing the complete solution for managing compute, control, and data

Unleashing the edge's full potential requires running existing and new enterprise-class business applications unmodified at the edge—not just pared-down "edge versions."

Workloads running in the data center or cloud must all run identically at the edge—whether containers, virtual machines, databases, software-defined storage, or something else. Running the same software stacks both in the cloud and at the edge affords cost savings, ease of management, and use of existing IT and operational technology (OT) skills. To achieve these benefits, edge systems are engineered with enterprise-class compute, storage, management, and security delivered in a rugged form factor to withstand harsh edge environments. In addition, converging OT with IT requires novel approaches.

There are three main categories of the OT-IT convergence value, as indicated in Figure 8-32:

- **Process convergence**—IT and OT teams agree to collaborate on end-to-end workflows and dataflows.

- **Software and data convergence**—Enterprise IT applications collaborating with OT applications are applied to both traditional enterprise data and data derived at the edge.

- **Physical systems convergence**—IT systems (compute, storage, management, and security) integrate in the same system chassis with OT systems (data acquisition systems, control systems, and industrial networks).

HPE Edgeline systems deliver on two fundamental promises of value:

- HPE Edgeline integrates and converges OT systems (control systems, data capture systems, industrial networks), in the same system chassis as IT systems.

- HPE Edgeline shifts uncompromised enterprise-class IT systems, from the data center out to the edge.

Examples of Edgeline systems include:

- EL300 Converged Edge System

- HPE Edgeline EL1000

- HPE Edgeline EL4000

The management engine built into each HPE Edgeline EL1000 and EL4000 system begins with the core capabilities of HPE iLO. Management is extended with edge-specific capabilities enabled by the HPE Edgeline Integrated System Manager (iSM)—embedded in the new HPE Edgeline EL300. Both HPE iLO and iSM provide local management of HPE Edgeline systems, supporting simple deployment and reliable operations. These management tools enable users to directly manage individual systems as well as consolidate management of multiple systems.

To successfully manage individual Edgeline systems, HPE iLO and iSM provide the following key capabilities:

- System configuration

- Health monitoring

- Event logging and alerting

- GUI and CLI for user access

- Remote virtual presence

- Redfish (REST) interface for programmatic access

- Security

- Wireless manageability

The HPE Edgeline Infrastructure Manager (EIM) enables administrators to manage multiple HPE Edgeline systems from a single pane of glass. With EIM, users no longer need to bounce from system to system when checking for issues or performing updates.

Note

Edge computing is a distributed, open IT architecture that features decentralized processing power, enabling mobile computing and Internet of Things (IoT) technologies. In edge computing, data is processed by the device itself or by a local computer or server, rather than being transmitted to a data center.

HPE Edgeline EL300 Converged Edge System

The HPE Edgeline EL300 Converged Edge System provides an effective way for your customers to connect and manage all their OT Systems such as control systems, data acquisition systems, and industrial networks with their existing IT infrastructure. The HPE Edgeline EL300 is a highly flexible, expandable, and customizable platform that can grow as your customer's needs evolve over time. Its modular design allows the device to incorporate expansion modules for a multitude of connectivity options. The HPE Edgeline EL300 device supports remote management over both wireless and wired networks. It also has a compact, ruggedized, fanless design that will withstand harsh environmental conditions with a wide operational temperature range of -30°C to 70°C and is ideal for embedded customer use cases.

HPE Edgeline EL1000

Figure 8-33 HPE Edgeline EL1000

HPE Edgeline EL1000, shown in Figure 8-33:

- True compute for edge use

- One cartridge box

- In field, near the source to collect the data

- Small-scale analytics

- Physically compact

- Ability to connect through Wi-Fi

HPE Edgeline EL4000

Figure 8-34 HPE Edgeline EL4000

HPE Edgeline EL4000, shown in Figure 8-34:

- True compute for edge use

- Four cartridge box

- Heavy analytics at the edge

- More of everything (compute, power, storage, internal PCI slots)

Scenario 10: HPE Reference Architecture for Oracle 18c OLTP and OLAP workloads on HPE Superdome Flex and HPE 3PAR Storage Reference Architecture

The wide HPE portfolio of data center products can be introduced using customer scenarios and recommended, validated configurations based on an HPE Reference Architecture or HPE Reference Configuration.

Businesses today demand faster transaction processing speeds, scalable capacity, consolidation, and increased flexibility. Traditional architectures with separate transactional and analytical systems are complex, expensive to implement, and introduce data latency. These challenges can be addressed by combining online transaction processing (OLTP) with online analytical processing (OLAP). Doing so requires a large, scale-up system architecture that can meet the demands of the combined workloads.

The HPE Superdome Flex sets a new standard for scalability and expandability while ensuring flexibility for all transaction, analytical, and data warehouse workloads. HPE Superdome Flex coupled with HPE 3PAR StoreServ storage arrays is an ideal scale-up configuration. The ability to scale-up to 32 CPU sockets, 48 TB of memory, and virtually unlimited storage capacity means that this solution can meet the needs of the most demanding Oracle Database workloads. The large memory capacity available with this server allows taking advantage of Oracle in-memory features, which can speed up analytical queries by orders of magnitude, while simultaneously processing transactions.

This HPE RA demonstrates that the HPE Superdome Flex is capable of simultaneously handling OLTP and OLAP workloads with minimal impact on transaction rates and query response times.

In addition, the HPE Application Tuner Express (HPE ATX) tool was utilized to provide optimal performance in a non-uniform memory access (NUMA) environment. Transaction throughput increased up to 67% when HPE ATX was used to align Oracle processes with their data in memory and evenly spread them across NUMA nodes on a 16-processor HPE Superdome Flex configuration.

Introducing the customer scenario

ZAIL company will be used as a storyline through this scenario. We will introduce the company using an interview:

- What is your primary business?

  - Large-scale, state-of-the-art drones for industrial purposes

- How many employees do you currently have?

  - Small high-tech company with 40 employees

- What does your selling and delivery channel look like?

  - Several government customer and large construction companies, no marketing, no sales force other than the owner

- Where are you currently storing data, and how do you access files?

  - Several NAS devices

- What does your server and network infrastructure look like?

  - Small computer room, 20 rack-based servers, open source shared block storage, two ToR switches, router

- What are your current plans?

  - Expansion to non-European markets

  - Consolidation of mission-critical database to highly available, scale-up, on-premise platform (moving from unstructured data in previous scenario to structured data)

Customer requirements

As a result of multiple interviews and gathering information about customer plans and the customer's current infrastructure, the following requirements emerged for the new solution:

- On-premise, mission-critical, scale-up hardware platform for Oracle 18c

- Support for up to 32 sockets and 48 TB of memory

- Compute platform capable of simultaneous OLTP and OLAP workloads

- Enterprise class all-flash array

    – Utmost performance of storage subsystem

- Array designed for 99.9999% availability

    – Full hardware redundancy

- Hardware requirements:

    – 16 sockets, Intel® Xeon® Platinum 8180

    – 16 Gb Fibre Channel (FC) host bus adapter (HBA), Emulex chip, two ports

Activity: Superdome information resources

1. Download these information resources:

    – HPE Reference Architecture for Oracle 18c OLTP and OLAP workloads on HPE Superdome Flex and HPE 3PAR Storage

       https://h20195.www2.hpe.com/v2/getdocument.aspx?docname=a00065205enw

    – HPE Superdome Flex QuickSpecs

       https://h20195.www2.hpe.com/v2/getdocument.aspx?docname=a00026242enw

    – HPE Superdome Flex server architecture and RAS

       https://h20195.www2.hpe.com/v2/Getdocument.aspx?docname=a00036491enw

2. Answer the following questions:

    a. How many sockets does the smallest Superdome Flex chassis have?

       _____

       _____

    b. What is the name of the external administrative node for the Superdome Flex?

       _____

       _____

    –   What are typical tasks of this management controller?

_____

_____

_____

_____

    –   When is the external controller needed?

_____

_____

_____

c.   What is the recommended processor for Oracle?

_____

_____

d.   What is an example of a high-availability feature related to memory?

_____

_____

e.   What is the highest bandwidth NIC supported by Superdome Flex?

_____

_____

f.   Under which condition(s) can be DIMM types mixed in the system?

_____

_____

_____

g.   What is the maximum weight of a single chassis?

_____

_____

Building blocks of the solution

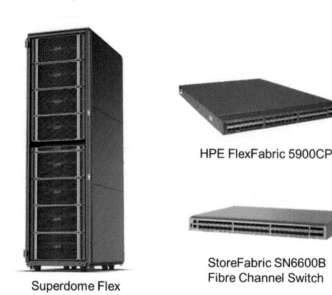

HPE FlexFabric 5900CP

StoreFabric SN6600B
Fibre Channel Switch

Superdome Flex

HPE 3PAR StoreServ 9450

Figure 8-35 Building blocks of the solution

In today's fully connected world, the exponential increase in data collection and management has never been higher. To keep up with this demand, businesses must constantly increase their database computing resources. Formerly, analytics was often limited to business data that provided only a historical snapshot of the business. Now tremendous growth comes from new real-time data sources such as IoT devices, social media, video, and so on. Analyzing data sources with business intelligence tools to create integrated intelligence is now needed to keep pace with change or to create a competitive advantage. To support these business intelligence capabilities in a near real-time fashion, a high-capacity OLTP system can help to feed these analytics, as indicated in Figure 8-35.

Running a mix of transactional and analytic workloads on the same Oracle database can be game changing. It can eliminate or reduce some of the issues inherent in maintaining separate systems for each workload, including:

- Extract, Transfer, and Load (ETL) processes to extract data from the OLTP environment, transport it to the OLAP environment, and load it into a data warehouse. In addition to the aforementioned latency, there can be challenges with transforming the data from the OLTP representation to the OLAP format.

- Using multiple systems for OLTP and OLAP may increase the number of Oracle licenses required.

- Each system must be configured to meet peak processing needs.

In addition to running multiple workloads on a single server, the ability to scale up capacity as requirements increase offers the following advantages over adding more servers (scaling-out):

- **Oracle database consolidation**—Over time, as Oracle database systems are deployed for departmental applications and projects, many companies find that they have an abundance of under-utilized systems that need to be maintained. With the ability to consolidate many systems into instances running on a scale-up platform, management and infrastructure costs can be reduced significantly.

- **Legacy applications**—Many older legacy applications simply do not have the out-of-the-box capability to run on a scale-out platform. Often the cornerstone of many IT infrastructures, these applications may require additional costly middleware applications or extensive-rewrites. Moving to a scale-up platform allows the application to scale without modifications.

- **Resource-demanding applications**—Applications such as OLTP require real-time processing ability. These capabilities, in turn, require large amounts of CPU, memory, and storage resources. Performing these operations on a single platform avoids the overhead of aggregating data across multiple systems/storage.

For mission-critical workloads, the HPE Superdome Flex provides the ease of scale-up combined with the capacity required to run mixed workloads. Since it is easily scaled by simply adding more chassis, there is no migration to a new server—you simply add the new resources to the existing partition. Mission-critical resiliency is provided through end-to-end implementation of processor RAS features, redundancy of key system components, and advanced system software, to help ensure the server is up and running 24 x 7. Additionally, in rare cases, where a problem happens that would typically bring down the entire server, the HPE Superdome Flex's modular design means that the problem can be remedied by modifying the existing partition to exclude the problem chassis, and then the server can be brought up (with reduced resources), to continue operations.

Management complexities are reduced as up to all eight chassis (32 processors) can be managed as a single entity. Unlike scale-out clusters, the HPE Superdome Flex provides great performance with minimal tuning.

To scale up a system such as the HPE Superdome Flex, a storage system with a similar, scale-up capability is required. The HPE 3PAR portfolio can scale to four controller nodes for the midrange products and eight nodes for the high-end products. In addition, capacity can be scaled from a few terabytes to over 80 PB in a four-system federation with a common OS, feature set, and management.

With HPE Infosight predictive analytics technology, and the ability to group arrays together for management and aggregation, these arrays are perfectly suited for mission-critical environments.

HPE Infosight not only monitors the environment for problems and potential hazards, but it also proactively predicts problems before they occur, and in some cases can resolve these problems without intervention. Infosight can see across your customer's entire infrastructure, giving them a view that they may have never had before, transforming their whole support model.

The testing highlighted in this RA details the OLTP and OLAP capabilities of a single, 16-processor HPE Superdome Flex configuration.

The solution presented in the RA includes the HPE Superdome Flex with HPE 3PAR StoreServ 9450 All Flash storage, running Oracle Database 18c. The HPE ATX software was utilized to achieve maximum performance in a NUMA environment.

HPE Superdome Flex

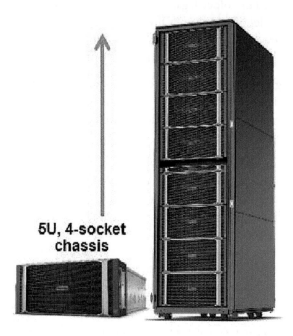

5U, 4-socket chassis

Figure 8-36 HPE Superdome Flex

HPE Superdome Flex server, as illustrated in Figure 8-36, delivers a unique and unprecedented combination of modularity, flexibility, scale, and reliability to deliver in-memory computing for businesses of any size. It is a mission-critical platform flexible and powerful enough to handle the massive and growing amount of business data. Its in-memory design and unparalleled scale provide the ability to analyze data from the digital core to the Intelligent Edge in real time. In addition, because the infrastructure is modular and cloud-ready, it is the right fit for any business of any size.

Your customers can keep pace with their evolving in-memory computing demands through a unique modular design: start small and grow as needed, flexibly scaling up or out. With superior RAS and end-to-end security, HPE Superdome Flex safeguards vital workloads. Our broad services portfolio and partner ecosystem, and mission-critical expertise help turn data into insight, so your customers can turn insight into action, and action into success—with peace of mind that their business will be always on.

HPE Superdome Flex includes:

- Proven RAS capabilities not available on other standard platforms.

- The best-in-class, predictive fault-handling Error Analysis Engine, predicts hardware faults and initiates self-repair without operator assistance.

- A firmware first approach to log analysis ensures error containment at the firmware level, including memory errors, before any interruption can occur at the OS layer.

- HPE Superdome Flex includes mission-critical resiliency from end-to-end implementation of processor RAS features, to redundancy of key system components to advanced system software.

- It is designed from the chipset up to provide up to five nines (99.999%) single-system availability.

HPE Superdome Flex is a flexible in-memory computing solution with a unique modular design that scales easily and economically for businesses of any size. It blends trusted HPE Superdome reliability with a standard x86-based design.

HPE Superdome Flex is designed around a 5U modular building block that can scale from four sockets up to 32 sockets in four-socket increments through a cabled crossbar interconnection fabric called the HPE Superdome Flex Grid. With this modular design flexibility, HPE Superdome Flex customers do not pay for infrastructure costs (that is, power capacity, Flex Grid cables, and more) above and beyond the system scale they require, but they can easily add capacity in the future as their application needs change.

Service access for the system is limited to the front or rear of the enclosure by way of forward and rearward sliding rails, and components like Bulk Power Supplies (BPS), fan assemblies, and boot drives can all be serviced while the mission-critical workloads and operating environments continue to run. Even HPE Superdome Flex Grid provides adaptive routing features designed specifically to enhance performance by routing traffic through the optimal latency path available and provides superior uptime by automatically routing traffic around failed components.

Superdome Flex benefits:

- Turn critical data into real-time insights

  - Unparalleled scale: 4 to 32 sockets as a single system

  - 768 GB to 48 TB shared memory

  - Highly expandable for growth; ultra-fast fabric

- Keep pace with evolving business demands

  - Unique modular 4-socket building block

  - Never outgrow, no over-provisioning

  - Open management for Hybrid IT consumption

- Safeguard mission-critical workloads

  – Proven five nines (99.999%) Superdome RAS

  – Mission-critical expertise with HPE Pointnext Services

World's most scalable and modular in-memory computing platform

Figure 8-37 HPE Superdome Flex can scale to 32 sockets as a single system

HPE OneView supports monitoring of HPE Superdome Flex, as illustrated in Figure 8-37. These are additional specifications of the platform:

- Unparalleled scale

  – Modular scale-up architecture

  – Supports both Gold and Platinum processors

  – Designed to provide 768 GB to 48 TB of shared memory

- – High-bandwidth (13.3 GB/sec- bidirectional per link)/low latency (<400 ns) HPE Flex Grid

  – Intel ® Xeon® Scalable (Skylake) processors with up to 28 cores

- Unbounded IO

  – Up to 128 PCIe standup cards, LP/FH PCIe

- Optimum flexibility

  – Four-socket chassis building blocks, low entry cost; HPE nPARs

  – Nvidia GPUs, Intel SDVis

  – 1/10/25 Gbe, 16 Gb FC, IB EDR/Ethernet 100 Gb, Omni-Path

  – SAS, Multi-Rail LNet for Lustre; NVMe SSD

  – MPI, OpenMP

- Extreme availability

  – Advanced memory resilience, firmware first, diagnostic engine, self-healing

  – HPE Serviceguard for Linux

- Simplified user experience

  – HPE OneView, HPE Remote Support, OpenStack

  – HPE Proactive Care

HPE Superdome Flex use cases

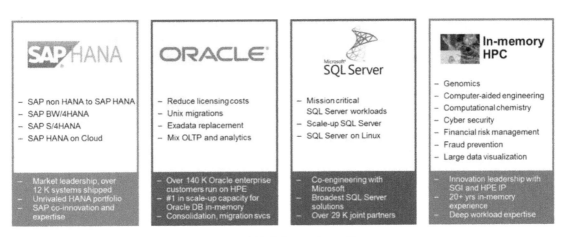

Figure 8-38 Typical HPE Superdome Flex use cases

Typical HPE Superdome Flex workloads include, as shown in Figure 8-38:

- **SAP HANA**—HPE Superdome Flex is ideal for in memory databases such as SAP HANA.

- **Oracle**—HPE Superdome Flex helps to reduce Oracle costs and complexity.

- **Microsoft SQL Server**—HPE Superdome Flex maximizes uptime and provides performance for mission-critical SQL servers.

- **In-memory HPC**—HPE Superdome Flex provides globally shared memory with seamless scale up capacity.

Management tools: Converged management for Superdome Flex

HPE Superdome Flex management tools and interfaces include embedded or external Rack Management Controller (RMC), HPE OneView, Redfish API, and OpenStack Ironic for OS provisioning.

HPE OneView support for HPE Superdome Flex

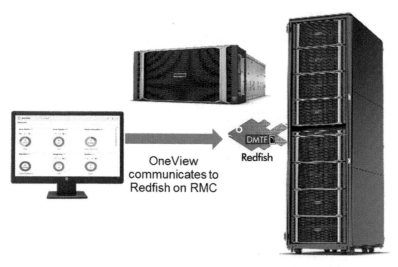

Figure 8-39 Converged management for Superdome Flex

In addition to CLI, SNMP, and IPMI, Superdome Flex can be monitored from HPE OneView, as indicated in Figure 8-39:

- New rack manager resource

    - Superdome Flex is monitored as Rack Manager (RM)

    - RM supports redfish multi-node devices

- Inventory support—rack manager
  - Individual chassis
  - RMC
  - HPE nPars (partitions)
- Health monitoring
  - Supports Redfish alerts related to fans, power supply, temperature, and chassis
- Unified RESTful API
- Maps, racks, data center, scopes

Activity: Designing a Superdome Flex solution

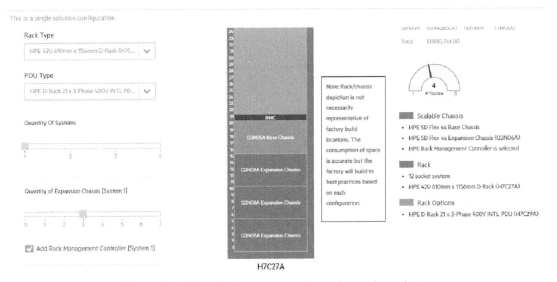

Figure 8-40 OCA—Designing a Superdome Flex solution

1. Access the One Config Advanced at Partner Ready Portal: **https://partner.hpe.com**

2. Design the Superdome Flex solution based on previous requirements, as shown in Figure 8-40:
   - Amount of sockets
   - Type of the processor
   - Type of FC HBA

- – 2x 480 GB SATA SSD
- – DVD-R drive
- – 11 TB of RAM

3. Prepare to present the BOM.

_____

_____

_____

_____

_____

_____

_____

_____

_____

_____

_____

_____

_____

_____

_____

_____

_____

_____

_____

_____

_____

_____

_____

Solution components

Qty	Part number	Description
		Rack Infrastructure
1	P9K16A	HPE 42U 800x1200mm Advanced Shock Rack
1	P9K16A 001	HPE Factory Express Base Racking Service
2	JG838A	HPE FlexFabric 5900CP 48XG 4QSFP+ Switch
		HPE Superdome Flex
1	Q2N05A	HPE Superdome Flex Base Chassis
2	Q2N43A³	HPE Superdome Flex 480GB SATA SSD
1	Q2N42A	HPE Superdome Flex DVD-R Drive
3	Q2N06A	HPE Superdome Flex 4s Expansion Chassis
16	Q6L90A	HPE Superdome Flex Intel Xeon-Platinum 8180 (2.5GHz/28-core/205W) Processor Kit
48	Q2N39A	HPE Superdome Flex DDR4 256GB (4x64GB) Mem Kit
4	Q2N08A	HPE Superdome Flex PCIe FH 12-slot 3 Riser Kit
16	Q0L14A	HPE SN1200E 16Gb 2p FC HBA
1	Q2N16A	HPE Superdome Flex 16-socket Interconnect and Scale Activation Kit
1	Q2N07A	HPE Superdome Flex Mgmt Controller
4	P9Q61A	HPE G2 Basic 3Ph 17.3kVA/C13 NA/JP PDU

Learning check

6. How many sockets does the Superdome Flex platform support?

_____

_____

7. Name two typical use cases for HPE's MCS flagship, HPE Superdome Flex.

_____

_____

_____

8. HPE OneView supports Superdome Flex in managed mode.

   ☐ True

   ☐ False

9. You are in a meeting with a customer, and they challenge you with a question: "I'm interested in a state-of-the-art, mission-critical, scale-up hardware with multi-terabyte capacity for RAM. I heard that the maximum number of processors for HPE ProLiant servers is four, and the memory scalability goes all the way to 6 or 12 TB of RAM. Is there any other platform that is more suitable to my needs?"

How should you respond?

_____

_____

_____

_____

_____

_____

_____

_____

_____

_____

Learning check

10. Write a summary of the key concepts presented in this chapter.

_____

_____

_____

_____

_____

_____

_____

_____

_____

_____

Summary

- High-Performance Computing is the key to continued business success.

- Big Data is growing at an exponential rate, and enterprises are seeking to translate Big Data Analytics into a competitive business advantage.

- The HPE Apollo family is a set of purpose-built compute offerings designed to address the needs of HPC workloads as well as Big Data Analytics, Object Storage, and Artificial Intelligence.

- HPE Superdome Flex Server is a compute breakthrough to power critical applications, enable real-time analytics, and tackle data-intensive HPC workloads.

Learning check answers

Chapter 1

1. What are the most important HPE components of the Reference Architecture for Oracle RAC 12c presented in this section?

   - **HPE Synergy Composer**
   - **HPE Synergy Image Streamer**
   - **HPE Synergy Gen10 Compute Modules**
   - **HPE 3PAR StoreServ 9450 all-flash storage**
   - **HPE Application Tuner Express**

2. You are in a meeting with a customer, and they challenge you with a question: "What are the most important barriers of transforming IT environment for an edge-centric, cloud-enabled, data-driven world?"

   How should you respond?

   - **Technology**
   - **People**
   - **Economics**

3. Match the customer need with HPE portfolio.

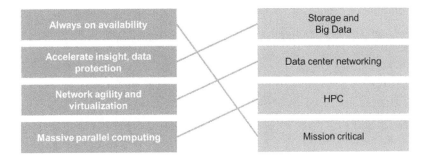

4. Name the consumption-based IT model from HPE Pointnext.

   - **HPE GreenLake Flex Capacity**

Chapter 2

1. Which hardware components can increase availability of the server?
   - **Redundant power supplies, fans, NICs**
   - **Redundant management modules (OA, FLM, Composer)**
   - **Storage subsystem—RAID**
   - **Memory subsystem (mirror, spare)**

2. HPE Reference Configuration is primarily targeted to business decision makers.
   - ☐ **True**
   - ☐ False

3. Which HPE ProLiant Gen10 series should you recommend to a customer requiring multiple general-purpose servers with traditional 1U/2U/4U form factors?
   - A. **DL servers**
   - B. Apollo servers
   - C. ML servers
   - D. CL servers

4. Which parameters can be used to select a network card for Gen10 DL server?
   - **Type of card (Ethernet vs. Converged)**
   - **Speed**
   - **Amount and type of ports (connector)**
   - **Chipset**

5. Match the amount of processor sockets to the HPE ProLiant Gen10 server.

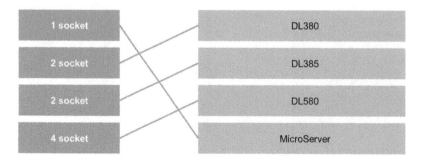

6. Which HPE ProLiant Gen10 series should you recommend to a customer requiring 6 TB of RAM and 10 PCIe 3.0 slots?

   A. MicroServer

   B. DL380 Gen10

   C. DL385 Gen10

   D. **DL580 Gen10**

7. Which Nimble storage solution should you recommend to a customer requiring 4 PB of effective capacity and 200,000 IOPS for random workloads?

   A. HPE Nimble AF20Q

   B. HPE Nimble AF60

   C. **HPE Nimble HF60**

   D. HPE Nimble HF60C

8. Which storage platform should you recommend to a customer requiring an affordable, entry-level primary storage?

   A. HPE Scalable Object Storage with Scality RING

   B. HPE 3PAR File Persona

   C. **HPE MSA**

   D. HPE 3PAR StoreServ

9. Which HPE networking device should you recommend for a customer requiring an affordable, data center switch supporting 1 Gb downlink ports and 40 Gb uplinks for a small-scale environment?

   A. **FlexFabric 5710**

   B. FlexFabric 5940

   C. Aruba 8325-32C

   D. HPE Altoline 9960

10. Which tool can you use to demonstrate the 3D model of a server solution to the customer?

   – **HPE Product Tour**

11. Describe the purpose and functions of the HPE OneConfig Advanced tool.

    - **Configuration tool accessible from HPE Partner Ready portal**
    - **Available both internally and for HPE Partners**
    - **Large configurations of multiples of rack/servers**
    - **Intuitive web-based interface**
    - **Includes latest products**

12. Proposal-ready content that is based on non-technical, external sources such as the HPE website does not require review by an SME.

    ☐ **True**

    ☐ False

13. Which resource contains installation steps required to set up an HPE device?

    - **Quick Start/Setup Guide**
    - **Installation Guide**

14. You are in a meeting with a customer, and they challenge you with a statement: "I heard that configuration process required to prepare a quote is time-consuming, with a high risk of errors and risk of ordering incompatible components".

    How should you respond?

    - **HPE provides a range of tools and resources for simplifying the configuration and quoting process. These include Reference Architectures, HPE Switch Selector, HPE Proposal Web, HPE OneConfig Advanced, HPE Power Advisor, HPE Synergy Planning Tool, HPE Server Memory Configurator, SSD Selector Tool, HPE iQuote Universal, and a range of HPE solution sizers.**

Chapter 3

1. You are attending a meeting with a banking customer to discuss their future data center modernization plans. They have been alarmed by reports of firmware-level security breaches, and they tell you that such an event in their infrastructure would cost them millions of dollars in fines. They tell you that they require FIPS-level security or higher, and ask you if HPE servers can deliver this level of security. They also ask what HPE offers in the Gen10 platform for protecting against firmware-level attack.

    - **HPE has implemented a Silicon Root of Trust in ProLiant Gen10 servers. This feature is anchored in the silicon and is unique in the industry, giving HPE impenetrable protection right through the entire supply chain. FIPS-level security, and the higher level CNSA (SuiteB), is available in ProLiant Gen10 servers.**

2. Match the controller family with available RAID levels and Boot mode support.

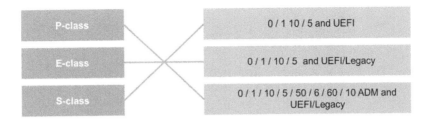

P-class	0 / 1 10 / 5 and UEFI
E-class	0 / 1 / 10 / 5 and UEFI/Legacy
S-class	0 / 1 / 10 / 5 / 50 / 6 / 60 / 10 ADM and UEFI/Legacy

3. HPE G2 Enterprise Rack Series support up to 3000 lbs. dynamic load.

   □ **True**

   □ False

4. Name five on-system tools for HPE ProLiant server management.

   – **UEFI**

   – **iLO 5**

   – **RESTful API, HPE RESTful Interface Tool, and other HPE scripting tools**

   – **Intelligent Provisioning**

   – **Smart Storage Administrator**

   – **HPE Smart Update and Service Pack for ProLiant**

5. What are the three benefits of using UEFI compared to legacy BIOS?

   – **Use drives larger than 2.2 TB**

   – **Enable Secure Boot to improve security measures**

   – **Take advantage of the UEFI shell and HPE RESTful API for scalable configuration deployment**

   – **Perform industry-standard server configurations with fewer reboots**

   – **Support new technologies—USB 3.0 stack, TPM 2.0, NVMe boot, iSCSI Software Initiator support, HTTP/HTTPs boot as a PXE alternative, and more**

6. Name three workload profiles configurable in Gen10 RBSU.

   – **General power-efficient compute, General peak frequency compute, General throughput compute, Virtualization—Power efficient, Virtualization—Max performance, Low latency, Mission critical, Transactional database, High-Performance Compute, Decision support, Graphic processing, IO throughput, Web/E-commerce, Extreme efficient compute, Custom**

7. Match the processor family with benefits.

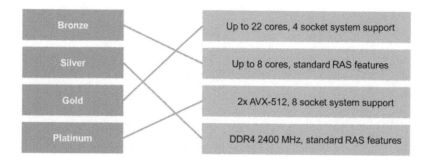

8. Name three components of HPE Intelligent System Tuning.

   – **Jitter Smoothing**

   – **Core Boosting**

   – **Workload Profiles (Workload matching)**

9. Memory controllers in HPE Gen10 ProLiant servers support up to four memory channels per CPU.

   ☐ True

   ☐ **False**

10. What are the three possibilities for connecting to iLO?

   – **Web-based interface**

   – **SSH**

   – **ROM-based configuration utility (initial setup from UEFI System Utilities)**

   – **iLO RESTful API**

   – **RESTful Interface Tool**

   – **iLO mobile app**

11. Which HPE tool can be used to configure Smart Array Controller?

   – **Smart Storage Administrator**

   – **UEFI Configuration tool for Array Controllers**

   – **REST API**

   – **PowerShell cmdlets**

12. Intelligent Provisioning allows administrators to perform assisted installation of an HPE ProLiant server.

   ☐ **True**

   ☐ False

13. You are in a meeting with a customer, and they challenge you with a question: "Is it possible to select the type of a local storage? Amount of drives, type of drive, and physical size?"

   How should you respond?

   – **Yes it is possible. The options available for each server model are documented in the QuickSpecs for that server.**

Chapter 4

1. Match the switch family with the description.

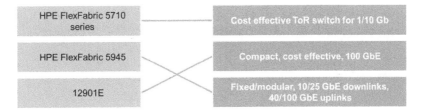

2. What is the typical speed of uplink ports on HPE FlexFabric 5710/594x/5980 series?

   – **40/100 GbE**

3. Your customer is interested in a network management software for a mixed environment with 30 devices. Which software will you recommend?

   – **HPE Intelligent Management Center Basic Software Platform**

4. You are in a meeting with a customer and they challenge you with a statement: "I heard that HPE data center networking devices only support a traditional core/aggregation/access layered architecture. This approach does not match my current modernization plans."

   How should you respond?

   – **HPE FlexFabric solutions offer the benefits of a leaf-spine architecture. HPE also offers SDN solutions as a result of their recent acquisition of Plexxi.**

Chapter 5

1. What is the default type of RAID at Nimble AF-Series?
   - **Triple parity plus with integrated spare**

2. When will you offer Nimble HF-Series over AF-Series?
   - **Higher effective capacity is preferred**
   - **Secondary storage workloads**

3. Match the Nimble model with max capacity.

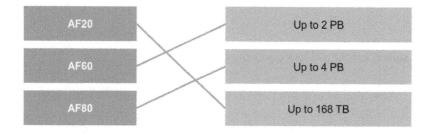

4. Match the data protection product/technology with its description.

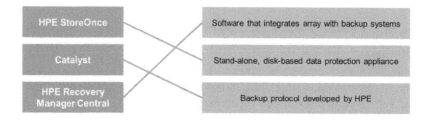

5. Name three features that are part of HPE 3PAR StoreServ.
   - **Synchronous replication**
   - **Asynchronous replication**
   - **Rapid provisioning**
   - **Maintain service levels**
   - **Replicate, snap, move, backup, and restore valuable data**
   - **Application-integrated snapshot management**

6. Match the HPE 3PAR StoreServ array with maximum front-end performance characteristics (IOPS) when RAID1 is used and 100% random read.

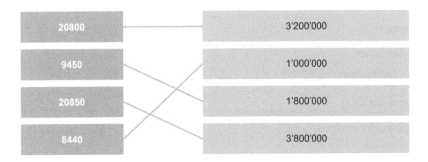

7. Select the management tool you will use for daily management tasks on 3PAR array, such as creating volumes?

   –   **A**

8. Which ports can be used to connect HPE 3PAR StoreServ 8000 to servers?

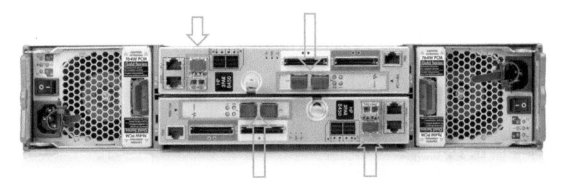

9. You are in a meeting with a customer, and they challenge you with a statement: "Data security and availability is my top concern. I was reviewing Nimble specifications, and I like the deduplication and compression capabilities, but I heard that HPE Nimble Storage can survive only a single drive failure per enclosure. This technology is not compatible with my views on enterprise-class storage." How should you respond?

   –   **The HPE Nimble triple+ parity can tolerate the simultaneous failure of any three SSDs.**

   –   **A 99.9999% availability guarantee is offered on the HPE Nimble Storage portfolio.**

Chapter 6

1. Name the components of the HPE Synergy management subsystem.
   - **Composer**
   - **Image Streamer**
   - **Frame Link Module**
   - **Management Ring**
   - **Management Network**

2. What is the total Ethernet throughput on uplinks on a single Synergy Virtual Connect master module (HPE VC SE 40 Gb F8)?
   A. 80 Gb/s
   B. 120 Gb/s
   C. **240 Gb/s**
   D. 2.56 Tb/s

3. What is the name of the configuration object inside HPE OneView that can be used to define server configuration?
   - **Server profile**

4. Which HPE storage products are supported by HPE OneView for automating volume provisioning?
   A. **HPE 3PAR StoreServ**
   B. **HPE Nimble Storage**
   C. **HPE StoreVirtual**
   D. HPE StoreEasy

5. Select the Synergy CNA.

6. What are the three required components for composable, local, in-frame storage in HPE Synergy solution?

    – **Mezzanine Array Controller**

    – **SAS interconnect module**

    – **D3940**

7. Select the Synergy local disk module.

8. Which HPE products or subsystems can be managed from PowerShell?

    – **OneView**

    – **iLO**

    – **Storage**

    – **OneSphere**

    – **BIOS**

    – **Smart Array**

    – **Onboard Administrator**

9. Which HPE solution can simplify private and hybrid cloud management?

    – **HPE OneSphere**

10. You are in a meeting with a customer, and they challenge you with a statement: "I heard that HPE specializes in traditional data center components and does not offer a software-defined platform, where hardware provisioning can be done from the management application." How should you respond?

    – **HPE Synergy with its embedded HPE Composer management solution is one example of an HPE software-defined architecture. It provides composable compute, fabric, and storage resources and is an ideal foundation for a software-defined data center.**

Chapter 7

1. Which typical data center components is HPE SimpliVity replacing?

   – **Servers/compute resources**

   – **Storage resources: shared storage, caching, backup, and deduplication, storage switch**

2. What is the maximum recommended amount of VMs for the SimpliVity platform?

   – **2000 to 2500**

3. What does the HyperProtected part of HPE SimpliVity HyperGuarantee stand for?

   a. Save 90% capacity across storage and backup combined

   b. Add or replace HPE SimpliVity systems with zero downtime for local or remote sites

   c. **Under 1 minute to complete a local backup or local restore of a 1 TB VM**

   d. Three clicks to back up, restore, move, or clone a VM from a single console

4. How is SimpliVity management implemented?

   – **SimpliVity management is integrated in virtualization management (HPE SimpliVity management plugin for VMware vCenter or HPE SimpliVity management plugin for Microsoft System Center)**

5. At which level does the data optimization happen in the HPE SimpliVity platform?

   a. CPU and memory

   b. Hypervisor (VMware vSphere or Hyper-V)

   c. **HPE OmniStack Accelerator Card**

   d. HPE OmniStack Virtual Controller

6. You are in a meeting with a customer, and they challenge you with a question:

   "I'm interested in a modern virtualization solution that will include all the resources needed for running virtual machines in a single building block. Is there anything HPE can offer in this space?" How should you respond?

   – **HPE offers a hyper-converged solution called HPE SimpliVity. HPE SimpliVity simplifies the data center by incorporating multiple functions into a single building block data center appliance that can be easily expanded, and includes all functionality managed through the native hypervisor management interface.**

Chapter 8

1. Which HPE platforms are part of the HPE Elastic Platform for Analytics?

   – **Edgeline 1000/4000**

   – **Apollo 2000/6500/Synergy/DL380**

   – **Apollo 4200/4510**

2. How many 2-socket servers will fit in the HPE Apollo r2000 Gen10 chassis, if no GPU support is required for a specific workload?

   A. 1

   B. 2

   C. 3

   D. **4**

3. Match the HPE platform for HPC with the description.

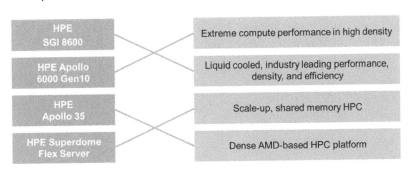

4. How many 2.5" (SFF) SSDs will fit into the Apollo 4200 Gen10 server?

   – **Up to 48 + 6**

5. Which HPE solution will you recommend or add to the quote for configuring and installing cluster environments, monitoring cluster and node metrics, and remotely managing resources?

    – **HPE Insight Cluster Management Utility**

6. How many sockets does the Superdome Flex platform support?

    – **4 to 32S**

7. Name two typical use cases for HPE's MCS flagship, HPE Superdome Flex.

    – **SAP HANA**

    – **ORACLE**

    – **MS SQL Server**

    – **In-memory HPC**

8. HPE OneView supports Superdome Flex in managed mode.

    ☐ True

    ☐ **False**

9. You are in a meeting with a customer and they challenge you with a question: "I'm interested in a state of the art, mission-critical, scale-up hardware with multi-terabyte capacity for RAM. I heard that the maximum amount of processors for HPE ProLiant servers is 4, and the memory scalability goes all the way to 6 or 12 TB of RAM. Is there any other platform that is more suitable to my needs?" How should you respond?

    – **The HPE Superdome Flex solution offers up to 32 processor sockets in a single system and up to 48 TB of shared memory. It also has proven five nines (99.999%) availability.**

Practice Test

INTRODUCTION

The HPE ASE—Hybrid IT Solutions Architect V1 certification validates a successful candidate's ASE level skills to plan, design, recommend, and demonstrate HPE Hybrid IT solutions and deliver a proof of concept for a solution.

Ideal candidate for this exam

A successful candidate will have the competence to:

- Demonstrate knowledge of HPE server, storage, networking, and management tools and their concepts and solutions.

- Identify and describe the components required for a Hybrid IT solution and explain the features, functions, and the benefits they provide.

- Demonstrate knowledge of data gathering, planning, sizing, and HPE configuration tools along with the related technical documentation to design, prepare, and evaluate Hybrid IT solutions.

- Given a set of customer requirements, validate that sufficient key information has been gathered and applied to design and/or implement an appropriate solution.

- Given a set of customer requirements, design a Hybrid IT solution for availability, resiliency, and data protection.

- Assess a customer environment and integrate an HPE Hybrid IT solution with the customer's existing environment.

- Contribute basic HPE design and product recommendations for individual building blocks as part of a team designing a complex HPE Hybrid IT solution.

- Share and explain installation and configuration requirements for a solution design to an integrator.

- Assess, explain, and propose appropriate HPE service offerings related to the HPE Hybrid IT solutions portfolio

Exam details

The following are details about the exam:

- Exam ID: HPE0-S57

- Exam Type: Proctored

- Number of items: 60

- Item types: Input text, input numbers, matching, multiple choice (single-response), multiple choice (multiple-response), and point and click

- Exam time: 1 hour 30 minutes

- Passing score: 68%

- Reference material: No online or hard copy reference material will be allowed at the testing site.

HPE0-S57 testing objectives

- 9%—Describe, differentiate, and apply industry-standard architectures and technologies

- 19%—Gather and analyze customer business and technical requirements

- 25%—Recommend and position HPE Hybrid IT products, solutions, tools, and appropriate services for customer use cases

- 38%—Architect and design an HPE solution based on customer needs

- 9%—Present and demonstrate the solution to the customer and advise implementation planning

Test preparation questions and answers

The following questions will help you measure your understanding of the material presented in this book. Read all the choices carefully, as there might be more than one correct answer. Choose all correct answers for each question.

Questions

1. Which processor family is suitable for mission-critical systems? (Select three).

   a. Bronze 3x00

   b. Silver 4x00

   c. Gold 5x00

   d. Gold 6x00

   e. Platinum 8x00

2. Match the HPE technology to its description:

Storage principle	Description
Workload matching	Maximizes the performance of all processor cores
Processor Jitter Control	Allows the user to tune servers either automatically or manually
Core boosting	Configuration option to deploy BIOS settings based on the application customer intends to run on the server

3. Which technology offers routing-like functionality based on best path for a specific source-to-destination traffic?

   a. STP

   b. TRILL

   c. LACP

   d. MLAG

4. Customers require a new backup solution for their VMware and Hyper-V environment, stored on a 3PAR 8400. They request a solution that will move the backup data across their storage network and allow for copying backup data to third-party cloud providers. Which two components should you recommend? (Select two.)

   a. Veeam Backup and Replication

   b. HPE StoreOnce 3540 with Catalyst

   c. HPE Recovery Manager Central

   d. Microsoft Data Protection Manager

   e. Microsoft Storage Spaces Direct

5. Match the appropriate server, storage, or networking platform to the workload:

Storage principle	Description
Aruba	High-performance computing and deep learning
Apollo 6000	Object storage
Apollo 4510	Campus and branch networking
FlexFabric	Traditional data center networking

6. What is the appropriate formula to calculate required primary storage capacity?

   a. Data x Growth rate x Years

   b. Data x (1+Growth rate) x Years

   c. Data/(Growth rate ^ Years)

   d. Data x (1+Growth rate)^Years

7. You are selecting an appropriate Nimble model for a customer requiring low capex and IOPS up to 100 thousands of IOPS. Which model will you recommend?

   a. HF20H

   b. HF20C

   c. HF40

   d. HF60

8. Which HPE networking device should you recommend to a customer requiring an affordable, data center switch supporting 10 Gb downlink ports and 40 Gb uplinks for a small-scale environment?

   a. FlexFabric 5710

   b. FlexFabric 5940

   c. Aruba 8325-32C

   d. HPE Altoline 9960

9. Which storage technology allows a customer to provision a group of servers with 20TB of storage from only 10TB of actual physical storage?

   a. deduplication

   b. space reclamation

   c. compression

   d. thin provisioning

10. A customer requires local access to the AHS log for their Gen10 servers. What is required to meet this need?

    a. an installed iLO Advance license

    b. a USB key

    c. Secure Boot enabled

    d. Two-factor authentication enabled

11. Match the backup-related factor to its description:

Term	Description
RTO (Recovery Time Objective)	How much data is allowed to go unprotected and how far back in time data must be recovered?
Retention	How long the customer is willing to wait for the data to be recovered and the maximum allowable downtime.
RPO (Recovery Point Objective)	How long the data needs to be kept available. Can range from seconds to decades, depending on company policies and government regulations.

12. A customer needs to implement an all-flash array with up to 2 PB of effective storage (5x data reduction is anticipated). Which model will you recommend?

    a. AF20Q

    b. AF60

    c. HF40C

    d. HF40

13. Which HPE management tool provides a single, integrated management environment for a converged infrastructure and provides storage provisioning functions?

    a. HPE 3PAR SSMC

    b. HPE Storage Operations Manager

    c. HPE OneView

    d. HPE InfoSight for HPE 3PAR

14. Match the HPE 3PAR StoreServ model to the description:

HPE 3PAR StoreServ model	Description
8200	Upgradable with up to 4 controller nodes
8450	Price is driving factor and capacity up to 1000TB is adequate
8400	All-flash with >1 million IOPS

15. Match the multimode 50 μm transceiver maximum length using OM4 with the FC speed:

Distance	FC speed
400m	32 Gbps
125m	16 Gbps
100m	4 Gbps

16. What is the switching capacity of the HPE FlexFabric 12900E series?

   a.   100 Gbps

   b.   125 Gbps

   c.   12 Tbps

   d.   120 Tbps

17. Match the network technology to the use case:

Technology	Use case
RoCE	Network overlays for an increased amount of separated Layer 2 segments, cloud providers, data center consolidation
VXLAN	Cloud computing, Microsoft SMB Direct, Microsoft SQL
DPDK	Improve performance of iSCSI (bandwidth, latency) and lower CPU utilization
ISER	Linux environments requiring fast packet processing, OpenStack, network function virtualization

18. A customer requires a budget-friendly switch to support out of band management connectivity, which model will you recommend?

   a.   HPE FlexFabric 5710

   b.   HPE FlexFabric 5945

   c.   HPE FlexFabric 12902E

   d.   HPE FlexFabric 12904E

19. Recommend a Synergy interconnect based on following requirements:

    – Software-defined infrastructure

    – Ethernet connectivity

    – Downlinks configurable by sever administrators

    – Configuration fully integrated with Synergy Composer

        a. HPE Virtual Connect SE 40 Gb F8 Module

        b. HPE Synergy 40 GB F8 Switch Module

        c. Mellanox SH2200 Switch Module for HPE Synergy

        d. HPE Synergy Brocade 16 GB FC Switch

20. What is the maximum amount of Synergy D3940 Storage Modules you can install to the Synergy 12000 frame?

    a. 2

    b. 4

    c. 5

    d. 8

21. What is the typical HPE SimpliVity configuration workflow?

Order	Step
1	Select services and support
2	Select software options
3	Select the hardware options
4	Select the base node

22. A customer requires a hyper-converged solution with hardware, PCIe-based deduplication acceleration. Recommend the HPE product that satisfies customer needs:

    a. HPE SimpliVity 170r

    b. HPE Synergy 480 Gen10

    c. HPE Apollo 2800

    d. HPE SimpliVity 380

23. Recommend an optional HPE management tool for a high-performance cluster based on Apollo 6000, which can meter server power consumption and aggregate dynamic power capping.

    a. HPE OneView

    b. Apollo Platform Manager

    c. Insight Cluster Management Utility

    d. SGI Management Suite

24. Which interfaces are commonly used in HPE StoreOnce environments? (Select two.)

    a. NTFS (New Technology File System)

    b. EXT4

    c. EXT3

    d. NFS (Network File System)

    e. CIFS (Common Internet File System)

25. Your need to architect an SQL Database consolidation solution, based on the HPE Reference Architecture for SQL 2017. Which server should you recommend?

    a. HPE DL560 Gen 10

    b. HPE DL360 Gen 10

    c. HPE ML30 Gen10

    d. HPE BL460c Gen10

26. A customer needs a VMware Horizon VDI solution for a space-constrained remote office. The solution must include deduplication and compression, and be simple to implement and manage. Which platform should you recommend?

    a. HPE Synergy 480 Gen10

    b. HPE SimpliVity 2600

    c. HPE DL380 Gen10

    d. HPE DL360 Gen10

27. A customer is looking for an ideal hardware platform for scale-up, in-memory high-performance cluster. Select the appropriate HPC platform.

    a. HPE Synergy 480 Gen10

    b. HPE SimpliVity 380

    c. HPE Apollo 2000

    d. HPE Superdome Flex

28. For a data consolidation project at a branch office, a customer requires an expandable, tower server with standard 3-1-1 warranty. Which platform will you recommend:

    a. HPE Synergy 480 Gen10

    b. HPE SimpliVity 380

    c. HPE ProLiant ML30 Gen10

    d. HPE Superdome Flex

29. A customer is considering a refresh of their data center switches to support the 25GbE connectivity. Which switch family should you recommend?

    a. FlexFabric 5710

    b. FlexFabric 5940

    c. FlexFabric 5945

    d. FlexFabric 5980

30. Which document can be used to define extra customer instructions, such as special packaging or BIOS configuration?

    a. BTO Part Number

    b. Customer Intent Document

    c. CTO Part Number

    d. Support Contract ID

31. You are presenting a UI of HPE InfoSight. Which menu option contains AI performance Recommendations?

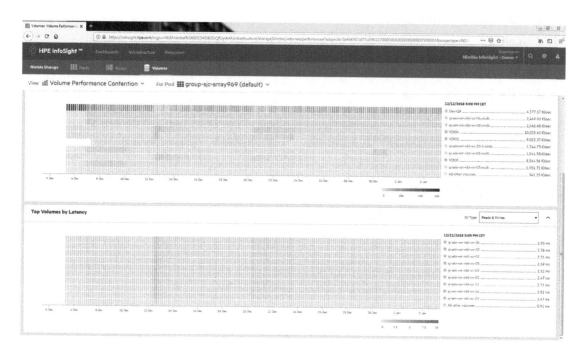

  a. Dashboards

  b. Infrastructure

  c. Resources

  d. Organization

32. You are demonstrating an HPE Synergy, HPE C-series FC switches, and HPE StoreServ integration.

  Which objects need to be configured in HPE OneView to provision host access to volumes on the storage system? (Select two.)

  a. Volume

  b. Volume template

  c. Server profile

  d. Server profile template

  e. Firmware bundle

33. You are demonstrating a StoreOnce NAS replication. Which object needs to be configured at the target appliance in order to enable replication?

   a.   StoreOnce Federation

   b.   StoreOnce VT Library

   c.   StoreOnce NAS share

   d.   Catalyst Store

Answers

1.   ☑ **C, D,** and **E** are correct. Only Gold and Platinum series contain advanced reliability, availability, and serviceability features.

   ☒ **A** and **B** are incorrect. Bronze and Silver processors contain standard RAS features.

   For more information, see Chapter 3.

2.   Correct matching is shown in the table below:

HPE technology	Description
Core boosting	Maximizes the performance of all processor cores
Processor Jitter Control	Allows the user to tune servers either automatically or manually
Workload matching	Configuration option to deploy BIOS settings based on the application customer intends to run on the server

   For more information, see Chapter 3.

3.   ☑ **B** is correct. With TRILL, Layer 2 forwarding is based on best path selection, very much like that of Open Shortest Path First (OSPF) or Intermediate System to Intermediate System (IS-IS). This provides actual best path selection while supporting a redundant, active-active topology.

   ☒ **A, C,** and **D** are incorrect. STP uses a single path in the network, which may not be the best path between specific source and destination. LACP and MLAG are used for link aggregation.

   For more information, see Chapter 4.

4.   ☑ **A** and **B** are correct. Veeam and StoreOnce will greatly complement the 3PAR solution with a backup functionality, including third-party cloud providers.

   ☒ **C, D,** and **E** are incorrect. You cannot create a working backup solution from these three components for both VMware and Hyper-V environment.

   For more information, see Chapter 4.

5. Correct matching is shown in the table below:

Platform	Workload
Aruba	Campus and branch networking
Apollo 6000	High-performance computing and deep learning
Apollo 4510	Object storage
FlexFabric	Traditional data center networking

For more information, see Chapter 2.

6. ☑ **D** is correct. Data x (1+Growth rate)^Years is the appropriate formula to calculate required primary storage capacity. Amount of data needs to be multiplied by 1+growth rate per each year.

☒ **A, B,** and **C** are incorrect.

For more information, see Chapter 2.

7. ☑ **C** is correct. HF40 can handle up to 110k IOPS and can be obtained at lower price point than HF60.

☒ **A** and **B** are incorrect. HF20 cannot handle 100k IOPS. **D** is incorrect, because a customer requires low capex.

For more information, see Chapter 5.

8. ☑ **A** is correct. The HPE FlexFabric 5710 can support both 10 Gb downlinks and 40 Gb uplinks at the lowest price point.

☒ **B, C,** and **D** are incorrect, as these switches are offered at higher price point than 5710.

For more information, see Chapter 4.

9. ☑ **D** is correct. Thin provisioning allows to provision more capacity than the array actually contain.

☒ **A, B,** and **C** are incorrect. Deduplication and compression provides higher effective capacity. Space reclamation can be used to reclaim back unused space, when thin provisioning is used.

For more information, see Chapter 5.

10. ☑ **B** is correct. Local USB key can be used to download the AHS log on Gen10 servers.

☒ **A, C,** and **D** are incorrect. AHS log is available even with standard license, Secure Boot is not affecting AHS log, and two-factor authentication will not help with local access to AHS log.

For more information, see Chapter 3

11. Correct matching is shown in the table below:

Term	Description
RTO (Recovery Time Objective)	How long the customer is willing to wait for the data to be recovered and the maximum allowable downtime.
Retention	How long the data needs to be kept available. Can range from seconds to decades, depending on company policies and government regulations.
RPO (Recovery Point Objective)	How much data is allowed to go unprotected and how far back in time data must be recovered?

For more information, see Chapter 5.

12. ☑ **B** is correct. AF60 supports up to 2 PB of effective storage under stated conditions.

   ☒ **A, C,** and **D** are incorrect. AF20Q supports up to 128TB under stated conditions. HF40C and HF40 are not all-flash arrays.

   For more information, see Chapter 5.

13. ☑ **C** is correct. HPE OneView is a single, integrated management environment for converged infrastructure and provides storage provisioning functions.

   ☒ **A, B,** and **D** are incorrect. SSMC can be used to manage 3PAR, InfoSight is not used for managing devices, and Storage Operations Manager is storage oriented, not a converged tool.

   For more information, see Chapters 5 and 6.

14. Correct matching is shown in the table below:

HPE 3PAR StoreServ model	Description
8200	Price is driving factor and capacity up to 1000TB is adequate
8450	All-flash with >1 million IOPS
8400	Upgradable with up to 4 controller nodes

For more information, see Chapter 5.

15. Correct matching is shown in the table below:

Distance	FC speed
400m	4 Gbps
125m	16 Gbps
100m	32 Gbps

For more information, see Chapter 5.

16. ☑ **D** is correct. HPE FlexFabric 12900E series provides up to 184 Tbps bidirectional switching capacity.

    ☒ **A, B,** and **C** are incorrect. HPE FlexFabric 12900E series provides higher capacity.

    For more information, see Chapter 4.

17. Correct matching is shown in the table below:

Technology	Use case
RoCE	Cloud computing, Microsoft SMB Direct, Microsoft SQL
VXLAN	Network overlays for an increased amount of separated Layer 2 segments, cloud providers, data center consolidation
DPDK	Linux environments requiring fast packet processing, OpenStack, network function virtualization
ISER	Improve performance of iSCSI (bandwidth, latency) and lower CPU utilization

    For more information, see Chapter 4.

18. ☑ **A** is correct. HPE FlexFabric 5710 is a perfect, budget-friendly switch to support out of band management.

    ☒ **B, C,** and **D** are incorrect. 5710 series can provide the functionality at lower price point.

    For more information, see Chapter 4.

19. ☑ **A** is correct. HPE Virtual Connect SE 40 Gb F8 Module is software-defined, Ethernet-based, and configurable by Synergy Composer.

    ☒ **B, C,** and **D** are incorrect. HPE Synergy 40 GB and Mellanox SH2200 cannot be configured by Synergy Composer. HPE Synergy Brocade 16 GB FC switch does not provide Ethernet connectivity.

    For more information, see Chapter 6.

20. ☑ **C** is correct. As D3940 is double-wide module, we can install five of these to Synergy 12000 frame and two compute modules to provide access to storage modules.

    ☒ **A, B,** and **D** are incorrect.

    For more information, see Chapter 6.

21. Correct order is shown in the table below:

Order	Step
1	Select the base node
2	Select the hardware options
3	Select software options
4	Select services and support

For more information, see Chapter 7.

22. ☑ **D** is correct. HPE SimpliVity 380 provides PCIe-based deduplication with Acceleration Card.

☒ **A, B,** and **C** are incorrect. Synergy platform, Apollo 2800, and SimpliVity 170r do not support the hardware-based deduplication.

For more information, see Chapter 7.

23. ☑ **B** is correct. Apollo Platform Manager can meter server power consumption and aggregate dynamic power capping.

☒ **A, C,** and **D** are incorrect. HPE OneView supports power consumption metering, but not the dynamic power capping. Insight Cluster Management Utility and SGI Management Suite do not meter the power consumption and do not support dynamic power capping.

For more information, see Chapter 8.

24. ☑ **D** and **E** are correct. HPE StoreOnce supports both NFS and CIFS with NAS Share targets.

☒ **A, B,** and **C** are incorrect. NTFS, EXT4, and EXT3 are filesystems.

For more information, see Chapter 5.

25. ☑ **A** is correct. HPE DL560 Gen10 is used as hardware platform by Reference Architecture for SQL 2017.

☒ **B, C,** and **D** are incorrect.

For more information, see Chapter 3.

26. ☑ **B** is correct. HPE SimpliVity 2600 is an ideal platform for VMware Horizon VDI and it includes deduplication and compression technologies.

☒ **A, C,** and **D** are incorrect. Synergy platform does not match the space-constrained remote office. HPE DL380 and DL360 are generic servers without deduplication and compression technologies.

For more information, see Chapter 7.

27. ☑ **D** is correct. HPE Superdome Flex is an ideal hardware platform for scale-up, in-memory high-performance cluster.

    ☒ **A, B,** and **C** are incorrect. Synergy supports maximum four processors in a system. SimpliVity is a hyper-converged solution, not HPC. Apollo 2000 supports maximum two processors in a system.

    For more information, see Chapter 8.

28. ☑ **C** is correct. HPE ProLiant ML30 Gen10 is a tower server suitable for a branch office.

    ☒ **A, B,** and **D** are incorrect. Synergy requires rack-based infrastructure; Superdome Flex and SimpliVity 380 are not tower servers.

    For more information, see Chapter 3.

29. ☑ **C** is correct. HPE FlexFabric 5945 supports the 25GbE connectivity.

    ☒ **A, B,** and **D** are incorrect. 5710/5940/5980 is used for 1/10 Gb environments on downlink ports.

    For more information, see Chapter 4.

30. ☑ **B** is correct. Customer Intent Document can be used to define extra customer instructions.

    ☒ **A, C,** and **D** are incorrect. Support ID is not BTO/CTO numbers are used for ordering.

    For more information, see Chapter 2.

31. ☑ **A** is correct. Dashboards menu option includes access to Labs and AI Performance Recommendations.

    ☒ **B, C,** and **D** are incorrect. AI performance recommendations are available from Dashboards menu option.

    For more information, see HPE InfoSight.

32. ☑ **A** and **C** are correct. Volume and server profile objects are needed for host access to volume.

    ☒ **B, D,** and **E** are incorrect. Volume template and server profile template can be used for creating volumes and profiles, but are not connected to the real hardware. Firmware bundle is not used for configuring storage access.

    For more information, see Chapter 6.

33. ☑ **C** is correct. NAS share needs to be configured at target appliance in order to set up replication.

    ☒ **A, B,** and **D** are incorrect. Federation is used for single-pane management. VTL and Catalyst stores cannot be used for NAS replication.

    For more information, see Chapter 5.

Index